D0163248

Cuban Rural Society
in the Nineteenth Century

Cuban Rural Society in the Nineteenth Century

The Social and Economic History of Monoculture in Matanzas

LAIRD W. BERGAD

PRINCETON UNIVERSITY PRESS

PRINCETON, NEW JERSEY

Copyright © 1990 by Princeton University Press
Published by Princeton University Press, 41 William Street,
Princeton, New Jersey 08540
In the United Kingdom: Princeton University Press, Oxford

All Rights Reserved

Library of Congress Cataloging-in-Publication Data

Bergad, Laird W., 1948–
Cuban rural society in the nineteenth century : the social and economic
history of monoculture in Matanzas / Laird W. Bergad.
p.   cm.   Bibliography: p.   Includes index.
ISBN 0-691-07816-5 (alk. paper)
1. Matanzas (Cuba : Province)—Economic conditions. 2. Matanzas
(Cuba : Province)—Social conditions. 3. Sugarcane industry—Cuba—
Matanzas (Province)—History—19th century. I. Title.
HC152.5.Z7M383 1990   89-36040

Publication of this book was made possible by grants
from the Publications Program of the National Endowment
for the Humanities, an independent Federal agency, and
the Research Foundation of the City University of New York

This book has been composed in Linotron Aldus and Palatino

Princeton University Press books are printed on acid-free paper,
and meet the guidelines for permanence and durability of the
Committee on Production Guidelines for Book Longevity of the
Council on Library Resources

Printed in the United States of America by Princeton University Press,
Princeton, New Jersey

10   9   8   7   6   5   4   3   2   1

Designed by Laury A. Egan

HC
152.5
.Z7
M37
1990

FOR MY MOTHER AND FATHER

CONTENTS

PART THREE

Matanzas between Rebellions: The Structures of Monoculture Transformed, 1878–1895

PART FOUR

Epilogue: The Social and Economic Impact of the War for Independence and Its Aftermath, 1895–1900

ILLUSTRATIONS

Figures

Maps

TABLES

PREFACE

Below the ruins of Monserrate, a nineteenth-century convent perched upon a gentle rise at the southwestern edge of the city of Matanzas, a diverse visual panorama unfolds. To the west the lush tropical landscape of the Yumurí Valley is striking for its rich verdant tones and textures. Río Yumurí meanders among royal palms, orange and breadfruit trees, thick pastures, irregular fields of yucca, *malanga*, banana, and plantain, and finally broadens only to disappear into the bay. Curling wisps of smoke rising from scattered *bohíos*, circling vultures, and chirping tree frogs lend an element of timelessness to the rural world of the valley.

To the east the city's stark images appear, softened somewhat by the fiery red of dozens of *flamboyanes* interspersed among drab concrete and asphalt. The modest skyline is highlighted by the rival towers of the old Alcaldía and nearby cathedral, mute testimony to the struggle between secular and clerical authorities for symbolic domination.

The town, dating from the late seventeenth century, is built on an elevated triangle of land lying between the banks of the Yumurí and San Juan rivers. Swampland was drained in the early nineteenth century, first to the north where barrio Versalles hugs the bay between the Yumurí and the San Severino fortress. Beyond the residential areas of Versalles, oil storage tanks and the vile pollution of a refinery accentuate the ecological realities of the late twentieth century, providing a sharp contrast with the bucolic Yumurí Valley.

The land to the south of the Río San Juan was drained in the 1820s, and Pueblo Nuevo was laid out in the traditional grid pattern. The old *almacenes* still snake along the river's south bank; further on, the railroad station, originally built in the late 1830s, stands at the crossroads leading to Cárdenas or Unión de Reyes. Modern high-rise housing projects complete the view, lending an aura of modernity to the eastern outskirts of town.

Most striking to the east is the bay itself, a wide expanse of water in the shape of a large boot, unprotected from the often rampaging Atlantic. Large cargo ships unload, enter, or move out to sea. With a little imagination one can conjure up the image of Piet Heyn, who drove the Spanish fleet into the bay in 1628 and seized the king's silver. The treasures of one silver ship lie buried somewhere beneath the silt along with the mysteries of more than three centuries.

The town, which became a veritable city in the nineteenth century, was supported by an agricultural economy revolving first around cattle ranching, timber, and tobacco exploitation. Although coffee cultivation spread in the late eighteenth and early nineteenth centuries, monocultural sugar production reduced every other rural activity to insignificance by the mid-1840s.

This has persisted through the 1980s. South of the port a small range of rolling hills runs east–west for several miles, but beyond them in every direction the terrain is monotonously flat. With the exception of the north coast road to Cárdenas, where henequen fields abound, the human and ecological landscape is overwhelmed by cane fields shimmering to the horizon in every direction. South, toward the great swamp bordering the Caribbean, the Ciénaga de Zapata; east, to the rival city of Cárdenas and beyond; southeast on the road to Cienfuegos all the way to the foothills of the Sierra Escambray, there is little but cane, cane, and more cane.

Although small *poblados* and provincial towns dot the countryside, it is the sugar mills that have defined the rhythm of provincial life for nearly two centuries. Their smokestacks interrupt the horizon, calling beacons which stubbornly persist despite periodic changes in the surrounding social, economic, and political environment. It once took more than 500 *ingenios* to complete the *zafra*, although 21 *centrales* now grind all of the province's cane. Their names have changed since the triumph of the revolution in 1959: España Republicana, Méjico, Sergio González, René Fraga, and Jesús Rabi were once known as España, Álava, Tinguaro, Santa Rita, and Por Fuerza. The old names are still faintly visible on smokestacks, and many elders continue to prefer the traditional nomenclature.

Others have faded from memory. On the road leading from the town of Colón to the northeast, two signs point to the small villages of Ponina and Flor de Cuba. Absolutely nothing suggests the tragic drama played out in these environs, for two of Cuba's most productive nineteenth-century ingenios once reigned supreme here. Now, but for two small road signs, not the slightest physical evidence survives of this former source of misery and suffering to a great African slave population, and fount of fortune to two planter families who preferred the comforts of Havana to the rural world of sugar.

This book is about the nineteenth-century social and economic development of the province of Matanzas. It is not about Cuban sugar production but, rather, the society produced by sugar. A diverse society, modern yet antiquated in many ways, the socioeconomic order was always shifting in response to a wide range of internal and external variables. European technological innovations and the price of sugar on foreign markets had as much impact on the region as the quality of the soil or the devastation wrought by hurricanes, epidemics, war, and revolution.

The historical characters forging the history of Matanzas offer an opportunity to examine a changing cross section of nineteenth-century Cuban rural society through the prism of local life. Every social sector was found in the province at one time: impoverished immigrants from the Canary Islands; counts and marquises; pirates and smugglers; merchants from the North Atlantic world; foreign and local entrepreneurs who built railroads and shipping lines; slave traders; slaves and free blacks in rural and urban zones; *cimarrones* and *palenques*; political revolutionaries; poor white and mulatto smallholders; Chinese contract laborers; and, above all, the planters who harnessed the resources to transform the environment from a densely forested frontier zone to the richest sugar-producing region of the world by the mid-nineteenth century.

The specific patterns of socioeconomic development in nineteenth-century Matanzas were unique in many ways, both within Cuba and when compared to neighboring Caribbean countries. However, long-term structural similarities with other monocultural economic systems in Latin America and the Caribbean stand out. In 1800, with a few exceptions, the province's small, scattered population struggled to eke out a living on fragmented farms. Some grew tobacco, others coffee or sugarcane, a few cut timber and raised cattle. There was no great urban market to sustain the province, as there was for Havana, and the sugar boom of the eighteenth century scarcely affected the region.

Within several decades, however, Matanzas became the center of Cuban sugar production. Matanzas sugar sweetened the diets of Europeans and North Americans for the remainder of the nineteenth century, and the local economy generated millions of pesos. The population grew to more than a quarter million by the early 1890s, but most of the province's inhabitants continued laboring in low-paying, unskilled occupations in urban or rural zones despite the opulence of elite groups. High rates of illiteracy, infant mortality, disease, and seasonal unemployment were accompanied by low levels of life expectancy. Persistent poverty and few prospects for social development were the legacies left by the sugar "prosperity" of the nineteenth century. In this sense the history of Matanzas is part of a broader story. Despite local variations—in chronology, geography, particular products, and ethnic and cultural mixtures—the peoples of Latin America and the Caribbean have had the misfortune of sharing similar experiences over the long haul.

The region considered for this book was not officially constituted as a province until 1878. The boundaries of the contemporary province remain very similar to those established in the late nineteenth century. Archival materials were examined for all Matanzas *jurisdicciones* and *partidos*, provincial administrative subdivisions. References in the text to the "province" refer to the region constituted in 1878.

Research was conducted in a number of archival collections; the most important were the Archivo Histórico Provincial de Matanzas and the Archivo Nacional de Cuba. The Matanzas archive, located in the center of the old city, is one of the best organized and most pleasant to work in throughout Cuba. I had the privilege of being the first foreigner to be permitted to examine systematically the various collections. Materials from Matanzas are contained in all of the vast *fondos* at the Archivo Nacional, and these were studied in as much detail as possible. The Biblioteca Nacional José Martí, in Havana, is another repository for primary documentary materials from Matanzas, as is the Biblioteca Gener y del Monte in Matanzas.

Cuban materials were also examined in the Ultramar collection at the Archivo Histórico Nacional, Madrid; the Biblioteca Nacional de España, Madrid; the Public Records Office, London; the Manuscript Division of the New York Public Library, which contains the rich Moses Taylor Collection; the Library of Congress; and the U.S. National Archives.

I have tried as much as possible to avoid repeating the findings of other scholars who have contributed to the rich historiography on sugar and slavery in nineteenth-century Cuba. Of course, I owe an intellectual debt to the many pioneering studies cited throughout this work.

ACKNOWLEDGMENTS

In a sense this book is the result of a collective effort from which I benefited over the course of the past six years. For their generous support, I owe many people and institutions my gratitude. I want to extend special thanks to my "socio" Armando Fernández Soriano, of Casa de las Américas, for his much-appreciated help in resolving so many details during my research trips to Cuba.

The old-style hospitality provided by the staff of the Archivo Histórico Provincial de Matanzas made research quite enjoyable. I want to thank Saúl Vento, the director, for sharing—on numerous hot, muggy afternoons when my eyes were too tired to go on reading—the knowledge and experiences garnered over a long life in Matanzas. Compañeras Graciela, Teresa, Olga, and Orquídea fulfilled many requests, always with graciousness and humor.

I thank Julio LeRiverend, director of the Biblioteca Nacional José Martí, for helping secure permission from the Cuban Academy of Sciences to work in the Archivo Nacional de Cuba in 1982. Efficient work there would have been impossible without the generous assistance of my good friend and colleague, Fé Iglesias García, the Cuban historian who is a one-person guide to the collections at the Archivo Nacional. I also thank her for the many stimulating hours we spent discussing and disagreeing on the themes and interpretations contained in this book. The staff of the Archivo Nacional went out of their way to make my work efficient and productive. My sincere thanks go to many unnamed people there who often wondered aloud why I was copying so many numbers.

I want to express my gratitude to Mirta Martínez, of the public library in Matanzas, the Biblioteca Gener y del Monte, for helping me track down nineteenth-century newspapers, and for her enthusiastic interest in my project. The "refrescos" that so often appeared made many a steamy afternoon more bearable.

The help of Israel Echeverría of the Biblioteca Nacional José Martí is greatly appreciated, especially his patience with my requests to photograph old maps. I also want to thank the staff of the Colección Cubana for their assistance.

I must thank the custodians and administrators of resources closer to home, especially the staff of the New York Public Library. Many anonymous librarians unknowingly contributed time and patience to the research for this book. I especially want to express my thanks to the personnel of the Manuscript Division for their help. The same acknowledgments are due to the staff of the National Archives of the United States.

The assistance of Olga Torres, of the Lehman College Library, was indispensable. My many requests for obscure nineteenth-century Cuban books were carefully researched, and almost always she was able to locate them and call them in via interlibrary loan. I thank her for so much patience.

I also want to thank my close friend Luis M. Rodríguez for a great deal. He was an adventurous companion and research assistant during the summer of 1986, and his artistic skills are responsible for the map reproductions contained in this book.

Stanley Engerman's detailed criticisms and suggestions were immensely helpful in fine-tuning the final version of this book, and I want to thank him for his meticulous efficiency and care in reading a very long manuscript. I also thank Rebecca Scott for her comments on the original draft of this book.

Charles B. Purrenhage copyedited the manuscript version of this book. The changes he made on nearly every page immensely improved the prose, and I want to express my gratitude for his professional dedication and careful editing.

Several institutions provided the financial assistance that made research and writing possible. I want to thank the City University of New York and the Professional Staff Congress for providing funds to support summer research trips to Cuba, England, and Spain. My thanks go, moreover, to Barbara Bralver, director of the Grants Office at Lehman College, for reading my proposals and facilitating administration of these grants. I also express my appreciation to María and Adelaide, who always helped with many requests. Brenda Newman and Miriam Korman of the CUNY Research Foundation efficiently answered many queries. The John Simon Guggenheim Memorial Foundation and the Latin American and Caribbean Program of the Social Science Research Council generously provided financial support for the final stages of research and the writing of this book. I want to thank both institutions, for without their support I would not have been able to complete this project. I also thank Lehman College for providing a one-year sabbatical leave.

Finally, and most sincerely, I wish to convey appreciation to my children for sometimes, certainly not always, attempting to understand why I devoted so much time and energy to this book, often at their expense. Yara and Alejandro have paid an emotional price for the time this project took their father away from them. I want them to know that even though it sometimes may not seem so to them, they are part of this book, and my thoughts of them are interwoven into every page. I hope my periodic lack of attention to their needs will be understood and forgiven some day.

My mother and father have continually provided unwavering and unselfish support in so many ways. They are unique people whom I admire, love, and respect. Thanks for so very much, especially your example.

Skyview Acres
Pomona, New York
May 1989

ABBREVIATIONS

AHN	Archivo Histórico Nacional (Madrid)
AHPM	Archivo Histórico Provincial de Matanzas (Matazas)
ANC	Archivo Nacional de Cuba (Havana)
DN	Nieto y Cortadellas, *Dignidades nobiliarias en Cuba* (1954)
DUSCC	Despatches of United States Consuls at Cárdenas
DUSCM	Despatches of United States Consuls at Matanzas
exp.	*expediente*—dossier or file
FO	Foreign Office
fol.	folio
HFC	Santa Cruz y Mallen, *Historia de familias cubanas* (1940)
leg.	*legajo*—box or bundle of papers
ME	Miscelánea de Expedientes
NYPL	New York Public Library
PN	Protocolos Notariales
PRO	Public Records Office (London)
RG	Record Group
SPSS	Statistical Package for the Social Sciences
USNA	United States National Archives (Washington, D.C.)

INTRODUCTION

CHAPTER 1

Matanzas before Sugar:
The Frontier Cattle and
Tobacco Economy

Early in the sixteenth century, twenty-seven weary shipwrecked Spaniards were ferried across a spacious bay called Guánima in the canoes of seemingly friendly indigenous peoples. All were brutally drowned but one. The lone survivor was discovered in 1513 by the Narváez expedition, and he told the story of the massacre that gave the future city and province its name—Matanzas.

The early explorers of the Spanish Main all entered the bay: Ocampo in 1508, Narváez in 1513, Grijalva in 1518, and the Adelantado Diego Velázquez in 1519. Two small native villages, located on the eastern shore near the mouths of the Guaybaca (Buey Vaca) and Caneymar (Canimar) rivers, were often requisitioned for provisions, but no permanent Spanish presence was established owing to the lack of placer gold deposits.

In 1532 the Oidor of Hispaniola, Juan de Vadillo, noted that settlers in the south-coast town of Trinidad voiced a desire to populate the land around Matanzas Bay. However, there is no record of settlement until the 1540s, when a number of colonizers abandoned Trinidad and Sancti Spíritus for the trek across the island to a place with a markedly contrasting spiritual ambience. They built rudimentary homes on high ground north and south of the San Juan River, fished the pristine waters of the bay, and planted a mixture of native and European fruits and vegetables with the help of Indian labor.

The fleet from Vera Cruz took refuge in the bay in 1555, and notices of corsairs were frequent. But in 1570, when the Obispo de Cuba, Juan del Castillo, traveled through his diocese to conduct a census, there were no towns in the Matanzas region. The infamous Sir Francis Drake, frustrated in his attempt to lay siege to Havana in 1586, retreated to Matanzas and reported that the shores were deserted.[1]

Although permanent settlements had not yet been established, in the mid-sixteenth century the area's natural resources attracted the attention of a small elite that was consolidating its political power in the incipient port of Havana. Endowed with rich natural pastures that could support an abundance of cattle, and with thickly wooded hardwood forests to provide timber for the city's construction and embryonic shipyards, legal rights to exploit the region were sought by wealthy *habaneros*, presaging future patterns of domination. This was accomplished by petitioning local authorities for usufruct rights over land through requests for *mercedes de tierra*.[2]

Two types of grants were sought, *hatos* for *ganado mayor* (bovine cattle); and *corrales* for *ganado menor* (pigs). Since population was scarce and land abundant, early grants did not specify land area but were designated by recognized geographical landmarks, usually rivers. By 1579, however, overwhelmed with petitions and conflicting claims, cabildos were ordered to fix the exact center of all prior and future awards. The *agrimensor*, or surveyor, became an indispensable functionary, and the confusing circular system of Cuban landed property emerged. (See Map 1 for hatos and corrales existing in 1800.)

At the center of each hato a *bramadero*, or marker, was fixed, the merced extending 2 leagues from that point in every direction. The center of a corral was marked by a *recogedor*, usufruct extending to the edges of a circle with a 1-league radius.[3] Hatos and corrales were both referred to as haciendas and later, when multiple heirs took possession, as "haciendas ganaderas." This circular character of landed property persisted through the early nineteenth century and repeatedly generated much confusion over property rights: centers were often established too close to existing grants, and sweeping arcs of land with few visible boundaries frequently overlapped.

Requests to the Havana cabildo for land in Matanzas were numerous from the mid-sixteenth through the seventeenth centuries. The first recipient was Inés de Gamboa, the widow of an early settler, Pedro Velázquez. In March 1558 she was awarded Hato Caneimar, which encompassed the fertile land around the Canimar River and extended west to the site of the future town. Gamboa was also granted a corral to the south of the bay, Macuriges, along the rudimentary east–west road, and after marrying for a second time in 1561 to the Regidor of Havana, Alonso Suárez de Toledo, another grant to the west of the bay, Puerto Escondido, was acquired.[4]

These early Matanzas entrepreneurs, absentees living in Havana, sought to capitalize on the opportunities offered by the gradual economic expansion taking place in the colonial capital during the second half of the sixteenth century. After the conquest of the Aztecs in the early 1520s, the Crown established a fleet system for the transatlantic crossing in order to protect its treasures from marauders. By the 1560s two fleets set sail from the Peninsula each year; one headed for Vera Cruz, the other bound for Panama. They met in Havana before embarking on the return voyage.

The establishment of Havana as a central cog in the colonial commercial

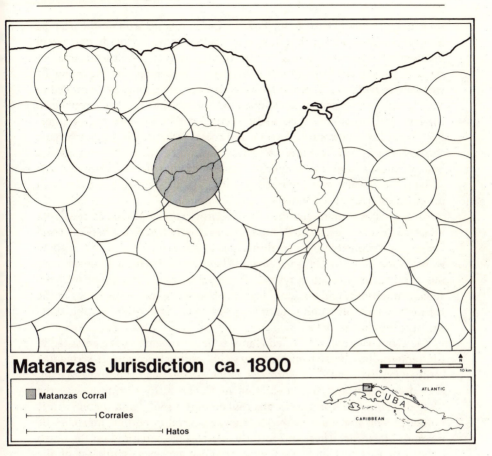

Matanzas Jurisdiction ca. 1800

Matanzas Corral
Corrales
Hatos

ATLANTIC
CUBA
CARIBBEAN

Map 1. Matanzas Hatos and Corrales, ca. 1800

SOURCE: Biblioteca Nacional José Martí, Colección Cubana, "Plano demonstrativo de la jurisdicción de Matanzas. Isla de Cuba. 25 de septiembre de 1800."

system heralded the development of numerous dynamic economic activities revolving around servicing and administering the fleet. Shipyards for construction and repair arose, demanding timber, a diverse array of hardware, skilled artisans, and a variety of other provisions. Transients traveling to the mainland colonies or returning to Europe, ship crews, and colonial bureaucrats and their retainers swelled the city's population when the fleet was docked. A diversified consumer market for food products developed in the growing port and stimulated the proliferation of vegetable and fruit farms in the surrounding countryside.[5]

Havana also consumed great quantities of salted beef or pork, and ships sought hides, tallow, or other cattle by-products to fill remaining space in their holds before departing for Europe. Cattle roamed wild on the island's natural pastures, and little effort was made to fence in herds or control breeding. Periodically animals were hunted, driven toward Havana, or slaughtered and stripped of hides, which were then shipped to the capital or transported overland. From as far away as Puerto Príncipe, cattle moved to the Havana market trudging along a road system that gradually connected the port with other Cuban population centers.[6] Well-traveled routes developed from Havana toward the southern coast, eastward on the north coast through the Matanzas region, southeast toward the cities of Trinidad and Sancti Spíritus, and on to Puerto Príncipe. Rudimentary overland roads serving the Havana-based market for cattle products linked Matanzas with other major areas of settlement.

An economic system emerged in sixteenth-century Matanzas revolving around a primitive cattle economy that was closely tied to the Havana market. It was dominated by a small nucleus of powerful families, all in some way connected to the Havana cabildo. They consolidated control over various rural zones through a system of mercedes based upon nepotism, personal connections, and no doubt bribery. Urban life was nonexistent in the future province, although fishermen and small-scale farmers inhabited areas near the expansive bay.

The Gamboa–Suárez de Toledo family does not seem to have persisted in the region after the sixteenth century, but another prominent sixteenth-century family, headed by Antón Recio y Castaños and his brother Martín, played an important role in subsequent Cuban history.[7] Antón was the "Regidor Perpetuo" of the Havana cabildo in the 1560s, and therefore it is not surprising that he was able to acquire several important mercedes de tierra in Matanzas. These included the corrales of Camarioca on the north coast, just east of Gamboa's Caneimar; Guanajayabos, southeast of the present city of Cárdenas; and Sabanilla de la Palma, contiguous to Guanajayabos.[8]

In the sixteenth century land itself was of little significance, and agricultural development was confined to the regions around major population centers. Labor was scarce. Few indigenous peoples remained in western Cuba by the second half of the sixteenth century, most African slaves were employed in urban rather than rural occupations, and Cuba could not compete with Mesoamerica and the Andean region for migrants to the New World. Mestizo frontiersmen living scattered about the countryside were supplemented by small numbers of slaves to meet the labor demands of a primitive cattle economy.

The legal rights to wild cattle roaming the countryside were the principal benefits derived from early land grants in the Matanzas region. Mercedes were sought in order to capitalize on commercial opportunities emerging with the impressive growth of transatlantic trade after the discovery of silver in Zacatecas and Potosí, and to take advantage of the central role Havana occupied in colonial commerce.

The Matanzas cattle economy supported a variety of ancillary economic activities in the late sixteenth and early seventeenth centuries. Foreign ships frequently appeared in the unfortified bay, and a flourishing contraband trade was nurtured by settlers in the interior or near the coast. Matanzas became a well-known port of call for French, Dutch, and British ships plying the Caribbean on official or more sinister missions. A small local market for produce, hides, and salted meat developed, and these were exchanged for European manufactured goods and sometimes slaves.

In the interior, along the east–west road crossing the island from Havana to Santiago, several population centers emerged. Small frontier inns lodged travelers and serviced the cattle drives moving toward the capital.[9] In Guamutas, on the road to Puerto Príncipe, a church was constructed in the late sixteenth or early seventeenth century. Guamacaro, a crossroads settlement with one *camino* leading north to Matanzas Bay while the other continued on to Havana, became another incipient town.[10]

By the early seventeenth century, not one but two roads extended east from Havana. One pushed along the northern tier of the island toward Matanzas Bay, then east past the future cities of Cárdenas and Sagua la Grande, directly through the area that would become Las Villas, and on to Puerto Príncipe. The other moved southeast through the Güines Valley, then crossed the vast plain to the north of the Ciénaga de Zapata, on through the rich land of the future Matanzas *partido* of Hanábana (where indigenous peoples by that name once thrived) and past Xagua Bay, which would become Cienfuegos, and finally on to Trinidad and Sancti Spíritus. Along this route the village of Macuriges became a resting point for travelers.[11]

The region around the Río Canimar, which runs from south to north and enters the east side of Matanzas Bay, was another center of early colonial settlement. Navigable for nearly seven miles inland by small boats or flat barges, it became a major trade route linking the timber-rich hardwood forests of the Matanzas interior to the bay and then the Havana shipyards. Along the banks of the Canimar, small subsistence farms flourished as well.

Rivers flowing into the western and southern perimeters of the bay also attracted settlers. Along the Yumurí, San Juan, and San Agustín, small farming settlements were established, distant enough from the coast to avoid frequent marauders, but close enough to trade with smugglers if conditions were favorable. The men who periodically rounded up cattle or pigs lived along the banks of these rivers.

Although several successful sugar mills were established around the port of Havana in the sixteenth century, there is no indication that sugarcane was grown or processed in Matanzas. It is likely that cane was planted as part of the general biological experimentation with the adaptability of European crops, and there may have been some primitive production of molasses. But it was not until the seventeenth century that the region's first *trapiches* appeared. Along the banks of the Río de Cañas, a tributary of the San Agustín which merges with the San Juan before it empties into the bay, Francisco Díaz Pimienta built Ingenio el Salto in the early 1620s, popularly referred to as Ingenio Viejo. Its grinding machinery powered by water, the mill gained notoriety in 1628 when the commander of the silver fleet, Juan de Benavides, sought refuge there after the Dutch drove his ships toward Matanzas.[12]

This enterprise seems to have met an early demise, for there are no notices of its survival by the late seventeenth century, although other attempts at fomenting sugar production followed. In 1667, Juan de Sotolongo, a Havana military official and noted entrepreneur, was granted a merced of 90 caballerías of land to construct an ingenio along the banks of the Canimar.[13] The fate of this mill is also unknown.

By the latter half of the seventeenth century, after a long period of official neglect, the region began to receive a great deal of notice. Royal attention had emphatically been drawn to Matanzas with the loss of the fleet in 1628, and although Cuba's seventeenth-century captains general were well aware of the contraband trade conducted from the region, they were powerless to intervene. Havana's critical role as the rendezvous point for the two fleets meant that revenues allocated to Cuba by the Crown were usually destined for the capital's fortifications and general maintenance.

However, the threat to Cuba posed by Spain's European rivals, whose trading presence in the Caribbean grew impressively during the seventeenth century, was underscored by the English seizure of Jamaica in 1655. Plans to fortify strategically located points throughout Cuba followed. With the urging of Captain General Francisco Xelder, the possibility of erecting a small fortress on the west side of Matanzas Bay, at Punta Gorda, was actively discussed in the late 1650s.[14] Although revenues were not forthcoming, a desire to impose control over the thriving contraband trade and to establish an official presence led to a formal plan for fortifications by the early 1680s.

In 1680 a map was prepared for insular authorities detailing the geography of the bay. It fixed the precise location and general plan for the construction of a fortress, and it designated the land between the Yumurí and San Juan rivers as ideal for the founding of an official town.[15] Although no one inhabited this land, the map indicates the presence of fishermen on the coast just to the north of the Yumurí and the existence of regular ferry service across the bay in local *lanchas*.

The Crown authorized construction of fortifications in 1684, and in 1690 issued orders that a town be founded at the precise location indicated on the 1680 map. The land on which the future town was to be erected was part of the Corral de Matanzas, acquired as a rural retreat by the Havana-based Convento de Santa Clara. Despite the fact that land was theoretically owned by the king, the Crown was obliged to pay 8,000 ducats (11,000 pesos) to the order for legal rights. A surveyor laid out the perpendicular streets and fixed the location of the church. Thirty immigrant families from the Canary Islands were recruited as "pobladores," who were sold urban plots "a censo" and awarded small parcels of land along the San Juan River. In October 1693 San Carlos y San Severino de Matanzas was officially founded.[16]

Formal establishment of a Spanish town did little to disrupt local life in the late seventeenth and early eighteenth centuries. The Canary Islanders settling Matanzas immersed themselves vigorously in the region's economy. By the 1690s the traditional dependence on cattle, wood, and subsistence farming, had given way to the widespread cultivation of tobacco. Supported by the thriving trade with foreign ships regularly appearing in the bay, tobacco was first planted in the 1630s on *vegas* established near the Río San Agustín.

Tobacco planting gradually spread along the fertile banks of the area's major rivers. Centers of tobacco cultivation were established in the Yumurí Valley, close to the river; along the San Agustín southwest to the incipient population center of Ceiba Mocha, whose original settlers were tobacco *vegueros*; south from the bay along the San Juan to the future interior town of Santa Ana; on the north coast west of the bay, along the Canasí River; and to the east on the flatland near the well-traveled Canimar.[17]

Matanzas tobacco was not used to manufacture cigars but to produce snuff (*rapé* or *polvillo* in the local lexicon), which enjoyed popularity among the nobility of northern Europe. The locally produced leaf was a light green variety, very different from the aromatic darker leaf later grown in the Vuelta Abajo. This type of tobacco assumed the name *verdín* for its color and was actively sought by the smugglers frequenting the bay. The Canary Islanders settling the region in the 1690s planted little but tobacco on the land bestowed them along the Río San Juan.

The local tobacco economy continued its growth in the early eighteenth century and resulted in a phenomenon unique to Matanzas: the construction of two "molinos de tabaco," or snuff mills, which stimulated the further spread of tobacco farming in the region. In 1715, Manuel José de Jústiz y Umpierrez requested permission to construct a tobacco mill on the San Agustín River, near the location of Ingenio Viejo built a century before. By 1717, despite the establishment of the first *factoría* (the royal monopoly on tobacco processing and marketing), the mill was operating, and shortly thereafter Jústiz financed the construction of a second mill, located at the junction of the Cañas and San Agustín rivers.

The entrance of Jústiz into the tobacco economy marks the beginning of an important new phase in the economic history of Matanzas. While habaneros had been drawn by the region's primitive cattle economy from the mid-sixteenth century, and although numerous mercedes had been awarded by the Havana cabildo, few families maintained a lasting presence. Havana capital developed the first sugar mill in the early seventeenth century, but this effort also failed to leave an imprint on Matanzas society.

From its origins in the 1630s, Matanzas tobacco cultivation had been based almost entirely on local efforts. Vegas were small-scale family-farm operations with little or no outside capital involvement, and there were no large landed estates. The economic lifeline of seventeenth-century Matanzas vegueros revolved around the regular contraband trade. In a sense, the official founding of the town was little more than a minor disruption of local autonomy. Royal officials were unable to alter substantially the firmly established patterns of illicit trade at the beginning of the eighteenth century.

But the appearance of Jústiz in Matanzas substantially changed the economic and political realities of the region. The snuff mill offered a relatively stable market for tobacco farmers and an incentive to expanded planting. Now, however, a monopoly was established on snuff production by a well-connected outside political figure, and this heralded the end of independent tobacco-leaf marketing to the smugglers who had traditionally fueled the local economy. After 1717, Matanzas vegueros had but one outlet for their principal product, an absentee with the power of colonial government behind his enterprise. In essence, Jústiz personified the tobacco monopoly. If the official founding of the town meant the entrance of external political forces intent on imposing the authority of the colonial state, the establishment of the snuff mills heralded the arrival of outside economic interests that would gradually overwhelm the region over the course of the next century.

Jústiz was a criollo, born in Havana in 1689. His father had come to Cuba from Guipuzcoa, Spain, sometime in the early 1680s, probably as a government official of some rank. Before his vocation as a tobacco entrepreneur, Manuel José rose through the Spanish military and held the positions of Coronel de los Reales Ejércitos, Sargento Mayor y Alcalde de la Fortaleza del Morro in Havana, and Governor and Captain General of San Agustín de la Florida.

His younger brother Juan José, born in 1691, was closely involved in the Matanzas tobacco enterprise, and he had served the Crown as the Alcalde Ordinario of Havana and Contador General de la Real Hacienda of Cuba. These were powerful men, connected to every echelon of the colonial bureaucracy, and it is not surprising that, notwithstanding the proclaimed tobacco monopoly, the Matanzas snuff mills remained in private hands. Manuel, who never married and left no heirs, died in 1750. Juan José's demise came in 1759, but preceding his death he was proclaimed Marqués de Jústiz de Santa Ana. One of his legacies was to have financed the construction of the Matanzas cathedral. The other was to bestow unknowingly the name "del Marqués" to the mill constructed in 1716.[18]

Sometime in the early 1720s Jústiz sold the second mill to another member of the powerful Havana nobility, the Conde de Jibacoa, whose descendants would establish modern sugar ingenios in Matanzas during the nineteenth century. This mill was distinguished from the Jústiz mill by its popular name, "del Conde."

Although the entrance of Havana-based entrepreneurs into the rural world of Matanzas agriculture in the early eighteenth century introduced the element of external control, local tobacco farmers gained several distinct advantages. The first, noted above, was a guaranteed market. The independence of unrestrained linkages with contrabandistas may have been compromised, but a reliable market at the local level offered a new type of stability to tobacco growers. Second, both the conde and the marqués thrust the double-edged sword of credit into rural Matanzas. Advances of cash or supplies could lead to land improvements, the use of better tools, and larger harvests. But the specter of mounting debt might mean ruin over the long term. Third, the presence of powerful, politically connected entrepreneurs at the local level in a sense shielded growers from other predators intent on controlling economic life.

The first royal tobacco monopoly lasted from 1717 through 1724 (it would be resurrected in 1761), but the major regions of Cuban tobacco culture were in the environs of Havana, in the Güines Valley, near Santiago in the east, and increasingly in Pinar del Río.[19] Tobacco may have sustained the Matanzas economy, but royal authorities were spread thin in their futile initial attempt to impose controls on tobacco cultivation and processing. The success of the two snuff mills rested upon tobacco supplies provided by Matanzas growers, and the count and the marquis used their political connections to keep authorities from unwarranted intervention in the Matanzas river valleys where tobacco flourished, at least in the first half of the eighteenth century. They also maintained complete control over their mills, despite the monopoly that theoretically should have precluded private ownership.

The role of mill owners as a buffer between expanding state authority in the region, symbolized by the official founding of the town, the construction of the San Severino fortress, and the imposition of the tobacco monopoly, should not be minimized. In 1741 another external threat appeared: a branch of the Real Compañía de Comercio de la Habana was opened in Matanzas, with the sole purpose of monopolizing the tobacco trade. The Real Compañía was backed by a powerful troika of shareholders that included the royal family, peninsular financiers based in Cádiz, and the wealthiest members of the Havana merchant class. The colonial governor of Cuba was a major shareholder.[20] Modeled on the Real Compañía Guipuzcoana of Caracas, which had been formed in 1728, the Havana-based company was granted a monopoly on all imports and exports from Cuba—difficult to enforce, however, because of the pervasiveness of smuggling in so many regions around the island's coast.

Once again the mill owners temporarily protected Matanzas vegueros from another group of outsiders intent upon profiting from the local tobacco economy. This was not an altruistic gesture but was based upon a desire to keep a viable system functioning with minimal disturbance. Tobacco farming was a delicate operation. Vegas had to be replanted each year, seedlings carefully nurtured and shaded from the sun, and the delicate harvest had to be collected at the precise moment of maturity to guarantee high quality. Although they cultivated tobacco, the mill owners were primarily processors and marketers. Dependent on local sources of labor, and to a great extent on the production of local vegueros, it was in their interest to ensure that tobacco supplies would be not be jeopardized. The Real Compañía and the millers struck a deal. Snuff would be purchased from the mills and exported by the company, according to its legal rights, but growers continued their economic linkages with the mills and would be disturbed as little as possible.[21] Additional credit was pumped into the local economy by the Compañía, and small numbers of slaves had to be introduced, but Matanzas tobacco culture was able to weather yet another intrusion by outsiders. This was an ephemeral situation.

By the mid-eighteenth century, Matanzas began to receive the attention of important Havana-based entrepreneurs who would effectively transform the economic and ecological landscape of the region over the next fifty years. Most functioned as absentees, but some families established a permanent presence in Matanzas. There was an initial interest in the thriving local tobacco culture, but several factors militated against any long-term investments in tobacco planting. The most decisive was the reestablishment of the factoría in 1761, which effectively destroyed Cuban tobacco culture over the next thirty years. By the 1790s Cuba was importing leaf from Virginia.[22]

The Jústiz brothers were both dead by the 1760s, and the descendants of the Conde de Jibacoa shifted their primary interests to sugar. This meant that there were no longer any local power brokers to stand between governmental officials, who gradually established a close relationship with the emerging sugar/slave trade economy and with the independent tobacco growers of the Matanzas river valleys.

To its satisfaction no doubt, the factoría was quite able to control Cuban tobacco production, processing, and marketing in the short term. Its bureaucratic shortsightedness, however, led to the gradual decline of tobacco farming in Matanzas. This was not simply an economic disaster. Independent, small-scale tobacco farmers could not survive in the new economic ambience of stringent controls, which were antithetical both to the product that sustained them and to their very existence as a social class. Their demise by the early nineteenth century meant a decisive end to anything resembling an independent yeoman peasantry in Matanzas.

Tobacco growers came under other pressures as well. The development of sugar culture in Havana after 1740 was disastrous for independent tobacco farmers in those regions coveted by the sugar planters. Vegueros waged a protracted struggle with cattle interests over land rights, but managed to hold their own in all regions of the island through the early eighteenth century. The cattle economy was primitively organized, capital investment was small-scale, and ultimately cattle and tobacco could coexist.

Not so with sugar. In the mid-eighteenth century, Havana's entrepreneurial elite began to construct ingenios in the outlying regions of the capital and slowly pushed southeast toward the fertile Güines Valley, long a center of tobacco production. Despite resistance, vegueros had little hope. They were aligned against powerful economic and political interests determined to reproduce the sugar-based wealth of Jamaica and Haiti. This was especially true after the English occupation of Havana in 1762, when slave imports and virtual free trade fueled the expansion of sugar, and coffee as well.[23] Sugar and coffee planters moved slowly toward zones with high-yielding virgin soils; they practiced a sophisticated type of slash-and-burn agriculture, although cycles of land use and abandonment were certainly not so short as those in subsistence societies having unrestricted land availability. Land contiguous to Havana had been exhausted by excessive exploitation, and the island's river valleys, where tobacco traditionally flourished, were to become the principal centers of cane cultivation until railroads opened up new land to the east in the 1840s.

By and large, Matanzas was on the periphery of this initial phase of sugar expansion, which was centered to the south and southeast of Havana. Coffee appeared in the late 1760s and early 1770s, but the establishment of *cafetales* in Matanzas would begin in earnest only after the Haitian revolution of 1792, which resulted in French immigration to the region. Nevertheless, numerous Havana-based entrepreneurs began to penetrate the future province. Although tobacco was the principal economic resource in the river valleys near the bay, the southern tier of Matanzas had maintained its traditional cattle economy through the end of the eighteenth century. Cattle products thrived on the strength of Havana's consumption, and the expansion of the sugar sector in the second half of the eighteenth century meant the emergence of a new dynamic market for Cuba's cattle ranchers.

Ingenios required a variety of cattle products, from tallow and hides to significantly increased supplies of salted meat for the maintenance of expanding slave populations. They also needed a large and stable supply of draft animals. Sugar-mill owners sought land not only for cane fields in river valleys, but also for *potreros,* or stock-raising farms, to nurture the animals that powered grinding machinery and hauled cane-filled carts from field to mill. The old practice of allowing cattle to run wild on natural pastures, now seen as potential cane fields, was gradually replaced by an orderly system complete with fences, concerted attempts at breeding, and the planting of artificial pastures. The frontier cowhand who occasionally participated in cattle slaughters or roundups was displaced by the *boyero,* or cattle tender, as the primitive cattle hacienda was supplanted by the organized potrero.

The Havana nobility built their mills near Santa María del Rosario, San José de las Vegas, Bejucal, Güines, and all the way to Batabanó on the south coast, following river valleys and existing roads. They also moved into the southern regions of Matanzas to establish control over cattle haciendas.[24]

Almost every powerful member of the Havana nobility had established a presence in Matanzas by the 1770s.[25] These are familiar surnames in Cuba: the O'Farrill, Montalvo, Calvo, Zequeira, Recio, Zayas, and Armenteros families were among the most prominent. The Conde de Macuriges is a case worth noting. The title was granted to Lorenzo Montalvo y Montalvo in 1765. Born in Valladolid in 1704, he came to Cuba as Intendente General de la Marina and became the patriarch to a large family that would become one of the most powerful in Cuba during the nineteenth century. Montalvo established the ingenios Santísima Trinidad and San Blas in the Havana partidos of Managua and Canoa. He also owned the following haciendas in the future Matanzas partido of Macuriges: Ranchuelo, El Ciego, La Güira, and remarkably the entire Ciénaga de Zapata. His son, Ignacio Montalvo y Ambulodi, became one of the most powerful men in late-eighteenth-century Cuba. Named Conde de Casa Montalvo in 1779, Ignacio was one of the founding members of the Real Consulado de Agricultura y Comercio; in 1794, along with Francisco Arango y Parreño, he embarked on the first official Cuban mission to study sugar technology abroad.[26]

The O'Farrills were among the first Havana families actually to establish sugar mills in Matanzas, near the town of Ceiba Mocha, which had been an early center of tobacco cultivation. The progenitor of the Cuban O'Farrills was Ricardo O'Farrill y O'Daly, who came to the island early in the eighteenth century. In 1713 the Crown granted a monopoly (*asiento*) on slave imports to the English South Sea Company, and O'Farrill, who was born in Monserrate, was designated as the company's Havana factor. The profits derived from the slave trade made O'Farrill's descendants some of the most powerful men in Cuba. His son, Juan José, married the daughter of the Marqués de Villalta, Luisa María Herrera y Chacón. In the 1780s Juan José owned the ingenio Santo Cristo de la Vera Cruz, one of the largest in Cuba. Their son, Juan Manuel O'Farrill y Herrera, born in 1756, was wed to María Luisa Montalvo, daughter of Ignacio Montalvo, the Conde de Casa Mon-

talvo. Juan Manuel and his brother Rafael established two of the first ingenios in Matanzas in the late eighteenth century. Their brother-in-law, Juan
Manuel O'Farrill y Arrendondo would establish the first steamship service
between Havana and Matanzas in 1819.[27]

Before such well-connected powerful clans the small-scale tobacco farmers and primitive cattle ranchers of Matanzas had limited possibilities of
maintaining their traditional frontier independence. While the early intrud-
ers, the Marqués de Jústiz and the Conde de Jibacoa, worked closely with
local residents in ventures benefiting all to some degree, the sugar-planting
nobility from Havana would prove to be insatiable. They would not rest
until every area of the future province was under their control, until Matanzas had been converted into the richest monocultural sugar-producing
zone in the world and a center of African slavery. The eighteenth-century
independence of the frontier would be a distant memory by the middle of
the nineteenth century.

Statistical data on Matanzas are available for the first time in 1774, when
an organized census was conducted throughout Cuba. Administratively,
Matanzas was part of the jurisdiction of Havana, although separate data
exist for the city and its surrounding rural areas.[28] The total population of
3,249 included 901 slaves, 27.7 percent of all inhabitants, but the rural/
urban population distribution is unknown. Luis de las Casas, the colonial
governor known for his support of the Havana nobility's efforts to modernize public administration and the economy, supervised another census in
1792 which revealed a 91.3 percent increase in the region's population since
1774. A total population of 6,216 was found, of whom 30.6 percent (1,900)
were slaves. These data are summarized in Table 1.1.

Data on rural Matanzas in the late eighteenth century indicate the state
of agricultural development. One of the most notable aspects was the persistence of small farms and tobacco vegas. In 1778 there were 306 farms
classified as "estancias y vegas," although there was no distinction made
between the two. By 1792, 515 farms fell into this category.

The establishment of stock-raising farms was another significant feature
of late-eighteenth-century rural life, reflecting the shift toward a more regularized and organized cattle sector in the economy. Three rural properties
were classified as potreros in 1778; twenty-two in 1792. These farms must
be carefully distinguished from the old haciendas on which cattle roamed
wild and were rounded up or slaughtered when needed.[29]

The sugar sector was of minor significance until the 1790s, when prices
soared on world markets owing to the withdrawal of Haitian sugar because
of the great slave rebellion. In 1766 there were only two ingenios in Matanzas; in 1778 there were five; and in 1792 the number stood at eight. But
between 1792 and 1796 another new phase in the economic history of the
region began. Ten new sugar ingenios were constructed in Matanzas, and

Table 1.1. Matanzas Population by Race, Legal Status, and Sex, 1774–1792

	1774		1792	
	Pop.	%	Pop.	%
Whites	2,017	62.1	3,418	55.0
Males	1,163		1,945	
Females	854		1,473	
Free Colored	331	10.2	898	14.4
Males	174		672	
Females	157		226	
Slaves	901	27.7	1,900	30.6
Males	515		1,156	
Females	386		744	
TOTAL	3,249	100.0	6,216	100.0

SOURCE: AHPM, ME, Estadística, leg. 1, no. 5.
NOTE: Pop. = population.

by 1796 eighteen ingenios produced 3,672 boxes of sugar.[30] Sugar planters were no doubt attracted to the region by the official opening of the port of Matanzas to foreign trade in early 1794.

Data for 1799 show that five ingenios in Macuriges utilized 661 slaves (132.2/ingenio). There were five ingenios directly to the south of the bay, in Santa Ana, but of a much smaller scale since they used a total of 125 slaves, or 25 per ingenio. In the Yumurí Valley nine ingenios utilized 381 slaves, or 42.3/ingenio.[31] No production data are known to exist.

Conspicuously, no coffee farms are indicated in the 1778 and 1792 agricultural censuses, although it is likely that some were included under the category of estancias. However, a contemporary description from 1797 notes that the old tobacco center of Ceiba Mocha was "surrounded by flat, picturesque coffee farms." In the partido of Canasí, on the north coast to the west of Matanzas Bay, there were two coffee farms in 1797: Mohá, with 20,000 matas worked by 19 slaves, and Bellavista with 36,000 matas and 28 slaves.[32] Coffee cultivation would spread rapidly in Matanzas in the first two decades of the nineteenth century.

Despite the incipient changes taking place in the region, statistical data for 1796 emphasize the predominance of traditional forms of land owner-ship and use. It was estimated that 2,000 caballerías in Matanzas were oc-cupied by ingenios, "sitios de labor," estancias, and potreros, while in Ma-curiges 1,000 caballerías fell into the same categories. However, the old circular haciendas occupied 4,107 caballerías in Matanzas, and there were 31,590 caballerías of land belonging to haciendas in Macuriges. Other regions of rural Matanzas dominated by traditional circular haciendas in 1796 include Guamacaro, with 5,054 caballerías; Guamutas, with 19,270 caballerías; and Hanábana, with 57,494 caballerías.[33] These patterns of land use indicate that the frontier was by and large intact by the turn of the nineteenth century. The availability of huge areas of underutilized land would attract powerful entrepreneurs to the region over the next several decades.

PART ONE

Sugar and Coffee Invade the Frontier: Matanzas before Railroads, 1800–1837

CHAPTER 2

Matanzas in the Early Nineteenth Century

Three factors pushed sugar from the environs of Havana toward frontier areas to the south, southeast, and east in the late eighteenth century. The first was soil exhaustion in the region surrounding the port city. Cane cultivation thrived on high-yielding virgin soils, but when fertility waned sugar production was no longer economically viable. By 1800 Havana was surrounded by small-scale truck farms and potreros geared toward provisioning the urban market.[1] There were no sugar-producing trapiches close to the colonial capital.

The second factor was related to the enormous demand for wood by the sugar sector and the destruction of forest reserves near Havana by the late eighteenth century. In 1796 José Ricardo O'Farrill estimated that each Cuban ingenio consumed three-quarters of a caballería of wood (25.2 acres) per *zafra*, and this was before the installation of steam engines, which used even greater quantities. On the eve of the nineteenth century there were approximately 400 ingenios in the jurisdiction of Havana, consuming 300 caballerías (10,800 acres) of woodland each year. The impossibility of transporting large supplies of timber from distant areas, because of a poor road system and reliance on oxcarts, meant that ingenios had to be relocated near forest reserves.[2]

The third factor was linked to the capital-accumulation process Cuba experienced in the latter half of the eighteenth century. Entrepreneurial inclinations were the hallmark of the Havana nobility, who in a sense mirrored the economic behavior of Europe's nascent capitalist class. Capital was a resource to be harnessed and employed in productive endeavors, not simply dissipated in conspicuous consumption.

Profits garnered during the initial phase of sugar expansion in the 1760s and 1770s were utilized to construct new ingenios and import greater numbers of slaves in the 1780s and 1790s. The sharp rise in world prices for sugar during the 1790s, which increased from 8 to 14 cents/pound at the local level between 1790 and 1795, meant huge profits for planters with established mills.[3] These profits, in turn, were invested in the further expansion of the sugar sector in the late 1790s and early 1800s, and were also used to finance slave trading and coffee cultivation.[4]

Endowed with all of the elements required for sugar production—forests, virgin land, natural pastures, and navigable rivers—Matanzas became a center of sugar and slavery in the early nineteenth century. Capital accumulated in the late eighteenth century by Havana-based entrepreneurs was used to purchase land, construct ingenios, and encroach upon the patrimony of earlier settlers.[5] In addition, the growth of sugar culture led to improvements in infrastructure, the appearance of local credit facilities, and the general economic development of the region which attracted substantial investments in coffee planting as well.

The First Ingenios and Factors
Favoring Economic Growth

The first important nuclei of Matanzas sugar production coalesced in areas close to the bay, along the region's many rivers. Eighteen ingenios were producing sugar in 1796, and by the early years of the nineteenth century twenty-five ingenios were in full production. Five were located in the Yumurí Valley, north of the river. Two of these were owned by old Havana families: one by the Marquesa de Jústiz, the great-niece of the tobacco entrepreneur; the other by Bernardo Junco, Capitán de Dragones y Alcalde Ordinario of Matanzas, who also served as administrator of the Real Aduana, the port's customshouse. The Junco family had settled in San Agustín de la Florida in the late sixteenth century, moved to Havana sometime in the mid-seventeenth century, and appeared in Matanzas toward the end of the eighteenth century.[6]

Five other ingenios were located to the southwest of the Yumurí Valley, north of the Río San Agustín and between the villages of Corral Nuevo and Ceiba Mocha. Two of these were owned by the Lamar brothers, José Ignacio and Luis; another was operated by Manuel del Portillo, José Ignacio Lamar's father-in-law, who was the factor of the royal tobacco monopoly in Matanzas. The Lamars originally hailed from Bordeaux, France, one branch settling in Louisiana and another in Havana in the mid-seventeenth century. The family was drawn to Matanzas through the activities of Luis Lamar, who in the 1780s was one of the first surveyors to practice his trade in the province.[7]

Farther west, along the north coast on the banks of the Canasí River, two ingenios were owned by well-established Havana families connected by marriage. The Zequeira family, who held the title Condado de Lagunillas, owned one; the Garros, intermarried with the Herreras and holding the title Condado de Fernandina, owned the other.[8]

South of the San Agustín, along the Río Cañas in the direction of the village of Santa Ana, officially established in 1794, there were ten ingenios. The Conde de Jibacoa, Gonzalo Herrera y Santa Cruz (whose son was married to a Garro), owned one mill near the family's old tobacco *molino*, and the Marqués de San Felipe owned another. The origins of the other eight families operating sugar mills are unknown.

Finally, the O'Farrill brothers, Rafael and Manuel, operated the two mills most distant from the port, southwest of Ceiba Mocha and geographically closer to sugar interests expanding from Havana rather than from the Matanzas bay area. (See Map 2 for these early nineteenth-century ingenios.)

Thus, the Matanzas sugar industry was initially developed in the 1790s and early 1800s by an elite having powerful political connections and a history of entrepreneurial activity in the jurisdiction of Havana. Sugar prospered in Matanzas not only because of ideal natural conditions, but also because of the capital and know-how accumulated over the previous half-century. The founders of ingenios in this early phase of sugar expansion were already familiar with productive methods and with the nuances of international markets. They were not faced with the traditional problems encountered by infant industries: experimenting by trial and error with relatively unknown methods, often resulting in innumerable and costly short-term errors. Access to markets had been opened from the 1760s; sources of foreign technology had been secured and broadened with the independence of the United States and the growth in trade with that new nation; techniques of production had been refined; a transatlantic slave trade guaranteed labor supplies and did not have to be developed from scratch; and institutional supports existed in Havana, such as the Real Consulado de Agricultura y Comercio and the Sociedad Económica de Amigos del País, established in the early 1790s.[9] In short, a productive system that had already resolved many initial difficulties was transferred from Havana to Matanzas and installed in an environment conducive to rapid growth.

Several other important factors provided conditions favoring the development of a sugar and coffee export economy in Matanzas during the first two decades of the nineteenth century. The first was the official opening of the port. In 1794 Matanzas was permitted to trade with Spanish ports of call; and in May 1809, while King Fernando VII was a French prisoner and revolutionary juntas were forming throughout colonial Spanish America, the Junta de Autoridades Superiores in Havana opened Matanzas to foreign shipping.[10] This simply legalized a de facto situation: commerce had been carried on from the port for years, and official trade data had even been collected beginning in 1806.[11] Nonetheless, an institutional obstacle had been removed from international trade, which now could be considered something other than smuggling or contraband. In 1818 all Cuban ports were opened to unrestricted trade with foreign nations.[12]

A second obstacle to economic expansion was eliminated with the 1815

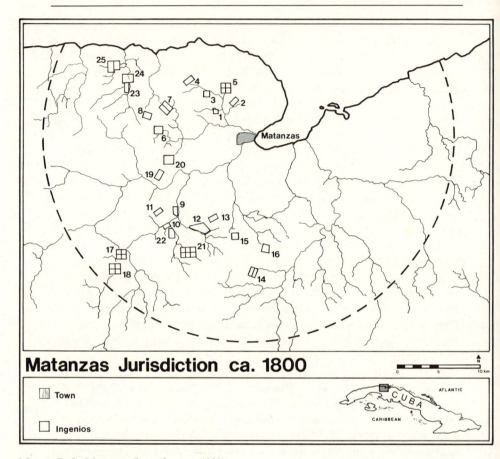

Map 2. Early Matanzas Ingenios, ca. 1800.

SOURCE: AHPM, Mapas y Planos, leg. 24, exp. 179, "Plano relativo a la jurisdicción de Matanzas, ingenios, poblaciones, y haciendas."

Guide to Owners: (1) Bernardo Junco, (2) Simón Rodríguez, (3) Bernardo Román, (4) Francisco Domínguez, (5) Marquesa Jústiz, (6) Luis Cavallero, (7) Ignacio Lamar, (8) Manuel Portillo, (9) Tomás Saldivar, (10) Manuel Guerrero, (11) Conde de Jibacoa, (12) Ignacio Álvarez, (13) Esteban Aguiar, (14) Francisco Gómez, (15) Agustín López, (16) Diego Mena, (17) Rafael O'Farril, (18) Manuel O'Farril, (19) Luis Lamar, (20) Gabriel Santoyo, (21) Marqués de San Felipe, (22) José de Castro, (23) José Zequeira, (24) Antonio Garro, (25) Teresa de Zayas.

promulgation of a royal *cédula* allowing landowners to cut wood freely within the boundaries of their properties—"Libertad de Montes y Plantíos." Crown control over Cuba's forests was established in the early colonial period because of the importance of Havana's shipyards. Timber could not be felled without an official license, and the deforestation taking place in the 1760s and 1770s near Havana prompted the founding of a Junta de

Maderas in 1776. Operating with customary bureaucratic inefficiency, requests for permission to clear land were often not considered or were routinely denied.

The creation of an institution representing the sugar interests in the early 1790s, the Real Consulado, was accompanied by an intense campaign to curb the authority of the Junta de Maderas. For in order to expand sugar production, woodland had to be constantly cleared and virgin land planted in cane. The authority of the junta was blatantly flouted, and the reality of unrestricted denuding of forestland was finally legalized in the 1815 decree permitting owners to cut and sell wood freely, thus eliminating another institutional restraint to agricultural growth.[13]

A third factor traditionally inhibiting the development of Cuban agriculture was the legal absence of private land ownership. Cabildos were permitted to grant land in usufruct from the early sixteenth century, until this right was stripped from them in 1729. The huge circular haciendas emerging in the sixteenth and seventeenth centuries were designed to serve a sparsely populated, primitive cattle economy. But as population expanded and multiple heirs claimed sections of old hatos or corrales, legal usufruct rights became chaotic. Undefined boundaries inhibited agricultural expansion; and with the spread of sugar cultivation after the mid-eighteenth century, colonial authorities were increasingly pressured to abolish the old system and institute inalienable land proprietorship.

Even though the process of "demolición," or breakup and conversion of haciendas into de facto private parcels, began in earnest in the late eighteenth century, it was not until 1816 that a royal decree officially sanctioned individual or corporate private property in Cuba. Four means could be used to make legal land claims: presentation to local authorities of documents specifying pre-1729 cabildo land grants; proof of actual family possession for 100 years on uncultivated and 50 years on cultivated land; the existence of legal instruments such as wills or land-sale documents; and the testimony of local cabildos.[14] Although a land market had developed in Cuba in the latter half of the eighteenth century, in the early nineteenth century another institutional obstacle to agricultural expansion was removed with the legal establishment of a modern private property law. (See Map 3 for an illustration of the "demolición" of the Corral de Matanzas.)

Finally, in 1815 Matanzas was declared "cabecera capital de un gobierno territorial," the administrative capital of an officially recognized Cuban jurisdiction. Although an *ayuntamiento* had been established in 1693 with the founding of the town, all of rural Matanzas remained legally part of the jurisdiction of Havana until 1815. Three lightly populated rural partidos theoretically administered a vast hinterland: Hanábana in the southeastern region of the province; Guamutas in the northeastern region; and Macuriges, extending south of Matanzas Bay to the Zapata swamp.[15] The 1815

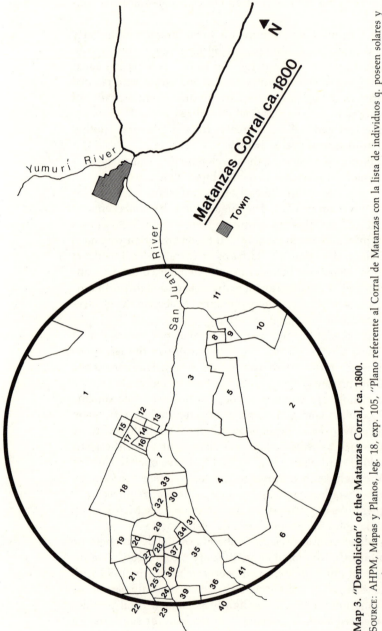

Map 3. "Demolición" of the Matanzas Corral, ca. 1800.

SOURCE: AHPM, Mapas y Planos, leg. 18, exp. 105, "Plano referente al Corral de Matanzas con la lista de individuos q. poseen solares y terrenos en el mismo. 14 de enero de 1801."

Guide to landowners and number of caballerías: (1), (2), and (3) Marquesa Jústiz, 248; (4) Conde de Jibacoa, 40; (5) Potrero de San Juan de Su Majestad, 8; (6) Potrero de Cañas de Su Majestad, 18; (7) Molino de Tabaco de Su Majestad, 5; (8) Francisco Campi, 1; (9) Manuel Antonio Pereira, 1; (10) Esteban Aguiar, 7; (11) José de la Guardia, 15; (12) Capitán de Morenos Gaspa, 0.5; (13) Juan Ávalos, 0.5; (14) Pedro Díaz, 1; (15) Antonio Díaz, 1; (16) Ignacio Olivera, 1; (17) Mariano Guillén, 1; (18) Ignacio Hernández, 18; (19) Unknown; (20) Gabriel Santoyo, 6; (21) José Benítez, 4; (22) José Aguiar, 1; (23) Juan Ávalos, 0.1; (24) Nicolás Benítez, 1; (25) Manuel Benítez, 1; (26) and (27) José de Fuentes, 2; (28) Manuel de Fuentes, 1; (29) Antonio Martínez, 4; (30) Josefa Collaso, 1; (31) Juan Casañolas, 0.5; (32) José Benavides, 1; (33) Ana Olivera, 2; (34) and (35) Juan Salinas, 2; (36) Feliciano del Junco, 10; (37) Bernardino Aguiar, 1; (38) Francisca de Fuentes, 1; (39) Cayetano Benítez, 1; (40) Bernardo Díaz, 0.17; (41) José Medina 3.

decree established local administrative control over an area extending for a radius of 6 leagues (nearly 16 miles) from the cathedral of Matanzas; included were the rural partidos of Yumurí, Ceiba Mocha, Santa Ana, Guamacaro, and Camarioca, the principal areas of settlement and agricultural production.[16] (See Map 4.) In this way, some administrative control over local life was transferred from Havana to Matanzas.

Economic growth in the early years of the nineteenth century was not only linked to investments by the Havana sugar sector. The expansion of production and the official opening of the port led to a substantial rise in international trade during the 1790s and early 1800s. In 1809, 162 ships officially entered the bay, a large number of U.S. origin. The forging of trade linkages between Cuba and the newly independent United States during the Napoleonic period, when European trade with the Caribbean declined owing to constant naval warfare, led to direct investments by U.S. citizens in the Matanzas region.[17] Capital was invested in four areas of economic activity: the establishment of merchant houses; slave trading; sugar production; and coffee farming.[18]

The first attempt to construct permanent dock facilities in Matanzas was undertaken in 1808 and 1809 by an early U.S. firm established in the port, Sres. Latting & Glen. Zacarías Atkins, progenitor of the Atkins family interests in Cuba, was an important Matanzas slave trader in the first two decades of the nineteenth century and was a landowner as well. By 1810 John Rhodes and Joseph Otis owned one of the region's largest coffee plantations, 24 caballerías (806 acres) along the Canimar River, with 56,000 coffee trees in full production. And John Forbes, a merchant established in the city of Matanzas, was co-owner of Ingenio Reunión Deseada in the partido of Santa Ana.[19]

Capital was also channeled into the local economy by Spanish commercial interests. Early-nineteenth-century chronicles note that a group of Spanish entrepreneurs permanently settled the Matanzas bay area after a return to the Peninsula was precluded by the French invasion of Spain in 1808. The most prominent appears to have been Joaquín Madan, a Matanzas merchant and slave trader, whose firm Ximeno y Madan rivaled Latting & Glen in the early nineteenth century. In addition, Matanzas was settled by French immigrants from Louisiana and Haiti in the 1790s and early 1800s. Numerous French surnames appear as owners of cafetales, and some sugar ingenios as well, in the first years of the nineteenth century.[20]

Thus, the early growth of the Matanzas economy was linked to three sources of capital investment. The Havana-based creole nobility became the most important sugar planters in the region, investing capital accumulated through the second half of the eighteenth century. Increased trading linkages with the United States led to the commercial and agricultural penetration of Matanzas by North American merchants, slave traders, and plant-

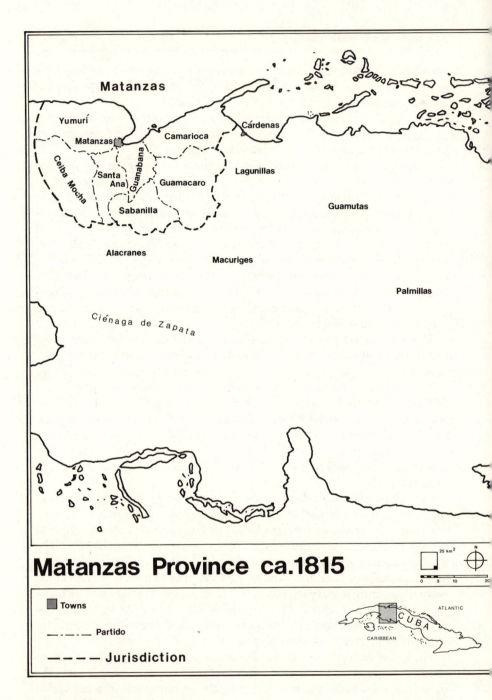

Matanzas

Yumurí

Matanzas

Cárdenas

Camarioca

Ceiba Mocha

Santa Ana

Guanabana

Guamacaro

Lagunillas

Guamutas

Sabanilla

Alacranes

Macuriges

Palmillas

Ciénaga de Zapata

Matanzas Province ca.1815

25 km²

0   5   10   20

N

▦ Towns

—·—·— Partido

— — — Jurisdiction

ATLANTIC

CUBA

CARIBBEAN

Map 4. Matanzas Province, ca. 1815

SOURCE: Esteban Pichardo, *Isla de Cuba. Carta Geotopográfica* (Havana: Dirección de la Capitanía Gener 1860–1872).

ers. Finally, European-based capital was invested in the Matanzas economy by Spanish commercial interests and French migrants who concentrated on agricultural endeavors.

Population Distribution and Agricultural Development

The first detailed quantitative data on Matanzas were generated by a census conducted in 1817 (see tables 2.1 and 2.2). Settlement patterns in early-nineteenth-century Matanzas reflected the region's geography of economic

Table 2.1. Matanzas, 1817: Population by Partido, Race, Legal Status, and Sex

	Whites			Free Blacks and Mulattoes						
				Creoles/Mulattoes			Africans			All Free Colored
	M	F	T	M	F	T	M	F	T	
Matanzas City	1,248	1,172	2,420	442	449	891	61	58	119	1,010
Yumurí	857	691	1,548	35	34	69	16	11	27	96
Ceiba Mocha	1,368	886	2,254	74	64	138	25	16	41	179
Santa Ana	1,083	813	1,896	64	35	99	3	4	7	106
Guamacaro	449	310	759	60	73	133	5	9	14	147
Camarioca	294	240	534	18	13	31	2	3	5	36
TOTAL	5,299	4,112	9,411	693	668	1,361	112	101	213	1,574

	Slaves								
	Creoles/Mulattoes			Africans			All Slaves	Total Pop.	%
	M	F	T	M	F	T			
Matanzas City	212	270	482	256	278	534	1,016	4,446	20.4
Yumurí	150	131	281	1,762	183	1,945	2,226	3,870	17.8
Ceiba Mocha	452	397	849	1,442	538	1,980	2,829	5,262	24.2
Santa Ana	268	175	443	1,292	264	1,556	1,999	4,001	18.4
Guamacaro	909	305	1,214	784	213	997	2,211	3,117	14.3
Camarioca	44	46	90	315	87	402	492	1,062	4.9
TOTAL	2,035	1,324	3,359	5,851	1,563	7,414	10,773	21,758	100.0

SOURCE: AHPM, ME, Estadística, leg. 1, no. 2, "Estadística de Matanzas y los cinco partidos de su jurisdicción. 15 de febrero 1817."
Note: M = males; F = females; T = total; Pop. = population.

development. The city itself was physically confined to the high land between the San Juan and Yumurí rivers in 1815. Although bridges had been
constructed crossing both in the 1780s and 1790s, the future barrios of Versalles and Pueblo Nuevo were still swampland.[21]

Demographic expansion of the city was hardly impressive between 1792
and 1817, when population increased from 3,418 to 4,446, or 1.06 percent
annually. In 1817 a numerous free-black and mulatto population, 22.7 percent of all inhabitants, lived in the town; slaves made up another 22.9 percent of the city's residents. Urban free-black and mulatto communities were
characterized by an equitable distribution of males (49.8 percent) and females (50.2 percent), which probably encouraged the evolution of Afro-
Cuban family life and natural reproduction. Among urban slaves, 53.9 percent were females and 46.1 percent were males. These data are in sharp
contrast with the five rural partidos, where the preference for males by
plantation owners resulted in a marked sex imbalance among slaves: in
1817, 73 percent of all rural slaves in Matanzas were males and 27 percent
were females.

The city's white population, 54.4 percent of all urban inhabitants, was
also characterized by an equitable pattern of sex distribution in 1817: 51.6
percent were males; 48.4 percent, females. While there were more white
males (57.9 percent) than white females in the five rural partidos, sex imbalance was not nearly so pronounced as it was for the slave population.

Table 2.2. Matanzas, 1817:
Number of Establishments, Farms, Operators, and Caballerías of Land

	City of Matanzas	Yumurí	Ceiba Mocha	Santa Ana	Guama- caro	Cama- rioca	Total
Pulperías	26	10	26	20	4	0	86
Almacenes	10	0	4	0	0	0	14
Tiendas	31	0	7	2	0	0	40
Ingenios	0	21	17	24	11	3	76
Cafetales	0	7	15	23	13	17	75
Potreros	0	18	46	35	30	9	138
Sitios	0	180	154	194	69	73	670
Landowners	0	268	230	230	122	97	947
Land Renters	0	122	35	33	0	5	195
Land Area	—	1,680	1,649	2,099	1,487	667	7,582

SOURCE: AHPM, ME, Estadística, leg. 1, no. 2, "Estadística de Matanzas y los cinco partidos de su
jurisdicción. 15 de febrero 1817."
NOTE: Pulperías were small stores, usually selling little more than food products; almacenes were
warehouses; tiendas were general stores, selling a wide variety of products; ingenios were sugar
farms and their mills; cafetales were coffee farms; potreros were stock-raising farms; and sitios
were subsistence farms. A caballería is 33.6 acres.

Southwest of the port along the old *camino real*, Ceiba Mocha had been a center of tobacco culture in the eighteenth century, but by 1817 coffee farms (15) and sugar plantations (17) dominated the local economic structure.[22] This partido was the oldest region of commercial agriculture in Matanzas and was the most densely settled. Nearly one-quarter of the jurisdiction's population lived there in 1817. Slaves accounted for 53.8 percent of Ceiba Mocha's people (2,829); while the free-black and mulatto population numbered a minuscule 179, or 3.4 percent of the partido's residents. The town was the only other urbanized center in Matanzas, supporting 4 warehouses, 7 general stores, and 26 *pulperías*, although only 304 people resided there.

The Yumurí Valley had long been a focal point of settlement in the Matanzas region, and it became a center of sugar and coffee production and African slavery in the early nineteenth century. Twenty-one ingenios were grinding cane in 1817; there were 7 cafetales; and 57.5 percent of the population were slaves, the vast majority (87.4 percent) of African rather than creole origin.

Santa Ana (today Cidra), a population center due south of the port along the old camino real, in the heart of the Magdalena Valley, also developed into a major sugar- and coffee-producing region. This was a relatively recent area of settlement, in contrast with Yumurí and Ceiba Mocha, and had all the characteristics of a frontier zone. Twenty-four ingenios and 23 cafetales had been established by 1817, and a population of 4,001 (50 percent slaves) lived there.

To the east, in the direction of Cárdenas, the partido of Camarioca ran along the Atlantic coast, and directly south was the partido of Guamacaro.[23] These were developing regions; a scant 4.9 percent (1,062) of Matanzas residents lived in Camarioca (46.3 percent slaves), although there were 3 ingenios and 17 cafetales in 1817. Guamacaro was larger, both in land area and population (see Table 2.2). Its ingenios (11) and cafetales (13) supported a substantial slave population, which accounted for 70.9 percent of the partido's inhabitants.

Over the next quarter-century the human and economic geography of the province was transformed. The city itself mushroomed across both rivers into the barrios of Versalles and Pueblo Nuevo, and by 1841 the urban population accounted for 13.1 percent of all *matanceros*.[24] Slaves constituted 30.2 percent of the city's inhabitants, and free blacks and mulattoes made up another 15.9 percent.

The expansion of sugar and coffee cultivation into frontier regions shifted the focus of the province's economy to the east, south, and southeast of the city. Within the confines of the 1817 jurisdictional boundaries, the number of ingenios increased from 76 in 1817 to 161 in 1841. Additionally, there were 183 sugar mills located in the partidos of Alacranes, Cimarrones, Guamutas, Lagunillas, Macuriges, and Palmillas, areas that had been largely undeveloped in 1817. The expansion of coffee production was equally impressive. There were 75 cafetales in 1817 and 175 in 1841 within the 1817 boundaries. In 1841 an additional 142 coffee farms dotted the countryside in the outlying partidos noted above.

The 1841 data reveal the importance of the sugar economy, since population by place of residence is indicated. More than one-third of all Matanzas inhabitants resided on ingenios in 1841, and in some partidos the percentage was strikingly higher. In Sabanilla 71.3 percent of the population lived on sugar plantations; 59.5 percent in Cimarrones; 52.3 percent in Yumurí; and 52.2 percent in Santa Ana. Nearly 14 percent of the total population lived on cafetales; and the most important center of coffee production was Guamacaro, where 44.9 percent of all inhabitants lived on coffee farms.

If the outlying partidos of Alacranes, Cimarrones, Guamutas, Lagunillas, Palmillas, and Macuriges are examined, the greater relative economic importance of the sugar sector is striking (see Table 2.3). Coffee was produced in the 1830s, but by and large commercial agriculture in the frontier areas of Matanzas was already dominated by the sugar entrepreneurs who would overwhelm these regions in the 1840s and 1850s.

A significant portion of the population (32.6 percent) lived and worked

Table 2.3. Matanzas, 1841:
Types of Farms and Percentage of Population on Each Type by Partido

	No. Ingenios	% Pop. on Ingenios	No. Cafetales	% Pop. on Cafetales	No. Other Farms	% Pop. on Other Farms
Yumurí	33	52.3	9	2.5	722	43.9
Ceiba Mocha	21	23.1	26	24.7	500	45.0
Santa Ana	37	52.2	29	18.8	269	27.7
Guamacaro	30	43.9	73	44.9	44	9.2
Camarioca	15	21.1	38	31.7	234	43.5
Sabanilla	25	71.3	0	0	97	23.9
Alacranes	34	43.4	14	7.6	367	45.0
Cimarrones	27	59.5	11	7.5	119	27.7
Guamutas	23	21.8	36	8.9	482	67.1
Lagunillas	38	39.7	40	19.1	253	22.6
Palmillas	14	22.8	1	0.4	259	70.5
Macuriges	47	46.3	40	14.6	441	37.6
TOTAL	344	36.4	317	13.9	3,787	32.6

SOURCE: AHPM, ME, Estadística, leg. 1, nos. 5, 7.

NOTES: Pop. = population. Percentages of people living on ingenios, cafetales, and other farms do not add up to 100; the remaining population lived in towns and villages.

on crop- and stock-raising farms in 1841. This was especially true on the edges of the frontier. In Guamutas and Palmillas, the farthest partidos from the city to the southeast, more than two-thirds of the population resided on these smaller units of production. The distribution of farms by partido and the percentage of population living on each unit of production is indicated in Table 2.3.

The most important demographic transformation occurring in Matanzas between 1817 and 1841 was the increase in the slave population, both numerically and as a percentage of all inhabitants. In 1841 there were 53,331 slaves within the Matanzas jurisdiction, 62.7 percent of all residents. This compares with 10,773 slaves in 1817, making up 49.5 percent of the total population. There were also 41,043 slaves in the six outlying rural partidos in 1841, and they were two-thirds of the total population. Some regions in rural Matanzas were predominantly African in their ethnic composition. The most extreme examples were Guamacaro, where 89.9 percent of all people were slaves; Guanábana, 83.8 percent; Sabanilla, 76.4 percent; Cimarrones, 74.7 percent; and Lagunillas, 73.3 percent. Exactly two-thirds of all slaves in 1841 were males. Population by partido, by different racial and legal categories, and by sex are shown in Table 2.4.

Thus, by the 1840s the frontier had been pushed to regions far from the bay area. The rural partidos that would form Cárdenas in 1843 and Colón in 1856 were colonized, and the transformation of these areas into sugar-producing zones had begun in earnest. During the 1840s these regions became the most important centers of sugar and slavery, not only in Cuba but in the entire Caribbean.

Ceiba Mocha in 1817: Land Use, Tenure, and Slavery

The manuscript census returns for Ceiba Mocha in 1817 permit detailed analysis of a Matanzas rural partido in the early stages of sugar and coffee export development.[25] It should be recalled that roughly one-quarter of the Matanzas population lived in Ceiba Mocha in 1817. Twelve rural properties were listed as ingenios in full production; 1 was "en fomento," or in the process of development; and 3 farms produced sugarcane but possessed no milling machinery. These 16 farms occupied 567 caballerías, or 32.1 percent of Ceiba Mocha's total land area, and they used 36.1 percent of the partido's slaves.

Ingenio San Miguel, owned by the Marqués de San Felipe, was the largest sugar plantation—100 caballerías worked by 163 slaves. Francisco Barba and Concepción Cavallería operated the second-largest ingenio, La Perla, with a slave population of 164 on 60 caballerías of land. Ingenio Buen Amigo, the property of Domingo Ugarte (a Havana resident), occupied 49

Table 2.4. Matanzas, 1841: Population by Partido, Race, Legal Status, and Sex

	Whites			Free Blacks and Mulattoes			Slaves			Total Pop.
	M	F	T	M	F	T	M	F	T	
Matanzas										
City	5,646	4,658	10,304	1,428	1,613	3,041	3,264	2,515	5,779	19,124
Guamacaro	782	414	1,196	73	65	138	7,532	4,290	11,822	13,156
Yumurí	2,710	1,994	4,704	251	165	416	6,131	2,839	8,970	14,090
Ceiba Mocha	2,308	1,835	4,143	209	225	434	4,056	2,322	6,378	10,955
Sabanilla	1,141	831	1,972	146	115	261	4,918	2,341	7,259	9,492
Camarioca	1,451	1,033	2,484	73	41	114	3,110	1,591	4,701	7,299
Santa Ana	985	689	1,674	67	40	107	3,101	1,557	4,658	6,439
Guanábana	416	255	671	30	29	59	2,453	1,311	3,764	4,494
Alacranes	1,849	1,377	3,226	90	70	160	3,905	1,683	5,588	8,974
Cimarrones	910	553	1,463	57	55	112	3,303	1,359	4,662	6,237
Guamutas	2,787	1,821	4,608	208	150	358	5,929	2,631	8,560	13,526
Lagunillas	2,013	1,354	3,367	77	72	149	6,638	2,974	9,612	13,128
Macuriges	2,246	1,600	3,846	233	189	422	6,956	3,327	10,283	14,551
Palmillas	1,156	834	1,990	300	273	573	1,677	661	2,338	4,901
TOTAL	26,400	19,248	45,648	3,242	3,102	6,344	62,973	31,401	94,374	146,366

SOURCE: AHPM, ME, Estadística, leg. 1, nos. 5, 7.
NOTE: M = males; F = females; T = total; Pop. = population.

caballerías and was worked by 141 slaves. These three mills accounted for more than one-third of all land controlled by the sugar sector and 46.3 percent of the 1,010 slaves working on ingenios in Ceiba Mocha.

Coffee production was an important component of the regional economy in 1817. Ceiba Mocha's 15 coffee farms were less extensive in size—the largest measured 21 caballerías—but coffee cultivation did not require economies of scale to be profitable. Coffee plantations occupied a total of 208 caballerías, 11.8 percent of Ceiba Mocha's land area. It is important to underline the fact that the coffee sector employed slightly more slaves than the sugar sector in 1817: 1,073, or 38.4 percent of the total slave population.

Although the average size of a Ceiba Mocha sugar ingenio was much larger than an average coffee farm in 1817, 35.4 versus 13.9 caballerías, the coffee sector utilized larger numbers of slaves per farm. The average work force of a cafetal included 71.5 slaves, while sugar ingenios used an average of 63.1 slaves. This suggests the intensive nature of Cuban coffee production and should be emphasized, since heretofore it has been assumed by scholars that sugar's labor demands were much greater than those of coffee. This was evidently not true during the formative phase of Cuba's early-nineteenth-century economy.

An additional 347 slaves (12.4 percent of the total) were utilized on potreros; and 367 slaves (13.1 percent of the total) lived and worked on *sitios*,
or small-scale crop farms. Table 2.5 indicates average farm size, number of
slaves, and number of slaves used per caballería on each type of farm.

Coffee farming attracted a variety of powerful entrepreneurs in the early
nineteenth century. Investments were drawn from Havana commercial interests, eighteenth-century sugar-planting families, and recently arrived
immigrants. James Drake, owner of the largest commercial house in Havana during the early nineteenth century, established Cafetal Carlota in
Ceiba Mocha on 21 caballerías worked by 157 slaves. Santiago Drake, as he
was called in Havana, came to Cuba in the late eighteenth century from the
English city of Ash; he established Drake Hermanos in Havana and also
operated a branch in Matanzas. He was married to Carlota del Castillo,
daughter of the Marqués de San Felipe after whom the cafetal was named.
The marqués owned Ceiba Mocha's largest sugar ingenio.[26] The O'Farrills,
eighteenth-century sugar entrepreneurs from Havana, owned two cafetales
extending for 33.3 caballerías and holding 68 slaves; and a recently arrived
German immigrant, Martin Averhoff, owned Cafetal Sociedad, with its 10
caballerías and 105 slaves.[27]

Ingenios and cafetales employed free labor as well. Ceiba Mocha's sugar
plantations utilized 145 white workers and 33 free blacks and mulattoes in
1817. Combined, these groups accounted for 15 percent of the total labor
force, slaves making up the remainder. Proportionally fewer free laborers
were employed on coffee farms. Of a total coffee labor force of 1,153, there
were only 76 non-slave workers (74 whites and 2 free blacks), 6.6 percent
of the total. Thus, the coffee sector exhibited a relatively greater dependence
on slave labor than the partido's sugar plantations.

A significant portion of the Ceiba Mocha slave population was employed
on other types of rural property. Stock- and crop-raising farms owned 25.5

**Table 2.5. Ceiba Mocha, 1817: Average Farm Size, Slaves per Caballería,
and Average Number of Slaves by Type of Farm**

	Cabs.	Slaves/Cab.[a]	Slaves/Farm
Ingenios	35.4	1.8	63.1
Cafetales	13.9	5.2	71.5
Potreros	14.0	0.5	7.5
Sitios	1.9	0.9	2.0

SOURCE: AHPM, ME, Estadística, leg. 8, no. 137, fols. 17–64.

NOTE: See note, Table 2.2. Cabs. = caballerías.

[a]Slaves/Cab. data must be viewed with caution, since they do not reflect slaves/cultivated
area ratios. Source does not indicate the extent of cultivated acreage.

percent of all slaves, although free labor clearly predominated. Of the 2,560 workers on potreros and sitios, 1,797 (70.2 percent) were white; 49 (1.9 percent) were free people of color; and 714 (27.9 percent) were slaves. (See Table 2.6.)

Land ownership was extremely concentrated even in this early phase of export-oriented economic development. Nine farms in Ceiba Mocha were 40 caballerías or larger in 1817 and constituted 3.4 percent of all rural properties; however, they occupied more than 30 percent of total land area. At the bottom of the landowning hierarchy, 59.5 percent of all farms were smaller than 3 caballerías in extension, but these accounted for only 10.9 percent of all land. (See Table 2.7.)

Slave ownership in Ceiba Mocha was also characterized by extreme patterns of concentration and fragmentation. Although slaveholding was ex-

Table 2.6. Ceiba Mocha, 1817: Land Use and Work Force by Type of Farm

	No. Farms	%	Cabs.	%	Total Slaves	%	African Slaves	%
Ingenios	12	4.6	460	26.1	972	34.8	650	33.2
Cafetales	15	5.7	208	11.8	1,073	38.4	850	43.5
Potreros	46	17.6	645	36.5	347	12.4	230	11.8
Sitios	184	70.5	345	19.5	367	13.1	194	9.9
Sitios/ Ingenio	3	1.1	67	3.8	34	1.2	28	1.4
Corte de Ingenio	1	0.4	40	2.3	4	0.1	4	0.2
TOTAL	261	100.0	1,765	100.0	2,797	100.0	1,956	100.0

	Creole Slaves	%	White Workers	%	Free Blacks	%
Ingenios	322	38.3	127	6.3	33	39.3
Cafetales	223	26.5	74	3.7	2	2.4
Potreros	117	13.9	371	18.4	16	19.0
Sitios	173	20.6	1,426	70.6	33	39.3
Sitios/ Ingenio	6	0.7	14	0.7	0	0.0
Corte de Ingenio[a]	0	0.0	4	0.2	0	0.0
TOTAL	841	100.0	2,021	100.0	84	100.0

SOURCE: AHPM, ME, Estadística, leg. 8, no. 137, fols. 17–64.
NOTE: There was also 1 "Molino del Rey" noted, with no land or slaves.
See note, Table 2.2. Cabs. = caballerías (33.6 acres each).
 [a] A corte de ingenio was a sugar estate in the process of development.

Table 2.7. Ceiba Mocha, 1817: Land-Tenure Structure

Farm Size[a]	No. Farms	%	Land (Cabs.)	%
.13–.99	37	14.3	17	1.0
1–1.99	75	29.0	82	4.6
2–2.99	44	17.0	93	5.3
3–4.99	26	10.0	93	5.3
5–9.99	27	10.4	176	10.0
10–19.99	26	10.0	345	19.6
20–39.99	15	5.8	407	23.1
40–59.99	5	1.9	229	13.0
60–99.99	2	0.8	120	6.8
100+	2	0.8	202	11.5
TOTAL	262	100.0	1,764	100.0

SOURCE: AHPM, ME, Estadística, leg. 8, no. 137, fols. 17–64.
NOTE: Cabs. = caballerías (33.6 acres each).
[a]The smallest farm size recorded was .13 caballerías.

Table 2.8. Ceiba Mocha, 1817: Slave-Ownership Structure

Slaveholdings	No. Slave owners	%	No. Slaves	%
1–5	93	58.1	261	9.3
6–10	25	15.6	192	6.9
11–20	13	8.1	182	6.5
21–50	11	6.9	342	12.2
51–100	9	5.6	628	22.5
101–150	6	3.8	708	25.3
151+	3	1.9	484	17.3
TOTAL	160	100.0	2,797	100.0

SOURCE: AHPM, ME, Estadística, leg. 8, no. 137, fols. 17–64.

tensive—61.1 percent of all landowners registered slaves—most owned 5 or fewer slaves. Nearly three-fifths of Ceiba Mocha's slaveowners fell into this category, but collectively they controlled only 9.3 percent of the total slave population. At the other extreme, 11.3 percent of all slaveholders (with 51 or more slaves) owned 65.1 percent of Ceiba Mocha's slaves in 1817. (See Table 2.8.)

Ceiba Mocha was the oldest region of settlement in Matanzas. As a small *poblado*, it served as a resting point for travelers on the camino real in the seventeenth century; tobacco cultivation supported the local population

through most of the eighteenth century. The first two decades of the nineteenth century heralded the end of the smallholder tobacco-growing society
that had flourished in the region. Sugar and coffee overwhelmed the economy and produced two fundamental changes. First, outsiders based in Havana established control over sugar and coffee production. Second, African
slavery became the dominant socioeconomic institution supporting local
economic life. In 1817 more than half of Ceiba Mocha's population was
enslaved, and 70 percent of that slave population was born in Africa.

Yet, Ceiba Mocha's economy was rather diversified in 1817. Monocultural sugar production was decades away, and the area's land was extremely
productive because of prior marginal use. Over the next three decades, however, Ceiba Mocha was gradually transformed. Soil fertility was depleted by
excessive exploitation and the absence of conservation. Forest reserves were
destroyed, and there was no effort at replacement. Sugar and coffee entrepreneurs subsequently moved to higher-yielding frontier zones; and the
local economy, central to Matanzas in the early nineteenth century, was
reduced to relative insignificance. Ceiba Mocha encapsulated in a short period of time the boom-and-bust cycles characterizing Cuba's economic history.

Camarioca, Alacranes, and Yumurí: Coffee and Sugar, 1817–1822

Before 1800 the areas to the south and west of Matanzas Bay were the principal centers of settlement and agricultural development in the province. To
the east, the fertile land around the Canimar River had been exploited for
its timber reserves in the early colonial period; a sugar mill was established
in the seventeenth century; and tobacco farming was prevalent in the eighteenth century. But, by and large, the area east of the Río Canimar, extending all the way to the future city of Cárdenas, was an unpopulated frontier
where cattle grazed on natural pastures and agriculture was almost nonexistent.

However, in the early nineteenth century this region, encompassing the
partido of Camarioca, became an important coffee- and food-crop-producing
zone. Although sugar ingenios were also established, Camarioca did not
attract the investments of the Havana oligarchy. A nucleus of U.S. citizens
established themselves around the Canimar and Camarioca rivers, and invested primarily in coffee cultivation.[28]

The first available statistical data for the Camarioca region are for 1816,
when 18 cafetales had already been established. They occupied 39.4 percent
of the partido's land and used 31.3 percent of its slave population. By way
of contrast, the sugar sector's 4 ingenios owned 12.3 percent of total land
and utilized 20.6 percent of all slaves. Small-scale sitios predominated, and

collectively they owned more slaves, 36.3 percent of the total, than either sugar or coffee plantations. (See Table 2.9.)

Yet, despite its mixed economy, land concentration was extreme in Camarioca. A French immigrant, Domingo Alers, owned 29 percent of the partido's total acreage, and the 8 farms, extending for more than 20 caballerías (4.6 percent of all farms), absorbed 46.4 percent of Camarioca's land. Other categories are indicated in Table 2.10.

Between 1816 and 1822 Camarioca experienced rapid economic growth revolving around coffee production. The number of cafetales doubled to 37 by 1822, and sugar ingenios increased to 8. In addition, nearly 1,000 slaves were introduced into the region, raising the slave population from 675 to 1,648. A fundamental redistribution of labor accompanied coffee-induced economic expansion. The coffee sector accounted for 56.3 percent of Camarioca's slaves in 1822; sugar plantations used 33 percent; and 10.1 percent of the slave population labored on cattle and small-scale crop farms.[29]

Slave-ownership patterns show the same type of concentration found in Ceiba Mocha. Most slaveholders (67.3 percent) owned fewer than 5 slaves, while only 5 slaveholders (5 percent of the total) controlled 31.3 percent of Camarioca's slave population. (See Table 2.11.)

The 1822 data provide an opportunity to examine the comparative internal dynamics of sugar and coffee production in early-nineteenth-century Cuba. Data on land cultivation, output, and gross income allow a crude calculation of productivity both for land and for slave labor. These statistics indicate why coffee cultivation in Cuba collapsed after 1840.[30] Gross income per slave and per caballería were so overwhelmingly higher in the sugar economy, compared with coffee, that it is exceedingly clear why entrepre-

Table 2.9. Camarioca, 1816: Land Use and Work Force by Type of Farm

	No. Farms	%	Cabs.	%	No. Slaves	%	No. White Workers	%
Ingenios	4	2.3	169	12.3	139	20.6	27	3.2
Cafetales	18	10.2	544	39.4	211	31.3	39	4.6
Sitios	134	76.1	469	34.0	245	36.3	704	83.4
Potreros	13	7.4	183	13.3	76	11.3	52	6.2
Solares	7	4.0	14	1.0	4	0.6	22	2.6
TOTAL	176	100.0	1,379	100.0	675	100.0	844	100.0

SOURCE: AHPM, ME, Estadística, leg. 6, no. 114, fols. 1–3, "Padrón gral. de los havitantes que contiene el partido Camina y Camarioca de los ingenios, cafetales, potreros, sitios de labor y cavallerías de tierra perteneciente a cada [illegible]. Año de 1816."
NOTE: See note, Table 2.2. Cabs. = caballerías (33.6 acres each). Solares were small parcels of land in cities or villages on which homes were built.

Table 2.10. Camarioca, 1816: Land-Tenure Structure

Farm Size (Cabs.)	No. Farms	%	Land (Cabs.)	%
.13–.99	5	2.9	3	0.2
1–1.99	40	22.9	40	2.9
2–2.99	42	24.0	85	6.2
3–4.99	27	15.4	100	7.2
5–9.99	25	14.3	163	11.8
10–19.99	29	16.6	348	25.2
20–39.99	4	2.3	101	7.3
40–59.99	1	0.6	40	2.9
60–99.99	0	0	0	0
100–199.99	1	0.6	100	7.2
200+	1	0.6	400	29.0
TOTAL	175	100.0	1,380	100.0

SOURCE: AHPM, ME, Estadística, leg. 6, no. 114, fols. 1–3, "Padrón gral. de los havitantes que contiene el partido Camina y Camarioca de los ingenios, cafetales, potreros, sitios de labor y cavallerías de tierra perteneciente a cada [illegible]. Año de 1816."
NOTE: Cabs. = caballerías (33.6 acres each).

Table 2.11. Camarioca, 1816: Slave-Ownership Structure

Slave-holdings	No. Slave-owners	%	No. Slaves	%
1–5	68	67.3	168	24.9
6–10	15	14.9	107	15.9
11–20	13	12.9	189	28.0
21–50	3	3.0	91	13.5
51–100	2	2.0	120	17.8
TOTAL	101	100.0	675	100.0

SOURCE: AHPM, ME, Estadística, leg. 6, no. 114, fols. 1–3. "Padrón gral. de los havitantes que contiene el partido Camina y Camarioca de los ingenios, cafetales, potreros, sitios de labor y cavallerías de tierra perteneciente a cada [illegible]. Año de 1816."
NOTE: 57.4 percent of all landowners owned slaves.

neurs west of Oriente province abandoned coffee cultivation en masse in the 1830s and 1840s. In Camarioca a single caballería of land planted in cane yielded two and a half times the gross income from a caballería planted in coffee (1,968 pesos versus 709 pesos). Each slave used on a sugar plantation generated more than three times the gross income generated on a cafetal (177 pesos versus 56 pesos). (See Table 2.12.)

Table 2.12. Camarioca, 1822: Economics of Sugar and Coffee Farms

	Sugar	Coffee
No. Farms	8	37
No. Cultivated Caballerías	49	74.25
Arrobas Produced	73,700	10,528
Arrobas/Caballería	1,504	142
No. Slaves[a]	544	938
No. Slaves/Farm	68	25.4
Gross Income in Pesos	96,304	52,640
Gross Income/Caballería	1,965	709
Gross Income/Slave	177	56
Gross Income/Productive Unit	12,038	1,423

SOURCE: AHPM, ME, Estadística, leg. 6, no.115, fol. 3.

NOTES: Gross sugar production was 73,700 arrobas (1 arroba = 25 pounds). It was indicated that two-thirds of production was "quebrado" at 3.75 cents/pound; and one-third was "blanco," at 5.75 cents/pound—yielding a total of 81,254.25 pesos. In addition, ingenios produced 21,600 barrels of molasses at 50 cents/barrel, or 10,800 pesos in all. Ingenios also produced 850 arrobas of coffee (212.5 quintales) at 20 pesos/quintal, or 4,250 pesos. Coffee farms produced 2,632 quintales at 20 pesos/quintal, or 52,640 pesos. A caballería is 33.6 acres; a quintal is 100 pounds.

[a]The number of working-age slaves is not known.

The sugar and coffee economy had another focal point of development in the early nineteenth century, along the southern tier of Matanzas province directly east of the Güines Valley. Güines had been one of the most productive centers of commercial development in the late eighteenth century and an important region of investment by the Havana *sacarocracía*. As land was occupied and cultivation spread, entrepreneurs began to move east from the valley in the direction of Alacranes, which administratively was part of Havana. While Cuban archives hold no manuscript census reports for early-nineteenth-century Alacranes, an excellent economic *informe* exists for 1822 which allows comparisons to be made with the Camarioca sugar and coffee economy.

Alacranes had 17 ingenios in full production in 1822, worked by 745 slaves, or 45.9 percent of the partido's total slave population. Thirteen cafetales used 436 slaves, or 26.9 percent of the total; 103 sitios utilized 272 slaves (16.8 percent); and 19 potreros owned 170 slaves (10.5 percent). There were significant differences in the amount of income produced per caballería of land compared with Camarioca. Ingenios in Alacranes produced less sugar per land unit (995 arrobas/caballería) than those in Camarioca (1,504 arrobas/caballería).[31] This was linked to the fact that the sugar sector was much older in Alacranes and completely new in Camarioca, where cane was planted on virgin soil. Coffee, however, yielded more production per land area in Alacranes (176 arrobas/caballería) compared with the 142 arrobas/caballería found in Camarioca.

It is striking, though, that the income per slave produced by Alacranes ingenios was precisely the same found in Camarioca, 177 pesos/slave. Slaves produced considerably more gross income per worker on Alacranes cafetales, 92 pesos/slave compared to the 56 pesos/slave noted for Camarioca. Since no age-distribution data exist for either partido in 1822, it is impossible to determine whether these data reflect real productivity differences or simply disparities in the ratios between productive versus nonproductive slaves. Tables 2.12 and 2.13 summarize these data.

The Yumurí Valley was perhaps the oldest area of settlement in the Matanzas region. Along the fertile banks of the Yumurí River, subsistence farming flourished in the seventeenth century, and the valley became a center of tobacco-leaf production in the eighteenth century. During the 1790s and the early years of the nineteenth century, sugar production spread methodically; by 1817, Yumurí's dependence on sugar made it the least-diversified partido in the jurisdiction of Matanzas. This early development of sugar monoculture was a precursor to the future of the entire province.

Although manuscript census data do not provide information on land use or tenure, an 1817 farm-by-farm slave census reveals the overwhelming predominance of sugar. While from one-third to one-half of all slaves were used on sugar estates throughout the rest of Matanzas, 85.7 percent of Yumurí's slaves worked on the partido's 23 ingenios in 1817.[32] Not only was there a sharp proportional contrast in the number of slaves utilized, but it is evident that Yumurí's ingenios were larger than the sugar plantations

Table 2.13. Alacranes, 1822: Economics of Sugar and Coffee Farms

	Sugar	Coffee
No. Farms	17	13
No. Cultivated Caballerías	98	45.5
Arrobas Produced	97,500	8,000
Arrobas/Caballería	995	175.8
No. of Slaves	745	436
No. Slaves/Farm	43.8	33.5
Gross Income in Pesos	131,994	40,000
Gross Income/Caballería	1,347	879
Gross Income/Slave	177	92
Gross Income/Productive Unit	7,764	3,077

SOURCE: AHPM, ME, Estadística, leg. 6, no. 115, fol. 4, "Estadística rural del distrito del ayuntamiento de Alacranes. Cultura e industria agrícola."
NOTE: An arroba is 25 pounds; a caballería is 33.6 acres.

found elsewhere in Matanzas. An average of 91.3 slaves were used on each farm, significantly higher than the average of 68 in Camarioca or the average of 63.1 found in Ceiba Mocha. It should be added that nearly all of Yumurí's slaves were adult workers, since nearly 90 percent were *bozales* (African-born slaves).

Six coffee farms using 14 percent of the slave population, an average of 57 slaves/cafetal, complete the economic panorama of the Yumurí Valley. Comparative data on the sugar and coffee economies of Yumurí, Ceiba Mocha, Alacranes, and Camarioca are provided in Table 2.14.

Control over the economy of the Yumurí Valley was similar in structure to that in other regions of Matanzas during the early nineteenth century. Old Havana-based families played the dominant role in the local economy, although recently arrived immigrants of peninsular or French origin also owned ingenios or cafetales. Juan Montalvo, who would inaugurate the first steamship service between Matanzas and Havana in 1819, owned one ingenio and a cafetal as well. He was the largest slaveholder in Yumurí with a total of 286 slaves on both farms. The Zequeira family, who held the title Condado de Lagunillas, owned three ingenios. María del Carmen Peñalver, the widow of José María Peñalver, the Marqués de Arcos, owned a cafetal. And Teresa de Zayas, of the powerful, Havana-based Zayas clan, operated an ingenio.[33]

Several government officials also owned ingenios in Yumurí. The "Auditor de Guerra" of Matanzas, Justo Ximénez, and Felipe Cicre, a coronel in the local militia, each operated a sugar mill in the valley. Ignacio Lamar, the

Table 2.14. Comparative Data on Sugar and Coffee in Camarioca, Yumurí, Ceiba Mocha, and Alacranes, 1817–1822

	Camarioca	Yumurí	Ceiba Mocha	Alacranes
SUGAR				
No. Ingenios	23	16	17	8
Avg. No. Slaves/Ingenio	91.3	63.1	43.8	68.0
% Slave Pop. on Ingenios	85.7	36.1	45.9	33.0
COFFEE				
No. Cafetales	6	15	13	37
Avg. No. Slaves/Cafetal	57.0	71.5	33.5	25.4
% Slave Pop. on Cafetales	14.0	38.4	26.9	56.3

SOURCES: AHPM, ME, Estadística, leg. 8, no. 137, fols. 17–64, and leg. 6, no. 115, fols. 3–4; AHPM, Gobierno Provincial, Esclavos, leg. 34.

NOTE: Data for Yumurí and Ceiba Mocha are for 1817; data for Camarioca and Alacranes are for 1822. Pop. = population.

Frenchman who owned a sugar plantation in Ceiba Mocha, also had established an ingenio in Yumurí.

The valley's prosperity in the early nineteenth century was ephemeral. Yumurí was the first Matanzas partido to become a monocultural sugar-producing zone, and the region mirrored the eighteenth-century pattern of development found in Havana. It also foreshadowed the process that other Matanzas partidos close to the bay would experience over the next several decades. Soil exhaustion and depleted forest reserves reduced the Yumurí sugar economy's importance by the 1840s; as planters pushed eastward, toward high-yielding virgin soils and abundant forests where the same process would routinely be repeated, the valley's land was fragmented into small-scale, crop-raising farms.

Toward the end of the second decade of the nineteenth century, small population centers began to appear in frontier regions far to the east and southeast of the city of Matanzas. Agricultural development began gradually in these areas during the 1820s, but it was not until the 1830s that sugar production invaded the eastern frontier on a significant scale.

A few poblados on the northern camino real coalesced in the late eighteenth century, but they were not important foci of economic growth until much later. Guanajayabo, to the southeast of Cárdenas, was officially established as a town in 1770; and Guamutas, an old area of timber exploitation, dated from 1778. Yet, even by 1826 there were no ingenios in Guamutas, although seven cafetales had been developed. The eastern edge of Matanzas sugar cultivation in the 1820s seems to have been the Cimarrones region, where eight mills ground cane in 1826.[34] Settlements, however, existed farther east. Palmillas, southeast of Colón, was officially founded in 1808, and Nueva Bermeja (Colón) was established in 1818.

To the south of Matanzas, the economic expansion of the first two decades of the century gave rise to new population centers. San Antonio de Cabezas appeared in 1822; and, much farther south, Corral Falso (near the old Hacienda Macuriges) celebrated its first Mass in 1825.[35]

The most important region of gradual settlement was the large bay area that became the future city of Cárdenas. There are no notices of Cárdenas as a population center before the nineteenth century, although the nearby natural salt flats of the Hicacos Peninsula were exploited from the early colonial period. In 1802, however, the Conde de Lagunillas, Juan Zequeira, petitioned colonial authorities in Havana for permission to divide his immense properties, the haciendas Lagunillas, Arroyo Bermejo, and Quebrada Grande. Small-scale *sitieros* and cattle ranchers settled these "haciendas demolidos," and an *embarcadero* seven miles to the north of Lagunillas came into use. This was the site of the future city of Cárdenas. A poblado appeared at the mouth of the Siguagua River, and took the same name; just to the east, the villages of Guásimas and Cantel were officially founded in 1817.

Scattered coffee farms were developed, and trade in salt, hides, coffee, and some timber was carried on from the embarcadero. It was not until 1828 that the town of Cárdenas was officially established, and even as late as 1833 it functioned as little more than a lightly settled trading center. There were only eight structures in that year, but three were warehouses owned by Rabel & Co., Maribona Pérez & Co., and A. Pallimonjo.

The coffee farms of Camarioca gradually spread along the north coast in the direction of Cárdenas during the 1820s, but it was not until the 1830s that sugar began its broad penetration of the Cárdenas region. This was paralleled by ambitious plans for railroad construction. By 1843, Cárdenas would be linked by rail to the richest sugar regions in Cuba; a separate *tenencia de gobierno*, or *jurisdicción*, was created that included the vast Colón region; the port was officially opened to foreign shipping; and Cárdenas was rapidly converted into the largest sugar-producing zone in Cuba.[36]

CHAPTER 3

Land, Sugar, and Commerce

The Matanzas Land Market

Despite the fact that inalienable property rights were not conferred in Cuba until 1816, land transactions were numerous in Matanzas from the early nineteenth century. Notaries routinely recorded land sales after 1800, although it was not until 1817 that the "Anotaduría de Hipotecas," which noted mortgage obligations, first appeared. Land values varied for many reasons, and among the most important variables affecting prices were the topography of the terrain, proximity to the bay or rivers, soil quality, timber reserves, whether land was cleared and planted, and contiguity with existing sugar or coffee farms.

Although transactions rarely recorded information beyond buyer and seller, the extension and price of the land, and whether liens existed on the property, existing documentation clearly denotes the differences between frontierland and functioning farms. If land was undeveloped, it would be recorded as a "venta de terreno," whereas land that had been improved was designated by type—estancia, sitio, cafetal, or ingenio.

One of the more remarkable aspects of the land market in Matanzas was the long-term price stability for undeveloped frontierland in the first four decades of the nineteenth century. Although land values rose markedly in regions of sugar and coffee cultivation, frontier terrain in locales without overland linkages to the port of Matanzas or Cárdenas fluctuated between 250 and 300 pesos per caballería from the early nineteenth century through the late 1830s.

In 1804, for example, Ignacio Álvarez purchased 13.5 caballerías on the old Corral de San Pedro (due south of the city of Matanzas) for 4,050 pesos, or 300 pesos/caballería.[1] In 1810, 13 caballerías were sold for 300 pesos/caballería in San Antonio de Cabezas, to the southwest of Santa Ana.[2] And in 1817 the standard price for undeveloped land in Corral Nuevo, to the southwest of the Yumurí Valley, was 250 pesos/caballería.[3] As the frontier moved east, land values remained the same in peripheral areas of agricultural development. In Lagunillas, to the south of the port of Cárdenas, undeveloped land was sold for 300 pesos/caballería in 1826. Throughout the 1830s and as late as 1840, even though land values soared in developed regions, the 300 pesos/caballería price for undeveloped land remained stable in frontier zones.[4]

The construction of railroads, which opened the southern and eastern frontiers in the early 1840s, would fundamentally change this situation; prior to railroad development, however, frontier land itself was not a commodity that fluctuated in value. It must be kept in mind that while the population around the Matanzas bay area increased notably before 1840, most of the province was characterized by sparse population and extensive land reserves. Land had value only if cleared and planted, and the labor and capital resources needed to put land into production were overwhelmingly greater than the value of land itself. Thus, the absence of demographic pressures and the availability of extensive land in the eastern and southern regions of the province kept frontier terrain at stable price levels for nearly four decades.

The value of improved land was considerably greater, and often improvements were worth much more than the land itself. While undeveloped plots in the Yumurí Valley were selling for 300 pesos/caballería, small-scale estancias were transacted at 1,000 pesos/caballería in 1804, and this price seems to have been standard in other regions as well. Ingenio land planted in cane was considerably higher in value. In 1809 Ingenio Jesús María's land planted in cane was valued at 1,300 pesos/caballería, and the cane planted on this land was assessed at an additional 540 pesos/caballería. That same year, Ingenio San Juan Bautista's cane fields were worth 1,500 pesos/caballería plus an additional 500 pesos/caballería for the cane that had been planted.[5]

By 1818 the price of land on crop farms had increased to 1,500 pesos/caballería in Yumurí, and in the Magdalena Valley, where sugar production was flourishing, cleared farmland was selling for as much as 2,250 pesos/caballería. For example, Felipe Mena, a peninsular official in the city of Matanzas, purchased a 6-caballería "sitio de labor" for 13,500 pesos in 1818.[6] In Canimar in 1821, a 6-caballería cafetal was sold for 10,333 pesos, or 1,722 pesos/caballería.[7]

The value of Matanzas coffee farms is indicated by the 1823 sale of a 10-caballería cafetal located near the Canimar River. José Arango purchased this land, which was contiguous to another property he owned. From 36,000 to 40,000 coffee trees were in full production, and 15 slaves working the farm were included in the sale. Average slave prices in Matanzas in 1823 were 441 pesos/slave; thus, the value of the farm's slave population was approximately 6,615 pesos. Since the total transaction was for 24,500 pesos, the land itself including coffee trees was worth 17,885 pesos, or 1,789 pesos/caballería.[8]

A more detailed portrait of a Matanzas cafetal in the mid-1820s is provided by the 1826 judicial assessment of Cafetal Laberius, owned by Esteban

Junco. This property extended for 6 caballerías, although it is apparent that only 4 had been cleared and cultivated. The land alone was valued at 2,900 pesos, but its improvements and productive capacity were worth much more: 37,000 coffee trees were assessed at 3,777 pesos (10.2 cents/tree); 8,000 coffee seedlings less than one year old were valued at 500 pesos; and the fruit trees, plantains, and tubers were worth 1,402 pesos. Thus, this coffee farm was valued at 1,430 pesos/caballería, although it should be stressed that one-third of the farm produced nothing. It is also important to underline the fact that land improvements were worth nearly twice as much as the land itself.[9] (See Table 3.1.)

Grazing land was valued at roughly 1,000 pesos/caballería in the mid-1820s. For example, in 1826 a potrero of 10.75 caballerías was purchased by Tomás Ortega for 10,375 pesos.[10]

In 1827 Matanzas produced 1,733,000 arrobas of sugar (19,410 metric tons), 21.4 percent of total Cuban sugar production. Havana's predominance as Cuba's major sugar-producing zone continued through the 1830s, but by the mid-1840s Matanzas ingenios had increased their gross production fivefold to 109,913 metric tons, more than 55 percent of Cuba's sugar output. This dramatic increase was closely linked to investments made in Matanzas by a new sector of the sugar-planting class, appearing in the province in the early 1830s.

The Transformation of the Sugar Sector in the 1830s

In the first three decades of the nineteenth century, the Matanzas sugar and coffee economy was established and developed by several distinct social groups. Most prominent was a nucleus of Havana-based families who had been present in Cuba at least from the beginning of the eighteenth century; some even traced their Cuban roots to the early colonial period. Many

Table 3.1. Assessment of Cafetal Laberius, 1826

	Value in Pesos	%
6 Caballerías Land	2,900	33.8
37,000 Coffee Trees	3,777	44.0
8,000 Coffee Seedlings	500	5.8
Fruit Trees, Plantains, and Tubers	1,402	16.3
Total	8,579	100.0

SOURCE: ANC, PN, Matanzas, Joaquín de la Fuente, 1826, fols. 191–191ᵛ.
NOTE: A caballería is 33.6 acres.

claimed noble titles as counts and marquises, and they were close to the center of colonial political power. Few were newcomers to the world of commercial agriculture. These were the same families, most of them linked by marriage, who in Havana province had initiated the transition from tobacco and cattle to large-scale sugar production during the second half of the eighteenth century. The experience and knowledge garnered in Havana was transferred to the Matanzas region, which attracted capital investment because of its immense forest reserves, natural pastures, and productive virgin soils. These families were all creoles; while they had linkages with Spain, their economic interests and social positions were insular, not peninsular.

A second group of sugar and coffee entrepreneurs was composed of peninsular Spaniards of more recent arrival. Most were either bureaucrats sent to Matanzas to administer colonial institutions or officers in the service of the Crown's military. Notaries, surveyors, customs officials, and ayuntamiento officers were prominent among this group. They often intermarried with previously established Matanzas families and were less influential in those Havana institutions close to the center of political power, such as the Sociedad Económica or the Real Consulado. They also resided in Matanzas and could rarely afford homes in the Cuban capital. This differentiated them from the Havana nobility who maintained sumptuous houses at the center of power and visited their estates only at harvest time. This second sector of the Matanzas entrepreneurial elite may have been of foreign origin, but they were more locally oriented than the absentee creole families from Havana with respect to the mundane routine of daily life in the province.

A third sector of the agrarian elite was also composed of newcomer families. This group was diverse. Many were North American and French immigrants who had already played a leading role in the coffee economy. Some were of peninsular origin with no official connections to the colonial government—small-scale entrepreneurs with a little capital accumulated in Europe who came to try their luck in the New World as so many of their predecessors had over the centuries. Without doubt, the Havana-based families were at the top of the social and economic hierarchy in early-nineteenth-century Matanzas, followed by the other groups noted above. Matanzas was a vast frontier, and the region was open and fluid enough to accommodate each group with minimal conflict.

However, in the 1830s still another group of entrepreneurs began to penetrate Matanzas. Largely, but not exclusively, of immigrant origin, these families would become the wealthiest and most powerful in Cuba by the mid-nineteenth century. The mills they established in the 1830s and early 1840s would become legendary, and some still grind cane in socialist Cuba.[11] The Poeys, Barós, Diagos, Zuluetas, Pedrosos, Torrientes, and other newcomers appeared in Matanzas, introducing an innovative dynamic element to provincial life. While these families established the most technologically modern mills in Cuba in the 1840s, 1850s, and 1860s, it should be stressed that they did not push aside the old Havana elite. Rather, they cooperated and coexisted with them in slave-trading expeditions and railroad building, the two most important activities supporting Matanzas sugar production after 1840. The descendants of the old Havana families remained, but they were challenged for dominance by this newer group of modernizing entrepreneurs who often had business interests extending to New York, London, Barcelona, and Seville. These two elite sectors would control Cuban sugar production until the 1880s, when the technological revolution and changing international market conditions of the last two decades of the nineteenth century resulted in a fundamental reorganization of the province's sugar industry.

Juan Poey was perhaps the best known of the entrepreneurs making their historical debuts in Matanzas during the early 1830s. By the 1860s his Ingenio Las Cañas was one of the most technologically modernized mills in Cuba. Poey was a creole, born in Havana in 1800. His father, Simón Poey Lacasse, migrated to Cuba in the late eighteenth century from Oléron, France, and was a notorious slave trader, one of Cuba's largest in the period of the legal *trata* during the first two decades of the nineteenth century.[12]

Las Cañas, located in Alacranes on the old Hacienda San Agustín de Alacranes, was established in 1825 by the parish priest Presbítero Francisco Rodríguez after he purchased the land from Rita González de la Barrera. González, who continued to own land in Alacranes, was heavily in debt, and the 16 caballerías that became Las Cañas were auctioned to pay outstanding debts.

By 1833 the farm was still in the process of development. It was classified as a sitio/ingenio, which meant that the mill was not functioning. Poey bought the farm in partnership with his father-in-law, Francisco Hernández, a slave-trading associate of his deceased father, and also acquired new milling machinery from Rodríguez that had been purchased but not assembled. The sale was effected because Rodríguez was unable to pay a 12,000-peso debt to a Havana merchant house, Sres. Ruiz y Menéndez, who held a mortgage on the harvests of 1833 and 1834.[13] A complete inventory accompanied the sale, which makes possible a detailed portrait of a Cuban ingenio in the early stages of development during the 1830s.

Las Cañas extended for 16 caballerías, but only 3 had mature cane ready to be harvested during the 1833 zafra. Three caballerías were recently sown in cane, and 5 more caballerías had been cleared of timber and cleaned, and presumably would be ready for planting for the harvest of 1834 or 1835. Another 5 caballerías were pasture and woodland.

A building measuring 66 varas by 24 varas (1 Cuban vara was equal to approximately 3 feet, 2 inches) and with a cedar roof was constructed for the trapiche, which had been delivered to the property but not installed. A small hospital to treat the slave population had been constructed, and living quarters for the owner (14 varas in length) were habitable. In addition there were assorted ancillary requirements for the production of sugar, such as machetes, *hormas* (conical molds used to purge sugar), and even a *campanario*, or bell tower, with its bell to call the slave population to and from the fields. The estate also included 24 pairs of oxen, 4 horses, and 24 slaves, of whom 10 were males and 14 females. Only 3 slaves were born in Cuba; from abroad came 1 Lucumí, 4 Mandingas, 5 Carabalís, 4 Gangás, 2 Congos, and 5 Minas.

The total sale price paid by Hernández and Poey for Las Cañas was 50,844 pesos: 11,844 pesos were paid in cash to Rodríguez; a debt of 12,000 pesos was assumed to Ruiz y Menéndez, who approved the transaction; and 27,000 pesos were to be paid to Rodríguez in the future. Four payments of 6,000 pesos would be made on January 1 of each year from 1834 through 1837, and a final payment of 3,000 pesos was due on January 1, 1838. No interest was noted in this transaction.

Poey evidently bought out Hernández in 1835 or 1836. In September 1835 he purchased 10 caballerías of land contiguous to Las Cañas from the same Rita González who had sold the original 16 caballerías to Father Rodríguez in 1825. This land was evidently undeveloped, for the purchase price was 4,000 pesos, or 400 pesos/caballería.[14] These 26 caballerías would form the nucleus of the great Ingenio Las Cañas, whose ruins are still visible today.

Another well-known entrepreneur appearing in Matanzas in the mid-1830s was Julián Zulueta y Amondo, who without doubt was the wealthiest and most influential man in Cuba by the 1860s. A notorious slave trader, respected railroad builder, importer of Chinese contract laborers, and owner of five of Cuba's most productive ingenios—Álava, Habana, Vizcaya, España, and Zaza—Zulueta was a millionaire many times over by the mid-nineteenth century. He was a man with an obvious sense of humor as well, facetiously boasting of fictional humble origins as a way of embellishing his image as self-made man.[15] In fact, Zulueta hailed from a wealthy Basque family with a history of large-scale commercial activity dating from the mid-eighteenth century. The Zuluetas were among the largest slave traders on the African coast well before the birth of Julián in 1814, and Zulueta & Company had been established in Seville since the 1770s and in London and Liverpool since 1824.[16]

Zulueta was born in Anucita, Álava, and arrived in Cuba in 1832. In 1835, at the age of twenty-one, he made his first appearance in Matanzas, purchasing Ingenio San Francisco de Paula, which was located in Corral Nuevo to the west of the city of Matanzas. (Zulueta would move his center of operations to Hacienda Banagüises, in the Colón region, during the early 1840s.) Julián purchased this ingenio as the representative of his uncle, Tiburcio Zulueta, who never appears in a Matanzas historical document before or after this transaction. He probably financed the deal and resided in Spain, while Julián supervised the operation of the ingenio. The purchase price of 228,048.37 pesos certainly calls into question Zulueta's claim to youthful poverty.

The history of Ingenio San Francisco reveals much about the economic fragility of undercapitalized Matanzas sugar producers in the early nineteenth century. The ingenio was one of the first to be constructed in Matanzas in the 1790s, and it appears on the earliest ingenio map drawn up for the jurisdiction (see Map 2). It was founded by Luis Ignacio Caballero, a regidor in the Matanzas ayuntamiento during the late eighteenth century who was probably of peninsular origin. The ingenio was partially inherited by his daughter, Manuela Teresa Caraballo, who purchased the shares of the other heirs in 1814. She was married to an officer in the local militia, Teniente Coronel Antonio de la Luz; sometime in the 1820s, she was widowed.

Toward the end of the 1820s, Caballero found herself in extreme financial difficulties. She was heavily in debt to the Havana merchants Gonzalo Alfonso (Juan Poey's brother-in-law and one of the wealthiest slave traders in Cuba), Joaquín Arrieta (who later founded Ingenio Flor de Cuba), and Joaquín Gómez, another notorious peninsular slave merchant. Allowing her to refinance an unspecified but substantial debt, they set up a long-term repayment schedule that included a mortgage on the ingenio's zafras. However, not only was Caballero unable to meet her payments, but disaster struck in 1833. A cholera epidemic swept through Matanzas and caused a catastrophic loss of slaves and draft animals, which left her completely unable to collect and process the harvest of 1834. To guarantee the harvest, over which they held a mortgage, her creditors provided slaves and oxen, but Caballero was forced to turn over the rights to Ingenio San Francisco so that a suitable purchaser could be found. Her debt had accumulated to 338,438.50 pesos.

The young Zulueta, with connections to these leading merchant/slave traders, was the buyer. Ingenio San Francisco was 36 caballerías in size and included 128 slaves. There were 11 creoles, 11 Mandingas, 3 Minas, 15 Gangás, 29 Congos, 23 Lucumís, 25 Carabalís, 3 Vivís, 1 Briche, 2 Macuás, 1 Popó, and 1 Arará. Males accounted for 73.4 percent of all slaves (94), and 26.6 percent (34) were females. Immediately after the plantation was purchased, 110 more slaves were added to the ingenio's *dotación*.[17]

Just when San Francisco was sold is unknown, but in the early 1840s, as railroad construction began from the cities of Matanzas and Cárdenas toward the fertile southern and eastern zones of the province, Zulueta began purchasing the land where his great mills would be constructed in the 1840s and 1850s. In 1842, prior to his move to Hacienda Banagüises, northeast of the town of Nueva Bermeja (Colón), he married Francisca de los Dolores

Samá y de la Mota, who hailed from Extremadura and was the daughter of Salvador Samá, a large-scale Cuban slave trader in the early nineteenth century.[18]

The Diago family, who would construct ingenios Tinguaro, Ponina, and Santa Elena in the same region as Zulueta's great mills, also began moving east to Matanzas from the Güines Valley in the 1830s. The Cuban Diagos originated with the migration of Pedro Diago y Baranda, a *gallego* from Coruña, who came to Havana in 1792 as director of the insurance firm Seguros Marítimos de la Habana. This company serviced transatlantic shipping in the late eighteenth century, and many of its "accionistas" were closely connected to the Cuban slave trade. Married in 1794 to Luisa Fato y del Castillo, the couple had five children: two daughters, Micaela and Luisa; and three sons, Pedro, Francisco, and Fernando, who by the mid-nineteenth century would become powerful sugar barons, railroad builders, and financiers.[19]

The senior Diago established two ingenios in the Güines Valley during the boom years of the 1790s. Ingenios Cambre and San José, known to as Diago Grande and Diago Chico, were the principal Diago family holdings in the early nineteenth century. When the three brothers came of age, they managed to acquire Ingenio Amistad (also in Güines), which was owned in partnership with a brother-in-law, Joaquín Ayestarán y Goicoechea, a Basque who was married to their sister Luisa Diago y Fato. (Fernando Diago would later wed the couple's daughter, his niece Luisa de Ayestarán y Diago.) Amistad had been the property of Ayestarán's father in partnership with the Governor of Cuba in the 1790s, Luis de las Casas.[20]

In the 1830s the Diago brothers began their expansion toward the frontier. Sometime early in the decade Pedro Diago y Fato acquired the 40-caballería Ingenio Santa Rita, located in Sagua La Grande in the region known as Sierra Morena. This ingenio bordered the Atlantic near a coastal embarcadero to the northwest of the village of Rancho Veloz.[21] In addition, the land that would be used to establish Tinguaro and Santa Elena on the Hacienda Banagüises was also purchased in 1838 or 1839, although these ingenios would not produce their first zafras until the early 1840s.[22]

Havana commercial capital also began to penetrate Matanzas in diverse capacities during the 1830s. In addition to financing ingenio construction and acting as factors for Matanzas sugar and coffee planters, merchant houses also acquired land and constructed mills. Representative of this sector is the Torriente family, who later would found the Banco de Santander in Spain with capital accumulated in Cuba. The Torriente y de la Gándara brothers, Antonio, Francisco, and Cosme, came to Cuba from Santander sometime in the early 1820s. Havana-based sugar brokers and small-scale financiers, they established a branch of Torriente Hermanos in Matanzas during the early 1830s and were destined to build and operate the largest warehouse in Matanzas by the mid-nineteenth century. Another brother, Vicente, remained in Santander, operating a merchant house that maintained close ties with the Torriente's Cuban operations. In February 1838 the brothers purchased 55 caballerías of land on Hacienda Macuriges, along the southern road between Havana and Cienfuegos. The land, which was adjacent to the Zapata swamp, was owned by the Conde de Casa Montalvo, Juan Montalvo y Castillo; and the purchase price was 16,400 pesos, less than 300 pesos/caballería. The Torriente brothers built Ingenio Cantabria on this land in the early 1840s, and a railway line connected the farm with Matanzas, Güines, and Havana by the middle of the decade.[23]

During the 1830s several interrelated transformations occurred in the structure and geography of the Matanzas economy. The first was linked to generational changes in the ownership of productive resources. Younger members of families pioneering the development of the province's sugar economy took over the operation of old mills and actively established new ones as well. And they in turn were challenged for control of the upper echelons of the socioeconomic hierarchy by a new generation of entrepreneurs, usually peninsular in origin, who penetrated the region during the decade. Both these sectors of the planter class were endowed with substantial resources. Some invested family capital accumulated through sugar production in the late eighteenth century and in the first three decades of the nineteenth century, as was the case with the Diagos. Others, such as the Zuluetas and Torrientes, brought coffers filled through slave trading and other commercial activities.

The ingenios they built were modern, capital-intensive mills for the epoch, utilizing the innovations in processing technology that emanated from the North Atlantic centers of industrialization. All installed steam engines in fully mechanized ingenios; old-style Jamaican trains were bypassed in favor of modern Derosne or Rillieux devices; the earliest centrifuges found in Cuba were first employed on their mills, which were stocked with enormous slave populations. By the late 1840s, every one of these new ingenios was connected by rail to Matanzas, Cárdenas, or Havana, and many developed railway transportation within the confines of their estates.

The appearance of this new generation of dynamic entrepreneurs did not mean the disappearance of the old families. They were not interested in taking over established mills in older areas of production, although on occasion such takeovers did occur. Their sights were trained on the high-yielding, forested land in areas to the south and east of Cárdenas and in the zone that would become the jurisdiction of Colón in the mid-1850s. There had been trapiches in these regions from the eighteenth century. Notices of sugarcane planting as far east as Guamutas and as far southeast as Palmillas and Hanábana were common before 1800, but these were marginal zones of colonization and production until the 1830s.

The main sugar-producing regions in the first three decades of the nine-teenth century were concentrated in the areas around the port—in the Yu-murí Valley and Ceiba Mocha to the west and southwest; in the Magdalena Valley in the Santa Ana region to the south; eastward in the direction of Cárdenas in Canimar and Camarioca; and, in the 1820s, farther southeast toward Guamacaro. The other major zone of sugar culture was along the southern tier of Matanzas, in the Alacranes region due east of the Güines Valley and directly south of the city of Matanzas.

During the 1830s, however, the frontier was redefined by the new gen-eration of sugar planters opening up unexploited land in the regions men-tioned above. Few bothered with coffee because the return on investments in sugar was so much greater. The land area in this new zone of expansion is immense by Cuban standards. Cárdenas, which became administratively independent from Matanzas in 1843, and Colón, which became a jurisdic-ción in 1856, were the centers of this zone; together, they extended for a total of 33,368 caballerías, compared with 8,772 caballerías in the jurisdic-tion (not province) of Matanzas.[24] Other regions of sugar production devel-oped around Cienfuegos and Trinidad on the south coast, in areas of Las Villas and Camagüey, and on the north coast in Sagua la Grande. However, the Cárdenas-Colón region remained the most important center of Cuban sugar production through the close of the nineteenth century.

The powerful entrepreneurs opening up the frontier were all involved in the railroad enterprises that were first planned in Cuba during the early 1830s. By 1837 the first Cuban railway line linked Bejucal and Havana, and the railroad was pushing on to Güines. In addition, a project to construct a line from Cárdenas to the interior had been granted approval by Madrid in 1837, and plans for two distinct lines from Matanzas had been drawn up and were awaiting official sanction.[25] Every member of this generation of sugar planters was not only well aware of plans for new infrastructural develop-ment, but was a heavy investor in railroad construction. Land purchases in the 1830s and the founding of ingenios were linked to the knowledge that the railroad was on its way.

The moving frontier meant the development of a land market in areas where property had rarely been bought or sold, and where land was hitherto virtually valueless. Yet, by the mid-1830s sales were numerous, and the principal beneficiaries were titled Havana families who had been awarded land grants in the eighteenth century or earlier. For generations, much of this land was not only underutilized, but had no market value. With the sudden shift of the frontier eastward, owing to the imminent development of railway lines and the expansion of the sugar industry, vast tracts of land on old corrales or hatos became marketable and were purchased by small-scale farmers with modest resources as well as by those with greater ambi-tions.

All this meant a substantial windfall for the marquises and counts who were able to convert unused land into capital that could be invested in more dynamic activities, among which railroad building and ingenio moderniza- tion or new construction were priorities. Capital was generated in two ways through these sales. Sometimes land was purchased outright with cash paid at the time of the transaction. More often, however, sales were effected "a censo," which meant that the purchaser needed to make only a small down payment. Usufruct was secured and could be maintained by the yearly pay- ment of 5 percent of the parcel's total value. In these transactions the prin- cipal remained the same, payments would usually be in perpetuity, and le- gal titles remained in the hands of the seller. Yet the transaction was recorded by the Anotaduría de Hipotecas, which functionally meant the public generation of a signed legal document that was in practice simply a rental contract. Thus, owners could generate rent, secure property improve- ments, and ensure the maintenance of indisputable property rights despite giving up usufruct. This practice of "ventas a censo" was widespread in the 1830s and would continue as a mechanism for developing frontierland and producing capital through the 1860s.

This could mean significant yearly revenues for landowners. Several ex- amples illustrate this process and indicate the value of land in new regions of colonization in the 1830s. The Conde de Casa Montalvo, Juan Montalvo y Castillo, actively sold parcels of land throughout the 1830s, either out- right or in "censo" arrangements. In 1832 and 1833, sections of Hacienda Macuriges were sold, the prices ranging between 200 and 500 pesos/cabal- lería. Eleven sales were made "a censo," and in this manner 92 caballerías of land were effectively rented to 11 families. The total nominal value of these transactions was 37,076 pesos, or 403 pesos/caballería.[26]

Two other examples are provided by the Conde de Fernandina and the Marqués de la Real Proclamación, who had jurisdiction over enormous land areas that originated in land grants made during the early colonial period. In 1838 the count was selling off land from Corral Santo Domingo. A total of 100 caballerías were sold "a censo" to 11 buyers for 35,044 pesos, or 350 pesos/caballería. The marquis sold 85 caballerías from Hacienda Guanajay- abo to 14 families for 41,400 pesos, or 437 pesos/caballería.[27] These are but a small fraction of the total sales made during the 1830s and 1840s.

Trade, Merchants, and Credit

The port of Matanzas was legally opened to foreign shipping in 1809, and this legitimized the smuggling that had traditionally been carried on from the bay area. It also removed a major obstacle to legal commerce and was followed by the establishment of foreign merchant houses dedicated to trade. A North American firm, Latting & Glen, was one of the first import-export houses to open a business in Matanzas, and they began a project to construct dock facilities in 1809.[28]

Trade data from Matanzas in the early nineteenth century indicate that sugar exports did not expand in earnest until after 1816. However, caution must be exercised here, for export statistics do not necessarily parallel the process of economic expansion. Many early-Matanzas ingenio and cafetal owners were Havana-based, and their lines of credit and access to foreign markets extended through Havana merchant houses. Until the major import-export firms of the capital opened branches in Matanzas in the late 1820s, many Matanzas planters marketed their crops through Havana. Thus, production increases in Matanzas were not always reflected in official export data.

After 1816, however, there was a more positive correlation between increases in sugar production and a rise in trade from the port. Although gross production data are available only for selected years, productive capacity can be roughly gauged by examining the number of ingenios in the province. Between 1817 and 1827 the number of sugar mills increased from 76 to 111 (46.1 percent), while the volume of sugar exports rose from 39,000 to 94,700 boxes (143 percent). (One box of sugar was equal to approximately 17 arrobas, or 425 pounds.)

The 1827 data indicate that, in addition to the 111 mills grinding cane, 93 more plantations were "en fomento," being cleared, planted, and prepared for production.[29] The meteoric rise in the sugar trade from Matanzas after 1827 was linked to the increase in the number of mills coming into production in the early and mid-1830s. Between 1827 and 1838, sugar exports from Matanzas more than doubled (see Figure 3.1). This was also related to the appearance of Havana-based import-export firms and foreign-owned merchant houses that established direct linkages with international markets from Matanzas.

The coffee trade was more erratic, as shown in Figure 3.2. In the short terms, the production of coffee is in many ways economically more complex than that of sugar, since there is a four- to five-year delay between planting and full productivity of individual bushes. Thus, there is substantial time lag between initial land-and-labor investment and the generation of income. On the other hand, coffee does not require much in the way of complex and costly processing machinery in order to prepare beans for marketing; it can therefore be produced by smallholders as well as on extensive plantations.

Coffee has other disadvantages. The drastic difference in income generated per slave and per land unit between coffee and sugar cultivation has already been discussed. Investments in sugar were overwhelmingly more lucrative, although the start-up costs for sugar were astronomically higher than those for coffee because of the need for expensive processing equip-

Sugar Exports

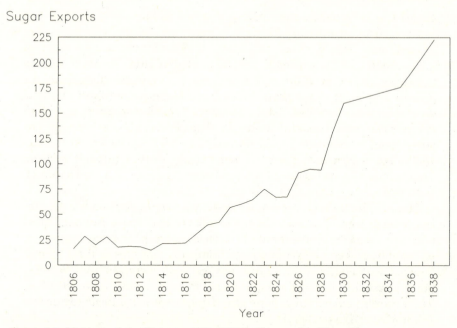

Figure 3.1. Matanzas Sugar Exports, 1806–1838 (in thousands of boxes)
SOURCES: Jacobo de la Pezuela, *Diccionario geográfico, estadístico, histórico de la isla de Cuba* (Madrid: Imp. del Establecimiento de Mellado, 1863), vol. 4, pp. 47, 58; AHN, Ultramar, leg. 4602.

ment. Coffee is also more susceptible to extensive damage by hurricanes or even by violent storms. Sugarcane can be likewise affected, but has more resiliency. Canes may be flattened by driving rains and strong winds, but usually they are not permanently damaged and still grow to maturity. Once coffee blossoms or the berries are knocked from trees, the harvest is lost. The problem is exacerbated by the fact that Matanzas coffee farms were established on flatlands that offered no natural protection. This is one factor that may help explain the radical fluctuations in coffee exports from Matanzas in the early nineteenth century.

Another possible explanation is the turnover within the ranks of coffee plantation owners, many of whom were foreigners. Investments to produce coffee were minuscule compared with the costs of founding a sugar mill. If things were going badly for whatever reason, coffee planters could sell off their slaves, sometimes at a profit, and abandon the island without sustaining cataclysmic losses. There is much evidence that many U.S. coffee planters remained in Cuba only for a short time in the early nineteenth century. Many names found among coffee planters in the 1810s are conspicuous for their absence in the 1820s. One thing is certain. After 1840, when railroad lines were rapidly developed throughout the province, production and ex-

Coffee Exports

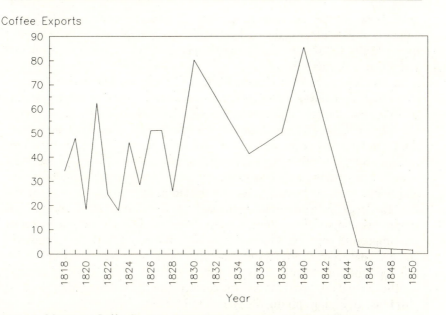

Year

Figure 3.2. Matanzas Coffee Exports, 1818–1850 (in thousands of quintales)

SOURCES: Pezuela, *Diccionario geográfico*, vol. 4, pp. 47, 58; *Balanza general del comercio de la isla de Cuba en el año de 1838* (Havana: Imprenta del Gobierno y de la Real Hacienda por S.M., 1839).

ports plummeted to insignificance, and coffee was never resurrected as a major resource in the Matanzas region (see Figure 3.2).

Reliable statistical data on shipping and the composition and origin of imports to Matanzas are lacking for the first two decades of the nineteenth century. Fragmentary data from the 1820s, however, reveal that U.S.-owned shipping nearly monopolized the import-export trade. In 1820 Washington established a Consular Commercial Agency in the port to look after U.S. commercial interests. A detailed account for 1823 indicates that of 197 ships entering the Matanzas harbor, 191 were U.S.-owned. By 1826, 226 ships entered the bay, and 209 were of U.S. origin. Only 4 flew the Spanish flag.[30] Spanish shipping in the early 1820s was occupied with the losing military effort to defeat the insurrection on the mainland and maintain the empire, which had been under siege since the Latin American wars of independence erupted in 1810. Commercial shipping was minuscule, and perhaps this is one reason why Spanish merchants did not play an important role in Matanzas until the late 1820s and early 1830s.

Piracy seriously disrupted Spanish shipping in the Caribbean. The U.S. consul in Matanzas reported extensively on attacks perpetrated against Spanish ships by pirates, many of whom were Argentine and Venezuelan revolutionaries harassing Spanish efforts at resupply through Caribbean ports.[31] By 1834, when reliable statistics on trade are again available, U.S. shipping still dominated the trade of Matanzas, though not to the extremes of the 1820s. Of 333 ships entering the bay in 1834, 226 were U.S.-owned and 79 were Spanish.[32]

In addition to the near monopolization of shipping, Matanzas importers in the 1820s purchased products almost exclusively from the United States. In 1826, for example, 91.3 percent of all imported goods (by value) originated in the United States. Consumer staples led the way. Rice, salted cod, flour, cooking fat, pork, and jerked beef were among the most important items.[33] By the 1830s other types of products were imported to meet the needs of the expanding sugar economy. Standard imports included staves and hoops for barrels; and, with the depletion of forest reserves near the bay, the large-scale importation of coal from the United States began. Coal imports would stoke the fires of many ingenios through the remainder of the nineteenth century. Moses Taylor & Company of New York regularly shipped coal from Pennsylvania's Lehigh Valley mines to Matanzas; with the beginning of railroad construction in the late 1830s, pig iron became another valuable import. Wood for construction from Maine lumberyards also filled U.S. ships plying the waters to Matanzas.[34]

Exports, however, were more diversified with respect to destination, even though a large share was carried by U.S. ships. In 1826 the United States consumed 39.2 percent of Matanzas exports; England, 14.9 percent; and the Netherlands purchased 15.8 percent of total export value. These exports consisted almost exclusively of sugar, molasses, and coffee. In 1823, the U.S. consul in Matanzas estimated that 80 percent of export value consisted of sugar products, while the remaining 20 percent was coffee. It is also worth noting that the balance of payments for Matanzas in 1826 was extremely favorable: a little more than 1 million pesos in goods were imported, while almost 1,900,000 pesos of sugar and coffee were exported.[35]

Data on shipping rates are available for the late 1830s. Sugar was shipped to New York for 1.50 dollars/box or 37.4 cents/hundredweight, and coffee was carried for the same price. A hogshead of molasses paid 4 dollars freight.[36]

Before railroad construction, products from Matanzas ingenios and cafetales moved overland to the bay or down the major rivers of the region in flat-bottomed barges, or "lanchas." The Yumurí River carried produce from the valley, the Cañas and San Agustín serviced Ceiba Mocha, and the Río San Juan provided transportation for the areas to the south of the bay from Santa Ana.

But as the frontier slowly moved east, the Canimar River became the most important shipping artery connecting the bay area to producing zones in the interior. Sometime in the second decade of the nineteenth century, construction began on a huge embarcadero on the banks of the Canimar, approximately five miles from the coast. This became the major warehouse and transshipment center for sugar and coffee outside the port itself.[37] Produce from as far away as Guamutas and Nueva Bermeja was shipped to the embarcadero, which was called Tumbadero by locals. Lanchas regularly moved from the warehouse down the river and across the bay to the docks of Matanzas. These boats, which could hold up to 100 boxes of sugar, charged 12.75 pesos for a round trip from Tumbadero to the mouth of the river, and smaller barges charged 8.50 pesos.[38] During the 1830s, plans were drawn up for a railroad line from Tumbadero to the interior. It was never constructed, however, and in the 1840s the railroad established direct linkages from the interior to the ports of Cárdenas and Matanzas. Tumbadero fell into disuse.

The banks of the Canimar also served as a summer retreat for city dwellers (and as a winter retreat for visitors from the States). A North American woman, Sarah Echevarría, established a guest house in the early 1830s and published announcements in the local paper, the *Aurora de Yumurí*, in both Spanish and English.[39]

The merchant class of Matanzas was composed of three definable groups. The first consisted of foreign firms established early in the nineteenth century. Most were large-scale importers of manufactured goods and basic consumer staples such as flour and salted fish, which provisioned ingenios, cafetales, and the province's other consumer markets. This sector of the merchant class also speculated in the local commodities market by purchasing sugar and coffee, which were then resold and shipped to export markets. They also acted as factors for plantation owners, collecting commissions on sales and fees for the transportation and warehousing of sugar and coffee. In addition, they sometimes supplied credit to planters in the form of working capital or supplies at harvesttime through "refacción" contracts.[40] Slave trading was also a major activity and one of the primary mechanisms of capital accumulation.

The second group appeared in the 1820s and 1830s. Composed largely of peninsular Spaniards acting in much the same capacities as the first group, they became more powerful because of their diversified activities. In addition to traditional merchant roles, they also established modern ingenios and invested heavily in railroad building.

The third group, also generally composed of peninsulares, was made up of smaller-scale shopkeepers who owned the many tiendas and pulperías in the city itself and in villages throughout the province. A wide variety of consumer goods was supplied to the local population through these retail outlets, but this sector did not provide credit to planters; nor did they act as sugar and coffee brokers or as slave traders.

Yet, one of the most important sectors of Cuban society was conspicuous for its absence in the commercial sector. The titled families with roots in the

eighteenth century or before, who played such a critical role as sugar entrepreneurs in Havana and later in Matanzas, shunned the world of commerce.
There are few examples of Cuban-born families in the early nineteenth century establishing merchant houses or participating in the import-export
trade. This is puzzling because these same families were not averse to risk
or economic diversification. They exhibited a marked entrepreneurial spirit
and were responsible for pushing the sugar economy into frontier regions,
importing the most advanced machinery from Europe or the United States,
and they were initiators and heavy investors in the first Cuban railroads. In
addition, some financed slave-trading expeditions to the coast of Africa. Yet,
with the exception of James Drake's Cuban-born sons and Cristóbal Madan,
the creole son of Joaquín Madan, there are no examples of Cubans participating in any important commercial capacity in Matanzas during the first
half of the nineteenth century. Why these families did not extend their
entrepreneurial spirit to commerce is puzzling, for foreign competitors were
thus allowed to establish an exclusive base of economic and political power
in Cuba's urban centers.

Specific data on merchant families are meager for the first two decades of
the nineteenth century. Two U.S.-based merchant houses seem to have
played dominant roles as import-export firms. George Latting headed one
of the most important companies early in the century, and his presence in
Matanzas continued through the 1820s. He was first in business as Latting
& Glen, which dated from at least 1809. By the early 1820s he was associated as Latting, Adams & Stewart, the largest consignees of merchandise
imported into Matanzas. One of his partners was Francis Adams, who
headed the U.S. Consular Commercial Agency in Matanzas in 1824; and
the other, William Stewart from Philadelphia, owned the sugar ingenio Carolina in Cienfuegos. By the late 1830s, however, Latting, Adams & Stewart
dissolved their business, sold their principal warehouse at the mouth of the
Yumurí River, and disappeared from Matanzas.[41]

The other principal North American merchant in early-nineteenth-century Matanzas was Zacarías Atkins, who owned Cafetal Especulación on the
banks of the Canimar River. Atkins's principal activity was slave trading,
although by the 1820s he operated an import-export house that carried a
diversified variety of merchandise.[42]

John Forbes, another North American who owned a cafetal along the
Canimar River, was a small-scale merchant of minimal economic importance.[43] Finally, during the early 1820s the U.S. firm Simpson, Tryon &
Company also acted as consignees for imported goods. Simpson owned a
cafetal in Canimar, but this farm seems to have flourished briefly, for there
is no evidence of its survival beyond 1825.[44]

The most important slave-trading merchant in early-nineteenth-century
Matanzas was Joaquín Madan, who first appeared in Cuba sometime during

the second half of the eighteenth century. Emigrating from Ireland, Madan established Madan Sobrino e Hijos in Havana. He became the first success-ful Havana merchant to open a branch in Matanzas and was without doubt the region's largest importer of bozales. Madan owned several ships; and the largest, the *San Joaquín*, regularly plied the Atlantic between the Afri-can coast and Cuba.[45] He was also linked by marriage to the most powerful Cuban slave-trading families. Madan's daughter Antonia was married to Julián Luis Alfonso, the son of the Catalán merchant and slave trader Gon-zalo Luis Alfonso. Joaquín's son Cristóbal Madan, who would become one of Cuba's most important railroad entrepreneurs, cemented the Alfonso-Madan linkage by marrying his niece, María Alfonso y Madan.[46]

Latting, Atkins, and Madan dominated commercial life in Matanzas until the late 1820s. After 1825, however, the expansion of sugar and coffee pro-duction and the continued growth of trade attracted a variety of merchants to the region. Many had been established in Havana for some time and opened branches in Matanzas in order to capitalize on the economic expan-sion taking place. Others were newcomers to Cuba, who could not compete with Havana merchants but understood that Matanzas offered bright pos-sibilities for the future.

Among the Havana merchants opening offices in Matanzas, the most im-portant were Eduardo Fesser, who founded Fesser Hermanos in the late 1820s, and James Drake's son, Santiago Drake y Castillo, who allied himself in the early 1830s with the North American merchant Henry Coit in Drake & Coit. Fesser came to Cuba from Andalucía in the early 1820s. His mar-riage in 1826 to Micaela Diago y Fato, the sister of Francisco, Fernando, and Pedro Diago, guaranteed entrance into the upper echelons of the Cuban so-cioeconomic power structure. He also gained access to elite political circles, for his brother-in-law Francisco Diago was married to María Josefa Tirry y Loinaz, the daughter of the Marqués de la Cañada Tirry, Juan Tirry y Lacy, the Governor of Matanzas.[47] Fesser became a merchant of considerable power, for it was he who built, owned, and operated the Almacenes de Regla in Havana, Cuba's largest warehouse, where an enormous share of Cuban sugar was stored before export to foreign markets.

Santiago Drake y Castillo was the son of the English merchant, James Drake, whose firm Drake Hermanos was one of the largest import-export houses in nineteenth-century Cuba. His Matanzas association with Henry Coit during the 1830s has its roots in the early nineteenth century. Coit's father, Levi Coit, was a New York merchant heavily involved in Caribbean trade during the 1790s.[48] The senior Coit had close business connections with the Howland brothers of New York, who owned a fleet of forty-two ships and traded extensively with Cuba. The Howlands never opened a branch of their New York–based business in Cuba, but they did purchase a sugar ingenio near Sagua la Grande—El Dorado—and they also owned two coffee plantations near Matanzas, Ontario and Mt. Vernon.[49] Henry Coit was a nephew of the Howlands, the son of one of their sisters, and while representing the company in Cuba he developed close business linkages with the Drakes. Drake & Coit operated in Matanzas from 1830 to 1838, when the firm split up because Santiago was called upon to take over the operations of Drake Hermanos in Havana. Coit returned to New York but actively continued commercial linkages with Cuba, and Drake Hermanos of Havana absorbed the Matanzas operation.[50]

Two North American merchants, Joseph Harris and George Bartlett, also established a presence as importer-exporters in Matanzas during the mid-1820s. They associated as George Bartlett & Company, but after Bartlett's death in the late 1820s Harris continued operating alone as Joseph Harris & Company. During the early 1830s Lewis Shoemaker, who had been named head of the U.S. Consular Commercial Agency in Matanzas, joined Harris. Shoemaker and Harris operated through the 1830s but did not maintain their business beyond 1840.[51]

The growth of sugar and coffee cultivation in Matanzas during the first three decades of the nineteenth century was financed largely by Havana merchant houses, many of whom were heavily involved in slave trading. The foreign commercial firms operating in Matanzas participated in all facets of trade, but they did not play a role as major creditors to the region's planters. Prior to 1830 almost every mortgage of land, slaves, or future harvests involved Havana merchants such as Drake Hermanos or Pedro Martínez y Cía., Cuba's largest slave-trading firm.[52]

However, in the early 1830s several Matanzas merchants began to finance sugar-producing enterprises. Drake & Coit were the first creditors of importance and were followed by Fesser. The appearance of the Torriente brothers in Matanzas during the early 1830s heralded the arrival of a large-scale commercial house that concentrated its activities in Matanzas. Torriente Hermanos became the principal warehousers and "refaccionistas" to Matanzas planters for the next three decades, although many plantation owners would continue their linkages with Havana firms. The Torrientes, from Santander, had migrated to Cuba in the 1820s and established a merchant house in Havana. Sometime in the early 1830s they moved the center of their activities to Matanzas, although their Havana branch continued operating.

The dramatic rise in sugar production during the late 1820s and early 1830s attracted many merchants to the province, and a new phenomenon developed—local competition to market the sugar produced by Matanzas planters. Sugar marketing was highly speculative, could be extremely lucrative, and was closely tied to the provision of credit. Although many of the old titled families, such as the Montalvos, O'Farrills, or Zequeiras, had the capacity to finance their own operations, most sugar planters required large infusions of outside capital. Slave populations had to be augmented or replenished; machinery had to be purchased, modernized, or maintained; a wide variety of manufactured goods and food products were needed to provision ingenios, especially during the zafra, which could extend from December through June.

The "refacción" contract became the mechanism through which planters acquired credit. Functionally, two broad purposes were served by these contracts. First, planters were provided with operating capital throughout the year, and there were usually special provisions for increased capital needs at harvesttime. Second, merchants were guaranteed sugar supplies for export, since all contracts required planters to sell their sugar to the creditors, usually at local market prices. Merchants gained other advantages as well. They usually provided transportation services to planters; sold "envases," boxes, and conical molds as part of the contract; collected interest as high as 1.5 percent monthly on outstanding debts; charged warehousing fees to planters from the date of delivery until the produce was loaded on ships; and collected brokerage fees for acting as middlemen between planters and foreign markets.

Merchants providing capital to planters through *refacción* contracts had an advantage over competitors who were exclusively importer-exporters. These other merchants actively purchased sugar from planters; but oftentimes, especially when ingenio owners felt prices would increase, supplies were withheld from market. The refacción contract did not afford planters such a luxury. They were obligated to deliver sugar as soon as it was refined; indeed, in cases of large loans, merchants often stationed a representative at the ingenio to oversee the harvest, to ensure that boxes were not artificially weighted by planters, and to make sure the sugar was promptly shipped. In almost all refacción contracts, zafra's were mortgaged, as were animals, slaves, and sometimes machinery. By law, until the 1850s, when the "privilegio de ingenios" was repealed, the ingenio land itself could not be mortgaged.

Through refacción contracts, the Torrientes were the principal local source of credit to Matanzas planters during the 1830s. An 1834 contract illustrates the numerous agreements recorded by Matanzas notaries. The Torrientes financed the 1834 zafra of Ingenio Esperanza, located in Guamutas. Esperanza was operated by Juan Peraza González, a Cuban who inherited the mill from his father. A debt of 42,981 pesos was acknowledged by González from previous loans, and an emergency loan of 5,250 pesos was made in January 1834 so that more slaves could be purchased for the harvest, which had just begun. The Torrientes also promised to provide capital for all of the food consumed on the ingenio during the zafra, to pay all local taxes incurred, and to provision the ingenio with everything needed to complete the harvest. In return, González mortgaged Esperanza's entire production to Torriente Hermanos: the ingenio's 45 slaves; its 38 "yuntas," or pairs of oxen; and its milling machinery. Unspecified interest would accumulate on the old debt as well as on any new debts incurred, and the Torrientes would be paid warehousing charges of 25 centavos for each box of sugar delivered, plus a commission of 2.5 percent on the sale of all sugar and molasses.[53]

This system established merchant economic control over the planters, and it would be perfected and broadened during the 1840s and 1850s. Many merchants also invested heavily in sugar production, as was the case with the Torrientes. When the "privilegio" was repealed, the avenue to foreclosure and accumulation of agricultural assets by the merchant class was opened. After mid-century, when the technological modernization of sugar production was mandated by increased international competition, the days of the independent planter were numbered. More merchant houses opened in Matanzas, and in Cárdenas as well, specializing in the financing of sugar production. This led to merchant domination over agriculture; the merchant class, it should be added, was almost exclusively composed of immigrant groups.

The lowest tier of the commercial hierarchy was occupied by small-scale shopkeepers and *pulperos*, found in the city and in the urban concentrations throughout the province. Once again, Cubans were conspicuously scarce among the ranks of this group. Several merchant census tracts (in manuscript) clearly illustrate the dimensions of immigrant control. In Ceiba Mocha there were 30 merchants operating different types of establishments in 1827. Twenty-three were of peninsular origin, and their businesses were collectively worth 53,446 pesos, or 92.4 percent of total commercial wealth. Seven Cubans owned small pulperías with an aggregate assessed value of 4,387 pesos, or 7.6 percent of the total. A similar situation was found in Santa Ana during the same year: 13 peninsular merchants owned businesses valued at 20,350 pesos, or 92.9 percent of all commercial resources; 10 Cubans ran very small pulperías worth 1,550 pesos, or 7.1 percent of the total. Finally, in Guamacaro, there were 13 tiendas with an assessed value of 20,300 pesos. Catalonians were dominant, and there were merchants from Vizcaya, Asturias, Galicia, Murcia, and Santander; not one Cuban owned a business.[54]

CHAPTER 4

Slavery

The dependence of sugar and coffee production on slave labor meant that, if economic expansion were to proceed in Matanzas, it was imperative for the slave population to increase constantly. Indeed, no other region in Cuba experienced such dramatic growth in the number of slaves during the first half of the nineteenth century. Between 1817 and 1827, when the overall Cuban slave population rose 37.9 percent, Matanzas slaves increased 146 percent (from 10,773 to 26,522). The slave population had doubled to 53,331 between 1827 and 1841, a period when the island experienced a 47.4 percent increase in total slaves. Additionally, the administrative partidos that were merged to form Cárdenas in 1843 and Colón in 1856, had an additional 41,043 slaves in 1841.[1]

Not only did the absolute number of slaves increase, but there was a marked proportional rise in slaves as a percentage of total population. In 1817 slaves constituted 49.5 percent of all Matanzas inhabitants; they were 57.9 percent in 1827 and 62.7 percent in 1841. In some rural partidos, where cultivation of sugar or coffee was the only economic activity, slaves accounted for an even greater share. The most extreme example is Guamacaro: in 1841 there were 30 ingenios and 73 cafetales, and 89.9 percent of the population was enslaved. In Guanábana 83.3 percent were slaves; in Sabanilla, 76.4 percent; in Cimarrones, 74.7 percent; in Lagunillas, 73.2 percent; and in Santa Ana, 71.8 percent.

Sex distribution among slaves was marked by the predominance of males. In 1817, 73.2 percent of all Matanzas slaves were males; in 1827, 63.3 percent; and in 1841, 66.7 percent. The 1817 data indicate that 68.8 percent of all slaves were Africans; and while there are no data on Cuban slave imports specifically for Matanzas, or on the national origins of Matanzas slaves after 1817, it is likely that the ratio of African to creole slaves remained above 60/40, since it is apparent that the slave population did not increase naturally in this period and that imports were largely responsible for slave population growth.[2] (These data are summarized in Tables 4.1 and 4.2.)

African culture in Matanzas was also nourished by a free-black and mulatto population that increased proportionally along with slaves. There were 854 free people of color in 1817, 2,602 in 1827, and 4,570 in 1841. Although free blacks and mulattoes were found everywhere in small numbers, two-

Table 4.1. Matanzas Slave Population by Partido, 1817–1841

	1817		1841	
	No. Slaves	% Total Pop.	No. Slaves	% Total Pop.
Matanzas City	1,106	22.8	5,779	30.2
Yumurí	2,226	57.5	8,970	63.7
Ceiba Mocha	2,829	53.8	6,378	58.2
Santa Ana	1,999	50.0	4,658	71.8
Guamacaro	2,211	70.9	11,822	89.9
Camarioca	492	46.3	4,701	64.4
Sabanilla	—	—	7,259	76.4
Guanábana	—	—	3,764	83.8
TOTAL	10,773	49.5	53,331	62.7
Alacranes	—	—	5,588	62.3
Cimarrones	—	—	4,662	74.7
Guamutas	—	—	8,560	63.3
Lagunillas	—	—	9,612	73.2
Palmillas	—	—	2,338	47.7
Macuriges	—	—	10,283	70.6
TOTAL			41,043	66.9

SOURCES: AHPM, ME, Estadística, leg. 1, no. 2, "Estadística de Matanzas y los cinco partidos de su jurisdicción. 15 de febrero 1817"; leg. 1, no. 7, "Población de Matanzas en el censo general de 1841," "Distribución de Habitantes 1841," and "Población de los partidos de la jurisdicción de la Habana (1841) que hoy (1846) pertenecen a la provincia de Matanzas," fols. 3–4ᵛ.
NOTE: Pop. = population.

Table 4.2. Matanzas Free-Black, Mulatto, and Slave Populations by Sex, 1817–1841

	Free Blacks and Mulattoes			Slaves		
	M	F	T	M	F	T
1817	805	769	854	7,886	2,887	10,773
1827	1,201	1,401	2,602	16,768	9,754	26,522
1841	2,277	2,293	4,570	34,565	18,766	53,331
1841ᵃ	965	809	1,774	28,408	12,635	41,043

SOURCES: AHPM, ME, Estadística, leg. 1, no. 2, "Estadística de Matanzas y los cinco partidos de su jurisdicción. 15 de febrero 1817"; leg. 1, no. 7, "Población de Matanzas en el censo general de 1841," "Distribución de Habitantes 1841," and "Población de los partidos de la jurisdicción de la Habana (1841) que hoy (1846) pertenecen a la provincia de Matanzas," fols. 3–4ᵛ.
NOTE: M = males; F = females; T = total.
ᵃThese data are for the partidos of Alacranes, Cimarrones, Guamutas, Lagunillas, Palmillas, and Macuriges.

thirds were concentrated in the city of Matanzas in 1841. The sex-distribution pattern among free people of color can be radically contrasted with
that among the slave population: in the former group, there were almost
exactly the same number of males as females in 1841. (See table 4.2.)[3]

The slave trade to Matanzas in the early nineteenth century had two
components. The first originated in Havana, where an important sector of
the Matanzas planter class resided. Credit and trade linkages to rural Matanzas extended from Havana merchant houses such as Drake Hermanos
and Pedro Martínez y Cía., and slaves were secured in the Havana slave
market financed by these same firms.[4] Many ingenio owners, especially titled families, had long-standing business connections with Havana slave
traders dating from the second half of the eighteenth century. Mechanisms
to secure labor supplies had been well developed and were extended from
Havana to the Matanzas frontier in the early nineteenth century.

There was also a local slave trade to Matanzas organized and financed by
the major merchants of the bay area, both before 1817, when the *trata* was
legal, and afterward when theoretically it was banned. Joaquín Madan, Zacarías Atkins, and George Latting not only purchased slaves from incoming
vessels, but also organized expeditions to the African coast on their own
ships. Madan and Atkins were the most active traders through the 1820s.
Madan owned the *San Joaquín*, which was regularly dispatched to Africa,
and Atkins's ship the *Serenade*, capable of transporting more than 500 bozales in one run, was a major carrier of slaves for Matanzas planters.[5]

Trends in slave prices in Matanzas, based on a sampling of transactions
recorded by Matanzas notaries, are indicated in figures 4.1 through 4.4.[6]
Trends in frequency of slave sales, by sex, origin, and age group, are shown
in Figures 4.5 through 4.8. The most important variable determining prices
among different slave categories was age. Prime-age slaves, fifteen through
forty years old, accounted for more than two-thirds of all slave sales in most
sample years between 1804 and 1837; and in many years more than 80
percent of all transactions involved this group (see Figure 4.7).

Although there seems to have been little variation in prices between
males and females or between creoles and Africans when all slave transactions are examined (Figures 4.1 and 4.2), among prime-age slaves creole
males and creole females were consistently more costly than prime-age Africans of either sex (Figure 4.4). This was directly related to the premium
placed on "seasoning" (the acculturation of slaves to forced labor and absolute domination) and to the scarcity of prime-age creoles. In all sample
years between 1804 and 1837, Africans were more frequently bought and
sold, and in many years they accounted for more than 70 percent of total
sales (see Figure 4.6).

An important factor influencing slave price trends seems to have been
fluctuations in the African slave trade to Cuba. Between 1804 and 1809

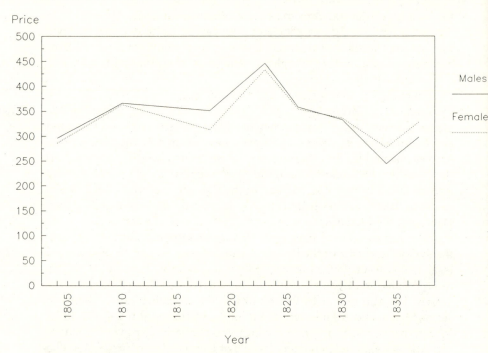

Figure 4.1. Matanzas Slave Sales, 1804–1837: Average Prices by Sex (in pesos)
Sources: See Chapter 12, note 21.

there was a major decrease in the annual number of slaves arriving in Cuba (see Figure 4.9).[7] This was paralleled by a fairly sharp rise in average prices for prime-working-age slaves. In 1804 the average price for slaves fifteen through forty years old of both genders was 299 pesos. By 1810 this same category had increased by 33.4 percent to 399 pesos/slave.

The Cuban slave trade recovered after 1810, and although there was some downward movement in the volume of landings in 1813 and 1814, by 1817 imports peaked for the period under consideration at 34,500 slaves. As slave supplies increased, prices softened. Between 1810 and 1818, prices for prime-working-age slaves declined 8.8 percent from an average of 399 pesos to 364 pesos/slave.

After 1818, slave prices rose considerably; and between 1818 and 1823 the average price of slaves fifteen through forty years of age had risen by 28 percent to 466 pesos. This was directly related to a sharp reduction in slave imports, which declined precipitously from the high of 1817 (34,500 slaves) to a meager 1,900 slaves in 1823. Once again, after 1823 increases in slave arrivals were accompanied by a downward trend in slave prices.

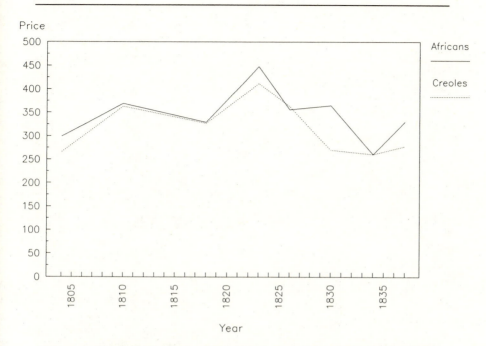

Price

Africans

Creoles

Year

Figure 4.2. Matanzas Slave Sales, 1804–1837: Average Prices by Origin (in pesos)
SOURCES: See Chapter 12, note 21.

Average prices for prime-working-age slaves declined by 20.4 percent between 1823 and 1826, from 466 to 371 pesos/slave.

The slave trade to Cuba fluctuated between 1823 and 1826, but after 1826
(until 1835) there was a gradual rise in the volume of imports, and it is not
surprising to find that the slave market reacted to the increase in supply
with lower prices. Between 1830 and 1834, average prices for prime-age
slaves decreased by 21.5 percent, from 382 to 300 pesos, and it should be
added that 1834 prices were 35.6 percent lower than the peak levels of 1823.

Once again, the decline in slave trading after 1835 was reflected by a substantial recovery of slave prices, which soared by 56.6 percent between 1834
and 1837 (from 300 to 470 pesos). It should be added that the late 1830s
were years of intensified demand for slaves because of the many new mills
established in Matanzas during this period.

Another important factor influencing demand for slaves during the mid-
1830s was the cholera epidemic of 1833 which swept through the Matanzas
slave population. Although general mortality rates are unknown, José Antonio Saco visited 18 ingenios in the Matanzas partido of Sabanilla and
found that, depending on the individual plantation between 23 percent and
60 percent of the slave population perished during the epidemic. For exam-

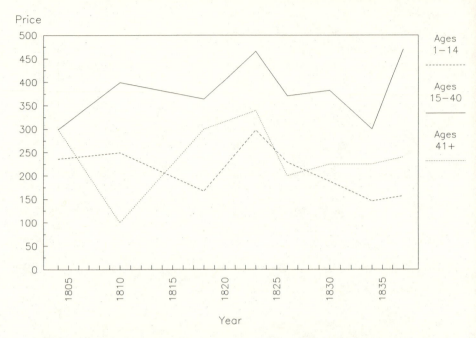

Figure 4.3. Matanzas Slave Sales, 1804–1837: Average Prices by Age Group (in pesos)
Sources: See Chapter 12, note 21.

ple, on Domingo Aldama's Ingenio Santo Domingo 75 slaves died out of a total dotación of 130.[8] With respect to the cost of slave labor, the epidemic meant a need to replace slave workers which contributed to the strong demand and upward trend in slave prices after 1834.

It is apparent that the Matanzas slave market responded closely to fluctuations in the volume of the Cuban slave trade. The short-term sensitivity of slave prices to import levels was linked to the extreme scarcity of creole slaves available for market in the early decades of the nineteenth century. Supplies of marketable slaves were largely determined by the volume of the trata. Demand for slave labor experienced short-term cyclical fluctuations, to be sure. By and large, however, this was a period of continuous economic expansion, which meant a consistently strong secular demand for slaves in the first four decades of the nineteenth century.

The profitability of sugar or coffee production was another factor influencing demand for slave labor. Throughout this period, prices for sugar in the Havana and Matanzas markets fluctuated between 4 and 7 cents/pound for the best quality white sugars, and quite often the slave market reacted in the short term to sudden shifts in local commodity prices. This is graphically underlined by the sharp rise in sugar prices that occurred between the

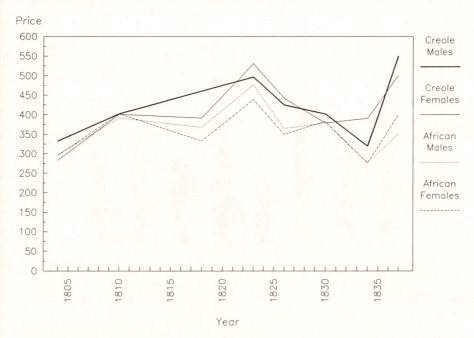

Price

Creole Males

Creole Females

African Males

African Females

Year

Figure 4.4. Matanzas Slave Sales, 1804–1837: Average Prices by Sex and Origin, Ages 15–40 (in pesos)

SOURCES: See Chapter 12, note 21.

harvests of 1835 and 1836. In 1835 white sugars were traded in Matanzas at between 5 and 5.5 cents/pound. By January 1836, prices had more than doubled to between 11 and 11.25 cents/pound and these higher prices prevailed through the 1836 zafra.[9] The rise in Matanzas slave prices after 1835 was probably connected to this sharp increase in sugar prices, which meant greater income and capital availability to planters.

Price differentials by sex for prime-age slaves were inconsistent over time. In some years, males were valued somewhat higher than females: by 11.2 percent in 1804; 2.2 percent in 1818; 6.7 percent in 1823; 3.3 percent in 1826; and 7.3 percent in 1837. Yet, in other years, prime-age females were marketed at higher average prices than males: 1.5 percent greater in 1810 and 10.9 percent greater in 1834. In 1830, average prices for prime-age males and females were equal (at 382 pesos). The same kind of inconsistency is found when controlling for place of birth. The relative average prices of creole males and creole females showed little consistency; nor did the average relative prices of African males and females. Nevertheless, prime-age creoles of both sexes almost always sold for more than prime-age Africans.

The scarcity of prime-age creoles in early-nineteenth-century Matanzas

Percentages

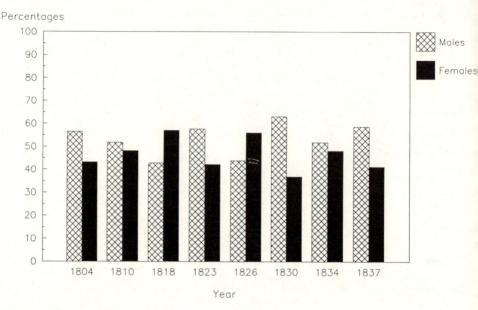

Figure 4.5. Matanzas Slave Sales by Sex, 1804–1837 (selected years in percentages)
Sources: See Chapter 12, note 21.

Percentages

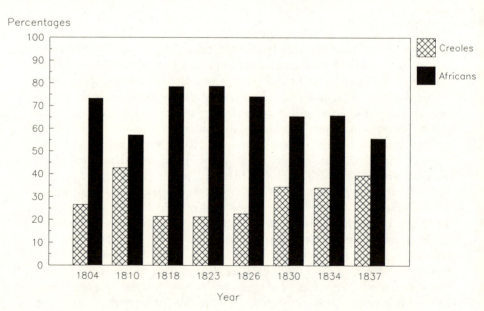

Figure 4.6. Matanzas Slave Sales by Origin, 1804–1837 (selected years in percentages)
Sources: See Chapter 12, note 21.

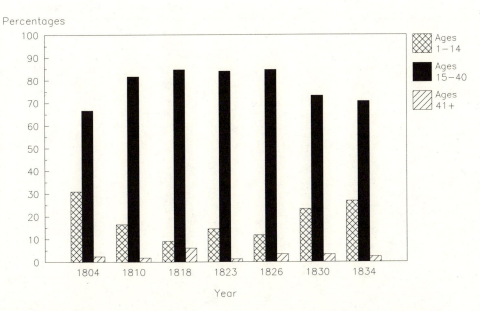

Figure 4.7. Matanzas Slave Sales by Age Group, 1804–1834 (selected years in percentages)
Sources: See Chapter 12, note 21.

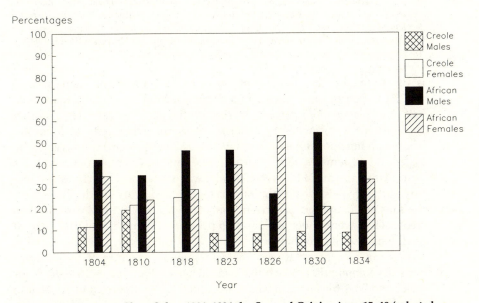

Figure 4.8. Matanzas Slave Sales, 1804–1834, by Sex and Origin, Ages 15–40 (selected years in percentages)
Sources: See Chapter 12, note 21.

Slave Imports

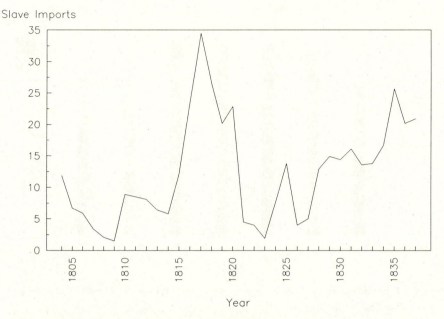

Year

Figure 4.9. Slave Imports into Cuba, 1804–1837 (in thousands)
Sources: David Eltis, "The Nineteenth-Century Transatlantic Slave Trade: An Annual Time Series of Imports into the Americas Broken Down by Region," *Hispanic American Historical Review* 67:1 (1987), pp. 122–123; David R. Murray, *Odious Commerce: Britain, Spain, and the Abolition of the Cuban Slave Trade* (Cambridge: Cambridge University Press, 1980), p. 18.

is illustrated by the manuscript slave-census returns for Camarioca in 1817.[10] Camarioca was primarily a coffee-growing region, and more than half of all slaves (56.3 percent) worked on the partido's cafetales. Another 20.7 percent were owned by small-scale sitieros, while only 15.5 percent labored on ingenios. Of 489 slaves in 1817, 88 (18 percent) were creoles, 40 males and 48 females. The mean age of Camarioca's creole males was 8.4 years; while the mean for creole females was 6.4 years. Thus, the age structure of the creole slave population was highlighted by its youth. These were the sons and daughters of Africans imported after 1800: 89.7 percent of all creole slaves were under age 15; 87.5 percent of all males and 91.7 percent of all females fell into this category.

This can be contrasted with the demographic structure of the African-born slave population, which had a mean age of 25.7 years: 26.4 years for males and 23.1 for females. Males accounted for 78.1 percent of all African slaves, and 80.2 percent of all the African males were of prime working age, between 15 and 40 years old. Among African females, 69.3 percent fell into this category, most of whom were clustered in the prime reproductive age group, between 16 and 25 years. Unfortunately, a lack of raw data on births or deaths makes it impossible to calculate fertility rates or population growth rates. The available data are summarized in Figures 4.10 through 4.12.

The life experiences of slaves were largely determined by where they worked and, in the case of rural slaves, by the size of the farms on which they lived. Before sugar monoculture overwhelmed Matanzas in the 1840s and 1850s, slaves labored on all types of farms. Even in regions of intense sugar production, such as Ceiba Mocha in 1817, the work and life situations of slaves were diverse. In that year the greatest number of Ceiba Mocha's slaves (38.4 percent) lived on coffee plantations, one-fourth worked on crop- or stock-raising farms, and approximately one-third lived on sugar plantations.[11] The rhythm of work and of life in general on cafetales and on crop- or stock-raising farms was less harsh than that on sugar estates where more regimented and disciplined labor systems prevailed. It should be stressed that the vast majority of all Matanzas slaves before the 1840s lived and labored on non-sugar enterprises.

Later in the century, most Matanzas slaves lived on extensive plantations where slave populations of 200 or more were common. In the early nineteenth century, however, small units of production prevailed, and slaves generally lived on farms or plantations with relatively modest dotaciones. In 1817 there were no Matanzas ingenios or cafetales with more than 200 slaves. The size of slave holdings was linked to the level of economic development in a particular region. In Ceiba Mocha, where the coffee and sugar economy was rather well developed by 1817, 42.6 percent of all slaves lived on farms having 101 or more slaves. This can be contrasted with Camarioca, where no farm was worked by more than 50 slaves and where 51.9 percent of the slave population lived on farms having 20 or fewer slaves. In Guamacaro, where sugar and coffee farms were being developed, 31.9 percent of all slaves lived with 20 or fewer fellow bondsmen, but another 38.3 percent of the slave population labored on farms with between 51 and 150 slaves. These data are summarized in Table 4.3. Thus, the experiences of slaves with respect to the size of the communities in which they lived, and with respect to social interactions with others who had the misfortune to share a similar fate, were diverse throughout Matanzas. Conditions were largely linked to the prevailing type of regional economic activity, which determined the size of each farm's slave population.

Before the 1830s there are no records of slave populations living in *barracones*, the jail-like slave quarters that became the rule in rural Cuba by the mid-nineteenth century.[12] While many slaves were concentrated close to each farm's center of operations—the ingenio on sugar plantations and the drying patios and *tahonas* on coffee farms—a large number also seem to have lived in traditional *bohíos*, clustered together to form small slave

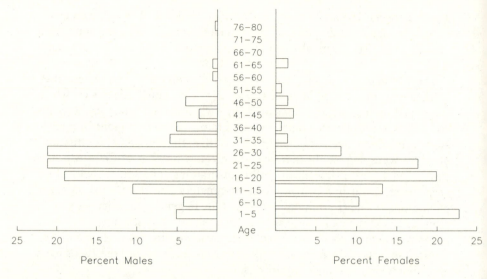

Figure 4.10. Age Pyramid of All Slaves in Camarioca, 1817
Source: AHPM, ME, Estadística, leg. 6, no. 114, fols. 4–20.

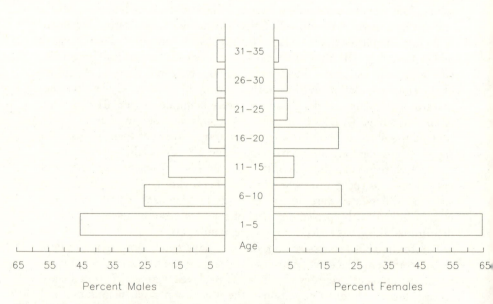

Figure 4.11. Age Pyramid of Creole Slaves in Camarioca, 1817
Source: AHPM, ME, Estadística, leg. 6, no. 114, fols. 4–20.

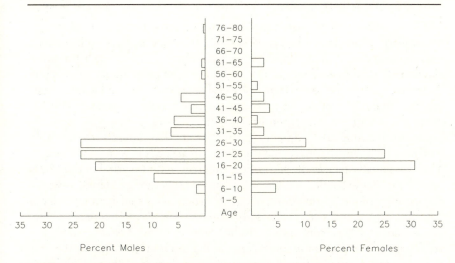

Figure 4.12. Age Pyramid of African Slaves in Camarioca, 1817
SOURCE: AHPM, ME, Estadística, leg. 6, no. 114, fols. 4–20.

Table 4.3. Ceiba Mocha, Guamacaro, and Camarioca, 1817:
Percentage of Slave Population on Farms by Size of Slaveholding

Slaveholdings	Ceiba Mocha	Guamacaro	Camarioca
1–5	9.3	10.3	13.9
6–10	6.9	10.5	17.1
11–20	6.5	11.1	20.9
21–50	12.2	29.8	48.1
51–100	22.5	19.5	0
101–150	25.3	18.8	0
151–200	17.3	0	0
TOTAL	100.0	100.0	100.0

SOURCES: AHPM, ME, Estadística, leg. 8, no. 137, fols. 17–64, and leg. 6, no. 114, fols. 4–20; AHPM, Gobierno Provincial, Esclavos, leg. 34 (no exp. no.), "Estado que manifiesta los esclavos de ambos sexos que se hallen en este partido de Guamacaro. 26 marzo de 1817."

villages. Slave access to "provision grounds" for the cultivation of food supplies seems to have been fairly extensive in the early decades of the nineteenth century.[13] It must be stressed that Matanzas was part of a frontier zone where land was plentiful and marginally exploited. Permitting slaves to cultivate their own plots resolved a fundamental problem, reducing capital expenditures and eliminating the logistical difficulties of securing and transporting bulky foodstuffs over poor roads.

The cultivation of provision grounds was an important part of slave life in the early nineteenth century, and while this aspect of servitude should not be exaggerated, it did function as a potential source of cash for some slaves and it did open doors to the wider world of petty trade. The degradation of slavery and the extreme physical and psychological brutality that was part and parcel of daily life for most slaves should be stressed. But for some slaves there were apparently mitigating factors.

Matanzas historical documents reveal not only that some slaves were able to secure cash, but that they had the ability to spend it in a variety of ways. This was equally true at the start of the nineteenth century and in the 1820s and 1830s. For example, in 1826 and 1827 the Governor of Matanzas wrote report after report complaining about taverners who sold liquor to slaves day and night, and who purchased produce from slave vendors.[14] Complaints about slaves consuming alcohol, generally *aguardiente* (cane-derived brandy), in rural or urban taverns were numerous throughout the first four decades of the nineteenth century. Even as late as 1836, official warnings were issued against the purchase of products from slaves, who sold a wide variety of merchandise illegally, some of it no doubt stolen from their masters. Implicit in these complaints is the fact that many slaves had not only secured cash, but had the mobility and maneuverability within the slave system to spend it.

An interesting case illustrating slave access to cash was the good luck that befell three African-born slave women, Candelaria, Carlota, and Merced, who won 625 pesos each in 1828 by playing the Real Lotería. This secured their freedom through the institution of *coartación*, which gave slaves the right of self-purchase.[15] If slaves were actively participating in officially sanctioned gambling, the implied access to specie contrasts with the image of slaves as victims totally without recourse to their own mechanisms of survival. It was surely a rarity that slaves were able to hit the lottery, but this case is indicative of slave participation in an activity that demanded cash. Slaves were obviously able to use their intelligence and ingenuity to participate as broadly as possible in a world that was theoretically forbidden to them, one that was much broader than the narrow confines of the farms or plantations on which they lived.

There were even cases of skilled slaves hiring themselves out for wages without the knowledge or permission of their owners.[16] Other examples show that slaves garnered valuable skills and were paid cash wages with the approval and encouragement of their masters. In 1830, for example, Francisca Morgado consigned her slave Felipe Neri, seventeen years old, to a four-year apprenticeship as a mason with the master craftsman Juan Dimas. Dimas was responsible for all maintenance expenses over the course of the contract, and in the final year Felipe would draw a salary of 1 peso daily.[17]

The scale of these kinds of activities is entirely unknown, but illegal practices were obviously pervasive enough to warrant official chastisement. Access to cash through the marketing of provision-grounds produce or other merchandise in small quantities explains to some extent how slaves could place down payments on their freedom through coartación contracts. By making a down payment on his or her freedom, any slave could become a *coartado*, thereby freezing the final price of freedom and also prohibiting the master from selling at a higher amount. Coartación contracts were transferable to other masters by law and had to be honored by slave purchasers.[18] While urban slaves may have had more flexibility to accumulate cash legally or surreptitiously, because of the relative anonymity of city life, provision-grounds cultivation and the possibility of marketing small quantities of produce evidently allowed rural slaves some access to the broader world of the marketplace and the possibility of freedom through self-purchase.

Manumissions and down payments on freedom were frequently recorded by Matanzas notaries. Most manumissions resulted from slaves completing payments on their freedom, although there were cases where masters bestowed freedom upon favored slaves through last wills and testaments.[19] In eight sample years between 1804 and 1837, 133 manumissions were recorded that permit a limited profile of Matanzas slaves who were able to secure their freedom.[20]

Males accounted for 44.4 percent of those freed, females making up the remaining 55.6 percent. There was a nearly equal division between Africans (51.2 percent of the sample) and creoles, who accounted for 48.8 percent of those freed. The age structure of manumitted slaves reveals the predominance of prime-age slaves: 70 percent were between fifteen and forty years old; 14.5 percent were forty-one years of age or older; 11.8 percent were between one and fourteen years old; and about 4 percent were newborn slaves whose freedom was purchased by their slave parents before baptism for 50 pesos.[21] Some young children had their freedom purchased by slave parents who remained in bondage. Though theoretically free, these children continued living within the confines of farms and plantations where slavery reigned, and they would reap the benefits of freedom only upon reaching adulthood. Yet, for slaves able to purchase the freedom of their children, the satisfaction of establishing a bridge to liberty must have been rewarding, even if it would never be crossed in their lifetimes.

There were also female slaves who became concubines to white masters and whose children acquired freedom because of legal recognition by their fathers. The case of Justa Gangá is apposite. She was an African slave owned by the Frenchman Luis Ángel Fonchar, who was born in Nantes and came to Matanzas as a coffee planter sometime in the early nineteenth century. Fronchar owned the small cafetal Descanso, which extended for 3.5 caballerías and was worked by 18 slaves, of whom 12 were African. In his will,

Fronchar legally recognized his three children with Justa—Luis, Josefa, and Micaela—and named Justa his sole and legitimate heir.[22]

These instances of slaves acquiring freedom were part of the slave experience, but they must be placed in their proper perspective. Despite the apparent access to small amounts of cash in the early nineteenth century, freedom was beyond the realm of real possibility for most slaves, who lived trying to survive somehow through the most degrading of all human conditions. Access to cash, small-scale involvement in surreptitious petty trade, stealing away at night to local taverns, and the theoretical possibility of making a down payment on freedom may have mitigated the harsh realities of slavery in some small way. But these aspects of servitude should not be used to argue that masses of slaves had genuine life alternatives or that, because of these possibilities, slavery was in any way humane. As the nineteenth century progressed, and as slaves were increasingly concentrated on large plantations where strict vigilance and discipline reigned, the alternatives noted above diminished considerably.

Although the Matanzas free-black and mulatto population increased from 1,676 in 1817 to 4,570 in 1841, along with the large-scale slave imports of the period, they decreased as a percentage of all people of color—from 17.6 percent in 1817, to 9.8 percent in 1827, to 8.5 percent in 1841. One thing remained stable, however, and that was the preference of free blacks and mulattoes for the city of Matanzas. In 1817, 64.2 percent of the free-black and mulatto population lived in the city; by 1841, this figure had risen slightly to 66.5 percent.[23]

Not only was there general disdain for rural labor among free people of color, but with the expansion of trade and growth of the city, employment possibilities existed in skilled and unskilled occupations alike. Slavery defined Matanzas rural society, and to be black or mulatto in the countryside no doubt meant being treated as a slave despite purported freedom. Urban Matanzas offered a refuge of sorts. The city held a large free population of color, and to be African or Afro-Cuban did not necessarily imply a priori identification as a slave. Sex distribution was well balanced, which meant the possibility of family life; in addition, "cabildos de nación" offered cultural linkages with African traditions as well as a measure of independent social cohesion for blacks and mulattoes.[24] Yet, to be black and free did not mean equality with whites by any means. Free people of color constituted a separate legal category, were watched closely by the authorities (especially during periods when slave rebellions broke out in the countryside), and were often the object of persecution and repression such as occurred during the hysteria surrounding the "La Escalera" slave conspiracy of 1844.

Freedom did not necessarily inspire sympathy for the plight of fellow countrymen who remained in bondage. There are numerous cases of freed slaves who were able to prosper modestly and who became slaveowners themselves. The case of Mariano Erice exemplifies this. Mariano was a Carabalí who acquired his freedom in Matanzas early in the second decade of the nineteenth century. He converted to Catholicism and married a free Carabalí woman, María de Jesús, who bore two children, José Pantaleon and María. Mariano ran a small business in the city of Matanzas, owned a single caballería of land on the city's outskirts, and had eight slaves, all of them Africans.[25] His last will and testament left the estate to María de Jesús and—going against custom—did not grant freedom to any of his slaves.

Freedom was legally beyond the reach of the slave masses, but that did not preclude the desperate quest for liberty which commonly resulted in maroonage. Slaves frequently deserted plantations and small farms for remote areas in the hill country, where they tended to coalesce in small *palenques*, or maroon communities. It is hardly surprising that a Cárdenas partido and small village bear the name Cimarrones, which means runaway slaves.[26]

Notices of palenques in Matanzas date from 1770, when local officials noted the existence of a small nucleus of runaways inhabiting the "los molinos" region near the juncture of the San Agustín and Cañas rivers. However, systematic data on cimarrones were not collected until 1817, when monthly notices of runaways were published by Matanzas officials. In one month alone in 1817, 133 slaves deserted their masters: 64 in Yumurí; 51 in Santa Ana; 23 in Ceiba Mocha; 13 in Camarioca; and 8 in Guamacaro. Only 3 were creoles, but that fact is of little significance because there were so few adult creoles inhabiting Matanzas in 1817.[27] There is absolutely no evidence to suggest that slaves deserted solely from sugar plantations because of comparatively worse conditions of life or poorer treatment. Runaways abandoned coffee farms and sugar plantations alike, and there are even notices of cimarrones deserting small sitios and potreros.

During the early 1820s a large palenque existed on the north coast, to the east of the city of Matanzas in the Puerto Escondido region, and there were notices of cimarrones inhabiting the area's coastal beaches as well. In 1829 an extensive maroon community occupied the hills of Nueva Florida to the south of Ceiba Mocha. It was reported that 300 runaways lived in hillside caves and that they were well armed with knives and machetes. There were also notices in 1830 of the growing number of cimarrones "apalancados" (living in palenques) in Santa Ana, in the Limones Grandes mountains near Guamacaro, and in the mountainous region between Ceiba Mocha and Aguacate.[28] The Zapata swamp was another natural refuge for runaways but there are no notices of large scale palenques in this inhospitable region.

The dynamics of daily life within Cuban palenques are entirely unknown. There is no doubt that animals were raised for slaughter, but independent agricultural production was probably marginal, given the uncertainty of long-term survival for any community. Notices of cimarrón raids on small farms and even large plantations for provisions were common. In 1830, for example, a *cuadrilla* (gang) of cimarrones, attacked the ingenio San Francisco in Corral Nuevo and made off with livestock and produce.[29]

Planters and local authorities organized *rancherías* to raid known palenques and capture runaways, especially after periods of frequent attacks or rebellions. *Rancheadores*, or slave bounty hunters, also roamed the Cuban countryside with attack dogs, but they were effective only against individuals or small nuclei of cimarrones, not against the larger palenques.[30]

The survival of maroon communities was closely tied to settlement patterns and population density. In the first three decades of the nineteenth century, despite continued agricultural colonization and economic expansion, vast areas of Matanzas province were still sparsely populated and were ideal locations for runaways to hide and defend themselves from recapture. By the 1830s, however, colonization accelerated, and all areas of the province were in the process of settlement and agricultural development. This meant that remote refuges were harder to find and that the possibility of establishing palenques was considerably diminished.

The powerful entrepreneurs moving into frontier areas in the 1830s and early 1840s were intent on providing security for their productive enterprises and determined to protect their capital investments. Concern for security intensified with the beginning of railroad construction in the late 1830s. Planters financed increased raids against known maroon communities, and independent bounty hunters combed the Matanzas countryside. During the early 1840s careful statistical data on maroons were maintained, and local-level officials, the *pedaneos* of each *cuartón*, or subdivision of a partido, were made responsible for capturing runaways. The campaign was effective. By the mid-1840s, notices of palenques disappeared from the historical record, although information on runaways did not. Perhaps the foreclosed possibility of establishing successful maroon communities was responsible for the large-scale recourse by slaves to other methods of resistance during the early 1840s.

There are no notices of slave rebellions in Matanzas until 1825, when a revolt broke out in Guamacaro that resulted in considerable violence and destruction. It should be noted that Guamacaro was the partido where close to 90 percent of the total population was enslaved, the vast majority of them Africans. There is no indication of organization or leadership, and the British consul in Havana reported that the revolt was spontaneous. More than 24 farms were sacked and burned; 15 whites were killed; 60 rebellious slaves were slain by authorities; and close to 200 slaves fled into the surrounding countryside, only to be captured by militiamen and bounty hunters. Most of those captured appear to have been murdered.[31]

One can only speculate on the impact this rebellion had on the white population of Matanzas and on the planter class in particular. There is no doubt that rural militia units were deployed more extensively and that increased vigilance and tightened security resulted within individual farms and plantations. In addition, a clear policy of separating Africans by tribal group was adopted, and creoles and Africans were also separated as much as possible. There would not be another rebellion until 1835, and that was confined to several farms in the interior partido of Macuriges, where slaves on the ingenio Carolina and the cafetal Burato revolted. The rebellion was contained, and there seems to have been little loss of life.[32]

It is not known whether these revolts had grand schemes or were spontaneous reactions to local-level brutality and hardship. Reports on conditions prevailing on slave plantations in the 1830s noted the extremes of degradation and good treatment. The British consul reported in 1836 that "there is no disposition on the part of the Negroes to disturb the public tranquility; they are an inoffensive people except when goaded to it [rebellion] by such cruelty as is rarely practiced in this Island."[33] An example of such cruelty is contained in an 1837 report on the conditions of slaves on the ingenio La Lima in Santa Ana. This report noted the "miserable condition in which the slave population of Ingenio La Lima is found, because of the fact that they are all naked and that there is an extreme shortage of food."[34]

Even if their daily lives were governed by physical conditions falling between the extremes of brutality and beneficent treatment, the absence of freedom was a perpetual incentive for resistance. Whether it took individual forms, such as flight, or more direct collective action such as rebellion, Matanzas slaves were loath to accept their fate as permanent. Revolts may have been few and far between in the 1820s and 1830s, but the rebellions and conspiracies of the 1840s would become legendary to future Cuban generations as symbols of resistance to oppression.

PART TWO

Monoculture: The Economic and Social Structures Wrought by Sugar in Matanzas, 1837–1878

CHAPTER 5

Demographic Trends

The social and economic development of Matanzas between 1837 and 1878 was paradoxical in a variety of ways, for transformation and dynamic growth were paralleled by elements of timeless stability and extraordinary stagnation. If it were possible to interview the historical actors combining to form the Matanzas social order in the mid-nineteenth century, descriptions of daily life would vary according to position in the social hierarchy. The planter/merchant/slave-trading elite would offer a very different view of sugar prosperity than the numerous owners of small, fragmented *sitios de labor*. Free blacks and mulattoes would tell a distinctive story, and the perspectives of plantation slaves would reflect cultural parameters so dissimilar from those of the rest of society that the object of description would be scarcely recognizable beyond superficialities. The lexicon used to describe this period—"prosperity," "economic growth," "progress," and "modernization"—had different meanings in the barracones where most plantation slaves were quartered by the 1850s and 1860s.

By the late 1830s a highly differentiated class structure had matured, and it remained intact with few variations through the late 1870s. The same families who established control over the developing sugar economy in the 1820s and 1830s consolidated their positions of power and wealth through the end of the Ten Years' War (1868–1878). Newcomers were integrated into elite ranks, to be sure, but the surnames of the great ingenio owners in 1878 were the same as in the early 1840s: Diago, Baró, Poey, Zulueta, Torriente, Aldama, Pedroso, Cárdenas, Herrera, Montalvo, Peñalver, and the rest.

The slave population increased through the mid-1860s because of an active slave trade to the province directed by these same families. But, despite the fortunes generated by sugar, the material conditions of Cuban slaves hardly improved in the decades preceding the abolition law of 1880. Free blacks and mulattoes fared no better, and the numerous impoverished smallholders farming inferior land, scattered among the sugar estates, derived few benefits from the dramatic growth of sugar production. The economy expanded dynamically, but the social structure was frozen as if in a time capsule. Although methods of producing sugar changed and imported technology from the North Atlantic nations made Matanzas one of the most

modern and prosperous regions in Latin America in many ways, social mobility was nonexistent and the distribution of wealth was fossilized. The
socioeconomic history of Matanzas province in the mid-nineteenth century
provides a classic example of economic growth without development. Quantitative transformations were not paralleled by qualitative improvements in
the lives of a broad cross section of the social order, and few stable foundations for future socioeconomic development were constructed.

Yet, there were dynamic transformations. Among the most prominent
was the increased productive capacity of the provincial sugar economy,
which was owing in part to new mill construction as well as to the adaptation of the industrial revolution's most advanced technological innovations.
The utilization of steam engines was generalized by the late 1850s; vacuum-
pan evaporators, Derosne or Rillieux devices, had replaced antiquated Jamaican trains on the most productive plantations; and modern centrifuges
were employed on capital-intensive estates by the early 1870s.

The development of the most extensive railway system in Latin America
revolutionized transportation and facilitated the geographical mobility of
the Matanzas sugar economy toward eastern and southeastern regions of
forest and virgin land. Every great estate was connected by rail to the ports
of Matanzas or Cárdenas by the mid-1850s. A few mills even used railroads
to transport cane from fields to ingenios, although this was not a generalized
phenomenon until the late nineteenth century.

Yet, the methods for producing cane hardly changed. Planters experimented with different varieties and fully understood the optimum desirable
chemical combinations needed to maintain or increase yields. Different
types of plows were utilized to prepare the soil, and some were even driven
by steam. But planting, weeding, harvesting, loading, and transporting cane
were accomplished the same way they had been for centuries. Extensive
slave labor gangs, working by hand and with machetes, hoes, and shovels,
toiled in the fields endlessly marking time, just as their kinsmen had in
Jamaica, Barbados, Haití, Brazil, and elsewhere in the Caribbean where
sugar "prosperity" degraded the lives of millions of African slaves and their
offspring.

The progressive mechanization of refining and the steady advance of
transportation technology raised labor demands, since increases in milling
capacity meant the need for more cane. The only way to produce more sugarcane was by expanding planting, and this meant a need for more labor.
Cuban planters were largely unsuccessful in their quest to diversify substantially the labor basis of sugar production. By the mid-1870s, despite the
chronological proximity of final abolition, ingenio owners remained as dependent on slave labor as they had been during the early nineteenth century
or before. While sugarcane processing was transformed, the methods and
techniques of producing cane were surrounded by an aura of timelessness,

impervious to the far-reaching changes experienced in other spheres of economic life.

Slave trading to Matanzas crested in the late 1850s but was finally curbed a decade later. Chinese contract laborers had been imported from 1847 to help meet sugar's insatiable labor needs, but dependence on slaves continued unabated. Notwithstanding, the legal abolition process began in 1870 with Spain's promulgation of the Moret Law, which freed all children born to slave mothers after 1868 and all slaves reaching sixty years of age.

The following pages of Part Two will argue that it was not the persistence of slavery into the early 1880s that caused the crisis in Cuban sugar production during the 1880s and 1890s, for evidence suggests that slave labor remained completely viable from a strictly economic point of view on the eve of emancipation. Rather, it was abolition that would contribute to the demise of the old planter class in the aftermath of the Ten Years' War. Former slaves were loath to work as laborers on the estates that represented tyranny and oppression, and the entire labor basis of sugarcane cultivation was transformed after 1880.

The old planters, so resilient and innovative in the decades before abolition, began to recede from the historical stage toward the late 1870s. Their offspring, long accustomed to lives of luxury, little effort, and the prerogatives of a wealthy elite could not or would not adapt to the radical changes in Cuban society wrought by abolition and shifting international market conditions.

Social and political rebellion plunged Matanzas into the age of revolution between 1837 and 1878. In the early 1840s a wave of slave revolts spread through the province, and in 1844 the slave and free Afro-Cuban populations were violently persecuted by colonial authorities because of a perceived conspiracy. "La Escalera," named for the ladders to which suspects were tied and flogged in order to extract confessions, led to increased vigilance and security measures that effectively curbed collective slave resistance until abolition began in 1870.

The insurrection of 1868, led by disaffected creole landowners in eastern Cuba, had a different class basis. Prominent Matanzas families were found among the Cuban-born planters leading the independence revolt. The ensuing revolutionary war (1868–1878) shifted the framework of political debate throughout Cuba; but the foundations of the Matanzas economic system were scarcely touched, since the war was largely confined to eastern Cuba. Revolutionary violence was met by brutal policies of repression on the part of the colonial government, and political turbulence swept through all layers of Cuban society. With respect to the routines of daily life, however, Matanzas social and economic structures were marginally affected by the rebellion, at least until the invasion of the province in 1875 and 1876. By and large, stability and order reigned during a period of revolutionary violence and ideological upheaval. The social and economic impact of abolition, which followed the war, would be much greater than the rebellion itself in Matanzas.

Multiple layers of transformation were part and parcel of this period, yet they gyrated around an extremely stable central aspect of provincial life. Sugarcane cultivation, sugar processing, and trade in sugar defined the lives of most matanceros throughout these four decades. The sugar culture spread relentlessly between 1837 and 1878, sometimes encouraged, other times slowed, but never hindered by the transformations occurring in other realms. The deep roots of monocultural sugar production were so firmly established in these decades that they have persisted through the post-1959 socialist period.

Cuban historiography has traditionally considered 1868 as a pivotal year, and indeed the beginning of the Ten Years' War marks a radical departure in the island's political history. Yet, from an economic perspective, the trends of development established in the 1840s, 1850s, and 1860s continued uninterrupted in Matanzas. The province's sugar economy expanded through the period of revolutionary war, new mills were constantly constructed, and the rebellion had only a marginal impact on investment patterns by elite groups. Radical transformations in the socioeconomic history of the province would come after the war. Accordingly, although the onset of the rebellion was a landmark in Cuban history, the story told in Part Two of this book continues through the conclusion of that rebellion.

By 1877 slightly more than a quarter of a million people lived in the province of Matanzas. A frontier zone with only several thousand inhabitants at the turn of the nineteenth century, the region's cities, towns, and countryside became centers of population rivaling Havana. The city of Matanzas itself mushroomed because of its role as an export center serving a productive hinterland: in 1846, the population was 17,860; by 1862, it had expanded to 30,539; and in 1877, more than 88,000 people lived there. Cárdenas, also became a city of note, its population increasing from only 1,731 in 1846 to 12,401 in 1862 and to 18,528 in 1877.[1] (See Maps 5 and 6 for the administrative subdivisions of Matanzas province in 1843 and 1856.)

Although the province's economic structure revolved around sugar production and related rural activities, cities and towns serving the agrarian economy attracted an ever-growing portion of the total population. Some 18 percent of all inhabitants lived in urban areas in 1846; 28 percent in 1862; and more than 37 percent lived in the cities of Matanzas and Cárdenas in 1877. Urbanization in the 1870s seems to have been related to two factors. Even though rural violence resulting from the Ten Years' War was minimal in Matanzas, the invasion of Las Villas and parts of Matanzas by rebel forces in late 1875 may have stimulated the rural-to-urban migration that swelled the region's cities in the late 1870s. Abolition, which began in

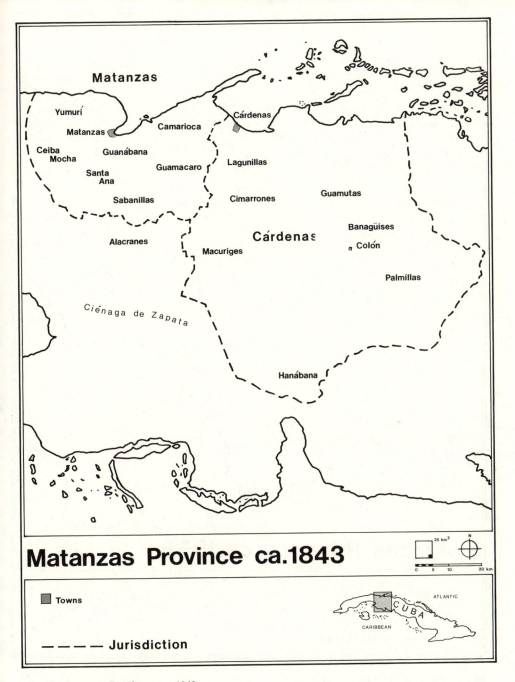

Matanzas

Yumurí

Matanzas   Camarioca   Cárdenas

Ceiba
Mocha   Guanábana   Lagunillas

Santa
Ana   Guamacaro

Sabanillas   Cimarrones   Guamutas

Banagüises

Cárdenas   Colón

Alacranes   Macuriges   Palmillas

Ciénaga de Zapata

Hanábana

Matanzas Province ca.1843

25 km²   N

0   5   10   20 km

▦ Towns

– – – – Jurisdiction

ATLANTIC

CUBA

CARIBBEAN

Map 5. Matanzas Province, ca. 1843

Source: Esteban Pichardo, *Isla de Cuba. Carta Geotopográfica* (Havana: Dirección de la Capitanía General, 1860–1872).

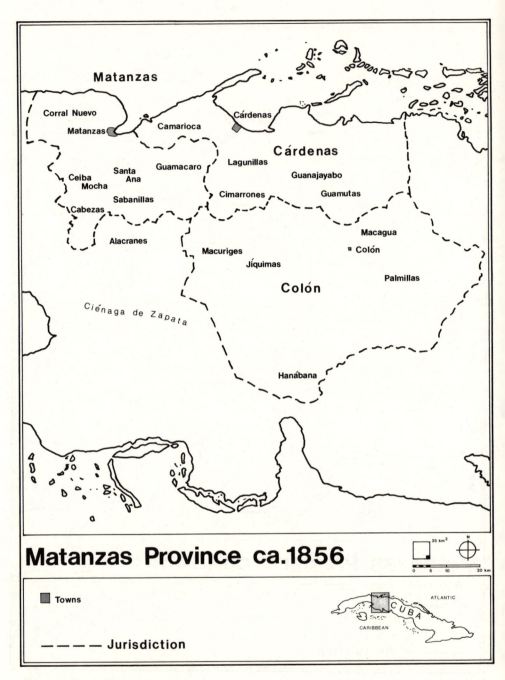

Map 6. Matanzas Province, ca. 1856

SOURCE: Esteban Pichardo, *Isla de Cuba. Carta Geotopográfica* (Havana: Dirección de la Capitanía General, 1860–1872).

1870 with the passage of the Moret Law, also may have prompted migration to urban areas. In 1877 blacks and mulattoes constituted 37.1 percent of Matanzas-city residents and 24.7 percent of the population of the city of Cárdenas. Almost one-third (32.8 percent) of all free blacks and mulattoes in the province lived in these cities.

Yet, urban centers were more heavily populated by whites than by any other racial or legal category. In 1862, for example, more than two-thirds of all urban residents were white; approximately one-fifth were slaves; and just over 12 percent were free blacks and mulattoes. In 1877, 64.3 percent of the population in Cárdenas was white, 58.6 percent in Matanzas.

Nearly 40 percent of all matanceros in 1846 and 1862 lived on sugar plantations, although geographically and among different sectors of the population there were significant variations.[2] In 1862, 73.6 percent of all slaves in the province lived on ingenios, but only 22.3 percent of all whites and 4.6 percent of all free blacks and mulattoes resided on sugar estates. In 1846, 9.1 percent of the total Matanzas population labored on coffee farms, but the collapse of the Cuban coffee economy after 1850 resulted in a drop to slightly more than 2 percent by 1862. Approximately one-third of all matanceros lived on other types of farms, primarily sitios de labor and potreros, although it should be noted that only 12.2 percent of the province's slaves labored on these farms in 1862.

In rural zones where sugar production was concentrated, the percentage of population living on ingenios was more extreme. For example, in Sabanilla 65.5 percent of all residents lived on sugar estates in 1846; in Guamutas, 59.2 percent; in Macuriges, 55.4 percent; and in the Yumurí Valley, 47.8 percent. There were also significant differences in settlement patterns between the more urbanized jurisdicción of Matanzas and the predominantly rural Colón and Cárdenas. In Matanzas, 31.8 percent of all inhabitants lived on ingenios in 1862; in Colón, 41.3 percent; and in Cárdenas, 48.3 percent. No comparable data are available for 1877.

Slaves as a percentage of the provincial population peaked in 1846 at 56.8 percent and declined to 46.1 percent in 1862. However, the demographic structure of the province's rural partidos continued to include much higher percentages of slaves through 1862. For example, while 56.8 percent of the Matanzas provincial population was enslaved in 1846, if predominantly rural Cárdenas is examined separately, 62.4 percent of all inhabitants were slaves. In 1862 slaves made up 72.5 percent of the total population in Sabanilla; 69.6 percent in Macagua; 66.9 percent in Lagunillas; 62.8 percent in Guamacaro; 62.7 percent in Cimarrones; and 56.8 percent in Guamutas. Moreover, the Chinese "coolie" trade to Cuba, which began in 1847, resulted in a substantial number of Asians inhabiting Matanzas: 7.8 percent of the total population in 1862; 8 percent in 1877.

When disaggregated by provincial subdivisions, the 1877 data are problematic, because the black and mulatto population is not divided into slave and free at this local level. However, broad racial categories can be ascertained, and the continued predominance of people of color in those rural partidos where sugar production was concentrated is evident. In Sabanilla, 68.9 percent of the total population was black or mulatto in 1877; in Macagua, 58.1 percent; in Lagunillas, 53.9 percent; in Guamacaro, 59.5 percent; in Cimarrones, 62.8 percent; and in Guamutas, 48.6 percent.[3] Most were undoubtedly enslaved. Tables 5.1 through 5.8 summarize all these data.

Among the white population of Matanzas in 1846, 22.7 percent were foreign-born; in Cárdenas, 16.5 percent. Most numerous were the Canary Islanders, who constituted 58.7 percent of all foreigners in Matanzas and 47.2 percent in Cárdenas. Peninsulares made up 35.3 percent of the foreign-born population of Matanzas in 1846; 41.7 percent in the case of Cárdenas.

In 1862, 26.5 percent of all whites in Matanzas were foreign-born; 24.1 percent in Cárdenas; and 15.2 percent in Colón. Again, Canary Islanders and peninsulares were the most numerous groups. Thus 70.6 percent of all such foreigners in Matanzas were *canarios*; 44 percent in Cárdenas; and 36.8 percent in Colón. Peninsulares made up 23.4 percent of the foreign-born population in Matanzas, 46.4 percent in Cárdenas, and 54.7 percent in Colón.

Rates of growth among the various sectors of the Matanzas population can be roughly ascertained using available data, although the statistical estimates that follow should be used with a great deal of caution. With the exception of data on the slave trade, there are no reliable data series on immigration for Matanzas, and information on births and deaths are fragmentary except for materials contained in the published 1862 census. There is no way, for example, to calculate any undercount of live births or infant deaths within any sector of the population.

Between 1846 and 1862 the overall population increased at an annual average of 2.7 percent; between 1862 and 1877, however, the annual rate of growth fell to 1.1 percent.[4] The likely cause of this decline was the end of the African slave trade to Cuba in the late 1860s. According to the most recent estimates, between 1846 and 1862 approximately 160,300 slaves were imported into Cuba.[5] Since approximately 25 percent of Cuba's slave population between 1846 and 1862 lived in Matanzas, it can be conservatively calculated that 40,000 slaves were imported to the province during that period. After 1862, only 8,700 slaves were imported to Cuba, or approximately 2,175 to Matanzas if it is assumed that one-fourth of all arrivals were destined for the province. Although loss of life in the province during the Ten Years' War is not known, it must surely have been minimal, given the absence of extensive combat in Matanzas. The war was not a significant cause of decline in the population growth rate. This suggests that

Table 5.1. Matanzas Population by Sex, Race, and Legal Status, 1846–1877

	1846			1862			1877		
	M	F	T	M	F	T	M	F	T
Whites	29,036	22,945	51,981	45,201	33,420	78,621	66,922	55,002	121,924
Asians	0	0	0	15,247	1	15,248	20,028	26	20,054
Yucatecos	0	0	0	49	23	72	0	0	0
Emancipados	0	0	0	577	182	759	189	270	459
Free Blacks and Mulattoes	3,919	3,867	7,786	4,931	5,321	10,252	18,717	19,184	37,901
Slaves	50,154	28,482	78,636	55,265	34,378	89,643	40,357	30,033	70,390
TOTAL	83,109	55,294	138,403	121,270	73,325	194,595	146,213	104,515	250,728

SOURCES: Cuba, Gobernador y Capitán General, *Cuadro estadístico de la siempre fiel isla de Cuba correspondiente al año de 1846* (Havana: Imp. del Gobierno y Capitanía General, 1847); Cuba, Centro de Estadística, *Noticias estadísticas de la isla de Cuba en 1862* (Havana: Imp. del Gobierno, Capitanía General y Real Hacienda, 1864); Spain, Instituto Geográfico y Estadistico, *Censo de la población de España según el empadronamiento hecho en 31 de diciembre de 1877* (Madrid: Imp. de la Dirección General del Instituto Geográfico y Estadística, 1883); Fé Iglesias García, "El censo cubano de 1877 y sus diferentes versiones," *Santiago* 34 (June 1979), pp. 167–214.

NOTES: The data for 1846 and 1877 include Alacranes, for which there were no disaggregated data by sex for 1862. However, the totals should be included in total population calculations, for the partido eventually became part of Matanzas. Alacranes had a total population of 16,690 in 1862: 6,894 whites (Asians and Yucatecos included); 861 free blacks and mulattoes; 8,853 slaves and 82 emancipados. These data must be added to the above totals to derive the total population of each category for 1862.

The population total for 1877 noted in the officially published census lists 288,868 total residents, transients, and absentees as the population of Matanzas. Different versions of the census have been published, and the data presented here are derived from the Iglesias article, which considers the data published in the *Boletín Oficial de Hacienda de la Isla de Cuba* for 1881 and 1882 as most reliable.

Table 5.2. Matanzas Population By Place of Residence, 1846–1862 (in percentages)

	1846	1862			
	Total	Total	Whites	Free People of Color	Slaves
Cities and Towns	18.4	28.3	43.5	64.0	11.6
Ingenios	38.5	39.0	22.3	4.6	73.6
Cafetales	9.1	2.2	1.9	1.5	2.6
Other Farms	34.0	30.5	32.3	29.9	12.2

SOURCE: See Table 5.1.

NOTE: Comparable data for 1877 are not available.

Table 5.3. Cárdenas, Matanzas, and Alacranes, 1846:
Population by Partido and Place of Residence

	City or Town	Ingenios	Cafetales	Other Farms	Total
MATANZAS					
City[a]	16,986			874	17,860
Yumurí	196	5,027	114	5,207	10,544
Guanábana	100	1,954	470	1,178	3,702
Camarioca	313	1,113	1,508	1,567	4,501
Guamacaro	428	4,416	2,990	1,261	9,095
Sabanilla	710	5,055	—	1,957	7,722
Santa Ana	233	2,886	365	1,995	5,479
Ceiba Mocha	919	1,329	1,050	4,544	7,842
Total	19,885	21,780	6,497	18,583	66,745
CÁRDENAS					
Lagunillas	3,251	4,480	1,972	2,943	12,646
Palmillas	432	3,360	—	4,182	7,974
Ceja de Pablo	55	1,499	—	2,709	4,263
Cimarrones	468	3,259	1,048	2,409	7,175
Hanábana	105	—	—	1,099	1,204
Macuriges	317	7,747	1,239	4,676	13,979
Guamutas	301	7,347	1,273	3,486	12,407
Guásimas	65	489	9	1,168	1,731
Total	4,994	28,172	5,541	22,672	61,379
ALACRANES	550	3,302	595	5,832	10,279
Total	25,429	53,254	12,633	47,087	138,403

SOURCE: Cuba, Gobernador y Capitán General, *Cuadro estadístico de la siempre fiel isla de Cuba, correspondiente al año de 1846* (Havana: Imp. del Gobierno y Capitanía General, 1847).
[a]Includes the urban barrios of Pueblo Nuevo and Versalles.

the dramatic decline in the annual rate of demographic increase after 1862 was linked to the curbing of the Cuban slave trade.

Between 1846 and 1862 the white population increased at an annual rate of 2.6 percent; the free-black and mulatto population increased at 1.7 percent; and the slave population at 1.4 percent. Published data from the 1862 census lends support to the hypothesis that the white population was expanding because of natural increase, although these rates do not reflect possible underrepresentation of infant mortality. The birth rate per thousand inhabitants in Matanzas during 1862 was 31.4 among whites, while the death rate was 17.6/thousand for that group. This compares to a birth rate of 26/thousand and a death rate of 22/thousand among the slave population. The free-black and mulatto population experienced the highest birth rate, 36.7/thousand, and the highest death rate as well at 26.7/thousand.

Table 5.4. Cárdenas, Colón, and Matanzas, 1862: Population by Place of Residence

	Cárdenas	Colón	Matanzas	Total	%
Cities and Towns	12,399	6,057	32,809	51,265	28.3
Ingenios	24,415	20,662	25,523	70,600	39.0
Cafetales	1,266	921	1,805	3,992	2.2
Haciendas	0	574	0	574	0.3
Potreros	3,467	4,839	2,536	10,842	6.0
Sitios	5,810	15,316	15,224	36,350	20.1
Estancias	18	0	165	183	0.1
Other Farms	1,924	602	861	3,387	1.9
Other	1,223	1,100	1,359	3,682	2.0
TOTAL	50,522	50,071	80,282	180,875	100.0

SOURCE: Cuba, Centro de Estadística, *Noticias estadísticas de la isla de Cuba en 1862* (Havana: Imp. del Gobierno, Capitanía General y Real Hacienda, 1864), "Distribución de la población en los pueblos y fincas de la isla."

NOTE: *Ingenios* were sugar farms and their mills; *cafetales* were coffee farms; *haciendas* were traditional circular forms of land tenure dating from the early sixteenth century; *potreros* were stock-raising farms; *sitios* were subsistence farms; and *estancias* were small farms growing a variety of products. Places of residence were unknown for 7,221 people in Cárdenas, 14,146 in Colón, and 147 in Matanzas.

Table 5.5. Matanzas Population by Race and Legal Status, 1846–1877
(in percentages)

	1846	1862	1877
Whites	37.6	40.4	48.6
Asians	0	7.8	8.0
Free Blacks and Mulattoes	5.6	5.3	15.1
Emancipados	0	0.4	0.2
Slaves	56.8	46.1	28.1

SOURCE: See Table 5.1.

For lack of documentary materials, there is no way to estimate these rates prior to 1862, but there are sufficient data to estimate crude death rates among slaves between 1846 and 1862. A slave population of 78,636 in 1846 rose to 98,496 by 1862. If we estimate that approximately 40,000 slaves arrived in Matanzas through the trata (i.e., one-fourth of all slaves arriving in Cuba), then *without* imports the slave population would have been 58,496 minus any deaths. The number of manumissions must also be calculated and *added* to this population in order to determine death rates, for these slaves disappeared from the census rolls as a group but had not died.

Table 5.6. Cárdenas, Matanzas, and Alacranes, 1846:
Population by Jurisdiction, Race, and Legal Status

	Whites	Free Blacks and Mulattoes	Slaves	Total
Matanzas	26,717	4,840	35,188	66,745
Cárdenas	20,620	2,469	38,290	61,379
Alacranes	4,644	477	5,158	10,279
TOTAL	51,981	7,786	78,636	138,403

SOURCE: Cuba, Gobernador y Capitán General, *Cuadro estadístico de la siempre fiel isla de Cuba, correspondiente al año de 1846* (Havana: Imp. del Gobierno y Capitanía General, 1847).
NOTE: There are no disaggregated data by partido for 1846.

The 1862 census estimated that an average of 1,900 slaves were manumitted yearly in all of Cuba between 1858 and 1862. Since Matanzas accounted for approximately one-fourth of total Cuban slave population, we can estimate that 475 slaves were freed each year. If we apply this number to the sixteen years between 1846 and 1862, we come up with a figure of 7,600 for the number of Matanzas manumissions. These calculations, both for slave imports to Matanzas and manumissions in the province, do not include deaths that may have resulted among these sectors of the population over time, since those data are not available.

If manumissions are not deducted and new slave arrivals are subtracted, the slave population (declining annually by 1.1 percent between 1846 and 1862) would hypothetically have been 66,096 in 1862. If manumissions are deducted, the slave population can be estimated to have declined 1.8 percent yearly in Matanzas between 1846 and 1862. This estimate is significantly lower (28 percent) than the 2.5 percent annual loss in slaves estimated both by Juan Poey in 1862 and by the British consul in 1848.[6]

It is nearly impossible to estimate real death rates either among the free-black and mulatto populations or among slaves between 1862 and 1877 because of the paucity of relevant data and the onset of the legal abolition process in 1870. Abolition had the effect of transferring former slaves to the free-black and mulatto categories in census counts. Additionally, it is impossible to determine how many slaves disappeared from slave rolls because of manumissions or death; nor can we discover the proportion of free blacks and mulattoes resulting from natural increase rather than from the addition of recently freed slaves.

One aspect of the slave population's decline should be emphasized. Even with the beginning of legal abolition in 1870, the overall annual rate of

**Table 5.7. Colón, Cárdenas, Matanzas, and Alacranes, 1862:
Population by Partido**

	Whites[a]	Free Blacks and Mulattoes	Emanpicados	Slaves	Total
COLÓN					
Macagua	3,556	165	78	8,699	12,498
Cabecera	1,409	187	8	603	2,207
Palmillas	3,041	509	22	2,833	6,405
Hanábana	2,196	311	—	893	3,400
Macuriges	7,837	287	147	8,640	16,911
Jíquimas	10,823	667	103	11,203	22,796
Total	28,862	2,126	358	32,871	64,217
CÁRDENAS					
Cabecera	8,116	641	86	3,558	12,401
Camarioca	4,096	195	14	2,613	6,918
Cimarrones	2,706	80	38	4,905	7,729
Lagunillas	2,558	136	9	5,468	8,171
Guamutas	5,220	229	102	7,307	12,858
Guanajayabo	4,943	89	26	4,508	9,566
Total	27,639	1,370	275	28,359	57,643
MATANZAS					
City[b]	18,583	5,036	34	6,886	30,539
Corral Nuevo	4,895	533	42	4,439	9,909
Cabezas	4,745	325	5	2,936	8,011
Guamacaro	3,380	222	—	6,083	9,685
Ceiba Mocha	3,843	335	11	1,426	5,615
Sabanilla	2,079	217	—	6,068	8,364
Santa Ana	3,062	270	39	4,641	8,012
Total	40,587	6,938	131	32,479	80,135
ALACRANES	6,894	861	82	8,853	16,690
TOTAL	103,982	11,295	846	102,562	218,685

SOURCE: Cuba, Centro de Estadística. *Noticias estadísticas de la isla de Cuba en 1862* (Havana: Imp. del Gobierno, Capitanía General y Real Hacienda, 1864), "Partidos pedaneos, con expresión de los cuartones que cada uno contiene y la particular de cada pueblo aldea y caserío que se halla en ella."
[a]Includes Yucatecos and Asians. The Asian population of Colón was 5,510; Cárdenas, 5,429; and Matanzas, 3,803.
[b]Distrito Norte and Distrito Sur combined.

decline among Matanzas slaves between 1862 and 1877 was 2.2 percent, although the rate was 1.3 percent between 1862 and 1871 and 3.5 percent from 1871 to 1877.[7] Narrative accounts of annual slave losses in the 1850s and 1860s routinely refer to a 2.5 percent annual decrease, although the slave-census materials analyzed above reveal a 1.8 percent rate of decline

Table 5.8. Matanzas, 1877: Population by Partido, Race and Sex

	Whites			Asians			Blacks and Mulattoes			Total Pop.
	M	F	T	M	F	T	M	F	T	
Alacranes	1,948	1,566	3,514	827	0	827	2,237	1,638	3,875	8,216
Bolondrón	997	653	1,650	613	0	613	4,951	2,551	7,502	9,765
Cabezas	2,950	2,533	5,483	545	0	545	1,639	1,238	2,877	8,905
Camarioca	3,004	1,986	4,990	161	0	161	548	481	1,029	6,180
Canasí	1,423	1,175	2,598	377	0	377	1,023	776	1,799	4,774
Cárdenas	6,763	5,154	11,917	2,039	0	2,039	2,141	2,431	4,572	18,528
Cimarrones	1,018	799	1,817	1,136	0	1,136	2,785	2,204	4,989	7,942
Colón	6,327	4,370	10,697	2,422	15	2,437	4,095	3,431	7,526	20,660
Corral Nuevo	3,384	2,997	6,381	65	0	65	764	524	1,288	7,734
Cuevitas	1,653	1,324	2,977	331	0	331	1,710	949	2,659	5,967
Guamacaro	1,896	1,377	3,273	648	1	649	3,217	2,546	5,763	9,685
Guamutas	3,697	2,215	5,912	1,412	0	1,412	4,535	2,388	6,923	14,247
Guanajayabo	1,167	1,191	2,358	498	0	498	1,780	1,569	3,349	6,205
Jovellanos	1,852	1,343	3,195	775	0	775	2,032	1,658	3,690	7,660
Lagunillas	1,390	1,187	2,577	465	0	465	1,989	1,564	3,553	6,595
Macagua	1,050	770	1,820	268	0	268	1,648	1,250	2,898	4,986
Macurijes	3,323	2,380	5,703	1,811	10	1,821	4,921	4,101	9,022	16,546
Matanzas	24,289	27,812	52,101	3,731	9	3,740	15,278	17,714	32,992	88,833
Perico	1,065	802	1,867	1,052	0	1,052	911	990	1,901	4,820
Roque	2,101	1,446	3,547	341	0	341	1,367	1,140	2,507	6,395
Sabanilla	921	723	1,644	864	0	864	3,133	2,429	5,562	8,070

	M	F	T	M	F	T	M	F	T	Pop.
San José de los Ramos	1,512	1,261	2,773	345	0	345	2,090	1,475	3,565	6,683
Santa Ana	2,511	1,979	4,490	96	0	96	2,105	1,306	3,411	7,997
Unión de Reyes	478	446	924	83	2	85	218	248	466	1,475
TOTAL	76,719	67,489	144,208	20,905	37	20,942	67,117	56,601	123,718	288,868

SOURCE: Spain, Instituto Geográfico y Estadístico, Censo de la población de España según el empadronamiento hecho en 31 de diciembre de 1877 (Madrid: Imp. de la Dirección General del Instituto Geográfico y Estadística, 1883), vol. 1.

NOTE: M = males; F = females; T = total; Pop. = population. In this census the population was divided into three major categories: "residentes presentes," "transuentes," and "residentes ausentes." Each of these groups were divided into "españoles," "extranjeros," "asiáticos," and "de color." The totals listed here were derived by adding all three major categories, which yields different totals from those listed in the document. The census listed two types of totals: "Población de hecho," which added "presentes" and "transuentes"; and "Población de derecho," which added "presentes" and "ausentes." Since the logic of arbitrarily excluding one or the other is unclear, I have added all categories. Thus, "españoles" and "extranjeros" have been added together to derive the white population. There were no separate data on slaves, although this category can be derived from other sources.

(including manumissions) between 1846 and 1862. This does not differ dramatically from the 2.2 percent rate of overall decrease between 1862 and 1877. It should be noted that the 3.5 percent rate of decline between 1871 and 1877 was nearly twice as high as the 1862–1871 rate. This was not the result of an internal transfer of slaves from Matanzas to other regions in Cuba.

It must be stressed that the abolition process initiated by the 1870 Moret Law only freed slaves reaching age sixty and newborns after 1868. These two groups of relatively unproductive slaves are included in the post-1871 rates of decline. If pre-1871 and post-1871 rates of slave-population decline are compared, and if the fact that unproductive slaves constituted the bulk of those freed after 1871 is taken into consideration, then it seems that the beginning of abolition did *not* seriously disturb core slave-labor forces. Although consistent age-structure data are not available, it is likely that rates of decline among prime-age slaves in Matanzas were similar before and after 1871. Labor supplies were seriously disrupted by the end of the slave trade in the late 1860s, not by any radical departure in demographic trends among the slave population after abolition began. Varied demographic data on different sectors of the Matanzas population from 1846 through 1877 are provided in Tables 5.9 and 5.10.

Settlement patterns in Matanzas underwent substantial changes between 1846 and 1877. Urbanization, discussed above, was one important trend. A second was the shift of population to frontier areas of economic development. Between 1846 and 1862 the rural areas of Matanzas jurisdiction (excluding the city) experienced a population increase of 15.6 percent, from 48,885 to 56,514 inhabitants.[8] When we examine the rural partidos comprising Cárdenas and Colón, frontier regions where new ingenios were established throughout this period, population increased by 87.4 percent, from 61,379 to 115,045 residents.[9]

Between 1862 and 1877 the economy of Matanzas jurisdiction, the oldest area of settlement in the province, stagnated while new ingenios were constructed in frontier zones. Accordingly, the rural population declined a significant 14.1 percent, from 56,514 to 48,571 inhabitants.[10] This probably contributed to the growth of the city of Matanzas, since the rural population moved to the city in search of employment as opportunities in the surrounding countryside contracted. Cárdenas, settled after the Matanzas bay area, also experienced a considerable decline of its rural population—8.9 percent between 1862 and 1877, from 38,424 to 34,989 residents.[11] Only Colón, a region still in the process of expansion through the 1870s, experienced demographic growth in its rural zones. Rural Colón's population increased 14.8 percent between 1862 and 1877, from 64,217 to 73,717 inhabitants.[12] These data are summarized in Table 5.11.

If the shifting geography of the sugar industry is examined, it is evident

Table 5.9. Matanzas Rates of Population Growth by Race and Legal Status,
1846–1877

	1846–1862	1862–1877
Whites	2.6	3.0
Free Blacks and Mulattoes	1.7	9.1
Slaves	1.4	−2.2
TOTAL	2.7	1.1

SOURCE: See Table 5.1.
NOTE: The slave population declined at an average annual rate of 1.3 percent between 1862 and 1871, and at 3.5 percent between 1871 and 1877.

Table 5.10. Matanzas, 1862: Birth, Death, and Fertility Rates by Race and Legal Status
(per thousand inhabitants)

	Birth Rate	Death Rate	Fertility Rate
Whites	31.4	17.6	226
Free Blacks and Mulattoes	36.7	26.7	585
Slaves	26.0	22.1	142

SOURCE: Cuba, Centro de Estadística, *Noticias estadísticas de la isla de Cuba en 1862* (Havana: Imp. del Gobierno, Capitanía General y Real Hacienda, 1864).
NOTE: The fertility rate has been calculated by dividing the number of births by the number of women between the ages of sixteen and forty, and then multiplying by 1,000. It should be emphasized that all of these rates are based on the number of *baptisms*, not live births, since this is the only information available. The number of deaths before baptism is not known.

that there was a very close correlation between trends in mill construction and patterns of internal migration, whether forced, as in the case of slaves, or otherwise. For example, between 1846 and 1862, when the rural zones of Matanzas jurisdiction experienced a 15.6 percent increase in population, the number of ingenios declined slightly, from 138 to 131. However, if we examine rural Cárdenas and Colón, where the number of ingenios increased by 42 percent in the same period, 200 ingenios in 1846 and 284 in 1862, population increase was a significantly higher 87.4 percent.

Between 1862 and 1877, differences in the rural zones of the three jurisdictions of Cárdenas, Colón, and Matanzas are more striking. Population declined 14.1 percent in Matanzas while the number of mills increased from 131 to 133. There was a 6.9 percent increase in the number of mills in Cárdenas (from 144 to 154), but population declined by 8.9 percent. Evi-

Table 5.11. Population Growth in Rural Areas of Matanzas, 1846–1877
(in percentages)

Jurisdiction	1846–1862	1862–1877
Matanzas	+ 15.6	− 14.1
Cárdenas	+ 87.4	− 8.9
Colón	—	+ 14.8

SOURCE: See Table 5.1.
NOTE: The 1846 data for Cárdenas are for Cárdenas and Colón combined; there are no separate
data for Colón.

dently, the construction of some new ingenios slowed the comparative rate
of population decrease. Only in Colón, where ingenio construction continued in frontier zones to the south (primarily in the partidos of Hanábana,
Palmillas, and Macuriges), did population increase dynamically by 14.8 percent, while the number of sugar mills rose by 27.1 percent, from 140 to 178
ingenios.

These data should be emphasized. Heretofore, changes in the demogra-
phy of Cuba in general, notably in the ratio of rural to urban inhabitants,
have been attributed to the revolutionary period from 1895 through 1898.
During the war for independence, the overall population of the island declined by more than 15 percent because of the violence and destruction
caused by the war. Rural inhabitants were reconcentrated in cities by Spanish counterinsurgency policies, or they fled the rural destruction for urban
areas. The radical economic reorganization following the U.S. occupation
after 1898 has also been cited as a fundamental cause of demographic shifts.

It should be stressed that, while these factors were critical in the later
nineteenth and early twentieth centuries, transformations in the demographic structure of Cuban rural society had an organic component derived
from the internal dynamics of economic development. Population increased
in regions of sugar expansion, but when land was exhausted and the frontier
was redefined eastward, population declined in the older productive zones.
The cycle was repeated in region after region so long as virgin land was
available for colonization in frontier zones. The war (1895–1898) and the
U.S. occupation accelerated a process of demographic change that had its
roots in the economic dynamics of the Cuban sugar economy.

CHAPTER 6

Railroads Open the Frontier

The spread of sugar through Matanzas province between 1837 and 1878 repeated previous cycles of Cuban sugar expansion. During the latter half of the eighteenth century, sugar had moved from Havana toward the southern coast and southeast through the Güines Valley. After 1800, mills were established near the city of Matanzas and gradually spread in an arc away from the bay: westward in the Yumurí Valley; southwest through Ceiba Mocha; south to the Magdalena Valley; and east through Camarioca toward Cárdenas. In the southern regions of the province, sugar moved east from Güines toward Alacranes. Declining yields in older areas of production, owing to soil exhaustion and the need for wood to fuel steam engines, were the driving force behind these waves of expansion.

During the 1830s, frontier regions in the southeastern areas of Matanzas, in the Colón region, were looked on by the entrepreneurial elite as the next major zone of colonization. Although distant from the great port of Havana, the construction of railroad lines in the 1840s and 1850s forged efficient linkages to this area. By mid-century, wealthy planters could breakfast in Havana and dine on their estates in distant Colón by early evening. Cuba's greatest nineteenth-century mills were constructed in Colón, which became the richest zone of Cuban sugar production by the mid-1850s.[1]

The difficulty of overland transportation by mule and *carreta*, together with the high cost of shipping products to Havana from interior zones, was a point of great concern to the Havana elite from the mid-eighteenth century. Penetration of frontier regions followed a precise pattern. The first interest was in forests and wood reserves. The wholesale reduction of woodlands around the capital by the 1760s meant the need to exploit forested areas to the south and southeast of Havana. After land had been cleared, smallholders usually moved in to cultivate subsistence crops or tobacco for export. Finally, the powerful sugar barons appeared, establishing mills and potreros until the land was exhausted and they were forced toward new regions where the same cycle was repeated. The time frame for this process could be half a century, as was the case with the Güines Valley between 1750 and 1800.

Two separate markets required substantial timber supplies. The sugar sector's boilers consumed vast quantities at harvesttime, and an urban mar-

ket for wood grew along with the mushrooming city of Havana. Havana
required wood for three related industries. The first was the construction of
urban housing and storage facilities. Second, in the aftermath of the English
seizure of the capital in 1762, a wave of fortification projects began. Third,
Havana shipyards required particular types of hardwood for boat construction and repair, many of which could be secured only from distant, interior
forests.

With the simultaneous expansion of these economic sectors, infrastructural improvements became a priority to private entrepreneurs and government officials alike. The traditional network of caminos reales and vecinales, or local roads, could not efficiently satisfy the transportation needs of
an expanding economy in the second half of the eighteenth century. Public-
works plans for widening and improving roads were drawn up and implemented, but transportation to the interior remained a major obstacle to economic growth. In 1767 the Intendente de la Marina, Lorenzo de Montalvo,
who also held the title Conde de Macuriges, proposed an ambitious plan to
squeeze though this bottleneck. He suggested the construction of a canal
between the Mayabeque River, near Güines, and the Almendares River,
which emptied into Havana Bay.[2] The project was studied, and military engineers even drew up plans; but when the count died in 1778, nothing had
been accomplished.

In the 1790s, interest in canal building was once again resurrected by
progressive planters and government officials. The Real Consulado, which
had assumed responsibility for infrastructural improvements, and Governor Luis de las Casas attempted to revive interest in the project early in the
decade. But the scale was so daunting that it was never initiated, despite
periodic discussion through the 1820s and early 1830s. Improvements of
existing roads were undertaken, but high transportation costs and the difficulty and unreliability of communications to and from the interior persisted. The rainy season created havoc, for the dirt roads often became seas
of mud—only to become deeply rutted when the sun later hardened the
clay.[3]

Linkages between Matanzas and the capital were improved considerably
in 1819 with Juan O'Farrill's inauguration of maritime service aboard the
steamship Neptune. By the early 1820s, competing shipping firms plied the
Caribbean daily between Havana, Matanzas, and the incipient port of Cárdenas. However, the problems of internal transportation remained as acute
as ever. With the continued construction of new mills, forests were receding
at an alarming rate away from the port cities; and as ingenios were founded
in more distant zones, the costs and difficulties of transporting supplies to
the mills and sugar to port were exacerbated.

The railroad, of course, changed this in many ways. For one, coal could
now be imported cheaply from the United States and shipped quickly to the

mills.[4] This alone transformed the parameters of sugar production; for, hitherto, a fundamental assumption was that the productive life of any mill was directly linked to the proximity of available timber reserves. The railroad ended this and allowed mill owners to contemplate the new concept of geographical permanence, providing some efficient way could be found to replenish the soil so that agricultural yields would not eventually decline to unprofitable levels.

Another impact of the railroad was to telescope the time frame for the exploitation of newly colonized regions. The timber–smallholder–ingenio sequence had been closely followed in Havana province and, during the late eighteenth and early nineteenth centuries, in the Matanzas bay area. For the interior of Matanzas province, however, the railroad allowed timber exploitation and ingenio construction to proceed simultaneously. The smallholder phase in the cycle of development was eliminated. Sugar planters and tobacco farmers waged a protracted struggle over land in the Güines Valley in the 1770s, 1780s, and 1790s, and this was repeated in the Yumurí Valley and in the Ceiba Mocha region during the 1790s and early 1800s. No such impediments stood in the way of sugar as it expanded into the area surrounding Colón in the 1830s and 1840s. Smallholders, never having established an extensive presence, did not have to be removed; they developed into a broadly based social group as appendages to the great estates.

Wealthy Havana- and Matanzas-based planters were able to accumulate vast quantities of largely virgin land with little opposition. The railroad transported milling equipment and supplies quickly from ports to production sites. Capital accumulated during the pre-railroad period; entrepreneurial skills honed over several generations; sophisticated linkages with international markets; labor derived from a well-oiled slave trade—all were applied quickly and efficiently to the Matanzas hinterland, which became the center of Cuban sugar production for the remainder of the nineteenth century. It is not surprising that the onset of railroad construction was paralleled by a peak in the slave trade to Cuba, between 1830 and 1840. The railroad opened new possibilities for sugar-related economic expansion, and the reverberations were felt all the way to the West African coast.[5]

The railroad age began early in 1830 with the opening of the first line connecting Manchester and Liverpool, England. The Cuban elite, so keenly aware of every technological innovation in the centers of industry and finance, immediately perceived the possibilities for revolutionizing the Cuban countryside. Within five weeks, Havana-based institutions representing the most prominent planters convened to consider the possibility of railway construction. In August 1830 the Junta de Caminos de Hierro was established by the Royal Governor. The junta included representatives from the Real Consulado, the Real Sociedad Patriótica, and the Ayuntamiento de la Habana and was chaired by the Conde de Villanueva, Claudio Martínez de Pinillos, who was Superintendente de Hacienda, President of the Junta de Fomento, a respected and well-connected political figure in Madrid, and an ardent enthusiast of railroad building.[6]

The junta set an initial goal of connecting the sugar-rich Güines Valley with Havana, and a formal petition for approval of this project was submitted to the Crown in April 1831. The proposal estimated that planters along the proposed route were paying 800,000 pesos each year to ship sugar to Havana and that the railroad would reduce the cost to 300,000 pesos annually.[7]

The principal obstacle, of course, was financing. Even the most powerful local merchants were unaccustomed to advancing the sum of money required, some 2 million pesos; nor was there any willingness to underwrite long-term loans. Cuban merchants may have had the financial capacity to finance such an endeavor, but they preferred to extend credit to operations having the potential of repaying loans within a year or two. In addition, the concept of corporate enterprises, the *sociedades anónimas* that the railroad itself would spawn, had not yet become customary in colonial Cuba. There was also trepidation caused by the uncertainty of the railroad's practical and financial utility.

The Junta de Fomento, headed by the Conde de Villanueva, built and initially operated the first Cuban railroad. Negotiations for financing were conducted in London, and the banking firm of Alexander Robertson & Company, with the guarantee of the Spanish Crown, provided the capital. The loan was approved in late 1834; a U.S. engineer, Alfred Kruger, was contracted to direct the project; construction began in November 1835; in November 1837, the first branch was opened to Bejucal, directly south of Havana; and one year later the railroad had pushed eastward and reached Güines.[8]

Although the first Cuban railway line was owned and operated by the state, it was privatized in 1842. But even before the first section from Havana to Bejucal was opened in 1837, competing merchants and planters had drawn up plans for the construction of three separate rail systems in Matanzas. The first would originate in the port of Cárdenas, follow a southeasterly trajectory through Contreras, swing due south of Cárdenas through Cimarrones, and proceed to Soledad de Bemba. After this initial line of 83 kilometers was completed, a new section would turn sharply to the southwest toward Macagua, which had become a region of ingenio development in the late 1830s.

The entrepreneurs organizing the Cárdenas–Bemba railroad, as it was originally called, were almost all creoles from old, Havana-based titled families who had purchased land and constructed mills in Matanzas province. Juan Montalvo y O'Farrill, the grandson of the Conde de Macuriges and the second-eldest son of Ignacio Montalvo, Conde de Casa Montalvo, was the first president and largest shareholder of the Empresa del Ferrocarril de Cárdenas, the project's official name. Joaquín Peñalver y Sánchez, the son of the Marqués de Casa-Peñalver, Sebastián Peñalver y Barreto, was the second-largest *accionista* and became president of the Cárdenas railroad in 1844.[9] Anastasio Carillo, the creole Auditor de Guerra and professor of political economy and law at the University of Havana, was vice-president. Domingo del Monte, the distinguished Havana lawyer, journalist, and poet was secretary. He was married to Rosa Aldama y Alfonso, the daughter of the planter/merchant/slave trader Domingo Aldama. Among other prominent shareholders were Wenseslao Villaurrutia, who had been one of the organizers of the Havana–Güines railroad as secretary of the Junta de Fomento; Carlos Drake, the creole son of Santiago Drake, the powerful Havana merchant who operated a branch of the business in Matanzas with Henry Coit; and Joaquín Pedroso y Echevarría, one of the wealthiest men in Cuba in the mid-nineteenth century.[10]

The Cárdenas–Bemba railroad was designed by its directors to connect the port of Cárdenas with the regions where they owned land and had begun to construct ingenios. However, the rich cane-growing districts to the southeast of Cárdenas would not be serviced by this line. The Colón region had been slowly colonized in the 1830s by powerful families who wanted to see their estates connected by rail with a major port as quickly as possible. In 1840, a petition was submitted to the Crown for permission to construct a second railroad from a point several miles to the east of Cárdenas, the embarcadero of Júcaro, southeast through the hacienda Banagüises (Colón), and then west to Macuriges. An extension to Sabanillas and a connection with the railway system pushing toward the south from Matanzas Bay were envisioned and eventually constructed.[11]

Nicolás Peñalver y Cárdenas, who was bestowed the title Conde de Peñalver in 1836, was a petitioner and the first president of the Empresa del Ferrocarril del Júcaro. Another major supporter of the project was Joaquín de Arrieta, a diversified entrepreneur who was building Ingenio Flor de Cuba, which would become one of Cuba's largest mills in the early 1840s. Arrieta had been the *contador* of the Banco de Fernando VII in the early 1830s and was a business partner with the British consul John Murphy as co-owner of La Consolidada, a copper-mining venture in Santiago del Prado.[12] Pedro Diago (hijo) was a third backer. His father owned the Amistad mill in Güines and, along with his two brothers, Francisco and Fernando, was in the process of establishing the ingenios Tinguaro, Santa Elena, and Ponina along the projected rail line. Tomás de Juara Soler, a business associate of the Diagos, a Havana merchant, and the founder of Ingenio Conchita in the Banagüises region, was the last petitioner. The Marqués de Villalta was also involved in the initial stages of the project.

Alexander Robertson, the banker who financed the Havana–Güines line, frequently traveled to Cuba and met in Havana with the Conde de Peñalver to negotiate the terms of the loan that financed the beginning of construction.[13] The Ferrocarril de Júcaro would play a central role in the economic development of the frontier in subsequent decades. It should be noted that two cousins, Joaquín and Nicolás Peñalver, were presidents of the competing railroads built from the port of Cárdenas.

The third line in Matanzas, the Ferrocarril de la Sabanilla, was begun in 1838, and again the role of creole entrepreneurs based in Havana and Matanzas was paramount. Officially sanctioned in 1840, the line moved east from the city of Matanzas for several miles before turning south to Guanábana and then on through Cidra to Sabanilla. In 1843, construction began on a major extension from the *paradero* of Guanábana east to Coliseo, and this branch of the Matanzas railroad was completed in 1848.[14]

Perhaps the most impressive aspect of early Cuban railroad building was the dynamism and entrepreneurial acumen manifested by the island's creole elite. Construction may have been financed by English banking firms, and the technology—including engineering supervision, railroad ties, rails, locomotives, and cars—may have been imported, but control over the Cuban railway system was exercised by Cubans. Slave trading, sugar planting, and now railroad building were under the domination of a Cuban-born elite who acted deliberately in their own interests despite operating within a colonial political framework that responded to their needs. Railroad routes were carefully designed to penetrate the zones where major shareholders owned land or had constructed mills. The counts and marquises who could trace their Cuban origins to the sixteenth, seventeenth, or eighteenth centuries were joined by the sons of more recent immigrants. Newcomers such as the Diagos, Drakes, Pedrosos, and Zuluetas worked together with the Montalvos, Peñalvers, and Herreras in joint enterprises closely linked to the needs of sugar. The Cuban railroad system, developed before Spain itself experimented with "caminos de hierro," was the most sophisticated in Latin America through the late nineteenth century. It was built because of sugar, and sugar made it economically viable.

The economic power and political clout of the island's creole elite was clearly manifested during the struggle for control over the Havana–Güines railroad. Although nominally built and initially operated by the Junta de Fomento, state ownership seems to have been designed as a temporary contingency in order to facilitate the acquisition of financing from the London banking firm of Robertson & Company. In 1838, before the final stretch to Güines was even opened, the colonial government announced intentions to transfer ownership to the private sector and a royal order in early 1839 authorized the sale.

Two competing groups emerged. One was a curious alliance between the old titled families and Cuba's most powerful immigrant merchants, all of whom were heavily involved in the slave trade. Pedro Martínez y Cía., Joaquín Gómez, Pedro Blanco, José Suárez Argudín, Pancho Marty, and the young Julián de Zulueta joined with the Conde de Peñalver, the Marqués de Arcos, the Condesa de Lagunillas, and others in a capital-rich company that raised 1.125 million pesos by issuing 2,250 shares.

The second consortium was led by Miguel de Herrera y O'Farrill, who would soon become the Marqués de Almendares. The Aldamas and Alfonsos, closely connected through marriage, were major shareholders, as was the powerful merchant Santiago Drake and the sugar planter Juan Poey. Conspicuous in their collective absence were the titled families of Havana, who were firmly allied with the first group.

The choice of the Junta de Fomento was surprising, given the configuration of the competing groups. Ownership of the railroad, the Compañía de Caminos de Hierro de la Habana, was awarded to the second group, which defied the perceived political influence of Havana's oldest families. The decision remains mysterious, and explanations are speculative at best. Colonial authorities were under increasing British pressure to curb the slave trade. A second Spanish-English treaty had been signed in 1835; slavery had been definitively abolished in the British Caribbean in 1838; and leading Cuban intellectuals such as José Antonio Saco had begun publicly to attack the slave trade.[15] The first group was openly led by Havana's principal slave-trade merchants, and colonial authorities may not have wanted to appear as if they were appeasing well-known *negreros*. Since a British banking firm was backing the project, perhaps this was a condition of approval for transfer of the mortgage note. Then again the Alfonsos, the second group's largest shareholders, were also notorious slave traders.

It is tempting to conclude that the vote was a victory of creole *hacendados* over a group of predominantly immigrant merchants.[16] But this ignores the fact that Santiago Drake, a prominent member of the second group, was one of Havana's leading immigrant *comerciantes*, while the titled families supporting the first group were creoles who generally owned mills in the sugar-producing zones crossed by the railroad. This is why, in the aftermath of defeat in their quest to acquire the Havana–Güines line, they immediately shifted their attention to the Matanzas and Cárdenas railways as objects of investment and influence. The decision of the Junta de Fomento to reject the titled Havana nobility remains enigmatic, but an important result of their decision was to transfer control over a critical resource to men who were the entrepreneurial driving force behind the Matanzas socioeconomic system.[17]

Railroad construction continued at a steady pace through the mid-1860s until every region of the Matanzas hinterland was connected by rail. Havana and Matanzas were first linked indirectly by the construction of a line pushing east from Güines toward Unión de Reyes, in the sugar-rich partido of Alacranes. There it connected with the Matanzas rail line that moved south from Sabanilla.

In the late 1850s, construction began on a route designed to form a direct link between Havana and Matanzas along the northern coastal road. The key organizers of this project were the owners of the Almacenes de Regla in Havana, led by Eduardo Fesser, the Andalucian merchant who was married to the Diagos' sister. Financed by an initial loan of 1.25 million pesos from the London banking firm J. Henry Schroeder & Company, the Ferrocarril de la Bahía de la Habana a Matanzas was completed in 1862.[18]

In 1858 the Cárdenas and Júcaro lines merged into the Ferrocarril de Cárdenas y Júcaro, and this line was linked with Coliseo and the Matanzas railroad system at Bemba. A final connection between the Matanzas and Cárdenas railways was completed in the early 1860s, when a line pushing southeast from Unión de Reyes joined the Cárdenas railroad at Corral Falso. An additional section was constructed south to the border of the Ciénaga de Zapata and then southeast to Cosme de la Torriente's Ingenio Cantabria.[19] (See Map 7.)

Despite elite rivalries over control of the different rail systems constructed during the mid-nineteenth century, there was a central unity of purpose in the goals of all these projects. The railroads were built to service sugar, and in this they were eminently successful. Virgin lands in frontier zones, which would slowly have been opened regardless of infrastructural improvements, were rapidly developed in the 1840s and 1850s. Sugarcane cultivation swept through previously uninhabited forest areas, transforming a varied ecological environment into a uniform sea of cane that extended horizon to horizon by the mid-1870s, from the Atlantic coast to the Zapata swamp. The human landscape was also transformed by the massive influx of African slaves who were brought to rural Matanzas for the single purpose of serving the demands of sugar monoculture. By the end of the Ten Years' War the railroad had pushed the frontier to Las Villas, where it would remain until the late nineteenth and early twentieth centuries.

Matanzas Province ca.1860

25 km²

0 5 10 20 km

- ● RR Crossing/Stop

••••••••••••• Railroads

Map 7. Matanzas Province Railroad System, ca. 1860

SOURCE: Esteban Pichardo, *Isla de Cuba. Carta Geotopográfica* (Havana: Dirección de la Capitanía General, 1860–1872).

CHAPTER 7

The Frontier Sugar Economy:
Development of Hacienda Banagüises

The railroad effectively removed the geographical constraints to sugar expansion by linking distant regions endowed with forest reserves and virgin soils to Cuba's major ports. A journey to Colón from Matanzas by horse or *volante* could take two days or more in the 1820s; and the slow-moving, oxen-drawn carts laden with sugar could spend a week or two completing the trip. Not only was transportation unreliable because of the poor condition of the island's caminos, but the cost of shipping sugar was extremely high. In addition, transportation capacity was severely limited by the relatively small size of the carretas and by the numbers of oxen, carts, and drivers employed.

By the mid-1840s, however, planters could expand planting and construct new mills with the assurance that sugar and supplies would be moved quickly, reliably, and cheaply to and from Havana, Matanzas, or Cárdenas. Communications with rural estates from urban areas were revolutionized, and mill owners could remain in the cities and still receive daily reports on the progress of the harvest. There was no longer the maddening look to the skies to see whether transportation would be feasible, for rain could wash out roads quickly and sabotage the most carefully laid plans for shipping products to or from the estates.

Prior to the wave of railroad construction that swept through rural Matanzas in the 1840s and 1850s, a productive system had been carefully nurtured. Land, labor, and capital resources were harnessed by a largely native-born elite that had established firm control over the Cuban countryside by the late 1830s. Even without the "caminos de hierro" that obsessively caught their imaginations, the continual expansion of sugar production would have ensued. The railroad, by removing the transportation bottleneck that hindered expansion, accelerated the process of economic growth and magnified the quantitative potential of sugar production throughout Matanzas rural society.

The numbers are impressive: 384 mills in 1846; 456 in 1862; and 516 in 1878, the peak year before the centralization of sugar processing began.[1] But the transformation of the Matanzas hinterland did not simply involve the installation of greater productive capacity through ingenio construction along rail lines. There was a qualitative dimension to the transformation; for not only were new mills built, but productive efficiency increased as well on the largest, capital-intensive estates.

Yet, despite such vigor, deep-seated debilities ultimately created instability. Above all, planter income depended on the price of sugar on foreign markets, over which there was no control. Dependence had other dimensions. Technology was imported, and there was little Cuban effort at creating a capital-goods industry. Profits were routinely plowed back into sugar production rather than used to diversify the Cuban economic base—a pattern of economic behavior relentlessly bred by monocultural structures of production. Credit ultimately was filtered through Cuban hands, but it originated in New York, London, Barcelona, or Seville. Labor supplies were linked to a slave trade whose very existence was tenuous and under constant siege throughout this period. Politicians from the North Atlantic nations, whose merchants had participated in the trata in a variety of ways, from supplying ships to financing ventures to the West African coast, were finally able to curb slavers coming into the Caribbean. Cubans possessed land, but every other factor of production hailed from the outside.

Yet, planters and merchants thrived, and the system remained fully operational through the 1870s. Only in the 1880s would the ultimate weakness caused by the multidimensional facets of dependence take its toll. The collapse of world sugar prices—owing to market saturation, the end of the slave trade in the late 1860s, and abolition in the 1870s and 1880s—would cause the downfall of a planter class that seemed impervious to danger in the heyday of railway construction. For the period between the inauguration of the first Cuban railroad line to Bejucal in 1837, and the end of the Ten Years' War, in 1878, represented the maturation of an economic system slowly crafted since the mid-eighteenth century. Cuba's powerful creole families reached the zenith of economic control in this period, only to see the system they created with such painstaking care (and at such a terrible human cost to the other sectors of Cuban society) unravel rapidly during the final decades of the nineteenth century.

Three cycles can be identified in the growth of Cuban sugar culture between 1837 and 1878. The first was ushered in by the railroad and was characterized by a wave of ingenio construction in the 1840s and 1850s, principally in frontier regions opened by "caminos de hierro."

The second cycle did not mark a radical break in development patterns. It began in 1857 with the rapid rise and subsequent meteoric decline in sugar prices on the world market in 1858. Its major characteristic was the formation of joint-stock companies by merchants traditionally serving the sugar economy who now moved to establish direct control over production. These companies, La Perseverancia, the Compañía Territorial Cubana, and the

Gran Azucarera, failed for a variety of reasons by the late 1860s, although this did not drive the families sponsoring them into ruin.

The third cycle began in the 1860s and early 1870s and was marked by the penetration of newly arrived commercial interests into the rural world of sugar production. Immigrant merchants who were relative newcomers to Cuba began to acquire mills, foreshadowing a trend that would develop on a broad scale in the 1880s. It should be stressed that the old creole, sugar-producing elite was not seriously weakened before the end of the Ten Years' War. This third cycle would set the stage for their collective retreat, although this could not have been predicted as the rebellion drew to a close in 1878.

The social and economic history of the area to the north of Colón, known as Banagüises, exemplifies the development of the frontier during the 1840s and 1850s. Banagüises was linked by the Ferrocarril de Júcaro to the port of Cárdenas and, by 1860, had been transformed into one of the richest zones of Cuban sugar production. Many families developed the region. Among the most prominent were the Diagos, who constructed the ingenios Santa Elena, Tinguaro, and Ponina; Julián de Zulueta, the founder of the Habana, Álava, Vizcaya, and España mills; the Arrietas, who developed Ingenio Flor de Cuba; Tomás de Juara Soler, who built the Conchita mill; and the Pedrosos, founders of the ingenios San Martín and Echevarría.

Although this area was referred to as Banagüises, it actually encompassed three old haciendas: San Juan de Banagüises, San Antonio de Gigues, and San Sebastián de Río de Piedras, all situated in the old partido of Guamutas. The Banagüises hacienda was originally granted by the Havana cabildo in 1629 to Juan de Arfián and Luis Rodríguez de la Soledad, who were also awarded Gigues in 1631 for cattle raising.[2] Sometime in the late seventeenth or early eighteenth centuries, Ana de Oquendo, who was linked to the family of the Marqués de la Real Proclamación, acquired all three haciendas. Although the mechanisms of transfer are unknown, in the late 1780s or early 1790s the Havana Licenciado, Lope José Blanco, gained possession of this vast area. It was then purchased by the Marqués de Arcos, José María Peñalver y Navarrete, in two transactions of 1794 and 1797. On his death, title passed to the daughter, María Peñalver y Peñalver, and her husband, the Conde de Peñalver, Nicolás de Peñalver y Cárdenas. As president of the Ferrocarril de Júcaro, the conde's short-term goal was to link Banagüises, which he largely owned, by rail with the port of Cárdenas.

The imminent connection of this distant interior zone with a major port, legally opened in 1843, made it a center of speculation and investment. The conde developed one of the largest mills along the railroad route, Ingenio Purísima Concepción, located in the Cárdenas partido of Guamutas bordering Banagüises to the north. He also capitalized on rising land values by selling off large parcels of his patrimony to key entrepreneurs. (For the location of the mills discussed below, see Map 8.)

An early major acquisition was effected by Joaquín de Arrieta, who purchased the 20-caballería nucleus of the great Ingenio Flor de Cuba on April 21, 1838, for 35,000 pesos.[3] As part of the mill's development in the early 1840s, Arrieta ordered a horizontal high-pressure steam engine from the West Point Foundry in New York and, shortly thereafter, installed 2 Derosne refining trains and 8 centrifuges.[4] The Arrietas tapped local Havana merchants for rather small amounts of credit in order to run Flor de Cuba, but their major creditor was the London banking firm Frederick Hut & Company, which financed the purchase of the mill's modern machinery.[5] The mill had one of the largest productive capacities in Cuba and continued to be owned by the Arrietas through the Ten Years' War. In 1859 it produced 200,000 pesos in gross income; in 1865, 228,000 pesos; and in 1876, 202,539 pesos.[6]

While the Arrietas utilized British capital to finance the development of Flor de Cuba, the Diagos were closely linked with North America capital through their extensive business dealings with the New York merchant house of Moses Taylor & Company. The family owned the Amistad, Cambre, and San José estates in Güines, mills that dated from the early nineteenth century, and they moved east in the 1830s by acquiring Ingenio Santa Rita in Sagua la Grande and Ingenio Cuanabaco near the Matanzas village of Canasí, on the north coast.[7] But with plans for railroad construction the Diagos looked to the Banaguises region as the future center of their operations.

During the late 1830s and early 1840s, they acquired the land where the Tinguaro, Santa Elena, and Ponina estates were developed. Eighty caballerías were purchased between 1838 and 1840 from the Conde de Peñalver, for Tinguaro and Santa Elena; and in 1843 an additional 34 caballerías were purchased farther to the east, for the construction of Ponina.[8] In April 1840, two sets of milling equipment were ordered from the West Point Foundry, through Moses Taylor & Company, and in December the Diagos placed an order for a steam-driven saw to mill the timber on the Tinguaro estate. The bill for the first set of machinery came to 7,822.35 dollars. A detailed invoice, sent for the second set, provides an example of the expenses involved in purchasing modern machinery for sugar production in the early 1840s (see Table 7.1). While the machinery was on order, land was being cleared and planted in cane. Tinguaro's first zafra was in 1840, and Francisco Diago estimated that enough cane was planted to produce 3,000 boxes of sugar, approximately 570 metric tons.

Yet, the cost of the most modern machinery available in the centers of industry and finance was small compared to the cost of labor. Although information on the initial labor force used on the three Banagüises mills is

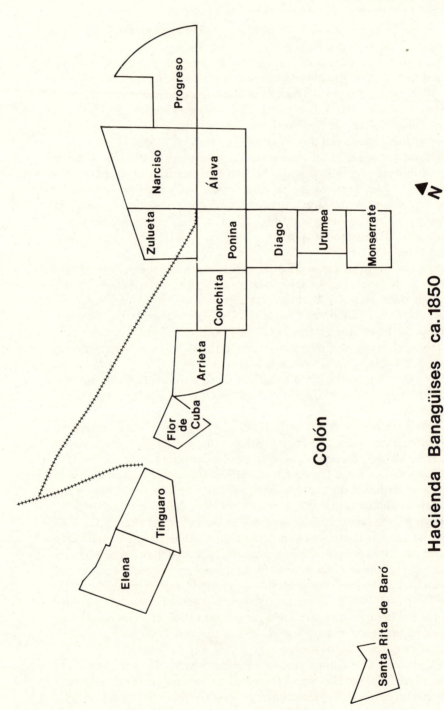

Hacienda Banagüises ca. 1850

+++++++ Ramal de Banagüises

Map 8. Hacienda Banagüises, ca. 1850

Table 7.1. Invoice for Milling Equipment from West Point Foundry to Francisco Diago for Ingenio Tinguaro, 1840 (in dollars)

One high-pressure horizontal steam engine cylinder 11-in. diam. 4-ft. stroke with iron boiler 50-in. diam. 22 feet long with wrought-iron heads, 2 wrought-iron flues connecting machinery with wrought-iron shaft for 10-ft. wheel. Horizontal sugar mill, rollers 24-in. diam. 4 feet long with square shafts.   6,000.00

1 set wheels for mill	89.40
Packing boxes and shipping	65.00
1 Swainson's piston	175.00
1 pinion for flywheel shaft	25.00
1 spur segment for 10-ft. wheel	11.50
1 square coupling box	22.50
2 cast-iron connecting shafts	20.00
1 set outside rings for Swainson's piston	35.00
1 secret safety valve with weight inside the boiler	80.00
1 set Smith tools and 500 fire bricks	431.75
1 cane carrier	250.00
TOTAL	7,205.15

SOURCE: Invoice of Apr. 10, 1840, from West Point Foundry to F. Diago, NYPL, Moses Taylor Collection, case B, drawers 2, and 3, box 6.

not available, in 1846 Francisco Diago purchased 195 slaves for Tinguaro for 72,900 pesos, or 373 pesos/slave, ten times more than the price of the processing equipment.[9]

The correspondence between the Diagos and Moses Taylor indicates the excitement stirred by the new project, especially the prospect of a railroad link to their mills. Pedro Diago wrote to Henry Coit in late 1840 expressing absolute marvel that, even though Tinguaro was more than 40 leagues from Havana, once the railway were built he could make the trip in 12 hours and ship sugar at a savings of 1 peso/box. But the new endeavor also meant that the Diagos reluctantly had to remain in the countryside to supervise the project. Francisco wrote in November 1840: "The development of my new ingenio this year has had me distracted from my usual activities." And, in February 1841: "The desire to increase our sugar harvests has obliged me to spend the greater part of the year in the countryside, often against my will, since I love my wife and daughters very much and I don't find it pleasing to be away from them."[10]

The dependence of Cuban planters on imported technology had other dimensions. No one in Cuba had the know-how or capability to install or service milling equipment. Nor is there evidence that planters ever had the foresight or willingness to have mechanics trained for their ingenios. Throughout this period they employed foreign "maquinistas" at harvesttime to ensure that machinery could be serviced immediately if problems arose.

Contracts to purchase new milling equipment from the United States or England were almost always accompanied by stipulations that skilled mechanics be sent to make sure the machinery was mounted correctly and operating efficiently. The owner of the West Point Foundry, a Mr. Kemble, sometimes had difficulties contracting mechanics to travel to Cuba. To the exasperation of Francisco Diago after the machinery for Tinguaro had arrived, there was no one to assemble and install his new equipment; he wrote to Moses Taylor, requesting that a mechanic be recruited as quickly as possible.[11]

Not only were mill owners dependent on foreign technicians to install and maintain equipment, but there were no local suppliers of spare parts in the event of malfunction or complete breakdown. This could be disastrous at harvesttime; for if milling equipment failed, the ingenios could be paralyzed at considerable financial loss. This was the case in March 1841, when Pedro Diago wrote in desperation to Moses Taylor & Company that a new roller shaft on one of his ingenios had broken beyond repair. He demanded that a replacement be sent immediately.[12] Although shipping service to New York had been regularized from Matanzas and Havana, it still took a week to make the journey under optimal weather conditions, once under way, and of course a week to return. After time had been spent processing the order in New York, acquiring the necessary parts, preparing a ship for departure, passing through Cuban customs, and transporting the parts to the mill site, a planter would be fortunate to secure replacement parts within two months. With so many ingenios installing new machinery, it is surprising that no Cuban entrepreneur developed a servicing-and-parts business in Havana or Matanzas. Merchants simply acted as middlemen, taking orders from planters and then forwarding them to the United States or Europe; or planters dealt directly with suppliers in foreign markets.

These, of course, were short-term problems characteristic of any business enterprise in the start-up phase of operations, and they were ultimately resolved. The Diagos' Banagüises mills were in full production by the mid-1840s, and in 1848 the railroad from Júcaro finally arrived at Ponina.[13] As part of a general survey of the most productive ingenios in Cuba, the British consul in Havana, Joseph Crawford, rendered an economic report to the Foreign Office on January 3, 1849, that provides valuable economic data on Ponina.

The estate extended for 75 caballerías: 35 were planted in cane by January 1849, but only 20 had been harvested during the zafra of 1848; 6 caballerías were dedicated to provision crops; and the rest of the estate was woodland. Ponina had no pastureland and rented nearby potreros for 300 to 500 pesos/caballería to graze its animals. The production for 1848 was 6,633 boxes of sugar (450 pounds each), or 1,337 metric tons, a yield of 66.9 metric tons/caballería of planted land. White sugars made up 32 percent of total production (2,120 boxes); yellow, or *quebrado*, sugars, constituted 65.3 percent (4,331 boxes); and browns, or *muscovados*, were 2.7 percent (182 boxes). Based on current prices of 4.75 cents/pound for whites, 3.5 cents/pound for yellows, and 2.5 cents/pound for muscovados, Ponina produced 115,576 pesos in gross income for 1848.

The estate possessed a slave population of 409 slaves, but Crawford made it clear that only 201 were part of the labor gang. There were 59 Chinese contract laborers, about whom the ingenio's administrator Ignacio Martínez stated: "they are very inferior as working hands to the Negroes." The work force at harvesttime was supplemented by 70 rented slaves, making an effective labor gang of 330. This meant that each worker produced 350.23 pesos in income, which suggests why slave labor was so desirable in mid-nineteenth-century Cuba. It should be recalled that Francisco Diago had purchased 195 slaves at 373 pesos each in 1846. Thus, one working slave could almost generate enough income to pay back the owner's investment in a little more than a year's time. Of course the 208 unproductive slaves had to be maintained; but if they are included in the calculation, the estate generated 214.83 pesos for each slave (productive and unproductive) in 1848.[14]

In May 1849 Francisco reported on the sugar production of his ingenios including the old Amistad mill in Güines, as follows:[15]

Ponina	2,000 tons
Santa Elena	1,325 tons
Tinguaro	1,250 tons
Amistad	1,100 tons

In 1850 a new steam engine for Ponina and three new milling devices were ordered from the West Point Foundry. The new engine was 18 inches in diameter, had a 4.5-foot stroke and a 22-foot wheel, and included connecting equipment. The total cost was 6,475 dollars. The three mills had top rollers that were 26 inches in diameter and 5 feet, 8 inches in length; the side rollers were 30 inches in diameter and 5 feet, 8 inches long. The price was 3,600 dollars for each mill, and the Diagos ordered unspecified spare parts at a cost of 1,108 dollars. The entire bill (18,383 dollars) was due six months from delivery, and there would be a deduction of 5 percent for prompt payment.[16]

The Banagüises mills financed lives of luxury for the Diago brothers and their children. Not only were magnificent homes maintained in Havana, but summers were spent traveling abroad. The United States was the preferred place to visit, and in 1850, after the completion of the harvest, an ailing Pedro Diago and his wife, María de la Trinidad de Zayas, embarked for the resort of Saratoga Springs, New York. From there they visited Albany, later traveled to Niagara Falls, and then went on to Boston and Portland, Maine. The crowning moment of this vacation was a trip to Washington, D.C., and a February 1851 audience with President Millard Fillmore. Pedro Diago remained in Washington through March 1851 while his brothers supervised affairs on Hacienda Banagüises. He wrote to Henry Coit in March from the U.S. capital: "Our life is like that of a court; little is thought of other than dances, parties, visits, sight-seeing trips, ministers, 'chargés,' 'attachés.' . . . [T]he white gloves are in constant exercise, and no one speaks of sugar or molasses."[17] No one may have spoken of sugar or molasses, but it was the mills in rural Matanzas that made it possible for Pedro Diago to rub elbows with the social elite of the antebellum United States.

Pedro Diago died sometime in the early 1850s, and his three ingenios continued in operation under the direction of Fernando and Francisco. By 1857 the brothers were caught up in the euphoria created by the doubling of sugar prices on the world market during the zafra of that year. Although prices were to retreat in 1858, the meteoric rise in capital availability resulting from the earlier windfall led to a wave of heretofore-unparalleled speculation. Elite groups invested astonishing sums to form joint-stock companies dedicated to agriculture, credit, insurance, shipping, and warehousing.[18]

The first Cuban "sociedades anónimas" had been formed for railroad construction in the 1830s and 1840s. While there were several unsuccessful attempts to establish banks as well, it was not until 1857 that corporate forms of ownership over ingenios became commonplace in Cuba, and these were especially pervasive in Matanzas. The emergence of corporate bodies that owned multiple mills should not be confused with centralization and concentration of production. Ingenio ownership continued to be dispersed, and milling capacity remained rather limited on individual estates. But the transfer of mill ownership over to joint-capital enterprises did appeal to some of the largest planters in the late 1850s and early 1860s.

One benefit of joint-stock companies was the possibility of raising substantial amounts of operating capital for investment purposes by pooling resources. Large fixed assets could also help secure ample loans because of the impressive collateral that could be posted in the form of multiple mills. But the principal allure to owners of large estates was simply that they could convert nonliquid assets, which had accumulated in previous decades, to capital that could be invested in secure, long-term interest-bearing bonds in the United States.[19]

The formation of joint-stock companies in the late 1850s did little to alter the productive parameters of Cuban sugar ingenios, and most of these agricultural "sociedades anónimas" had failed by the mid-1860s. The technological limitations of processing meant that the only way to expand production substantially was to construct new mills and to plant more land in cane. There was no elastic capacity to raise the output of any given mill. Those who were investing capital speculatively hoped that inflated sugar prices would maintain high income levels and ensure substantial returns on their investments. In addition, by directly owning mills, merchant houses were guaranteed supplies of sugar for export and did not have to negotiate with planters to purchase sugar at prevailing or projected market prices. However, sugar prices dropped in 1858 as sharply as they had increased in 1857, and prices remained relatively stable through the 1860s.

The surviving Diago brothers clearly had capitalization in mind in 1857, when they formed La Perseverancia, which consisted of the ingenios Ponina, Santa Elena, and Tinguaro. Documentation on the initial offering has not been located, but the company lasted for only six years and was dissolved in 1862 and 1863. Of 2,431 outstanding "acciones" in 1863, the most prominent shareholders were Pedro Martínez y Cía. of Havana (663 shares); Rafael Rodríguez Torices, who made his fortune in the Chinese contract-labor trade (527 shares); and Francisco Diago, who was the company's director throughout its existence (378 shares). María de la Trinidad de Zayas, the widow of Pedro Diago, owned 145 shares.[20]

Although La Perseverancia ultimately failed, it appears to have been innovative in one respect. Faced with the incessant problem of restricted labor supplies, owing to constant threats to end the slave trade, the company seems to have conducted the first serious experimentation with the *colono* system. An economic report sent to the Crown by Cipriano del Mazo, concerning the failure of Cuban joint-stock companies, noted that La Perseverancia had rented a significant portion of land for cane cultivation to white and colored freemen without subdividing its property. In total, 26 caballerías of land were parceled out to 12 colono families, who received 2 percent of the net yield of the sugar as payment. It was generally assumed that planters derived a 6 percent net yield. Nevertheless, slaves continued to constitute the most important sector of the work force through the early 1870s.[21]

Although the precise reasons for the failure are unclear, the Diagos managed to maintain possession of Tinguaro and Santa Elena after the demise of La Perseverancia. When Francisco died in 1865, the Tinguaro mill passed on to his daughter, María Luisa Diago y Tirry, the Marquesa de la Cañada Tirry, who was married to the Conde de Armildez de Toledo, Isidro Wall y Alfonso. But by 1878 the enterprise was a mere shadow of its former grandeur. It had produced 237,250 pesos in gross income in 1865; in 1878, however, it generated only 70,287 pesos.[22]

Ownership of Santa Elena was transferred to Joaquín Diago y Zayas, the son of Pedro Diago and María de Trinidad de Zayas. But it too experienced collapse, probably because of the lack of continued capital investment. In 1865 the mill had produced 201,964 pesos, but gross income plummeted to 78,100 pesos in 1878.[23]

The Diagos' jewel, Ponina, was purchased by Rafael Rodríguez Torices in 1863, when La Perseverancia folded. He paid 592,650 pesos for the ingenio, of which 375,000 pesos were disbursed in cash to the company's shareholders. The Sociedad del Crédito Territorial Cubano, directed by Julio Ibarra, financed the remaining debt of 217,650 pesos, which would be paid over ten years (1863–1873) together with 12 percent annual interest on any outstanding balance. Ponina was purchased at the peak of its productive life. Although the mill produced 149,000 pesos in gross income in 1865, it turned out to be a poor investment for Torices, generating only 67,726 pesos in 1876 and a mere 1,500 pesos in 1878.[24] Once the pride of rural Matanzas, it then disappeared as so many other mills would over the next two decades. Outside of Colón there is a road sign pointing in the direction of a place called Ponina. In July 1986 I asked no fewer than two dozen people in the immediate area of the old mill if they had heard of anyone named Diago or of a sugar mill named Ponina. Not one could make any such associations.

After the failure of La Perseverancia, the Diagos ceased to be a dynamic force in rural Matanzas; and with the death of Francisco in 1865, the old mills were reduced to economic insignificance. However, the career of Julián de Zulueta, one of the more remarkable entrepreneurs in Cuban history, markedly contrasts with the decline of the Diagos after the mid-1860s.

Zulueta, whose uncle and first cousins operated Zulueta & Company of London and Seville, arrived in Cuba in 1832 at age eighteen (see Chapter 3). In 1835 he acquired Ingenio San Francisco de Paula, in Corral Nuevo, and by 1836 he was marketing sugar via Drake Hermanos to Moses Taylor & Company of New York.[25] Zulueta was also involved with the consortium of slave traders and Havana-based titled families who unsuccessfully attempted to purchase the Havana–Güines railroad from the Junta de Fomento in the late 1830s.[26] He was a notorious slave trader and operated a merchant house in Havana during the early 1840s.

In 1844 Zulueta began the development of an enterprise on the Hacienda Banagüises that would become the largest slave/sugar complex in nineteenth-century Cuba. Well aware that the railroad line from Júcaro was projected to push through the region, Zulueta on October 26, 1844, finalized the purchase of 60 caballerías of undeveloped land from the Conde de Peñalver, Nicolás Peñalver y Cárdenas, the president of the Júcaro railway. The purchase price was 44,974 pesos, or 750 pesos/caballería.[27] It was on this parcel, just to the south of Peñalver's Ingenio San Narciso, that Zulueta's slaves began clearing land and constructing the mill which would become Ingenio Álava, Cuba's largest producing mill in the 1850s and 1860s.

Zulueta set out to establish the most modern mill in Cuba, and he was successful in every respect. Álava was the first Cuban ingenio to employ the triple-effect vacuum evaporator. Ten centrifuges were utilized for processing; a sophisticated network of gaslights illuminated all sections of the mill; and Zulueta was the first Cuban planter to build an elaborate network of internal railway systems, which would connect the cane fields with Álava and the other mills he was to acquire or construct in the 1850s.

More than 600 slaves cleared land, planted cane, and constructed the mill in 1844, 1845, and 1846. Álava's first zafra in 1847 produced 6,000 boxes of sugar—in Zulueta's words, "a total that has not been attained by any other mill in Cuba." In addition, he estimated that half of the cane planted for the 1847 zafra could not be transported to the mill because of heavy rains.

In 1847 the Júcaro railway reached the paradero of Banagüises, which was adjacent to Álava, and in 1848 Zulueta became one of the first hacendados to construct a railway line to his ingenio. It passed through rich cane fields, thus serving the double function of transporting cane to the mill and sugar to the Banagüises paradero, from which it was shipped to Cárdenas for export. This contributed to a dramatic rise in production to 9,000 boxes in 1848 and 20,000 boxes in 1849. Álava had a slave population of 565 in 1848, and there were also 35 Chinese contract laborers. The estate extended for 148 caballerías, 42 planted in cane and 13 in provision crops. The British consul, Joseph Crawford, estimated that 370 slaves and Chinese made up the effective labor gang, or 8.8 workers/caballería of planted cane.[28]

In 1850 Zulueta completed the construction of a long stretch of rail northwest of Álava to the cane fields designated La Marquesita; in 1856, an addition extended this line farther to the north into new areas of cane planting. In the early 1850s, just to the east of Álava, Zulueta had also begun the construction of a second mill, which became Ingenio Vizcaya. A rail line was constructed in 1857 between Vizcaya and Álava, and a spur extended southeast of Vizcaya to recently planted cane fields. In 1856 Ingenio San Narciso, adjacent to Álava and Vizcaya and one of Cuba's leading ingenios in the 1840s and early 1850s, was purchased from the Conde de Peñalver. Renamed Ingenio Habana, this last mill completed a conglomeration of three ingenios that together made up the largest sugar enterprise in Cuba. (See Map 9.) The harvest of 1859 was worked by a combined labor force of 1,465 slaves and 162 Chinese contract laborers; it produced 459,000 pesos in gross income.[29]

Zulueta was not content simply to own the largest sugar/slave complex in Cuba. Sometime in the early 1860s he acquired an undeveloped parcel of land to the northwest of Colón, due south of Guanajayabo, and began development of Ingenio España. By 1865 the first zafra had been produced, and his four mills were collectively worked by 2,184 slaves and generated 605,811 pesos in gross income.[30] No other entrepreneur in Cuba could boast of such wealth.

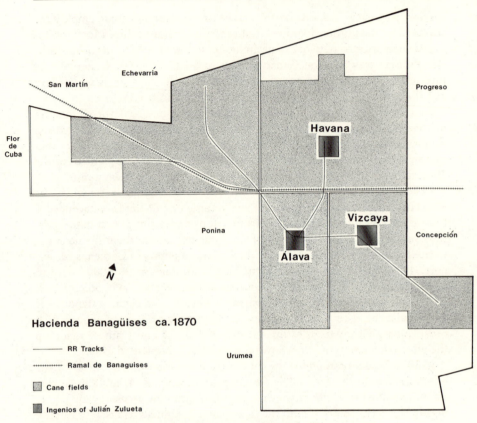

Map 9. Ingenios of Julián Zulueta on Hacienda Banagüises, ca. 1870
SOURCE: AHN, Ultramar, Sección de Fomento, leg. 67.

The capital to finance the construction of new mills derived not only from the profits of prior investments in sugar production, but also from capital accumulated in the slave trade to Cuba. Zulueta was known as the leading Cuban slave trader at the middle of the nineteenth century, but he went to great lengths to obscure his role in this illegal activity. He was even arrested once, in 1853, by the zealous Captain General Valentín Canedo, who was futilely determined to enforce the ban on the illegal trata. For lack of evidence, the charges were eventually dropped.[31]

Zulueta owned the steamship *Noc Daqui*, capable of carrying more than 1,000 slaves. He was identified by the British consul as the importer of 935 slaves through Cárdenas on June 14, 1858, and of 903 slaves on September 8 of the same year. The latter mission had been reported to the governor by local authorities after the slaves had disembarked near Cárdenas. It was difficult to hide such a large contingent of slaves, not to mention the 200 armed men who escorted them overland to Álava.[32] Yet, no charges were brought against this man, regarded as the wealthiest and most influential in Cuba.

In 1864, Zulueta and the Governor of Colón, José Agustín Argüelles, were caught smuggling more than 1,000 slaves, of whom 250 were sold for the benefit of Argüelles as a bribe. He eventually had to flee to the United States, but was extradited at the request of Spanish authorities and sentenced to life imprisonment for his crime.[33] Zulueta remained untouched. During November 1865 Zulueta was again caught transporting more than 400 slaves without "empadronamiento" papers. By law all slaves had to be registered in 1857, and those not registered were declared *emancipados*. He claimed that the slaves were from his dotaciones in Colón, had been rented out to ingenios in Cienfuegos, and were being transported back to Colón. Once again, he was not prosecuted; nor were the slaves freed as required by the legal code.[34]

Zulueta was marginally involved in the importation of Chinese contract laborers. He owned one ship involved in the Chinese trade, the *Paquita*, but the major importers of "coolies" were Rafael Rodríguez Torices, José María Morales, the Drakes, and Pereda & Company of Havana.[35]

Although Zulueta is identified in Cuba with his great Banagüises mills, Álava, Habana, Vizcaya, and España, toward the end of his life the great entrepreneur began to pave the way for the future by moving farther east. He was obviously an astute student of the history of sugar in Cuba and of the march eastward in search of virgin lands. Sometime in the 1870s he acquired a large tract of land to the south of Remedios and began an ambitious project of mill construction; he also began to develop a railway line from Placetas (east of Santa Clara) north through Remedios and Caibarién to a coastal embarcadero. The construction of the railway would, in Zulueta's words, break the isolation of Caibarién and "give life to a region that, while fertile, is mountainous and almost completely without means of communication at the present."[36]

The initial result of the project was the founding of Ingenio Zaza, designed to evolve into one of Cuba's giant mills with all of the modern equipment available from the industrial nations. It should be emphatically noted that Zulueta began this project in the middle of the Ten Years' War. Confined largely to the east, that war evidently did not lead to a climate of political instability threatening investments. Unfortunately, Zulueta underestimated or overlooked the possibility of the *insurrectos* carrying the war west of the *trocha*; this huge armed ditch, manned by the Spanish military, ran the width of the island and cut off Camagüey and Oriente from western Cuba. Early in 1875, revolutionary forces led by Máximo Gómez succeeded in crossing the trocha and brought the war to the Sancti Spíritus region. Eighty-three plantations were burned, including Zulueta's Zaza.[37]

Nevertheless, he continued with the project, evidently rebuilding Ingenio

Zaza after the Spanish counteroffensive drove the rebels back toward the east. He also requested official permission from the Crown to construct the railway system he envisioned. Although the project was eventually completed, apparently built entirely with Zulueta's capital, he did not live to see it bear fruit. The dynamic Marqués de Álava and Viscount of Casa-Blanca, titles bestowed in 1875, was not to die in bed of old age or lingering illness. In 1878, while inspecting one of his plantations, Zulueta was thrown from a horse and struck his head. He was president of the Círculo de Hacendados at the time of his death, which was described by the British consul, Augustus Cowper, as "a national calamity at a crisis like the present."[38]

More than any other figure in nineteenth-century Cuba, Zulueta personified the entrepreneurial spirit pushing the sugar economy forward. However, the wealth derived from rural Matanzas benefited him and his family alone. Quantitatively, Hacienda Banagüises was transformed in a variety of ways by Zulueta and his sugar-producing compatriots during the 1840s and later. But the qualitative aspects of life for the thousands of people who worked on the region's plantations did not improve. Their collective health was no better, they were not educated, and the material dimensions of their lives were not ameliorated. Zulueta's wealth, grew but there was a costly human toll: the unmitigated suffering and exploitation of the African slaves and Chinese workers who toiled in his fields and mills. The ingenios and railroads he built may have been the most modern in colonial Cuba—and, in a perverse way, they did represent technological progress and economic growth—but if the British consul regarded Zulueta's death as a "national calamity," his concept of "nation" was very narrow indeed. For inside the barracones on Álava, Zaza, España, Habana, and Vizcaya, there must have been great rejoicing at the death of a man who was little more than a tyrannical exploiter of other men and women.

Bordering Álava, Ponina, and Conchita to the north were the ingenios San Martín and Echevarría, whose histories exemplify the experience of large-scale, capital-intensive Cuban mills in the 1850s, 1860s, and 1870s. Administratively, these ingenios were in the Cárdenas partido of Guamutas; ecologically and economically, however, they were part of the Banagüises region. Slightly more than three miles from the Banagüises railroad station, they were connected to the paradero by rail.

Both mills were constructed in the early 1850s, somewhat later than the ingenios bordering them to the south. They were nominally owned by Francisca Pedroso y Herrera, the widow of Martín Pedroso y Echevarría (b. 1794, d. 1848), after whom San Martín was named. She was the sister-in-law of Joaquín Pedroso y Echevarría, banker, mill owner, and railroad builder. Antonio González Solar, a peninsular merchant based in Havana, acted as Doña Francisca's commercial agent and was in charge of finance, marketing, and day-to-day operation of the mills.[39] González was Joaquín

Pedroso's business partner and the director of Pedroso y Cía. of Havana which owned nearby Ingenio Descanso. Pedroso was also the owner of the Santa Gertudis estate.

The development of San Martín began in 1851, and the mill's first harvest was attempted in 1854.[40] It was an unmitigated disaster. González Solar had purchased the machinery for the mill from the West Point Foundry, as had most of the other mills in the Banagüises region. Moses Taylor was the middleman in the transaction, and he subsequently extended a 25,000-dollar line of credit to finance expenses for San Martín's first harvest. The milling machinery did not arrive at the site until January 17, 1854, when the harvest was already to have been under way. It took a little more than a month to install, and on February 24 grinding began. Within three weeks, everything came to a halt. Nothing worked properly. The grinding equipment had not been calibrated correctly, and no one on the estate could fix the machine. González Solar complained to Taylor that the cane was emerging from the grinding equipment "casi entera" (almost whole) and that one-half of the *guarapo* was lost. In addition, the pumps that moved the syrupy liquid to the modern, triple-effect vacuum evaporators were not working. Three-quarters of the cane that had been planted and was ready for harvest was not ground. González wrote in frustration to Moses Taylor: "We are regretful of having become involved with these vacuum apparatuses because of our bad experiences with them and because of the difficulty of finding skilled people capable of fixing them."

Although vacuum evaporators were theoretically the most efficient mechanisms available for sugar processing, San Martín's initial experiences underscore the extent of external dependence with respect to the most elementary aspects of Cuban sugar production. Hundreds of thousands of pesos had been invested in land, slaves, and the most advanced machinery; but, for lack of a skilled mechanic with the ability to service the modern equipment, virtually an entire harvest was lost.

The machinery was repaired during the summer of 1854, and González Solar wrote to Taylor with great optimism of the coming zafra. But once again, misfortune struck—a prolonged drought that lasted from September through December 1854. The 1855 harvest was one-half the volume projected in late 1854. During the fall of 1855, González Solar, ever enthusiastic despite his misfortunes, wrote once again to Taylor with an optimistic forecast for 1856: "The fields of both ingenios are beautiful, and I can assure you that they are the most vast and in the best condition of all the ingenios in Cuba. If I grind all of the cane that I have on both farms and prices continue as expected, I believe I am going to produce brilliant results during the coming year."

Finally, there was good fortune. San Martín had its first successful harvest in 1856, when 15,000 boxes of sugar were produced, while Echevarría (part of the same complex) produced 17,000 boxes, elevating the two mills to the top of the Cuban sugar-producing hierarchy. Only Flor de Cuba, Tinguaro, and Álava, all contiguous to San Martín and Echevarría, produced more sugar.[41]

The fortunes of San Martín and Echevarría improved during 1857 because of the dramatic increase in the price of sugar on international markets. With the emergence of joint-stock companies for agricultural exploitation, such as the Diagos' enterprise La Perseverancia, the two mills became objects of acquisition by a newly formed company, La Gran Azucarera. The history of the latter enterprise exemplifies certain aspects of the speculative boom ushered in by the sugar price inflation of 1857, notably the monumental mismanagement that drove it, and similar companies, into bankruptcy proceedings by the mid-1860s.

The Gran Azucarera was owned and operated by the Havana merchant establishment Sociedad Benítez, Dirón y Cía., which is believed to have been financed in part with capital invested by Spain's Queen Mother María Cristina, the mother of Isabel II. The principal partner in Benítez and Dirón was Antonio Benítez y Pérez de Abreu (b. 1812, d. 1864), a criollo whose family had migrated to Cuba from the Canary Islands in the first half of the eighteenth century.[42] In 1848 his sister, Susana Benítez, was married to Antonio Parejo y Cañero, a native of Córdoba, Spain, and a confidant of the royal family. Parejo had established Ingenio Santa Susana, named for Susana Benítez, in the partido of Lajas, Cienfuegos, during the early 1850s, and this mill became part of La Gran Azucarera along with another of his ingenios, Santísima Trinidad.

Negotiations for the purchase of San Martín and Echevarría were conducted in late 1857 and early 1858. This represented an excellent opportunity for the Pedrosos and González Solar to convert fixed assets to capital; in hindsight, it was a brilliant financial decision, for they sold these mills at the precise top of the market, just before sugar prices plummeted and the value of mills also declined. On May 5, 1858, the two mills were sold to Benítez, Dirón y Cía. for the sum of 2 million pesos in gold. An 800,000-peso cash down payment was made by the purchaser, and the remaining balance was to be paid in three equal yearly payments plus 4 percent annual interest on any outstanding amount.[43] There were additional expenses of more than 1 million pesos because of taxes, commissions, and insurance, and including more than 117,000 pesos invested immediately for the purchase of new machinery. The Havana merchant house Noriega, Olmo y Cía. financed at least part of this transaction, for they acted as guarantors of the outstanding balance to the sellers. The problems encountered in 1854 and 1855 seemed insignificant in light of the profits that were realized by this transaction.

At the time of its sale, San Martín extended for 167 caballerías and possessed a dotación of 428 slaves (229 males and 199 females). Ingenio Echevarría was 91 caballerías in size with a slave population of 340 (186 males and 154 females). Both mills combined were worked by 206 Chinese contract laborers for a total work force of 974 men and women.

The complex financial interactions among merchant houses, and between merchants and planters, are indicated by the peripheral transactions that preceded the purchase of San Martín and Echevarría by La Gran Azucarera. These illustrate the beginning of merchant penetration into the realm of sugar agriculture as direct owners of mills on a significant scale, rather than as marketers and financiers. In January 1858 Noriega, Olmo y Cía. borrowed 1 million pesos as operating capital from three Havana merchant houses. Eduardo Fesser's companies, the Almacenes de Regla and the Banco de Comercio, lent Noriega 578,947.37 pesos; the Sociedad Crédito Industrial, directed by Fernando Ylluz, was tapped for 157,894.75 pesos; and, interestingly, Antonio González Solar, who ran San Martín and Echevarría, provided 263,157.87 as director of Pedroso y Cía.[44] This capital was then advanced to Benítez y Dirón to purchase the two ingenios. González Solar thus made the transition from administrator of the mills to a role as one of their principal creditors.

Noriega, Olmo & Company borrowed this money because they had recently formed an agricultural holding company, the Compañía Territorial Cubana, which had accumulated 11 ingenios, a cafetal, and an urban warehouse in the city of Matanzas. Ingenios Noriega, Andrea, and Purísima Concepción were mortgaged as collateral for the loan, although these three mills were not included in Territorial Cubana, but remained titled solely to the parent company, Noriega, Olmo y Cía.[45]

The Compañía Territorial Cubana began accumulating mills in the aftermath of the 1857 sugar harvest. Flush with capital because of the inflation of 1857, the firm purchased 7 mills in late 1857 and early 1858. Ingenio Belfast (40 caballerías in Jíquimas adjacent to Tinguaro) was purchased for 250,000 pesos on November 3, 1857; Arco Iris (54 caballerías in Alacranes) was bought on November 11 for 457,480 pesos; La Perla (88 caballerías in Guamacaro) was purchased on November 20; Victoria (38 caballerías in Lagunillas) and Socorro (93 caballerías in Ceja de Pablo) were acquired on December 1; Fundador (86 caballerías in Macuriges) was purchased on December 18 for 298,000 pesos; and Santa Cruz (49 caballerías in Corral Nuevo) was bought on March 24, 1858, for 275,112 pesos.[46] Ingenios Apuros, Chumba, San Joaquín, and Destino were also purchased. By the early 1860s, the Compañía Territorial Cubana had accumulated 769 caballerías of land, 2,247 slaves, and 462 Chinese contract laborers.[47] All were in Matanzas province, most clustered in or around the Banagüises region.

Thus, in the late 1850s, several fundamental changes occurred in the linkages between sugar production and finance capital. Large-scale merchant establishments, which had previously provided credit, transportation, warehousing, factoring, and marketing services to planters, began to establish direct ownership over the largest and most productive sugar mills in the Matanzas region. Not only were joint-stock companies formed, but for the first time in Cuban history there was a concerted attempt to concentrate ownership over multiple enterprises in different economic sectors through interlocking directories of various companies. Noriega, Olmo & Company not only owned the Compañía Territorial, but helped finance La Gran Azucarera, thus exerting influence and a measure of control over a rival company. In addition, José Noriega was one of the principal shareholders in the Sociedad General de Crédito Mobiliario y Fomento Cubano. His partners included Rafael Rodríguez Torices, who purchased the Diagos' Ingenio Ponina, and Julián de Zulueta's brother-in-law, Salvador Samá, a notorious slave trader. Noriega, Olmo & Company was also the largest creditor to the Banco Español de la Habana during the crisis of late 1857 and early 1858 when the bank borrowed 6 million pesos from Havana merchants in order to remain solvent. Noriega lent the Banco Español 500,000 pesos, and Pedroso y Cía., which helped finance Noriega's extension of credit to La Gran Azucarera for purchase of the ingenios San Martín and Echevarría, lent 400,000 pesos to the beleaguered bank.[48]

Benítez, Dirón, y Cía. were also rather diversified. They owned a controlling interest in La Gran Azucarera, 2,639 "acciones" worth 1,319,950 pesos in 1863. They also had 399,324 pesos invested in four railway companies, the Trinidad, Cárdenas–Júcaro, Marianao, and Oeste lines. In addition, they owned shares worth 44,800 pesos in La Alianza, a rural credit and insurance company controlled by Julián de Zulueta, José Baró, Francisco Rosell, and Santiago Sánchez.[49] The old Havana titled nobility forged linkages and cemented business alliances by intermarrying. In the mid-nineteenth century a more modern approach to business relationships was effected by relative newcomers to the island. Interlocking directorships, mutual guarantees of credit by multiple companies, and shareholding in diverse business enterprises created ties among the Havana and Matanzas commercial elites.

The formation of agricultural holding companies such as La Perseverancia, the Compañía Territorial Cubana, and La Gran Azucarera by powerful commercial and agricultural entrepreneurs was the first large-scale attempt to concentrate resources in the Cuban sugar economy. However, this should not be confused with concentration of production, which took place later in the nineteenth century. The specialized division of sugar production into its industrial and agricultural phases would be initiated only with the appearance of the first *centrales* in the mid-1870s. The accumulation of mills by particular companies in the late 1850s did little to alter the productive parameters of the sugar economy. Dependence on slave labor was not mitigated, and the manner in which sugarcane was produced hardly changed at all. Industrial yields improved somewhat, but the major characteristics of the sugar economy remained intact during the 1860s. Production was dispersed, and the debacle experienced by all of these companies by 1865 ensured the continuation of minimal concentration in ownership. In retrospect, the formation of these agricultural companies for sugar production represented little more than simple speculation bred by the inflation of 1857 and the sudden rise in cash flow to merchant houses and large-scale planters who derived the principal economic benefits from the sugar economy.

Nevertheless, the formation of corporate enterprises devoted to agricultural exploitation represented a more modern approach to business. In part this reflected a fundamental shift in the legal code governing the credit mechanisms utilized by ingenios and their creditors. Prior to 1852, sugar plantations enjoyed protection by a 1529 royal decree known popularly as the "privilegio de ingenios." This law made mills and all of their property inalienable by forbidding the mortgage of fixed assets in the sugar sector. Loans could be secured only through establishing liens on production and slaves, not on land or machinery.[50] By the 1840s this prohibition was becoming an obstacle to the extension of rural credit. Merchants were reluctant to extend long-term loans to planters without the security of fixed assets as collateral. In 1852 a royal decree rescinded the "privilegio" for all new mills, and existing ingenios had the prerogative of renouncing the "privilegio" and mortgaging their property. Indeed, after 1852, merchants refused to lend large amounts of working capital, including the traditional "refacción" contracts, unless planters mortgaged their mills and land.[51] The "privilegio" was completely abolished in 1865.

By forming corporate bodies that legally owned mills, the merchant establishments of Havana, such as Noriega, Olmo & Co. and Benítez, Dirón & Co., maintained financial control over their agricultural assets, while partners in the firms were legally beyond the reach of creditors as individuals. While this had already been an accepted business practice in the industrial nations, it was the first Cuban manifestation of a modern corporate approach to economic enterprises. When they formed the Compañía Territorial Cubana, Noriega and Olmo wisely excluded their three previously owned mills (the ingenios Noriega, Andrea, and Concepción) from the corporation. Bankruptcy proceedings against the Compañía Territorial were initiated in 1863, but only the assets of Territorial were affected. The parent company and the three mills it owned could not be held legally accountable for the financial liens incurred by the agricultural holding company. Thus, the rush to form agricultural "sociedades anónimas" in 1857 and 1858, by the Diagos and others, was not only linked to capital availability because of sugar price inflation. It was also a concerted effort by entrepreneurs to maximize the credit potential of ingenios, through the new possibility of mortgaging valuable assets, while minimizing personal liability through the formation of corporate enterprises.

All three major holding companies were plunged into bankruptcy proceedings in the early 1860s. It should be emphasized that they were owners of some of the largest and most productive Cuban sugar ingenios. The reasons are not completely clear, but it seems that mismanagement, rather than a lack of economic viability, played the leading role in the demise of these enterprises. Without a personal stake in each mill, corporate owners seem to have been lax and perhaps negligent in controlling operating expenses and profitability. Their experience as corporations stands in sharp contrast to individually owned complexes that thrived during the same period. For example, Julián de Zulueta's three mills, Álava, Habana, and Vizcaya, prospered during this same period, as did José Baró's Luisa, Olimpo, and Santa Rita estates.

Detailed accounts that were part of the bankruptcy proceedings against La Gran Azucarera allow some insight into the operating expenses and profitability of the company's four mills. As early as 1861 the firm was heavily in debt. Pedroso y Cía. acted as the principal "refaccionista" for the ingenios San Martín and Echevarría, providing operating expenses of 546,631.50 pesos between September 1861 and October 1862 at 10 percent annual interest. It is clear that the Gran Azucarera had difficulties making payments on this debt, and that Benítez, Dirón y Cía. was unwilling to commit itself further in any attempt to make the mills more viable. Essentially, the parent company was reluctant to throw good money after bad. The situation deteriorated to the point that the slaves on both mills were not being fed and had few provisions to sustain them by late 1863.[52] Because of the large outstanding debt the company had accumulated, creditors were unwilling to extend themselves by providing capital for even the most basic provisions. These ingenios, two of Cuba's largest producing mills in the late 1850s, were now being neglected to the point of disaster several years later. What was wrong?

First, it should be underlined that there was little fluctuation in sugar prices during these years. Thus, income was not affected by radical shifts in international market conditions. Table 7.2 shows the stability in prices received for different grades of sugar produced by Ingenio San Martín from 1862 through 1866.

In their publicly printed explanation of why the Gran Azucarera was not solvent, the directors emphasized the fact that none of the mills was producing anywhere near its installed productive capacity. The principal cause of this, according to the company, was the fact that capital resources and credit were not available to purchase more slaves. Labor shortages resulted in an inability to utilize the productive potential of the firm's mills. The company wrote: "The resources of this Society have not yet permitted the

Table 7.2. Prices Received by Ingenio San Martín for Different
Grades of Sugar, 1862–1866
(in cents per pound)

	Whites	Yellows	Browns
1862	6.5	5.0	3.1
1863	6.5	5.3	4.0
1864	6.7	5.8	5.1
1865	5.6	4.8	4.6
1866	6.8	5.8	4.3

SOURCE: Sociedad en Comandita La Gran Azucarera. *Balanza general y memoria* (Havana: Imp. La Universal, 1866).

NOTE: Whites were "blancos"; yellows, "quebrados"; browns, "cucuruchos."

expenditures needed to increase the slave population of the estates to the number required by the extension of land, cultivated acreage, and the power of their refining machinery in order to arrive at maximum productive capacity."[53]

This explanation is somewhat suspect, and it was probably used by Gran Azucarera's directors to obfuscate their negligent management of the company. Even in 1866, 1,101 slaves were owned by the four mills, and there were 187 Chinese contract laborers working on the estates. In addition, substantial slave labor gangs were rented at harvesttime. One of the largest disbursements for operating expenses was payment for slave rentals at the rate of 20 pesos/month/slave. In 1863, 18.6 percent of refacción credit on San Martín was used to rent slaves; 19.4 percent was used in 1864, 21.7 percent in 1865, and 20.6 percent in 1866. Table 7.3 indicates the types of refacción expenses incurred by San Martín between 1863 and 1866.

When the profitability of the four mills is examined, it becomes exceedingly clear why the company was not solvent. Accounts were kept separately for San Martín/Echevarría and for Santa Susana/Santísima Trinidad. In 1863, San Martín and Echevarría derived profits of 8.3 percent on invested capital, but this declined to 7.7 percent in 1864 and to only 3.1 percent in 1865. Santa Susana and Santísima Trinidad's economic performance were much worse: 2.8 percent in profits were recorded in 1862; 1.6 percent in 1863; 7.4 percent in 1864; 0.9 percent in 1865; and 3.6 percent in 1866.[54] (See tables 7.4 and 7.5.) However, the economic difficulties of these enterprises were much more serious than profits indicated, for interest and principal payments on outstanding debt were not listed as part of operating expenses. There is no question that the slim profit margins indicated above could hardly cover these expenses, which were linked to the total purchase price of nearly 6 million pesos paid for the four mills. It should also be

Table 7.3. Operating Expenses for Ingenio San Martín, 1863–1866
(in pesos)

	1863	1864	1865	1866
Slave Rentals	32,933	45,194	49,072	53,667
Salaries				
Asians	9,516	10,936	14,244	18,060
Employees	25,274	41,565	34,021	39,486
Food				
Tubers	3,344	4,663	5,134	3,143
Jerked beef	2,014	8,045	5,564	5,941
Rice	16	976	3,254	3,325
Corn	2,473	9,522	8,246	15,453
Clothing	929	3,410	5,091	3,384
Medical Expenses	1,459	1,611	1,710	1,663
Leather	3,626	4,680	2,366	3,418
Hardware	7,999	16,207	11,367	17,459
Containers, Transportation, Freight, and Warehousing	75,191	68,083	61,523	69,379
Animal Carbon	1,745	3,159	6,686	0
Gas Carbon	1,428	3,312	963	2,949
Wood	792	1,257	789	974
Miscellaneous	7,260	10,328	15,748	22,400
TOTAL	176,449	232,948	225,778	260,701

SOURCE: See Table 7.2.

underlined that capital could yield much greater returns if utilized in other capacities. Loans to planters generated a minimum of 10 percent interest—and produced other revenues, since "refacción" contracts stipulated that lending companies provide transportation, warehousing, and marketing services paid for by planters.

La Gran Azucarera was caught in an unresolvable economic dilemma. The company owned extensive resources, but could not turn a profit. There is no question that the purchase price of the four mills was partially responsible. These ingenios were acquired during the speculative hysteria resulting from the sugar price rise of 1857. This had the effect of inflating the value of sugar mills well beyond their real worth when international sugar prices retreated in 1858 and 1859. There may have been difficulties linked to labor shortages, as suggested by management, but the crux of the problem was economic overextension resulting from the inflated purchase price of the four ingenios. Liens on the properties resulting from the purchase made future creditors reluctant to risk extensive loans, since existing mortgage notes would be honored first in the event of a failure. Service on the

Table 7.4. Income, Expenses, and Profits on Ingenios San Martín
and Echevarría: Harvests of 1863–1865
(in pesos)

	1863	1864	1865
Income	473,116	536,358	388,302
Expenses	221,494	302,857	294,330
Net Income	251,622	233,501	93,972
Return on Investment (%)	(8.3)	(7.7)	(3.1)

SOURCE: See Table 7.2.
NOTE: Return on investment was calculated by dividing the net income by the original purchase price of 3,032,046 pesos.

Table 7.5. Income, Expenses, and Profits on Ingenios Santa Susana and
Santísima Trinidad: Harvests of 1862–1866
(in pesos)

	1862	1863	1864	1865	1866
Income	256,016	180,160	330,626	189,076	259,360
Expenses	177,190	136,347	124,368	164,221	158,622
Net Income	78,826	43,813	206,258	24,855	100,738
Return on Investment (%)	(2.8)	(1.6)	(7.4)	(0.9)	(3.6)

SOURCE: See Table 7.2.
NOTE: Return on investment was calculated by dividing the net income by the original purchase price of 2,797,598 pesos.

original contracted debt of La Gran Azucarera was overwhelming, and it is likely that lack of careful management exacerbated the financial dilemma faced by the company.

All three major agricultural holding companies failed. The Diagos' La Perseverancia was broken up in the early 1860s. By 1863, the Compañía Territorial Cubana's mills were being sold. And La Gran Azucarera's properties were involved in extended litigation that lasted until 1878. In that year, Santa Susana and Santísima Trinidad, which had been purchased for 2,797,598 pesos in 1857, were assessed at 560,614 pesos gold and were auctioned to Eugenio Moré for two-thirds of that amount.[55]

Notwithstanding these failures, it should be emphasized that by the mid-1850s the region surrounding Hacienda Banagüises had been converted into the richest zone of Cuban sugar production. Eight of the ten leading ingenios of the island were located there, as shown in Table 7.6.

While the lives of the people inhabiting rural Matanzas were largely de-

Table 7.6. Largest-Producing Cuban Ingenios, 1856

	Boxes of Sugar	Owner
Álava[a]	20,000	Zulueta
Flor de Cuba[a]	18,000	Arrieta
Tinguaro[a]	18,000	Diago
Concepción[a]	17,000	Pedroso
Ponina[a]	15,000	Diago
San Martín[a]	15,000	Pedroso
Santa Susana	15,000	Parejo
Narciso (Habana)[a]	10,000	Peñalver
Urumea[a]	10,000	Zuasnavar
Unión	10,000	Fernández

SOURCE: Félix Erenchún, *Anales de la isla de Cuba. Diccionario administrativo, económico, estadístico, y legislativo* (Havana: Imp. de la Antilla, 1855–1857), p. 1963.

NOTE: Concepción was adjacent to Vizcaya to the east; San Martín was adjacent to La Ponina to the northwest; Urumea was adjacent to Álava to the southeast; Santa Susana was in Cienfuegos; and Unión was close to Banagüises in the Colón partido of Jíquimas.

[a]Banagüises ingenio.

fined by the sugar plantations, to focus on ingenio life as representative of the experiences of nineteenth-century matanceros would be erroneous. The historical record left by the great sugar estates allows a more complete reconstruction of their histories than we can accomplish for any other segment of the Cuban socioeconomic hierarchy. Yet, if we examine the changing pattern of land use, ownership, and income distribution, it is immediately clear that the vast majority of landowners were smallholders, living on fragmented farms scattered among or nearby the sugar mills.

CHAPTER 8

Land Use, Tenure, and Production

The utilization of land in Matanzas between 1837 and 1878 was closely linked to the shifting geography of the provincial sugar industry (see Map 10). Before railway construction, the frontier moved slowly to the south and southwest, and land-use patterns evolved to serve the needs of sugar. In the 1840s and 1850s the pace of change quickened. Frontier regions were rapidly developed by plantation owners, and land use was transformed from extensive underutilization to intensive exploitation in a relatively short period of time. Hatos and corrales grazed by cattle and pigs were planted in cane; forests succumbed to the same fate.

From the mid-eighteenth century, sugar expansion had been paralleled by a great deal of social conflict and economic dislocation. Planters waged a protracted struggle to remove vegueros from the fertile lands of the Güines Valley during the second half of the eighteenth century; and, to a lesser degree, this same process was repeated in the Yumurí Valley and the Ceiba Mocha region during the 1790s and early nineteenth century. But the spread of sugar toward Cárdenas in the 1820s, and to Colón after railway construction began, was not accompanied by the same kinds of social and economic conflict. These were sparsely populated areas with vast reserves of unexploited land, and there was no need to remove an independent peasantry that had established firm roots in an earlier period. The obstacles to sugar had to do with the question of how to harness the resources needed to clear land, plant cane, and construct mills. Once these barriers were removed, the spread of sugar monoculture was relentless. A population of fragmented smallholders did not precede sugar, but developed along with the spread of ingenios.

Land-Use Patterns

Documentary materials on Matanzas land use are lacking for the 1840s and fragmentary for the early 1850s; they become abundant in the late 1850s, when a reliable series of statistical data are available and extend through 1878. Sugar's domination of land-use patterns in the early 1850s is indi-

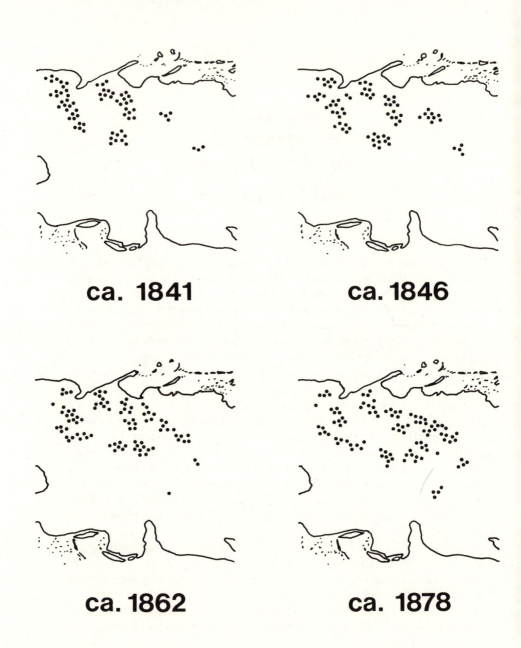

ca. 1841

ca. 1846

ca. 1862

ca. 1878

Each dot (•) approx. 5 Ingenios

Map 10. Expansion of the Matanzas Sugar Economy, 1841–1878

Source: AHPM, ME, Estadísticas, leg. 1, no. 7; Cuba, Gobernador y Capitán General, *Cuadro estadístico de la siempre fiel isla de Cuba correspondiente al año de 1846* (Havana: Imp. del Gobierno y Capitanía General, 1847); Cuba, Centro de Estadística, *Noticias estadísticas de la isla de Cuba en 1862* (Havana: Imp. del Gobierno, Capitanía General y Real Hacienda, 1864); "Noticias de las fincas azucareras en producción que existían en toda la isla de Cuba al comenzar el presupuesto de 1877–1878," *Revista Económica*, June 7, 1878, pp. 7–24.

cated by data on the Matanzas partidos of Sabanilla, San Antonio de Cabezas, and Corral Nuevo. Sabanilla and Cabezas, due south of Matanzas Bay, were contiguous to one another. The Matanzas railroad passed directly through Sabanilla on its way to Unión de Reyes, and the rail system that was constructed east from Güines crossed San Antonio de Cabezas as it pushed to join the Matanzas line at Unión. Thus, both of these partidos were linked by rail to the ports of Havana or Matanzas by the late 1840s.

In 1852 there were 20 ingenios in San Antonio de Cabezas, 5 cafetales, 342 sitios de labor, and 20 potreros, although the sugar estates (5.2 percent of all farms) occupied 43.7 percent of the partido's total land area. Concentration of land use by the sugar sector was even more extreme in Sabanilla. In 1852, 20 ingenios occupied 59.6 percent of all land; and in 1855, after 4 new mills had been constructed, sugar estates controlled 68.8 percent of Sabanilla's land.[1]

By way of contrast, small-scale subsistence farms made up 59.1 percent of all rural properties in Sabanilla in 1852, but occupied only 6 percent of the partido's total land area. In 1855 the amount of land utilized by sitios declined to 4.9 percent of the total. Stock-raising farms in Sabanilla occupied 27.3 percent of all land in 1852 and 26.4 percent in 1855. These potreros served the needs of sugar. The oxen, beef, or milk cattle that grazed their pastures were utilized by sugar estates, which devoted their own arable land to cane planting rather than to pastures or food-crop production. It was common for planters to lease potreros for their cattle or to pay potrero owners for the service of cattle tending. Thus, although sugar plantations did not directly own all the land, the portion of land actually used to serve the sugar economy was well above 90 percent of the total.

Corral Nuevo was a more established area of Matanzas sugar culture compared with Sabanilla or San Antonio de Cabezas. That partido encompassed the Yumurí Valley, which had been the earliest zone of ingenio construction in the province, and extended westward along the Atlantic coast from Matanzas Bay. The region's sugar economy remained surprisingly resilient throughout the 1850s, although its locus shifted from the Yumurí Valley east toward the village of Canasí, where some of Cuba's most powerful sugar entrepreneurs constructed ingenios. Joaquín Pedroso y Echevarría built Ingenio Santa Cruz, which became part of the Compañía Territorial Cubana in the late 1850s; the Diagos owned the Cuanabaco mill; the Conde de Fernandina operated Ingenio San José; and Francisco Torriente also owned an ingenio in the partido. In addition, the old Ingenio San Francisco de Paula, the first sugar mill purchased by Julián de Zulueta in the 1830s, had been broken up into 20 sitios, which were leased by Zulueta to smallholders.[2]

Yet, despite the age of Corral Nuevo's sugar economy, relative to that of the partidos which were developed largely as a result of railroad construction in the 1840s and 1850s, ingenios dominated land use in much the same way. In 1854 there were 29 sugar mills (5.4 percent of all rural properties), and they occupied 53.1 percent of the partido's land area. Cattle ranches controlled another 18.2 percent of the land, while fragmented sitios accounted for roughly one-quarter of Corral Nuevo's total acreage. Land-use patterns for Sabanilla, San Antonio de Cabezas, and Corral Nuevo are shown in Tables 8.1 through 8.3

A series of local-level manuscript census reports for Colón, between 1859 and 1876, reveal the statistical details of changing land-use patterns. In 1859 sugar estates occupied 46.4 percent of all land in Colón, and this increased slightly to 49.8 percent by 1865. Stock-raising farms serving the sugar economy accounted for 20.4 percent of total land area in 1859 and for exactly the same percentage in 1865.

However, between 1865 and 1876 the sugar sector increased its control over land in Colón to 71 percent of total acreage. Another 14.6 percent was owned by the potreros that were so closely linked to the sugar economy. This rise in direct land ownership by sugar planters during the Ten Years' War was connected with the development of frontier regions far to the south and southeast of the cities of Matanzas and Cárdenas. The increase was *not* caused by any spatial expansion of individual estates, for the technological parameters of production made it difficult to enlarge a given plantation complex. The average size of a Colón sugar estate remained rather stable, 54.8 caballerías in 1860 and 55.8 caballerías in 1878.[3] By the mid-1870s, it should be stressed, 85 percent of all land in Colón was utilized in some capacity by the sugar economy.

This new zone of sugar production included the southern regions of Macuriges and the entire partidos of Hanábana and Palmillas. A map of Colón rendered in 1858 described this area as "a region almost completely uninhabited all the way to the southern coast, but suitable for development because of its soils."[4] In the latter half of the 1860s and in the early 1870s, a wave of ingenio construction swept through the region. Hanábana and Palmillas had been a haven for a small, scattered population of subsistence farmers. In 1859, for example, 68.9 percent of all acreage in Hanábana was occupied by sitieros. In Palmillas the land classified as sitios was less extensive, but still substantial at 29.5 percent of the total.

Sugar altered the ecology and rural socioeconomic structure of these partidos in much the same way that it had in regions just to the north. The Banagüises area and surrounding partidos had been the center of sugar development in the 1840s and 1850s; however, investment shifted to virgin territories during the 1860s and 1870s. There were only 3 mills in Hanábana in 1865; but 17 new ingenios were built by 1876, and land controlled by the sugar sector increased from 261 to 864 caballerías. In Palmillas 6 new mills were constructed between 1865 and 1876, and land owned by ingenios

Table 8.1. Sabanilla Land Use by Type of Farm, 1852–1855

| | 1852 | | | | 1855 | | | |
	No. Farms	%	Cabs.	%	No. Farms	%	Cabs.	%
Ingenios	20	15.7	761	59.6	24	19.0	1,030	68.8
Cafetales	1	0.8	91	7.1	0	0	0	0
Sitios	75	59.1	77	6.0	71	56.3	73	4.9
Potreros	31	24.4	348	27.3	31	24.6	395	26.4
Total	127	100.0	1,277	100.0	126	100.0	1,498	100.0

Sources: AHPM, ME, Estadística, leg. 6, no. 116; leg. 8, no. 145, fols. 28–31.
Note: *Ingenios* were sugar farms and their mills; *cafetales* were coffee farms; *sitios* were subsistence farms; and *potreros* were stock-raising farms. Cabs. = caballerías (33.6 acres each).

Table 8.2. San Antonio de Cabezas, 1852: Land Use by Type of Farm

	No. Farms	%	Cabs.	%
Ingenios	20	5.2	460	43.7
Cafetales	5	1.3	17	1.6
Sitios	342	88.4	405	38.5
Potreros	20	5.2	170	16.2
Total	387	100.0	1,052	100.0

Source: AHPM, ME, Estadística, leg. 6, no. 116.
Note: See note, Table 8.1. Cabs. = caballerías (33.6 acres each).

Table 8.3. Corral Nuevo, 1854: Land Use by Type of Farm

	No. Farms	%	Cabs.	%
Ingenios	29	5.4	1,136	53.1
Cafetales	2	0.4	42	2.0
Sitios	473	87.4	564	26.4
Potreros	36	6.7	390	18.2
Tejares	1	0.2	7	0.3
Total	541	100.0	2,139	100.0

Source: AHPM, ME, Estadística, leg. 6, no. 118, fols. 1–42, "Padrón de predios del partido de Corral Nuevo formado en 17 de noviembre de 1854."
Note: See note, Table 8.1. *Tejares* are small-scale brick-making workshops. Cabs. = caballerías (33.6 acres each).

increased from 629 caballerías to 1,100 caballerías. In Macuriges the number of mills rose from 34 to 44, while ingenio land increased by 19 percent.

If data on land use are analyzed at the partido level, the impact of sugar monoculture on usufruct patterns is equally striking. For example, in 1859 sugar plantations occupied one-half of all land in the entire jurisdiction of Colón. But in Macuriges, estates owned 64.3 percent of total acreage and potreros accounted for another 18.1 percent. In Macagua, ingenios directly occupied 80.1 percent of all land, and stock-raising farms another 13.4 percent. In 1859 only 6.4 percent of total land area in Macagua was utilized by non-sugar-sector rural landowners. These same kinds of partido-level data prevailed through 1876 and are summarized in Table 8.4.

Land-use data for Cárdenas in 1867 and 1875 further illustrate the impact of sugar monoculture on landed property. In 1867, 63.7 percent of the jurisdiction's land was directly owned by ingenios; in 1875, the figure was 67 percent. Stock-raising farms tied to the sugar estates occupied approximately 15 percent of all land in both years. Thus, nearly 80 percent of all land in Cárdenas was used to serve the sugar economy in some capacity from the late 1860s through the mid-1870s, a situation that paralleled land-use patterns in Colón. These data should be stressed, for sugar monoculture's absolute control over land did not result from the centralization of production and the substantial increases in sugar output that occurred in the 1880s and in the early twentieth century. The industry underwent radical shifts in its productive structure with the appearance of centrales and colonos in the late nineteenth century and with the penetration of U.S. capital in the aftermath of the war for independence. However, in the broadest terms, sugar monoculture's domination over land was established well before the centralization of sugar processing and the comparative fragmentation of cane cultivation.

If analyzed by partido, the Cárdenas data on land use demonstrate even more graphically the dimensions of the sugar sector's control over land. Camarioca, on the north coast between the cities of Cárdenas and Matanzas, had been an important provincial center of coffee production in the early nineteenth century. In 1816 nearly 40 percent of all land was owned by the region's cafetales. By 1867, not one cafetal remained, even though the partido's rocky and sandy soils did not permit the large-scale development of sugar. In that year only 31.1 percent of all land was owned by ingenios, and this decreased to 28.1 percent in 1875.

This can be contrasted with land-use patterns prevailing in the partidos of Cimarrones, Guanajayabo, and Guamutas. These areas, to the south and southeast of the city of Cárdenas, had been penetrated by different railroad lines in the 1840s. The Cárdenas–Bemba railway system crossed through Cimarrones on its way to Soledad de Bemba in the early 1840s, and along this line some of Cuba's largest ingenios were constructed. José Baró built

Table 8.4. Colón Land Use by Type of Farm and Partido, 1859–1876

1859

	Jíquimas		Macuriges		Hanábana		Macagua		Palmillas		Total	
	Cabs.	%	Cabs.	%	Cabs.	%	Cabs.	%	Cabs.	%	Cabs.	%
Ingenios	2,070	47.8	1,936	64.3	307	14.2	2,189	80.1	676	21.0	7,178	46.4
Cafetales	60	1.4	10	3.3	0	0	0	0	0	0	70	0.5
Potreros	1,385	32.0	544	18.1	366	24.5	366	13.4	499	15.5	3,160	20.4
Sitios	814	18.8	520	17.3	1,494	68.9	175	6.4	949	29.5	3,952	25.6
Hatos	0	0	0	0	0	0	0	0	66	2.0	66	0.4
Haciendas	0	0	0	0	0	0	0	0	1,030	32.0	1,030	6.7
TOTAL	4,329	100.0	3,010	100.0	2,167	100.0	2,730	100.0	3,220	100.0	15,456	100.0

1865

	Jíquimas		Macuriges		Hanábana		Macagua		Palmillas		Total	
	Cabs.	%	Cabs.	%	Cabs.	%	Cabs.	%	Cabs.	%	Cabs.	%
Ingenios	2,358	52.3	2,011	68.7	261	11.6	2,131	77.4	629	26.2	7,390	49.8
Cafetales	98	2.2	10	0.3	0	0	0	0	0	0	108	0.7
Potreros	817	18.1	329	11.2	909	40.3	340	12.4	630	26.3	3,025	20.4
Sitios	1,233	27.3	515	17.6	1,083	48.1	274	10.0	539	22.5	3,644	24.5
Haciendas	0	0	0	0	0	0	0	0	600	25.0	600	4.0
Tejares	5	0.1	63	2.2	0	0	7	0.3	2	0.1	77	0.5
TOTAL	4,511	100.0	2,928	100.0	2,253	100.0	2,752	100.0	2,400	100.0	14,844	100.0

1876

	Cabecera		Macuriges		Hanábana		Macagua		Palmillas		Total	
	Cabs.	%	Cabs.	%	Cabs.	%	Cabs.	%	Cabs.	%	Cabs.	%
Ingenios	198	85.3	2,395	78.7	864	39.6	2,261	86.2	1,100	72.2	6,818	71.0
Cafetales	0	0	16	0.5	0	0	0	0	0	0	16	0.2
Potreros	2	0.9	318	10.4	777	35.6	166	6.3	140	9.2	1,403	14.6
Sitios	32	13.8	316	10.4	498	22.8	195	7.4	279	18.3	1,320	13.7
Haciendas	0	0	0	0	42	1.9	0	0	3	0.2	45	0.5
TOTAL	232	100.0	3,045	100.0	2,181	100.0	2,622	100.0	1,522	100.0	9,602	100.0

SOURCES: ANC, ME, leg. 4120, no. M, "Repartos municipales de la jurisdicción de Colón, 1859"; ANC, Gobierno General, leg. 405, no. 19209, "Padrón de fincas rústicas de la jurisdicción de Colón, 1865"; ANC, Gobierno General, leg. 945, no. 16724, "Padrón general de la riqueza rústica para regir en los años económicos de 1866 a 1867"; ANC, Gobierno General, leg. 270, No. 3563, "Padrón general de fincas rústicas de este distrito, año de 1875 a 1876."

NOTE: Cabs. = caballerías (33.6 acres each). See note, Table 8.1. *Hatos* are Crown land; *tejares* are small-scale brick-making workshops; *haciendas* are traditional circular forms of land tenure dating from the early sixteenth century. There were no data for Jíquimas for 1876. For comparative purposes, an analysis was made of the 1859 and 1865 data excluding Jíquimas, and the percentage of land occupied by ingenios was almost exactly the same as that for the data including Jíquimas: 44.3 percent in 1859 and 47.5 percent in 1865. Thus, the 1876 increase in the percentage of land controlled by ingenios was *not* the result of any statistical distortion owing to an absence of data for this partido.

the Luisa and Olimpo mills, and the Conde de Peñalver founded Purísima Concepción. In 1867, 93.8 percent of the partido's land was directly owned by sugar ingenios; in 1875, 94.6 percent was so owned.

Guanajayabo was the first destination of the Júcaro railroad in the early 1840s, and this line continued southeast through Guamutas. In Guanajayabo 70.3 percent of all land was directly controlled by sugar plantations in 1867, and this had increased to 78.7 percent by 1875. Guamutas, where the ingenios Echevarría and San Martín were constructed in the 1850s, had 68.2 percent of its land under the control of sugar plantations in 1867 and 73.6 percent in 1875. Table 8.5 shows land-use patterns in Cárdenas partidos during this period.

Land-Tenure Structures

Within the plantation structure that dominated rural Matanzas during the mid-nineteenth century, it is hardly surprising that land ownership was concentrated in the hands of a small, sugar-planting elite. However, the image of slave-based ingenios as truly representative of agrarian Cuba in the nineteenth century distorts the human experience of that society. To be sure, the productive structures and great slave populations of the ingenios were economically and demographically dominant. But most of the land-holding sector within Cuban rural society was made up of smallholders, scratching out a living on fragmented farms interspersed among the ingenios, usually on inferior lands. Almost all were connected to the mills in some way, raising cattle or growing a portion of the food consumed by the sugar sector. Others were independently impoverished.

Sitieros accounted for approximately three-quarters of all landowners in rural Matanzas from the early 1850s through the late 1870s. In regions where sugar culture expanded, however, there was a rather dramatic decrease in the amount of land they controlled. In more established areas of the sugar economy, there was relative stability in land-ownership patterns. For example, landholding patterns in Cárdenas had been firmly established in the 1840s and 1850s and were not in flux during the 1860s and 1870s. Accordingly, land under the domination of these fragmented subsistence farms decreased only marginally between 1867 and 1875, from 19.4 percent of total acreage to 16.9 percent.

In Colón, however, where the rural landscape was still in the process of transformation, the changes were much more devastating to this smallholding sector of society. In 1859 sitieros controlled 27.5 percent of all land, and this declined slightly to 24.5 percent in 1865. But the expansion of the sugar economy between 1865 and 1876 was accomplished at the expense of these subsistence farmers. During this period the sugar estates increased their control over land to 71 percent of all acreage in Colón, while the percentage of land owned by sitieros plummeted to 13.7 percent. Accompanying this

Table 8.5. Cárdenas Land Use by Type of Farm and Partido, 1867–1875

1867

	Camarioca		Cimarrones		Guamutas		Guanajayabo		Lagunillas		Total	
	Cabs.	%	Cabs.	%	Cabs.	%	Cabs.	%	Cabs.	%	Cabs.	%
Ingenios	401	31.1	1,193	93.8	1,939	68.2	957	70.3	812	57.5	5,302	63.9
Cafetales	0	0	18	1.4	0	0	33	2.4	20	1.4	71	0.9
Potreros	615	47.7	8	0.6	191	6.7	74	5.4	288	20.4	1,237	14.9
Sitios	272	21.1	49	3.9	701	24.6	286	21.0	250	17.7	1,613	19.4
Tejares	2	0.2	4	0.3	14	0.5	11	0.8	41	2.9	72	0.9
Total	1,290	100.0	1,272	100.0	2,845	100.0	1,361	100.0	1,411	100.0	8,295	100.0

1875

	Camarioca		Cimarrones		Guamutas		Guanajayabo		Lagunillas		Total	
	Cabs.	%	Cabs.	%	Cabs.	%	Cabs.	%	Cabs.	%	Cabs.	%
Ingenios	391	28.1	1,304	94.6	1,888	73.6	1,042	78.7	904	59.8	5,548	67.0
Cafetales	0	0	0	0	0	0	11	0.8	0	0	11	0.1
Potreros	623	44.8	0	0	196	7.6	38	2.9	351	23.2	1,252	15.1
Sitios	368	26.4	74	5.4	456	17.8	233	17.6	223	14.8	1,402	16.9
Tejares	10	0.7	0	0	24	0.9	0	0	32	2.1	66	0.8
Total	1,392	100.0	1,378	100.0	2,564	100.0	1,324	100.0	1,510	100.0	8,279	100.0

Sources: ANC, Gobierno General, leg. 945, No. 16724, "Padrón general de la riqueza rústica para regir en los años económicos de 1866 a 1867"; ANC, Gobierno General, leg. 269, no. 13554, "Jurisdicción de Cárdenas. Padrón general de la riqueza rústica de esta ciudad y su jurisdicción formado para los años económicos de 1875 a 1876."

Notes: Cabs. = caballerías (33.6 acres each). See note, Table 8.1. *Tejares* are small-scale brick-making workshops. The total column for 1867 includes 61 caballerías in potreros and 55 in sitios located in "Rastro de la Villa." For 1875, the total includes 19 caballerías in ingenios, 44 in potreros, and 48 in sitios, also in "Rastro de la Villa."

decrease in land control was further fragmentation. In 1859 and 1865 the average size of a sitio in Colón was approximately 3.3 caballerías. But by 1876 this had dropped by more than 40 percent to an average of 1.9 caballerías per sitio, comparable to the 1.8-caballería average found in Cárdenas in 1875.[5]

The small sitios dotting Colón's countryside were surprisingly diverse. Many were family-operated subsistence farms with little commercial orientation. Others, despite their small size, relied on slave labor for the production of food crops consumed by owners and laborers or marketed to ingenios. This was the case with a 1-caballería sitio located in Macuriges in 1872 and owned by María Narcisa Hernández, who lived there with her husband and five children. The farm grew an assortment of vegetables, but most of the land was dedicated to the production of plantains, which were marketed to nearby sugar plantations. The land, houses, fences, and equipment were valued at 2,500 pesos. Hernández also owned 10 slaves, who along with 2 pairs of oxen and 1 horse were assessed at 5,665 pesos, more than the land itself. Slavery (to be discussed in Chapter 12 below) was an all-encompassing institution not simply confined to the dominant sugar sector.[6]

Functionally, stock-raising farms were appendages to the sugar economy. Cattle from ingenios grazed their pastures; and if they were independent operations, products were marketed to the great estates. These rural landowners accounted for approximately 10 percent of all farmers in Cárdenas between 1867 and 1876, and they occupied 15 percent of all landed property. Their average size was approximately 12 caballerías in both years.

There was relative stability in Colón's cattle sector from 1859 through 1865. Potreros constituted 12 percent of all farms and occupied 20.4 percent of rural land in both 1859 and 1865. But the expansion of sugar affected ranchers in much the same way as it did subsistence farmers. Their numbers plummeted to 8.5 percent of all rural property owners by 1876, and their control over land dropped to 14.9 percent of total acreage. However, the average size of this reduced number of *potreros* rose slightly from 16.4 caballerías in 1859 to 17.5 caballerías in 1865 and 19 caballerías in 1876.

With landholding polarized between the extensive sugar plantations and the fragmented food-crop farms, potreros became in effect the middle sector of Matanzas rural society. A portrait of this social stratum is provided by an 1868 inventory of the potrero Matilde, located in the Colón partido of Macuriges. Two brothers, Juan Francisco and Silvestre Anastacio Placencio, owned this average-size farm which extended slightly in excess of 19 caballerías. One-third of the land was classified as *monte* (scrub); another third was sown in *pastos artificiales* (planted pasture); and the final third was covered with natural pastures, royal palm trees, and plantains. Matilde counted on the labor of 12 slaves (9 males and 3 females), and a variety of animals grazed the farm's pastures. There were 39 pigs, 100 chickens, 20 turkeys, and a few horses, colts, and oxen. Most of Matilde's pastures were rented to nearby ingenios for cattle grazing. In addition, the farm used a well with a pump and had two houses, one for its owners (13.57 x 7.68 meters) and another for its slaves (13.57 x 5.95 meters). The total value of this farm was 34,380 pesos, of which 20,900 pesos was in land and 8,100 in slaves.[7]

Thus, land tenure in Matanzas rural society was both concentrated and fragmented in the mid-nineteenth century, as one would expect in an economy dominated by plantation agriculture, regardless of principal crop. In 1859, for example, nearly 50 percent of all farms in Colón were less than 2 caballerías in extension, but they occupied only 3.9 percent of all rural property. At the other extreme, 1.7 percent of total farms (all ingenios) were larger than 100 caballerías and controlled 29.5 percent of all land. By 1876, 54.5 percent of all farms were smaller than 2 caballerías and occupied 3.8 percent of total land, a situation similar to the prevailing tenure pattern of seventeen years earlier. Plantations extending for more than 100 caballerías were 1.9 percent of all rural properties, but absorbed nearly one-quarter of total land area. Land-tenure structures for Cárdenas in 1867 and 1875 reveal similar profiles. These data, disaggregated for greater detail, are included in Tables 8.6 and 8.7.

In the sugar sector itself, the size of individual plantations varied within the province by locale. Between 1860 and 1878, when comparative data are available, the average size of an ingenio remained stable in the jurisdiction of Matanzas: 40.1 caballerías in 1860 and 40.2 caballerías in 1878. In Cárdenas, though, there was a significant spatial expansion of individual ingenios; the significance of this fact should be minimized, however, since the average number of caballerías cultivated in cane remained stable during the same period. Cárdenas ingenios increased in average size from 33.9 caballerías in 1860 to 43.1 caballerías in 1878; but cultivated acreage in the same period increased only slightly, from 18.9 to 19.5 caballerías.[8]

Ingenio land tenure in Colón also remained stable between 1860 and 1878, but it should be emphasized that in this frontier zone the average size of sugar estates was significantly larger than those found in Matanzas, Cárdenas, or even Alacranes. Colón's plantations extended for an average of 54.8 caballerías in 1860 and 55.8 caballerías in 1878.

Although the average size of ingenios remained relatively stable in Colón between 1860 and 1878, a clear pattern of land concentration was manifest among the largest estates in the sugar sector. Ingenios greater than 50 caballerías in size constituted 29.5 percent of all provincial milling complexes in 1860, and they occupied 50.8 percent of the total land area controlled by ingenios. By 1878, 35.5 percent of all plantations extended for more than 50 caballerías, but this sector of the planter class increased its control of land to 61.5 percent of the total owned by plantations. It should be stressed, however, that the trend toward land concentration did not result in any increase in average cultivated acreage per ingenio. It is striking that between 1860 and 1878 the average number of caballerías cultivated in cane on each ingenio remained absolutely stable: 21.8 caballerías in 1860 and 21.7 in 1878. This phenomenon will be considered in more detail below. Provincial land-tenure patterns in the sugar sector between 1860 and 1878 are shown in Table 8.8.

Sugar Production

The amount of land sown in cane on individual plantations was closely linked to several limiting factors. First and foremost was the productive ca-

Table 8.6. Colón Land-Tenure Structure, 1859–1876

Farm Size (Cabs.)	1859				1865				1876			
	No. Farms	%	Land (Cabs.)	%	No. Farms	%	Land (Cabs.)	%	No. Farms	%	Land (Cabs.)	%
.13–.99	342	21.7	159.8	1.0	204	14.8	104.3	0.7	250	29.0	118.3	1.2
1–1.99	407	25.9	449.5	2.9	333	24.2	383.6	2.6	220	25.5	247.8	2.6
2–2.99	202	12.8	421.5	2.7	179	13.0	380.0	2.6	104	12.1	221.3	2.3
3–4.99	163	10.4	576.0	3.7	185	13.4	647.3	4.4	54	6.3	183.3	1.9
5–9.99	159	10.1	1,049.2	6.8	171	12.4	1,122.4	7.6	66	7.6	444.7	4.6
10–19.99	121	7.7	1,582.5	10.2	120	8.7	1,560.1	10.5	50	5.8	686.5	7.2
20–39.99	68	4.3	1,907.9	12.3	79	5.7	2,104.7	14.2	36	4.2	1,052.5	11.0
40–59.99	53	3.4	2,484.7	16.1	51	3.7	2,517.3	17.0	30	3.5	1,500.8	15.6
60–99.99	32	2.0	2,269.5	14.7	35	2.5	2,547.5	17.2	36	4.2	2,774.3	28.9
100–199.99	21	1.3	2,767.0	17.9	16	1.2	1,935.8	13.0	15	1.7	1,846.0	19.2
200+	6	0.4	1,791.0	11.6	4	0.3	1,540.0	10.4	2	0.2	525.0	5.5
TOTAL	1,574	100.0	15,458.5	100.0	1,377	100.0	14,842.8	100.0	863	100.0	9,600.3	100.0

SOURCES: ANC, ME, leg. 4120, no. M, "Repartos municipales de la jurisdicción de Colón, 1859"; ANC, Gobierno General, leg. 405, no. 19209, "Padrón de fincas rústicas de la jurisdicción de Colón, 1865"; ANC, Gobierno General, leg. 270, no. 13563, "Padrón general de fincas rústicas de este distrito, año de 1875 a 1876."

NOTE: Cabs. = caballerías (33.6 acres each).

Table 8.7. Cárdenas Land-Tenure Structure, 1867–1875

Farm Size (Cabs.)	1867				1875			
	No. Farms	%	Land (Cabs.)	%	No. Farms	%	Land (Cabs.)	%
.13–.99	191	20.3	89.0	1.1	288	27.5	129.5	1.6
1–1.99	235	25.0	265.0	3.2	268	25.6	294.3	3.6
2–2.99	124	13.2	260.7	3.1	115	11.0	248.1	3.0
3–4.99	89	9.5	310.6	3.7	82	7.8	294.4	3.6
5–9.99	95	10.1	663.8	8.0	84	8.0	556.3	6.7
10–19.99	80	8.5	1,039.1	12.5	89	8.5	1,146.1	13.9
20–39.99	64	6.8	1,791.0	21.6	64	6.1	1,833.8	22.2
40–59.99	37	3.9	1,633.3	19.7	30	2.9	1,377.5	16.6
60–99.99	19	2.0	1,403.0	16.9	21	2.0	1,597.5	19.3
100–199.99	6	0.6	838.0	10.1	6	0.6	799.5	9.7
TOTAL	940	100.0	8,293.5	100.0	1,047	100.0	8,277.0	100.0

SOURCES: ANC, Gobierno General, leg. 945, no. 16724, "Padrón general de la riqueza rústica para regir en los años económicos de 1866 a 1867"; ANC, Gobierno General, leg. 269, no. 13554, "Jurisdicción de Cárdenas. Padrón general de la riqueza rústica de esta ciudad y su jurisdicción formado para los años económicos de 1875 a 1876."
NOTE: Cabs. = caballerías (33.6 acres each).

Table 8.8. Matanzas, 1860–1878: Ingenio Land-Tenure Structure

Ingenio Size (Cabs.)	1860				1878			
	No. Ingenios	%	Land (Cabs.)	%	No. Ingenios	%	Land (Cabs.)	%
1–10	20	5.0	159	0.9	31	7.2	189	1.0
11–20	65	16.3	1,019	6.0	65	15.2	1,043	5.3
21–50	197	49.3	7,160	42.3	180	42.1	6,376	32.3
51–100	112	28.0	7,862	46.3	129	30.1	8,836	44.8
101–200	6	1.5	767	4.5	21	4.9	2,718	13.8
201+	0	0	0	0	2	0.5	578	2.9
TOTAL	400	100.0	16,967	100.0	428	100.0	19,740	100.0

SOURCES: Carlos Rebello, *Estados relativos a la producción azucarera de la isla de Cuba* (Havana: Imp. del Gobierno, 1860); "Noticias de las fincas azucareras en producción que existían en toda la isla de Cuba al comenzar el presupuesto de 1877–1878," in *Revista Económica*, June 7, 1878, pp. 7–24.
NOTES: Cabs. = caballerías (33.6 acres each). There were 3 ingenios for which data on land tenure were not available in 1860, and 85 such ingenios for 1878.

pacity of the milling complex. Matanzas ingenios were the most modern in Cuba by 1860, and more than 90 percent used grinding machinery powered by steam engines. However, 87 percent of all Matanzas mills still employed antiquated, open-air Jamaican trains for clarification and evaporation of guarapo, and this severely limited productive capacity.[9] Derosne and Rillieux vacuum evaporators were employed on roughly 13 percent of the province's mills. In Colón, however, where the more capital-intensive estates were concentrated, one-quarter of all ingenios (33 of 128 mills) processed sugar with vacuum apparatuses.

The significantly larger productive capacity prevalent on Colón ingenios resulted in substantially greater average areas of planted cane. For example, in the jurisdiction of Matanzas, where only 5.5 percent of all ingenios utilized vacuum evaporators, an average of 19.5 caballerías were planted in cane on each ingenio. In Cárdenas, 8.8 percent of the mills used this modern equipment, and the average was 18.9 cultivated caballerías/ingenio. But in Colón the average extension of land planted in cane in 1860 was 27.6 caballerías/mill. Thus, the type of processing equipment, or the installed productive capacity at the mill, was the single most important variable affecting how much land area was sown in cane.

Industrial yields, of course, varied by the type of processing equipment employed, and this was of critical importance in maintaining economic viability during the 1860s and 1870s. There is clear evidence that agricultural yields in the province, or cane production/caballería, dropped considerably in these two decades.[10] But modern, fully mechanized mills that utilized steam engines for grinding, and vacuum evaporators and centrifuges for processing, made up for these agricultural declines by producing significantly higher sugar yields from the cane they processed, compared with the yields from mills using the older Jamaican trains. In 1843 a detailed statistical report on industrial yields was written by Wenceslao de Villaurrutia, concerning the harvests produced by his Ingenio San Juan de Nepomuceno (or La Mella, as it was popularly called) from 1830 through 1843. Between 1830 and 1836, with oxen-driven grinding equipment and Jamaican trains, sugar yields averaged 3.91 percent of cane by weight. Villaurrutia installed a steam engine that was employed in zafras from 1837 through 1840, but he derived lower yields that averaged 3.46 percent of cane by weight. By the harvest of 1843, a Derosne vacuum evaporator was installed, and yields increased by 71 percent to 5.91 pounds of sugar for each 100 pounds of cane.[11]

Not only did yields improve, but the ratio between more costly white sugars and the cheaper yellow or quebrado sugars changed significantly. During the harvests of 1837 through 1840, 36 percent of the sugar produced by La Mella was white, the rest quebrado. When the Derosne equipment was employed, 75 percent of the sugar produced was white, more than double the portion produced by Jamaican trains.[12] Thus, while agricultural yields may have been declining after 1860, higher industrial yields and the production of better-quality sugar offset the apparent poor performance of the sugar economy's agricultural sector.

Through the 1860s and 1870s centrifuges were increasingly employed on the most modern mills, especially in the Banagüises region. But by 1878 there had been no substantial change in land-use patterns or in the productive potential of individual mills. The sugar industry expanded through the construction of new ingenios and by planting new cane fields, not by any overall increase in the efficiency of existing units of production (although there were exceptions). In the eighteen years between 1860 and 1878 the average number of caballerías sown in cane on plantations in all regions of Matanzas province remained relatively stable. Matanzas jurisdiction mills cultivated an average of 18.9 caballerías in 1860 and 19.5 in 1878; Cárdenas ingenios experienced a slight decrease from an average of 19.5 to 18.3 caballerías/ingenio; and in capital-intensive Colón 27.6 caballerías/ingenio were cultivated in 1860, 26.7 caballerías in 1878.

Another factor determining levels of production on individual estates was the number of laborers employed in sugarcane agriculture. Despite improvements in the methods and techniques of sugar processing, there were few transformations in the way cane was cultivated through the nineteenth century. There was experimentation with different cane varieties, and an ambitious project to mechanize plowing was attempted in the 1860s by Guillermo Fowler, a Matanzas mill owner who developed a steam-driven plow.[13] But, by and large, cane cultivation remained labor-intensive, and there was little mechanization through the end of the century.

It should also be emphasized that sugar agriculture's dependence on slave labor gangs diminished only marginally, even in the 1870s after the onset of the legal abolition process.[14] Despite the fact that large numbers of Chinese contract laborers were employed, by the late 1870s slaves made up more than 70 percent of the total work force on Matanzas sugar estates. Approximately seven full-time workers were needed at harvesttime for each cultivated caballería of sugarcane in 1878. In Cárdenas the average number of slaves employed on each ingenio was 97.7; in Matanzas the corresponding figure was 103.3; but in Colón, where there was greater average cultivated land area per ingenio, an average of 126.5 slaves were employed on each estate. Thus, not only were productive levels on individual ingenios linked to the type of processing technology employed, but there was a direct correlation between the numbers of slaves working on each ingenio and the productive output.

The widespread absence of internal transportation systems also inhibited the spatial expansion of sugar plantations between 1837 and 1878. A small number of estates utilized costly rail systems to transport cane from the fields to the ingenios, and this allowed the development of *cañaverales* in areas distant from mills. Cane must be transported quickly to the processing area once cut, for sucrose content declines rapidly within a day of harvesting. Most plantations used traditional oxcarts to move cane from field to mill, and this imposed specific limits to the distance cane fields could be located from mills, and thus limitations on the potential extent of cultivated acreage. Railroads altered the governing concepts of transportation time and distance, although it should be underlined that internal rail systems were few and far between in the late 1870s.[15] When they were used, though, productive potential soared. For example, in Colón the average cultivated area on each sugar estate was 26.7 caballerías in 1878. But on Julián de Zulueta's ingenios, which utilized railroads to move cane from the fields to the mills, substantially more acreage was sown in cane: 70 caballerías on Álava; 50 on Habana; 57 on Vizcaya; and 79 on España.[16]

Not only did milling capacity, labor supplies, and internal transportation systems determine the extent of cultivated acreage, but these three factors closely interacted to govern the productive potential of each plantation. It was absurd to install modern machinery with large productive capacities if not enough cane could be harvested and transported to the mills to keep the ingenios grinding and producing sugar. Yet, the extent of cultivated acreage was directly tied to the number of laborers employed on each estate, and labor shortages became acute with the abolition of the Cuban slave trade in the late 1860s and the difficulty of substituting wage labor for slavery. Without railroads, there were rigid barriers to the distance cane could be planted from mills.

Given these productive parameters, it is hardly surprising that average cultivated acreage on Matanzas plantations did not change between 1860 and 1878. The key to a breakthrough in productive potential was capital availability. Modern machinery could be installed, railroads could be constructed, and laborers would be forthcoming if wages were high enough. But the old planter class, who had reached the zenith of their power and influence on the eve of the Ten Years' War, would not live to see the concentration of production and the spatial expansion of cane fields. Others, with access to greater capital resources, would oversee the transition to the concentration of processing and the more efficient division of production within the sugar economy.

In the 1860s and 1870s sugar production was characterized by its dispersal. In 1860 approximately one-quarter of all estates cultivated fewer than 10 caballerías of cane each, but only 8.2 percent of the province's total cultivated land area. At the other end of the productive hierarchy, 22.1 percent of all sugar plantations planted more than 30 caballerías of cane, and they accounted for 42.7 percent of all acreage cultivated in sugar. By 1878 there had been insignificant changes: 28.2 percent of all ingenios planted 10 caballerías or less, only 8.4 percent of the province's cultivated land—almost exactly the same situation as in 1860. Strikingly, 22 percent of all ingenios planted cane on more than 30 caballerías, exactly the same portion as in 1860. Collectively they planted 46.6 percent of all acreage in cane, slightly more than in 1860. Thus, between 1860 and 1878 there was absolutely no trend toward a greater concentration of production. These data, disaggregated into jurisdictions, are summarized in Table 8.9.

Table 8.9. Matanzas, 1860–1878: Cultivated-Acreage Structure of Ingenios by Jurisdiction

Matanzas Province

Ingenio Size (Cabs.)	1860				1878			
	No. Ingenios	%	Land (Cabs.)	%	No. Ingenios	%	Land (Cabs.)	%
1–5	24	6.0	101	1.2	40	9.4	139	1.5
6–10	73	18.3	611	7.0	80	18.8	644	6.9
11–20	124	31.1	1,937	22.3	132	31.0	2,066	22.3
21–30	90	22.6	2,372	27.3	80	18.8	2,112	22.8
31–40	57	14.3	2,065	23.7	50	11.7	1,824	19.7
41–50	19	4.8	869	10.0	25	5.9	1,168	12.6
51–100	12	3.0	748	8.6	18	4.2	1,220	13.1
101 +	0	0	0	0	1	0.2	108	1.2
Total	399	100.0	8,703	100.0	426	100.0	9,281	100.0

Jurisdiction of Matanzas

Ingenio Size (Cabs.)	No. Ingenios	%	Land (Cabs.)	%	No. Ingenios	%	Land (Cabs.)	%
1–5	6	4.7	23	0.9	8	7.8	28	1.5
6–10	27	21.1	231	9.2	25	24.5	207	10.8
11–20	50	39.1	779	31.1	33	32.4	521	27.2
21–30	25	19.5	674	26.9	21	20.6	571	29.8
31–40	13	10.2	455	18.2	11	10.8	398	20.8
41–50	5	3.9	221	8.8	4	3.9	191	10.0
51–100	2	1.6	119	4.8	0	0	0	0
Total	128	100.0	2,502	100.0	102	100.0	1,916	100.0

Jurisdiction of Cárdenas

Ingenio Size (Cabs.)	No. Ingenios	%	Land (Cabs.)	%	No. Ingenios	%	Land (Cabs.)	%
1–5	13	8.8	57	2.1	15	10.2	54	1.9
6–10	32	21.8	266	9.6	33	22.4	266	9.3
11–20	50	34.0	781	28.2	50	34.0	758	26.5
21–30	27	18.4	683	24.6	25	17.0	665	23.2
31–40	20	13.6	729	26.3	15	10.2	545	19.0
41–50	3	2.0	140	5.0	4	2.7	184	6.4
51–100	2	1.4	118	4.3	4	2.7	284	9.9
101 +	0	0	0	0	1	0.7	108	3.8
Total	147	100.0	2,774	100.0	147	100.0	2,864	100.0

Jurisdiction of Colón

Ingenio Size (Cabs.)	No. Ingenios	%	Land (Cabs.)	%	No. Ingenios	%	Land (Cabs.)	%
1–5	5	4.0	21	0.6	11	8.7	32	0.9
6–10	14	11.3	114	3.3	16	12.6	119	3.5
11–20	24	19.4	378	11.0	33	26.0	551	16.3
21–30	38	30.6	1,015	29.6	23	18.1	593	17.5
31–40	24	19.4	881	25.7	18	14.2	665	19.6
41–50	11	8.9	508	14.8	15	11.8	700	20.7
51–100	8	6.5	511	14.9	11	8.7	728	21.5
Total	124	100.0	3,428	100.0	127	100.0	3,388	100.0

Sources: See Table 8.8.
Note: Cabs. = caballerías (33.6 acres each).

CHAPTER 9

Agrarian Income Distribution

Perhaps the most salient feature of monocultural societies is their absence of diversity in every sense of the word. The landscape of rural Matanzas was monotonously uniform by the late 1870s, its ecology harnessed to serve the needs of one crop. Although diverse with respect to ethnicity, the people inhabiting the province had the most fundamental aspects of their daily lives defined by the great sugar estates. Infrastructural improvements served the sugar economy. Technological progress was applied exclusively to ingenios or activities supporting them. Above all, agrarian wealth was so concentrated that, if income distribution is used as our criterion to measure social stratification, only the tiniest fraction of Matanzas rural society can be classified as falling between the two extremes rich and poor.

The Matanzas domestic market revolved entirely around sugar. There was simply no other sector of the socioeconomic order with enough income to create any demand at all for the development of a diversified consumer market. Thus, it is hardly surprising that sugar gave rise to few ancillary industries having the potential to satisfy the basic needs of a rather large population. There is no evidence of even the most elementary cottage production of fundamental consumer goods. Almost every manufactured product consumed was imported from the industrial nations where the sugar produced in rural Matanzas was marketed. The dependence created by sugar was multidimensional.

When income-distribution data are examined, the numbers are dramatic indeed. But a qualitative dimension to the wealth produced by sugar must also be carefully recognized. Not only was sugar income heavily concentrated in the hands of a few, but a large share of this income was controlled by absentees—not foreign absentees, as would be the case after 1898, but domestic entrepreneurs living in Havana who made use of their incomes in a variety of ways having little to do with improving the quality of life in the province that produced their riches. The wealth generated by the Matanzas sugar economy was systematically drained from the region to support lavish homes in the capital, international business investments, costly educations for sons and daughters of the sugar elite, and exotic vacations abroad.

Spanish colonialism alone was not responsible for the export of capital from Matanzas. The means of production in Matanzas province between

1837 and 1878 were largely owned by native-born Cubans, although there was certainly an important immigrant presence. Matanzas was exploited by a criollo elite acting in their own class interests within the political parameters defined by colonialism. Much historical literature blames imperialism for Latin America's persistent poverty, chronic underdevelopment, and utter economic dependence. Clearly capital and technology from the centers of industry and empire played an important role in the development of Matanzas sugar culture; but it was upper-class Cubans who were responsible for utilizing the resources of the developed world to further their own interests at the expense of a broad spectrum of Cuban rural society. Even if Cuba had been politically independent, it is highly unlikely that the socioeconomic impact of monocultural sugar production would have been very different. Property and income would have been monopolized by the same sector of society regardless of political forms.

Data on agrarian income distribution are available from 1859 on. In Colón and Cárdenas, ingenios consistently earned more than 90 percent of total rural income—with the exception of 1876, when Colón sugar mills received 88.9 percent of gross revenues deriving from agriculture. These data are summarized in Table 9.1.

Table 9.1. Colón and Cárdenas, Income Distribution by Type of Farm, 1859–1876 (in hundreds of thousands of pesos)

| | Colón | | | | | | Cárdenas | | | |
| | 1859 | | 1865 | | 1876 | | 1867 | | 1875 | |
	Income	%	Income	%	Income	%	Income	%	Income	%
Ingenios	7,776	90.6	8,614	95.8	7,616	88.9	8,036	94.9	7,053	92.0
Cafetales	73	0.9	24	0.3	2	—	39	0.5	9	0.1
Potreros	348	4.1	153	1.7	366	4.3	120	1.4	190	2.5
Sitios	353	4.1	177	2.0	563	6.6	245	2.9	392	5.1
Others	29	0.3	19	0.2	18	0.2	27	0.3	22	0.3
Total	8,579	100.0	8,987	100.0	8,564	100.0	8,468	100.0	7,666	100.0

Sources: ANC, ME, leg. 4120, no. M, "Repartos municipales de la jurisdicción de Colón, 1859"; ANC, Gobierno General, leg. 405, no. 19209, "Padrón de fincas rústicas de la jurisdicción de Colón, 1865"; ANC, Gobierno General, leg. 945, no. 16724, "Padrón general de la riqueza rústica para regir en los años económicos de 1866 a 1867"; ANC, Gobierno General, leg. 270, no. 13563, "Padrón general de fincas rústicas de este distrito, año de 1875 a 1876."

Notes: Ingenios were sugar farms and their mills; cafetales were coffee farms; potreros were stock-raising farms; sitios were subsistence farms. The data for Colón in 1876 do not include the partido of Jíquimas. All income statistics have been rounded off to the nearest thousand; percentages are based on the actual statistics.

Not only was income overwhelmingly concentrated in the sugar sector, but *within* the planter class income was heavily concentrated in the hands of mill owners who did not reside in the province. In Colón 16 ingenios earned gross incomes of more than 100,000 pesos in 1859, 13.1 percent of all ingenios. They derived 38.1 percent of the total income flowing to the sugar sector. A large number of these plantations were concentrated in the Banagüises region. Julián de Zulueta's ingenios Álava, Habana, and Vizcaya reported a combined gross income of 459,000 pesos; Joaquín Arrieta's Flor de Cuba earned 200,000 pesos; the Marqués de Arco's Ingenio Progreso declared an income of 130,000 pesos; the Marquésa de Urria's mills, Concepción and Santiago jointly earned 181,000 pesos; the Diagos' Tinguaro, Santa Elena, and Ponina estates (Sociedad Perseverancia) earned 429,614 pesos; José Baró's Santa Rita mill produced 151,555 pesos; Cosme de la Torriente's Ingenio Isabel generated 120,000 pesos; Noriega, Olmo y Cía.'s Ingenio Andrea had a gross income of 109,550 pesos; and the Sociedad Territorial Cubana's San Joaquín and Fundador mills earned 170,000 pesos.

By 1865, income concentration within the planter class in Colón was even more extreme: 26 ingenios (21.5 percent of all mills) controlled 47.1 percent of total income flowing to the sugar sector. By 1876 there was a drop in these figures. Nevertheless, sugar income remained extremely concentrated: 19 mills (16.2 percent of the total) earned 38.9 percent of all sugar-related income in Colón.[1]

The income-distribution profile within the Cárdenas sugar sector was similar. In 1867, 13.4 percent of all ingenios (19) earned more than 100,000 pesos—38.2 percent of total gross income derived from sugar. By 1875 only 12 mills, or 8 percent of all ingenios, fell into this category, but they controlled 32.3 percent of all sugar income. Included in this group were José Baró's Ingenio Luisa, 284,445 pesos in 1867 and 220,000 pesos in 1875; the Conde de Peñalver's Purísima Concepción, 218,887 pesos in 1867 and 432,305 pesos in 1875; Ignacio Montalvo y Calvo's ingenios Peñón and Jesús María, 219,869 pesos in 1867 and 246,412 pesos in 1875; Joaquín Pedroso y Echevarría's Ingenio Santa Gertudis, 113,700 pesos in 1867 and 145,000 pesos in 1875; Teresa Herrera de Melgares's (the daughter and heiress of the Marqués de Almendares) San Luis mill, 195,599 pesos in 1867 and 204,737 pesos in 1875; and Nicolás Martínez y Valdivieso's Ingenio Aurora, which earned 131,598 pesos in 1867 and 131,598 pesos in 1875.[2]

Planter income was directly linked to the prices for sugar on the international market. Although there were repeated short-term fluctuations in sugar prices—the most dramatic occurring in 1857 and 1858—the long-term trend in prices between 1840 and 1878 was upward. Prices were extremely erratic in the 1840s and 1850s, but from 1861 through 1873 the price of white and quebrado sugars moved gradually higher in an orderly and stable fashion. The trend in prices paid for sugar on the Matanzas sugar market between 1840 and 1878 is shown in Figure 9.1.

This relative stability in the upward curve of sugar prices during the 1860s encouraged investment and new mill construction in frontier regions, despite the turmoil and upheaval occurring throughout Cuban social, economic, and political life. Not only had the slave trade to Cuba been effectively curbed by the mid-1860s, but the definitive end of slavery was heralded by the passage in 1870 of the Moret Law, which freed all children born to slave mothers after 1868 and all slaves reaching sixty years of age. Above all, the political instability caused by the insurrection in eastern Cuba should have affected investment patterns in the rich sugar-producing districts of Matanzas.

Sugar, however, seemed impervious to these potential threats to its well-being during the 1860s and 1870s. New mills were continually constructed, and even more significantly there was a substantial increase in planter income, especially in regions of recent ingenio development. For example, in the Colón partidos of Macuriges, Hanábana, and Palmillas (the frontier area colonized by sugar planters in the 1860s and 1870s), gross income increased a dynamic 71.9 percent, from 3.2 to 5.5 million pesos, between 1865 and 1876.[3] Although sugar-output statistics are not available for each ingenio, one can say beyond doubt that the Ten Years' War scarcely affected produc-

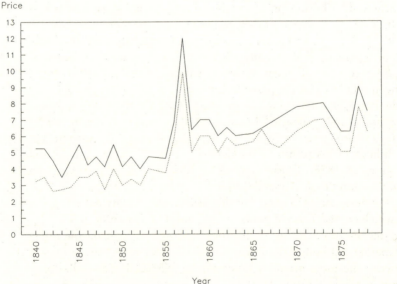

Figure 9.1. Sugar Prices in Matanzas, 1840–1878 (in cents per pound)
SOURCE: *Aurora de Matanzas.* 1840–1878.

tion in Matanzas province. To the contrary, this revolutionary period was paralleled by a growth in income for the planter class, especially among the highest-income-earning ingenios discussed above. Indeed, the prosperity of the early 1870s for Matanzas planters may have made the abolition process more acceptable to them.

The dazzling sums of capital generated by the sugar sector had little effect on the rest of Matanzas rural society. A handful of planters were economically nurtured by sugar, but there was no trickle-down effect; the absence of a domestic market was paramount, minimal economic development took place, and widespread poverty was persistent.

An abundance of smallholders struggled to maintain their dignity and eke out a living on fragmented subsistence farms or cattle ranches. Landowners with annual incomes below 500 pesos owned 71.4 percent of all farms in Colón in 1859, but they earned a meager 2.3 percent of total income. In 1865 this sector made up 72 percent of landed society, but accounted for only 1.5 percent of gross income; in 1876, they garnered only 0.8 percent of total income in Colón. The situation was equally extreme in Cárdenas, where in 1867 nearly half of all landowners earned less than 500 pesos, or 0.6 percent of the jurisdiction's total income. In 1875, nearly 60 percent of Cárdenas landowners fell into this category, and they derived 1.1 percent of all income. Income was so concentrated at the top of the landowning hierarchy that there was little social stratification. Middle sectors with the disposable income and capacity to create a domestic market were insignificant. Salaried employees could earn more than landowners. A *mayordomo*, or ingenio foreman, was paid 816 pesos annually; a *boyero*, or cattle tender, earned 420 pesos; and a skilled mechanic was paid 2,040 pesos in 1871.[4]

Income-distribution data for Colón and Cárdenas are presented in Tables 9.2 and 9.3 and are disaggregated for greater detail. It is unfortunate that systematic data on income are not available for the jurisdiction of Matanzas through this period; for the region was the oldest area of sugar culture in the province, and income-distribution patterns were probably distinct. Some idea is provided by a farm census conducted in the partido of Ceiba Mocha in 1865. Along with the Yumurí Valley, the Ceiba Mocha region had been the oldest area of settlement and agricultural exploitation in the province of Matanzas. During the eighteenth century, tobacco culture flourished; and in the late 1790s and early nineteenth century, sugar plantations and coffee farms were developed. There had been 17 ingenios and 15 cafetales in 1817 (see Table 2.2), but by 1865 both activities had declined. There were only 5 ingenios in Ceiba Mocha, all of them small-scale mills, and only 1 cafetal remained. The area had been turned over to fragmented subsistence farms and cattle ranches. These two categories of rural property owners controlled three-quarters of all land in the partido and more than 60 percent of total agrarian income in 1865.

Table 9.2. Colón Agrarian-Income Distribution Structure, 1859–1876
(in pesos)

Income Level	1859				1865				1876			
	No. Farms	%	Income	%	No. Farms	%	Income	%	No. Farms	%	Income	%
1–50	142	9.1	5,366	0.1	101	10.2	3,916	0.1	1	0.1	50	0
51–100	294	18.9	24,246	0.3	191	19.2	16,257	0.2	39	4.5	3,900	0.1
101–150	182	11.7	24,706	0.3	85	8.6	11,396	0.1	67	7.7	8,413	0.1
151–200	199	12.8	38,059	0.4	131	13.2	25,713	0.3	63	7.3	12,079	0.1
201–300	149	9.6	40,230	0.5	107	10.8	29,668	0.3	98	11.3	25,735	0.3
301–500	144	9.3	60,195	0.7	99	10.0	43,688	0.5	142	16.4	61,445	0.7
501–1,000	154	9.9	111,847	1.3	83	8.4	63,514	0.7	124	14.3	99,815	1.2
1,001–2,000	108	6.9	164,735	1.9	58	5.8	86,576	1.0	112	12.9	168,878	2.0
2,001–5,000	53	3.4	162,215	1.9	25	2.5	75,550	1.8	77	8.9	246,432	2.9
5,001–10,000	22	1.4	150,864	1.8	4	0.4	28,051	0.3	27	3.1	191,455	2.2
10,001–20,000	22	1.4	330,319	3.9	8	0.8	111,898	1.2	27	3.1	379,178	4.4
20,001–50,000	36	2.3	1,288,521	15.0	38	3.8	1,341,902	14.9	29	3.4	976,344	11.4
50,001–100,000	32	2.1	2,283,473	26.6	39	3.9	2,775,743	30.9	38	4.4	2,691,853	31.4
100,001 +	18	1.2	3,894,202	45.4	25	2.5	4,373,102	48.7	21	2.4	3,698,421	43.2
TOTAL	1,555	100.0	8,578,978	100.0	994	100.0	8,986,974	100.0	865	100.0	8,563,998	100.0

SOURCES: ANC, ME, leg. 4120, no. M, "Repartos municipales de la jurisdicción de Colón, 1859"; ANC, Gobierno General, leg. 405, No. 19209, "Padrón de fincas rústicas de la jurisdicción de Colón, 1865"; ANC, Gobierno General, leg. 270, no. 13563, "Padrón gral. de fincas rústicas de este distrito, año de 1875 a 1876."

Table 9.3. Cárdenas Agrarian-Income Distribution Structure, 1867–1875
(in pesos)

Income Level	1867				1875			
	No. Farms	%	Income	%	No. Farms	%	Income	%
1–50	34	3.6	845	0	55	5.3	2,465	0
51–100	114	11.9	5,602	0.1	144	14.0	13,888	0.2
101–150	37	3.9	2,567	0	27	2.6	3,868	0.1
151–200	126	13.2	12,410	0.1	220	21.3	43,774	0.6
201–300	50	5.2	6,566	0.1	64	6.2	18,062	0.2
301–500	113	11.8	23,040	0.3	107	10.4	43,103	0.6
501–1,000	132	13.8	49,696	0.6	115	11.2	87,282	1.1
1,001–2,000	105	11.0	77,233	0.9	95	9.2	152,560	2.0
2,001–5,000	82	8.6	133,320	1.6	58	5.6	189,601	2.5
5,001–10,000	23	2.4	78,720	0.9	28	2.7	215,905	2.8
10,001–20,000	11	1.1	83,414	1.0	31	3.0	515,882	6.7
20,001–50,000	32	3.3	579,387	6.8	42	4.1	1,478,792	19.3
50,001–100,000	41	4.3	1,477,701	17.5	33	3.2	2,309,002	30.1
100,001 +	57	6.0	5,937,101	70.1	12	1.2	2,591,438	33.8
Total	957	100.0	8,467,602	100.0	1,031	100.0	7,665,622	100.0

Sources: ANC, Gobierno General, leg. 945, no. 16724, "Padrón general de la riqueza rústica para regir en los años económicos de 1866 a 1867"; ANC, Gobierno General, leg. 270, no. 13563, "Padrón general de fincas rústicas de este distrito, año de 1875 a 1876."

Accordingly, the income-distribution structure of Ceiba Mocha in 1865 was markedly different from that of the sugar centers of Cárdenas and Colón. Nearly 90 percent of all farmers reported gross incomes below 500 pesos yearly, and they controlled one-third of total agricultural income. Four small sugar mills reported incomes greater than 5,000 pesos, and these also accounted for roughly one-third of all income.[5] The sectors falling in between are shown in Table 9.4.

Although there was a more equitable distribution of income in Ceiba Mocha, with its predominant cattle and food-crop economy, the poverty of the region should be stressed. A diversified domestic market could not have been supported by the income levels prevailing in Ceiba Mocha during the 1860s. It is likely that most of the small farms in the region had only a marginal commercial orientation and were self-sustaining operations that could do little more than support subsistence-level peasant families. Yet, these sparse data from Ceiba Mocha suggest something of the socioeconomic reality of a region in the aftermath of an export boom. Sugar and coffee had generated a measure of prosperity for elite groups during the

Table 9.4. Ceiba Mocha, 1865: Agrarian-Income Distribution Structure
(in pesos)

Income Level	No. Farms	%	Income	%
1–50	61	18.0	1,949	1.7
51–100	87	25.7	6,183	5.2
101–150	57	16.8	6,893	5.9
151–200	28	8.3	4,622	3.9
201–300	33	9.7	7,777	6.6
301–500	29	8.6	11,045	9.4
501–1,000	29	8.6	22,414	19.0
1,001–2,000	7	2.1	9,650	8.2
2,001–5,000	4	1.2	10,111	8.6
5,001–10,000	3	0.9	23,947	20.3
10,001–20,000	1	0.3	13,200	11.2
TOTAL	339	100.0	117,791	100.0

SOURCE: AHPM, ME, Estadística, leg. 9, no. 148, fols. 26–42.

early nineteenth century, but had left little in the way of permanent improvement within the region. By the 1860s, this period was a distant memory. Those who dwelled in Ceiba Mocha after the sugar and coffee economy had run its course lived no better than the impoverished inhabitants preceding the export boom. Daily material life for most people in the 1860s was probably much the same as in the eighteenth century.

CHAPTER 10

Commerce and Credit

By the early 1840s sugar alone defined and sustained the Matanzas economy. Coffee exports declined precipitously in the first half of the decade, and frontier regions opened by the railroad were converted into monocultural, sugar-exporting zones. Cárdenas was opened to international commerce in 1843, although the port never developed into a major Cuban export center. Sugar from the Matanzas hinterland was exported from the bay itself or transported by rail to Havana.

Export statistics from the port of Matanzas reveal sharp fluctuations in the volume of the sugar trade, although it must be emphasized that these data do not reflect levels of production. The leading merchants of Matanzas, such as the Torrientes, Drake Hermanos, and Fesser & Co., centered their operations in Havana, and often sugar was transported from Matanzas ingenios to Havana for export. In addition, many Matanzas planters were financed by Havana merchants through "refacción" contracts that required sugar or molasses to be delivered to the capital.

Rail travel was extremely efficient. The Ferrocarril de la Bahía de la Habana a Matanzas made two round trips each day between Matanzas and the Almacenes de Regla in Havana. In the late 1850s the train left Matanzas at 10:30 A.M., stopped in each major town, and arrived in Havana at 12:20 P.M. Another run was made in the afternoon, the train departing Matanzas at 3:30 P.M. and arriving in Havana at 5:22 P.M. From the interior, the Ferrocarril de Coliseo left Soledad de Bemba at 7:15 A.M. and arrived in Matanzas at 9:30 A.M. The Júcaro railroad departed from the Banagüises station at 5:51 P.M. and arrived in Cárdenas at 7:22 P.M.[1] Distance, rainfall, the condition of old "caminos reales," and the limited capacity of oxendrawn carretas no longer governed the possibilities of internal transportation and shipping.

The railroad also revolutionized communications—not only by dint of the relatively short time it took to journey from the capital to zones of sugar production, but also because telegraph lines were constructed along railroad routes in the early 1850s. Samuel Morse first experimented with his telegraph communications system in Puerto Rico during the 1840s, and in 1844 a functioning network was operational between Baltimore and Washington, D.C. The first Cuban telegraph lines were installed on an experimental basis in Havana in 1851; and by 1853 Batabanó, on the south coast, had been connected with the Cuban capital. By the end of the decade, Cuba was criss-crossed with telegraph lines linking every major zone of production with the island's principal ports. In 1867 a telegraph cable connected Cuba to the U.S. mainland, effectively inserting the island into the network of tele-graphic communications that was revolutionizing international commercial relations.[2] Thus, not only could produce be moved quickly from zones of production to ports, but weather, local market conditions, and price struc-tures in the consumer markets could be communicated rapidly to rural areas once considered hopelessly distant and remote from the centers of com-merce.

Although much of the sugar produced in Matanzas was transported by rail to Havana and exported from the capital, the bay itself was also con-verted into a thriving port. Direct steamship service was established with U.S. ports by the largest Matanzas import-export merchants, who often acted as consignees for merchandise imported from the United States and as factors for Matanzas sugar planters. Ships also sailed directly from Matan-zas to European ports, although they often called there only to fill remain-ing cargo space after their principal stop in Havana.

The export market for Matanzas sugar was rather diversified. The United States and Great Britain consistently imported the greatest share of the sugar exported from Matanzas, although between 1843 and 1851 other countries directly imported a significant portion of the region's sugar. Ger-many, Holland, Italy, Belgium, and France were among those that con-sumed Matanzas sugar, but these market areas did contract considerably in the 1850s, 1860s, and 1870s. Spain was never a major importer of sugar from Cuba, although it should be noted that Spanish shipping participated in the sugar trade to Europe. After 1851 England and the United States consistently imported two-thirds or more of the sugar exported from Ma-tanzas.[3] Figures 10.1 and 10.2 show the fluctuations in the Matanzas sugar trade between 1843 and 1872 and the principal consumer markets importing sugar from the region.

The Matanzas merchant class was composed exclusively of foreign im-migrants and their offspring throughout the entire nineteenth century. There are few examples of Cubans acting as merchants, even in the most marginal village pulperías. Although newly arrived groups of immigrants often appeared in the port with aspirations of carving out a niche for them-selves in the merchant hierarchy, there was remarkable social stability within the merchant community. The most important firms established in the late 1820s and early 1830s operated through the 1870s. Obvious exam-ples are Drake Hermanos and the Torriente brothers, who were the princi-pal Matanzas warehousers, exporters, and local sources of credit to regional planters.

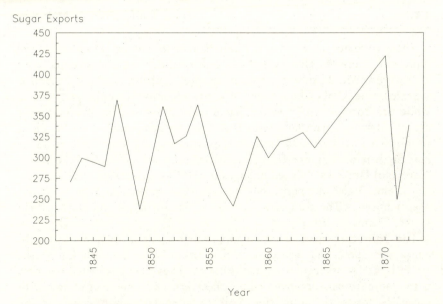

Sugar Exports

Year

Figure 10.1. Sugar Exports from Matanzas by Quantity, 1843–1872 (in thousands of boxes)

SOURCES: *Mercantile Weekly Report*, 1843–1872, in NYPL, Moses Taylor Collection, case C, drawers 3 and 4, box 10.

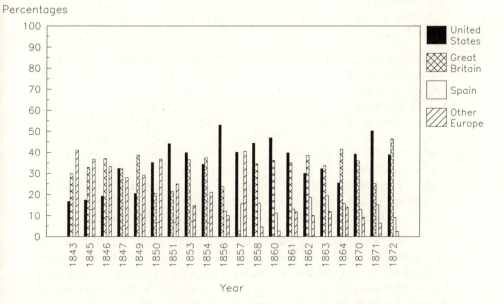

Percentages

United States

Great Britain

Spain

Other Europe

Year

Figure 10.2. Sugar Exports from Matanzas by Destination, 1843–1872 (selected years in percentages)

SOURCES: *Mercantile Weekly Report*, 1843–1872, in NYPL, Moses Taylor Collection, cases B and C, drawers 3 and 4, boxes 7, 8, 10.

These were not mere provincial merchants with narrowly conceived local economic interests. They were highly diversified, family-run enterprises that were vertically integrated economically. Both firms owned Matanzas ingenios: the Drakes had established the ingenios Saratoga and Júcaro, while the Torrientes owned the Isabel and Cantabria estates. They were shareholders in Cuban railway lines and also backed Havana financial institutions such as the Banco Español. International investments were also a part of their operations. Through marriage to Carlota del Castillo, James (Santiago) Drake established linkages to the Castillo interests in New Orleans, and Drake Hermanos had business investments in New York and Massachusetts. The company was also a part owner of the London firm Drake, Kleinwort & Cohen.[4]

The Torrientes operated an import-export house in their home city of Santander, Spain, and had extensive dealings in London with Baring Brothers, a large British banking establishment. They also transacted business with Hamburg bankers, from whom they secured ample lines of credit. In the early 1860s, in conjunction with investments made to construct the largest warehouse in Matanzas, the Torrientes borrowed 100,000 British pounds sterling (500,000 pesos) from Baring Brothers and an additional 50,000 pounds (250,000 pesos) from the Hamburg firm of Tok, Berenberg, Gossler & Company. Ingenios Isabel and Cantabria were mortgaged to secure these loans.[5]

Describing the warehouses of Matanzas in the early 1860s, Jacobo de la Pezuela wrote:

> [A]mong the warehouses of Matanzas none can compare with the warehouse for depositing produce built a few years ago along the banks of the San Juan River by the opulent hacendado and merchant Cosme de la Torriente. . . . His warehouse is in the form of an irregular pentagon divided in eight parts. . . . The principal warehouse has two floors. . . . The capacity of the building has been calculated to hold 80,000 boxes of sugar and 20,000 hogsheads of molasses, which enter and leave by rail. . . . For the maritime service of the warehouse complex, Torriente's warehouse serves the same function for Matanzas that the Almacenes de Regla fulfill for Havana. . . . [T]he cost of construction of the buildings alone was more than 600,000 pesos.[6]

A third powerful Havana-based group operating in Matanzas was the Fesser brothers of Andalucía. Eduardo Fesser built and operated the Almacenes de Regla in Havana, established the Banco de Comercio, also in the Cuban capital, and was heavily invested in railway enterprises. He was connected to the Diago brothers through marriage to their sister Micaela. Edward was in charge of the family's Cuban operations, while his three brothers, Adolphus, Joséph, and John, tended a merchant house at 12 Leadenhall St., London, and one in Seville. Fesser & Company was active in Matanzas through the 1870s.[7]

Employment in these firms also led to independent commercial careers. The best-known case is that of José María Morales y Sotolongo, who began working as an employee of Drake Hermanos in Havana early in the nineteenth century and who later became a wealthy entrepreneur. He founded J. M. Morales & Company, which had branches in Havana and Cárdenas by the early 1850s, and also established the slave-insurance company La Protectora. William Schweyer, a U.S. citizen, worked for Drake in Matanzas between 1832 and 1839 before launching his own Matanzas business with Joseph Day of Portland, Maine, in 1839.[8] Maine lumberyards supplied shooks and staves for the barrels and boxes used to ship Matanzas sugar, and these business ties led to investment in Cuba by Maine merchants.

Other North American merchants with small-scale import-export houses in Matanzas during the 1840s and 1850s included James & John Bayley, established in 1839 (although it is evident that they had been operating from Havana earlier in the decade); Charles Parkinson, who joined the Bayleys as a partner in 1855; and James Knight and his son George, who opened a firm in the mid-1840s. Charles Traub, a native of Nassau and the British vice-consul in Matanzas in the early 1850s, was the only English merchant operating in Matanzas during the mid-nineteenth century. He associated with the Bayleys from 1853, in Bayley & Traub, and later (from 1859) with Parkinson in Traub & Parkinson. James Burnham & Company, which had operated in Havana during the early 1840s, opened a branch in Matanzas in 1849. The North Americans William Safford, E. Marshall & Company, Smith & Company, and Rabel & Company of New Orleans operated in Cárdenas in the 1840s.

Several German firms were also present in Matanzas. Brodermann & Company was in business in the mid-1830s, but disappeared shortly thereafter. Augustus Kobbe & Company opened in 1845 and remained through the 1860s. Uhrbach & Lunschen appeared in the mid-1850s and also remained through the 1870s. Other European firms established in Matanzas included the French company D. F. Roget y Cía., which opened in the mid-1830s and remained though the 1860s. C. F. Poujaud y Cía. was first noted in the early 1850s and also persisted through the 1860s. Picard y Albers, another French firm, operated in the 1840s but had disappeared by the 1850s.[9]

These smaller North American, German, or French merchant houses did not play a role in the Matanzas economy as major creditors or warehousers. They were primarily small-scale middlemen in the sugar export trade. At harvesttime they bid for sugar or molasses from those independent planters who were not encumbered by the "refacción" contracts that obligated others to deliver sugar to specific merchants. Relatively small amounts of credit were extended, through provisions advanced to planters. Contacts were maintained with import houses in the major consuming centers of New York, London, Hamburg, or Bremen, and sugar was exported to these market areas. But smaller merchant establishments did not command sufficient capital resources to play an important role in the financing of ingenio construction, slave purchases, or the substantial sums of working capital required by the largest mills during the yearly zafra. Yet, they sometimes irked the principal houses by competing to purchase sugar supplies for export from independent planters. Cornelius O'Callaghan, an aspiring Cárdenas merchant, wrote to Moses Taylor in late 1851: "I shall not be surprised if some of the heavy dealers, whose animosity appears very strong against the new competition which have sprung up here in their line since last season, determine by and by to sell molasses very low, to injure the latter if possible."[10]

Credit for the Matanzas sugar economy took a variety of forms and experienced a number of transformations between 1837 and 1878. Although the Havana-based titled families built ingenios and financed railroad construction, they rarely acted as merchants, and there are no examples of commercial firms operating with capital provided by these politically powerful family groups. However, such clans as the Montalvos and Peñalvers controlled huge Matanzas land areas because of grants they received from cabildos before 1729, when the power of local authorities to award land was curbed. Some had also purchased vast tracts of land at low prices during the eighteenth century.

As settlement patterns shifted and the geography of the provincial sugar economy moved toward southern and eastern frontier regions, lands controlled by these families became the object of acquisition by sugar planters and smallholders alike. By financing land sales "a censo," these noble families provided an important form of credit to the local economy.[11] This type of credit must be distinguished from the finance capital supplied by merchants to construct ingenios, import machinery, and purchase slaves—although, in the development of frontier regions, that too was important.

Land transactions financed by titled families from Havana continued through the 1870s. The Peñalvers were instrumental in the sale of the Banagüises region to the Arrietas, Diagos, and Zuluetas in the late 1830s and early 1840s. They also provided land to the Torrientes farther to the south for the construction of Ingenio Cantabria. The Conde de Casa Montalvo continued to sell frontierland "a censo" in the 1840s and 1850s to planters and smallholders alike. In the 1850s, for example, land in the southern regions of Macuriges was coveted as a future area of sugar development. The Montalvos owned two large haciendas in the area, Francisco López and Tabaco, which bordered Hanábana. In May 1855, 130 caballerías were sold to Rafael Saavedra for 18,200 pesos, or 140 pesos/caballería. Saavedra was obligated to pay 5 percent of this value annually to Montalvo in perpetuity.[12] In 1857 and 1858 numerous small parcels, ranging in size from 2 to 10 caballerías, were sold by Montalvo to various purchasers, always with "a censo" credit arrangements, which required little or no down payment.[13] In the 1860s, as the frontier shifted farther to the south and east, the hacienda Amarillas in the Jagüey Grande region was sold "a censo," and the same sort of sales were taking place in eastern Palmillas.[14] In this manner titled families, who by and large did not engage in commerce, played an important role in stimulating the land market in the province.

However, large-scale Havana merchants with international connections financed the most important aspects of the Matanzas sugar economy. In the 1840s the principal firms were Drake Hermanos, Pedro Martínez y Cía., the Fessers, and the Alfonsos, all of immigrant origin. They had played a leading role in the expansion of sugar culture in Havana province during the late eighteenth and early nineteenth centuries, and most were closely connected to the Cuban slave trade. Having accumulated vast sums of capital, a sophisticated knowledge of international markets, and extensive shipping and marketing linkages with major consuming regions, this Havana-based merchant class efficiently shifted capital investment to Matanzas on an ever-increasing scale as railroads honeycombed the province's interior. During the 1840s, 1850s, and 1860s powerful newcomers appeared in Matanzas, although this did not mean the demise of established merchant families. Noriega, Olmo & Company; Benítez and Dirón; the Pedrosos and the Torrientes; José and Salvador Baró; and Julián Zulueta all became important merchants. But the Cuban sugar economy expanded sufficiently to accommodate these newer clans without displacement of older commercial interests.

Although most merchants were originally immigrants and maintained close connections with Spain or some other European country, it should be stressed that the capital used to develop sugar monoculture in Matanzas was generated and accumulated in Cuba. Foreign firms, such as Moses Taylor of New York and Baring Brothers of London, may have played a leading role in supplying lines of credit to merchants and to some planters as well. But, by and large, the capital utilized to finance sugar production in Matanzas was controlled by Cuban-based financial interests with long experience and finely honed entrepreneurial skills. Profits derived by this merchant class may have been consumed conspicuously in many instances, and a portion may have been repatriated to Spain; but, for the most part, accumulated capital was employed productively and efficiently within Cuba to promote economic expansion. Profits were plowed back into productive endeavors in the same way that the bourgeoisie of the North Atlantic nations utilized their capital. The difference was that investments revolved around one central economic resource, the structures of monoculture were deepened, and economic diversification was negligible. Yet, while capital may have been utilized efficiently to maximize profits for elite groups, the Cuban economic system revolved exclusively around export markets for sugar. The absence of domestic demand, because of extreme income concentration, could hardly encourage diversified investment patterns. Capital flowed to sugar, merchants and planters prospered, and the rest of society derived few lasting benefits from economic growth.

The "refacción" contract was the chief economic and legal means through which credit was extended to planters by the merchant class. Capital for purchase of land and machinery was usually secured through conventional loans, or "obligaciones," which were similar to "refacción" contracts in many ways, since harvests, slaves, machinery, and land were mortgaged to guarantee debts. The "refacción" contract, however, addressed the particular financial needs of each harvest. These contracts were routine for most mill owners, although the largest ingenios rarely secured operating capital that way. This is because there were distinct disadvantages to planters. Not only were they bound to sell their products to particular merchants, sometimes at fixed prices, but a further array of stipulations was forced upon planters.

A contract drawn up in 1852, between the Cárdenas merchant house Queipó, Vidal y Cía. and the owners of Ingenio Conclusión, Julio Marcel and Francisco Scull, was typical. The Conclusión estate, located in Palmillas, extended for 34 caballerías and had a slave population of 166 men and women. Its owners resided in Havana. In October 1852, Marcel and Scull urgently needed capital to prepare for the coming harvest, which in effect put them at the mercy of whatever terms might be imposed by their creditors. Queipó and Vidal agreed to provide 20,000 pesos, but the estate's owners virtually had to relinquish control over Conclusión. All sugar produced on the ingenio had to be delivered to Queipó and Vidal; the purchase of all *envases* was mandated; 50 cents in warehousing charges were collected on each *bocoy* of sugar; a 2 percent commission was paid on all sales; a 1 percent monthly interest on all outstanding debts was collected; and transportation costs via railroad to Cárdenas were the responsibility of Marcel and Scull. In addition, irrespective of the market price for muscovado sugars at harvesttime, the price paid to Conclusión's owners was fixed at 12 pesos/bocoy. Each bocoy held approximately 1,000 pounds of sugar; thus, Queipó and Vidal paid only 1.2 cents/pound for Conclusión's production. During the harvest of 1853 the actual market price of muscovado sugars fluctuated at slightly above 2 cents/pound. The difference accrued to Queipó and Vidal. For providing operating capital these merchants derived more gross income than the mill owners themselves. The harvest of 1853 and all subsequent harvests were mortgaged until the debt and related charges were paid.[15] This arrangement typified the dilemma of small, undercapitalized estates. There were few alternatives but to accept the conditions imposed by merchants. If not, the mature cane simply could not be harvested.

There was little variation in the terms of "refacción" arrangements over time, although with the repeal of the "privilegio de ingenios" in 1852 accruing debts could lead to foreclosure. Prior to 1852, only future harvests could legally be mortgaged to creditors; afterward, however, merchants refused to enter into "refacción" arrangements unless ingenios themselves were mortgaged as collateral. It was through such a contract that Noriega, Olmo & Company acquired the Macuriges ingenio Andrea when its owner could not meet his obligations. Andrea was a relatively small estate, extending for 30 caballerías. José Jauregui purchased the plantation in 1845 from Juana Josefa Rodríguez, and its zafras were financed by Noriega and Olmo with the usual stipulations. In 1853, Jauregui recognized a debt of 31,573 pesos that spiraled to 165,203 pesos by 1855. In September 1856, unable to make significant payments, Jauregui was forced to cede Andrea to Noriega and Olmo—a timely deal for the Havana merchants, since sugar prices soared shortly thereafter.[16]

The terms of "refacción" contracts were onerous, to be sure, but most middle-size or smaller planters had little choice. These marginal ingenio owners did not produce enough income to finance production through their own revenues. Large-scale planters, however, either had the capability of self-financing or they dealt directly with foreign sources of credit in the principal market areas consuming Matanzas sugar. There are no instances of the old nobility entering into "refacción" contracts with the merchant class. Relative newcomers—the Poeys, Barós, Diagos, Torrientes, Zuluetas, and others—dealt directly with foreign creditors, imported materials such as staves and shooks needed for packaging, maintained urban warehouses where produce was stored for export, and generally avoided middlemen to their economic advantage.[17]

Significant advantages were derived by planters who could avoid pre-harvest contractual commitments to deliver sugar to creditors. Sugar prices fluctuated weekly, and with the advent of the railroad in the 1840s and the telegraph in the 1850s, information on changing conditions in export markets could be readily secured by planters and merchants alike. Drake Hermanos published the English-language *Mercantile Weekly Report* from Havana, reporting every nuance of changing production and market conditions. Rainfall patterns during the growing season were carefully documented; the condition of cane in the fields was reported regularly; notices of when grinding had begun on individual estates were supplied; the quality of the first boxes of sugar was noted; factors affecting prices in foreign markets, such as the progress of the beet sugar harvest in Germany and Russia, were reported.[18]

Although these reports were directed at English and U.S. sugar importers, they were used by planters as well. The slightest hint that international or local conditions could result in price increases for sugar led independent planters to withhold supplies from market until price trends were defined. For example, rumors of instability in European supplies and of a drought in Cuba over the summer of 1848 resulted in high prices being asked by planters without "refacción" contracts when the harvest began in early 1849. In April 1849, the *Mercantile Weekly Report* noted that planters were holding out for relatively high prices and that merchants were refusing to purchase sugars until they declined. In May, there was "more firmness on the part of our planters." But by June the pressure was reversed when Drake reported that "the stock here [Havana] and in Matanzas is large and it is evident that the accounts of the shortness of our crop have been much exaggerated." Yet, as late as August 1849 "several planters still withhold their crops from the market in expectation of higher prices, but European limits are too low for our actual rates and from the U.S. there is no demand whatsoever." Even in November, "planters continue to ask rates which could not be afforded."[19]

Independent planters could also exert upward pressures on prices when the ports were filled with ships awaiting cargo for voyages to Europe or the United States. In early 1853 Matanzas Bay was filled with ships awaiting supplies, and planters refused to market sugar to local merchants until better prices were received.[20]

Yet, planter leverage on the sugar market should not be exaggerated. Plantation owners with "refacción" contracts were obligated to deliver sugar or molasses soon after it was processed. In the case of large debts, merchants stationed representatives on plantations to ensure that there would be no attempt to market sugar with rivals. "Refacción" contracts were a key mechanism that merchants used to secure supplies; and if prices were fixed in credit arrangements, substantial profits could result whenever there was the slightest upward movement in sugar prices on the international market. Still, planters maintaining independence from creditors were also ultimately accountable to global supply-and-demand trends. Even a reduced harvest, resulting from drought, hurricanes, or blight, could do little to affect the price structure on an international sugar market that was shifting in the mid-nineteenth century because of an upsurge in European beet sugar output. Independent planters may have fared better than those whose harvests were encumbered through contracted debts; but in the long term, dependence on factors beyond local control defined the overall direction of the nineteenth-century Matanzas sugar economy.

Large Havana and Matanzas merchant houses with guaranteed supplies of sugar; smaller merchants who operated as factors for planters on commission or who purchased sugar independently—both had to deal ultimately with import houses in the sugar-consuming nations. Sugar importers in New York or London derived profits that dwarfed those reaped by Havana or Matanzas merchant houses. One of many transactions recorded by Moses Taylor in 1861 was typical, and it illustrates the way in which the profits generated by Cuban sugar contributed to the capital-accumulation process in the United States.

In a transaction effected in April 1861, Taylor purchased 250 boxes of sugar weighing 4,333 arrobas (108,325 pounds) at 3 cents/pound. The boxes themselves were purchased for 3.25 dollars each, making the total bill 4,062.25 dollars. In addition, charges had to be paid in Cuba before the ship could be cleared for departure. An export duty of 7 reales/box (.875 dollars) was paid; shipping charges of 2.5 reales/box (.3125 dollars) were disbursed; lighterage, brokerage, and a consular certificate cost 47 dollars; a commission charge of 2.5 percent (110.15 dollars) was paid to the factor handling the transaction; and another 1.75 percent (80.58 dollars) was paid for "negotiations," probably as a bribe to Spanish officials to ensure that things went as smoothly as possible. The total cost of the sugar in Cuba, including all charges, came to 4.2436 cents/pound, 29.3 percent of which consisted of expenses involved in exporting the sugar from the island. The total price was 4,596.86 dollars. On arrival in New York, this sugar was never transported to Taylor's warehouses but was sold on the New York wharf to a Brooklyn refiner for 7.3101 cents/pound. There had been a 3.5 percent loss in weight during the voyage owing to evaporation. The net weight of the sugar sold came to 104,534 pounds, for total revenues of 7,641.54 dollars; thus, a net profit of 66.2 percent was made on this transaction.[21]

These profit possibilities led major Havana and Matanzas merchant houses to open branches in the United States, Great Britain, or Spain in order to eliminate the middlemen standing between them and even greater revenues. Julián Zulueta, for example, owned a merchant establishment in Liverpool, and a branch of his business was located in Andoain, Spain.[22] In 1859, José Baró and his brother Salvador opened a firm in New York under the name R. Herques & Company "with José Baró of Havana as the principal partner." Baró was a silent partner in a number of firms throughout Cuba. Along with his brother he was the principal backer of Salvador Baró y Cía., based in Havana with branches in Matanzas and Cárdenas. In 1852 he had been a partner in Fermin, Santos y Cía. of Cárdenas. He became the "comanditario" (silent partner) of Padró, Serra y Cía., also of Cárdenas, formed in 1871. He was also the principal backer of F. Baró y Cía. of Caibarién, formed in 1872 with his sons Federico, José N., and Andres Baró. Salvador Baró was a principal partner in Chartrand, Gavilán y Cía. of Havana in 1873.[23]

Goicouría y Cía. was established in Havana and New Orleans in the 1850s. In 1861 the firm moved to New York, and in 1863 a branch was opened in Matanzas. Charles Traub, the British merchant from Nassau, was associated with Richard Fritze (in the port of Trinidad), whose brother owned N. A. Fritze & Company of Bremen, Germany. The Fessers operated in London and Seville; the Drakes in London; and Federico Altes, a Cárdenas merchant, opened a New York branch of his business in 1864, under the charge of Charles Maden.

There are many more examples revealing the international character of the merchant class that operated in nineteenth-century Matanzas. Owners of seemingly modest operations in the port cities of Matanzas or Cárdenas had impressive connections with international markets, permitting them to reap spiraling profits from the sugar produced in rural Cuba. Although no account books have been located for the major merchants or planters of nineteenth-century Matanzas, it is certain that Cuban sugar production generated substantially more profits for brokers than for growers. Naturally those merchants/planters who were vertically integrated, such as the Torrientes, Zuluetas, Barós, or Pedrosos, derived greater profits from the sugar produced on their own estates.

The control over credit and marketing exercised by the merchants of Havana, Matanzas, or Cárdenas continued through the Ten Years' War, despite the advent of banking institutions and insurance companies in the mid-1850s. The first Cuban bank, El Banco de Fernando VII, was founded by the colonial government in 1832 under the auspices of the Intendant Claudio Martínez de Pinillos, Conde de Villanueva. The bank's resources were modest, since it was not financed with private capital but rather with revenues generated by the Real Hacienda. It lasted for eight years, had limited available capital, accumulated an onerous debt of some 6 million pesos by the early 1840s, and did little to alter either the fundamental dynamics of credit or the circulation of specie on the island.[24]

Two subsequent institutions—the Cuban-based Caja de Ahorros, Descuentos y Depósitos, formed in 1840, and the peninsular-based Caja Real de Descuentos—hardly affected the island's monetary system, agricultural credit, or the vicissitudes of international commerce.[25] Havana merchants continued their monopoly over rural credit, were intimately linked with U.S. merchant houses or British banking institutions, and utilized widely recognized letters of credit drawn on these foreign firms (e.g., Baring Brothers and Moses Taylor) to negotiate international transactions.

In 1855, however, the Crown authorized the creation of the Banco Español de la Habana, supervised by the colonial government but financed principally by private shareholders.[26] The Banco Español was authorized to issue paper currency in Cuba, but this was closely tied to the amount of gold and silver on deposit in the bank. It established individual savings accounts, paid interest on deposits, could issue letters of credit, and had the authority to make loans. Its major function, though, and the reason it was supported by the principal merchants of Havana, was to regulate the circulation of currency on the island (this was an exclusive power) and to issue and negotiate international letters of credit that would be uniformly recognized by merchant houses of different countries.

Although the Banco Español never provided rural credit on a significant scale, its establishment in 1855 heralded the appearance of other institutions that played an important role in supplying credit to the sugar planters of rural Matanzas. La Alianza, whose initial purpose was to provide insurance on slaves and shipping was established by Julián Zulueta, José Baró, Francisco Rosell, and Santiago Sánchez. During the monetary crisis of 1857 La Alianza absorbed the Caja Central de Comercio, the Crédito Agrícola de Cárdenas, La Positiva, and the Banco de Pinar del Río, and it became an institution supplying rural credit.[27] El Crédito Mobiliario y Fomento Cubano was another important credit company, and it was closely involved in financing the agricultural holding enterprises the Compañía Territorial Cubana and La Gran Azucarera. Its principal accionistas were José Noriega, of Noriega, Olmo y Cía.; Rafael Rodríguez Torices, the owner of Ingenio Ponina; and Salvador Samá, Julián Zulueta's brother-in-law. Other important financial institutions established in the mid-1850s included La Protectora, José María Morales's insurance company, and La Providencia, a rival firm.

The emergence of corporate enterprises dedicated to finance, insurance, or agricultural exploitation in the mid-1850s did not alter the fundamental parameters governing the economy of Matanzas rural society. There is little evidence that the mechanisms of rural credit were transformed in any way, and interest rates experienced no decline. Nor was the role of merchants who traditionally financed sugar production diminished. The advent of banks did not supplant the Drakes, Barós, Zuluetas, Torrientes, or Pedrosos; and their connections with English- and U.S.-based sources of credit were not mitigated.

Banking establishments financed ingenios, to be sure, but the "refacción" contract remained the prime mechanism linking mill owners with capital. "Refacción" contracts continued to secure credit for planters and to ensure sugar deliveries for the merchants to export, as they had since the early nineteenth century. They may have used the nomenclature of modern banking establishments, but Cuban banks in the mid-nineteenth century functioned exactly in the same way as rival merchant houses and did little to alter the economic structures of rural society.

In Matanzas itself, the Banco de San Carlos de Matanzas was founded, and it became an important local source of credit and eventually an owner of ingenios through foreclosures. The director of San Carlos was the Catalán Francisco Gumá y Ferrán, who typified the new group of immigrants arriving in Cuba during the 1860s and 1870s. His father, Sebastián Gumá y Soler, had come to Matanzas in 1816 and established Gumá, Ferrer y Compañía. Although he returned to Catalonia in 1843, two decades later his son

Francisco was drawn to Matanzas after a career as a railroad entrepreneur in Spain, where he had constructed the railway line between Barcelona and his native town of Villanueva y Geltrú.

Seeking vertical integration in much the same way as traditional merchants, under Gumá's supervision the Banco de San Carlos extended loans via "refacción" contracts that included mortgages as guarantees for credit. Thus did San Carlos acquire the overextended Ingenio Nuestra Señora del Carmen in 1866. This Guamacaro estate extended for 50 caballerías, was worked by 89 slaves and 27 Asian contract laborers, was completely irrigated with 12,000 feet of iron tubing, and even had a small internal railroad system. Its owners, José Gener and Pedro Domínguez of Havana, had accumulated a debt of 116,830 pesos with the bank through a series of "refacción" contracts that had never been liquidated. In addition, debts of 67,284 pesos to ten other merchants had been assumed by San Carlos when the estate was purchased for 334,562 pesos.

Two other ingenios were acquired that same year. Licenciado Carlos Ortíz had accumulated a debt with the bank of 113,735 pesos through the "refacción" of his Macuriges ingenio San Carlos, which was adjacent to the Torrientes' Cantabria estate. Unable to pay, he agreed to sell the plantation to the Matanzas bank for 143,735 pesos. The bank also acquired Ingenio Reforma, 60 caballerías in Caibarién, but sold it for 118,000 pesos to Sres. Setién Hermanos shortly after its acquisition.[28]

The advent of banking institutions in the 1850s heralded a gradual shift in the composition of the Matanzas merchant elite. Again, it should be reiterated that the old families and their firms did not disappear before the end of the independence rebellion in 1878. But newcomers appeared with markedly different sets of interests. Most conspicuous were Spanish immigrant merchants having extensive capital resources but with little previous involvement in the development of the Cuban economy.

The merchant/planter families who heretofore controlled credit were involved in all of the great dramas of Cuban economic growth. They founded innovative ingenios and experimented with new technologies: steam engines, vacuum evaporators, and centrifuges. They helped finance the impressive network of railway and telegraph lines that crisscrossed the Matanzas hinterland. Although many were of immigrant origin, these families planted firm roots in Cuba. Fortunes were made on the island, not abroad. Their children were born and raised in Cuba, and social and economic interests were by and large insular. They looked upon the Cuban economy from two perspectives. Cuba offered a road to wealth through ruthless exploitation, it is true; but it was also home, and there was a concern to mold colonial society so that elite groups would be better served.

Recent immigrants shared no such preoccupations. Capital had already been accumulated abroad before arrival in Cuba, and there was little interest in the island other than as an object of investment. The director of the Banco de San Carlos, Francisco Gumá, was representative. Those penetrating Matanzas in the 1860s and 1870s were the advance guard of the new group of merchants who would gradually dominate the region in the 1880s and 1890s. Their interests were peninsular, not insular, and Cuba would never be home. They coexisted with the traditional elite until after the Ten Years' War, when so many old families were relentlessly swept from the historical stage. Yet, no romantic images should cloud our view of these older families. They were all slave traders to varying degrees and ruthless exploiters of men and women.[29] Newcomers arrived after the demise of the Cuban trata, and they would operate in a society that was developing new forms of labor exploitation.

Credit transactions recorded by Matanzas notaries in the 1860s and 1870s indicate the presence of these newer merchants, although there are few biographical details available. The case of Grande Hermanos was typical. This was a heavily capitalized firm operated by three brothers, José, Francisco, and Juan Grande, natives of Asturias. The firm was established in Cuba in 1872 with capital resources of 434,037 pesos. A tienda was purchased on Calle de la Salud in Havana, and a branch of the business was opened in Matanzas on Calle Magdalena. In addition, the brothers acquired Ingenio Santa Ana in Bolondrón. They appear as "refaccionistas" to many smaller-scale ingenios in the 1870s.[30] Another Matanzas merchant of Asturian origin who appeared in the 1870s was Francisco Rionda y Polledo, who also acted as a "refaccionista." He married into the Torriente family, wedding the daughter of Cosme de la Torriente, Elena Torriente y Hernández.[31] The Grande family survived the Cuban war for independence (1895–1898) and operated an important sugar mill in Canasí, Central Elena, in the early twentieth century. Rionda was a partner in one of the largest Spanish-owned sugar brokerages in Havana, Rionda, Ceballos & Company.

The resiliency and entrepreneurial acumen of the merchants financing the development of rural Matanzas throughout most of the nineteenth century should be emphasized. They rapidly adjusted to changing situations and were quick to seize upon new opportunities for profit maximization. Routine economic behavior was not their way. Rather, dynamism and flexibility were the hallmarks of their collective socioeconomic history, despite the fact that the Matanzas economy revolved around monocultural sugar production. Sugarcane cultivation may have been the only option for planters, but for merchants there were diverse investment opportunities. Railroad building; import-export activities; construction of warehouses; direct ownership over ingenios; provision of rural credit; establishing branches in consumer markets; ownership of shares in banks, the founding of insurance companies; investments in long-term, interest-bearing bonds in Europe or the United States; and, until the mid-1860s, clandestine slave trading were activities pursued by established merchants and newcomers alike.

This paradox must be carefully recognized. For within a predominantly monocultural plantation society there was a social class with broadly diversified economic interests. Yet, despite the fact that investment patterns were so extensive, capital was almost exclusively channeled into activities closely linked to sugar production and export. There was no Machiavellian conspiracy to reinforce the structures of dependence and monoculture, for these resulted from rational economic considerations on the part of the social sector controlling capital. Investments were geared toward profit-maximizing activities, and these revolved in some way around sugar. The cycle was insidious. Capital may theoretically have been available for investment in any number of economic activities, but the structures of a plantation society effectively eliminated any possibility of developing a broad economic base. The virtual absence of a domestic market for anything beyond the needs of sugar precluded sectoral economic diversification. Sugar monoculture was perpetuated by the inability of capital to generate profits on a significant scale in activities linked to any other economic activity. Export markets ultimately supported the Cuban economy, and the environment of rural Cuba was harnessed to meet external demand. Internal demand unrelated to the sugar complex was rudimentary.

CHAPTER 11

The Socioeconomic Impact
of the Ten Years' War

In terms of productive capacity, the Matanzas sugar economy was scarcely affected by the insurrection between 1868 and 1878. In a communiqué written in 1880, the British vice-consul in Matanzas noted that "the country round Matanzas has suffered little from the late insurrection, and . . . the sugar industry there is in a comparatively thriving condition."[1] Sugar and molasses exports from the port of Matanzas did not depart from their normal pattern of cyclical fluctuation (see Figure 11.1). A downturn in exports during 1871 had little to do with the revolutionary war, but was related to

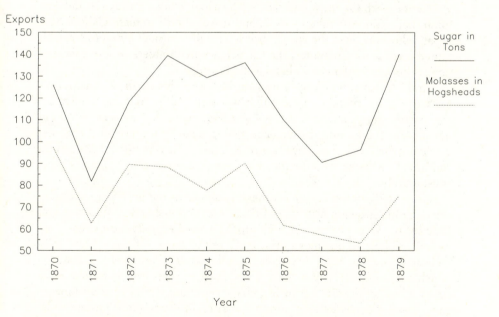

Figure 11.1. Sugar and Molasses Exports from Matanzas, 1870–1879 (in thousands of tons or hogsheads)
SOURCE: PRO, FO 72/1550, letter of Consul D'Costas of Matanzas, Oct. 2, 1880.

a poor harvest caused by meteorological conditions.[2] The weather improved after 1871, and exports recovered in the mid-1870s.

Although the rebel army crossed the trocha in 1875 and invaded some sections of Matanzas (notably the area contiguous to the Ciénaga de Zapata, south of Colón), the drop in sugar exports in 1876 was again closely linked to adverse climatic conditions rather than to rural violence. Matanzas suffered from a prolonged drought, lasting from November 1875 through May 1876, that resulted in a reduced harvest and declining exports.[3] However, rebel activities probably affected the harvest of 1877, even though recovery began in 1878 and the harvest of 1879 returned to previous levels. In short, the province emerged from this period of political upheaval with its mills and productive capacity intact.

This does not imply that Matanzas was totally unscathed or unaffected by the war. There were scattered attempts at local insurrection in the early stages of the rebellion. A conspiracy was discovered in Ceiba Mocha in February 1869, and there is evidence of a plan to promote an antigovernment rising in the city of Matanzas early in 1869.[4] However, the only actual armed revolt in the province took place on February 12, 1869, on Ingenio Australia, near the town of Jagüey Grande in the partido of Hanábana. This was a recent area of colonization and ingenio construction, and the railroad would not reach the town until 1878. The Mora brothers, Máximo and Antonio, had built Australia in 1862, and it was their foreman, Gabriel Menocal, who organized the revolt. It was brutally crushed by a pro-Spanish armed force from Guamutas, the Chapelgorris volunteers, who recognized none other than Julián de Zulueta as their leader.[5]

Rural Matanzas was largely undisturbed after this small skirmish, until 1875 when the invasion of Las Villas was initiated by Máximo Gómez. In the intervening years the war may have been a source of concern, but it did not disrupt the economic expansion taking place in undeveloped regions. The construction of new ingenios in Palmillas, Hanábana, and Macuriges continued unabated, and the income flowing to the region's planters grew substantially.

In late 1875, however, the southern extremes of the province, especially the rich cane-growing districts of Colón, were seriously affected for the first time by the war. Led by "El Inglesito," Henry Reeve, bands of rebels attacked and burned ingenios to the south of the town of Colón in late 1875 and early 1876, the most spectacular assault occurring on Ingenio Los Alpes, which was completely destroyed. Combat took place on José Baró's Santa Rita mill in April 1876, but little damage was done. There were also incursions into Cárdenas by rebel forces operating in the Sagua la Grande area, and many cane fields were burned during late 1876, although few milling complexes were attacked.[6]

Revolutionary activity in the province seems to have created a heretofore-unknown phenomenon: the emergence of widespread rural banditry perpetrated by gangs of runaway slaves and Chinese contract laborers. Small-scale palenques had existed in the province during the early nine-teenth century; with the expansion of sugar culture into frontier regions and with the general population growth taking place, however, few inaccessible areas offering natural protection to cimarrones remained by the mid-1870s. The exception was the inhospitable Zapata swampland, which consistently attracted small groups of runaways.

Although the insurrection was not clearly abolitionist until 1871, after this date the offer of emancipation to slaves who would abandon plantations and join the rebel forces was evidently well known among dotaciones in the cane-growing regions of Matanzas. But rebel activity was an abstraction in faraway Camagüey and Oriente, and any possibility of actually crossing overland to rebel lines was remote. Deterrents to plantation desertion were strong. Pro-Spanish mercenaries such as Zulueta's Chapelgorris volunteers were little more than private armies organized and financed by planters to patrol the countryside and ensure minimal disruption of economic life. These armed groups were widespread throughout the province, and they were supplemented by the official presence of Spanish regulars who were garrisoned in strategic locations in order to protect railways and sugar estates.

The passage of the Moret Law in 1870 also mitigated to some extent the willingness of individual slaves to risk their lives in an attempt to join the rebellion. Yet, the onset of the legal abolition process and the inability of Spain to contain a rebellion that had become openly abolitionist by the mid-1870s resulted in a substantial shift in plantation discipline. Slaves were more assertive, and the parameters of social control were in the process of redefinition by the actions, or threats of action, of the slaves themselves.[7]

The invasion of Las Villas and the penetration of Matanzas by rebel units composed in part by ex-slaves, who had deserted plantations and farms in eastern Cuba, converted the abstract into the real for the slave population and Chinese contract laborers of Matanzas. The Moret Law had generated high hopes among slaves, but by the mid-1870s impatience with any real progress toward final abolition for the majority of working-age slaves induced an upsurge in desertions whenever rebel units operated near ingenios; or slaves simply fled for maroonage and freedom. The rebel presence in rural Matanzas created a new type of social and political space—which, to the dismay of planters, was rapidly taken advantage of by the slaves.

The peak of desertion and rural banditry in Matanzas took place in late 1876 and early 1877. Captain General Joaquín Jovellar issued a decree in January 1877 authorizing all white males to "scour the woods round about their several dwellings, in order to capture all black and Mongolian runaways, whether slaves or temporarily bound to servitude." Rewards of 102 pesos in gold would be paid for every slave and 34 pesos in gold for every Chinese captured.[8] Britain's Consul General Cowper visited the Colón district in early 1877 to survey the situation, and he reported that many planters were paying bribes to rebels to ensure that their plantations would not be burned. He also reported that much destruction was clearly being carried out by local runaways who were quite familiar with the districts in which they operated. Yet, he voiced doubts about whether they were directly linked with the political goals of the rebellion, for

> how far these bandits are really connected with the insurrection is unknown. . . . [T]hey burn and murder and ravish in such small parties that they baffle the troops sent against them. They are undoubtedly composed in a great measure of runaway negro slaves and contracted Chinamen, and it is certain that all incendiarism is done by this class of men, their knowledge of the localities enabling them to do so with impunity, one man being sufficient to burn an estate.[9]

Whether inspired by a sympathy for separatism or by a desire to determine their own destinies, the slaves of rural Matanzas in the final stages of the Ten Years' War had changed in ways that heralded the end of absolute control by the planters. Restlessness, rebelliousness, and impatience with the abolition process made slaves more assertive and more willing to resist actively the perpetuation of servitude. The proliferation of rural banditry that coincided with the rebel invasion of Matanzas was the most blatant manifestation of this new spirit of resistance.

After the arrival in Cuba of General Arsenio Martínez Campo in late 1876, the Spanish counterinsurgency effort was revitalized. Matanzas was pacified, rebel forces were effectively driven toward the east, and rural banditry ceased because of a well-organized military effort to pacify the countryside. The sugar economy had experienced a short-term threat to its well-being; but, in retrospect, the rebel invasion did little to damage the productive infrastructure of the province. There was not one recorded attack on the railways, those vital transportation links which sustained sugar and military troop movements alike. With some exceptions, damage to milling complexes was minimal.

Yet, a great impression had surely been left among the province's slaves. In their efforts to inspire revolt, rebels directed appeals to slaves to abandon plantations, join the rebellion, and thus become free through their own actions. This brush with social and political revolution must have imbued a certain spirit of resistance in the barracones of the great mills. There was little patience to be found when peace was reestablished. Slaves were anxious to determine their own destinies and were restless over the terms of the 1880 abolition law that established the *patronato*—little more than the continuation of slavery by other means. Abandonment of plantations became epidemic in the early 1880s; in a sense, slaves were acting on the exhortations of the rebel army made several years earlier.

Although sugar-sector income was scarcely affected by the rebellion, the specter of potential long-term political instability led some planters to place their capital in the relative security of U.S. government bonds. The inflationary surge taking place in Cuba, where the Banco Español was printing large quantities of paper currency to finance the counterinsurgency effort, was also no doubt a motivation to export capital. This was effected by purchasing U.S. government bonds, which paid 6 percent annual interest rates in the early 1870s. The records of Moses Taylor & Company of New York reveal the regular purchase of these bonds by Matanzas planters from the early 1870s on. In November and December of 1870, for example, José Baró invested 259,000 *dollars* in such notes. Among other planters purchasing bonds in the United States were the Conde de Peñalver, the Montalvos, the Zayas family, and Tomás Terry of Cienfuegos.[10] In all likelihood planters with commercial connections in Europe probably exported their capital to these more stable areas of investment, although it should be noted that systematic data in this regard are lacking.

The political disposition of Matanzas planters toward the rebellion in the east was almost unanimously pro-Spanish. Nonetheless, many planters were sympathetic to some of the reformist goals of the revolution. Indeed, among the ranks of the Círculo Reformista, which addressed the issue of slavery in the mid-1860s, many Matanzas planters were to be found.[11] But reformism was one thing and a rebellion threatening huge economic assets was quite another. Within two weeks of the Grito de Yara of October 10, 1868, leading Matanzas planters, including Julián Zulueta and Miguel Aldama, appealed to Captain General Francisco Lersundi to permit open public debate on issues facing Cuba, as a means of defusing the rebellion and promoting reform. They were rebuffed, and the planter class was effectively polarized. Among the most prominent ingenio owners backing the rebellion was Aldama, who fled to New York and whose family's mills were seized by the colonial government in accord with a policy of embargo placed on the assets of all planters sympathizing with the rebels.[12] Zulueta, of course, backed colonialism, as did most of the other large-scale mill owners throughout rural Matanzas.

Although the war itself did little to disrupt economic trends and tendencies that had been developing in Matanzas province throughout most of the nineteenth century, in its aftermath slavery was abolished. The abolition process was complex, and its causes were multifaceted. The British campaign to end the trata was finally successful by the late 1860s, but even then enough working-age slaves inhabited Cuba to prolong the institution indefinitely if natural reproduction were encouraged. Just as the abolition of the slave trade to the United States in 1808 did little to bring about the end of slavery, likewise the termination of the Cuban slave trade did not mean a coup de grace to the institution itself.

It will be argued later that, from a strictly economic point of view, there was no compelling reason to turn to free wage labor in the 1860s or 1870s. Despite assertions to the contrary, slavery did not collapse because of its lack of economic viability or internal contradictions. Nor were the vast majority of planters swayed by ideological arguments revolving around morality or the rights of man. Investments in slaves were enormous, and economic interests superseded liberal pretensions, even if they were in vogue.

The rebellion, however, changed the parameters of debate on the slavery question. Spain could not afford the luxury of a prolonged discussion after 1868; nor, for that matter, could the planters of the major sugar-producing regions of western Cuba after the invasions of 1875 and 1876. The insurrection, above all, raised the political stakes of maintaining slave labor in Cuba: so long as slavery persisted, a substantial sector of Cuban society served as potential raw recruits for the rebels. Appeals to slaves to desert their plantations and torch the cane fields were a central aspect of the invasions of Las Villas and Matanzas in 1875 and 1876. The ensuing destruction was costly in Sagua la Grande, Trinidad, Cienfuegos and, to a much lesser extent, in the southern regions of Matanzas province. In antislavery, elite groups leading the rebellion also had an issue that garnered a great deal of international support, since by the late 1870s Brazil and Cuba were the only slaveholding societies remaining in the Americas. European powers led by Great Britain and France had long since officially condemned slavery and the slave trade, and the Civil War had abolished servitude in the United States.

Planters were appalled by the rebellion's appeal to their dotaciones whenever rebel armies drew close, and the specter of the Haitian revolution was once again raised in rural Matanzas. Rafael Torices wrote with alarm that the rebellion was in reality a race war, feasting on the discontent of slaves who wanted nothing less than to create "another Santo Domingo," the recurring nightmare of planters throughout Cuba.[13] If Spanish officials arrived at the conclusion that slavery had to be abolished so that colonialism in Cuba could survive, Matanzas planters gradually accepted the inevitable demise of slavery as the price of their own economic survival. The state, and the planters underwriting Spanish colonialism, had to defuse the appeal of rebellion to such a substantial sector of Cuban society. Although there were disputes and struggles within the general acceptance of abolition's inevitability, there is no question that the major impact of the rebellion was to raise the issue of slavery in graphic rather than abstract terms for the elite groups influencing political decisions.

The Ten Years' War transformed the slaves of rural Cuba from objects of policy and legal codes to active participants in the colonial political arena.

Those joining the insurrection, or who fled plantations for banditry and maroonage, in a sense forced the colonial government's hand. For if their fury were unleashed en masse, the great slave population of rural Cuba would do more than sweep away Spanish colonialism.

Abolition was, no doubt, the single most important outcome of the war, and its impact would be devastating to the planters—who, by and large, were unaware of their own vulnerability. There was no orderly transition to free labor in the aftermath of emancipation, although the attempt was certainly made through a variety of institutional mechanisms. Most of the great families who constructed the plantation economy of rural Matanzas were swept away in the 1880s and 1890s, in part because of the abolition of slavery. In a sense, this was the most important impact of the war. Though indirectly, and not as the result of fighting or destruction, the war affected a broad cross section of the social order, from the barracones to the great houses of rural Matanzas.

CHAPTER 12

Slavery

Between 1837 and 1878 slavery reached the zenith of its socioeconomic importance in Cuba. The sugar economy was constructed on the foundation of slave labor, and this fundamental aspect of rural life continued through the end of the Ten Years' War. Yet, despite its centrality to the Cuban economic system, slavery began to unravel for a variety of reasons in the 1860s. The slave trade was the first casualty. Abolitionism and the end of the U.S. Civil War in 1865 resulted in increased pressure upon Spain—under constant assault from Great Britain since the early nineteenth century—to enforce the theoretical ban on the trata to Cuba and to begin rigorous international cooperation to end slaving in the Caribbean.[1] The Cuban trade, which had crested in the late 1850s, was effectively curbed within a decade.

Although the end of the slave trade did not herald the demise of slavery itself, the revolutionary upheaval of October 1868 in eastern Cuba did hasten the beginning of the legal abolition process. The insurrection for Cuban independence was not definitively abolitionist until 1871, but from its onset the rebellion's leaders focused on slavery as an issue that was part and parcel of the colonial problem addressed by the uprising. Spain's inability to contain the revolt forced colonial authorities to act on the issue of servitude. For fear of rebels in Oriente and Camagüey was not nearly so pervasive as the terror inspired by the specter of a massive slave uprising.

Colonial officials in Madrid and Havana recognized that the island's slave population constituted the raw recruits for rebellion, and it was necessary to answer the revolution's abolitionist declarations. The Moret Law of 1870 stole the rebellion's antislavery thunder, for it initiated the process of emancipation by declaring that all offspring born of slave women after 1868 would henceforth be free, and that all slaves reaching age sixty would also become free men and women.[2]

The final abolition law was not promulgated until 1880, and emancipation was not consummated until 1886. Abolition was a gradual process, and slavery was dismantled slowly in Cuba throughout the 1870s.[3] But the erosion of slavery was not paralleled by the step-by-step substitution of new labor alternatives for sugar planters, despite their persistent and sometimes frantic efforts. Above all, it should be emphasized that dependence on slaves as the core labor force on nearly all Matanzas plantations continued through the 1870s. Slave labor supported the sugar economy, yet it was slowly being eradicated even if new sources of labor were not emerging at the same pace as slavery's demise. There may have been a gradual process to slavery's legal abolition, but the transition to new forms of labor force organization was far from smooth or orderly.

Planters had an extremely difficult and sometimes impossible time finding alternative labor sources. The inability of plantation owners to substitute free labor for slaves as abolition progressed led to fundamental shifts in economic and social organization. These resulted in the restructuring of the island's sugar industry rather than the methodical substitution of freemen for slaves within existing structures of production. Processing and growing cane were eventually separated, resulting in a more productive and economically efficient utilization of resources. But this was paralleled by a fundamental reorganization within elite groups. Although production statistics convincingly demonstrate that abolition did not affect the long-term upward curve in Cuban sugar output, social evolution did not follow such a smooth trajectory. The planter class that had prospered in the heyday of slavery was unable to survive emancipation and the difficult transition to new forms of labor exploitation.

Slave Demography

The growth of the Matanzas slave population was closely linked to the curve in the slave trade to Cuba. Trends in slave imports to the island are shown in Figure 12.1. Although periodic fluctuations can be noted, the general movement between 1838 and 1846 was downward, while between 1846 and the late 1850s the tendency was toward higher levels of imports, which crested in 1859. Accordingly, between 1846 and 1857, when reliable slave-census materials are available, Matanzas slaves increased from 78,636 to 104,519, an average yearly growth rate of 2.6 percent.[4] The importance of Matanzas as the principal center of Cuban slavery in the 1850s is apparent, for during the same period the slave population in all other Cuban regions increased at a much lower rate, 0.8 percent annually.

The subsequent decline in the trata to Cuba was followed by a decrease in the slave population, and this was reflected in Matanzas. Matanzas slaves decreased to 102,562 by 1862 (-0.3 percent annually from 1857) to 87,858 in 1871 (-1.7 percent annually from 1862) and 70,390 in 1877 (-3.6 percent annually from 1871). The overall rate of decline between 1862 and 1877 was 2.6 percent yearly, which is considerably lower than the many exaggerated estimates of a 5 percent annual decrease. The decline in the 1870s was closely linked to the abolition process, which precluded the possibility of natural increase by freeing newborns.

It should be noted that the Matanzas province rate of decline was not as

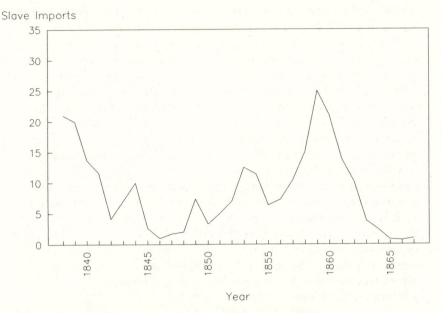

Slave Imports

Year

Figure 12.1. Slave Imports into Cuba, 1838–1867 (in thousands)
SOURCE: David Eltis, "The Nineteenth-Century Transatlantic Slave Trade: An Annual Time Series of Imports into the Americas Broken Down by Region," *Hispanic American Historical Review* 67:1 (1987), pp. 122–123.

rapid as that in the rest of Cuba. Between 1862 and 1871 the Matanzas slave population decreased at a rate of 1.7 percent annually while non-Matanzas slaves declined each year by 3.1 percent. Between 1871 and 1877 Matanzas slaves decreased by 3.6 percent yearly while the slave population in the rest of Cuba dropped at an average yearly rate of 7.1 percent.

Slavery declined at a slower pace in Matanzas compared with other regions in Cuba, and as the abolition process deepened Matanzas slaves accounted for a progressively greater portion of the total Cuban slave population. In 1846 Matanzas slaves constituted 24.3 percent of all Cuban slaves; in 1857, 28 percent; in 1862, 27.8 percent; in 1871, 30.5 percent; and in 1877, 35.3 percent.[5] These data underline the centrality of slave labor to the Matanzas sugar economy, even in the 1870s after abolition had begun, and suggest the probable transfer of slaves from other regions in Cuba to Matanzas during the 1860s and 1870s.

The close linkage of slave-population growth rates to the Cuban slave trade also suggests that Cuban slaves were not experiencing a positive rate of natural increase. It should be stressed that broadly based demographic data on births and deaths have not been located in Cuban archives. The 1862 census materials suggest higher birth rates (26 per thousand) than death rates (22 per thousand) for slaves. But such a slight difference could not have resulted in significant demographic expansion through natural repro-duction. One significant reason is that the slow rate of slave-population in-crease revealed by these data was more than offset by manumissions through coartación and grants of freedom by masters in last wills and tes-taments.

Other circumstantial evidence also supports the conclusion that Matanzas slaves were not reproducing in significant numbers. The overall ratio of male to female slaves hardly changed between 1846 and 1871, remaining almost completely stable at 3:2. This reflected a pattern of slave imports in which males were more numerous than females. Had the population been increasing through natural reproduction, a more equitable sex-distribution pattern among the slave population would have resulted over time.

Province-wide data on the age structure of the slave population also but-tress the argument that any increase in the Matanzas slave population was linked to imports rather than to reproduction. The age pyramid of Matanzas slaves in 1862 reflects the prevalence of working-age slaves. More than 50 percent of all males and females were between the ages of sixteen and forty, and an additional 21 percent were older than forty. Had the slave population been growing through natural increase, a substantially greater portion of all slaves would have fallen into lower age categories. (See Figure 12.2.)

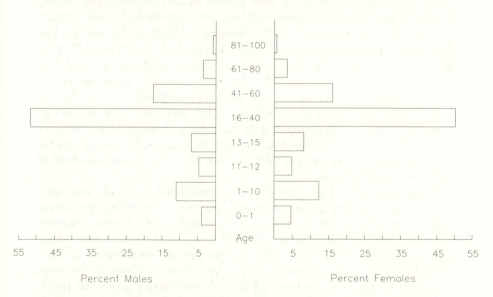

Figure 12.2. Age Pyramid of All Slaves in Matanzas, 1862
SOURCE: Cuba, Centro de Estadística, *Noticias estadísticas de la isla de Cuba en 1862* (Havana: Imp. del Gobierno, Capitanía General y Real Hacienda, 1864).

Other types of fragmentary data support the same conclusions. The 1854 plantation records of Ingenio San Juan, located in Sabanilla, are most dramatic. The San Juan estate was owned by Ángel Zapatín, who maintained his principal residence in Havana. Ingenio San Juan was inhabited by 700 slaves, of whom 503 were African-born and the remainder were creoles. Among the African slaves there were 176 Lucumís, 160 Gangás, 82 Carabalís, and 64 Congos. The mean age of all slaves on the plantation was 36.1 years (39 for males and 32.1 for females). More than 70 percent of the total slave population were above the age of thirty-five. No African slave was younger than thirty, and 90 percent of all Africans were between the ages of thirty-six and fifty, suggesting that there were few purchases of Africans in the years prior to 1854. As expected, creole slaves were much younger, having a mean age of 15.9 years. There are no data on births and deaths, but it should be stressed that as the African population was aging it was not replacing itself through natural reproduction. These data are depicted in Figures 12.3 through 12.5.

Demographic data from another Matanzas ingenio, Nuestra Señora de la Paz, illustrate the continued aging of the Matanzas slave population and reinforce the general conclusion that reproduction could not possibly have maintained labor force levels in the 1850s and 1860s. This estate, located in Guamacaro, was owned by María Eugenia Álvarez de Marrill. It extended for 42 caballerías, 27 of which were planted in cane in 1867. The milling complex was semi-mechanized, with two Jamaican trains but no vacuum evaporators or centrifuges. In 1867 Nuestra Señora de la Paz was worked by an aging population of 197 slaves: 123 males and 74 females; 121 Africans and 76 creoles. The mean age of all slaves was 38.8 years, and 75.6 percent of the dotación were older than thirty-six. The mean age of the female slaves was 41.2 years, which implies that reproductive possibilities were limited, since birth rates must have been exceedingly low in this age category. Without supplementing its labor force through the purchase of recent African imports, this estate's years as a slave-labor-based ingenio were numbered. (See Figures 12.6 through 12.8 for the age structure of slaves on this plantation.)

The priority on both the plantations just considered was clearly the maintenance of slave populations composed primarily of working-age slaves. Data on fertility and birth rates are not available, and it is also unknown whether younger creoles were marketed in order to reduce maintenance costs for unproductive slaves. Without the constant importation of Africans, however, it was impossible to replace prime-age slaves in the short run, and the apparent low levels of natural reproduction meant the inevitable secular decline of slave populations after the trata was curbed. Data from the Cárdenas partido of Guanajayabo, an intensive sugar-producing region, clearly indicate this. There were 31 ingenios located there in 1862,

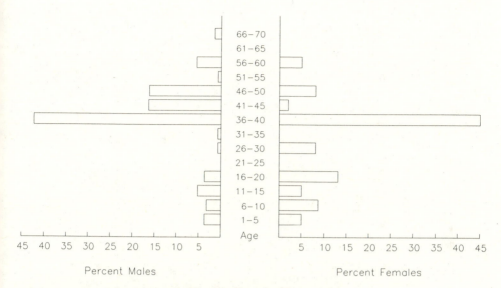

Figure 12.3. Age Pyramid of All Slaves on Ingenio San Juan, 1854
SOURCE: AHPM, Gobierno Provincial, Esclavos, leg. 6 (no exp. no.).

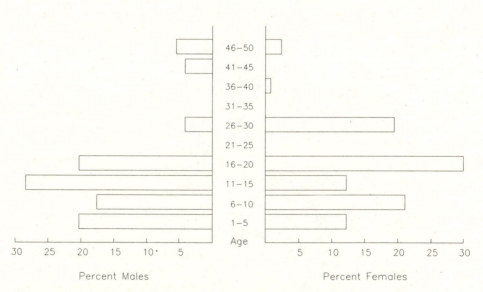

Figure 12.4. Age Pyramid of Creole Slaves on Ingenio San Juan, 1854
SOURCE: AHPM, Gobierno Provincial, Esclavos, leg. 6 (no exp. no.).

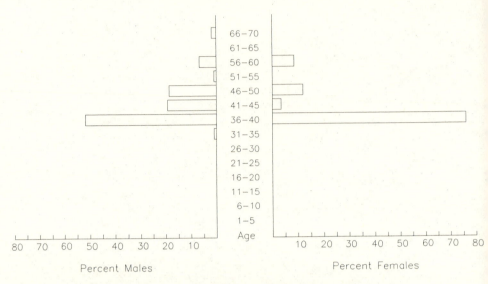

Figure 12.5. Age Pyramid of African Slaves on Ingenio San Juan, 1854
SOURCE: AHPM, Gobierno Provincial, Esclavos, leg. 6 (no exp. no.).

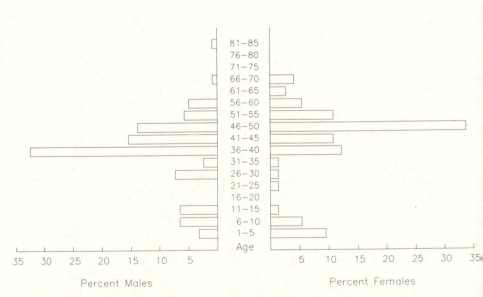

Figure 12.6. Age Pyramid of All Slaves on Ingenio Nuestra Señora de la Paz, 1867
SOURCE: AHPM, Gobierno Provincial, Ingenios, leg. 3, no. 40.

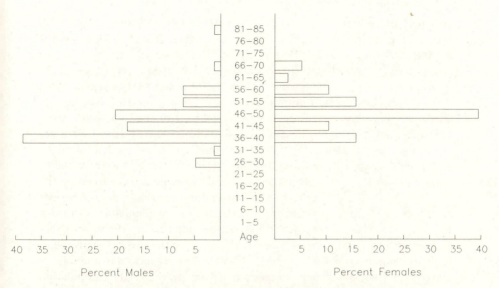

Figure 12.7. Age Pyramid of African Slaves on Ingenio Nuestra Señora de la Paz, 1867

SOURCE: AHPM, Gobierno Provincial, Ingenios, leg. 3, no. 40.

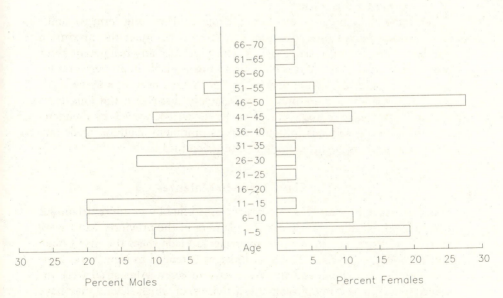

Figure 12.8. Age Pyramid of Creole Slaves on Ingenio Nuestra Señora de la Paz, 1867

SOURCE: AHPM, Gobierno Provincial, Ingenios, leg. 3, no. 40.

and the partido had a slave population of 4,943 men and women. But with the curbing of the slave trade and the emancipation law of 1870, there was a precipitous decline to 2,107 slaves by 1871.[6]

The demographic characteristics of Guanajayabo's slave population in the final decade of Cuban slavery are interesting for a number of reasons. First, a more equitable sex-distribution pattern was evident, since 43.6 percent of all slaves were females and roughly three-quarters of all slave women were younger than thirty. More than 40 percent of all female slaves were between the ages of fifteen and thirty, when fertility rates are generally highest. Second, with the drastic decline in African imports by the early 1860s, aging African slaves had begun to die off, or were nominally freed by the Moret Law, and thus the African-born component of slave dotaciones declined. In 1871 three-quarters of Guanajayabo's slave population were Cuban-born, and this meant a generally younger population. The mean age of Guanajayabo's slaves was 22.4 years, in sharp contrast with the profile of the two plantations discussed above. These combined factors resulted in an age pyramid which strongly suggests that Guanajayabo's slave population was reproducing naturally. Whether this was the result of better treatment or of the encouragement of reproduction is unknown. Yet, it should be stressed that when the importation of prime-age Africans declined and slave populations were demographically undisturbed by new arrivals, the possibility of natural patterns of reproduction is apparent.[7] Figures 12.9 through 12.11 summarize these data.

Yet, most plantations were either oblivious to these long-term possibilities or simply acted on short-term concerns to maintain the maximum number of economically active slaves. This precluded any real potential for reproduction. So long as African imports were available in prime-working-age groups, natural increase does not seem to have been encouraged. Although plantation owners may have belatedly discovered the long-term possibilities of slave reproduction after the slave trade waned, by then survival of slavery itself was in doubt and its imminent abolition made any concerted attempts at encouraging reproduction futile.

The Slave Trade to Matanzas

The slave trade to Matanzas was largely controlled by immigrant families who were the leading merchants and planters in the province. Most were based in Havana, although their investments made them the first Cuban multinational enterprises. Financial linkages extended to New York, London, Seville, Barcelona, and the West African coast. Almost all were involved in a diverse array of economic activities, of which slaving may have been the most lucrative. Investments in railroads, banks, insurance companies, sugar estates, shipping, import-export firms, and later the legal trade

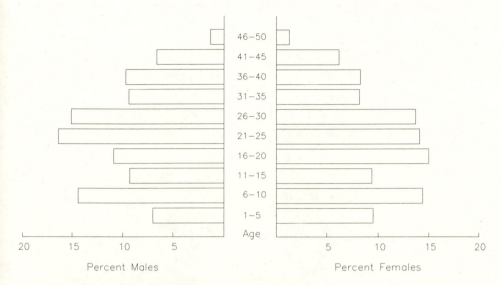

Figure 12.9. Age Pyramid of All Slaves in Guanajayabo, 1871
SOURCE: AHPM, Gobierno Provincial, provisional leg. 60, exp. 1731.

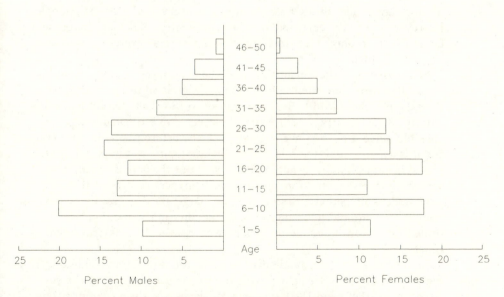

Figure 12.10. Age Pyramid of Creole Slaves in Guanajayabo, 1871
SOURCE: AHPM, Gobierno Provincial, provisional leg. 60, exp. 1731.

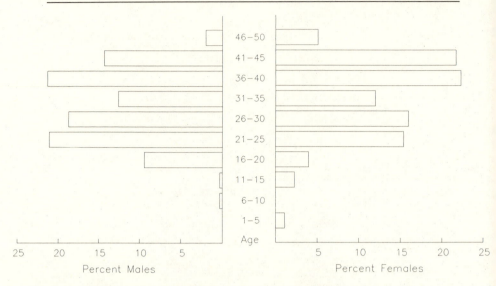

Figure 12.11. Age Pyramid of African Slaves in Guanajayabo, 1871
SOURCE: AHPM, Gobierno Provincial, provincial leg. 60, exp. 1731.

in Chinese contract labor were common among the major importers of slaves to Matanzas sugar estates. Julián Zulueta, long recognized as Cuba's leading slave trader in the mid-nineteenth century, is the classic example. However, it should be noted that the Torrientes, Aldamas, Barós, and Drakes—all leading Matanzas merchants/planters—were in the same league as Zulueta.

Many aspects of the Cuban slave trade have been revealed by recent historical literature, but often information is generalized rather than specific. For example, the role of U.S. shipping prior to 1862 has been recognized as critical. Most recently, North American slavers are estimated to have provided 90 percent of the slave shipping to Cuba before the U.S. Civil War, and it is apparent that the role of U.S. finance capital was important in the 1850s, if not crucial in sustaining the trata.[8] But the details remain vague, and the impression that foreign firms and shippers controlled the Cuban slave trade is altogether misleading. By and large, the organization of slave-trading expeditions, financing, disembarkation, and marketing was controlled by Cuban-based family groups who reaped the principal financial benefits.[9]

Accommodations with and adaptations to the fluctuating conditions of the slave trade were frequent. With the constant expansion of the sugar sector in the 1840s and 1850s, demand for slaves was always rather strong. However, efforts at enforcing the official ban on slaving shifted according to the attitudes of particular colonial governors with respect to enforcing the treaties of 1817 and 1835, and according to the intensity of Spanish and British patrols off the Cuban coast. Slavers had to adapt by changing disembarkation sites and raising the level of bribes to local officials.

In the 1840s and early 1850s the major points of slave smuggling in Matanzas were all located on the north coast. Five areas constituted rendezvous spots for ships arriving from the African coast and importers waiting to conduct bozales to prearranged places from which they would be distributed to purchasers. Two of these were to the west of the bay: one at Puerto Escondido and the other located about a mile to the east at Bacunayagua. Few people lived along the rocky coast between these two points, and small embarcaderos were located at the mouths of the narrow rivers used to move slave cargoes inland in flat lanchas. The populated Yumurí Valley was skirted, and slaves landing in this region were distributed in the rich plantation zones of Aguacate, Ceiba Mocha, and areas farther south.

Three principal points were located to the east of Matanzas Bay. The most distant was in the Sierra Morena region of Sagua la Grande, far to the east and an area of ingenio development by many Matanzas planters. This was an ideal zone for smuggling. There are literally hundreds of small keys just off the coast that afford natural protection, and the coastline is generally rocky and inhospitable. Few people lived in this remote region, which was not connected by road to Cárdenas or Matanzas in the 1840s and 1850s. However, there were roads to the Colón region through sparsely populated areas, thus permitting large numbers of newly arrived slaves to be moved to Colón's sugar plantations with little notice.

In the bay area itself the most common point of disembarkation was at the mouth of the Río Camarioca, which facilitated rapid transportation inland since the river is navigable for some seven miles to the south. The Camarioca River reaches the rich, cane-growing Cárdenas partido of Guamacaro, where many slave cargoes were marketed to plantations. The other distribution point required much daring, coordination, and probably hefty bribes. This was on the eastern shore of the bay itself, at the mouth of the Canimar River, which was the oldest inland trading route in Matanzas. The river was navigable for about five miles to the old embarcadero (Tumbadero), which had been neglected after the advent of railway lines. But it remained an important distribution point for slave smugglers, precisely because of its official neglect.[10]

These locations were used by Matanzas slavers through the end of the trata. In the late 1850s, however, expeditions were increasingly routed through the remote and sometimes treacherous Ciénaga de Zapata, which borders the south coast of Cuba. Noriega, Olmo y Cía., the Havana merchant house that established La Compañía Territorial Cubana, operated a major slave-smuggling operation using the Zapata swamp as a receiving point for recently arrived slaves. As the slave trade intensified after 1855, local authorities were deluged with circulars from Havana urging them to enforce the laws that prohibited slaving and to report suspected landings. In April 1856 Matanzas authorities received an order from Havana requesting information on those responsible for the upsurge in reported disembarkations along the coast of the Ciénaga de Zapata. Although there is no evidence that local officials complied, in July 1857 a communiqué was received from Havana detailing aspects of Noriega and Olmo's operation.

The company dispatched a number of their slaves, under the guise of runaways, to the Ciénaga de Zapata in order to construct *ranchas* and *barracas* to receive shipments of slaves from the African coast. There were several locations where slaves could be temporarily quartered and fed before being sold and shipped to plantations. It is also evident that prospective purchasers could visit these transshipment centers to inspect newly arrived bozales. If they were caught, the slaves in charge of the operation were to claim they were cimarrones from La Compañía Territorial's plantations.[11]

Subsequently, a small contingent of 33 Africans was seized by authorities on Ingenio Susana. They included 28 males with an average age of eighteen years and an average height of 57.3 inches (1.457 meters). The 5 females in this group averaged fifteen years in age and 55.4 inches (1.407 meters) in height.[12] The discovery of the Zapata swamp operation and the seizure just noted did not deter Noriega and Olmo from further slaving. In June 1859 Havana authorities issued a notice of a slave disembarkation under the firm's direction at Puerto Escondido. The slaves were transported overland at 4:00 A.M. to Ingenio Santa Cruz and were later distributed to various plantations in the immediate zone.[13]

Another prominent Matanzas merchant/planter involved in slaving via the Zapata swamp was Cosme de la Torriente, patriarch of the leading merchant family in the city of Matanzas. His Ingenio Cantabria was contiguous to the swamp, which functioned as a convenient conduit for supplying both the estate and neighboring plantations. In November 1864 colonial authorities managed to capture one of Torriente's employees, José González, who confessed to participation in a plan to smuggle slaves. González was sent by Torriente to meet a contingent of 600 slaves who were scheduled to disembark from the brigantine *Flora*, captained by Ramón Aguizne and piloted by Salvador de Pozas y Cueta. In Batabanó, on November 19, 1864, González met with four men led by Andrés Miró, a Catalán residing in Havana. Along with the slaves, 4 trunks filled with shotguns, 36 pistols, 36 muskets, and 36 dozen rounds of ammunition were to be transported overland, all escorted by an armed contingent.[14]

Bribery was the key to maintaining high levels of slave imports in the late 1850s. Havana authorities may have given the appearance of trying to curb slaving, by issuing regular circulars exhorting local officials to more vigilance, but these were largely designed to placate British antislaving officials stationed in Havana and patrols cruising the Caribbean. Slavery was the foundation on which the sugar economy rested, and plantation dotaciones could be maintained only by continuing imports. It would have been relatively easy for authorities to station permanent garrisons in places of repeated landings. This was never done, however, and such obvious and well-known locations such as the mouths of the Canimar and Camarioca rivers continued as key disembarkation points for slave smugglers till the end of the trata. Most local officials were in collusion with the wealthy and powerful Matanzas merchants/planters who ran the key slaving operations.[15] All these men were well known to Havana officials.[16]

Even if apprehended, slave traders rarely suffered severe consequences, nor did they curb their activities. The case of Zulueta and the Governor of Colón has already been discussed. Colonial officials (and this had been the case since the sixteenth century) were too underpaid to refuse the offering of rather large sums of money simply to turn their backs on an activity that maintained the Cuban economy.

This does not mean that British, and sometimes Spanish, efforts at seizing slave ships and their cargoes was nonexistent or unsuccessful. At least 107 slave ships were seized on the Cuban coast between 1824 and 1866, with a total of 26,024 Africans on board.[17] This represented approximately 5.7 percent of the total number of slaves successfully landed between these years, according to the most recent estimates.[18] A yearly breakdown of seizures is provided in Table 12.1.

Africans seized by authorities were theoretically to be freed under the terms of the 1817 and 1835 treaties banning the slave trade to Cuba. They were classified as "emancipados," but absurdly their fate was the responsibility of Spanish colonial officials.[19] In most cases, they were entrusted to planters who were obliged to enter into contracts guaranteeing maintenance and wages. Matanzas planters were among those to whom emancipados were most frequently assigned; and, once on plantations, these Africans were treated exactly as ordinary slaves.[20] Thus, even if Africans were seized upon disembarking on the Cuban coast, they still became part of the sugar plantation labor force and their fate was hardly different from that of their legally enslaved brethren.

Price Trends on the Matanzas Slave Market

The price structure of the Matanzas slave market fluctuated considerably between 1840 and the mid-1870s. Slave prices for both males and females exhibited marked downward trends in the first half of the 1840s. Average prices for males declined 19.5 percent between 1840 and 1846 (from 328 to 264 pesos), while average prices for females fell 29.4 percent (from 316 to 223 pesos).[21] This decline was in all likelihood linked to the surge in African

Table 12.1. Seizures of Africans on the Cuban Coast, 1824–1866

Year	No. Ships	No. Slaves
1824	1	150
1826	6	1,131
1828	2	619
1829	4	853
1830	2	293
1832	3	976
1833	1	490
1834	3	1,091
1835	8	2,056
1836	4	1,216
1841	1	411
1842	8	706
1843	1	85
1846	1	10
1847	1	134
1848	1	130
1849	2	257
1851	1	402
1852	1	25
1853	4	477
1854	11	2,684
1855	4	234
1856	1	49
1857	10	1,672
1858	4	1,663
1859	1	438
1860	6	2,387
1861	5	1,175
1862	1	281
1863	4	2,018
1864	3	1,493
1865	1	140
1866	1	278
TOTAL	107	26,024

SOURCE: AHN, Ultramar, Cuba, Esclavitud, leg. 3549, exp. 181.

imports to Cuba during the 1830s that saturated the Cuban slave market, thus exerting downward pressure on prices. These price declines were also the probable cause for the downturn in imports during the first half of the 1840s.

Price differentials between males and females indicate no discernible trend before 1846. Females sold at 96 percent of male prices in 1840 and 84 percent in 1846. Yet, in 1843 females were priced at 111 percent of the value of males. From 1846 to 1854, average prices for male slaves recovered (+30.3 percent) and slightly surpassed 1840 levels (328 pesos in 1840, 344 pesos in 1854). However, price differentials between males and females widened considerably. Females were sold at 65 percent of the average price for males in 1850 and at 81 percent in 1854. In addition, by 1854 average female prices (278 pesos) remained lower than in 1840 (316 pesos), although there was a 24.7 percent increase from 1846.

Between 1846 and 1854 two factors exerted upward pressure on male slave prices. First was the strong demand for labor accompanying the constant construction of new ingenios and the resulting increase in sugar production.[22] Second was the decrease in slave supplies owing to a downturn in African imports which began in 1841 and continued to 1847. Between 1834 and 1841 an average of 18,713 African slaves landed in Cuba each year. But between 1842 and 1852 annual imports averaged only 4,654 slaves.[23]

Average prices for all slaves increased sharply after 1855—soaring in Matanzas to 581 pesos in 1857, softening to 558 pesos in 1860, and peaking at 600 pesos in 1865. These prices were more than double those before 1850.

In Colón, prices reached their highest levels somewhat later—in 1870, when the average price per slave was 673 pesos—after which there was a gradual decline as the onset of the legal abolition process heralded the end of slavery.[24] The willingness of Colón planters to pay the highest prices of the century for slaves, at the precise historical moment when the end of slavery was no longer in doubt, suggests the continuing economic viability of slave-based sugar production. In 1872 Colón planters continued to purchase slaves actively, and they paid an average price (630 pesos) that was only slightly lower than the 1870 peak.

In Matanzas after 1855, sex differentials in slave prices were insignificant, and no discernible trend can be noted until 1870. In some years, females sold at slightly lower average prices, at 98.2 percent of the price for males in 1860 and at 93 percent in 1870. But in 1857 and 1865 female slaves sold for higher average prices (104 percent) than males.

However, a significant divergence in slave prices by sex took place in Matanzas after the promulgation of the 1870 Moret Law. In 1875 males sold at an average price of 518 pesos; females at 247 pesos, or 47.7 percent of male values. Under pressure to maximize productivity and to extract optimum labor from slave populations in the short term, owing to the imminent end of slavery, planters placed a greater premium on males, more so than at any other time during the nineteenth century. Although not so extreme, the same phenomenon occurred in Colón, where 1875 prices for males averaged 391 pesos and prices for females averaged 344 pesos, 88 percent of male values.

The declining value of female slaves was related to the fact that newborns had no future economic value, since they were theoretically free under the terms of the 1870 Moret Law. Slaveowners may also have viewed females as less viable economically: those bearing children would become a liability because of lost labor time, and the children themselves would have to be supported by masters under the terms of the 1870 law. (See Figures 12.12 and 12.13 for a representation of price differences by sex in Matanzas and Colón.)

What factors supported significantly higher slave prices after 1855, and what does the willingness of plantation owners to purchase slaves at relatively high prices through the early 1870s say about the economics of slave labor? On the supply side, a resurgence of the slave trade from the mid-1850s to the early 1860s meant an abundance of bozales landing in Cuba. According to British consular estimates, imports between 1853 and 1857 averaged 9,600 slaves per year, while from 1858 to 1864 more than 90,000 Africans were brought to Cuba, 13,014 annually.[25] Only after 1863 did a variety of factors combine to limit, then eliminate, the Cuban slave trade.

Not only were slave supplies abundant, but slave prices on the African coast seem to have remained remarkably stable from the 1840s through the mid-1860s, although shipping and operating costs for slave traders seem to have risen considerably. In addition, increased bribes to Spanish colonial officials effectively raised the operating costs for slavers.[26] These factors did not restrict the number of Africans that were shipped to Cuba, nor can they alone explain why Cuban slave prices rose so much in the late 1850s and early 1860s.

Three interacting factors produced the overwhelming demand for slaves that was responsible for pushing prices to the high levels noted above. First was the uncertainty surrounding the future of the slave trade itself. The long and persistent British campaign to force an end to the Cuban trade had traditionally been circumvented by collusion between Spanish colonial officials and Cuban slave traders. An additional obstacle to British efforts was the unwillingness of the United States to permit the search of United States vessels suspected of slave-trade involvement.

However, U.S. policy concerning the Cuban slave trade shifted as the Civil War deepened. Washington began to support British efforts to curb slaving in the Caribbean, and Spain was increasingly pressured to patrol the Cuban coast effectively. The result was a reduction of slave landings by 1865 and the trade's virtual elimination by 1867.[27] Thus, from the beginning of the U.S. Civil War, Cuban planters experienced increasing uncertainty on the critical question of future labor supplies. The planter response was to stock ingenios with large numbers of slaves, thus exerting upward pressure on prices because of increased market demand.

The Cuban slave market was also transformed after 1855 by a second factor, the sharp upward trend in sugar prices on the international market and the maintenance of those higher prices through the early 1870s (see

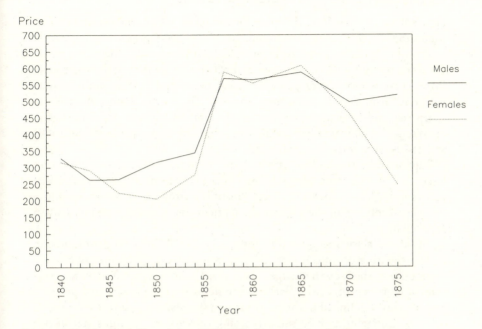

Figure 12.12. Matanzas Slave Sales, 1840–1875: Average Prices by Sex (in pesos)
SOURCES: See note 21, above.

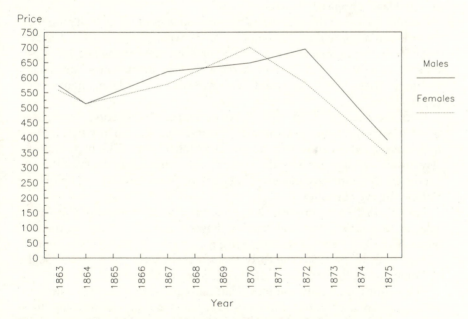

Figure 12.13. Colón Slave Sales, 1863–1875: Average Prices by Sex (in pesos)
SOURCES: See note 21, above.

Figure 9.1). In May 1855 the price for top-grade white sugar in the port of Matanzas was 4.63 cents per pound. By March 1856 prices were quoted at 6.88 cents per pound (+ 48.6 percent), and by August 1857 Matanzas planters were receiving 12 cents per pound for top-grade (*florete*) white sugar. Prices retreated to an average of 6.47 cents per pound in 1858, but remained at 6 cents or more per pound through 1870. Thus, even though there was a sharp rise and subsequent decline in sugar prices between 1855 and 1857, the overall trend from 1855 to 1873 was upward. Sugar prices in the 1860s and 1870s were considerably higher than in the 1840s.[28]

Supported by the highest prices of the century, Cuban sugar production increased 51.8 percent between 1855 and 1870, from 462,960 to 702,974 metric tons.[29] The growth in income resulting from price rises and productive expansion meant that higher slave prices could be supported by Cuban sugar planters.[30]

The third factor was related to the mechanics of Cuban sugar expansion during the nineteenth century. Despite innovative, capital-intensive refining methods, the growth of sugar output was heavily dependent on the constant integration of newly planted cane fields into the productive process. In part, this was linked to the need for ever-increasing quantities of cane in order to utilize efficiently the processing capacity of the mills. However, unlike its industrial counterpart, the agricultural phase of sugar production experienced few technological transformations, remaining both land-extensive and labor-intensive through the 1870s.

Despite constant efforts to find alternative sources of labor, including the importation of more than 120,000 Chinese between 1848 and 1874, Cuban sugar production remained as dependent on slave labor in the late 1860s as it had been a century before.[31] To increase sugar production new cane fields had to be planted, and this meant that slave labor had to be maintained or expanded.

With the relatively high sugar prices of the post-1855 period, new mills were constructed, land was cleared and planted, and ingenio owners continued actively purchasing slaves despite the higher cost.[32] The high cost of slave labor was supported by the evident profitability of a dynamically expanding, labor-intensive industry, one that exhibited few signs of contraction on the eve of abolition.

Prior to 1850, African-born slaves accounted for a majority of the slave sales in Matanzas. After mid-century, however, sales of creoles outnumbered Africans by ever-increasing margins, despite the vigor of the transatlantic trade in the 1850s and early 1860s. Creoles were more actively sold in Colón during the 1860s as well. (See Figures 12.14 and 12.15.)

The reasons are hardly complex. Natural reproduction patterns, though not leading to demographic growth, still resulted in a significant creole-to-African ratio by the 1860s.[33] In addition, it is likely that the high price struc-

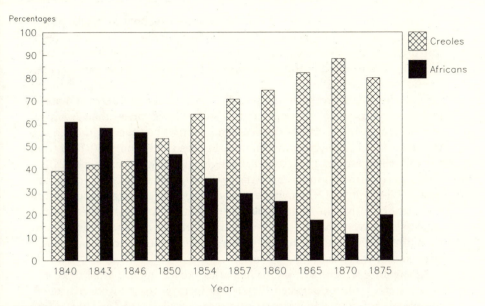

Figure 12.14. Matanzas Slave Sales by Origin, 1840–1875 (selected years in percentages)
SOURCES: See note 21, above.

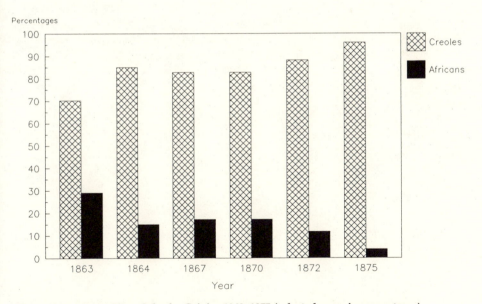

Figure 12.15. Colón Slave Sales by Origin, 1863–1875 (selected years in percentages)
SOURCES: See note 21, above.

ture of the slave market after 1855 induced some slaveholders to take profits on prior investments, especially those who had purchased young creoles at low prices in the 1840s or who owned creole slaves born on their estates. These factors resulted in the abundance of Cuban-born slaves being placed on the market after 1855.[34]

Until the price increases of the post-1855 period, the data seem to indicate that in Matanzas creole slaves generally sold at lower prices than Africans. (see Figure 12.16). This is a distorted impression, however. Although age information is fragmentary in Matanzas between 1840 and 1860, data from the 1830s suggest that it is likely that a high percentage of marketed African slaves were between fifteen and forty years old, the highest- priced age category. (See figures 12.17 and 12.18 for slave prices by age group in the jurisdictions of Matanzas and Colón.) In addition, a greater percentage of creole slaves were in the lowest-valued age group, younger than fifteen. Combined, these factors effectively lowered the average price of creoles relative to that of Africans.[35]

As the price structure of the slave market moved upward after 1855, and as more creole slaves between fifteen and forty years old were marketed, the overall differential in prices by origin narrowed. In 1857 and 1860 there was very little difference in average price between creoles and Africans; and

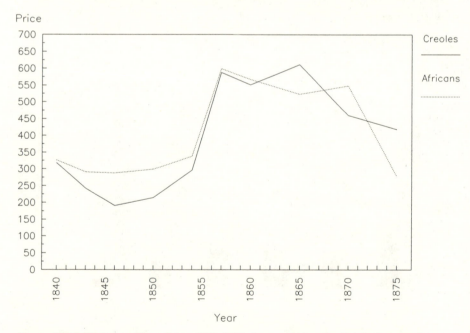

Figure 12.16. Matanzas Slave Sales, 1840–1875: Average Prices by Origin (in pesos)
SOURCES: See note 21, above.

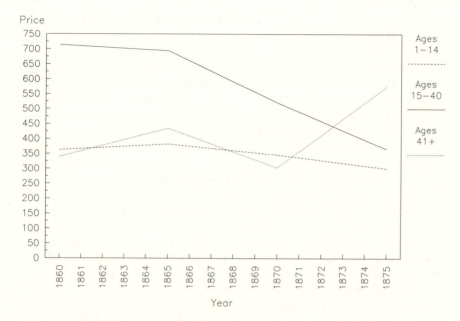

Figure 12.17. Matanzas Slave Sales, 1860–1875: Average Prices by Age Group (in pesos)
Sources: See note 21, above.

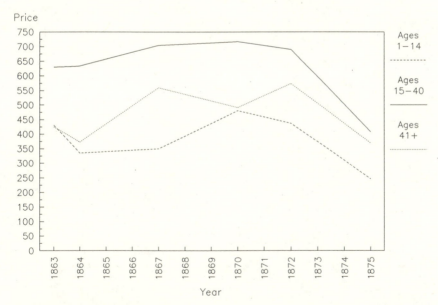

Figure 12.18. Colón Slave Sales, 1863–1875: Average Prices by Age Group (in pesos)
Sources: See note 21, above.

by 1865 Cuban-born slaves not only overwhelmed the Matanzas slave market (83 percent of all sales), but they sold at higher average prices than Africans, 611 versus 523 pesos.

This marked increase in the sale of higher-priced creoles was linked to the changing age structure of the slave population. The offspring of the voluminous African imports of the 1830s and early 1840s were just entering the prime-working-age group in the 1850s and early 1860s. Despite continuing imports, the African-born slave population was generally much older, which meant declining market values. For example, in Guanajayabo, the Cárdenas partido referred to above, the 1871 slave census revealed the mean age of Cuban-born slaves to be 19.3 years, while the African-born slave population had a mean age of 32.2 years.[36]

The data for Colón with respect to slave prices by origin indicate no discernible trend (see Figure 12.19). The higher price structure of the overall slave market in the 1860s and early 1870s is confirmed, but the comparative market values of Africans and creoles are inconsistent over time. In 1863, 1864, and 1870 creoles sold at average higher prices. But in 1867, 1872, and 1875 Africans were more costly, even though most transactions involving creoles consisted of prime-age slaves.

By the mid-1860s, with the waning and collapse of the Cuban slave trade,

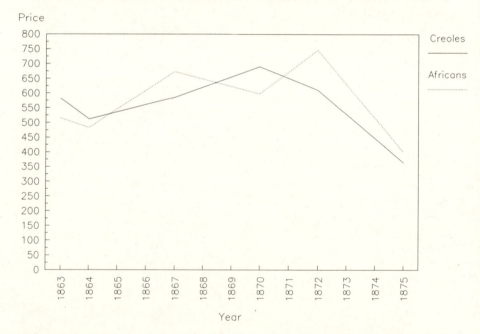

Figure 12.19. Colón Slave Sales, 1863–1875: Average Prices by Origin (in pesos)
SOURCES: See note 21, above.

sales of non-prime-age slaves declined notably. Although the slave market remained surprisingly active in the early 1870s, buyers were principally interested in working-age slaves of either sex. In Matanzas, 1860 data reveal that 39.6 percent of all sales were of prime-age slaves, but in 1865 that figure stood at 66.7 percent; in 1870 it rose to 74.3 percent and in 1875, 80.8 percent. In Colón a similar pattern can be discerned; more than two-thirds of all slave sales after 1863 were of prime-working-age slaves.[37] (See Figures 12.20 and 12.21.)

Prices for prime-age slaves in the 1860s and 1870s peaked at different times in Matanzas and Colón. In Colón, where almost all slaves worked on sugar plantations, average prices for this group reached their apex in 1870 at 717 pesos. In more urbanized Matanzas, where it is likely that a significant portion of marketed slaves were destined for non-sugar-sector occupations, prices for prime-age slaves peaked a decade earlier (in 1860, when they reached 714 pesos). It is also conspicuous that the average price for prime-age slaves in Matanzas had fallen to 521 pesos in 1870, a decline of 27 percent from 1860, and that this price was at 72.7 percent of the average value of Colón's prime-age slaves. The importance of these comparative data is worth stressing. They indicate the persistence of strong demand for working-age slaves in a major Cuban plantation zone (Colón) up to the very beginning of the legal abolition process.

When prime-age slave sales in Colón are disaggregated by sex and national origin, the strong demand for slaves is apparent—even in 1872, when the end of slavery was no longer in doubt. Prime-age creole males sold for an average price of 737 pesos in 1870 and for exactly the same price in 1872. The average price for prime-age African males increased from 638 pesos in 1870 to a peak of 837 pesos in 1872. It should be underlined that in Colón the price for male slaves peaked in 1872, at an average of 694 pesos. Demand for males was so strong in this major sugar-producing zone that prices continued to rise after legal abolition began in 1870. Moreover, it is interesting to note that labor demand also pushed prices higher for slaves forty-one years of age and older, in both Matanzas and Colón, between 1870 and 1872 (see Figures 12.17 and 12.18).

Creole females sold for an average price of 738 pesos in 1870, almost exactly the price for males, but declined to 634 pesos (86 percent of male values) in 1872. African females, like African males, increased in value from 1870 to 1872, from 550 to 700 pesos.

If slave labor was no longer economically viable by the 1860s and 1870s, it is puzzling that Colón's sugar planters would underwrite the highest prices in the history of Cuban slavery for prime-age slaves, even after final abolition was no longer a theoretical debate. In fact, the continuing rise in sugar prices up to 1873 evidently meant that slave-based sugar production

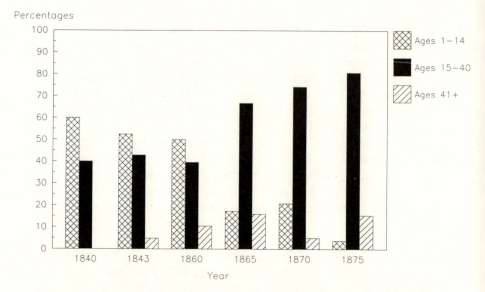

Figure 12.20. Matanzas Slave Sales by Age Group, 1840–1875 (selected years in percentages)
SOURCES: See note 21, above.

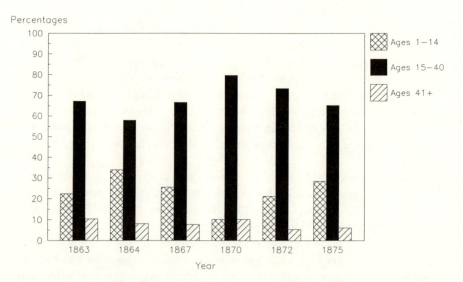

Figure 12.21. Colón Slave Sales by Age Group, 1863–1875 (selected years in percentages)
SOURCES: See note 21, above.

continued to remain viable despite the highest labor-replacement costs of the nineteenth century.

It was only after 1873, when sugar prices declined sharply, that demand for slaves softened and prices plummeted. Inflation, the political uncertainty caused by the Ten Years' War, and the imminence of final abolition were other critical factors. In 1875 the average price of prime-age slaves of both sexes and national origins was 366 pesos in Matanzas (-29.8 percent from 1870) and 408 pesos in Colón (-43.1 percent from 1870).[38] (See Tables 12.2 and 12.3, Figures 12.22 and 12.23.)

Thus, the movement of slave prices in Cuba between 1840 and 1875 can be broken down into two broad periods. During the first, from 1840 to 1855, prices seem to have responded exclusively to fluctuations in the supply of newly arrived Africans. The Cuban slave trade's high level of activity in the late 1830s drove down prices in the 1840s. The contraction of African imports through the early 1850s was followed by a recovery of slave prices. There seems to have been a time lag in the response of the slave market to changes in supply; prices shifted after supply levels had been clearly defined over several years. Since slaves represented the principal source of labor on

Table 12.2. Average Prime-Age Slave Prices in Colón, 1863–1875
(in pesos)

	1863	1864	1867	1870	1872	1875
Creole Males	698	628	714	737	737	440
Creole Females	653	662	692	738	634	380
African Males	557	533	653	638	837	400
African Females	520	—	850	550	700	—

Source: AHPM, PN, Manuel Vega Lavarría, Colón, 1863–1875.
Note: Prime-age slaves are those between fifteen and forty years old.

Table 12.3. Average Prime-Age Slave Prices in Matanzas, 1860–1875
(in pesos)

	1860	1865	1870	1875
Creole Males	775	706	517	547
Creole Females	759	708	499	200
African Males	500	641	677	263
African Females	725	475	500	308

Source: ANC, PN, Matanzas, 1860–1875.
Note: Prime-age slaves are those between fifteen and forty years old.

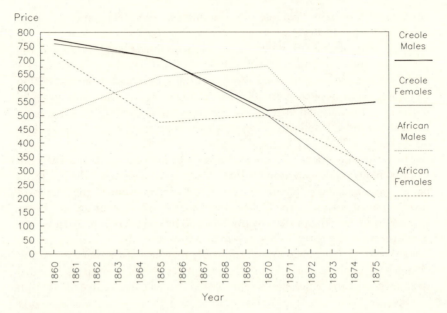

Figure 12.22. Matanzas Slave Sales, 1860–1875: Average Prices by Sex and Origin, Ages 15–40 (in pesos)

SOURCES: See note 21, above.

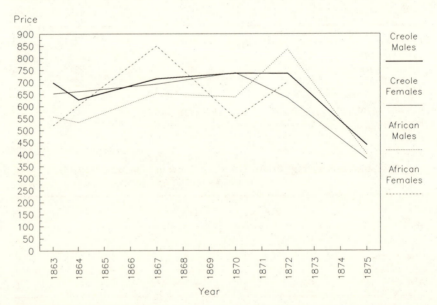

Figure 12.23. Colón Slave Sales, 1863–1875: Average Prices by Sex and Origin, Ages 15–40 (in pesos)

SOURCES: See note 21, above.

almost all sugar plantations, and since Cuban sugar production increased steadily during this period, strong demand for slaves was constant or increasing.

During the second period, from 1855 to 1875, other variables exerted more influence on slave prices than the supply of newly arrived bozales. The most important factor was the rise of sugar prices on the world market. Sugar prices fluctuated wildly between 1855 and 1857, but settled at substantially higher levels in the early 1860s and moved gradually upward between 1865 and 1872. Even though the slave trade reached its highest nineteenth-century level in the late 1850s and early 1860s, slave prices soared on the strength of an intense labor demand linked to rising sugar prices. A new plateau was reached in the early 1860s, and prices for males even increased in the sugar-producing region of Colón during the early 1870s. Other factors included a reduction of African imports after 1862, the effective end of the Cuban slave trade after 1867, and planter uncertainty over future labor supplies because of the specter of abolition.

Sugar price levels played a critical role in sustaining high slave prices, even after the onset of the legal abolition process. Between 1870 and 1872, when sugar prices continued to rise gradually, prices for male slaves increased in Colón, prices for creole males rose in Matanzas, and prices for males older than forty moved upward in both regions. It was only after 1872, when sugar prices dropped, that slave prices declined precipitously.

The strong demand for slave labor in the 1860s and early 1870s, reflected by the high price structure of the Cuban slave market, seems to indicate the continuing viability of slave-based sugar production. Cuban sugar planters were hardly naive, nor did they have any illusions about the long-term future of slavery by the late 1860s, and certainly not after 1870. Yet, they continued to support high slave prices.

Planters apparently acted on the basis of short-term economic considerations, which revolved around maximization of income by producing as much sugar as possible in order to take advantage of high prices on the world market. Construction of new mills, clearing and planting of virgin land, and maintenance of slave labor were all part of this strategy. Although plantation owners attempted to diversify their work forces, dependence on slave labor continued through the mid-1870s.[39]

The Economic Viability
of Slave-Based Sugar Production

From the mid-1840s, planters avidly sought to transform the labor base of Cuban sugar production by diversifying their work forces away from a dependence on slave labor. This was especially true from the late 1860s on, when several factors forebode the end of slavery. African imports had virtually ceased; the specter of large-scale slave desertions was raised by the deepening insurrection in eastern Cuba; and the legal abolition process was initiated in 1870 with Spain's enactment of the Moret Law.

Yet, despite efforts at broadening their labor forces, the planters were largely unsuccessful. Matanzas sugar production remained nearly as dependent on slave labor in the 1870s as it had been in the 1850s or 1860s. In 1877, for example, slaves accounted for more than 70 percent of all workers on ingenios in Matanzas.[40] Thus, while manufacturing and transportation were modernized at considerable cost, traditional methods and forms of labor-force organization stubbornly persisted in the labor-intensive agricultural phase of sugar production.

A series of questions central to modern nineteenth-century Cuban historiography have been generated by this seeming paradox. Did continued planter reliance on slaves make sugar production less profitable and lead directly to the crisis of the 1880s, when manufacturing was centralized and production was structurally divided into its two components, cane production and sugar processing?[41] Was abolition a response to internal contradictions in the industry, having to do with the persistence of slavery in an age of costly technological innovation?[42] Did sugar planters use abolition to reduce labor costs by creating a free labor market that would lead to greater productivity and higher profits?

Although planters sought the diversification of their labor forces, and finally recognized abolition as inevitable, their efforts were not necessarily prompted by the decreasing economic viability of slave labor. Planters may have been reacting to predominantly exogenous factors, such as the externally imposed end of the slave trade and Spain's determination to impose legal abolition. While some progressive planters were opposed to slavery on humanitarian grounds, and while small-scale or inefficient operations may have found it difficult to meet labor needs because of high slave prices in the late 1850s and 1860s, that does not mean that slave-based sugar production was no longer extremely lucrative. Sugar-sector economic variables indicate no compelling need for planters to abandon slavery as a labor system in the 1860s or 1870s. To the contrary, modernization of processing and transportation made slave labor more efficient and higher yielding in terms of income per slave. The economic viability of slave labor was related to two important factors that determined planter income and labor expenses: the price of sugar and the price of slaves. The price structures of both acted to sustain a slave/sugar complex that continued its dynamic expansion through the end of the Ten Years' War.

To examine the economic viability of slave-based sugar production in Matanzas, we shall use the manuscript farm-census returns for the jurisdiction of Colón in 1859, 1865, and 1876; those for Cárdenas in 1867 and 1875; and the province-wide ingenio census of 1877/78.[43] Standard information was recorded in each census. All listed the extension of individual plantations in caballerías, the number of slaves, and the gross income by farm. The Colón census of 1859 also noted the number of rented slaves and Chinese contract laborers on each farm, thus permitting a calculation of the total work force. In addition to the standard data on farm size, slave population, and total income, the 1876 Colón census listed the number of caballerías cultivated in sugarcane. The 1867 and 1875 Cárdenas censuses also added the extent of land planted in cane, and the 1875 census noted the different components of plantation labor forces. The 1877/78 data are the most complete and include all the jurisdictions of Matanzas province: Colón, Cárdenas, Matanzas, Alacranes, and Jovellanos. Plantation workers are disaggregated into different categories; cultivated acreage is indicated; and net income is calculated by estimating the costs of "refacción" contracts, or plantation credit and supply expenses, and deducting them from gross income.[44]

The most important indicator concerning the economic viability of slave labor was the income generated per slave: gross income, or net income when this was available, divided by the total number of workers. Since available data do not permit estimates of the relative income productivity of different types of workers, the calculations presented here examine the total income productivity of all workers. Thus, income per worker, as it is considered here, is equal to income per slave, despite the fact that labor productivity may have differed by category of worker. Unfortunately, there are no documentary materials that permit the measurement of labor productivity by different types of worker.

It was important to determine whether data on gross income were in constant values or in current values reflecting inflation. This is a critical problem because inflation was rampant in the 1870s. The Banco Español of Havana was directed by colonial authorities to print enormous quantities of paper money during the Ten Years' War in order to finance the Spanish military effort to defeat the rebellion.[45] During this period planters and merchants strove to retain fiscal control over their accounts by noting whether transactions used *billetes* (paper money), which was inflated, or gold, which denoted real values. Legal contracts recorded in the notarial protocols of the 1870s usually referred to the two types of currency.

The documentary materials utilized did not indicate whether income values were in paper or gold. However, the data clearly show that gross income figures were *not* listed in inflated paper currency and that they can be used with confidence to trace real income. This was determined by examining the number of producing ingenios and comparing them with gross income. In Colón, for example, total income for all sugar ingenios (125) in 1859 was 7,692,883 pesos. In 1876, when inflation was at its height, total sugar-sector

income (117 mills) was 7,616,361 pesos. The average gross income per plantation had changed only slightly upward, 5.8 percent.

To verify this, sugar prices must be examined as well, since planter income was ultimately determined by the price of sugar on world markets.
The most notable aspect of sugar prices between 1859 and 1878 was their
long-term stability. There were short-term fluctuations, to be sure. However, in 1859 best-grade white sugars were marketed at 7 cents/pound in
Matanzas, while quebrados were sold for 6 cents/pound. In 1876 white sugars brought 7.5 cents/pound, and quebrados were quoted at 6.25 cents/
pound.[46] Thus, income did not fluctuate in any of these years because of
price changes. If inflation were a factor, a radical change in income would
have been forthcoming between 1859 and 1876, and since this did not occur
it is assumed that income data reflected relatively constant prices. The 1877/
78 data for Colón confirm the accuracy of this observation. At 7,863,017
pesos, income was only slightly higher than for 1876, and production varying insignificantly.

The Cárdenas data provide further evidence that inflation was not a factor
in determining income recorded in the documentary sources used here. In
1867, prior to the outbreak of the insurrection, the sugar sector (142 ingenios) generated 8,036,190 pesos. By 1875, after inflation rates had soared,
Cárdenas mills (150) produced less value, 7,053,459 pesos. Again, if inflation were a factor in gross income data, much higher figures would have
been likely. It can be concluded that since local sugar prices were tied to
prices on the international market, they were not quoted in inflated local
currency, which would have reflected an inflationary process specific to
Spain and Cuba because of monetary policies adopted during the Ten Years'
War. It is certain that sugar prices were quoted in gold, which did not reflect
the inflation of paper money.

Since slaves were not the exclusive source of labor on Cuban sugar estates
in the 1860s and 1870s, it was important to determine the ratio of slaves to
total work force. To calculate income per slave, gross or net income must be
divided by the total number of laborers, not by the total number of slaves.
The 1859 data for Colón's plantations noted all categories of workers, and
81 percent were slaves.[47]

However, the 1865 Colón census listed only the number of slaves, and
there was a 1.5 percent (−425) decline from 1859. Since the number of
slaves was relatively constant between 1859 and 1865, and since there were
no factors in the social and economic structure of the region that would have
substantially increased the number of non-slave workers, slaves were estimated to constitute 81 percent of the sugar plantation work force in 1865.
Accordingly, the number of total workers was ascertained by dividing the
number of slaves by .81, and the result was divided into gross income to
determine income per worker.

The 1876 data for Colón also noted only the number of slaves on each estate. By this date, factors had changed decisively to reduce the ratio of slaves to total workers. The slave trade had been curbed, and the legal abolition process had begun in 1870. Slaves on ingenios in Colón declined from 22,534 in 1865 to 14,532 in 1876. In order to determine the total work force on sugar plantations in 1876, the 1877/78 sugar-census data were examined. In that year 69.3 percent of workers on Colón estates were slaves, and it is assumed that approximately the same percentage was valid two years earlier in 1876. Thus, to determine the total Colón work force in 1876, the number of slaves was divided by .69. The result, total workers, was divided into gross income to calculate income per worker.

The Cárdenas data for 1867 also listed slaves only. To calculate total workers, it was assumed that slaves as a percentage of total workers would be similar to the percentage for Colón in 1865, or 81 percent. Cárdenas is contiguous to Colón and shares the same ecological characteristics; moreover, patterns of economic development were similar in the mid-nineteenth century. Boundaries were fixed for administrative purposes, and do not reflect economic differences. Thus, the number of total workers for Cárdenas in 1867 was derived by dividing the number of slaves by .81, and the result was divided into gross income in order to determine income per worker. The 1875 Cárdenas data include all categories of workers, and slaves accounted for 74.9 percent of the total work force on ingenios.

The 1877/78 data for the entire province of Matanzas divide the sugar plantation work force into its components. This allows a reasonably accurate calculation of slaves as a percentage of all workers, and of income per slave. In Colón 69.3 percent of the work force was enslaved; in Cárdenas, 71 percent; in Alacranes, 67.6 percent; in Matanzas, 83.5 percent; in Jovellanos, 68 percent; and in the entire province of Matanzas 72.2 percent.[48]

Several factors suggest that planter efforts to increase efficiency by investing in sophisticated transportation and milling technology were successful. One indicator is the decreasing number of workers used for each cultivated caballería of sugarcane. The 1867 data for Cárdenas reveal that planters utilized 9 workers/caballería of cane. In 1875, this had decreased by a significant 17.8 percent to an average of 7.4 workers/cultivated caballería.

Although no comparable data exist for Colón in the 1850s or 1860s, in 1876 Colón's ingenios utilized 6.7 workers/caballería of cane. The 1877/78 data confirm the accuracy of the data for Cárdenas and Colón in the mid-1870s. Colón's ingenios (116) utilized 6.8 workers/cultivated caballería, and the corresponding figure for the 154 Cárdenas estates was 7 workers/caballería. The entire province of Matanzas (516 ingenios) employed 7 workers/cultivated caballería of cane.

The second variable, gross income per worker, is an even more persuasive indicator of greater efficiency. In Colón each worker on a sugar plantation generated an average gross income of 275.2 pesos in 1859; 309.6 pesos in 1865; 361.6 pesos in 1876; and 368.9 pesos in 1878. This represented a 34 percent increase in income per worker between 1859 and 1878.[49]

Comparable data for Cárdenas confirm the probable accuracy of the Colón data for 1865, 1876, and 1878. Each worker on a Cárdenas sugar plantation produced an average of 349.4 pesos of gross income in 1867; 353.9 pesos in 1875; and 312.6 pesos in 1878. There were differences between the two jurisdictions. The increase in the average income per worker in Colón between 1865 and 1876 was 16.8 percent; in Cárdenas, between 1867 and 1875, the increase was a mere 1.3 percent. In addition, income per worker increased in Colón between 1876 and 1878 by 2 percent, while in Cárdenas it fell 11.7 percent between 1875 and 1878. The precise reasons for these differences are not known. Colón, however, was a more recent area of sugar plantation development, and its soils may therefore have produced higher yields of cane. Still, the comparative similarities in income per worker for both jurisdictions, the data for which were derived from documentary sources generated by authorities who were administratively independent from one another, confirm the probable reliability of these data. (See Tables 12.4 and 12.5.).

In order to arrive at crude estimates of the economic viability of slave labor, slave prices must be compared with the income generated per slave. In 1859 the average income per worker on Colón ingenios was 275.2 pesos. The highest average price for a prime-age slave in 1860 was 775 pesos on the Matanzas slave market. If each worker produced 275.2 pesos in gross income, the labor of a newly purchased slave would pay for him/herself in 2.8 years, minus maintenance and depreciation expenses.

By the fourth zafra, the cost of slave labor would be confined to maintenance and depreciation expenses. The average working life of each slave is unknown, but if we conservatively estimate five years of labor per slave at constant income per worker, slaves in the 1860s would have generated 1.8 times their purchase price in gross income after five harvests.

It is probable that by the 1860s the average number of years of labor per slave was greater than five, although there are no reliable studies that estimate the productive lives of Cuban slaves. However, in the extremely cautious formula offered above, each additional year beyond five translates into greater income over the productive life of an individual slave.

To repeat, the above estimates are extraordinarily conservative. In reality, not only did income per slave increase over time, but the number of years of labor may have been as high as fifteen or twenty.[50] This means that far greater income would have been produced over the life of a slave purchased in 1860 if he/she continued working through 1875, when more than

Table 12.4. Colón Income per Worker by Partido, 1859–1878
(in pesos)

	1859[a]	1865[a]	1876[a]	1878[a]	1878[b]
Jíquimas	336.5	354.1		339.8	129.2
Macuriges	250.1	249.1	301.9	338.6	122.1
Hanábana	104.3	580.1	778.8	422.7	147.8
Macagua	254.2	293.1	348.0	387.0	134.9
Palmillas	227.9	346.9	434.4	395.6	138.4
Town of Colón			288.4	164.6	57.6
TOTAL	275.2	309.6	361.6	368.9	130.3

SOURCES: ANC, ME, leg. 4120, no. M, "Repartos municipales de la jurisdicción de Colón, 1859"; ANC, Gobierno General, leg. 405, no. 19209, "Padrón de fincas rústicas de la jurisdicción de Colón, 1865"; ANC, Gobierno General, leg. 270, no. 13563, "Padrón general de fincas rústicas de este distrito, año de 1875 a 1876"; "Noticias de las fincas azucareras en producción que existían en toda la isla de Cuba al comenzar el presupuesto de 1877–1878," *Revista Económica*, June 7, 1878, pp. 7–24.
[a]Gross income per worker.
[b]Net income per worker.

Table 12.5. Cárdenas Income per Worker by Partido, 1867–1878
(in pesos)

	1867[a]	1875[a]	1878[a]	1878[b]
Camarioca	300.4	317.8	278.5	128.3
Cimarrones	336.9	322.4	337.2	147.4
Guamutas	377.2	414.3	331.8	145.8
Guanajayabo	446.9	386.0	299.9	125.9
Lagunillas	254.5	249.4	202.4	82.0
Town of Cárdenas		258.1		
TOTAL	349.4	353.9	312.6	132.6

SOURCES: ANC, Gobierno General, leg. 945, no. 16724, "Padrón general de la riqueza rústica para regir en los años económicos de 1866 a 1867"; ANC, Gobierno General, leg. 269, no. 13554, "Jurisdicción de Cárdenas. Padrón general de la riqueza rústica de esta ciudad y su jurisdicción formado para los años económicos de 1875 a 1876"; "Noticias de las fincas azucareras en producción que existían en toda la isla de Cuba al comenzar el presupuesto de 1877–1878," *Revista Económica*, June 7, 1878, pp. 7–24.
[a]Gross income per worker.
[b]Net income per worker.

350 pesos were produced by each slave on Colón and Cárdenas sugar plantations.

Even when the average price for a prime-age slave peaked in Colón in 1870, the increased income per slave meant that purchase prices were recouped in a relatively short period of time. It can be estimated that Colón sugar ingenios produced 333.1 pesos/worker in 1870.[51] The most expensive prime-age slaves sold at an average price of 738 pesos in 1870. If we use these data, planters would recover purchase prices in 2.2 years, and after 5 years of labor slaves would have generated more than double their purchase prices. Maintenance costs must be deducted from all years if we are to arrive at accurate estimates of annual income per slave, but each additional year beyond the 2.2-year period translated into greater income over the productive life of a slave.

By 1876, when the cost of slave labor had collapsed because of the imminent end of slavery, each newly purchased slave generated the income to pay for him/herself in 1.1 years. Slaves produced 361.6 pesos/year income, and the most expensive average price for a prime-age slave was 390 pesos.[52] Thus, even in the waning years of Cuban slavery, it seems to have been economically viable in the short term to continue slave purchases.

There is no formula for readily converting the gross income generated per slave into profitability. Sufficient data are not available to estimate accurate rates of return on slave labor over time. For that, a different series of data would be needed: prices, depreciation, and replacement costs for machinery, tools, animals, and slaves; land values and depreciation; maintenance costs of slaves; costs of supplies, warehousing, commission fees, and taxes; and the reproductive rate of the slave population.[53]

A number of factors make it difficult to compare the economic viability of salaried labor on sugar ingenios with that of slave labor. The most important is the average productive work life of slaves. Another is the number of workers needed throughout the year. By the 1860s and 1870s the Cuban sugar harvest was completed in six or seven months on most estates, from December through June. A labor force at full strength was needed during the zafra, but an undetermined number of workers also had to be employed throughout the year on a variety of tasks such as weeding, replanting, clearing new land, repairs on machinery and structures, and stockpiling timber reserves.

In the late 1860s and early 1870s, the standard wage rate for unskilled labor was 25 pesos/month. Additionally, slaves could be hired for 17 pesos/month, but maintenance costs were assumed by the renters, probably raising the labor costs of rented slaves to 25 pesos/month.[54] Accordingly, the cost of one worker for seven months was 175 pesos in the 1860s and 1870s. From the available evidence it does not seem that salaries rose, even though plantation income per worker clearly increased throughout this period.

If we examine the peak year of slave costs in Colón—1870, when the highest average price of a prime-age slave was 738 pesos—a slave would have to labor for 4.2 seven-month harvests in order to make the cost of a free worker over 4.2 seven-month harvests equal to that of a slave. Other unknown factors must be factored into this equation. One such is the cost of slave maintenance, which is impossible to determine precisely. However, these costs were offset in this comparative example by the fact that masters derived twelve months of labor from slaves, not seven. Thus, the estimate of 4.2 years of labor from a slave purchased for 738 pesos as the point of comparable costs for slave versus salaried labor is extremely conservative. Any labor derived by masters beyond the 4.2 seven-month harvests would constitute an economic advantage of slave over free labor.

If the actual twelve months of labor extracted from each slave is substituted for the seven-month harvest, economic calculations change decisively. One year of salaried labor at 25 pesos/month would mean the same cost to planters whose slaves, purchased at 738 pesos, had labored for 2.5 years. After 2.5 years, the economic benefits of slave over salaried labor would begin to accrue.

Only the peak year in slave prices has been considered for the most expensive slaves. Prices for prime-age slaves fluctuated, while salary rates did not, during the 1860s and 1870s. This means that the economic break-even point between slave and free labor was much shorter in those years when slave prices were lower.

This evidence suggests that there was a continuing economic advantage of slave over free labor, even toward the end of Cuban slavery, and that this is why planters were willing to underwrite the comparatively high costs of slave labor even after legal abolition had begun in 1870. In addition, investments in slaves offered other advantages. Reliability was one. There was no guarantee that a free worker would work over the entire course of the seven-month harvest, while most slaves had no alternative. Slaves could also be used as collateral to obtain credit and could generate substantial income if rented. Free labor offered none of these possibilities.

The economic dynamics of slavery have been considered only for average ingenios. When we examine the most productive, capital-intensive mills, those with incomes exceeding 100,000 pesos yearly, and compare them with estates having gross incomes below 100,000 pesos, we find that the economics of slavery was even more favorable in terms of income yield per worker. For example, in 1859 Colón mills with less than 100,000 pesos in gross income produced 235.4 pesos/worker. On the 20 estates that generated more than 100,000 pesos in gross revenues, however, income per worker was 362.8 pesos, or 54.1 percent greater than that for the smaller mills. In 1865 Colón's 26 mills having incomes greater than 100,000 pesos produced 45 percent more income per worker than the smaller mills produced; in 1876, 28.9 percent more; and in 1878, 31.2 percent more.

The Cárdenas data confirm the tendency of larger estates to produce more efficiently and productively in terms of income per worker. In 1867, while Cárdenas mills earning less than 100,000 pesos in gross income produced 291.1 pesos/worker, those ingenios earning gross incomes more than 100,000 pesos produced 430.4 pesos/worker, or 47.9 percent more. The 1875 data are the most telling of all: the 100,000-pesos-plus mills earned 107 percent more in terms of income per worker than smaller mills. These data are summarized in Table 12.6.

This information is striking, for it shows that the utilization of more sophisticated technology at the ingenio, which was the case in all the large-income-earning mills, led to greater levels of economic output per worker. Rather than making slave labor less viable, the exact opposite was true (at least given the prevailing prices for sugar and slaves on local markets in the 1860s and 1870s). The idea that the progressive adoption of advanced transportation and processing technology led to the economic obsolescence of slave labor is not supported by the available data.

Two separate methods have been used to examine the economic viability of slave-based sugar production in Cuba during the 1860s and 1870s. The first was to study the income yields per worker on sugar plantations and to compare these with prevailing slave prices. Between 1859 and 1878 the average income produced by each worker on all sugar estates rose considerably. Even more impressive was the comparatively greater efficiency found on the highest-income-producing plantations (100,000+ in gross annual income). When income per worker is compared to the highest average prices for prime-age slaves, the time frame over which a slave's labor would pay for him/herself was less than five years for average mills, and considerably less than that on the largest plantations.

The second method was to compare the cost of slaves with the price of salaried labor. Irrespective of income per worker, sugar estates had to meet only minimal labor requirements in order to remain in business. The estimate of 25 pesos/month as the prevailing wage for unskilled labor in the 1860s and 1870s is reliable. By comparing this rate with the price of slaves, it has been shown that even when slave prices were at their peak, the cost of slave labor and the cost of free wage labor would have been the identical after two or three years.

Although the average productive work life of a slave on Cuba's sugar plantations is not known, any labor derived beyond three years meant an economic advantage of slave over free wage labor. This was irrespective of income per worker and is based only on a comparison between slave prices and wage rates for unskilled salaried workers.

These data challenge the conclusion that abolition in Cuba resulted from

Table 12.6. Colón and Cárdenas, 1859–1878:
Gross Income per Worker on Mills with More than 100,000 Pesos Gross Income
Compared with Gross Income per Worker on Mills with Less
than 100,000 Pesos Gross Income

| | Colón | | | Cárdenas | | |
Mill Income	No. Ingenios	Income/ Worker	Mill Income	No. Ingenios	Income/ Worker
1859			1867		
Less than 100,000	101	235.4	Less than 100,000	110	291.1
100,000 +	20	362.8	100,000 +	19	430.4
Difference (%)	(+54.1)		Difference (%)	(+47.9)	
1865			1875		
Less than 100,000	91	257.8	Less than 100,000	125	285.2
100,000 +	26	373.8	100,000 +	12	590.3
Difference (%)	(+45.0)		Difference (%)	(+107.0)	
1876					
Less than 100,000	92	322.9			
100,000 +	20	416.2			
Difference (%)	(+28.9)				
1878			1878		
Less than 100,000	52	320.5	Less than 100,000	127	269.4
100,000 +	18	420.4	100,000 +	12	418.0
Difference (%)	(+31.2)		Difference (%)	(+55.2)	

Sources: ANC, ME, leg. 4120, no. M, "Repartos municipales de la jurisdicción de Colón, 1859"; ANC, Gobierno General, leg. 405, no. 19209, "Padrón de fincas rústicas de la jurisdicción de Colón, 1865"; ANC, Gobierno General, leg. 270, no. 13563, "Padrón general de fincas rústicas de este distrito, año de 1875 a 1876"; ANC, Gobierno General, leg. 945, no. 16724, "Padrón general de la riqueza rústica para regir en los años económicos de 1866 a 1867"; ANC, Gobierno General, leg. 269, no. 13554, "Jurisdicción de Cárdenas. Padrón general de la riqueza rústica de esta ciudad y su jurisdicción formado para los años económicos de 1875 a 1876"; "Noticias de las fincas azucareras en producción que existían en toda la isla de Cuba al comenzar el presupuesto de 1877–1878," *Revista Económica*, June 7, 1878, pp. 7–24.

Note: In order not to distort these data, only mills for which there was information on the number of slaves are shown here. If the 1878 data on Colón are compared with the 1876 data, there seems to be a drop in the total number of ingenios. This is illusory, since there was a large number of mills for which data on the labor force were missing for 1878; thus, they were not included in these calculations.

slavery's increasing economic inefficiency or lack of viability. There is no evidence to support the notion that slavery collapsed under the weight of its own economic obsolescence. In fact, with the prevailing prices of sugar and slaves in the 1860s and 1870s, slave labor became *more* viable economically. Improvements in processing and transportation technology applied to the sugar sector were responsible for making slave labor more efficient in terms of the income produced by each slave.

From a strictly economic point of view, based on the data presented here, abolition made little sense for planters in the 1870s or early 1880s and seems to have resulted from a series of noneconomic factors. The slave trade had been abolished almost exclusively because of external pressures. There is little evidence that very many planters welcomed the enforced end of the trata. The Moret Law of 1870 had been imposed by Spain largely in response to the political crisis posed by the insurrection, which offered freedom for slaves fighting with the revolutionary forces. The Ten Years' War may have altered the political framework of the Cuban debate over slavery from 1868 on, but in reality the insurrection had little economic impact on sugar production in the slave-based producing regions of Matanzas.

Had slave imports been permitted through the 1870s and into the early 1880s, there is little reason to believe that sugar production would not have continued to flourish on a foundation of slave labor. By the late 1880s and early 1890s, however, slave labor would have become economically untenable. This was because of the substantial decline in sugar prices on international markets—an event that would have radically reduced the income generated by each slave. During the harvest of 1883, planters received up to 9 cents/pound for top-grade white sugar, which certainly softened the blow of ongoing abolition after the 1880 law established the patronato.

During the harvest of 1884, though, as the economies of the North Atlantic consuming markets contracted, sugar prices began to drop. By September 1884 best-grade whites had declined to 6.75 cents/pound, and although prices stabilized at between 4.5 and 5.5 cents/pound through 1889, by the harvest of 1890 Cuban sugar producers were receiving a top price of 2.88 cents/pound. By 1895, on the eve of the war for independence, sugar prices were 1.82 cents/pound for best-grade centrifuge sugar.[55] The correlation between insurrection and the fall in sugar prices should be noted. Had slavery not been abolished, it might indeed have collapsed by the early 1890s owing to reduced planter income. That, however, was not a possibility during the 1860s, 1870s, or early 1880s.

Slave Living Conditions

The relentless spread of sugar monoculture in rural Matanzas after the onset of railroad construction during the late 1830s radically altered the patterns of daily life for the slave population of the province. Changes were linked to shifting residential and occupational patterns. Although sugar production was dependent on slave labor before the 1840s, the majority of Matanzas slaves lived and worked on non-sugar-sector farms or in urban centers. But with the spatial expansion of the sugar economy and the constant construction of new ingenios, there was a significant shift of the Matanzas slave population to plantations in the 1840s and 1850s. The collapse of coffee was responsible for channeling slaves from cafetales to sugar estates. Even urban slaves were increasingly sent to rural areas in order to serve the needs of sugar. Changes in the urban-transport sector of the Matanzas economy offer an example of this process. In the late eighteenth and early nineteenth century, carting in urban centers was an occupation worked almost exclusively by slave labor. But by the 1840s the British consul in Havana noted that these drivers were increasingly sent off to work on estates and were being replaced by free labor in most of the island's cities.[56]

Local-level archival materials clearly indicate the shift of slaves over to ingenio labor. The Matanzas partido of Sabanilla, due south of the bay, was crossed by a railroad line in the 1840s, and this was followed by a wave of ingenio construction. Some of Cuba's largest plantations were located there, among them Domingo Aldama's Santa Rosa, Santo Domingo, and San José mills, the Drakes' Saratoga estate, and Gonzalo Alfonso's Ingenio San Gonzalo. In 1852 Sabanilla slaves numbered 5,568, of whom nearly 65 percent worked on ingenios. Three years later, in 1855, there had been a 10 percent increase in the slave population, but this was paralleled by a significant shift of labor resources. Four new mills had been constructed, and slaves were transferred from sitios, potreros, and cafetales to sugar plantations: 89.9 percent of Sabanilla's slaves worked on ingenios in 1855. (See Table 12.7.) There had also been a significant growth in the number of slaves on each estate. In 1852, ingenios utilized an average of 181 slaves, but this had increased to 231 slaves/ingenio by 1855.[57]

Data for 1854 from San Antonio de Cabezas, contiguous to Sabanilla to the east, and from Corral Nuevo, east of Matanzas Bay, reveal similar dimensions of slave utilization by the sugar sector. In Cabezas 77.3 percent

Table 12.7. Sabanilla Slaves by Type of Farm, 1852–1855

	1852		1855	
	No. Slaves	%	No. Slaves	%
Ingenios	3,614	64.9	5,536	89.9
Cafetales	748	13.4	0	0
Sitios	870	15.6	100	1.6
Potreros	336	6.0	526	8.5
Total	5,568	100.0	6,162	100.0

Source: AHPM, ME, Estadística, leg. 6, no. 116; leg. 8, no. 145.

Note: Ingenios were sugar farms and their mills; cafetales were coffee farms; sitios were subsistence farms; and potreros were stock-raising farms.

of all slaves resided on ingenios, and the corresponding figure for Corral Nuevo was 83 percent.[58]

The 1862 census indicates that approximately three-quarters of all provincial slaves lived on sugar estates. In rural Colón 82.2 percent worked on sugar plantations; in Cárdenas, 74.3 percent of all slaves lived on the ingenios; and in Matanzas, where more than 20 percent of the slave population lived in the city, 63.3 percent labored on ingenios. These data are summarized in Table 12.8.

With the decline of the Cuban slave trade in the early 1860s, its curtailment after 1867, the onset of abolition in 1870, and continued high levels of labor demand by the sugar sector, the transfer of slaves to ingenios accelerated considerably in the late 1860s and early 1870s. More than 90 percent of the Cárdenas slave population worked on ingenios in 1867, and this figure increased to 92.8 percent by 1875. In the central sugar-producing jurisdiction of Colón, 83 percent of the slave population lived on estates in 1859; 86.1 percent in 1865; and 94 percent in 1876 (see Table 12.9). This was a substantial reorganization of labor resources, evidence that once again calls into question the mistaken conclusion that slavery was not economically viable. Estate owners were under great pressure to operate rationally from an economic point of view, and they would not have sought more slaves without economic justification. The rhythms of daily life and the working conditions of slave populations were in large part determined by the type of farm on which they labored. It has been generally recognized that the most degrading and brutal conditions existed on sugar plantations at harvesttime, when slave populations were driven ruthlessly to maximize

Table 12.8. Matanzas, 1862: Slaves by Place of Residence

	Cárdenas		Colón		Matanzas		Province	
	No. Slaves	%	No. Slaves	%	No. Slaves	%	No. Slaves	%
City	3,032	12.3	631	1.9	6,751	20.7	10,414	11.6
Ingenios	18,290	74.3	27,019	82.2	20,629	63.3	65,938	73.2
Cafetales	381	1.5	627	1.9	1,297	4.0	2,305	2.6
Potreros	1,240	5.0	2,187	6.7	1,241	3.8	4,668	5.2
Sitios	916	3.7	1,738	5.3	1,490	4.6	4,144	4.6
Others	754	3.1	669	2.0	1,187	3.6	2,610	2.9
TOTAL	24,613	100.0	32,871	100.0	32,235	100.0	90,079	100.0

SOURCE: Cuba, Centro de Estadística, *Noticias estadísticas de la isla de Cuba en 1862* (Havana: Imp. del Gobierno, Capitanía General y Real Hacienda, 1864), "Distribución de la población en los pueblos y fincas de la isla."
NOTE: See note, Table 12.7.

Table 12.9. Cárdenas and Colón Slaves by Place of Residence, 1859–1876
(in percentages)

	Cárdenas		Colón		
	1867	1875	1859	1865	1876
Ingenios	90.2	92.8	83.0	86.1	94.0
Cafetales	1.4	0.1	1.0	1.3	0.3
Potreros	2.5	1.5	7.8	5.3	1.7
Sitios	5.5	5.5	6.3	6.9	4.0
Others	0.3	0.1	1.9	0.3	0.0
Total	100.0	100.0	100.0	100.0	100.0

Source: ANC, ME, leg. 4120, no. M, "Repartos municipales de la jurisdicción de Colón, 1859"; ANC, Gobierno General, leg. 405, no. 19209, "Padrón de fincas rústicas de la jurisdicción de Colón, 1865"; ANC, Gobierno General, leg. 270, no. 13563, "Padrón general de fincas rústicas de este distrito, año de 1875 a 1876"; ANC, Gobierno General, leg. 945, no. 16724, "Padrón general de la riqueza rústica para regir en los años económicos de 1866 a 1867"; ANC, Gobierno General, leg. 269, no. 13554, "Jurisdicción de Cárdenas. Padrón general de la riqueza rústica de esta ciudad y su jurisdicción formado para los años económicos de 1875 a 1876."
Note: See note, Table 12.7.

production. Eighteen-hour days were routine on the great estates by the 1850s, and in all likelihood conditions worsened as abolition neared.[59]

In addition, the size of the productive units determined fundamental aspects of life for slave populations. On smaller rural properties with few slaves, there was more flexibility and less supervision because of the greatly diminished need for massive security precautions. On such farms, usually sitios or potreros, regimentation was minimal, and without doubt slaves enjoyed better living conditions. These slaves often lived in small bohíos rather than in closely guarded barracks; usually, sex-distribution patterns were more equitable; and family life was a possibility.

The breadth of social interaction was also governed by the number of slaves on a given farm or plantation. On the large-scale plantations that dominated the slave experience by the 1850s and 1860s, life took on the characteristics of a collective. Slaves lived together in close, cramped quarters. They marched to and from the fields jointly, worked in labor gangs, and generally shared the most intimate aspects of daily existence. How this type of regimentation affected the culture, political attitudes, and social psychology of Afro-Cubans before and after abolition is a topic hardly explored by scholars.

Yet, it must be stressed that the number of slaves living on small farms decreased considerably as the nineteenth century progressed. It was rare to find slave dotaciones exceeding 150 or 200 slaves in the early nineteenth century. But by the 1850s most slaves lived on plantations where more than 200 slaves was common. In Sabanilla, for example, more than 70 percent of the total slave population in 1855 lived on estates having more than 200 slaves.[60] Although this is an extreme example, in Cárdenas more than half of all slaves resided on plantations having more than 200 slaves in 1867; and in Colón more than 60 percent of the slave population labored on ingenios having more than 200 slaves in 1859 and 1865, although this figure stood at 56.1 percent in 1876. Table 12.10 shows the size of slaveholdings in different Matanzas partidos and jurisdictions.

Plantation slaves worked in a variety of occupations, and although the prevailing image is of masses of cane cutters, in the late 1840s only about one-quarter of all slaves actually cut cane. Sugar production required a great many tasks. Full-time workers were needed to load cane on carts or, later, railway cars; to transport it to the mill; to feed the cane stocks into grinding equipment; to haul away *bagazo*; to stoke fires; to oversee the boiling and

Table 12.10. Various Partidos and Jurisdictions, 1852–1876:
Percentage of Slave Population on Farms by Size of Slaveholding

Slave-holdings	Cama-rioca (1852)	Saba-nilla (1855)	S. Antonio Cabezas (1852)	Corral Neuvo (1854)	Cár-denas (1867)	Cár-denas (1875)	Colón (1859)	Colón (1865)	Colón (1876)
1–5	5.8	1.1	11.7	5.2	2.3	2.2	2.9	3.1	2.7
6–10	10.2	1.6	7.0	5.8	2.4	2.1	3.6	3.5	1.4
11–20	8.1	2.1	3.6	4.7	2.3	1.8	4.6	3.5	2.2
21–50	38.8	5.6	15.4	2.9	7.1	8.7	6.0	4.6	5.5
51–100	17.2	3.4	7.2	9.9	13.9	13.2	6.8	6.0	7.1
101–150		9.8	34.7	28.5	8.6	13.0	9.7	8.3	12.6
151–200		3.1	9.3	7.5	12.9	22.9	5.9	8.9	12.4
201–300	19.9	37.6	11.1	35.5	21.3	19.8	13.3	22.0	27.7
301–400		16.7			14.2	4.8	15.2	14.7	13.7
401–600		7.1			8.5	2.5	12.4	5.3	6.4
601 +		11.8			6.7	8.9	19.7	20.0	8.3
TOTAL	100.0	100.0	100.0	100.0	100.0	100.0	100.0	100.0	100.0

SOURCES: AHPM, ME, Estadística, leg. 6, no. 116 (Camarioca, 1852; San Antonio de Cabezas, 1852); leg. 6, no. 118, fols. 1–42 (Corral Nuevo, 1854); leg. 6, no. 145, fols. 28–31 (Sabanilla, 1855); ANC, ME, leg. 4120, no. M, "Repartos municipales de la jurisdicción de Colón, 1859"; ANC, Gobierno General, leg. 405, no. 19209, "Padrón de fincas rústicas de la jurisdicción de Colón, 1865"; ANC, Gobierno General, leg. 270, no. 13563, "Padrón general de fincas rústicas de este distrito, año de 1875 a 1876" (Colón 1859, 1865, and 1876); ANC, Gobierno General, leg. 945, no. 16724, "Padrón general de la riqueza rústica para regir en los años económicos de 1866 a 1867"; ANC, Gobierno General, leg. 269, no. 13554, "Jurisdicción de Cárdenas. Padrón general de la riqueza rústica de esta ciudad y su jurisdicción formado para los años económicos de 1875 a 1876" (Cárdenas, 1867 and 1875).

evaporation trains; to pack drying molds; to tend cattle; to keep the boiling and purging houses clean and orderly; and finally crate sugar for export.

In 1849 Joseph Crawford, the British consul in Havana, sent a report to the Foreign Office detailing slave occupations on a hypothetical 40-caballería estate on which 20 caballerías were planted in cane. Such a plantation was expected to produce 500 boxes of white sugar and 1,500 boxes of muscovados and quebrados (at 425 pounds/box). The total dotación was estimated to consist of 200 slaves, although only 116 were workers. The remainder were children, the aged, nurses, cooks, and invalids. The following were listed:[61]

28	cutting cane and loading carts	24.1%
14	cartmen	12.1
10	cane carriers [from carts to grinding machinery]	8.6
2	feeders	1.7
4	trash cartmen	3.4
16	boiling house including stokers for two sets of coppers [trains]	13.8
10	purging house	8.6
8	drying depot and packing	6.9
4	tending cattle	3.4
10	spreading and carting trash	8.6
6	house servants	5.2
4	disposable	3.4
116	*Total*	100.0%

The healthiest slaves were employed cutting cane and loading carts, while children above age twelve and older slaves were utilized in less strenuous tasks. It is likely that by the 1860s, as acreage planted in cane on the larger plantations expanded and as processing became more mechanized because of the widespread use of centrifuges, a greater portion of plantation slaves worked in fields as cane cutters, loaders, and haulers.

Occupations on smaller productive units (food-crop farms and cattle ranches) were less diverse and the work regime not so regimented. Although slaves were increasingly concentrated on large ingenios, it should be noted that the vast majority of slaveholders were owners of relatively few slaves. Sitieros made use of slaves on farms of all sizes, and their utilization as domestic servants was common at every level of Matanzas landholding society. For example, in Colón 44.9 percent of all slaveholders owned five or fewer slaves in 1859; the figure was 52.9 percent in 1865 and 54.8 percent in 1876. Yet, these small-scale slaveowners controlled but a tiny fraction of Colón's slave population: 2.9 percent in 1859; 3.1 percent in 1865; and 2.7 percent in 1876.[62]

The opening of the frontier on a massive scale because of railroad construction in the 1840s and 1850s produced fundamental transformations in land-use patterns throughout Matanzas. Forest and savanna succumbed to cane; and improved processing technology, which increased the productive capacity on the great estates, allowed more extensive planting within individual plantations. This had a substantial impact on a fundamental aspect of life for the province's slave population.

In the early decades of the nineteenth century the cultivation of *conucos*, or provision grounds, was a basic fact of slave existence on most ingenios. Before their concentration in barracones, slaves lived scattered about in bohíos, around which a variety of fruits and vegetables were grown and animals were raised. In addition, plantation owners with extensive acreage usually designated a sector of the estate for food-crop production. Slaves devoted much time and energy toward the careful nurturing of their own food supplies, and there is evidence that part of provision-grounds production was independently marketed by the slaves themselves. This provided access to cash and the possibility of participation in a broader economic system outside the narrow confines of the plantation. It also provided the means for making down payments on freedom through coartación contracts.

Plantation owners permitted slaves to cultivate their own food supplies for a number of reasons. First and foremost, the productive capacity of the ingenio was limited by technological parameters. Cane fields could be located only so far from mills, or sucrose yields would be minimal because of the lengthy transportation time needed to move the cane to the processing area. In addition, before the employment of centrifuges and other advances in refining, productive capacity was rather limited. All of this meant that there were definite limits to the amount of land that could be planted in cane. Thus there was enough forest, pasture, and even potential cropland for slaves to cultivate their own food supplies. Food to sustain slave dotaciones did not need to be purchased. Imported food was expensive, and the transportation of bulky foodstuffs by oxcart along rudimentary roads to the interior was both time-consuming and costly.

However, from the 1840s on, the economic factors that had permitted Matanzas slaves to cultivate their own food supplies changed decisively. For one thing, the productive capacity of the industry as a whole increased significantly with the constant technological modernization of processing. With respect to land use, this meant that more land could be planted in cane within individual plantations. Also, with the expansion of planting there was a need for more draft animals to transport cane to the mills. In the late eighteenth century and in first decades of the nineteenth century, plantation owners permitted slaves to cultivate food on land deemed unsuitable for cane. With the growth of the animal population, however, these lands were converted to pastures. In addition, when soil fertility and productive yields of cane fields declined to untenable levels, land was converted to pasture rather than turned over to slaves for food-crop cultivation. Fodder could not be imported; food could. In essence, with expanding slave and draft-animal populations, slaves competed with animals for land. In 1846 there were 30,805 oxen in rural Matanzas; by 1862, they had more than doubled to 63,865.[63] This in turn doubled the amount of grazing land needed to maintain such an important factor of production.

Yet another factor was the revolution in transportation wrought by railroad construction. Railroads made it possible to transport bulky food items (such as rice, flour, and beans) efficiently and cheaply from Havana or the city of Matanzas to ingenios in the distant interior. Before the advent of the railroads, it was essential for plantations to produce a substantial share of their own food supplies because of the difficulty and unreliability of transportation from port cities to faraway ingenios. Plantation owners had little choice but to permit, if not encourage, food production by their slave populations for purely economic reasons. But railroads, together with the other factors noted above, altered the possibilities of land use. It had become more economically advantageous to plant land in cane and import food to sustain the dotaciones.

Most plantations continued to produce plantains, but food staples such as rice, beans, flour, and salted cod were imported. The curbing of food-production privileges for Matanzas slaves reduced the prerogatives of slave existence. Authorities in the 1820s and 1830s, noting that slaves were marketing food throughout the Matanzas countryside, constantly complained about slaves purchasing liquor illegally in rural and urban taverns. This meant access to petty cash and expanded opportunities for a sector of the slave population, although this feature of slave life should not be overly exaggerated. By the 1840s and 1850s, these options were effectively closed.

Not only was food-crop acreage reduced to insignificance, thus eliminating surreptitious marketing possibilities for slaves, but new security precautions on the plantations also foreclosed the possibility of stealing away at night to towns or taverns. Slave settlement patterns within estates shifted from the scattered bohíos of the late eighteenth and early nineteenth centuries to clustered dwellings in the 1820s and 1830s and, finally, to the barracones so common in the 1840s and after.[64] Slaves were sometimes locked inside these concentration-camp-like barracks, and were carefully watched by guards to preclude the possibility of undetected activity. Security precautions were linked to the need to manage a growing slave population and to the fear of rebellions spawned by the slave conspiracies and actual revolts that took place in the early 1840s.

Thus, the closing of the frontier in Matanzas during the 1840s substantially changed the dynamics of slave existence. Slaves were concentrated on ingenios and in larger conglomerations. Slave life became more regimented, and there was comparatively less flexibility and maneuverability than had existed in the early nineteenth century. Increased processing capacity by the sugar industry led to greater work demands, and at harvesttime milling complexes operated round the clock. Settlement patterns shifted from dispersed dwellings to highly concentrated clusters for greater security. Access to land for food-crop cultivation diminished.

These conditions governed slave existence throughout the 1850s and 1860s. However, with the beginning of the independence insurrection in 1868 and with the Moret Law of 1870, fundamental changes slowly occurred in master/slave relations on Matanzas plantations. The ironfisted policies of plantation owners began to wane for several fundamental reasons. First was a gradual (yet stubborn) acceptance of the inevitability of slavery's demise. Second, and more important, was the increased rebelliousness of slaves themselves, which forced masters to shift strategies in order to ensure the continued functioning of their estates. Cuban slaves in western zones distant from the rebellion were well aware that the insurrection had proclaimed the abolition of slavery, and they were increasingly loath to accept their immediate conditions.[65] Emboldened by the apparent imminence of freedom, slaves began to resist the continuation of absolute and arbitrary domination by their masters.

Caution must be exercised here, for no actual rebellions by Matanzas slaves were recorded in the 1870s. In the wake of the independence insurrection, security precautions were paramount and rebellion would have been suicidal. Nevertheless, there was active resistance and frequent disruption of plantation life by slaves who, in effect, demanded a new compact between master and bondsman. This took two fundamental forms: desertion of plantations and work stoppages. In the 1870s, notices of slaves leaving the fields en masse were common throughout the province; and, even more serious, slaves frequently refused to leave the barracones to go to work.[66]

Traditionally, this kind of insubordination would have been dealt with harshly and effectively by whippings, jailings, and placing slaves in stocks or irons. But by the 1870s the slave resistance was so extensive that plantation owners would have defeated their own purpose by disciplining so many slaves. In the face of widespread sabotage to production, threatened or effected in the 1870s, when labor shortages were perhaps the greatest problem faced by sugar planters, it would have been impossible to complete harvests by resorting to old mechanisms of repression.

Wage labor made inroads on Matanzas plantations in the late 1860s and early 1870s, ingenio owners seeking the diversification of their work forces as abolition became inevitable. Still, slaves accounted for 70 percent of the sugar labor force even late in the decade. But the appearance of wage earners in increasing numbers on Matanzas plantations meant new dissatisfactions for slaves. Gangs of Chinese workers and white or mulatto freemen received wages for the same work done by slaves. This led to growing demands for nominal cash wages by slaves themselves, and this became the principal reason for work stoppages. Gradually masters realized they would have to compromise with their dotaciones if the sugarcane was to be harvested. As the 1870s progressed, minimal wages were more frequently and routinely paid to slaves for a variety of tasks.[67] Without these incentives, the increasing militancy of slaves would have made zafras impossible to complete.

Thus, slaves were able to widen the dimensions of their lives substantially by demanding and gaining access to cash in the 1870s. They also hastened the transformation of slavery in its waning days and played an active role in the transition to new forms of labor exploitation. Plantation owners were forced to adapt to new socioeconomic parameters. Rather then simply resorting to repression and harsh punishment in order to extract labor from their slaves, now impossible because of the scale of resistance, positive incentives were utilized to accomplish the same ends. Wages were paid in cash, but mill owners took to running plantation stores in order to recuperate specie by selling products to their increasingly diversified labor forces. In this way, more modern forms of exploitation paralleled the deepening abolition process and the growing assertiveness of slave dotaciones.

More than any other demand, with the exception of freedom, access to cash was the most coveted prerogative for Matanzas slaves in the 1870s. This was not only because of the flexibility and increased consumption potential that cash offered, but also because of the possibility of making down payments on freedom through coartación contracts. The Moret Law freed all children born of slave women after 1868, and this placed many slaves in the painful predicament of having nominally free children who in reality were condemned to live in servitude until their parents could attain freedom. Although the insurgents held out hope, and legal abolition had begun for the old and young, freedom for most slaves was remote in the 1870s and, because small children hindered mobility, maroonage was nearly impossible. But the road to freedom was theoretically possible for those with access to cash. Coartación contracts with masters offered hope for the future, and that is why wages were the single most important demand motivating work stoppages in the 1870s.

It is impossible to quantify manumissions in Matanzas without reading the notarial protocols of every notary operating in the many towns and villages of this vast area, and that is a daunting task. But a sampling of manumissions effected from 1840 through 1878 provides a profile of those who were able to obtain freedom. Letters of freedom were largely issued on completion of payment of coartación contracts or, in the 1870s, by grants of freedom made by slaveholders (these do not include slaves freed under the terms of the 1870 Moret Law).

A sampling of 302 manumissions in the jurisdiction of Matanzas between 1840 and 1875 revealed that 63.6 percent were females, the remainder males. More than two-thirds of these slaves were creoles, the rest Africans. A substantial portion, 43.1 percent, were prime-age slaves between fifteen and forty years old; 22 percent were forty-one or older; and 34.8 percent were younger than fourteen.

Data from Colón are similar. Between 1864 and 1878, of 208 manumissions examined, 58.7 percent were females; 41.3 percent were males. Creoles accounted for 72.6 percent of the sample, and Africans the remaining 27.4 percent. Prime-age slaves were 38.5 percent of the total; slaves older than forty-one made up 34.4 percent; and those younger than fourteen were 27.1 percent of this sample.[68]

Yet, despite the theoretical possibility of freedom offered by the institution of coartación, this option led to liberty for only a small fraction of the slave population. There are no data on the number of coartados—those making down payments on freedom who actually were able to complete payment and buy freedom. More than likely, the percentages were very small, for the free-black and mulatto population of Matanzas did not grow significantly until the 1870s. Between 1846 and 1862 their numbers increased from 7,786 to 11,295, or 2.4 percent yearly.[69] Since sex-distribution patterns were equitable, most of this annual increase was probably owing to natural reproduction rather than to manumission. Coartación and the possibility of emancipation may have meant hope and an abstract link to freedom for those able to make down payments, but the real prospects of consummating these contracts seem to have been minimal.

By 1877, when the next reliable data are available, there was a significant increase in the Matanzas free-colored population to 37,901. However, this was by and large linked to the Moret Law of 1870, which bestowed liberty on slaves reaching sixty years of age and newborns. It is impossible to determine whether it was easier for prime-age slaves to consummate coartación contracts in the 1870s, although this is doubtful since evidence indicates that core labor forces were maintained on ingenios through the decade.

Free blacks and mulattoes were concentrated in the province's urban centers: more than 50 percent lived in the cities of Matanzas and Cárdenas, both in 1846 and in 1862. Employment opportunities were extensive in skilled and unskilled occupations, and culture was nourished in their communities by *cabildos de nación*, authorized to function legally but carefully watched by provincial authorities. Women worked largely as laundresses and seamstresses. In 1846, 71 percent of Matanzas *lavanderas* and 30 percent of *costureras* were free-black or *mulata* women. Men worked as masons (45 percent of the profession), carpenters (20 percent), urban day laborers (47 percent), cigar rollers (20 percent), tailors (56 percent), and shoemakers (25 percent). These same professions prevailed through the 1860s.

Conspiracies, Rebellions, and Resistance

The most common form of resistance to servitude practiced by Matanzas slaves in the early nineteenth century was flight. While the province was still part of a shifting frontier, vast areas were unpopulated and largely inaccessible. These regions became destinations for cimarrones, and often large palenques were established by tenuous communities of runaways.[70] Yet, even in remote areas, palenques were always vulnerable to attack by rancheadores, the bounty hunters who combed the Matanzas countryside with bloodhounds and shotguns. Few cimarrón communities were self-sufficient in food or livestock production, never having the defensive capabilities or stability to establish permanent agricultural systems. Ultimately, food and supplies were acquired by hit-and-run raids on small sitios, or by the theft of cattle from potreros or ingenios. These activities signaled the proximity of runaways, and were usually followed by the organization of successful rancherías to hunt down cimarrones. However, the cycle was continuous. One group of runaways would be rounded up, but slaves elsewhere in the province would flee. So long as remote areas existed where slaves could find temporary refuge, abandonment of plantations continued.

Violence directed at property and against oppressive *mayorales* or *contramayorales* was less frequent. In 1825 there was a large-scale violent revolt in Guamacaro; twenty-four farms were looted and burned, and some fifteen whites were killed. Again, in June 1835, violent uprisings took place on Ingenio Carolina and Cafetal Burato. These were ruthlessly crushed by Spanish militiamen and were followed by strict vigilance.[71]

The last gasp of violent collective slave resistance took place in the early 1840s, culminating in the massive repression unleashed in Matanzas during 1844 and known as the conspiracy of "La Escalera." Colonial authorities in Havana and planters and their mayorales in the Matanzas countryside were increasingly fearful about the possibilities of a large-scale slave rebellion during the late 1830s and early 1840s. Their fears were nurtured by several factors.

First was the virtual Africanization of rural Matanzas. Slaves, of course, had been an important part of rural life since the late eighteenth century. But the rapid growth of sugar culture in the 1820s and 1830s, and the large-scale slave imports accompanying ingenio development, radically shifted the ratio of slaves to other sectors of the population. In every rural partido, slaves were in the majority—and, in most cases, overwhelmingly so. In 1841 slaves were nearly 90 percent of Guamacaro's population; 84 percent in Guanábana; 76 percent in Sabanilla; 75 percent in Cimarrones; 73 percent in Lagunillas; 72 percent in Santa Ana; 70 percent in Macuriges; and 64 percent in the Yumurí Valley. The terror of the Haitian slave rebellion was an ever-present nightmare in the minds of Cuban planters and colonial bureaucrats. When planters journeyed from the comfort of their Havana homes to rural Matanzas and found themselves immersed in a virtual sea of Africans, it is no wonder that fear took such a hold on planter social psychology. Greed motivated the slave trade; yet fear of revolt haunted the psyches of those who depended so heavily on slaves for their wealth.

Second was the growing perception that English abolitionist conspirators were encouraging and organizing the slave rebellion that was so dreaded. The activities of David Turnbull, who first visited Cuba in 1838 and returned in 1840 as the British Consul in Havana, exacerbated the fears of officials and planters who loathed English meddling in Cuban affairs.[72] Intent on curbing the Cuban slave trade, Turnbull devised intricate plans for yearly slave registries designed to free illegal imports and emancipados (Africans seized by Spanish or British patrols on arrival in Cuba). To the chagrin of British authorities, the emancipados, though theoretically free, were in reality enslaved. Turnbull was accused of inciting rebellion among the island's slaves. He journeyed to Matanzas in November 1841, but was forbidden by local authorities to visit any estates. So pervasive was anti-British sentiment in Cuba during the early 1840s that it is no surprise that English planters and mechanics working on sugar estates were a major target of the repression launched in March 1844.[73]

Third, the fear manifested by Cuban elite groups was not irrational or ill-founded. A series of rebellions in the early 1840s intensified the rising level of apprehension and the perception that somehow the English were behind this slave discontent. Many feared that a major conspiracy was brewing. In October 1841 Lucumí slaves, working in Havana on the construction of a sumptuous palace for the Matanzas merchant/planter Domingo Aldama, were involved in a confrontation with foremen supervising the project. This was a labor dispute, highlighted by a sit-down strike of slaves who refused to work, although their grievances are unknown. Ended by armed authorities, who fired on the defenseless slaves and killed a good number, this incident was widely trumpeted as a "rebellion" and as evidence of Turnbull's insidious effect on Cuban slaves.[74] The realities were unimportant. The image of rebellious slaves threatening the public order was disseminated throughout the island.

Although the "Palacio Aldama" incident seems to have been a case of insubordination rather than a genuine revolt, on March 26, 1843, there was a large-scale violent rising by slaves in rural Matanzas. It began on Joaquín Peñalver's Ingenio Alcancía and rapidly spread to contiguous estates in the Bemba-Cimarrones region of Cárdenas, a center of the provincial sugar industry. José Baró's La Luisa mill was attacked and burned. Ingenios Trinidad, Nieves, and Aurora were looted and torched, as was the cafetal Moscú and the potrero Ranchuelo. More than 200 slaves laboring on the Júcaro railway were jailed in Cárdenas as a precautionary measure. However, all of them escaped and joined the rampaging rebels. Local military units were supplemented by 400 troops sent by steamship from Havana, and within days the rebellion was quelled. The repression was ghastly. Spanish regulars massacred fleeing slaves and captives alike; many slaves committed suicide rather than be captured alive. Joseph Crawford, the British consul, reported that of 950 rebel slaves, more than half died, "the woods being filled with hanging victims." Captives were viciously flogged. Only five whites are known to have died.[75] Despite this debacle, in November 1843 slaves on the Triunvirato and Ácana estates revolted, only to be crushed immediately.

But even before the Alcancía and Triunvirato uprisings, rural Matanzas was terrorized by a band of cimarrones led by the legendary José Dolores. Between February 1843 and March 1844, José Dolores and his cuadrilla roamed the Matanzas countryside attacking ingenios, sitios, and potreros with impunity. Rancherías were organized repeatedly, and although several members of his gang were captured, Dolores was never apprehended. His activities ceased only with the massive repression and province-wide campaign to heighten security ushered in with La Escalera.[76] The presence of a gang of rebel slaves who could not be caught must have exacerbated the fears, by now approaching hysteria, shared by Matanzas whites.

There has been some discussion among scholars on whether there was an actual slave conspiracy in Matanzas during early 1844.[77] Almost nothing concrete is known about the participation of the British, whom Spanish authorities were quick to blame, or about the role of the Matanzas free-black and mulatto community, who bore the brunt of the repression. Nor is there any knowledge of conspiratorial activities on the part of the slaves themselves, although the 1843 rebellion indicates probable widespread plotting. Yet, no uprising took place, and whether one was in the offing is largely irrelevant. The importance of La Escalera for the history of rural Matanzas lay in the long-term success of the repressive policies surrounding the incident. After 1844 no slave rebellions are recorded in the Matanzas historical record, notices of palenques disappear, and the number of cimarrones drastically decline. Until the 1870s, when abolition had already begun and slaves were testing the limits of maneuverability within a decaying system, Matanzas planters lived among a controlled slave population. The repression accompanying La Escalera was largely successful in intimidating slaves and their free supporters alike in the near and long term. This outcome should be emphasized.

Methodical repression was directed against three sectors of Matanzas society in early 1844. Slaves had demonstrated fearlessness and a propensity for rebellion in 1843, and a clear message was directed at rural slave dotaciones. Attempted revolt would be met by ruthlessness and brutality, the high value of slaves notwithstanding. But potential rebels were not the only targets. A clear message was sent to crusading English abolitionists. International efforts by the British to end slavery could not be curbed, but there would be no toleration of internal threats to the Cuban slave/sugar economy à la Turnbull and his activities. This was perhaps the most pointed message of La Escalera, and it was not abstract. There were many British machinists working in rural Matanzas, and they were suspected for some time of abolitionist activities if not outright conspiratorial planning. Almost all British residents of Matanzas and Cárdenas were rounded up and jailed during March and April 1844, and most were locked in stocks and chains and treated with extreme harshness.[78] North American *maquinistas* were also incarcerated, since all foreigners were suspected of harboring antislavery sentiment.[79]

The testimony of Theodore Phinney, a British citizen who owned Ingenio Sonora in Cárdenas, reveals much about the resentments of Spanish authorities toward the English. Phinney wrote to Crawford, the British consul, describing the events on Sonora during La Escalera. Phinney had contracted a Cuban mayoral in 1841, Agustín Contrera, but after two years he was discharged for incompetence. The day after Contrera was fired, one of Phinney's cane fields was set ablaze. Despite this, after begging for his job, Contrera was rehired in August 1843, only to be fired once again after numerous complaints of cruelty by the estate's slaves. At this point, the military governor of Cárdenas visited the plantation and urged Phinney to rehire Contrera. Upon Phinney's refusal, the governor threatened to come to the plantation and "cut down every man on it if there should be any disorder."

In early 1844 the Governor General of Cuba ordered a military commission to scour the island in search of a slave conspiracy, and Cárdenas authorities began circulating rumors that the slaves of Ingenio Sonora were deeply involved. Phinney interpreted this as pure vindictiveness linked to the incident with Contrera and the local military governor. Troops came to the estate on the afternoon of March 17, 1844, and in the evening Contrera appeared as their aide. On the morning of the eighteenth, the troops began the systematic torture of selected slaves, designated by Contrera, in order to extract confessions of involvement in a conspiracy. They were tied to ladders and brutally whipped. Seven slaves were killed, 30 were disabled for two months, another 5 slaves could not work for three months, and 3 more were jailed at Matanzas along with two Englishman, an engineer and a blacksmith.[80] These kinds of activities were widespread throughout rural Matanzas.

In urban areas free blacks and mulattoes were viciously attacked, and jailed, and foreign people of color were summarily expelled from the island.

It has been estimated that some two thousand free blacks and mulattoes were arrested in the city of Matanzas alone; many, including the famous Afro-Cuban poet Plácido, were tortured and shot. All free blacks and mulattoes born outside of Cuba were ordered to be deported within fifteen days. Urban labor was seriously disrupted by the repression. The U.S. vice-consul reported on the huge number of arrests in June 1844 and of how the Matanzas docks were virtually paralyzed, since nearly all of the stevedores were free blacks and mulattoes who had been jailed.[81]

La Escalera, rather than being interpreted as a slave conspiracy, should be viewed as the brutal unleashing of state power to preclude any possible momentum from building toward a future rebellion. Colonial authorities, in collusion with local elite groups, reacted to fears of massive slave revolt spawned by intensified English abolitionism during the late 1830s and early 1840s, the recent importation of large numbers of Africans to Matanzas, and actual rebellions occurring between 1841 and 1843.

In addition, an overarching concern by elite groups was the long-term protection of investments that were spiraling upward as the province's interior was developed. La Escalera must be placed within this context. In the Banagüises region during the early 1840s, millions of pesos were being invested by the most powerful members of Cuba's socioeconomic elite, and thousands of slaves were purchased to stock the area's capital-intensive mills. Even more capital was being invested in railroad construction throughout Matanzas province at precisely this point in history.

Within these broader parameters, the instability caused by the fear of slave conspiracy and rebellion was untenable. Those threatening the process of investment and economic growth had to be dealt with harshly and their activities halted, even if there were substantial short-term costs. In retrospect, La Escalera was a brilliant coup from the Matanzas elite's point of view. It not only precluded any real conspiracy that may have been brewing, but it destroyed the potential for future slave rebellions. Foreign abolitionists were effectively intimidated, and their activities in rural zones were curbed. Free blacks and mulattoes, whose own fragile positions and prerogatives in urban centers were viciously attacked, lost their most articulate members through deportation or murder. Slaves themselves experienced the brutality and repression perpetrated by an organized military machine on a large scale. Masters and mayorales were abusive, to be sure. Jailings, whippings, and many other forms of degrading punishment were perpetrated within plantations. But another dimension to brutality was introduced by the unleashing of the Spanish militia, who took sadistic delight in an opportunity to vent their racist rage against the slave population they despised. For Matanzas slaves, La Escalera had effectively raised the stakes. Attempts at rebellion would be crushed with little mercy. In the aftermath of the repression, rural zones were heavily garrisoned on a long-term basis;

a peace of sorts prevailed, allowing the elite to continue plundering the human and natural ecology of rural Matanzas with little disruption over the next several decades.

This does not imply that slaves were passive or resigned to servitude. Logistically, however, it was nearly impossible to coordinate any widespread conspiracy. Not only were troops garrisoned throughout the province, but an administrative reorganization of rural areas effectively contributed to greater security and vigilance. Jurisdictions such as Matanzas, Cárdenas, and Colón had traditionally been subdivided into partidos, and these were further fractionalized into cuartones. After 1844, cuartones were subdivided into barrios, and at the head of each cuartón was a pedaneo responsible for keeping a careful monthly record of runaways and for reporting any disturbances or rumors of impending mischief by slave dotaciones. Rancheadores, who either had been hired by plantation owners or roamed the countryside on their own, were placed under the authority of these local pedaneos. Cimarrones decreased to insignificance in the mid-1840s, compared to their number only a decade earlier, and there are no notices of palenques after 1844.[82] Early in the nineteenth century the frontier had offered refuge; but by the 1840s it had been effectively closed, and there were no longer remote areas that could shelter large groups of cimarrones.

Yet, many isolated acts of resistance took place. For example, in 1851 3 slaves on Ingenio Trinidad were executed for murdering the estate's mayoral. In 1854, 54 slaves rented out to work on the Clara Luz estate fled back to their master, Charles Booth, the owner of Cafetal La Arcadia, claiming abusive treatment. Cane fields were torched now and again.[83] But no conspiracies or widespread collective actions were discovered until the 1870s. Then slaves tested the limits of the abolition process by refusing to work unless paid, abandoning plantations (especially when rebel troops moved into Matanzas in 1876), and generally disrupting life on the estates in any way possible. However, the historical record shows that during this transitional period in the history of Cuban slavery, slave-perpetrated collective violence was virtually nonexistent.

CHAPTER 13

Non-Slave Labor

From the late eighteenth century, sectors of the Cuban planter class voiced repeated interest in shifting the labor basis of Cuban agriculture toward free-white labor. The colonial elite, motivated by the Haitian slave revolt and the fear of a similar destiny for Cuba if slave imports were not checked, considered the need to maintain racial balance by encouraging immigration.[1] A Junta de Población Blanca was organized in 1817, with the goal of encouraging white-labor migration from the Peninsula; and an ambitious plan to create a class of yeoman farmers, La Cuba Pequeña, was launched shortly thereafter by the energetic Intendant Alejandro Ramírez.[2] But these early-nineteenth-century efforts succumbed by the 1820s. The lure of wealth through slave trading and slave-based sugar production sabotaged any serious attempts at diversifying the forms of labor exploitation, despite fears of Africanization and slave rebellion. Slavery remained the principal system of labor for Matanzas estate owners through the end of the Ten Years' War, although non-slave labor was used for certain tasks and became increasingly important in the 1870s with the onset of the legal abolition process.[3]

On early nineteenth-century Matanzas sugar plantations or coffee estates, the use of freeman as laborers was marginal. The sparsely populated frontier possessed no exploitable labor reserves for the Havana entrepreneurs developing rural Matanzas, and labor had to be imported. Free workers were difficult to recruit. Cuba enjoyed an abundance of available land outside of its sugar- and coffee-producing enclaves. Free men and women had little difficulty securing small sitios or potreros for modest sums, or they simply occupied unused land titled to others.[4] With Cuba's eastern frontier open and fluid, it was virtually impossible to attract freemen to work on plantations, which were associated with slavery and human degradation, and dependence on slaves remained paramount.

Yet, as Matanzas frontier regions were gradually opened and settled in the 1820s and 1830s, a narrowly based labor market slowly evolved to supply ancillary labor for the developing plantation economy. Before railroads crossed the Matanzas hinterland in the late 1830s and 1840s, transportation of supplies to ingenios and sugar to ports was almost entirely controlled by white, black, and mulatto free workers. Some labored as independent teamsters, others as employees of the merchant houses that supplied these services to planters.

Free workers performed other tasks as well. In 1848 the British consul Joseph Crawford reported that gangs of free workers were commonly hired to clear frontierland of forest or brush, difficult but lucrative work. It took a three-man crew forty days to clear and plant a single caballería of land, but they were paid 525 pesos for this task. Salaried workers were also contracted as ploughmen, at 20 pesos per month plus a daily food ration. By comparison, woodsmen who cleared and planted land derived monumental wages.[5] The fact that slaves were not used for such tasks is indicative of the scarcity of labor despite the substantial importation of African slaves in the 1830s. The labor demands of the developing plantation economy seem to have outstripped the Cuban slave market's supplies.

With the generalized installation of steam engines on Matanzas estates in the 1840s and 1850s, there was also the need for skilled mechanics to service and maintain machinery. Almost every mill employed foreigners as maquinistas, usually from the United States, England, or Scotland, and sometimes from Spain. Often, contracts for the purchase of equipment included clauses for skilled mechanics to be sent along with new machinery in order to supervise installation and ensure proper maintenance at harvesttime. Salaries were comparatively high. In 1871, for example, Cosme de la Torriente paid 170 pesos in gold monthly for the services of the mechanic Santiago Backman on Ingenio Isabel.[6]

Supervisory personnel and skilled workers on estates were also generally free wage laborers, although slaves often worked as blacksmiths, coopers, carpenters, or masons, and sometimes as contramayorales in charge of labor gangs. Each estate was administered by an *encargado*, usually a well-paid and trusted associate of the plantation owner. There were also a number of chief foremen, or *mayordomos*, responsible for the supervision of different tasks. In the 1860s and 1870s, salaries of between 50 and 75 pesos monthly were common. These foremen were assisted by mayorales or contramayorales, lower-level supervisors paid according to experience or age. Contramayorales drew wages as low as 17 pesos monthly, while experienced mayorales were paid as much as 50 pesos a month. Each estate also had a resident master carpenter paid according to experience. Cattle tenders, or boyeros, were almost always free workers who were paid between 35 and 50 pesos monthly.[7]

The construction of railroads also demanded an array of skilled workers, usually subcontracted by the firms constructing the different lines. Engineers, mechanics, metalworkers, and foremen were recruited from abroad to supervise grading, drainage, bridge construction, laying of rail, assembly of hauling and dumping cars, and locomotive operation and maintenance. Unskilled labor was usually composed of slave cuadrillas; after slaves work-

ing on the Sabanilla railroad rebelled in 1843, however, there was a concerted effort by railroad builders to contract peninsular white labor. Investments in railroads were astronomical, and entrepreneurs were increasingly
wary about sabotage to such important and costly assets.

A contract drawn up in May 1844 between Joaquín Peñalver, the president of the Compañía Ferrocarril de Cárdenas, and José María Fato, a Havana merchant and the father-in-law of Pedro Diago, is revealing. Fato was
commissioned to contract forty laborers between the ages of twenty and
forty years old. They had to be single, without families, and from the *interior* of the Spanish province of Galicia. This was a quest for uneducated
peasants with a history of docility and stoicism. The terms of the contract
and the conditions in rural Cuba no doubt tested their legendary patience
and resolve. The workers would be sent by ship to the port of Cárdenas to
serve as laborers for three full years. They were to be paid wages of 10 pesos
monthly, plus 5 pesos per month as a food allowance. Medical care would
be provided free during the first year, but if a worker died the costs of the
funeral and burial were the dead worker's responsibility! In the last two
years of the contract, the first three days of hospitalization were free, but
additional sick time would be billed to the worker at the rate of 25 centavos
daily.

The railroad company promised to advance the costs of transportation
from Galicia to Cárdenas up to a maximum of 40 pesos for each worker.
But, of the 10 pesos salary per month, 6 pesos would be withheld until the
cost of transportation was paid. In addition, the company would deduct 4
additional pesos monthly for the entire three-year duration of the contract
in order to create a fund under the control of the company. This money
would be deposited in an interest-bearing account at the discretion of the
railroad line. The proceeds would be paid to the workers only upon completion of the three-year term. Any worker abandoning the project before then
received absolutely nothing from this fund. In addition, if the company decided to fire a worker, for whatever reason, he would have the right to collect only one-half the amount deposited.[8]

The Cuban elite were fond of writing about labor shortages, the need to
promote white immigration, the high price of slaves, and the unwillingness
of the island's white population to work on plantations. The above contract
is a mute testimony to the difficulty of attracting free-immigrant labor under such abusive terms. Unwritten, of course, is that these white gallegos
would be subjected to a harsh work schedule and treated little better than
slaves.

Field labor was the exclusive domain of slaves. But with the scare induced
by the revolts of the 1840s, and the stubborn and persistent British campaign to enforce the ban on slaving, farsighted planters began a serious
search for alternative supplies of field labor. Numerous schemes were pro-

moted to entice Spanish or Canary Island colonos to rural Cuba.[9] However, Cuban planters had been so acculturated into a system of production that gave them arbitrary and absolute control over slave labor that it was nearly impossible to stimulate the widespread migration of contract workers from Spain. Freemen were loath to accept the onerous terms of contracts such as those offered by the Sabanilla railroad. Plantation work was associated with slavery; and, regardless of their humble origins, white Spaniards were reluctant to labor in an environment that was associated both with despised Africans and with abusive masters and overseers.

If free-white workers scorned plantation labor, an additional problem for planters was the specter of unreliability. The lure of the east—Las Villas, Camagüey, and Oriente—where land was available in abundance, made it nearly impossible to keep freemen bound to estates without paying exorbitant salaries. Work on sugar plantations was largely seasonal, the peak labor demands falling between December and June during the harvest. Without such mechanisms as enforceable labor contracts to bind free workers to individual plantations, there was no guarantee that workers would appear at harvesttime without the enticement of lucrative wages. Land availability in frontier zones and the continuation of slavery meant the virtual absence of a broadly based labor market in rural Cuba. In this economic environment planters had few choices. If they had to disburse large quantities of cash in salaries to lure free workers—the only way to attract labor in a rural ambience characterized by the unwillingness of freemen to labor en masse on plantations—it was more advantageous to purchase slaves. This allowed discipline to be arbitrarily imposed and ensured a comparatively reliable labor supply. Without a radical change in the factors governing rural life, planters had little choice but to continue their historical reliance on slave labor. Or substitutes for slaves would have to be found in order to guarantee planters their traditional prerogatives to impose discipline by force and ensure labor reliability.

Planters in the 1840s were not concerned with developing a real labor market in rural Cuba or with furthering a transition to free labor. The large, slave-based plantations of Matanzas established in the early 1840s—Flor de Cuba, Álava, Tinguaro, Ponina, Santa Elena—were testimony to the internal economic viability of slavery. But international pressures were threatening to curb the trata, and the future availability of slaves from the West African coast was increasingly uncertain. The overriding problem now was to supplement slave labor.

It is within this context that the Chinese contract-labor trade began in the late 1840s. The initiator was none other than Julián de Zulueta, who in collaboration with the Junta de Fomento's Comisión de Población Blanca, organized the first expedition in 1847 for the importation of 600 Chinese.[10] The junta subsidized the endeavor by paying Zulueta 170 pesos for every Chinese landed in Cuba. The notorious London slave-trading firm run by

Zulueta's cousin, Pedro de Zulueta, was placed in charge of organizing the logistics of the first expeditions, which utilized British shipping. With characteristic hypocrisy, the British crusaded against African slaving but lauded and applauded the importation of Chinese colonos, who were treated no better, and perhaps worse, than slaves. The British, after all, had sanctioned contract labor by importing hundreds of thousands of Hindus to their American colonies of Trinidad, Jamaica, and Guyana after slavery was abolished in the British Caribbean.

Thus, a temporary solution to the dilemma faced by Cuban planters was discovered. Chinese could be imported without the opposition of the British; once on Cuban plantations, under a thin façade as contract labor, they had little recourse for appealing their de facto condition as virtual slaves. The slave trade was not abandoned, but the planters had discovered an alternative source of labor if needed. Between 1847 and 1873 more than 120,000 Chinese contract laborers disembarked in Cuba. By way of comparison, approximately 168,000 Africans were imported in the same period.[11] (For a comparison of Chinese and slave imports from 1853 to 1873, see Figure 13.1; for a yearly breakdown of Chinese imported into Cuba, see Table 13.1.)

The Chinese trade was a complex international venture involving British agents in Manila and Amoy, who organized the recruitment and embarka-

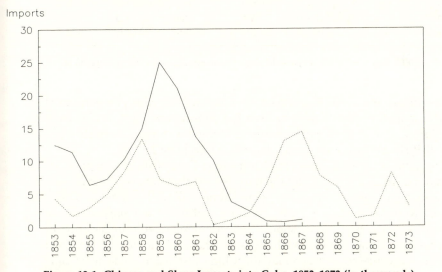

Figure 13.1. Chinese and Slave Imports into Cuba, 1853–1873 (in thousands)

SOURCES: David Eltis, "The Nineteenth-Century Transatlantic Slave Trade: An Annual Time Series of Imports into the Americas Broken Down by Region," *Hispanic American Historical Review* 67:1 (1987), pp. 122–123; PRO, ZHCI/3831, p. 6.

Table 13.1. Chinese Imported into Cuba, 1847–1873

	No. Ships	Tonnage	Chinese Embarked	Chinese Died	Chinese Landed	% Deaths
1847	2	979	612	41	571	6.7
1853	15	8,349	5,150	843	4,307	16.4
1854	4	2,375	1,750	39	1,711	2.2
1855	6	6,544	3,130	145	2,985	4.6
1856	15	10,677	6,152	1,182	4,970	19.2
1857	28	18,940	10,101	1,554	8,547	15.4
1858	33	32,842	16,411	3,027	13,384	18.4
1859	16	13,828	8,539	1,332	7,207	15.6
1860	17	15,104	7,227	1,008	6,219	13.9
1861	16	15,919	7,212	290	6,922	4.0
1862	1	759	400	56	344	14.0
1863	3	2,077	1,045	94	951	9.0
1864	7	5,513	2,664	532	2,132	20.0
1865	20	12,769	6,810	407	6,403	6.0
1866	43	24,187	14,169	1,126	13,043	7.9
1867	42	26,449	15,661	1,247	14,414	8.0
1868	21	15,265	8,400	732	7,668	8.7
1869	19	13,692	7,340	1,475	5,865	20.1
1870	3	2,305	1,312	63	1,249	4.8
1871	5	2,820	1,827	178	1,649	9.7
1872	20	12,886	8,914	766	8,148	8.6
1873	6	4,786	3,330	209	3,121	6.3
TOTAL	342	249,065	138,156	16,346	121,810	11.8

SOURCE: PRO, ZHCI/3831, P.6, Report of British Consulate General, Havana, Sept. 1, 1873.

tion of the Chinese, and shippers of other nationalities who were contracted to transport the laborers to Cuba. Tait & Company and Syme & Company conducted most of the Asian recruitment operations; French, Spanish, U.S., and British ships were the principal carriers (see Table 13.2).

It should be stressed, however, that it was in Cuba that the Chinese trade was designed and financed, by the most powerful members of the island's socioeconomic and administrative elite. Almost all of the organizers were linked to the Cuban slave trade, and they welcomed this opportunity to capitalize on the legal importation of semi-slave labor with the blessings of the ever-meddling British. While Zulueta organized the first mission, and played an active role throughout the Chinese trade, Havana merchants closely linked to the Matanzas sugar economy became heavily involved. Two firms, Villoldo, Wardrop y Cía. (based in Havana and Glasgow) and Pereda, Machado y Cía. were the most important concerns in 1852 and 1853, when the trade began in earnest after a six-year hiatus. While Pereda continued as an important trader, the largest importer was Rafael Rodríguez

Table 13.2. Chinese Imported into Cuba by Nationality of Carrier, 1847–1873

	No. Ships	Tonnage	Chinese Embarked	Chinese Landed	Chinese Died	% Deaths
British	35	27,815	13,697	11,457	2,240	16.3
U.S.	34	40,576	18,206	16,419	1,787	9.8
Austrian	3	1,377	936	864	72	7.7
Belgian	3	2,482	1,199	1,182	17	1.4
Chilean	4	1,702	926	743	183	19.8
Danish	1	1,022	470	291	179	38.0
Dutch	19	14,906	8,113	7,132	981	12.1
French	104	64,664	38,540	33,795	4,745	12.3
German	8	4,207	2,176	1,932	244	11.2
Italian	5	5,586	2,832	2,505	327	11.2
Norwegian	5	2,296	1,366	1,104	262	19.2
Peruvian	6	4,979	2,609	1,999	610	23.4
Portuguese	21	15,847	8,228	7,266	962	11.7
Russian	12	9,857	5,471	5,093	378	6.9
Spanish	78	47,604	31,356	28,085	3,271	10.4
San Salvadoran	4	4,145	2,031	1,943	88	4.3
TOTAL	342	249,065	138,156	121,810	16,346	11.8

SOURCE: See Table 13.1.

Torices, who organized the Empresa de Colonización, also known as La Colonizadora, in 1854. (He would later purchased the Diagos' Ingenio Ponina in Banagüises.) The Drakes also became principal consignees, and during the 1850s Torices, Pereda, and Drake Hermanos imported more than 70 percent of the Chinese who disembarked in Cuba.[12] Zulueta, through his firm La Alianza, was an importer, as were José María Morales, owner of La Providencia, and Joaquín Pedroso, the planter, merchant, banker, and railroad builder whose principal interests were in rural Matanzas.[13]

Each Chinese laborer entered into an eight-year contract containing a variety of stipulations. Salaries were set at 4 pesos monthly and, through the 1850s and 1860s, rarely varied from this norm. Despite the fact that food and maintenance were provided, this rate was absurdly low, since wages for unskilled labor ranged between 17 and 25 pesos per month. In addition, the costs of transportation were the responsibility of the unfortunate colonos. In the mid-1850s Joaquín Pedroso advanced 8 pesos for each colono's transportation expenses and, on arrival at his estates, provided clothing worth 2.50 pesos. One peso in salary was deducted each month until this initial debt was paid off. Under no circumstances could contracts be broken, and a clause authorized the legitimate sale of labor contracts.[14] Through this legal mechanism, a market in Chinese contract laborers developed parallel to the Cuban slave market. The Chinese were openly traded, and this was accepted with little objection by nearly every sector of Cuban society, domestic or foreign, despite violations of the intent and letter of the labor contracts.

Matanzas planters enthusiastically embraced this experiment in Chinese labor. Of the 34,050 Asian inhabitants of Cuba enumerated in the 1861 census, 44.8 percent worked on estates in Matanzas province. By 1877, after the Chinese trade had ceased, 42.6 percent of the 47,116 Chinese in Cuba labored in Matanzas.[15] While slaves were still the core of plantation labor, Chinese workers made up a significant portion of the province's ingenio work force. In 1859, for example, Chinese contract laborers accounted for 15.5 percent of the total 27,959 workers on Colón's sugar estates.

Many planters actively attempted to escape their traditional dependence on slaves by substituting Chinese workers. The Diagos' Perseverancia mills are a prime example. In 1859, the Tinguaro, Santa Elena, and Ponina estates utilized a work force totaling 1,580, of whom 583 (36.9 percent) were Chinese. The Sociedad Territorial Cubana's Ingenio San Joaquín counted on a labor force of 233 slaves and 107 Chinese laborers, 31.5 percent of the total. The Arrietas' Flor de Cuba had a total work force of 643, of whom 30 percent were Chinese. On smaller, less capitalized mills, the proportions of Chinese were sometimes much higher. Juan Bautista Sanz, a planter whose Ingenio La Chucha in Jíquimas extended for 42 caballerías, utilized 130 Chinese and 133 slaves in 1859. Juan María Ponce de Leon's Ingenio Escorial, at 70 caballerías, used 130 Chinese and 170 slaves. Ingenio Santo Domingo, 50 caballerías in Macagua owned by Domingo García Capo, utilized 150 Chinese workers and 60 slaves. Julián de Zulueta, however, Cuba's largest slave trader in the 1850s, continued his traditional reliance on slaves. His Álava, Habana, Vizcaya complex in Banagüises had a total work force of 1,627, of whom 9.9 percent (162) were Chinese.[16]

Data from Cárdenas for 1875 show the continued importance of Chinese laborers for the regional sugar economy. Of a plantation labor force of 19,931, Chinese made up 12.9 percent (2,579 workers). Slaves still constituted the core labor force on most estates, although there were exceptions. Ingenio Santa Rosa, 80 caballerías in Cimarrones (46 planted in cane) had 283 workers, of whom 154 were Chinese (54.4 percent). Yet, many traditional slave-based plantations continued to rely on slave labor, although Chinese colonos met important labor demands. José Baró's Luisa and Olimpo mills had a combined labor force of 973, of whom 20.2 percent were Chinese, while La Gran Azucarera's San Martín and Echevarría estates employed only 37 Chinese, 7.1 percent of all workers.[17]

The province-wide sugar census of 1877/78 revealed the presence of 8,648 Chinese working on ingenios. They accounted for a significant portion of the labor force, 13.3 percent of 64,993 total workers. An average of 20 Chinese were employed on each ingenio throughout the province.[18]

Few Chinese were imported after 1873, when the Chinese Passenger Act forbade North American and British shipping from continued participation in the *trata amarilla*. Finally, a treaty signed between Spain and China in 1877 ended yet another sad chapter in the history of human abuse that accompanied the development of Cuba's sugar economy. Nearly 12 percent of all the Chinese that left their homes had perished on the voyage to the Caribbean, a terribly high death rate. Mortality rates within Cuba are unknown, and the collective fate of Chinese survivors in the late nineteenth and early twentieth centuries remains a topic to be explored by future scholars. Some were able to return to China after the termination of their contracts, but no systematic data are known to have been collected. Others remained as wage laborers or migrated to cities where they lived in segregated communities. Many were press-ganged by the government for labor on public-works projects or, during the Ten Years' War, for service in the Spanish military. Crawford, the British consul general, reported in 1873 that Chinese who fulfilled their contracts were being sent by the colonial government to labor on the "segunda trocha," a second armed ditch being constructed to sever western Cuba from the rebellious east. This trench was projected to extend from Bagá, on the Bay of Nuevitas, to Santa Cruz.[19]

The Chinese could be violently rebellious. Planters reported that physical abuse by mayorales was simply not tolerated by the Chinese, who often murdered those attempting to enforce discipline by use of the whip. The Chinese believed that this kind of retribution was justified if sanctioned by a number of people. Accordingly, in the aftermath of any such violence perpetrated by one of their number, all the Chinese on an estate would confess, thus frustrating any attempt by planters to punish individuals. Another common response to unjustified punishment was the torching of cane fields or the abandonment of plantations for maroonage. Suicide to escape the unhappiness and misery of isolation on oppressive plantations was also widespread.[20] During the insurrection of 1868–1878, Chinese sometimes made their way to rebel lines; and with the breakdown of absolute control on plantations during the 1870s, they tested the limits of the new socioeconomic milieu in the same way that slaves sought new prerogatives.[21]

Although the Chinese were an important component of rural labor in Matanzas from the early 1850s through the late 1870s, their utilization as workers did little to alter the fundamental structure of labor relations in the plantation zones of the region. It is impossible to argue that Chinese labor represented the beginning of a transition to free labor and that dependence on forced labor decreased. The use of Chinese may have heralded a transition away from total reliance on slave labor; that, however, is not the same thing as a step toward free wage labor. The composition of coerced labor on Matanzas plantations was altered, but the importation of Chinese did little to foster the growth of wage labor or to decrease the dependence of Matanzas planters on external labor supplies. The Chinese were paid nominal wages according to contracts, but their utilization represented the continuation of coerced labor in another form. Certainly the flexibility and adaptability of Cuban planters is underlined by their willingness and enthusiasm to attempt a change in the labor foundations of sugar production. But, this was a reaction to external threats to the future of the African trata, rather than to any lack of economic viability of slave labor or to any real possibility of fomenting a broadly based labor market in rural Cuba. Had there been no British pressure to abolish the transatlantic slave trade, there would have been no Chinese contract-labor trade.

Thus, the ethnic shift in the composition of forced labor on Matanzas plantations had little short-term effect on the structure of labor-force organization. Any long-term impact was impossible. Not only did labor contracts expire after eight years, but there was no possibility of the Chinese population reproducing naturally. Practically no females were imported. In 1862 there was only 1 Chinese woman living in Matanzas, and by 1877 there was a grand total of 26 females. Death from old age and extreme exploitation, together with the infrequency of intermarriage, meant that without the maintenance of import levels, the Chinese population of Cuba would inevitably disappear. Thus, there could have been absolutely no long-term contribution of the Chinese to the formation of a Cuban labor market. Other than scattered, abstract declarations (which should not be taken at face value) there was little desire or willingness on the part of planters to effect the transition to free labor; nor was this the purpose of importing Chinese "colonos." They were imported to continue the survival of forced labor and to maintain the traditional prerogatives of planters in a period of uncertainty concerning the future of the African trata. The reality of eventual abolition was gradually accepted by the planters of rural Matanzas; structurally, though, Chinese contract labor represented little more than the maintenance of old forms of labor-force organization.

With the curbing of the African slave trade in the late 1860s, the beginning of legal abolition in 1870, and the cessation of Chinese imports in 1873, Matanzas planters faced the beginning of the acute labor crisis they had dreaded for so long. In the early 1870s core slave-labor forces were not seriously disturbed by the terms of the Moret Law. But with the inability to replenish slave supplies through imports, and with the increasing rebelliousness and resistance to absolute domination on the part of slave dotaciones by the mid-1870s, a plantation labor crisis began to unfold that would severely weaken the planters of Matanzas by the close of the decade. Complaints of labor shortages were widespread by the mid-1870s. Rafael Rodríguez Torices, then the owner of Ingenio Ponina, informed Moses Taylor in 1876 that the harvest would be only half of what was expected, solely because of a lack of workers to harvest cane.[22] This situation was generalized.

Planters responded with three fundamental strategies. The first was the development of various schemes to import "free" contract labor from different regions. Most of these plans were desperately farfetched, and all were ultimately unsuccessful. In 1873 a company was formed to recruit purportedly free workers from Africa and the "East Indies" (read: China). Remarkably, the company proposed the payment of only 4 pesos in monthly wages but would (magnanimously, in their view) create a fund of 384 pesos for each laborer, payable at the conclusion of an eight-year contract. This money would ostensibly cover repatriation costs for these "free" workers.[23] This dreamlike attempt to resurrect the past testifies to the failure of Cuban planters to internalize intellectually the process unfolding before their eyes. Absolute domination over rural labor was ending, but planters continued to believe that the same forms of control could be maintained under new guises.

This absurd plan was followed by more desperation. In 1877, under the leadership of Julián de Zulueta, now the Marqués de Álava, the Círculo de Hacendados formed the Planters' Colonization Company. This company planned to raise 2 million pesos for none other than the importation of "free" Chinese laborers, despite the fact that Spain and China had abolished the Chinese slave trade earlier in the decade. Zulueta, seeking approval for this backward-looking attempt to resolve the labor crisis of the 1870s, informed the British consul Augustus Cowper on the terms of this "new" plan. A fair proportion of women would be recruited; the Chinese would be imported without contracts so that they could negotiate terms with masters (!) of their choice; they would be sent back to China after a certain, yet undefined, period of service; and the Chinese government would be asked to appoint a consul to look after the rights of the Chinese.[24]

That same year, the Company to Import Free Laborers was established, with the goal of enlisting immigrants from the Canary Islands. However, these too would be contract workers subject to severe stipulations designed to convert them into semi-slave labor on the Chinese model. Wages of 8 pesos monthly would be paid.[25]

The search for labor in Africa, China, and the Canary Islands was little more than a desperate attempt to maintain old structures of labor exploitation at the precise moment when these were passing from the historical stage. A hallmark of the Cuban planter class, from the eighteenth century on, had been their flexibility and innovative response to the availability of new technology, or to any shift in international conditions affecting the Cuban sugar economy. But the absolute domination of field labor was apparently so deeply ingrained within the social psychology of Cuban planters that they were blinded to the coming end of their traditional prerogatives and to the impossibility of effecting utopian schemes designed to resurrect the past. The world was changing rapidly and decisively around them, and their failure to understand and adapt to the new socioeconomic environment was ultimately fatal.

The second alternative was more realistic, albeit marginally pursued and difficult. In recognition that the shortage of labor stemmed in part from the stubborn unwillingness of planters to acknowledge that labor availability was increasingly subject to the laws of the marketplace, wages were raised on some estates. Without substantial salaries, free workers would not labor on sugar estates. Accordingly, those planters with liquid capital at their disposal were willing to pay higher wages to ensure adequate labor supplies. In 1877 Ignacio Montalvo y Calvo, one of the wealthiest merchants/planters/noblemen in Matanzas, was contracting Chinese workers whose initial eight-year contracts had expired—at salary rates of 30 pesos monthly and without stipulations.[26] Indeed, 25–30 pesos monthly for field labor—unheard of only a few years before—was common in the mid-1870s. Yet, salaried workers could not meet the labor demands of the plantation economy. In 1875, with its labor force shrinking, free salaried workers on Cárdenas plantations constituted only 12.2 percent of all workers.[27]

Two factors were responsible for the inability to develop a free, salaried work force on a broad scale in the mid-1870s. First was the general unwillingness of freemen to labor on sugar plantations. Rural Cuban social relations in the mid-1870s were still defined primarily by the arbitrariness and harshness of slavery. The rebellion in the east, the increasing testing of the chains of bondage by the slaves themselves, and fears of a complete breakdown of plantation discipline on the part of planters resulted in the maintenance of extreme controls by overseers and mayorales. Despite the beginning of legal abolition, there was little change in the psychology or reality of labor relations. Workers were treated with suspicion, arbitrariness, and continued degradation, whether slave, Chinese, or free. So long as slavery defined attitudes toward labor, freemen were unwilling to work en masse on sugar plantations, salary increases notwithstanding.

A second constricting limitation to the development of salaried labor on a broad scale was linked to the economic dynamics of Cuban sugar production. Most planters did not have the cash or credit resources at their disposal to make the short-term transition to a system requiring significant payroll disbursements. Traditionally, merchants had advanced limited quantities of specie to planters for payment of skilled labor, but most of the economic mechanisms connecting planters with merchants and their capital revolved around credit based on the exchange of products. Provisions were advanced to ingenios, and sugar or molasses was delivered to square accounts at harvesttime. In the absence of banking institutions and with the continued predominance of credit facilities designed for an earlier era, it was nearly impossible to retool quickly the mechanisms of credit in order to meet the cash requirements mandated by salaried labor.

Some planters were able to raise liquid capital quickly, but for most this was a daunting task. Planters were virtual prisoners of the traditional credit system and, even though it was rapidly becoming outdated, of a labor system that made few ready-cash demands. Free workers would neither labor for promises of future wages nor accept scrip designed to bind them to individual plantations—at least in the 1870s. It must be underlined that a genuine labor market had not yet developed. Slave labor predominated on most plantations, and frontier regions still offered the lure of land availability as a survival alternative. There was no compelling need for large numbers of free workers to seek employment on estates in order to survive, especially given the multiple meanings of "labor" on Cuba's slave-based plantations. There would be no orderly transition to free, salaried labor even though the most farsighted planters may have seen this as inevitable, if not desirable.

The third strategy followed by planters attempting to find alternative sources of labor was the renting of sections of their estates. The idea of plantation subdivision, renting to colonos, was not new. As early as 1836, in the aftermath of the second Spanish-British treaty to enforce the abolition of the Cuban slave trade, a plan was proposed to the Sociedad Patriótica de la Habana for the development of a colono system of cane production.[28] The Diagos began to experiment with renters on their Tinguaro, Santa Elena, and Ponina estates in the early 1860s. But the real origins of the modern Cuban "colonato"—which grows cane but does not produce sugar—are found in the early-1870s response of planters to the labor shortages that accompanied the abolition of the Cuban slave trade and the ban on the importation of Chinese contract laborers.

Cuban colonos developed in the late nineteenth and early twentieth centuries as a diverse group, and they can in no way be considered a uniform social class.[29] Many were independent landowners, ranging from owners of fragmented small farms to hacendados with veritable estates and large numbers of employees. Others rented the land of plantation owners through contracts (whose arrangements varied). The colonos were bound together by one common characteristic. Cane was grown and marketed to processors for conversion into sugar. Yet, even the smallest and most dependent colonos, those renting small portions of existing plantations, had little in common with day laborers. A parcel of land was held in usufruct, and the benefits extracted from cane growing were linked to the individual effort of the colono and his family. For sugar producers, the incentive of material gain replaced the need for labor regimentation and control.

The use of colonos was marginal in the early 1870s and generally coincided with the establishment of ingenios designated as centrales, which specialized in processing cane rather than growing it. This was the first real division of labor and production in rural Cuba, but these centrales are not to be confused with the modern central factories that appeared in the early twentieth century. The technology employed was modern for the time to be sure, but production was limited. The types of processing equipment and the productive capacity of these mills differed little from the slave-based estates struggling to survive in rural Matanzas. They were distinguished by their specialization in sugar production and by their minimal labor demands, a response to new conditions of labor scarcity.

Eight Matanzas mills were designated as "centrales" in the mid-1870s. Five were located in frontier regions still in the process of development, four in Hanábana and one in Palmillas. The other three were in older areas of sugar production. It is conspicuous that almost all these mills were owned by relative newcomers to rural Matanzas. Older entrepreneurs were wed to traditional methods of productive organization; they found it difficult to make the transition to the new form of specialization that would become widespread in the 1880s. Most of these centrales had little land under direct cultivation and purchased cane from surrounding independent farmers, or colonos, who rented parcels from plantations in the process of subdivision. Table 13.3 describes centrales extant in rural Matanzas in 1875 and 1876.

Although there are few systematic data on these early Matanzas colonos, several scattered documentary references tell us something of the *colonato* in this formative phase. In 1873 Francisco Barreto sold Ingenio Pilar, located on the old Hacienda San Antón de la Anegada in Guanajayabo, to Francisco Fernández Piloto. Part of the sale noted the existence of three colonos on the estate. They were in charge of planting, cutting, and carting cane to the milling complex and were paid a piece rate of 2.25 pesos for each 2,500

Table 13.3. Centrales in Rural Matanzas, 1875–1876

	Partido	Owner	Cabs.	Culti-vated Cabs.	Workers Slaves	Workers Colonos	Workers Free
Central Oriente	Guamutas	Eduardo Zumarada and Francisco Gómez	14	1	1	10	7
Central Anita	Lagunillas	José (?) y Rivas	1	0	0	0	15
Central Victoria	Hanábana	Juan F. Casas y Cía.	23	4	12	0	0
Central Perla	Hanábana	José María González	42	14	22	0	0
Central La Paz	Hanábana	José Perera y Negrín	30	7	18	0	0
Central Sta. Petrona	Hanábana	Marcos Sardiña	25	2	12	0	0
Central Batalla	Macagua	Favio y Hermanos	11	5	18	0	0
Central Loreto	Palmillas	Agustín Rebolledo	2	2	0	0	0

SOURCE: ANC, Gobierno General, leg. 270, no. 13563; leg. 269, no. 13554.
NOTE: Cabs. = caballerías (33.6 acres each).

pounds of cane (100 arrobas) delivered to the ingenio.[30] No land extension is noted, but two contracts effected in 1870 by José Perera, the owner of Central La Paz, indicate the varied dimensions of *colono* land use. In one contract, Emilio Noda was ceded 1 caballería of land for a period of nine years. During this time, he was to plant the land in cane and was responsible for its harvesting and delivery to the mill during the zafra. Enrique Meloun, however, was given 9 caballerías, 8 of which were to be sown in sugarcane; the remaining caballería could be used at his discretion. Meloun was also responsible for the harvesting and delivery of this cane to the mill, although there is no indication of the economic compact between these colonos and the mill owner.[31]

The colonato was to become the most important labor system utilized by the Matanzas sugar economy in the period preceding the insurrection of 1895. In the aftermath of the Ten Years' War, the abolition law of 1880 established the patronato, which eased the end of forced labor. But this by no means paved the way for the formation of a labor market in the sugar-producing regions of rural Cuba. Cultural perceptions of plantation labor among free people—whether white, mulatto, or black—precluded attempts to expand the wage-labor force. Migration to the east or the anonymity of city life was preferred to the human degradation associated with plantation work.

Nor could the old planter class be weaned from their felt need to control, dominate, and discipline field labor. Slavery governed the psychology of labor relations, and it was nearly impossible for planters whose economic lives and social interactions had been defined by slavery for generations to adjust to a milieu in which attitudes toward labor required a completely different set of economic, social, and cultural criteria. In a socioeconomic environment where free people could survive through other means, the stubborn insistence on maintaining slavelike conditions foreclosed the possibility of any widespread development of a free labor market. Slavery may have been abolished legally by the mid-1880s, but transformation of the social psychology engendered by centuries of human bondage would be more difficult to eradicate, both in planters and in ex-slaves. The failure to adapt to abolition, among other factors, would mean the decline of the social group that had developed the plantation economy of Matanzas. Most of the prominent families who had built ingenios, constructed railroads, imported slaves and Chinese, and modernized mills would be vague memories by the early twentieth century. Their places were taken by newcomers whose attitudes toward labor were flexible, adaptive, and not weighed down by an institution legally relegated to history. The Diagos, Arrietas, Pedrosos, Montalvos, Aldamas, and others had built their lives around African slavery. Now its abolition was directly related to their downfall as Cuba's dominant social class.

PART THREE

Matanzas between Rebellions: The Structures of Monoculture Transformed, 1878–1895

CHAPTER 14

The Aftermath of War and the Impact of Emancipation

Matanzas emerged from the Ten Years' War with its productive infrastructure virtually intact. Yet, while physical damage to the province's mills and cane fields had been minimal, planters, merchants, and colonial officials were imbued with an overwhelming sense of crisis. The insurrection had hastened the beginning of legal abolition and had politically mobilized heretofore-dormant sectors of the social hierarchy. Matanzas sugar planters structured their economic lives around slave labor, but in the aftermath of the rebellion slaves refused to accept prewar conditions of plantation life. Insurgent slaves had gained their freedom as part of the Peace of Zanjón, which ended the war in 1878. Many blacks were unable to consummate the freedom nominally gained under the terms of the 1870 Moret Law. Restlessness was rife and eventually led to a complete breakdown of plantation discipline. Slaves fled, refused to work, demanded wages, and actively sabotaged production in a variety of ways. In short, the foundation upon which sugar monoculture in Matanzas had been built crumbled before the eyes of disbelieving and desperate planters.

Although the abolition law of 1880 attempted to stem the labor crisis by establishing the patronato, a system designed to maintain the old prerogatives of planters while easing the path to complete emancipation, it had little success in the face of a mobilized slave population determined to break the chains of human bondage. Planters unsuccessfully sought to maintain old productive structures, and the labor crisis deepened. Alternative sources of field labor could not be found in sufficient quantities to support a sugar economy that was beginning to disintegrate along with the institution on which it was based. Within three years of the war's end, more than eighty provincial mills had ceased grinding cane. Abolition may have been piecemeal and gradual from 1870 on, but it was cataclysmic for the old productive system—which, far from being incompatible with slave labor, was dependent on servitude and could not function in any other way. Slavery did not cause the crisis of the 1880s; abolition did.

The complete reorganization of productive structures began in the 1880s, continued into the 1890s, and was interrupted by the 1895–1898 rebellion, the coup de grace to the old planter class. Sugar production was increasingly concentrated, surviving mills were technologically modernized, and the division of the industry into its agricultural and industrial components was begun in earnest. With the short-term absence of labor replacements for disappearing slaves, processors had to find other mechanisms for securing cane to supply their mills. Four fundamental strategies were pursued by a constantly declining number of mill owners. The first was to continue the direct cultivation of cane on estates by employing wage labor. This had only limited success and drained resources, for capital that might have been used to modernize processing had to be devoted to salary disbursements.

A second alternative was to subdivide estates into *colonias*, rented to individuals who would be obligated to grow cane for the mills. The lack of a labor market in rural Matanzas made this a viable system of producing cane within the confines of sugar-processing estates. Since renters earned incomes according to the quantity of cane delivered to mills, a powerful incentive existed for efficient cane cultivation. A third possibility was to lease neighboring sugar estates whose owners no longer processed cane and did not have the capital or the will to continue agricultural exploitation. These, in turn, were usually subdivided into colonias.

The fourth alternative was to purchase cane from surrounding independent farmers. As ingenios became modernized centrales, grinding capacity increased markedly and demand for cane superseded the possibilities of agricultural production within existing plantations. Mill owners specialized in sugar production, not in cane growing. Even when surrounding land was available for purchase, labor-market limitations made it impossible for processors to cultivate sufficient quantities of cane to supply the ever-increasing demands of their mills. This developing market for sugarcane stimulated the proliferation of independent growers throughout Matanzas. Many were former mill owners who did not have the resources to modernize antiquated ingenios. Now they specialized in producing sugarcane, and since resources could be devoted to agriculture without the preoccupation and financial drain of manufacture, they increased production. Others were smaller farm owners with new incentives to convert land from food-crop production or pasture to sugarcane. Central factories provided the stability of a guaranteed market, which stimulated the development of cane cultivation on farms of all sizes throughout rural Matanzas.

Mill owners pursued all four strategies to varying degrees. This was not a linear process, accomplished with order and regularity. Sugar survived the crisis of abolition and the transition to new forms of productive organization, but a great deal of social dislocation accompanied the economic transformations of the 1880s and early 1890s. Some families withdrew from sugar production to live in Havana, Madrid, Paris, or New York on the capital accumulated over the previous period. Others adapted to the changing economic realities by becoming cane growers. Many marginal producers were ruined by bankruptcy, and their offspring were to live in relative poverty.

Above all, the end of the Ten Years' War not only heralded the demise of slavery, but it also marked the passing away of many slaveholding and sugar-producing families who had created sugar monoculture in Matanzas. The patriarchs of the leading entrepreneurial families had all died by the early 1880s. Although there were exceptions, their sons and daughters were of a different ilk. Most had studied abroad, in the United States, France, or Spain, and had embarked upon professional careers. Some preserved an emotional attachment to the estates of rural Matanzas that had defined their parent's lives, but for many there was no pressing economic reason to maintain a presence. Nor was there the drive to carve out new forms of wealth and exploitation from a virtual wilderness as their parents had done. Notable families remained, but many sold their interests to newcomers, mostly immigrants, who had the same kind of ambition possessed by the creators of Matanzas sugar monoculture.

Elite groups in the social hierarchy were redefined in the 1880s and 1890s. New merchant houses appeared in the cities of Matanzas and Cárdenas, and a progressively reduced number of modernizing mill owners tied to commercial capital became the largest sugar producers. Caution must be exercised here. The old planter elite was not entirely swept away. Some family groups did persist into the twentieth century; but they were joined by newly arrived immigrants, largely from Spain.

Transformations were not confined to elite groups. The entire social structure was overhauled by the economic changes taking place in the production of sugar. Former slaves or indentured Chinese fled rural zones for the cities and towns—or for the eastern frontier, where land and new economic possibilities were developing. Others took advantage of opportunities to cultivate small tracts of land, owned or rented, as colonos, and this was a major attraction for rural working-class immigrants from Spain.

For the first time in the history of rural Matanzas, numerically significant social groups developed between the elite and the toiling masses of slaves or Chinese. This phenomenon should not be exaggerated though. Middle sectors may have appeared in the 1880s, but they scarcely had time to consolidate positions in the newly emerging socioeconomic order before the devastation of the war for independence abruptly halted their development.

The previous period (1837–1878) in the development of Matanzas monoculture was characterized by the physical and economic transformation of the environment. Yet, there was little change in the social order. Sugar production expanded by constantly shifting toward new frontier regions where the same methods and techniques were reapplied to high-yielding virgin lands. Extant social and economic structures in older areas of production were re-created in new areas with little variation. This pattern of development was altered substantially after 1878.

Above all, the frontier had moved eastward. In some regions of Matanzas, bordering the Zapata swamp and far to the southeast in Palmillas, there was still room for development. But the end of the insurrection, which had created a great deal of instability in *Las Villas* province because of constant occupations by insurgent and Spanish armies, meant that in 1878 political conditions had been created for the expansion of sugar into the heart of this frontier. Thus, the fundamental condition that had guaranteed high yields and the spatial expansion of sugar in Matanzas, the existence of productive frontier land, was coming to an end.

This does not mean that the possibilities for sugar were exhausted. Any further growth of the Matanzas sugar economy, however, rested not only on a more productive division of labor, but on the intensification of production rather than on its extensive expansion. Higher yields of sugarcane would have to be extracted from the land, and greater yields of sugar had to be forthcoming from cane in order for the industry to maintain its economic viability. This required the intensive capitalization of processing and growing, the application of new techniques, and the reorganization of the labor base of cane cultivation.

The level of capital accumulated by the Matanzas sugar economy justified a move in this direction. A sophisticated infrastructural system serving sugar had been unscathed by the war, and thousands of acres of land were already planted in sugarcane. The human resources of the province had been honed to serve sugar in some capacity. The old Matanzas elite could not lead the required transformation alone, and this set the stage for the penetration of capital and entrepreneurial skills from outside the province. Thus, while production was reorganized, and as the social structure began to shift along with the ensuing economic transformation, one aspect of provincial life was unyielding. Monocultural sugar production remained resilient, enduring, and all-encompassing.

Demographic Changes to 1894

Between 1877 and the eve of the Cuban war for independence, the Matanzas population ceased its dynamic growth. The slave trade had been ended and, more important, the economy was no longer expanding to act as magnet for migrants from abroad or other regions within Cuba. Slightly more than a quarter-million people inhabited the province in 1877; nearly 260,000 lived there in 1887; and approximately 254,000 were counted in a local survey of 1894.[1]

With the abolition of slavery, the Matanzas black and mulatto population began to decline. There was a 5 percent overall decrease in their ranks between 1877 and 1887, in all likelihood reflecting a gradual migration away from the province. Nevertheless, proportionally there was little change; people of color accounted for roughly 43 percent of all matanceros in 1877 and 45 percent in 1887. (See Tables 14.1 and 14.2.)

Between 1877 and 1894, population growth patterns in rural zones continued the trends established during the 1860s and early 1870s. These were characterized by the decline of population in older areas of sugar production and by demographic expansion in zones of new ingenio construction. Rural partidos in the jurisdiction of Matanzas lost 2.7 percent of their total inhabitants between 1877 and 1887, and experienced another 2.7 percent overall decrease between 1887 and 1894. In Cárdenas the total decline was 8.8 per-

Table 14.1. Matanzas, 1887: Population by Partido, Race, and Sex

	Whites			Blacks and Mulattoes			Total Pop.
	M	F	T	M	F	T	
Alfonso XII	2,493	1,856	4,349	3,512	1,850	5,362	9,711
Bolondrón	3,064	2,024	5,088	4,303	2,425	6,728	11,816
Cabezas	3,575	3,275	6,850	1,089	863	1,952	8,802
Canasí	1,702	1,433	3,135	767	622	1,389	4,524
Cárdenas	8,633	6,947	15,580	3,763	4,011	7,774	23,354
Cervantes	824	628	1,452	1,060	692	1,752	3,204
Cimarrones	1,210	943	2,153	2,857	1,869	4,726	6,879
Colón	5,779	4,243	10,022	3,837	2,820	6,657	16,679
Cuevitas	1,968	1,480	3,448	1,692	1,183	2,875	6,323
Guamacaro	3,060	2,211	5,271	2,898	2,076	4,974	10,245
Guamutas	3,192	2,151	5,342	3,702	2,545	6,247	11,589
Guanajayabo	1,884	1,483	3,367	2,855	1,910	4,765	8,132
Jovellanos	1,966	1,522	3,488	2,735	2,295	5,030	8,518
Lagunillas	1,443	1,184	2,627	1,735	987	2,722	5,349
Macagua	1,626	1,218	2,844	1,531	1,035	2,566	5,410
Macuriges	3,388	2,312	5,700	4,722	2,952	7,674	13,374
Matanzas	21,554	19,391	40,945	7,195	8,239	15,434	56,379
Palmillas	2,398	1,480	3,878	3,513	1,427	4,940	8,818
Roque	2,152	1,635	3,787	3,126	1,303	4,429	8,216
Sabanilla	2,061	1,483	3,544	3,084	2,243	5,327	8,871
San José de los Ramos	2,267	1,607	3,874	3,167	1,990	5,157	9,031
Santa Ana	1,797	1,322	3,119	1,983	1,117	3,100	6,219
Unión de Reyes	1,327	850	2,177	4,388	1,570	5,958	8,135
TOTAL	79,362	62,678	142,040	69,514	48,024	117,538	259,578

SOURCE: Spain, Instituto Geográfico y Estadístico, *Censo de la población de España según el empadronamiento hecho en 31 de diciembre de 1887* (Madrid: Imp. de la Dirección General del Instituto Geográfico y Estadístico, 1892), vol. 1.

NOTE: M = males; F = females; T = total; Pop. = population.

Table 14.2. Matanzas Population, 1894

Municipal District	Population
Alfonso XII	9,523
Bolondrón	11,436
Cabezas	8,758
Canasí	4,139
Cárdenas	22,945
Cervantes	3,133
Cimarrones	6,792
Colón	15,974
Cuevitas	6,359
Guamacaro	9,626
Guamutas	11,528
Guanajayabo	8,028
Jovellanos	8,177
Lagunillas	5,308
Macagua	5,307
Macuriges	12,761
Matanzas	56,065
Palmillas	8,184
Roque	8,089
Sabanilla	8,773
San José de los Ramos	8,808
Santa Ana	6,019
Unión de Reyes	7,884
TOTAL	253,616

SOURCE: AHPM, ME, Estadística, leg. 9, no. 171, fol. 2.

cent between 1877 and 1887, although this slowed significantly to a 0.9 percent total population loss in the seven years between 1887 and 1894. Rural Colón, which had demographically expanded with the wave of in-genio construction in the 1860s and early 1870s, continued to increase between 1877 and 1887, experiencing a total population expansion of 5.5 percent. However, with the continuing sugar-production crisis of the early 1890s, when prices collapsed on international markets, Colón's rural population finally began a process of contraction. Between 1887 and 1894 the population of the jurisdiction's rural partidos dropped a total of 2.6 percent, Colón's first demographic decrease in the nineteenth century.[2] (See Table 14.3.)

As the frontier was moving to the east, slaves or *patrocinados* were emancipated and enjoyed freedom of movement on a heretofore-unparalleled scale. The changing economic order created new opportunities, while old restrictions governing the lives of a broad cross section of the provincial population were removed. Population shifts were gradual, although this pe-

Table 14.3. Population Growth in Rural Areas of Matanzas, 1877–1894
(in percentages)

Jurisdiction	1877–1887	1887–1894	1877–1894
Matanzas	−2.7	−2.7	−5.4
Cárdenas	−8.8	−0.9	−9.7
Colón	+5.5	−2.6	+2.6

Sources: Spain, Instituto Geográfico y Estadístico, *Censo de la población de España según el empadronamiento hecho en 31 de diciembre de 1877* (Madrid: Imp. de la Dirección General del Instituto Geográfico y Estadística, 1883), vol. 1; Spain, Instituto Geográfico y Estadístico, *Censo de la población de españa según el empadronamiento hecho en 31 de diciembre de 1887*, vol. 1; AHPM, ME, Estadística, leg. 9, no. 171, fol. 2.

riod of slow demographic reorganization in Matanzas was short-lived. The war for independence would result in a demographic disaster of unparalleled proportions for the provincial population. Between 1895 and 1898, more than one-third would die—casualties of combat, murder by opposing armies, or the widespread starvation induced by the Spanish policy of concentrating the rural population in cities and towns.

The Crisis of the Early 1880s

Even though the last two years of the Ten Years' War were marked by the beginning of serious strains on the Matanzas sugar economy, 1878 was bountiful for provincial mill owners despite continual complaints about the labor crisis. During the zafra 516 mills ground cane producing nearly 27 million pesos in gross income. Although no specific output data are available for Matanzas, in the immediate aftermath of the war Cuban sugar production soared. In 1879 the island's harvest surpassed 775,000 metric tons, the largest of the nineteenth century to that year. However, in 1880 sugar production declined, and in 1881 the harvest was smaller in volume than most zafras during the insurrection.[3]

This was the beginning of the crisis long dreaded by the planter elite, and its impact was swift in Matanzas. Between 1878 and 1881 the number of provincial mills grinding cane decreased by more than 16 percent, from 516 to 431 ingenios. Gross income to the sugar sector suffered a decline of 27.5 percent. What caused this sudden transformation of the region's sugar economy after the dynamic expansion of the war years?

First of all, it must be underlined, there was no dramatic shift in the price structure of the international sugar market. Prices received by Matanzas planters actually increased between 1879 and 1881. Top-grade white sugars were marketed at slightly more than 6 cents/pound in 1879, at 8 cents/

pound in 1880, and at 8.25 cents/pound in 1881. Quebrado sugars followed
the same price trend. (See Figure 14.1.) While there are no available data
on Matanzas sugar output for these years, if we compare gross income statistics with the aforementioned data on price trends, a significant decline in
production is obvious.

Available evidence indicates that this decline was closely linked to serious
difficulties in the agricultural phase of sugar production. Not only did the
number of mills decrease significantly in Matanzas between 1878 and 1881,
but land area sown in cane by mill owners also declined: 11,286 caballerías
were planted in 1878 and 9,909 caballerías in 1881, although the average
extension of land planted in cane on each estate changed only slightly. In
1878 an average sugar plantation cultivated 21.9 caballerías, while in 1881
this had increased to 22.9 caballerías. However, there was a significant
change in output per caballería of land. In 1878 each caballería of cane
planted in Matanzas produced 2,383 pesos in gross income; by 1881, this
had declined by more than 17 percent to 1,967 pesos.

Mills in older areas of production suffered significantly more than those
in regions of more recent development. Estates located in Colón still had
the capacity to expand internally. But in the jurisdictions of Matanzas and
Cárdenas, the oldest areas of sugar exploitation in the province, there was
little room for spatial growth. For example, the average number of culti-

Figure 14.1. Sugar Prices in Matanzas, 1876–1895 (in cents per pound)
SOURCE: *Aurora de Matanzas*, 1876–1895.

vated caballerías on Colón ingenios increased from 26.1 to 29 (11.1 percent) between 1878 and 1881. In Cárdenas there was a slight decline from 19.6 to 18.7 caballerías/ingenio, while in Matanzas there was a small increase from 18.8 to 19.9 caballerías of cane on an average sugar plantation. These data are summarized in Table 14.4.

Data on production for twelve mills in the Alacranes partido of Bolondrón

Table 14.4. Selected Characteristics of the Matanzas Sugar Economy, 1878–1881

Region	No. Mills	Total Cabs.	Avg. Cabs./ Mill	Culti- vated Cabs.	Avg. Culti- vated Cabs./ Mill	Gross Income in Pesos	Avg. Gross Income/ Mill	Gross Income/ Culti- vated Cab.
1878								
Colón	178	9,835	55.3	4,641	26.1	11,642,493	65,407	2,508
Cárdenas	154	6,694	43.5	3,016	19.6	6,276,143	40,754	2,081
Matanzas	131	5,538	42.3	2,458	18.8	5,945,090	45,382	2,418
Alacranes	53	2,110	39.8	1,171	22.1	3,033,816	57,241	2,591
Province	516	24,177	46.9	11,286	21.9	26,897,542	52,127	2,383
1881								
Colón	137	8,149	59.5	3,972	29.0	8,547,431	62,390	2,152
Cárdenas	131	5,891	45.0	2,445	18.7	3,949,581	30,149	1,615
Matanzas	106	4,502	42.3	2,114	19.9	3,914,864	36,932	1,852
Alacranes	57	2,398	42.1	1,378	24.2	3,080,638	54,046	2,236
Province	431	20,940	48.6	9,909	22.9	19,492,514	45,226	1,967

SOURCES: "Noticias de las fincas azucareras en producción que existían en toda la isla de Cuba al comenzar el presupuesto de 1877–1878," *Revista Económica*, June 7, 1878, pp. 7–24; Provincia de Matanzas. Excma. Diputación Provincial, Sección de Fomento y Estadística, *Censo agrícola. Fincas azucareras. Año de 1881* (Matanzas: Imp. Aurora de Yumurí, 1883). This last document is found in manuscript form in AHPM, ME, Estadística, leg. 7, no. 126, "Provincia de Matanzas. 1881. Estado de las fincas azucareras que se hallan en su territorio."

NOTE: Cabs. = caballerías (33.6 acres each). For 1878, the municipal districts of Jíquimas and Roque, which were listed with Jovellanos, are included in the calculations for Colón, since they are part of the 1881 data base. Data for total caballerías and cultivated caballerías were available for only 432 of the 516 ingenios listed in the 1878 census. The totals listed here are reliable estimates of the 516 ingenios. They were derived by multiplying the number of ingenios for which data were missing by the average number of caballerías of land (total or cultivated) in each of the municipal districts composing these partidos. Income data were available for 493 of the 516 ingenios. Total gross income was derived for the missing ingenios by multiplying the number of ingenios for which data were missing (33) by the average income of known ingenios (493).

All data were available for the 1881 census. In that document, Sabanilla and Cabezas were part of Alacranes (which was denoted as Alfonso XII). Since in 1878 these partidos were part of Matanzas, for comparative purposes their data were included in the calculations for Matanzas.

These data are only for mills grinding cane and do not include colonias.

illustrate the dramatic fall of sugar production in the early 1880s. Output of white sugar on twelve Bolondrón ingenios dropped 83.9 percent between 1879 and 1884; quebrado production declined 28.4 percent; and molasses output decreased by 38.9 percent.[4] (See Figure 14.2.)

The crisis of the early 1880s was widespread, swift, and merciless. Although its causes were multifaceted and manufacture was affected as well as agriculture, the decline in sugarcane production was closely linked to the inability of Matanzas planters to find substitutes for the slave laborers who had supported the sugar economy throughout its various phases of development. Above all, the crisis was a labor crisis of unforeseen dimensions. The abolition law of 1880 heralded the definitive end of slavery by establishing the patronato, which theoretically freed a portion of total slaves each year beginning in 1884. However, patrocinados were obligated to enter into contractual arrangements with former masters which left the legal prerogatives of slavery intact.[5] The transition to free wage labor was to be gradual, and planters would have time able to substitute wage laborers for former slaves.

But that is not what happened. The number of Matanzas slaves and patrocinados declined by 9.6 percent yearly between 1877 and 1883, but they were not replaced by wage workers.[6] In addition, plantation discipline eroded, and it was impossible to impose former work schedules upon field

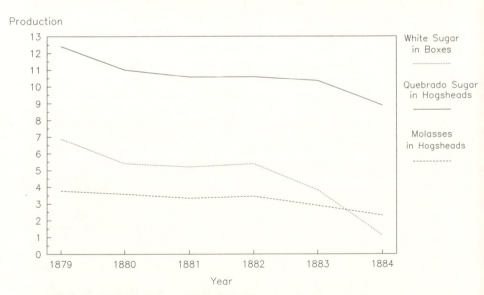

Figure 14.2. Production on Twelve Bolondrón Ingenios, 1879–1884 (in thousands of boxes or hogsheads)

Source: AHPM, ME, Estadística, leg. 9, no. 166, fol. 2.

laborers who resisted continued arbitrary domination at every turn. Agricultural yields declined not only because slave or patrocinado labor was disappearing and not being replaced, but also because remaining field labor was not so productive as such labor had been during the 1860s or 1870s. Galvanized by abolitionism, the possibilities for action carved out by the insurrection, and growing resistance to servitude, plantation slaves impeded agricultural production by refusing to respond to work demands.[7]

This phenomenon reflected the general militancy emerging among all sectors of labor, rural and urban. In Cuba's major cities a trade-based urban labor movement was developing, and there is no doubt that former slaves with ties to plantations played an important role. Tobacco workers had begun organizing guilds from 1865, when the Asociación de Tabaqueros de la Habana was first established, and this was followed by the formation of *gremios* representing different sectors of the tobacco working class.[8] Other tradesmen were also involved in incipient working-class organizations. In February 1886 there was a successful island-wide strike of coopers who were demanding wage increases. Two weeks later lightermen, weighmen, and longshoremen, following the lead of the coopers, struck over wages in every major port on the island. The U.S. consul in Matanzas reported the impressive unity among Matanzas dock workers in these strike movements, noting that Cubans, Spaniards, blacks, and mulattoes fraternized and acted in unison without allowing national or racial divisions to interfere in their movement.[9]

It is within the general context of this breakdown of old, absolute controls by elite groups that the disruption of sugar agriculture must be considered. The Ten Years' War unleashed heretofore-dormant forces in the social order. Sectors of the island's elite led the rebellion and demanded far-reaching political changes. But the masses were mobilized as well, even if large numbers of rural or urban slaves and workers did not directly take part in the revolt. In the aftermath of the insurrection, the reestablishment of the pre-1868 order was impossible. Above all, the abolition of slavery created an immediate labor crisis in the early 1880s from which the old planter class would not recover.

The economic problems faced by the planters of rural Matanzas were not confined to labor shortages and the falling productivity of existing labor. A variety of additional factors militated to drive large numbers of planters to bankruptcy and ruin by the end of the 1880s. Plantation owners were resigned to the inevitability of abolition, but they were not prepared for the rapid collapse of slave labor and of the old system of production after the insurrection. There was a startling lack of foresight on the part of the Matanzas elite and little meaningful preparation for the labor crisis of the 1880s. Intellectually, perhaps, planters could not come to grips with the reality of a drastic change in the relations of production. Many looked to the maintenance of old prerogatives and social controls in new forms, despite increasing evidence of a different future. The sugar economy had been so resilient, adaptive, and above all omnipotent that it was inconceivable to them that the social order built around sugar could come crashing down.

In part, this failure to recognize and adapt to the far-reaching changes occurring in the world around them was linked to the generational shift taking place. The old, innovative planter elite was disappearing from the scene, and their heirs were unaccustomed to dealing with the complexities of shifting markets, changing technological parameters, and scientific innovations. Nor did they possess the entrepreneurial acumen needed to revitalize a decaying system. There were exceptions, of course, but by and large the sons and the daughters of the old elite had little interest, aptitude, or need to continue the enterprises started by their parents.

Many were victims of economic routinization and collective paralysis when it came to innovation. In a detailed report on the provincial economy, submitted in late 1883, David Vicker, the U.S. consul in Matanzas, noted with marvel that in this "age of fertilizers" they were not being employed in Matanzas on a significant scale, even though the land was exhausted, agricultural yields were declining notably, and the sugar economy was falling apart. In another letter, he wrote that although the days of cheap labor were gone, "planters of the generation now passing away find it difficult to recognize the necessity of adopting new ideas and new customs. . . . [A] better and more thorough organization of labor is not practically accomplished."[10]

Difficulties begot more difficulties. The decline in production of the early 1880s was accompanied by the inability to make payments on outstanding loans. The sugar-producing elite was losing its labor force, yields and production were declining, and debt was mounting. Interest on unpaid debts accrued at rates upward of 12 percent yearly, and as debts increased merchants were no longer willing to risk further loans to planters. Future harvests, land, and machinery were already mortgaged to the hilt, and planters no longer possessed collateral that could secure additional loans.[11] The demand for capital and the contraction of credit markets pushed up interest rates to 24 percent yearly by the mid-1880s. This was an impossible financial burden for mill owners, for it meant that unpaid obligations would increase at faster rates than ever before.

Solvent planters attempted to deal with the crisis by the installation of modern processing equipment designed to increase the industrial yields of sugar. But the credit crunch made this difficult and, even when successful, it was sometimes an exercise in futility. One estate had installed new machinery at a cost of half a million pesos in the early 1880s, but could not borrow the 25,000 pesos needed to commence grinding during the 1883/84 harvest. Others, with older technology but considerable productive capacity, were not maintained because of the inability to acquire loans. Often, sales of wood, oxen, or horses raised cash to feed or pay laborers, but this further depleted productive resources needed in the long term.[12]

Mill owners also had to meet onerous tax burdens. Six percent of net income was paid to the municipal government. Another 2 percent was levied by the colonial government in Havana, and a surcharge of 16 percent was added onto this amount. Net income was calculated by deducting 60 percent from gross revenues, when in actuality production expenses were considerably more. Export duties amounted to .4 cents per pound of sugar, and there were transportation costs, warehousing fees, commissions, lighterage charges, loading charges, and bribes to avert unforeseen difficulties along the way.[13] These kinds of expenses were always part of the sugar economy, but they were extremely burdensome in the context of the general crisis experienced in the early 1880s.

Thus, in addition to the labor crisis, there was a credit crisis of considerable dimensions precisely at a time when cash-flow demands were raised. To attract labor, plantations had to pay wages; thus, they needed liquid capital during the zafra. Slaves were disappearing, but how could the transition to wage labor begin in earnest if it was so difficult to command the resources to meet the payrolls free labor mandated?

Two other factors dealt fatal blows to a large sector of the old elite. The first was short-term, but devastating nonetheless. A prolonged drought in Matanzas, during the summer and fall of 1883, resulted in heavily damaged cane fields and a harvest diminished by one-third from the previous year. The reduced zafra meant that few planters managing to grind cane during the winter of 1884 were able to pay their constantly increasing debts. Bankruptcies were widespread by the summer of 1884, and progressively more and more mills ceased producing sugar.

The second factor sounded the death knell for the structure of the Matanzas slave-based sugar economy and spurred a more productive division of labor. Sugar would remain, and in fact prosper, but the industry would be reorganized socially and economically. After the harvest of 1883, sugar prices on the international market fell almost continuously to 1895, when they reached a low of slightly under 2 cents/pound for the best-grade Cuban white sugars. European beet sugar claimed an increasing share of the world market; as supplies increased, prices declined. Against the backdrop of the general crisis of the early 1880s, this meant the final destruction of many old planter families. The capital requirements for remaining in business foreclosed the possibility of continued production to all but those with extensive lines of credit or accumulated capital. Commercial interests began to dominate rural Matanzas, processing was centralized, and the labor basis of sugar agriculture was completely transformed.

CHAPTER 15

Labor Reorganization:
Colonias and Wage Workers

As the economic crisis deepened in the early 1880s, it was paralleled by the reorganization of Matanzas social and economic structures. Several simultaneous processes began in the early 1880s, and these continued up to the eve of the insurrection in 1895. The labor basis of sugar production was completely transformed, resulting in a more efficient system of land use. A more productive division of resources resulted from the ongoing separation of processing and growing, and this was accompanied by the reorganization of landholding and by changes in the social composition of sugar-producing elites. Finally, the old commercial class of Matanzas province was replaced by relative newcomers whose access to extensive capital resources enabled them to take advantage of the dislocation caused by the crisis.[1] By 1895 the structures of sugar monoculture had been overhauled, and new levels of productivity were attained. The result was the survival of sugar and the emergence of a social order markedly different from the rural society that had flourished before the Ten Years' War.

Labor experienced the most far-reaching changes. The colonial elite had hoped to regularize the disintegration of slavery with the 1880 abolition law. Patrocinados were to be paid wages as an incentive for continued labor while slavery was being legally dismantled. But the patronato was little more than a hopelessly doomed attempt to slow the rapidly deteriorating labor situation by maintaining forced labor within new legal parameters. Patrocinados were to be paid 3 pesos monthly in gold—certainly attractive from the planter point of view, since free labor commanded salaries of 17 pesos monthly in gold during the *tiempo muerto* and 20 pesos gold each month at harvesttime in the mid-1880s.[2] Those who remained enslaved drew no wages.

Slaves and patrocinados responded to the continuation of servitude, legal or otherwise, with varied forms of resistance and sabotage. Forty slaves on the Torrientes' Ingenio Cantabria left the estate spontaneously in May 1880 because they were not permitted to sing in the fields while working. In the early 1880s, slaves on the Zuluetas' ingenios España and Álava regularly refused to leave their barracones to work. Francisco Feliciano Ibañez reported that slaves on his Ingenio San Joaquín would not follow any orders. Abusive mayorales on the ingenios Soledad and Arco Iris were attacked and gravely injured when they tried to discipline field laborers. Patrocinados left estates whenever they pleased and disobeyed work orders at their whim. If they did labor in the fields, they did not work as long or as hard as before, when mayorales patrolled the cañaverales on horseback with whips poised to meet insubordination.[3] The *látigo* was banned by the emancipation law of 1880, and now its use brought swift retaliation by slaves—either through physical attack on the abuser, or through protest to local juntas, which were charged with overseeing the rights of patrocinados and which could free them if the letter of the law was not followed.

The labor dilemma faced by planters was monumental. To continue the direct exploitation of estates, a free labor market would have to emerge, something progressive planters had been calling for since the 1840s. Theoretically this may have been attractive as an alternative to slavery, but when historical conditions made free labor a reality, planters were rudely awakened to the cold objectivity of emerging capitalist relations of production. Real market conditions for labor developed in rural Matanzas; but labor costs, rather than decreasing, skyrocketed. Workers were in short supply, demand was broadly based, and labor was costly. Planters unable to pay workers 20 pesos monthly in gold at harvesttime, the terms of the free labor market in the mid-1880s, could not continue to produce sugar. The generalized crisis of the early 1880s left many planters without the realistic possibility of meeting such stringent cash requirements. In order to survive, mechanisms to reduce the capital requirements of production would have to be found.

Plantation owners able to weather the storm pursued two strategies. The first was to specialize in cane production while abandoning processing. Cane was grown and sold to the emerging central factories, which concentrated on processing rather than growing. The second path was to divide estates into colonias of varying sizes and then rent them to colonos.

The term "colonia" had three distinct meanings in late-nineteenth-century rural Cuba, and these should be made clear. One referred to communities of immigrants who were recruited to populate sparsely populated frontier zones by settling on subdivided estates or unused *haciendas comuneras*. The classic example of this is the "colonia blanca" recruited to settle the Xagua Bay (Cienfuegos) region early in the nineteenth century.[4]

The second referred to groups of renters who were recruited to grow cane on estates that, because of the labor and credit shortages of the post-1878 period, were no longer able to cultivate the land directly. These colonos leased sections of varying sizes on already existing plantations. Rental arrangements were diverse in the early 1880s. Some colonos paid cash rents; others delivered predetermined quantities of cane to the mills at harvesttime. Most, however, were obligated through written contracts or oral agreements to cultivate cane on stipulated pieces of land and were paid a fixed volume of sugar for every hundred arrobas of cane delivered to the mills. By the mid-1880s, this second type of colonia was the most widely employed means of maintaining Matanzas sugar cane production. Although estate owners with capital reserves continued to exploit their plantations directly, these planters were few and far between in rural Matanzas by the end of the 1880s. Almost all plantations leased portions of their cane fields to colonos, thus reducing labor costs and shifting the burden of cane production to a newly emerging social sector.

The third meaning of "colonia" had to do with a separate social class distinguished by the fact that they were not renters, but actually owned the land on which cane was cultivated. This sector of rural society, though highly stratified, shared one fundamental economic reality. They specialized in cane cultivation and were dependent upon processors for the marketing of their product. These colonos might be former mill owners no longer capable of manufacturing sugar competitively. Many of their estates were quite large, and they too were almost always subdivided into colonias.

Thus, some colonos in this third category used another type of colono to produce cane. Others, owners of more modest estates, were simply independent farmers taking advantage of new opportunities to cultivate a different cash crop with a relatively guaranteed market.

The second and third types of colonia were the ones most commonly found throughout rural Matanzas in the 1880s and 1890s. Some colonos, then, owned the means of production; others, a renter class, did not. This dichotomy in the emerging class structure of Matanzas rural society is well worth noting.

It is impossible to quantify precisely the various types of colonos existing in rural Matanzas before the war began in 1895. Official documentation referred to "colonias" universally, without distinguishing whether they were owned or rented. One undated land census, however, probably preceding the 1895 insurrection, offers a very precise image of land-tenure patterns among farms designated as colonias. A highly stratified system of land control is clearly evident. Of the 1,257 colonos, 37.5 percent occupied less than 2 caballerías of land and accounted for only 2.7 percent of all land owned by this class. Another 25 percent owned between 2 and 5 caballerías, and they farmed only 6.2 percent of total colono land. Thus, more than 60 percent of all colonos worked tracts of land less than 5 caballerías in extension, but controlled a mere 8.9 percent of the 14,004 caballerías in the hands of colonos. Land concentration was extreme at the top of the colono hierarchy: 99 colonos, or 7.9 percent of the total, occupied farms larger than 40 caballerías and accounted for 52.7 percent of all colono land. Thus, the division of the sugar industry into its agricultural and industrial components did not lead to a more equitable system of land ownership, although it should be noted that all colonos were supported by a rather stable market. Table 15.1 summarizes these data.

Although not specified in the census, it is likely that the above data refer to owners rather than to renters. The 1899 census conducted under the auspices of the U.S. War Department counted 1,109 farms growing sugarcane that were owned and an additional 1,024 that were leased in the province of Matanzas.[5] The figure for owners is close enough to the figure in Table 15.1 to allow the conclusion that the land-tenure structure discussed above was almost certainly for landowning colonos.

The very existence of this new class of sugarcane producers was predicated upon close economic linkages with sugar processors and finance capital. By the early 1890s, contracts between growers, millers, and lending merchants became so widespread that a special commercial notary was established in Matanzas with the sole task of recording the numerous colono contracts. Colonos faced certain initial capital requirements regardless of the size of the farm. The smallest colonias employed family labor, but most colonos had to employ a work force determined by the size of the individual farm. Thus, capital was needed for salary disbursements and for other factors of production. Agricultural implements, carts, animals, and packing materials had to be acquired and their levels maintained. With the emer-

Table 15.1. Colonias in Bolondrón, Cárdenas, Colón, Guamutas,
Jagüey Grande, and Macuriges, ca. 1895:
Land-Tenure Structure

Farm Size (Cabs.)	No. Farms	%	Land (Cabs.)	%
.13–.99	227	18.1	104	0.7
1–1.99	245	19.5	278	2.0
2–2.99	170	13.5	358	2.6
3–4.99	145	11.5	510	3.6
5–9.99	141	11.2	919	6.6
10–19.99	139	11.1	1,880	13.4
20–39.99	91	7.2	2,573	18.4
40–59.99	50	4.0	2,319	16.6
60–99.99	31	2.5	2,264	16.2
100–199.99	15	1.2	1,897	13.5
200 +	3	0.2	902	6.4
TOTAL	1,257	100.0	14,004	100.0

SOURCE: AHPM, Gobierno Provincial, Ingenios, leg. 7, no. 122, fols. 1–40, "Relación de las colonias de caña existentes."
NOTE: Cabs. = caballerías (33.6 acres each).

gence of centrales in the late 1880s and early 1890s, the quality of sugar produced in rural Matanzas was improved; now, a greater portion consisted of light-brown crystallized sugars, rather than the darker, moister muscovados that had predominated before. This resulted in a substantial change in packing materials. The bulky wooden *cajas* gave way to sacks holding 13 arrobas (325 pounds) of sugar each, and these had to be purchased at colono expense.

A reduced number of merchant houses operating in Matanzas financed the colonias of the province. Surviving contracts illustrate the varied arrangements used by colonos to secure capital, and by merchants to guarantee sugar supplies for export. In October 1892, before the beginning of the 1892/93 harvest, Manuel López, owner of Colonia Santa Clara in Santa Ana, entered into a typical contract with one of the principal new merchant houses of Matanzas, Sres. Dubois y Compañía. In return for a guarantee that the first 300 sacks of centrifugal sugar produced by the colonia would be delivered to the company's warehouse, 2,000 gold pesos were lent at 12 percent annual interest. The value of the sugar would be determined by the current market price in the port of Matanzas at the time of delivery. Each sack, which measured 28 x 48 inches, would have to be purchased from Dubois at 40 centavos each. While the 300 sacks of sugar guaranteed the loan, the contract also allowed Dubois the right to purchase all sugar produced by the colonia at his discretion.[6]

But securing finance capital and a marketing outlet was not the only problem faced by landowning colonos such as Manuel López. Whereas the terms of their contracts required sugar deliveries, they only produced cane; An entirely separate arrangement had to be made to convert cane into sugar.

These were made with nearby ingenios or central factories. Informal agreements required colonos to deliver cane to the mills at their expense. Traditional oxcarts were often used for transportation, but internal railroad lines increasingly conducted cane to the mills from paraderos, where growers could deliver their harvested crop. Colonos were almost always paid in sugar rather than cash. The common rate was 5 arrobas of sugar for every 100 arrobas of delivered sugarcane. This arrangement provided advantages for both parties. The colono did not have to bear the expenses related to processing and could concentrate on raising the productivity of his land. The miller extracted somewhere between 9.5 and 10 arrobas of sugar from each 100 arrobas of delivered cane; thus, he kept roughly 45–50 percent of extracted sugar. Since the volume paid to colonos was fixed, processors had an incentive to increase industrial yields through the modernization of refining equipment.[7]

The overriding impression is that only the largest colonos had operating expenses justifying direct credit linkages with merchants, as was the case with the Colonia Santa Clara. More commonly, growers were financially linked with ingenios or centrales. Most mills paid a fixed number of arrobas in sugar for each 100 arrobas of cane delivered by independent landowners, regardless of actual yields.

Renting colonos, however, had completely different arrangements. For example, the La Paz estate, which produced no sugar and was thus classified as a colonia, was subdivided into twenty smaller colonias. Each colono received 1.5 caballerías of land and a bohío. By oral agreement, these colonos were required to maintain 1 caballería in cane, harvest the crop, and deliver it to a nearby mill. The remaining land (.5 caballerías) could be used at the colono's discretion. Each caballería was expected to yield 80,000 arrobas and the colono would be paid 5 arrobas of sugar for each 100 arrobas, of delivered cane. No separate rent was required.[8] If sugar sold at .03 pesos per pound, a gross income of 3,000 pesos per colonia would be produced. This was considerably more than could be earned through wage labor, and it certainly explains the broad-based proliferation of colonias during the 1880s and 1890s.

Other colonos paid rent in kind to landowners. On the Maravilla estate, most paid 1 arroba of sugar in rent for every 100 arrobas of cane produced; for income, they received the balance of the standard 5 arrobas of sugar for each 100 arrobas of cane. Inexplicably, others on the same estate paid rents of 1.25 arrobas of sugar for each 100 arrobas of cane.[9]

Some colonos paid a combination of cash and cane as rent. The Havana merchants Sres. Fernández y Valdez, who owned Central Destino in Macagua, rented 5 caballerías to Miguel Errandoca and José Bravo in 1880. A cash payment of 450 pesos was required annually plus all the cane produced on 1.33 caballerías of the land. The renters derived the full value of production on the remaining acreage.[10]

Others paid rents strictly in cash. In 1892 the Catalán María Francisca de Lora, leased 9 caballerías of land in Macagua to Leonardo González y Fernández (from Oviedo, Spain) and Eusebio Bello (a Cuban). These renters were obligated to plant 8 caballerías in cane and 1 in *viandas*. Rent would be paid at the rate of 25 centavos for every 100 arrobas of harvested cane.[11]

The varied arrangements linking different types of colonos to sugar processing make it difficult to describe the colonato of the late nineteenth century as anything like a homogeneous social class. Most independent landowning colonos were minifundistas. Renters might be those living within the confines of former large estates that had been subdivided into small plots because of labor shortages. Or they may have leased much larger tracts of land that were formerly small-scale sitios, or portions of ingenios that were being broken up and were no longer directly cultivated by the owners. Some even leased large estates from former mill owners who lacked the capital or resolve to keep operating.

This last group grew significantly in the 1880s and early 1890s, and was often made up of speculative entrepreneurs who wanted to capitalize on the reorganization of the sugar industry. By leasing land under contracts that called for rental payments at harvesttime, potentially valuable productive land could be acquired while large capital disbursements were avoided. In this way, land already planted in cane was secured with only a small capital investment. The agricultural productive capacity of these estates was by and large intact, although some neglected cañaverales did need to be weeded, cleaned, and sometimes drained. This was often a daunting task, but putting these estates into production was still not a question of clearing forest and undergrowth and then planting a first crop. Capital and labor had to be applied in order to restore these former plantations to production, to be sure, but the investments were small compared with the start-up costs of carving a sugar plantation from the wilderness. Those with ambition, capital resources, and entrepreneurial acumen were able to take advantage of these conditions and prosper.

An example is provided by the case of the young Havana lawyer José Mariano Crespo. Crespo was the heir to a veritable fortune. He was the son of León Crespo de la Serna, an early Matanzas merchant/planter who emigrated to Cuba from Santander in the late 1830s. León Crespo owned a prosperous merchant house in Matanzas and three estates in the province (ingenios Nuestra Señora del Carmen, Teresita, and Dolorita), and he was a senator to the Spanish parliament in Madrid. He left an estate worth more than 1 million pesos upon his death in 1885.[12] His son José was evidently imbued with the entrepreneurial spirit of his father. Not only did he continue the exploitation of the family plantations, but in the early 1890s he leased bankrupt farms at cut-rate prices. In 1894 Ingenio San José, 39 caballerías in Alacranes, was rented for six years at 4,000 pesos annually. The nearby El Tiempo estate, 25 caballerías, was rented from the heirs of Fulgencio García for seven years at 7,000 pesos annually.[13] In this way, production was revived on plantations that had been virtually abandoned, although the war would terminate this process abruptly.

Whether on small-scale colonias, owned or rented, or on larger cane-growing estates, the labor demands of sugarcane cultivation were great. Although the industrial capacity of Matanzas mills was considerably raised in the late 1880s and early 1890s by the capital-intensified processing, there was no such transformation of sugar agriculture. Colonia development decentralized agricultural labor problems, transferring the burden of resolution away from the processors to the growers. Yet, there was still no fundamental change in the productivity of field labor. A key question concerning the socioeconomic development of rural Matanzas in the aftermath of abolition has to do with the composition of the post-abolition labor force.

It is clear that the sugar industry's global labor demands in the 1880s and

1890s were reduced or mitigated. One factor was the mobilization of family labor accompanying the proliferation of fractionalized colonias, whether owned or rented. Colono family income was linked to agricultural productivity, and this was a powerful stimulus to mobilize heretofore-marginal family labor.

Another labor-saving development was linked to the ongoing transportation revolution wrought by the construction of private railway lines to individual centrales and by the use of public railroads to transport cane from colono fields to mills. The dramatic reduction in the price of steel rails during the mid-1880s facilitated the widespread construction of private railroad systems.[14] Although no quantitative data are available, it is certain that the number of full-time workers needed to transport cane to mills and sugar to ports fell considerably.

Finally, there was the capital intensification of processing, which significantly decreased industrial labor requirements. Although some traditional ingenios continued producing until the beginning of the revolutionary war in 1895, with the secular decline in sugar prices only the more efficient mills could remain solvent. Centrales installed expensive equipment: triple-effect vacuum evaporators, quadruple-effect evaporators, hydraulic regulators, grinding and regrinding machines, 600-gallon capacity *defecadoras*, all of which significantly reduced labor demand.[15]

Yet, despite these developments, cane was still cut by labor gangs of *macheteros*, and there was no reduction in the number of workers needed to harvest a caballería of cane. In addition, although railway dump cars carried cane to mills, those cars had to be loaded manually, another labor-intensive task. The structure of the Cuban sugar industry was substantially altered during the 1880s, and in this reorganization process gross production initially declined. Late in the decade, however, recovery began, and during the early 1890s production soared. In 1892, and again in 1894, Cuba produced more than 1 million tons of sugar. A broad-based labor force was needed to support this expansion, alterations in the structure of production notwithstanding. Which social sectors, then, combined to form this emerging rural proletariat?

Above all, significant numbers of these field laborers were emancipated slaves. Scholars attempting to reconstruct the immediate post-abolition experiences of freed men and women have become acutely aware of the paucity of public historical sources that refer specifically to blacks and mulattoes. When enslaved, the object of public policy, and valued economic resources, an abundant historical record was maintained. Upon final emancipation, though, blacks and mulattoes were no longer a legal category; thus, no special documentation was maintained on their individual or collective destiny.[16]

Although during the early 1880s many former slaves fled rural areas associated with oppression and human degradation, it is evident that a great many also remained to labor in a social and economic environment that was familiar to them. It is also likely that many who had fled rural areas in the late 1870s or early 1880s returned in the late 1880s and early 1890s because of the economic renewal taking place. The patronato of the early 1880s was intolerable—not only because the fundamental conditions of slavery remained, but because the terms of the 1880 law forced patrocinados to accept wages having little relation to the emerging labor market. Standard wages paid to patrocinados were 3 or 4 pesos monthly at a time when free labor received between 15 and 20 pesos. But by 1886, when the patronato was ended and final emancipation decreed, the labor shortage was acute. In order to lure workers, plantation owners or smaller colonos either had to pay reasonable wages in gold specie or face the hostile unwillingness of potential laborers to work in rural Cuba. When the euphoria caused by final emancipation subsided and ex-slaves had to face the stark realities of survival within a decaying socioeconomic milieu, steady wages on plantations, even if only during the harvest, probably lured a great many back to the environs in which they had previously labored.

There were other incentives as well. Not only were comparatively substantial wages paid, but the reorganization of the sugar economy meant that former slaveholders were disappearing from the scene. Many plantations had gone bankrupt and had been taken over by newcomers having few ties to slavery. There is no question that the newly emerging elite of white landowners was permeated with racist attitudes toward blacks and mulattoes. But economic life in rural Cuba was increasingly shaped by the impersonal forces of the marketplace. Laborers were needed to produce sugarcane, and wages were paid irrespective of race. The old prerogatives of arbitrary discipline had been banned; workers in general, rural and urban alike, were more militant and less likely to accept abusive treatment. Slaves had taken an active role in the emancipation process through varied forms of resistance and would not see the clock rolled back to pre-emancipation conditions of degradation. In short, labor relations in the Cuban countryside were changing substantially from those existing during slavery's heyday.

It should also be noted that no dramatic decline occurred in the Matanzas black and mulatto population between 1877 and 1887; the decrease of 5 percent paralleled the general decline in population. The real drop came in the 1890s. By 1899, the provincial black and mulatto population had declined by more than 30 percent from that of 1887.[17] However, most of this decrease was linked to the devastation, destruction, and mass starvation of the war years (1895–1898). In the late 1880s and early 1890s there was undoubtedly a process of rural-to-urban migration, as well as flight to the eastern frontier, but many blacks and mulattoes remained in rural zones where they continued to labor in agriculture.

Few were able to become colonos. The 1899 census distinguished owners and renters of rural properties by race. Of 1,109 owners of sugar-producing farms, only 5.4 percent were people of color. Among renters, 18.6 percent were blacks and mulattoes. There is also little evidence that freed men and women were able to acquire any other type of rural property. In 1899, of all rural landowners in Matanzas (1,955 total), only 6.6 percent were blacks and mulattoes. And only 20 percent of all 2,052 renters were people of color.[18]

Most black and mulatto men worked as day laborers and, because of the general shortage of labor, were probably afforded small incentives such as access to plots of land analogous to the provision grounds of slavery.[19] It must be kept in mind that a broad-based labor maïket had not yet developed in rural Matanzas, nor had huge plantations spread throughout the province. Labor in the 1880s and 1890s could not be taken for granted, and workers had to be lured to colonias and plantations with wages and other incentives. In 1899, 77.9 percent of all provincial black and mulatto males worked as laborers. Additionally, 36.6 percent of all black and mulatto women workers were classified as laborers. These census data imply agricultural labor, for urban occupations were usually denoted by trade or task.[20] The manager of Colonia Guabairo reported to the U.S. military authorities in 1899 that during the zafra a work force of 350 full-time workers was needed to harvest 33 caballerías of cane. This came to slightly more than 10 workers per caballería, which was almost exactly the same ratio found during the 1860s and 1870s in Colón and Cárdenas. The bulk of the labor force was composed of former slaves. Black males constituted 60 percent of all workers, black females made up another 10 percent and native-born whites were 20 percent; immigrants accounted for the remaining 10 percent of the work force.[21]

In the Matanzas cane fields, then, the first major sector of the post-abolition working class was made up of ex-slaves. The second-largest sector was composed of immigrants from Spain or the Canary Islands. In the aftermath of abolition, the changing structure of the sugar industry acted as a powerful magnet for Spanish migrants seeking opportunities to acquire land as colonos or to secure employment as salaried laborers. The number of migrants arriving in Cuba between 1882 and 1894 was substantial. More than 250,000 nonmilitary Spanish migrants disembarked in Cuba during this period, an average in excess of 19,000 per year. By way of comparison, the slave trade to Cuba between 1850 and 1860 averaged approximately 12,000 imports yearly.[22] Because of peculiar conditions within Cuba, highlighted by land availability in eastern frontier regions, labor for the expansion of the sugar economy had always been imported. The Cuban slave and Chinese contract-labor trades supported Matanzas sugar through the 1860s. In many ways the migration of Spanish free labor continued this dependence on external labor into the 1880s and 1890s.

Trends in sugar output and migration patterns were closely linked. The number of yearly Spanish migrants to Cuba increased significantly between 1885 and 1894, a period that was marked by fluctuations in Cuban sugar production but that enjoyed a definitive upward trend after 1889. The million-ton-plus zafras of 1892 and 1894 were paralleled by the highest levels of Spanish migration to the island. (See Figures 15.1 and 15.2.)

Not only were migration patterns closely associated with the yearly curve of sugar output in the 1890s, but monthly migration statistics within each year reveal a very close association with the rhythms of the Cuban sugar harvest. Data on monthly arrivals are available only for the years between 1882 and 1886, but the trend is unmistakable. The number of arrivals increased between September and a November peak, just as the zafra was getting under way. There was a sharp drop in immigration after March, as the harvest was drawing to a close, and significantly lower numbers of arrivals during the first half of the tiempo muerto to August, after which the cycle was renewed. Additionally, as the harvest was ending in April and May, the number of Spaniards departing Cuba for Spain increased dramat-

Figure 15.1. Spanish Immigrants to and Emigrants from Cuba, 1882–1894 (in thousands)
SOURCE: Spain, Instituto Geográfico y Estadístico, *Estadística de la emigración y inmigración de España en el quinquenio 1896–1900* (Madrid: Instituto Geográfico y Estadístico, 1903).

Production

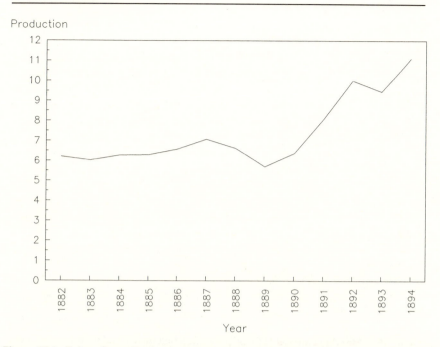

Figure 15.2. Cuban Sugar Production, 1882–1894 (in hundreds of thousands of metric tons)
SOURCE: Manuel Moreno Fraginals, *El Ingenio. Complejo económico social cubano del azúcar* (Havana: Ed. de Ciencias Sociales, 1978).

ically. (See Figure 15.3.) Without question, these data indicate that a large number of Spanish migrants to Cuba in the late nineteenth century were seasonal, journeying to work during the sugar harvest and returning to Europe at its conclusion. Although there was constant movement back and forth across the Atlantic, more than 100,000 of the quarter-million migrants coming to Cuba between 1882 and 1884 remained on the island. It should be noted that this was not family migration. More than 90 percent of all civilian migrants remaining in Cuba were males.[23]

Although native-born white Cubans undoubtedly worked in many occupations associated with the sugar industry, field labor seems to have been dominated by free blacks and mulattoes and by immigrants from Spain, seasonal or permanent. Some indication of the relative size of each group is provided by the 1899 census. In Matanzas nearly 26,000 foreign-born whites, blacks, and mulattoes between the ages of fifteen and sixty-four labored in agriculture. Cuban blacks and mulattoes made up 82.7 percent of the total, foreign whites the remaining 17.3 percent.[24]

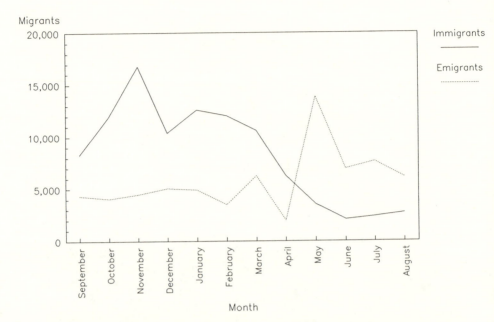

Figure 15.3. Monthly Patterns of Spanish Immigration to and Emigration from Cuba, 1882–1886

SOURCE: Spain, Instituto Geográfico y Estadístico, *Estadística de la emigración y inmigración de España en los años de 1882 a 1890* (Madrid: Instituto Geográfico y Estadístico, 1891).

CHAPTER 16

Sugar-Producing and Commercial Elites

Among the fundamental changes occurring in the socioeconomic structure of rural Matanzas during the 1880s and 1890s was the quantitative and qualitative transformation of sugar processing. The number of mills began declining in the immediate aftermath of the Ten Years' War and continued to fall until the onset of the second great insurrection for Cuban independence. Documentary sources on the rate of decrease in the number of functioning mills are scarce. No provincial-level agricultural censuses were conducted between 1881 and 1899, although in the aftermath of the war a detailed inventory on the state of the sugar industry was prepared by the Office of the Matanzas Secretary of Agriculture, Commerce, and Industry under the auspices of the U.S. Military Government. According to this report (*Report of the Work Accomplished by This Department during the Fiscal Year Which Commenced on the 1st of July 1899, and Ended on the 30th of June, 1900*), a total of 271 mills were still in existence before the war, although 121 were classified as "demolido," or no longer grinding cane. Thus, in all likelihood there were 150 functioning mills on the eve of the war for independence, a drop of nearly two-thirds from 1881.[1]

Modernization and the increased processing capacity of surviving mills meant a qualitative transformation as well. The appearance of mills designated as centrales characterized this period, although caution should be exercised here. Most central factories of the 1880s and 1890s continued to exploit their own estates directly; their internal productive structures were strikingly similar to those of other mills, although they clearly had greater processing capacity than mills classified as ingenios. Land was generally divided into colonias, and large quantities of cane were purchased from independent landowning colonos in the surrounding area. But these capital-intensive mills should not be confused with the productive units that emerged with the onslaught of U.S. investment capital in the twentieth century. Although many may have been incipient latifundia, they did not control vast extensions of land on the eve of the war for independence. In 1899 there were no farms classified as centrales that owned more than 200 caballerías of land.[2]

Nevertheless, a process of land accumulation by central factories was evidently under way before it was interrupted by the insurrection of 1895. Even though there were no centrales owning more than 200 caballerías, their average size was 80.8 caballerías while those farms designated as ingenios averaged 44.4 caballerías in extension. Ingenios were distinguished by smaller land areas and comparatively smaller processing capacities. Many ingenios were also subdivided into colonias, and in a sense they were reduced versions of the newer central factories, both having remarkably similar productive structures but on different scales. The land-tenure structure of the different types of Matanzas sugar mills in 1899 is shown in Table 16.1.

There was, however, a progressive concentration of land within the Matanzas sugar sector during the second half of the nineteenth century which can be traced by comparing data for 1860, 1878, and 1899. Over this four-decade period, the continual accumulation of land in estates greater than 50 caballerías is evident. In 1860 such estates constituted 29.5 percent of all sugar-producing farms and occupied 50.9 percent of total ingenio-controlled

Table 16.1. Matanzas Centrales and Ingenios, 1899:
Land Tenure Structure

Mill Size (Cabs.)	Centrales				Ingenios			
	No. Mills	%	Land (Cabs.)	%	No. Mills	%	Land (Cabs.)	%
1–10	1	4.0	10	0.5	23	12.2	133	1.6
11–20					23	12.2	363	4.3
21–50	6	24.0	246	12.2	74	39.4	2,610	31.3
51–100	11	44.0	761	37.7	71	32.4	4,089	48.9
101–200	7	28.0	1,003	49.7	5	2.7	668	8.0
201+					2	1.1	485	5.8
TOTAL	25	100.0	2,020	100.0	188	100.0	8,348	100.0
AVG. SIZE			(80.8)				(44.4)	

SOURCE: AHPM, ME, Estadística, leg. 7, no. 128, fols. 12–23, 34–35; no. 130, fols. 1–15, 40–58; no. 131, fols. 25–91; no. 132, fols. 1–19.

NOTE: Cabs. = caballerías (33.6 acres each). These data on ingenios are part of the contradictory record on the number of mills grinding cane in the late nineteenth century. In contrast to the Matanzas Department of Agriculture, Commerce, and Industry report (*Report of the Work Accomplished by This Department during the Fiscal Year Which Commenced on the 1st of July 1899, and Ended on the 30th of June, 1900* [n.p., 1900]), it is likely that one-third of the ingenios noted here were not grinding cane when this census was taken. Nevertheless, these data are the only statistical information available on land tenure within the sugar-processing sector for this period. *Centrales* were central factories that specialized in sugar production, not in sugarcane cultivation; *ingenios* were sugar farms and their mills.

land. In 1878, 35.5 percent of all ingenios fell into this category, while their land control increased to 61.5 percent of total land. By 1899, 49.7 percent of all ingenio estates were larger than 50 caballerías, and they controlled 67.5 percent of total sugar-sector property.[3]

Thus, while the separation of the agricultural and industrial sectors of the sugar industry did begin in the aftermath of the Ten Years' War, the process was only in its initial phase. Traditional forms of resource exploitation remained, and almost all mills, whether centrales or ingenios, continued to combine growing and processing—although the colono structure of cane cultivation substantially altered the socioeconomic organization of sugarcane agriculture.

The absence of extraordinary land concentration before the war, despite the other structural shifts occurring within rural society, is revealed by examining land-tenure patterns among all farms. The province-wide agricultural census of 1899 revealed the persistence of traditional patterns of fragmentation and concentration, but not the formation of the large-scale latifundia that would emerge early in the twentieth century. Of 2,912 total farms only 31 were larger than 100 caballerías, and while these rural estates controlled 16.5 percent of all Matanzas land, there is evidence of much greater land concentration in the 1860s and 1870s. For example, in Cárdenas and Colón, farms greater than 100 caballerías controlled well over 20 percent of all land in these decades (see Tables 8.6 and 8.7 for precise data). Table 16.2 summarizes provincial land-tenure patterns in 1899.

Table 16.2. Matanzas, 1899: Land-Tenure Structure

Farm Size (Cabs.)	No. Farms	%	Land (Cabs.)	%
.13–.99	778	26.7	343	1.2
1–1.99	597	20.5	688	2.4
2–2.99	338	11.6	716	2.5
3–4.99	237	8.1	833	2.9
5–9.99	327	11.2	2,172	7.5
10–19.99	231	7.9	3,103	10.7
20–39.99	189	6.5	5,381	18.5
40–59.99	101	3.5	4,861	16.7
60–99.99	83	2.9	6,138	21.1
100–199.99	27	0.9	3,612	12.4
200+	4	0.1	1,185	4.1
TOTAL	2,912	100.0	29,032	100.0

SOURCE: AHPM, ME, Estadística, leg. 7, no. 128, fols. 12–23, 34–35; no. 130, fols. 1–15, 40–58; no. 131, fols. 25–91; no. 132, fols. 1–19.

NOTE: Cabs. = caballerías (33.6 acres each).

The preconditions for the emergence of extensive latifundia were created in the 1880s and 1890s with the widespread construction of internal railroad systems on modernizing estates. These railways revolutionized the relationship between the agricultural and industrial phases of sugar production by permitting the transportation of cane from distant fields to mills quickly and without any extraordinary drop in sucrose content. Cane fields could be located farther from the mills than ever before, and this effectively increased the *potential* extension of individual estates. In the 1880s and 1890s, however, the result was the numerical and spatial expansion of the different types of colonos, rather any real increase in the direct cultivation of larger land areas by individual ingenios or centrales. The emergence of a veritable sugar latifundia system would be tied to the development of a broad-based rural labor market that allowed mill owners and colonos to expand planting with assurances of harvest labor. This was not the case in the prewar period. Railroads revolutionized productive possibilities, to be sure, and established the economic conditions for land accumulation. But in the 1880s and 1890s the railroad's principal social impact was to facilitate the development of the colonato.

There are no surviving data on the gross productive capacity of the Matanzas sugar industry, although it is evident from island-wide data that by the early 1890s there was an enormous rise in output per mill. Cuba produced 1 million tons of sugar in 1892, nearly twice the output of 1878 with less than half as many mills. In order to remain in business as prices continued to fall in the late 1880s and early 1890s, mills—whether classified as ingenios or centrales—either had to produce sugar more efficiently or go into bankruptcy.

The concentration of production was paralleled by the social reorganization of the Matanzas sugar-producing elite. Caution is important here, for this did not mean the wholesale disappearance of the old planter families. Many were forced from rural Matanzas by the shifting social and economic parameters of the post-1878 period and by the unwillingness or inability of family heirs to continue sugar production. The drastic decline in producing mills certainly took its toll on the old elite, although a number of mill-owning families from the 1860s or before remained important sugar producers through the close of the nineteenth century.

Analysis of the ownership of the 150 mills still grinding cane on the eve of the 1895 war of independence reveals this important element of social continuity. It is possible to identify the owners of 120 of these mills in 1878 and in 1895. Of this total, 55 percent (66 mills) were owned by the same families in both years, while the remaining 45 percent (54 mills) had changed owners.[4]

Long-time residents of Cuba (creoles and immigrants) who had conserved capital through the crisis of the early 1880s were able to survive as sugar producers. By and large, this sector was composed of diversified entrepreneurs with commercial and agricultural interests, and with substantial liquid assets accumulated during the previous period of sugar expansion. The Zuluetas are one example. The family patriarch, Julián de Zulueta, died in 1878, but his heirs were able to continue producing sugar into the twentieth century. Of the four mills in Banagüises, Habana and Viscaya ceased operations in the early 1880s, but España and Álava were modernized and continued grinding cane as centrales. Portions of the old estates were subdivided: España rented 50 caballerías to twenty-five colonos who produced 3 million arrobas of cane in 1899; Álava was exploited directly by means of wage labor, although there were also three colonias within the estate.[5]

The case of Francisco Rosell y Malpica offers another example. Rosell was born in Matanzas in the early 1850s but was educated in the United States and became a naturalized U.S. citizen in 1880, a commonplace occurrence among the sons of the Matanzas elite. By the mid-1870s he had acquired three estates, the ingenios Agüedita, Dolores, and San Salvador. Rosell also ran a merchant house in Matanzas and probably was involved in Havana commerce as well. During the crisis of the early 1880s, Rosell's capital reserves allowed him to take advantage of the depressed conditions by purchasing bankrupt plantations or underutilized land. He acquired the 42-caballería Colonia Desquite, adjacent to the Agüedita plantation in Palmillas. Colonia Estrella, 92 caballerías in Macuriges (next to Ingenio Dolores) and Colonia Progreso, 52 caballerías in Macagua, were also purchased. By 1895 Rosell had become one of the largest planters and sugar processors in the province, owning more than 325 caballerías of land with a gross productive capacity of nearly 9 million arrobas of cane.[6]

There was also the case of Carlos de la Rosa (a.k.a. Charles Rosa). Rosa was born in Hannover, Germany, in 1834 and migrated to the United States sometime in the 1850s. He maintained a residence in New York and became a naturalized U.S. citizen in 1869. His business and personal interests, however, were in Cuba. He first appeared in Cárdenas in the early 1860s as the representative of a German manufacturing firm that was marketing machinery to the ingenios of the region. Shortly thereafter he married Isabel Hernández, from an old Matanzas family that had settled the province in the late 1770s.[7] His foray into sugar production began with the acquisition of the Isabel estate in 1870. Two adjacent parcels were acquired in 1875, and the plantation sprawled to 87.5 caballerías, of which 74 were planted in cane. In June 1877 Rosa purchased the Diagos' Tinguaro mill and the contiguous Potrero Constancia, a total of 115 caballerías, for 500,000 pesos. Tinguaro was modernized at considerable cost. In 1883 and 1884, when the Cuban sugar economy was severely depressed, Rosa drew on his extensive capital reserves and installed new machinery on Tinguaro at a cost of half a million pesos, as much as the original purchase price. He also purchased a

20-caballería parcel of land in Calimete, in 1882, and the San Agustín plantation, 15 caballerías, in 1883.[8]

Another important family maintaining a presence in rural Matanzas were the heirs of the Catalán entrepreneur José Baró y Blanxart, the Marqués de Santa Rita and Viscount of Canet de Mar. Baró founded the Santa Rita, Luisa, Olimpo, and Conchita estates in the 1830s and 1840s and also established the first steamship service between Cuba and Spain. He was a notorious slave trader. One of his daughters, Cristina Baró, married the Conde de Diana, Juan Antonio Soler y Morell; her sister Clara Baró wed the count's brother, Leandro Soler y Morell. A third sister, Concepción Baró, married Juan Pedro y Roig, a native of Catalonia. These three sisters continued the family patrimony into the 1890s. Ingenio Santa Rita was run by Cristina, who with her husband also owned the Diana and Manuelito mills. Concepción operated the Conchita estate; Clara and her husband owned the Santa Filomena mill; and a fourth sister, Amalia, owned Olimpo. Ingenio Luisa, however, was sold to a peninsular Spaniard, José Menéndez Junquera.[9]

There are many more examples of older Matanzas families, creoles and immigrants, who maintained an important presence in the province. The Torrientes, the extensive clan of planters, merchants, and warehousers from Santander, were able to maintain possession of the ingenios Amistad and Carlota and of a newer mill, Central María. But their Elena, Isabel, Progreso, and San Pablo plantations were acquired by newcomers in the 1880s. The Fernández family, founders of Ingenio Unión in 1838, continued owning the mill through 1895. Families with noble titles, among them some of the earliest ingenio owners in the province, also remained. The Montalvos continued operating Ingenio Desquite; the Conde de San Fernando Peñalver did not give up the Alcancía estate; María Teresa Herrera, the daughter of the Marqués de Almendares, and her husband, José Melgares, continued to exploit Ingenio Atrevido; and the Calvos' ingenios San Luis and Dolores remained with the family through the 1890s.

Yet, many of the old families disappeared from rural Matanzas. The Poeys were gone, their legendary Ingenio Las Cañas having been acquired by a Havana immigrant merchant, Adolfo Muñoz Mendoza. The Diagos left no family members as mill owners. The Arrietas, who constructed Flor de Cuba, disappeared from Matanzas. The Aldamas, who had recovered their estates from the embargo placed by the Spanish government on insurgent properties during the Ten Years' War, were no longer sugar producers in the 1880s.

Formerly majestic ingenios faded from the physical landscape; and their owners, once energetic entrepreneurs who altered the provincial socioeconomic order, were a distant memory after the war for independence. The fate of the ingenios Echevarría, San Martín, and Dos Hermanos was typical.

These mills were the most modern in rural Matanzas in the 1850s and 1860s. All were built by Joaquín Pedroso y Echevarría, who in the mid-1850s sold Echevarría and San Martín to La Gran Azucarera, a company that was plunged into bankruptcy proceedings in the early 1860s. By 1885, Ingenio Echevarría had long been abandoned and, in a public auction held to pay some of the estate's debts, was acquired by Gregorio de Armas, who hailed from Sagua la Grande. The Armas family were not newcomers to Matanzas. They owned the Santa Rosalía, San Miguel, La Flor, and Socorro estates in the 1860s and 1870s and continued operating these mills through the 1890s. The Echevarría estate no longer produced cane, and its once rich cane fields were now turned over to Antonio Fernández Criado of Havana, for 4,000 pesos annual rent, to be used as a cattle ranch.[10]

San Martín had also been virtually abandoned. A peninsular merchant established in Havana, Agustín Anozarena y Ordaniz, acquired the estate in 1885 through public auction and proceeded to partition it into small parcels, which were leased. Twelve caballerías were rented in 1888 to a French immigrant, Armand Dahetz, who converted this land into the cane-producing Colonia Francesa. The contract was for eight years and called for 700 pesos annual rent in gold. In addition, Dahetz was obligated to construct fences around the property and to maintain them for the term of the rental agreement.[11]

The fate of Ingenio Dos Hermanos was similar. By the 1890s it had been subdivided into colonias. Hopelessly in debt, it too was placed on the auction block in the mid-1880s and was acquired by a peninsular Spaniard, Juan Ramón Zapatero of Asturias. Zapatero rented sections of the farm to a number of Canary Island immigrants, who were obligated to sell all harvested cane to Zapatero's Ingenio/Central Felicia.[12]

Over and again the story is similar. Old mills were abandoned or fell into disrepair, production plummeted or ceased, debts accrued, and properties were auctioned to the highest bidder. Most members of the old elite or their offspring had exhausted cash reserves or credit possibilities by the mid-1880s. Some not only abandoned their estates, but left Cuba as well. The employees and foremen of Ingenio Santiago, owned by the Marqués de Uña, filed a complaint with the Colón "depositario judicial" in 1885, claiming that they had not been paid in four months. In the deposition, they noted that the marqués had been on the plantation, abruptly left for Havana, and then without notice sailed for Europe, leaving word that "it will be impossible to pay them because he possesses neither cash nor products to effect payment."[13]

With the demise of entrepreneurial patriarchs, many heirs of the old elite had no interest in maintaining family patrimonies. Having inherited fortunes derived from the heyday of slaving and sugar prosperity, they lived lives of luxury and little effort; although some were forced to return to

Cuba to look after inheritances, most estates were disposed of rather than modernized. The case of Cristóbal Alfonso exemplifies this. Cristóbal was the son of the notorious slave trader Julián Luis Alfonso. He had married his cousin, Florinda Aldama y Fonts, daughter of the exiled revolutionary leader Miguel de Aldama. In 1859 Cristóbal was sent by his father to study in the United States, and he spent two years living in Stamford, Connecticut, and Washington, D.C. Throughout most of the Ten Years' War he resided in New York, becoming a naturalized U.S. citizen in 1870. In 1877 he and his wife journeyed to Paris, where they remained until 1886, when he returned to Cuba to look after the family estate, Central Triunvirato. However, Cristóbal Alfonso knew little about the economics of sugar production in rural Matanzas, having lived a life of idle luxury in the United States and France. Triunvirato was run by a succession of managers and was finally sold to his brother-in-law, Eduardo Echarte, thus remaining within the extended family.[14]

The depressed conditions of the sugar industry, widespread capital shortages, and the inability of many among the old elite to deal effectively with the crisis of the 1880s paved the way for the appearance of a new group of entrepreneurs in rural Matanzas. This coterie was composed primarily of peninsular immigrants drawn to Cuba precisely because of the economic opportunities presented by the crisis. These men were largely unaffected by gyrations in the Cuban economy, for their primary investments prior to the 1880s were in Barcelona, Santander, or Seville. Thus, they were able to draw on capital reserves and credit lines far removed from the island's economic cycles.

There are numerous examples. The history of the Isabel estate, established by the great Matanzas merchant and warehouse owner Cosme de la Torriente, was typical. Isabel, one of the province's most prosperous ingenios in the mid-nineteenth century, had gone bankrupt by the early 1880s; it was purchased from Torriente's heirs in early 1885 by a young Andalusian lawyer, the thirty-three-year-old Demetrio Pérez de la Riva who practiced his profession in the Havana suburb of Marianao. Pérez de la Riva was technically a colono, since Isabel's grinding equipment had long since fallen into disrepair. Cane was marketed during the harvest of 1885 at .02 pesos/ arroba to neighboring Ingenio Elizalde, an estate that continued processing through the 1880s.

Pérez de la Riva was unique, however: he did not divide Isabel into colonias but, rather, exploited it directly through the use of wage labor. The estate was evidently solvent and had an ample line of credit with the Asturian merchants Guillermo Escobedo and Juan Viña, young men in their mid-thirties who had recently established a business in Havana. Isabel was managed by one of Torriente's nephews, Leandro José de la Torriente, who drew a monthly salary of 250 pesos. There were two mayorales, paid 50 pesos monthly, and a North American carpenter, Charles Wilson, who drew 60 pesos a month in wages. From June through October, the estate employed 50 full-time workers at salaries of 17 pesos monthly in gold. Once the harvest began in December, the work force was raised by 60 percent to 80 full-time laborers, and wages increased to 20 pesos monthly in gold through the end of the harvest in May. Viña and Escobedo supplied the capital needed to run the estate and charged 1.5 percent monthly interest on outstanding debts. This system was evidently successful, for Isabel continued producing under the same owner until the war; although it was destroyed during the insurrection, Isabel was reconstructed and continued producing cane into the twentieth century.[15]

Several important points should be stressed concerning the reorganization of the 1880s. First, there was absolutely no penetration of rural Matanzas by U.S. investors before the end of the war in 1898. Nor is there any evidence that levels of U.S. commercial capital increased significantly from prior periods of development. Dependence on the U.S. market became almost total in the 1890s because of the McKinley Tariff Act, which removed U.S. import duties on Cuban raw sugar, but this was not followed by direct capital investments on the part of U.S. entrepreneurs. The only investments by U.S. citizens were those effected by Cubans who had attained U.S. citizenship. Most of these men and their families had been present in Cuba from early in the nineteenth century. Additionally, no merchant houses owned by U.S. nationals were operating in Matanzas and Cárdenas other than those which had operated there from the middle of the nineteenth century.

Second, the role of merchant capital in sugar agriculture or manufacture during the 1880s and early 1890s was no greater than it had ever been before. This period is generally portrayed as one in which foreign merchants moved en masse into the Cuban countryside, acquiring bankrupt mills and estates as the crisis deepened. An examination of the 120 known mill owners in 1895, however, reveals that this was not the case. Most mills grinding cane in 1895 were owned by family groups who had been established in Matanzas for some time. Most combined investments in agriculture with merchant activities, and many had initially accumulated capital as slave traders. The most powerful planters of rural Matanzas in the 1860s and 1870s were diversified investors, and these groups generally survived the crisis.

During the 1880s and 1890s there was no alteration in this fundamental aspect of the Matanzas sugar economy. Modernizing mill owners, some of them recent peninsular immigrants, were closely linked with commercial capital and merchant activity. But this had always been the case among the provincial elite. From the 1830s, ingenio owners had invested in railway companies, financed slave-trading missions, run merchant houses of various sizes, and often operated small warehouses. The most powerful entrepreneurs controlling the sugar economy of rural Matanzas were vertically integrated economically, and in this sense the 1880s did not herald a radical departure from past patterns of investment activity.

Finally, while newcomers to Cuba made important investments in the Matanzas sugar economy during the 1880s and early 1890s, their roles should not be exaggerated. Most of the mills that changed owners between 1878 and 1895 were acquired by entrepreneurs who had been operating in Cuba for some time. Of the 54 mills secured through sale, auction, or foreclosure in the 1880s and 1890s, at least two-thirds came under the ownership of individuals or companies present in Cuba since the 1870s or earlier. Only one-third were acquired by recent immigrants. Thus, while the sugar-producing elite shrunk considerably and production in general was reorganized, there was no overwhelming penetration of foreigners into rural Matanzas. The real shock would come after 1898, when absentee U.S. companies purchased mills, bought up extensive tracts of land, and became the most important creditors servicing the sugar economy.

There was continuity in other ways, too. Most of the large-scale planters controlling the provincial sugar economy from the early nineteenth century were absentees whose principal residences were maintained in Havana. There is not one instance of a titled family maintaining a permanent home in the province, nor did the other major entrepreneurial families live on their estates. In the early phases of development during the 1830s and 1840s, much time was spent supervising operations; ultimately, though, plantations were run by managers, foremen, and overseers. Communications from Havana were extremely efficient because of the modern railroad network constructed in the 1840s, when it became possible to journey to the most remote rural zones in less than one day.

By and large, absentee dominance over the Matanzas economy meant that net revenues derived from sugar production were systematically drained from the province into Havana, where they were allocated in a variety of ways. Some capital was invested in Cuban infrastructural development—more railroads, new mills, improved communications. Funds were also placed in high-yielding U.S. savings bonds, or profits were exported to home regions within Spain. Notwithstanding the structural changes in the sugar economy experienced in the 1880s and 1890s, this basic pattern of absentee control changed hardly at all. Locally based institutions lost control over the Matanzas economy when sugar began expanding early in the nineteenth century, not when the sugar economy was restructured in the 1880s.

Thus, while the concentration of processing brought far-reaching changes in the structures of production and in the social order, many aspects of provincial life demonstrated a measure of continuity. Social Darwinism governed the reorganization of the sugar-producing elites; the weaker, capital-deficient sectors of the planter class fell by the wayside. Enough of the older planter families survived, however, to lend an element of stability to the process of social and economic reorganization, despite the profound changes wrought by emancipation and the shifting structure of the sugar economy.

This measure of continuity among sugar producers can be contrasted with the social history of the provincial merchant elite. Numerous banking and commercial establishments failed during the crisis of the early 1880s, and traditional credit sources disappeared. The Caja de Ahorros, Banco Industrial, and Banco de Comercio were liquidated by the middle of the decade.[16] Drake Hermanos, the principal Havana commercial house from the beginning of the nineteenth century, disappeared. Noriega, Olmo y Cía., one of the most prestigious trading firms of the capital, folded as well. Benítez y Dirón, Pedro Martínez y Cía., and Salvador Baró y Cía. were no longer in business by the early 1880s.

Traditional local sources of Matanzas credit also faded into history. The Torrientes, for example, had been leading creditors and warehousers to provincial planters from the 1840s, but they ceased merchant operations after the Ten Years' War despite maintaining ownership over several estates. The Fessers, founders of the Havana Almacenes de Regla and major creditors to Matanzas planters, disappear from the historical sources in the 1880s. The Banco de San Carlos of Matanzas, run by the Gumá family, also fell victim to the crisis. The plethora of small-scale, foreign sugar brokers and creditors who flourished in the cities of Matanzas and Cárdenas at mid-century disappeared as well. These names are the parenthetical asides of local history, men who came and remained only long enough to accumulate a little capital, or to fail, and who then moved on: Poujaud, Burnham, Parkinson, Bayley, Traub, Kobbe, Urbach, Roget, Picard, Quiepó, Altes, Schweyer, Day, and many more—fleeting figures leaving no lasting imprint on provincial life.

New merchants took their places, almost every one of peninsular origin. Typical of these newcomers was the firm of Bea, Bellido y Compañía, chartered in Matanzas in 1883. Eduardo Bellido y Delgado, a native of Cádiz, was the principal partner in the firm along with two brothers, Pedro and Tiburcio Bea y Orquipo, from Vizcaya. An uncle of the Beas, Demetrio Manuel Bea y Marurí, had been a long-time Matanzas resident and in 1888 was granted the title Conde de Bellamar, although there is no evidence of family commercial investments prior to the 1880s.[17]

This company became one of the most important creditors to Matanzas sugar producers. The traditional mechanism of securing sugar with "refacción" contracts continued through the early 1890s, even though the reduced number of Matanzas merchants and the capital shortages following the crisis of the 1880s meant that credit terms were virtually dictated to sugar producers. A contract with the Armas family in 1885 was typical. Florencio, Agustín, and Antonio Armas operated Ingenio La Flor, 35 caballerías in Alacranes that they acquired in 1865, as well as a neighboring estate, the 40-caballería Ingenio San Miguel de Caobas. The Armas borrowed an unspecified sum from Bea, Bellido y Cía. prior to the 1885 harvest and agreed to deliver the first 8,000 sacks of centrifugal sugar to the company, which acted as factor for the Armas family. If the sugar was delivered before February 20, 1886, Bea and Bellido would collect a 10 percent commission on the resale value of the marketed sugar. After that date, a 20 percent commission would be collected from the Armas brothers, who were responsible for transportation charges, warehousing fees, and interest payments on outstanding debts.[18]

Bea and Bellido specialized in factoring, exporting, and supplying credit to processors and cane growers. They were not interested in agricultural investments and did not acquire any mills or colonias. This was also the case with the other four major export merchants of Matanzas—Sixto Lecuona, Dubois y Cía., Galván y Cía., and J. Lombard y Cía—and with the principal merchants of Cárdenas—Echevarría y Cía., Lluria, Freire y Cía, Pedro Huici, and Rosell, Gastón y Cía.[19]

Yet, other merchants specializing in loans to colonos or mill owners utilized legal obligations as inroads to acquire the properties of financially extended planters. The case of José Sainz y Sainz, a native of Santander, exemplifies this. Sainz appeared as a creditor to Matanzas planters just as the Ten Years' War was drawing to a close. One of his first major deals was to finance the purchase of Ingenio San Vicente in 1877 for Ramón Rodríguez y Gutiérrez, an immigrant from Asturias. San Vicente had been owned by Gavino Juncos y Morejón, from an old Matanzas family, and it extended for 36 caballerías in Jovellanos. Rodríguez operated the estate with capital furnished by Sainz, but he could not extricate himself from debt. As a result, in 1880, three-fifths ownership was transferred to Sainz while Rodríguez continued to manage the plantation. San Vicente operated through the crisis years of the early 1880s, but Rodríguez still could not extricate himself from his financial obligations to Sainz. In 1885 he was forced to cede the remaining two-fifths of the estate to his creditor.[20]

Sainz continued exploiting San Vicente to the eve of the insurrection in 1895, and he also operated another mill, Ingenio San Florencio. In 1890 he acquired the Cuabalejos estate, a colonia that had ceased grinding cane during the early 1880s. This Cimarrones property was not directly farmed but was rented for four years at 1,750 pesos annually to a peninsular immigrant, Manuel Miranda.[21]

Sainz was typical of the new class of merchants who were attracted to Matanzas because of the opportunities so prevalent after the Ten Years' War. Not only were there numerous cases of former planters losing properties to creditors because of an inability to amortize loans, but there was also the widespread embargo of rural estates by the colonial government because of a failure to pay taxes. Tax arrears were often ridiculously small fractions of the assessed value of plantations, but demoralized and bankrupt planters often were unable to generate the minimal capital necessary to hold on to their properties. For speculators with capital resources, this situation was ideal.

Most of these government-imposed embargoes were effected on ingenios that had ceased grinding cane and whose milling equipment had long been in disrepair. Cane fields were abandoned, overgrown with weeds, or flooded, and roads for hauling cane to the paraderos had not been maintained. In order for owners to restore these estates to productivity, outstanding taxes had to be paid; but these were the least of the capital requirements. Substantial investments were needed to hire labor for general rehabilitation of the property. Marginal growers, having ceased producing sugar, could not meet these demands and lost their estates. Such plantations were acquired for a tiny fraction of their nominal value, often by immigrants with comparatively extensive capital reserves.

The activities of the Bangos of Asturias exemplified this process. José Bango y Bango appeared in Matanzas during the 1870s as the co-owner of a commercial establishment that acquired the small, 11-caballería Ingenio San Francisco. In 1880, Francisco González y Bango, a partner in the firm, appeared at a public auction held by the government to pay the tax arrears of 21,389.11 pesos of the embargoed and abandoned Ingenio Concepción. This plantation was nominally valued at 487,421.77 pesos, not taking into account the investment needed to restore productivity. González Bango successfully bid for the property, acquiring it for a small fraction of its potential value.[22] A decade later, in 1890, José Bango made the only bid for the 15-caballería Ingenio Angelita, in Alacranes. Angelita had been seized by the government in 1889 for failure to pay taxes of 11,533.25 pesos. When Bango appeared at the auction and submitted an offer of 3,881.48 pesos, it was accepted.[23]

In the 1880s and 1890s, the sugar-producing and commercial elites of Matanzas were a combination of older families, able to weather the crisis because of extensive reserves of accumulated capital, and newcomers who were exploiting the opportunities presented by an economy in transition. The older families were represented by the heirs of those great entrepreneurs who had carved the provincial sugar economy from virgin forests and rolling savannas. The newcomers had few previous links with Cuba, and most probably aspired to remain only long enough to accumulate enough wealth to return home.

Together they helped reshape the structures of Matanzas sugar monoculture toward the concentration of manufacture and the dispersion of agriculture. They were the entrepreneurial heirs to a socioeconomic system that had prospered on the twin foundations of African slavery and constant expansion into new frontier areas, even during the tumultuous decade of war and revolution of the 1870s. Both of these fundamental pillars were gone by the 1880s. Slavery had disintegrated, and new labor systems for cane cultivation and sugar production heralded the first steps toward the formation of a rural labor market. The Matanzas frontier was virtually closed, and cane cultivation could no longer rely upon expansion into high-yielding virgin lands. The difficulty of dealing with both these changes simultaneously was exacerbated by the downward trend of sugar prices on the world market, which meant the need for greater efficiency and radical, cost-reducing measures.

In order to maintain sugar monoculture in the 1880s and 1890s, a series of obstacles had to be addressed in the short term. Those obstacles, though fundamentally different from the ones faced by previous entrepreneurial groups, were just as daunting. The old elite had created an economic system and a social order from a largely uninhabited frontier and with little in the way of a productive infrastructure. This creation was inherited, albeit virtually moribund, by the next generation, who either had to refurbish it or preside over its demise. The entire system needed to be overhauled; transformations had to be intensive and internal, not based on the extensive re-creation of existing forms of production and social organization. The old elite was innovative and dynamic, to be sure, but by and large they simply transferred methods and techniques from established areas of production over to frontier regions. But this was by no means a stagnant system, for its very existence had rested upon geographical mobility and continued investment of capital in new regions.

The elite of the 1880s and 1890s, however, could not afford the luxury of replicating extant structures of production or social organization. In many ways, the new generation faced even greater difficulties, trying to find wealth-producing formulas that could function in an altogether different socioeconomic milieu, insular and international. They were remarkably successful, given the breadth of transformation required, but scarcely had time to consolidate their position within Cuban society.

Although the war of 1895–1898 did not destroy sugar monoculture in Matanzas, it did end the specific process of elite class formation that had begun with the conclusion of the Ten Years' War. Few immigrant merchants would survive the war years, and the descendants of the old planter families who had met the challenges of the 1880s and early 1890s were by and large stretched beyond their capacity to survive, such was the devastation wrought by the renewed insurrection. The war marked the end of sugar monoculture's post-abolition reorganization in Matanzas. Renewed intensive growth would follow. For the structures of monoculture were too firmly rooted to be eradicated, even by the massive devastation caused by the Cuban war for independence.

PART FOUR

Epilogue: The Social and Economic Impact of the War for Independence and Its Aftermath, 1895–1900

CHAPTER 17

Demographic Disaster and Agricultural Collapse

The Matanzas sugar economy successfully weathered the crisis of the 1880s. The capital and labor foundations of the industry were structurally reorganized, and production surged during the early 1890s despite the steep fall in sugar prices on the world market. Sugar processing was concentrated, and cane cultivation was dispersed across a broad spectrum of the social hierarchy, from fragmented renters to owners of large colonias.

Economic reorganization was paralleled by social dislocation, especially among elite groups. Old planter families with limited capital resources ceased producing sugar, although many continued growing cane as colonos. Immigrants with access to extensive credit resources penetrated rural Matanzas and displaced many former mill owners. Again, some of the newcomers also became cane-growing colonos. Yet, enough older families survived the crisis to lend a measure of continuity at the top of the social hierarchy, the radical changes occurring in productive structures notwithstanding.

The merchant elite was fundamentally transformed by the virtual disappearance of firms that had traditionally operated in the ports of Matanzas or Cárdenas, or that had financed the provincial economy from Havana. Although there was a short-term contraction of credit during the crisis of the early 1880s, the shift in the social composition of the provincial commercial elite had no substantial, long-term impact on the rest of society. The functional mechanisms of credit that bound cane producers or sugar processors to finance capital were virtually unchanged in the 1880s and 1890s, despite the social reorganization of the merchant class. The refacción contract between merchant and planter remained a permanent fixture, providing another element of continuity within the parameters of economic reorganization.

Final abolition resulted in a labor crisis of considerable proportions in Matanzas, and contributed in large part to the extreme economic difficulties of the early 1880s. Initially, former slaves and Chinese abandoned the plantations for frontier regions to the east or for cities and towns, but many remained in rural zones or returned to labor on the sugar estates. The emergence of a genuine labor market in rural Matanzas during the 1880s and

1890s meant the first opportunities for former slaves to earn wages that reflected the market value of labor.

Freedmen often leased small portions of cane-growing estates as colonos or worked as wage laborers. They were joined in the province's rural partidos by peninsular immigrants who labored for salaries at harvesttime and then returned to Spain (or remained permanently on owned or rented colonias). The restructuring of sugar production and the development of a highly stratified colonato resulted in the partial opening of the socioeconomic hierarchy. For the first time in the history of sugar monoculture's development in Matanzas, significant numbers of people emerged between the elite groups and the masses of unskilled labor.

These processes were still taking form when the second Cuban war for independence erupted in February 1895, far to the east in Oriente province. During the Ten Years' War, the Matanzas economy had been largely untouched until 1876. Now, however, rebel armies invaded en masse in December 1895, and Matanzas was quickly converted from the center of Cuba's sugar economy to little more than an extensive battleground. For the next three years, conflicting armies crisscrossed the province, causing a human tragedy of unmitigated proportions. No corner was unscathed, death and destruction were sown everywhere, and Matanzas emerged from the war devastated and in absolute ruin. The crisis of the early 1880s was of minor significance to provincial history when compared with the horrendous suffering that accompanied the second revolutionary war.

Demographic Disaster

The invasion of Matanzas by the armies of Máximo Gómez and Antonio Maceo during Christmas week, 1895, has been described as one of the "most glorious pages in Cuban history."[1] From the political point of view of the rebel leadership, this was no doubt true. During the Ten Years' War insurgent armies had failed to confront Spanish power in the economically dominant western half of the island. The foundations of Spanish colonialism, its rich slave-and-sugar economy, had scarcely been affected in the most important regions of Cuban sugar production. Cuba's revolutionary leaders were determined not to repeat the strategic mistakes of the first independence struggle. Before launching the invasion of the western provinces in late 1895, Gómez, commander in chief of the insurgent armies, decided that this time the economic base of the colonial system had to be destroyed without exception. Orders were issued to lay waste to everything linked with sugar production: homes, warehouses, factories, fields, and railroads. The rebel army followed these orders to the letter and was eminently successful.

Gómez's loyalist counterparts—first General Martínez Campos, the Spanish hero of the Ten Years' War; then the ruthless General Valeriano Weyler y Nicolau, who assumed command of the Spanish armies in February 1896 after Martínez Campos had been routed by rebels in Matanzas—developed counterinsurgency tactics that had the same effect. By late 1896, orders had been issued by the Spanish military command prohibiting all unauthorized agricultural activities. Fields were to be torched or otherwise spoiled, and all cattle were to be driven into Spanish-controlled cities and towns in order to deprive rebels of potential food supplies. The most destructive of all policies, however, was the order to concentrate rural inhabitants in fortified villages and towns. The intent was to deprive the insurgents of logistical support from a rural creole population whose hatred toward Spaniards was exacerbated by the horrendous abuses committed by Spanish troops on their first forays into rural Cuba.

It would have been difficult to persuade the people of Matanzas that these were years of glory. Herded into towns, denied access to land to raise food crops, barely provisioned by Spanish authorities, and forced to live in terribly unsanitary conditions, matanceros also lost their homes and farms to destroying armies. Repeated epidemics of infectious disease, widespread malnutrition, and mass starvation were the fundamental realities experienced by the broad masses of people during the war. Between 1895 and 1898, it has been estimated, 24–30 percent of the provincial population died as a result of these conditions. This estimate excludes casualties suffered by armies in combat; nor does it take into account unreported deaths in rural areas outside the official control of colonial authorities. The actual death toll was probably higher than the recorded 60,000-plus civilian matanceros who perished between 1895 and 1898.[2] (See Table 17.1 and Figure 17.1.)

The reconcentration of the rural population had the most lethal impact on the people of Matanzas. This strategy for depriving the insurgents of logistical support had been discussed by Martínez Campos in mid-1895 but was not effected until autumn 1896.[3] But even before reconcentration was implemented as a systematic counterinsurgency policy, the province had endured to widespread political repression, the abandonment of the countryside by swarms of frightened people fleeing for their lives, and generalized economic and social dislocation. There had been an abortive uprising in February 1895 in Ibarra, some ten miles southeast of the city of Matanzas, and it was followed by a wave of violent repression. Martial law was declared on February 27, and anyone remotely suspected of pro-rebel sympathies was rounded up and jailed. Spanish officials feared a general uprising in Matanzas, and suspected rebel leaders were summarily executed.[4]

Repression was accompanied by Spanish military looting of rural zones. Animals were arbitrarily requisitioned and slaughtered to feed troops. Farms purported to harbor rebel sympathizers were destroyed: the buildings and homes were burned, the fields were trampled by horses or cattle, or were torched, and stockpiled food was consumed or carted off. Such incidents were not yet systematic in mid-1895, but they were precursors to activities that would become standard practice on both sides after late 1895.

Table 17.1. Deaths in Matanzas by Partido, 1889–1898

	1889	1890	1891	1892	1893	1895	1896	1897	1898
Alacranes	237	261	272	307	281	231	437	1,351	875
Amarillas	135	123	116	119	130	106	272	710	403
Bolondrón	301	439	381	393	404	346	368	897	800
Cabezas	198	226	155	196	214	191	382	1,652	732
Camarioca	37	42	62	62	61	48	13	53	5
Canasí	84	87	84	100	101	113	164	35	—
Cárdenas	676	711	638	730	722	751	1,233	3,112	2,132
Ceiba Mocha	142	150	135	166	125	128	207	1,218	538
Cimarrones	184	179	139	215	172	163	132	269	161
Colón	261	301	269	363	449	574	1,219	1,358	967
Cuevitas	130	129	141	165	125	132	283	539	246
Guamacaro	295	310	226	300	268	197	119	163	643
Guamutas	206	262	202	202	211	191	98	398	304
Guanajayabo	137	176	157	187	198	163	296	889	339
Jagüey Grande	111	136	145	141	134	147	395	1,119	288
Jovellanos	297	357	317	405	316	331	490	1,004	670
Lagunillas	129	105	97	122	104	126	42	38	25
Macagua	103	102	117	104	158	114	212	170	160
Macuriges	428	483	379	379	362	357	467	691	546
Matanzas	1,289	1,168	1,180	1,353	1,326	1,408	2,327	6,729	5,972
Manguito	182	183	128	158	145	140	140	416	264
Palmillas	53	60	75	88	88	77	57	14	29
Perico	90	99	132	100	101	132	137	361	241
Roque	184	168	142	129	106	119	50	145	156
Sabanilla	120	155	141	220	195	247	189	623	438
Santa Ana	94	109	85	128	151	98	81	317	250
San José de los Ramos	153	182	151	201	199	217	356	208	326
Unión de Reyes	111	115	136	148	171	161	328	868	578
TOTAL	6,367	6,818	6,202	7,181	7,017	7,008	10,494	25,347	18,078

Source: USNA, RG 140, Military Government of Cuba, Letters Received, 1899, no. 2594.
Note: These data were compiled by Spanish authorities and transcribed by U.S. authorities after the occupation.

In the wake of rural repression, inhabitants of small villages and rural zones began to flee.[5] The trickle of refugees into the towns became a veritable flood nearly a year before the enforced reconcentration began. In early January 1896, in the aftermath of the rebel invasion of the province, the U.S. consul in Matanzas wrote: "Great destitution exists among the country people who are crowding into the larger towns by the thousands. Business in this city is at a standstill."[6]

The city of Matanzas was inundated with migrants from rural areas who constructed makeshift shantytowns along the city's low-lying river banks. Population swelled from approximately 40,000 to 60,000 residents during

Births and Deaths

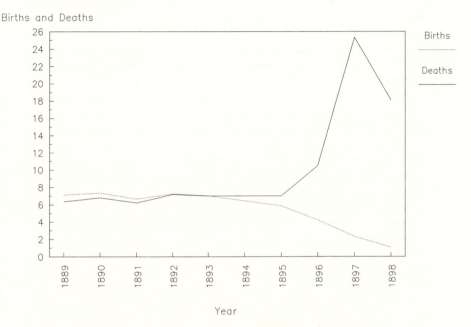

Figure 17.1. **Births and Deaths in Matanzas, 1889–1898 (in thousands)**
Source: USNA, RG 140, Military Government of Cuba, Letters Received, 1899, no. 2594.

the war, but more than 15,000 deaths were recorded between 1895 and 1898, largely owing to malnutrition, diseases resulting from poor diets and unsanitary conditions, and starvation. Ceiba Mocha, a small village of 600 people on the eve of the insurrection, was overwhelmed with 4,500 *reconcentrados* in late 1896 and early 1897. Only 1,280 emaciated, starving souls were alive when shocked U.S. military authorities entered the town in early 1899.[7]

Spanish atrocities perpetrated against these defenseless villages were frequent, especially in the aftermath of prolonged fighting or bitter defeat at the hands of insurgent forces. The U.S. consul reported in detail on a massacre at Sabanilla in January 1896, following the initial invasion of the province by Maceo and Gómez. Referred to by Spanish troops as "Little Africa" (two-thirds of the population were black or Chinese), Sabanilla had been occupied by insurgents who could not dislodge the Spanish garrison from their fortified emplacements. Merchant establishments were looted, and food was carried off or distributed to destitute townspeople. The rebels finally withdrew, and when the Spaniards emerged from their bunkers they embarked upon a systematic campaign of revenge against the unarmed civilians. All of those murdered over the next two days were blacks or mulattoes.[8]

Starvation because of Weyler's reconcentration policies was the most widespread cause of death. Spanish military authorities, with hatred and contempt for the overwhelmingly black and mulatto population of rural Matanzas, made little effort to alleviate the extreme human misery within fortified villages. Resources were strained, and often there was barely enough food to provision Spanish armies in the field. For the masses there was absolutely no way to secure food independently. Agricultural production ceased in Matanzas. It was impossible to return to the farms, for any Cuban civilian caught in a countryside deserted except for warring armies was considered a rebel and subject to execution. Insurgent armies could do little to alleviate the plight of their brethren, nor was this a fundamental concern of the rebel leadership. It was a time of war, and the priorities of Cuban insurgents revolved around military and political matters, not around the hopeless degradation, despair, and death that afflicted hundreds of thousands of Cubans caught in a situation over which they had no control.

The worst year was 1897. Between 1889 and 1893 the number of deaths in Matanzas averaged 6,717 yearly; in 1897, more than 25,000 civilians perished. The following year, 18,000 died, the decrease owing to emergency relief measures implemented toward the end of the year by the occupying U.S. military authorities. To be sure, the occupation of Cuba by the U.S. Army was part of a broad imperial design having sinister intent and far-reaching implications for Cuba and the rest of the Caribbean. This notwithstanding, the occupation staved off what could have been a population collapse analogous to the demographic disaster experienced by the Arawak Indians during the late fifteenth and early sixteenth centuries. General James H. Wilson, the military governor of Matanzas in 1899, may have been an instrument of imperialist policy, but he was deeply moved by the breadth of the human disaster he observed firsthand. In a lengthy report written in August 1899, he estimated that had food not been provided to the starving reconcentrados precisely when it was, three-fourths of the provincial population would have died.[9] There is no reason to doubt this speculation. Additionally, the number of births plummeted during the war (see Table 17.2).

Agricultural Collapse

Despite the onset of the insurrection in the east and the official repression and vigilance taking place in the province, Matanzas mill owners and colonos prepared for the harvest of 1896 as usual, with little premonition of the imminent disaster to come. The rebel assault was carefully planned to coincide with the beginning of the 1895/96 zafra, in order to strike a decisive blow at the economic foundations of the colonial system, and the first insurgent penetrations followed the invasion routes of 1876. In September 1895 small bands of rebels appeared unopposed in the Colón region, this

Table 17.2. Births in Matanzas by Partido, 1889–1898

	1889	1890	1891	1892	1893	1895	1896	1897	1898
Alacranes	283	307	308	424	355	313	170	88	48
Amarillas	189	229	211	245	226	187	100	55	41
Bolondrón	399	473	342	428	318	226	84	66	37
Cabezas	344	437	323	396	322	342	198	70	24
Camarioca	53	60	124	110	99	85	9	1	0
Canasí	147	128	141	129	198	167	102	41	—
Cárdenas	700	702	652	557	667	590	550	331	223
Ceiba Mocha	297	291	285	291	281	271	201	60	18
Cimarrones	150	179	153	176	142	82	14	17	5
Colón	205	194	193	240	253	207	204	130	84
Cuevitas	130	159	122	205	127	95	107	74	21
Guamacaro	375	303	348	306	294	147	29	20	18
Guamutas	332	255	232	258	182	143	58	127	36
Guanajayabo	211	208	187	238	208	159	92	12	19
Jagüey Grande	157	238	232	291	287	253	140	59	19
Jovellanos	256	298	294	274	297	184	129	91	43
Lagunillas	141	124	125	155	103	126	35	19	7
Macagua	119	105	125	136	99	68	58	12	6
Macuriges	468	464	395	394	394	175	64	51	45
Matanzas	963	961	899	921	957	980	1,441	589	379
Manguito	197	164	99	162	158	132	59	63	16
Palmillas	63	120	89	121	101	103	25	12	5
Perico	102	122	92	97	105	82	50	34	20
Roque	207	232	168	113	193	129	56	17	3
Sabanilla	170	139	201	201	239	222	86	115	65
Santa Ana	153	177	51	95	199	108	21	6	13
San José de los Ramos	188	160	114	145	110	158	32	78	26
Unión de Reyes	121	131	153	139	125	125	123	64	45
TOTAL	7,120	7,360	6,658	7,247	7,039	5,859	4,237	2,302	1,066

SOURCE: See Table 17.1.

advance guard having been sent by Maceo to test the Spanish military response. There was surprisingly little opposition, and in mid-December a
full-scale invasion of 10,000 men began. Gómez led 4,000 infantry and
2,000 cavalry in the northern tier of the province, and Maceo led 4,000 well-
armed troops in southern Matanzas. Within days, major population centers
were occupied, and the rebels roamed the countryside at will. The U.S. consul estimated that some 8,000 matanceros joined the invading rebel armies.[10]

Martínez Campos had been forced to shift his general headquarters from
east to west as the rebels advanced, and on December 23, 1895, his forces
were routed by insurgent armies at Coliseo, southwest of the city of Cár-

denas. The general then withdrew to Havana, his days at the head of Spanish colonialism's last redoubt numbered. On the insistence of Cuban and immigrant planters, Martínez Campos had allocated large contingents of Spanish troops to garrison duty on the principal Matanzas sugar estates in order to protect against expected rebel attacks. With his withdrawal from the province, any continued official protection rested upon private agreements between mill owners and Spanish officers in the field, who extracted large payments in return for their services. Weyler's arrival in February 1896 officially ended this policy. Resolved to wage a vicious war of attrition against the insurgents, the new commander of the Spanish forces removed all troops previously assigned to protect property and deployed them to fighting units.[11] Planters were authorized to hire private mercenaries in order to protect their estates, although many of these "private" guards were in reality Spanish officers and soldiers out to capitalize on the desperate need of mill owners for protection.

Caught between the strategic designs of the insurrectos and those of the Spanish military leadership, Matanzas agriculture was virtually destroyed in early 1896. Insurgent armies systematically burned plantations; destroyed fields, tools, machinery, and standing structures; and slaughtered cattle indiscriminately, both for food and as part of a general policy of wrecking the colonial economy. When rebels withdrew in the face of pending counterattacks, Spanish armies engaged in precisely the same activities to deprive the insurgents of logistical support. The scorched-earth policies of both armies effectively ended almost all agricultural activity until the conclusion of the war. The military campaigns in Matanzas between late 1895 and 1898 involved few clashes between opposing armies. Both military machines concentrated their efforts on the systematic destruction of all productive resources, and both operated with equal efficiency and success in this endeavor.

After the war, testimony before the Spanish Treaty Claims Commission—mostly by Cuban-born, naturalized U.S. citizens seeking economic reparations from Spain—provided ample description of the process of destruction. The case of Antonio Carillo de Albornoz is typical. Carillo and his brothers Isaac and Francisco, had inherited the 45-caballería Jicarita estate from their father in 1866. Isaac, a Havana lawyer, was married to Dolores Aldama, daughter of the deceased revolutionary leader Miguel Aldama. Such a distinguished family lineage notwithstanding, rebel troops arrived on December 29, 1895, and burned most of Jicarita's cane fields (although this time buildings were spared). On March 4, 1896, however, insurgents returned to finish the job. All of the estate's structures and machinery were destroyed, and any remaining cañaverales were torched. Rebel leaders then ordered all employees and laborers to abandon the estate. Having nowhere to go, they were forced into Weyler's emerging fortified towns. Since cane is a perennial, it began to grow on its own despite the lack of attention. Thus, in late 1896 and early 1897, Spanish troops passing by the estate fired the cane fields once again, repeating the deed in late 1897 and 1898.[12]

Ingenio Precioso, the property of Francisco J. Larrieu and his wife, Rosalía Torres, suffered a similar fate, but at the hands of the Spanish military machine. Precioso was a conglomeration of four farms that extended for 137 caballerías, 69 of which were planted in cane. Larrieu was suspected of rebel sympathies, and his estate was occupied by Spanish troops from November 1895 until May 1896. On May 15, 1896, he was arrested and subsequently imprisoned for 102 days in Cárdenas, having been accused of complicity with the insurgents. Spanish troops had lived off the farm, consuming its food crops and slaughtering its cattle for meat. Now, with Larrieu's arrest, the cane fields were burned, laborers were threatened and driven off the estate, other fields were trampled and destroyed, the plantation was systematically looted, and finally everything was torched. Periodically Spanish columns would return to fire regrown cane. Larrieu claimed damages of more than 1 million dollars in gold.[13]

The Diagos' old Tinguaro mill, which had been acquired and modernized by Carlos de la Rosa, was destroyed by both armies. Tinguaro had been garrisoned by the Spanish army under Martínez Campos's policy of protecting valuable property. With the arrival of Weyler and the redeployment of Spanish troops in February 1896, the proprietor was left to his own resources. On February 20, 1896, a band of insurgents arrived and set fire to several cane fields. Five days later, another gang of insurrectos appeared and burned more cane; and on March 3 Máximo Gómez himself stopped at the estate. Another rebel party continued torching Tinguaro's fields on March 8; finally, on August 3, 1896, several buildings with valuable machinery were destroyed, although the dwellings of the estate's colonos were spared. From then on, whatever remained of Tinguaro was demolished by Spanish columns. In October 1896 all of the colono bohíos were set ablaze, and on January 25, 1897 a Spanish garrison destroyed all remaining buildings and machinery. More than 1.7 million dollars in damages were done.[14]

By the war's end, only 20 of the 271 rural properties classified as ingenios had not been destroyed.[15] These were owned by wealthy families—some present in the province from early in the nineteenth century, others relative newcomers. All had sufficient capital to hire the private armies so necessary to protect their mills from attack. A typical mercenary band, hired to guard Francisco Rosell's Ingenio Dolores, commanded a total monthly salary disbursement of 2,030 pesos in gold: 100 pesos to the commanding officer; 50 pesos to the sergeant; 40 pesos each to two corporals; and 30 pesos each to sixty soldiers. During the war Rosell spent 99,630 pesos to protect Dolores and Agüedita and the San Lorenzo and Desquite colonias.[16]

Only the wealthiest families or merchant firms commanded the resources to pay such substantial salaries over the three-year course of the war. Among the mills not destroyed during the war were the Zuluetas' Ingenio Álava, the Torrientes' Central María, the Barós' Ingenio Santa Rita; the Armas family's Socorro estate, Pedro Fernández's Ingenio Unión, Leandro Soler's Santo Filomena, and the Sardiñas' Ingenio Reglita. All these mills were established by families who had been some of the most important entrepreneurs in Matanzas since the middle of the nineteenth century or earlier. Among the newcomers to the province who were able to protect their estates, most were merchants. Their properties included the Casañas brothers' Ingenio Dos Rosas; the Moras' old Central Australia, which had been purchased by a Spanish immigrant merchant house, Álvarez, Valdez y Cía.; Ingenio Progreso, owned by Suárez y Ruíz; José Sainz y Sainz's Ingenio San Vicente; and Antonio Gómez Araujo's Ingenio Nena. Families or firms that owned multiple mills had to decide which properties to protect. For example, the Zuluetas defended Álava, while España was destroyed, although this mill was reconstructed after the war. The heirs of Cristina Baró preserved Ingenio Santa Rita, but her husband, the Conde de Diana, lost Ingenio Diana. Table 17.3 lists mills grinding cane on the eve of the insurrection and shows their condition after the war.

Sugar mills and their cañaverales were not the only properties targeted for destruction by the opposing armies. Landowners large and small saw their properties destroyed, and every type of provincial farm was indiscriminately ruined. Of 318 colonias, only 36 emerged from the war with minimal damages. More than 95 percent of all the small-scale sitios and potreros in Matanzas were devastated. Houses and bohíos were torched, fences wrecked, fields were trampled by cavalry, and weeds and brush reclaimed previously cultivated land. Tables 17.4 and 17.5 indicate the extent of the destruction among different types of rural property.

In addition to the damage done to agricultural production, the war exacted a heavy toll upon the province's animals. Draft animals were decimated. The U.S. military authorities estimated that there were 50,000 yoke of oxen before the war and only 5,500 by mid-1899, after imports had begun from the United States. The count of horned cattle dropped from 298,391 head in 1894 to 8,800 in 1899. The number of horses fell from 102,268 before the insurrection to 3,700 at its end. Mules declined from 7,725 to 803. No poultry were to be found in Matanzas after the war; all hens, roosters, chickens, and ducks had been consumed by hungry armies and a starving populace.[17]

The provincial infrastructure was virtually destroyed. Railroad tracks were torn up, locomotives wrecked, dump cars demolished, and railroad ties burnt for fuel. The road system was nearly useless, for maintenance had not even been attempted during the war. Principal routes were rutted and

Table 17.3. Matanzas during and after the War for Independence:
Mills, Owners, and Postwar Status

Mill	Owner in 1895	Postwar Status
Admiración	Duquesne, Rita	Reconstructed
Agüedita	Rosell y Hijos	Reconstructed
Agüica	Perfecto Lacoste	Destroyed
Álava	Zulueta, Heirs of	Not Destroyed
Alcancía	Condesa de San Fernando	Reconstructed
Algorta	Sociedad Anónima	Reconstructed
Amistad	Ulacia, Sebastián	Reconstructed
Amistad	Torriente, Heirs of P.	Destroyed
Andrea	Peralta, Manuel	?
Andrea	?	Destroyed
Angelita	Delgado, Francisco	Destroyed
Anguila	Castillo, Rafael del	Destroyed
Antonia	Roque Escobar, José	Destroyed
Arco Iris	Ulzurrun, Luis D.	Destroyed
Armonía	Cuadra, Francisco	Reconstructed
Arroyo	Ulacia, Sebastián	Destroyed
Asunción	Ortia, Angel	Reconstructed
Atrevido	Melgares, José	Destroyed
Aurora	Gobel, Antonio	Destroyed
Australia	Alvarez, Valdéz y Cía.	Not Destroyed
Bolois	?	Reconstructed
Buenaventura	Samá, Heirs of	Destroyed
Caney	Fernández Mederos, Heirs of	Reconstructed
Carámbola	Suárez y Ruiz	Reconstructed
Carlota	Torriente hermanos	Destroyed
Carmen	?	Reconstructed
Carmen	?	Reconstructed
Cataluña	Oliver hermanos	Reconstructed
Central Batalla	Tavio, Pablo	Destroyed
Central Dolorita	Marquetti, Antonio	Destroyed
Central María	Torriente, Francisco M.	Not Destroyed
Coliseo	Amblard, Arturo	In Reconstruction
Coloso	Sánchez, Teodoro	Destroyed
Conchita	Baró, Concepción	Reconstructed
Confianza	Faret, Ricardo	Destroyed
Conquista	Torralba Pérez y Cía.	Destroyed
Cuatro Pasos	Martínez Alfonso, A. and M.	Reconstructed
Delirio	Hernández Piloto, J.	Reconstructed
Desempeno	Larrea, Joaquín	Reconstructed
Desquite	Montalvo, Sebastián	Reconstructed
Diana	Conde de Diana	Destroyed
Dichoso	Armas, Antonio	Destroyed
Dolores	Calvo y Herrera, Widow of	Reconstructed
Dolores	Rosell y Hijos	Reconstructed
Dolorita	Marquetti, Antonio	Destroyed
Dos Hermanos	Sardiña, Marcos	Reconstructed

Table 17.3. (*cont.*)

Mill	Owner in 1895	Postwar Status
Dos Rosas	Casañas hermanos	Not Destroyed
Dulce Nombre	Fáez, Perfecto	Reconstructed
El Carmen	Ballester, Patricio	Reconstructed
El Feliz	Piedra y Cía.	Reconstructed
Elena	Grande, Solaun y Cía.	Reconstructed
Elizalde	Elizalde, S. (Paris)	Reconstructed
España	Zulueta, Heirs of	Reconstructed
Esperanza	Santa Cruz de Oviedo	Reconstructed
Esperanza	?	Destroyed
Eugenia	Ruiz, Lorenzo	Destroyed
Feliz	Piedra y Cía.	Reconstructed
Flora	Armas, Agustín	Reconstructed
Fortuna	?	Destroyed
Gonzalo	Morejón, Ambrosio	Destroyed
Guamutica	Santiuste, J. M.	Destroyed
Guerrero	Elizalde, Juan B.	Destroyed
Helvecia	Ulacia, Sebastián	Destroyed
Isabel	Esnard hermanos	Reconstructed
Isabel	Arenal y Sáez, Pedro	Reconstructed
Jesús María	Montalvo, Marqués de	Destroyed
Jesús María	Serra, José, Heirs of	Destroyed
Jicarita	Piedra, Joaquín	Reconstructed
Juanita	?	Destroyed
Juguetillo	Belausteguigoitia, Domingo	Reconstructed
La Paz	Negrín, José P.	Reconstructed
La Rosa	Madan, Hijos de A.	Reconstructed
La Vega	Mesa, Tirso	Reconstructed
Las Cañas	Muñoz, Adolfo	Reconstructed
Limones	Terry y Dorticos, Emilio	Not Destroyed
Los Angeles	Cruz Gutiérrez, José	Reconstructed
Luisa	Menéndez Júnquera, José	Reconstructed
Majagua	?	Reconstructed
Manuelito	Conde de Diana	Destroyed
Maravilla	?	Destroyed
Merced	Manual y Vidal, A. J.	Destroyed
Mercedes	Hernández Ríos, Pablo	Not Destroyed
Monserrate	?	In Reconstruction
Nena	Gómez Araújo, Antonio	Not Destroyed
Nudorra	?	Reconstructed
Occitanía	Himely, Heirs of	Reconstructed
Olimpo	Baró, Amalia, Heirs of	Reconstructed
Otoño	Quintana, Felipe	Destroyed
Palestina	Sobrado, Gabriel	Destroyed
Perseverancia	Matas, Cándido	Destroyed
Perseverancia	Viera Montes, Manuel	Destroyed
Por Fuerza	Gómez, C.	Reconstructed
Precioso	Hoyo, Hipólito	Destroyed

Table 17.3. (*cont.*)

Mill	Owner in 1895	Postwar Status
Progreso	Suárez y Ruiz	Not Destroyed
Puerto	Fernández Blanco, José	Reconstructed
Recreo	Marqués de Villalba	Destroyed
Reglita	Sardiña, Cesáreo	Not Destroyed
San Agustín	Arcos, Ángel A.	Destroyed
San Antonio	Fernández, Merce y Rita	Destroyed
San Cayetano	Alfonso, Julio y Gonzalo	Reconstructed
San Felipe	Delgado, Felipe	Destroyed
San Florencio	Sainz y Sainz, José	Destroyed
San Francisco	Servia y González, Sres.	Destroyed
San Ignacio	Fernández López, José	Not Destroyed
San Joaquín	Pedroso, Gonzalo Joaquín	Destroyed
San José	Bea, Zábala	Destroyed
San José	Díaz Bolaño, José	Reconstructed
San José	Gálvez, José María	Reconstructed
San Juan	?	Reconstructed
San Juan Bautista	Ramos, Laureano	Reconstructed
San Lorenzo	?	Reconstructed
San Luis	Herrera, Serafín	Reconstructed
San Luis	Calvo, Catalina, Heirs of	Reconstructed
San Martín	?	Destroyed
San Miguel	Miró, Salvador	Destroyed
San Pablo	Bango, Pablo, Heirs of	Destroyed
San Rafael	Jorrín, Gonzalo	Reconstructed
San Vicente	Sainz y Sainz, José	Not Destroyed
Santa Amalia	Morgan, Thomas	Not Destroyed
Santa Ana	Grande, José	Destroyed
Santa Ana	?	Reconstructed
Santa Bárbara	Castañer, Joaquín	Reconstructed
Santa Catalina	Coffigny Ortíz, Heirs of	Destroyed
Santa Elvira	Perovani, Elvira	Destroyed
Santa Gertudis	González Mendoza, Antonio	Reconstructed
Santa Isabel	Menéndez, Teresa	Destroyed
Santa María	Ponce, Marcial, Heirs of	Destroyed
Santa Rita	Baró, Cristina, Heirs of	Not Destroyed
Santa Rita	José Carol Hermanos	Destroyed
Santa Rosalía	Castañer, Salvador	Destroyed
Santa Sofía	Díaz, José Lucas, Heirs of	Destroyed
Santiago	Tavio, José	Destroyed
Santo Domingo	García Serra y Cía.	Destroyed
Santo Domingo	?	Reconstructed
Santo Filomena	Soler, Leandro	Not Destroyed
Saratoga	Drake hermanos, Heirs of	Reconstructed
Serafina	?	Destroyed
Socorro	Armas, Socorro de	Not Destroyed
Soledad	Secada, Francisco G.	Not Destroyed
Telégrafo	?	Destroyed

Table 17.3. (*cont.*)

Mill	Owner in 1895	Postwar Status
Tinguaro	de la Rosa, Carlos	Reconstructed
Trinidad	Argüelles, J.	Not Destroyed
Triunfo	Hevia y Pérez, Heirs of	Destroyed
Triunfo	Ruiz, Pilar S.	Destroyed
Triunvirato	Echarte, Eduardo	Reconstructed
Unión	Ulacia, Sebastián	Destroyed
Unión	Fernández, Pedro	Not Destroyed
Valiente	García Bango, Silvestre	Reconstructed
Victoria	Ugarte, Widow of	Reconstructed

SOURCES: The names of mills and their postwar fates are recorded in Military Government of Cuba, Department of Agriculture, Commerce, and Industry, *Report of the Work Accomplished by This Department during the Fiscal Year Which Commenced on the 1st of July 1899, and Ended on the 30th of June, 1900* (n.p., 1900), pp. 240–242. Mill owners were identified in J.C. Prince, *Cuba Illustrated* (New York: Napoleon Thompson & Co., 1893–1894), pp. 124–174.

NOTE: Not every mill grinding cane in 1895 could be identified. Those listed as "reconstructed" were not necessarily rebuilt as sugar-producing estates; most were reestablished as cane-growing colonias.

Table 17.4. Matanzas after the War for Independence:
Status of Farm by Type of Farm

	Destroyed	Not Destroyed	Total
Potreros	821	53	874
Ingenios	251	20	271
Colonias	318	36	354
Sitios	3,512	144	3,656

SOURCE: Military Government of Cuba, Department of Agriculture, Commerce, and Industry, *Report of the Work Accomplished by This Department during the Fiscal Year Which Commenced on the 1st of July 1899, and Ended on the 30th of June, 1900.*

NOTE: *Potreros* were stock-raising farms; *ingenios* were sugar farms and their mills; *Colonios* were sugarcane farms that did not produce sugar; and *sitios* were subsistence farms.

overgrown with brush. Not only was it impossible for carts or wagons to move overland, but even horses and mules had difficulty traversing the province's best prewar roads and trails.[18]

As the war drew to a close, the people of Matanzas were broken. A handful of wealthy planters and merchants who had withdrawn to Havana, the United States, or Europe were prepared to resurrect the provincial econ-

Table 17.5. Matanzas after the War for Independence:
Status of Ingenios and Colonias by Partido

Partido[a]	Ingenios					Colonias					Total Culti-vated Cabs.
	A	B	C	D	Cabs.	A	B	C	D	Cabs.	
Alacranes	9	0	9	3	392	30	2	32	8	479	407
Bolondrón	18	0	18	5	1,039	3	1	4	2	87	309
Cabezas	27	0	27	0	729	24	15	39	11	314	253
Canasí	14	0	14	2	622	2	0	2	2	24	87
Cárdenas	2	2	4	0	154	2	0	2	2	30	61
Carlos Rojas	5	0	5	4	315	18	8	26	9	626	141
Cidra	6	0	6	5	262	13	0	13	0	306	65
Colón	9	0	9	3	392	16	8	24	13	288	138
Corral Falso	8	2	10	4	715	34	0	34	15	1,286	321
Cuevitas	2	2	4	1	607	2	0	2	2	117	123
Jagüey Grande	2	1	3	0	308	20	0	20	17	317	138
Jovellanos	10	2	12	0	540	10	0	10	9	79	173
Limonar	32	3	35	1	1,475	0	0	0	0	0	117
Macagua	3	0	3	2	242	13	0	13	11	433	124
Manguito	7	3	10	4	889	30	0	30	20	729	267
Martí	17	0	17	4	1,324	4	0	4	3	276	317
Matanzas	6	0	6	0	184	1	0	1	1	58	360
Máximo Gómez	25	0	25	3	983	8	0	8	8	112	393
Méndez Capote	13	2	15	1	578	4	0	4	2	42	311
Perico	2	0	2	2	183	16	2	18	15	287	85
Roque	8	2	10	3	837	45	0	45	17	383	129
Sabanilla	12	0	12	2	726	9	0	9	6	116	103
San José de los Ramos	11	1	12	2	707	3	0	3	3	194	116
Unión de Reyes	3	0	3	2	140	11	0	11	7	189	53
Total	251	20	271[b]	53	14,343	318	36	354	183	6,772	4,587
Avg. Size			(57.1)					(21.3)			

Source: See Table 17.4.
Note: A = destroyed; B = not destroyed; C = total mills (A + B); D = reconstructed. Cabs. = caballerías (33.6 acres each); Total Cultivated Cabs. = sum of cultivated land on ingenios and colonias.
[a]Before the war, Carlos Rojas was called Cimarrones; Cidra was Santa Ana; Corral Falso was Macuriges; Limonar was Guamacaro; Manguito was Palmillas; Martí was Guamutas; Máximo Gómez was Guanajayabo; and Méndez Capote was Lagunillas.
[b]Of these, 121 were listed as "demolido," which means they had ceased grinding cane.

omy. Most of the surviving population, however, emerged from the war weary, starving, and shell-shocked; they had little hope or plan, and little possibility of controlling their individual or collective destiny. The world around them had been destroyed, and the future held little beyond a struggle for survival.

CHAPTER 18

The Aftermath of War

The war began to end in late 1897, but it would take more than a year for the fighting to cease. Opposition at home, increased diplomatic pressures by the United States, and above all inability to defeat the Cuban insurgents forced the Spanish government to extricate itself gradually from the ghastly mire of war and revolution in rural Cuba. The blood-drenched General Weyler was recalled in October 1897 and replaced by the more moderate General Ramón Blanco. Charged with overseeing the transition to home rule in a last-ditch attempt to defuse the rebellion and preserve Spanish influence, Blanco inaugurated a Cuban government in January 1898 under the autonomy decree that had been issued for both Cuba and Puerto Rico. The rebels refused to consider this as anything more than it was, a veiled attempt to maintain the old structures of power, and they continued fighting. The U.S. invasion began in April, and in July 1898 Spain surrendered to U.S. forces.[1]

With the cessation of hostilities, all Spanish authorities in Matanzas resigned their offices and were replaced with Autonomist Party officials appointed by peninsular military commanders. These men had taken no part in the rebellion. The Spanish army began evacuating interior towns on November 15, and by December 28 all troops were on the coast awaiting ships to carry them home. On January 12, 1899, more than 13,000 Spanish soldiers disembarked from the port of Matanzas, and a huge celebration took place in the city from January 20 to 22.

With the withdrawal of Spanish troops, between November 1898 and January 1899, the Cuban rebel army occupied major population centers and removed Autonomist political figures from local positions of power. In January the U.S. armed forces began to garrison the province with more than 6,700 troops. Exhausted by war, with few resources at its disposal and overwhelmed with the logistical problems of administering a population literally starving before its eyes, the Cuban army cooperated fraternally with the U.S. occupation and coordinated relief efforts to provision desperate reconcentrados. Food rations were distributed during most of 1899.

Throughout the occupation, Matanzas rebel leaders enjoyed cordial relations with U.S. military authorities in the province. General James H. Wilson, the military governor, firmly believed that the Cuban civil government in the process of formation should be staffed by revolutionaries who had fought for Cuban independence, rather than by opportunistic political aspirants who suddenly appeared to vie for salaried positions.[2] This was the beginning of the maddening *empleomanía* that would afflict Cuba into the twentieth century. Cuban insurgent leaders were doubtless impatient and unhappy at not assuming full political power, but Wilson's desire to turn over as much authority to Cubans as possible was conducive to the development of amiable and constructive provincial-level relations between U.S. and Cuban officials.

War-weary matanceros greeted peace with hope, yet exhaustion. People were starving, the countryside lay ruined, few agricultural implements were available to the general populace, and draft animals were under the control of a handful of wealthy planters. Captain Fred S. Foltz, the acting inspector general for Matanzas, described the situation of early 1899 in graphic terms:

At the beginning of the American occupation . . . agriculture was practically dead. The laborers that had survived the starvation of the Reconcentration were still cowering in their palm huts on the outskirts of the towns and villages, living on rations issued by the Government and begging in the streets and at the railway stations. These people were too weak and anaemic to venture away from the centers of American charity and relief, or to make any attempt to redeem their fields.

Between the towns, the country was a deserted wilderness; the roads were overgrown with rank vegitation [*sic*], and neither cattle nor human beings were to be met with. All farm houses, not of sufficient size or importance to be turned into forts and regularly garrisoned, had fallen into ruin, and had been robbed of all valuable material, or burned.[3]

First Lieutenant Ralph Harrison, of the 2nd Cavalry, was sent on a reconnaissance mission through the province which yielded the following first-hand report:

Unión. A distance of twenty-one miles (Matanzas to Unión de Reyes) through as desolate although fertile a region as can be found. Except right near Unión, I doubt if I saw more than ten acres in cultivation. . . . There was nothing but high grass and bush everywhere. The march over what had evidently been a royal road, but it was badly overgrown and nothing but a dim trail remained. . . .

There was evidence of former prosperity in abandoned sugar mills and in cane fields that had been smothered out by weeds and morning glories.

I saw a few oxen grazing about two miles from Mocha, but saw no other animals except a cow and a calf. This was the first cow I had seen. It would be a most extravagant exaggeration to say that there were the least signs of any kind of revival of industrial prosperity along the route taken by me from Mocha to Unión. . . .

Guamacaro. The soil in the Guamacaro valley is black and most fertile. The valley is simply magnificent, but it appears that there is hardly an acre in cultivation. . . . I saw two or three ox teams in the valley, but no other animals of any kind, except the usual pig.

. . .

I did not see half a dozen animals of any kind between Camarioca and Matanzas. . . .

I was struck by the entire absence of oranges, limes, and cocoanuts [sic] in the region visited by me.[4]

By mid-1899, however, significant changes had occurred. Starvation had been eradicated by relief efforts, and as the population regained strength a return to the countryside ensued. The task of agricultural reconstruction was daunting, but there were few alternatives for survival. Smallholders trickled back to ruined farms and began to clear the land, plant subsistence crops, and construct rudimentary bohíos. Larger landowners, having little capital and no credit to generate the cash to pay salaries, offered small parcels to renters in exchange for labor commitments. Through rental arrangements, land could be rehabilitated and labor secured. The 1899 census, conducted under the auspices of the U.S. War Department, found 2,052 renters on fractionalized holdings; nearly 80 percent farmed plots less than .75 of a caballería in size.[5] This rental class exploited one-third of the 4,902 caballerías of cultivated land in Matanzas in 1899.

The census found that cultivated acreage in the province had decreased by 55.8 percent between 1895 and 1899, but these data should be viewed with caution. The actual decline was more severe, since the census enumerators counted land planted in cane that had grown on its own, without methodical care or minimal maintenance. Of 4,902 caballerías of land in cultivation, 79.9 percent was sown in cane and another 13.5 percent in bananas, plantains, and sweet potatoes. Table 18.1 indicates the wartime decline in land cultivation, by municipal district and according to official statistics.

Several fundamental, short-term problems stood in the way of agricul-

Table 18.1. Matanzas Farms, Land Area, and Cultivated Acreage by
Municipal District, 1895–1899

Municipal District[a]	No. Farms	Cabs.	Cultivated Cabs.		% Change
			1895	1899	
Alacranes	219	1,500	575	392	−31.8
Bolondrón	165	2,429	1,056	301	−71.5
Cabezas	189	1,050	237	216	−8.9
Canasí	30	616	195	74	−62.1
Cárdenas	17	202	59	80	+35.6
Carlos Rojas	78	825	353	96	−72.8
Colón	300	1,620	499	245	−50.9
Cuevitas	274	1,553	470	254	−46.0
Guamacaro	73	1,461	522	137	−73.8
Jagüey Grande	508	1,714	394	252	−36.0
Jovellanos	90	658	399	178	−55.4
Macagua	93	1,356	248	81	−67.3
Macuriges	282	2,107	948	425	−55.2
Martí	113	1,835	461	236	−48.8
Matanzas	624	2,682	863	309	−64.2
Máximo Gómez	135	906	373	154	−58.7
Méndez Capote	100	727	234	133	−43.2
Palmillas	162	2,311	726	310	−57.3
Perico	56	509	196	142	−27.6
Roque	208	1,675	729	254	−65.2
Sabanilla	150	1,216	708	224	−68.4
San José de los Ramos	96	678	305	217	−28.9
Santa Ana	75	736	387	75	−80.6
Unión de Reyes	46	251	152	116	−23.7
Total	4,083	30,617	11,087	4,902	−55.8

Source: United States War Department, Office of the Director of the Census of Cuba, *Report on the Census of Cuba, 1899* (Washington, D.C.: Government Printing Office, 1900).

[a]Carlos Rojas was formerly Cimarrones; Martí was Guamutas; Máximo Gómez was Guanajayabo; Méndez Capote was Lagunillas.

tural reconstruction. The scarcity of draft animals because of the general devastation of the war was severe. General Wilson recognized this and, as part of his rehabilitation effort, began to introduce oxen, cows, hogs, and even chickens from the United States. There was also a dearth of agricultural implements. Along with animals, provincial authorities made the importation of plows and machetes a priority. Reports from rural zones by military authorities in late 1900 reveal that small farmers had some access to imported animals and tools.[6] But, by and large, the efforts of the U.S.

Military Government revolved around the rehabilitation of the sugar industry.

Two major problems plagued the revitalization of sugar. The most serious was the extreme shortage of agricultural credit. The prewar Spanish merchant class of the province was a casualty of the insurrection and subsequent intervention, and during the transition to U.S. neocolonial control new credit institutions had not yet emerged. This was resolved with the onslaught of speculative U.S./Canadian banking and commercial interests that descended on Cuba in the early twentieth century. However, sugar rehabilitation in the short term was stymied by an acute capital scarcity. Wilson had proposed using the provincial military government as a quasi-lending agency for supply of emergency credit to planters and smallholders alike.[7] But this smacked of direct government participation in economic matters, and was unlikely to be implemented by the U.S. military governors John R. Brooke or Leonard Wood, both fervent believers in the free hand of the marketplace.

The economic vacuum created by the virtual absence of credit institutions would provide an opening for large-scale penetration of rural Matanzas by North American capital. The process was initiated in the immediate aftermath of the occupation. Manufacturers of sugar-milling equipment appeared in Matanzas in early 1899 to reconnoiter the financial situation.[8] U.S. capitalists began purchasing bankrupt properties. The Hires Sugar Company acquired twenty three farms, including the future Central Dos Rosas, previously owned by the Casañas brothers, peninsular merchants/planters who had been in Matanzas since the 1860s.[9] Francisco Gustavo de la Rosa, a resident of New York and the heir of Charles Rosa, sold Tinguaro to the Cuban-American Sugar Co., headed by the former Republican congressman from Texas, R. B. Hawley.[10] These were the initial investments in Matanzas sugar by U.S.-based firms.

Shortages of credit, animals, and tools were aggravated by an upsurge in 1900 of rural banditry directed against sugar estates. Insurrection and war tend to erode existing mechanisms of social control. Cuba's two great revolutionary struggles of the nineteenth century may have been led by disaffected sectors of the insular elite, but armed bands of insurrectos were composed primarily of the most exploited members of Cuban rural society. The class dimensions of both rebellions are underscored by the military objectives of the revolutionary armies when they swept into Matanzas. In 1876 the principal activity of insurgent bands was the firing of ingenio cane fields. Between late 1895 and 1898, though, the total destruction of the sugar industry was the focal point of the rebel armies.

Assaults on the property of the rich were thus legitimized, and this attracted all kinds of people to the rebel cause—including social bandits, outlaws driven to attack wealth largely because of an inability to break the perpetual cycle of poverty. Often, links between rural bandits and the rebellion were tenuous at best, and many supposed rebels were simply common criminals. Purported revolutionary activity could be little more than a convenient way to legitimize robbery, pillage, and general destruction. For criminal groups, the ritualized attacks on the rich that had generally been accepted throughout the war were now treated as illegal and disruptive acts. What had been considered "revolutionary" between 1895 and 1898 was classified as common criminality in 1899 and 1900. Attacks on property had become institutionalized by these bandits: they had conveniently called themselves revolutionaries, but they were never really subordinate to the political leadership of the insurrection; and their activities could not be curbed with the end of the rebellion.[11]

In the immediate aftermath of the war, banditry was virtually nonexistent—simply because of the devastation and destitution endemic to all parts of rural Matanzas. The year 1899 was relatively quiet, but by 1900 the gradual reconstruction of mills, rehabilitation of cane fields, and renewed sugar production were accompanied by an upsurge in rural banditry. Four basic activities were pursued: cattle rustling, extortion of mill owners, kidnapping for ransom, and the burning of cane fields when demands were not met.[12] The shortage of oxen and cattle and the general failure to use brands meant the development of a lucrative market for these animals and widespread theft. Extortion was carried out through kidnapping and demands for ransom, or mill owners received anonymous letters threatening that cane fields would be torched if payments were not made. The González Mendoza brothers, owners of the Santa Gertudis mill in Banagüises, received the following letter in December 1900:

> I expect of you that you will promptly and with your accustomed generosity remit to me the two hundred centenes of which I find myself in need. . . .
>
> I beg that you will send a person in your confidence on the 27th of this month, at ten o'clock in the evening, over the "Sordo road" so that, going or coming, we shall see each other.
>
> He must ride a grey horse and smoke a cigar; at the signal of the lighting of a match he must stop and dismount, placing on the beaten trail the money wrapped in white paper so that I may see it. He will then mount and go on; if he makes no suspicious movement, his life will be safe.

And you, sir, if you try any tricks with me, you will be roughly handled, and your cane will be fired at the four corners of the estate. Your crop will be ruined in this case or in [any] case of your failing to satisfy me.

Perhaps tomorrow I shall be compelled to double the amount of the contribution.[13]

Such activities continued into the early years of the twentieth century.[14] With the general breakdown of traditional mechanisms of social control by elite groups—first because of abolitionism in the 1880s, then because of war and revolution in the 1890s—it was extraordinarily difficult to reimpose order, especially in rural zones where the insurrection had bred rebelliousness and disdain for wealth.

These problems notwithstanding, the Matanzas sugar economy was revived in the closing years of the nineteenth century. For entrepreneurs who had conserved capital throughout the war, or newcomers intent on exploiting the depressed conditions of the immediate postwar period, there were few investment alternatives. The industry may have been destroyed during the insurrection, but the physical and human landscape of the province had been molded over a century to serve the needs of sugar. Matanzas capitalists, whether creoles or immigrants, did not pause to consider options after peace had been established. Sugar had sustained previous generations of elite groups, and it was routinely looked on as the key to future wealth. Thus, the revival of sugar monoculture began with a vengeance as the nineteenth century drew to a close.

The immediate task for sugar producers was to restore prewar installed capacity, both in the agricultural and the industrial sector. Because processing was concentrated in so few mills after the war, industrial reconstruction was an intensely focused task under the management of a small number of entrepreneurs. Mill owners who had accumulated capital during previous periods of sugar growth, or immigrants not affected by the insurrection, were able to begin the process of rebuilding damaged buildings and machinery, importing new equipment, repairing internal rail systems, and rehabilitating cane fields. During the harvest of 1898/99, forty mills ground cane and produced 110,000 metric tons of sugar, which was slightly more than half of the 202,000 metric tons produced in 1881.[15]

Repairing the damage done to cane fields required more extensive effort and involved larger numbers of people, since cane cultivation was so dispersed. Prior to the war, a large portion of the cane processed by Matanzas mills was acquired from colonos, who generally lacked the capital resources to reestablish production quickly. Thus, in the immediate aftermath of the

war, sugar producers generally harvested cane growing on their own properties (although some was acquired from larger colonos who were able to
hire laborers to cut cane that had regrown by itself). Fields had to be
weeded, drained, tended, and replanted, but there was enough cane standing
to produce a crop in 1899.

Rehabilitation efforts proceeded steadily through 1899 in preparation for
the first harvest of the new century. More than 1,400 caballerías of land
were replanted in cane; more than 10,000 oxen were purchased; 1,375
plows were imported, along with thousands of hoes, machetes, and axes;
and 43,000 laborers were employed and paid salaries of between 60 and 80
centavos daily.[16] But 1899 was an exceedingly dry year, and the prolonged
summer drought resulted in a harvest of only 99,200 metric tons in 1900,
smaller than the previous year.

By 1901, however, the Matanzas sugar industry was well on the way to
full recovery. A zafra of 219,862 metric tons was produced, more than double the preceding year's harvest. Because of the lack of reliable prewar statistical data, no comparisons can be drawn with the record harvests of the
early 1890s; but the dramatic improvements in the industrial sector compared with the sugar output from the 1881 zafra are worth noting. In 1881,
the 431 mills grinding cane in Matanzas produced an average of 471 metric
tons of sugar each. Forty-seven mills operated in 1901, producing an average of 4,678 metric tons per mill.

This tenfold increase in sugar production per mill was linked to two sets
of factors. The first was a series of processing innovations, developed since
the early 1880s, that increased installed industrial capacity. Massive double-
pressure grinding machines, regrinding equipment to extract the maximum
volume of guarapo from cane, triple- and quadruple-effect vacuum evaporators, and huge crystallizing vats were standard equipment employed on
mills after the close of the rebellion. One example was Ingenio Álava, run
by Julián Zulueta's sons. This was the largest producing mill in 1901, and
it utilized 3 hydraulic grinding machines with rollers 6 feet long; 2 regrinding machines with 7-foot rollers; 2 triple-effect vacuum evaporators with a
capacity of 3,000 gallons each; and 3 crystallizers that could hold a total of
31,200 gallons.[17] Modern machinery not only revolutionized grinding capacity, but also dramatically increased sugar yields. During the zafra of
1901, Matanzas sugar mills extracted industrial yields of 9.6 percent sugar
per arroba of sugarcane by weight. We have no analogous data for the 1870s
or 1880s, but by way of comparison the most capital-intensive, fully mechanized mills in 1860 produced yields of between 4.5 percent and 5.5 percent.[18]

The second series of factors had to do with the transportation revolution wrought by railroad construction. Public railroads had been built from the late 1830s and were used by the industry in a variety of ways. In the initial phase, however, railroad construction had little impact on the internal dynamics of sugar agriculture, since private use of public railway lines to transport cane to mills did not begin on a significant scale until the 1870s. The wealthiest mill owners constructed lines within their estates in the 1850s, but it was not until the 1880s and 1890s that this became a routine part of sugar production. Internal railway lines dramatically increased the possibilities for capital intensification and concentration of processing, and for a more productive specialization and division of resources. Central factories could now process cane grown in distant cañaverales without suffering a substantial loss in sucrose content. This increased enormously the quantity of cane that could be absorbed by individual mills.

The transportation revolution, however, did not result in a dramatic spatial expansion of estates during the 1880s and 1890s; rather, what followed was a proliferation of the colonato. Capital limitations, labor shortages, and the continuing poor performance of the agricultural sector (see below), prohibited the emergence of estates any larger than those found at mid-century. The railroad was a prerequisite to the centralization of processing, but it led simultaneously to the decentralization of cane production in the 1880s and 1890s.

Innovations in transportation may have revolutionized the production of sugar and the ties between sugar agriculture and industry, but they did not lead to improvements in agricultural productivity. Although there were significant structural shifts in the organization of cane production, the productivity of sugar agriculture exhibited a contrasting timelessness. Yields of sugarcane per caballería of land actually declined during the very same period when sugar production was transformed. At the turn of the twentieth century, sugarcane yields were no greater than the average in 1830—and substantially less than the yields on the most productive estates at the middle of the nineteenth century.

During the zafra of 1901 the best-quality land yielded 72,727 arrobas of cane per caballería; second-grade land generated 42,181 arrobas/caballería; and third-grade land produced 32,826 arrobas/caballería. By way of comparison, agricultural yields in 1830 were estimated to be nearly 75,000 arrobas/caballería, and in 1850 the most productive mills in the Banagüises region produced more than 100,000 arrobas/caballería. For example, San Narciso, which became Julián Zulueta's Ingenio Habana, produced 110,993 arrobas/caballería; Urumea, 105,286; and the Diagos' Santa Elena, 103,567. In the mid-1880s, agricultural yields were estimated at between 75,000 and 80,000 arrobas of cane per caballería.[19]

The development of the Matanzas sugar industry through the nineteenth century revolved around the continual expansion into frontier regions with high-yielding, virgin soils. By the 1870s, however, the provincial frontier was virtually closed, and the problem of declining yields was addressed by means of capital intensification of processing, not by any concerted effort to improve the agricultural sector's performance. Since the mechanization of cane cutting was virtually impossible because of technological limitations, the intensive application of new fertilizers was the only possible way to improve sugar agriculture. Capital resources, however, were devoted almost exclusively to the modernization of processing, and the agricultural sector was neglected. Undoubtedly, the greater profit margins that entrepreneurs perceived in industrial investments explain this asymmetry.

The proliferation of the colonato exacerbated the problem of constantly declining agricultural yields. Colono incomes were linked to agricultural production; thus, there was a built-in incentive to increase productivity. But most colonos suffered from capital shortages, which meant the impossibility of importing and applying the fertilizers needed to increase cane production. The fact that most colonos were paid in sugar according to the industrial yields of central factories allowed the colonato to benefit to some extent from the technological improvements taking place at the mill. The long-term responses of the Cuban sugar industry to this dilemma was the ritual repetition of eighteenth- and nineteenth-century patterns of development. In the twentieth century, sugar continued expanding into frontier regions with high-yielding virgin soils; Las Villas, Camagüey, and Oriente provinces became the most important producing regions.

Not only was there no improvement in agricultural yield, but the evidence suggests that labor productivity in the agricultural sector experienced little amelioration despite the abolition of slavery. In the mid-nineteenth century, sugar agriculture employed roughly 9 people per caballería of cultivated land. During the harvest of 1899 the ratio worsened, although this may have been the result of an increase in labor demand mandated by the daunting task of rural reconstruction. The U.S. military authorities estimated a total of 43,000 workers laboring on 3,839 caballerías of planted cane at harvesttime—11 workers/caballería.[20]

If we are to understand the economics of sugar production, it is extremely important to separate the industrial and agricultural sectors for analytical purposes. The yields of sugar per caballería of land are valid as a measurement of general productivity only in the absence of a change in industrial yields. However, through the second half of the nineteenth century, when processing innovations raised sugar-to-sugarcane yields, sugar production per caballería of land is meaningless as a measure of agricultural productivity, since increases were linked solely to improvements in the industrial sector.[21]

Detailed data on the 1901 zafra permit a glimpse of the economic and social dynamics of Matanzas sugar monoculture in the aftermath of the war and at the dawn of the twentieth century. Mills secured cane in a number of ways, and few generalizations may be applied to the industry as a whole. Some directly exploited their own land by hiring wage workers. This was the case with Ingenio Conchita (in Alacranes), which cultivated 123 caballerías of cane, none of which were leased to colonos. Conchita was one of the province's largest producers of sugar in 1901. But another large-scale mill, Ingenio Santa Gertudis, subdivided its 70 caballerías of cane among ten colonos and purchased an additional 6 million arrobas of sugarcane from surrounding independent growers. Thus, mills pursued a variety of strategies to secure cane, including direct cultivation, rental of parcels to colonos, and purchase from independent landowners also classified as colonos.

One of the more salient social dimensions of sugar production after the war was the dominant role assumed by the heirs of the men who had been the most important Matanzas entrepreneurs during the 1830s and 1840s. The children of José Baró continued to operate three mills, Conchita, Olimpo, and Santa Rita, all founded by their father in the first half of the nineteenth century. Julián Zulueta's children by his different wives continued to own Álava and España, whose combined production accounted for 11.7 percent of provincial sugar output in 1901. The Alfonsos owned Ingenio San Cayetano; the Solers ran Santa Filomena; and Joaquín Pedroso y Echevarría's son-in-law, Antonio González Mendoza (a Havana judge who became the first head of the Cuban Supreme Court), operated the Pedroso family's Santa Gertudis mill in Guamutas, now called Martí. Together, these old Matanzas families controlled one-third of total Matanzas sugar production in 1901.

Other families, who had arrived in the 1860s and 1870s, were also important producers early in the twentieth century. Examples include Francisco Rosell, the firm of Grande y Solaun, the Sardiñas brothers, Sainz, Martínez y Cía., the Casañas brothers, and the heirs of José Fernández Blanco. Still other mills were acquired in the aftermath of the war by newcomers to Matanzas. The U.S.-based Cuban-American Sugar Co. acquired Tinguaro; Pedro Arenal, a peninsular Spaniard, purchased the Armas family's old Ingenio Socorro; another peninsular merchant house, Botet Sociedad en Comandita, acquired the Montalvos' old Jesús María mill, one of the earliest founded in Matanzas; the Feliz Sugar Company, chartered in New York in 1898 and controlled by the Spanish sugar brokers Rionda,

Ceballos & Company, purchased Ingenio Feliz.[22] Among the casualties of the late nineteenth century were the titled families who had played such an important role as innovative mill owners and railroad builders during the formative period of the Matanzas sugar economy. Not one remained as a mill owner at the dawn of the twentieth century. Table 18.2 offers an overview of the sugar economy between 1899 and 1901.

Table 18.2. Matanzas Sugar Mills, Owners, and Production, 1899–1901

Mill	Municipal District	Owner	Sacks Produced (1899)	Sacks Produced (1900)	Sacks Produced (1901)	Cabs. Directly Cultivated	No. Colonias	Colonia Production
Agüedita	Palmillas	Rosell, Francisco	17,100	18,000	28,463	22	16	600,000 @
Álava	San José de los Ramos	Zulueta y Gámiz, hermanos	51,000	63,202	121,850	69	3	—
Algorta	Máximo Gómez	Montalván, José	0	14,000	37,583	35	0	0
Angelita	Martí	Delgado y hermano	0	0	22,795	12	10	500,000 @
Armonía	Bolondrón	Arrechaleta y Cuadra	0	0	21,257	37	11	800,000 @
Australia	Jagüey Grande	Alvarez Váldez, Antonio	0	8,000	24,892	10	20	—
Central Luisa	Carlos Rojas	Rivas de Castañer, Josefa	0	0	44,277	0	1	300,000 @
Conchita	Alacranes	Baró, Concepción	81,300	67,000	102,774	123	0	0
Condesa	Jovellanos	?	2,744	2,000	←——— ceased production ———			
Dolores	Macuriges	Rosell, Francisco	0	0	23,500	50	0	0
Dos Rosas	Cárdenas	Casañas y Casañas	3,000	1,900	9,016	22	1	18 Cabs.
Dulce Nombre	Macagua	Arrendondo, Luis; Pando, Francisco	0	6,000	20,100	3	4	200,000 @
Elena	Canasí	Grande y Solaun	3,600	4,000	4,091	12	4	6 Cabs.
España	Perico	Zulueta y Samá, Heirs of	26,000	30,069	54,374	50	25	3,000,000 @
Esperanza	Palmillas	Carreño y Arias	28,500	26,400	48,020	12	17	5,500,000 @
Féliz	Bolondrón	Feliz Sugar Co.	15,000	17,261	31,854	25	5	25 Cabs.
Flora	Bolondrón	Sainz, Martínez y Cía.	14,000	20,279	30,500	50	0	0
Guipuzcoa	Martí	Arocena, Manuel	7,000	8,500	23,795	—	—	—
Jesús María	Santa Ana	Botet S. en C., S.	0	0	9,000	12	2	3 Cabs.
Jicarita	Bolondrón	Díaz y Olivera	9,000	8,945	15,566	35	10	1,000,000 @
Julia	Limonar	?	2,000	1,500	←——— ceased production ———			
La Paz	Colón	P. de Monte y Cía.	0	0	0	0	0	0
Las Cañas	Alacranes	Muñoz, Adolfo	16,101	15,141	34,980	47	0	0
Limones	Guamacaro	Terry y Dórticos, Emilio	0	0	5,736	24	4	200,000 @

Mill	Municipality	Owner						
Los Angeles	Santa Ana	Cruz Gutiérrez, José, Heir of	3,800	1,700	6,000	0	16	17 Cabs.
Luisa	Guamacaro	Menéndez, José, Heirs of	0	0	27,886	40	9	900,000 @
Nena	Palmillas	Gómez Araújo, Antonio	17,506	11,995	19,408	50	0	0
Olimpo	Carlos Rojas	Baró, Amalia, Heirs of	9,000	5,960	7,493	9	0	0
Por Fuerza	Colón	P. de Monte y Cía.	26,300	30,069	45,868	9	0	Buys cane
Precioso	Cárdenas	Smith, Castro y Cía.	0	0	20,101	37	3	27 Cabs.
Progreso	Cárdenas	Suárez y Ruiz	15,738	10,850	15,311	6	8	1,049,728 @
Puerto	Canasí	Fernández Blanco, José, Heirs of	1,592	3,246	3,743	4	0	0
Reglita	Cuevitas	Sardiñas y hermano	28,200	18,868	46,600	25	3	359,000 @
San Cayetano	Santa Ana	Alfonso y Aldama, Julio	12,000	3,800	16,400	4	5	2 Cabs.
San Gonzalo	Unión de Reyes	Guell, G.; Diago, B.	0	0	16,700	0	8	2,340,000 @
San Ignacio	Cuevitas	Urbistondo, B., Heirs of	18,000	16,600	21,519	30	2	310,000 @
San Juan Bautista	Canasí	Cía. Central S. J. Bautista	0	1,113	10,431	5	36	1,300,000 @
San Rafael	Bolondrón	Moliner y Alfonso, Julia	0	0	35,909	50	3	1,060,000 @
San Vicente	Jovellanos	Izaguirre, Heirs of	12,000	8,000	21,394	12	2	500,000 @
Santa Amalia	Carlos Rojas	Guerendiain y Badiola (renters)	5,890	4,320	18,749	15	0	0
Santa Filomena	Macuriges	Soler, Leandro	38,235	34,840	50,425	59	1	1,000,000 @
Santa Gertudis	Marti	González Mendoza, Antonio	70,000	75,000	110,000	70	10	1,000,000 @
Santa Rita	Cuevitas	Baró, Cristina, Heirs of	16,000	13,087	43,267	15	8	1,305,000 @
Santo Domingo	Unión de Reyes	García Blanco, José	5,500	10,000	38,850	30	17	3,000,000 @
Saratoga	Sabanilla	Paillet, Ernesto	0	0	2,600	2	8	2,475,000 @
Socorro	Macuriges	Arenal, Pedro,	50,764	51,700	77,106	70	0	0
Soledad	Jovellanos	Pérez de Fernández, Dolores	16,000	16,800	43,600	40	0	0
Tinguaro	Perico	Cuban-American Sugar Co.	0	0	50,000	18	18	6,000,000 @
Unión	Cuevitas	Lezama Larrea, José	26,000	36,000	19,000	65	0	0
Valiente	Alacranes	García, Llana y Cía.	21,171	15,543	27,162	20	0	0
TOTAL			670,041[a]	681,688	1,509,945	1,335	290	

SOURCES: Military Government of Cuba, Department of Agriculture, Commerce, and Industry, *Report of the Work Accomplished by This Department during the Fiscal Year Which Commenced on the 1st of July 1899, and Ended on the 30th of June, 1900* (n.p., 1900); Junta de Agricultura, Comercio e Industria de la Provincia de Matanzas, *Memoria descriptiva de los trabajos realizados durante el año fiscal de 1900 a 1901* (Matanzas: Lib. La Pluma de Oro, 1901); USNA, RG 140, Military Government of Cuba, Letters Received, 1902, box 244, no. 1074.

NOTE: A sack is 13 arrobas, or 325 pounds. @ = arrobas; Cabs. = caballerías (33.6 acres each).

[a]Total production was 757,401 sacks; seven mills producing in this year did not grind cane again, and their production is therefore not shown here.

CHAPTER 19

Conclusions

At the dawn of the nineteenth century, Matanzas was little more than an appendage to the economic system that revolved around the port city of Havana. In the sixteenth, seventeenth, and much of the eighteenth centuries, Matanzas functioned as a strategic-reserve area for the Cuban capital. Cattle roamed wild on natural pastures, and periodically herds were driven toward Havana to provision the city with food or to supply urban-based industries with cattle by-products. Timber was sometimes cut from the province's forests, but this activity was restricted to regions near navigable rivers, since it was impossible to transport bulky hardwoods overland. Matanzas was in all respects an undeveloped, lightly populated frontier.

All this began to change in the second half of the eighteenth century. Two general factors attracted entrepreneurs to the province. The first was linked to the expansion of sugar and coffee cultivation outside the immediate environs of Havana. The spread of commercial agriculture southeast toward the Güines Valley, and south toward Batabanó from the 1740s on, meant that ancillary activities in support of the Havana-based agricultural export economy were pushed toward Matanzas. Cattle used by sugar mills for food or for draft purposes were pastured there. And as forests in areas of sugar expansion were depleted, Matanzas woodlands were increasingly coveted by the Havana sugar-producing elite. Thus, the process of economic development that was taking place in Havana province led to the penetration of Matanzas by entrepreneurs seeking resources to support their primary activities.

The second factor was linked to the possibility of capitalizing on a locally produced product. Small-scale tobacco agriculture had flourished in Matanzas river valleys from the mid-seventeenth century, largely supported by a thriving contraband trade with the non-Spanish ships that regularly called on the unfortified and officially neglected bay. The emergence of the Marqués de Jústiz and the Conde de Jibacoa, who constructed tobacco mills in the late eighteenth century, and the appearance later on of the factoría or royal tobacco monopoly, heralded the beginning of organized export agriculture under the control of outside entrepreneurs.

This would become a fundamental structural aspect of provincial economic organization. Capital, entrepreneurial skills, technology, labor, and nearly every other factor of production came from outside the province through the nineteenth century. The first entrepreneurs to establish control over productive resources in Matanzas were the titled families of Havana who initiated the transition to an agricultural export economy in the eighteenth century. Without exception, each of these families established a presence in the province, although not one ever shifted their principal residences from the Cuban capital. The Montalvos, Calvos, O'Farrills, Herreras, Peñalvers, Recios, Cárdenases, and Pedrosos all constructed important sugar ingenios in Matanzas early in the nineteenth century, and most of these remained in production until the aftermath of the Ten Years' War.

Although this entrepreneurial elite operated within the context of a colonial polity characterized by numerous short-term conflicts over a variety of issues, their activities were pursued with almost complete long-term independence. There may have been disputes with the Crown over tariff policies, access to foreign markets, or other matters of considerable importance, but Cuba's colonial status did not seriously hinder the relentless development of sugar monoculture in Matanzas through the nineteenth century. A native-born insular elite orchestrated and guided the Cuban economy through various phases of export-oriented growth and crafted an economic system that served their specific class interests. Had the island been an independent nation controlled by this elite, economic developmental patterns and the process of class formation would not have been very different at all. This is one reason that I have avoided any discussion of short-term political disputes between sectors of the insular elite or between that elite and the peninsular colonial authorities. The long-term processes discussed here were not seriously affected by the political economy of colonialism.

Cuban entrepreneurs may have drawn on credit lines established with British or North American banks or merchant houses, and may have purchased machinery from factories in England, France, or the United States, but this made them no more economically dependent than London or New York capitalists who used the same sources of credit and technology. It was Cubans who organized and financed mill construction, imported the technology, controlled the slave trade, and owned nearly every factor of production. The largest planters were even self-sufficient with respect to investment capital. Thus, the economic development of Matanzas province was above all in Cuban hands. The fact that U.S.-based merchant houses appeared in the cities of Matanzas and Cárdenas, that credit lines extended through New York and London, or that French and U.S. citizens established coffee farms in the province and sometimes owned sugar mills did not mitigate this overarching aspect of provincial economic life. This Cuban-based entrepreneurial elite was joined in Matanzas by immigrant families appearing in the 1830s and 1840s. Some, such as the Diagos, the Ayestaráns, and the Poeys, had participated in the Havana boom of the late eighteenth cen-

tury. Others were relative newcomers, such as the Zuluetas, Barós, Torrientes, or Arrietas. All were in some way connected to the Cuban slave
trade, and although there were rivalries among newer family groups, and
between older and more recent entrepreneurs, they had blended by mid-
century into a new elite class that put disputes aside to cooperate in joint
endeavors. The most important and extensive of those enterprises were railroad construction and slave trading.

The appearance of immigrant entrepreneurs in the 1830s and 1840s heralded few shifts in the local social structure. Newcomers were Cuban-based,
and although many were diversified entrepreneurs with investments in Europe or the United States, they had made Cuba their home. They continued
the patterns of economic and social development established by the eighteenth-century Cuban nobility. All maintained lavish homes in Havana,
and none ever moved to Matanzas on a permanent basis. Thus, the Matanzas economy was controlled by outsiders despite the shifting composition
of the entrepreneurial elite. There were no foreign villains here, ransacking
the local economy and repatriating profits to their countries of origin. Matanzas was pillaged by a Cuban-based elite operating from Havana. The
profits produced throughout the nineteenth century in Matanzas were systematically channeled out of the province. This contributed to the distorted
pattern of Cuban socioeconomic development that, in part, gave rise to the
revolutions which began in 1868, 1895, 1933, and 1953. In no small measure, those revolts were the reactions of provincial groups to the ostenta-
tious wealth and political monopoly of Havana-based power brokers.

Under the control of these two elite sectors, Matanzas was converted
from a sparsely populated frontier to the axis around which Cuba's sugar
economy turned. The colony's largest and most productive mills were located there until late in the nineteenth century; the island's principal railroad lines were constructed in Matanzas; and the province was a major destination of the slave trade and, later, the Chinese "coolie" trade to Cuba.

The Matanzas sugar economy's insatiable demands for masses of unskilled labor led to the long-term development of an extremely polarized
class structure. There were only fragmentary sectors of society between the
Havana-based elites and the masses of slaves and Chinese workers who labored to produce the province's wealth. Small-scale landowners proliferated
in rural zones along with plantation development, and the social structure
of urban areas was rather more complex than in rural zones. The income
generated by the provincial economy, however, was so extremely concentrated in the hands of elite groups that the development of a domestic market was negligible. Consumption patterns were dictated by the needs of
sugar, and the entire structure of the provincial economy was honed to serve
monoculture.

Capital was invested solely in activities linked to sugar production. Although one of the most modern railroad and communications systems in all of Latin America and the Caribbean crisscrossed the Matanzas hinterland, this must not be mistaken for economic diversification. The total lack of domestic demand precluded the possibility of diversified investment patterns, and this buttressed monocultural economic structures. Investors saw no profit possibilities in anything unrelated to sugar, and capital was routinely directed into deepening and broadening the sugar economy until there were no alternatives for economic development. The legacy created by this nineteenth-century system has endured. Thus, despite the radical changes in economic structures and in the distribution of wealth wrought by the socialist revolution of the 1960s, sugar monoculture remains in Matanzas.

Although uncounted hundreds of millions of pesos were generated by the Matanzas economy, there were virtually no improvements in the standard of living for the vast majority of matanceros. Masses of slaves, forced to live and labor in the most extreme human degradation because of sugar, experienced no long-term improvement in their lives, material or otherwise. Free whites, blacks, or mulattoes could perhaps contrast their experiences with the unfortunate conditions of those enslaved, but over the long haul they fared no better. Sugar may have generated fortunes for the elite of Havana, but by the end of the nineteenth century most people in Matanzas lived no longer, their health was no better, their diets no richer, their homes no sturdier; they remained largely illiterate, and they entered the twentieth century having enjoyed few improvements in their collective condition.

The socioeconomic history of Matanzas echoes that of many other regions of Latin America and the Caribbean where similar cycles of economic growth have left little in the way of long-term improvement in the lives of the common people. The structures of production and monopolization of resources by elite groups eliminated any possibility that social and economic development could accompany impressive cycles of economic expansion and the generation of extraordinary wealth. Cuban elites in the nineteenth century were imbued with the spirit of capitalism, and Social Darwinism ran rampant. There was no concept of society as a community, only the narrowly defined interests of class. This dynamic was no doubt nurtured by virulent racism, for the slaves whose labor produced wealth for Cuba's elites were despised and sometimes feared. These elites had no notion whatsoever of any obligation to oversee the development of a viable social system, with decent housing, medical care, education, and collective security for a broad cross section of the social order. Such concerns would come in another era, in many ways a reaction to the social and economic structures created by monocultural sugar production.

There is no question that a multifaceted dependence was part and parcel of the Matanzas economy in the nineteenth century. Planters and merchants had no control over the price structure of sugar and molasses on the world market. Labor supplies were linked to the constant importation of slaves and Chinese and, in the aftermath of abolition, to immigration from Spain. Technology was entirely imported—from such basic items as staves and shooks, used to construct barrels and boxes, to the sophisticated machinery needed to process sugar or power locomotives.

But it must be underlined that this dependence was created by Cubans responding to their own carefully defined class interests. Cuba may have repeated many of the historical aspects of sugar and slavery found in Jamaica, Haiti, and Barbados during the eighteenth century, but there were fundamental distinctions with respect to ownership structures and entrepreneurial skills. French and British planters and merchants developed their colonial possessions to serve the needs of domestic capital. But in Cuba there was a fundamental difference. Despite the island's colonial status, sugar monoculture was developed to serve the needs of a creole elite. Unlike the carefully designed activities of Britain and France in their Caribbean possessions, Spain did little to initiate economic development in Cuba but, rather, followed the lead of Cuban entrepreneurs. There was no Machiavellian conspiracy to create structures of dependence or monoculture on the part of peninsular officials or speculators, or for that matter by Cubans. Cuban entrepreneurs took advantage of opportunities to create wealth and maximize profits resulting from a complex combination of forces, domestic and foreign. These ultimately led to a single product that yielded the highest return on invested capital. Monoculture developed in Matanzas because of the objective conditions of the marketplace and for no other reason.

The Matanzas sugar economy was built on the twin pillars of African slavery and high-yielding virgin soils. The sugar economy relied on continued slave imports through the 1860s, despite attempts to diversify plantation labor forces. In addition, the locus of provincial sugar production shifted constantly toward frontier areas. When soil was exhausted in older areas of exploitation and agricultural yields declined, profitability waned. Planters responded by pursuing two strategies. Mills were modernized so that industrial yields could be increased to offset falling agricultural productivity. Or new areas with high-yielding virgin soils were colonized, and the same productive structures were routinely re-created.

By the 1870s, the entire system was threatened owing to the end of the slave trade and the closing of the frontier. Sugar's expansion into new areas continued through the Ten Years' War, but slavery's days were numbered and there were no more regions in Matanzas to be colonized. The patriarchs of old elite families also disappeared as the relentless course of nature took its toll. Planters inheriting the Matanzas sugar economy were faced with two huge problems. The entire labor base of the industry had to be overhauled because of abolition and the lack of any measures to maintain agricultural productivity; moreover, the industrial phase of sugar production had to become more efficient in order to guarantee economic viability. These problems were exacerbated in the 1880s and 1890s by the beginning of a steep fall in sugar prices on the world market.

The interlude between Cuba's independence insurrections was accompanied by far-reaching transformations in the Matanzas sugar economy. A series of fundamental changes were effected in the organization of production, resulting in a more efficient and productive division of labor. The manufacturing sector was concentrated and modernized, in many ways a response to the agricultural sector's poor performance. The capital intensification of processing resulted in greater efficiency and renewed profitability, despite the crisis of the early 1880s and the secular decline in sugar prices through 1895.

The agricultural sector was entirely overhauled, but the ensuing transformation did not result in any general improvement of agricultural yields. The development of central factories allowed agriculturalists to concentrate on cane production without the preoccupation or financial drain of investments in manufacture. It also permitted processors to begin freeing themselves from the concerns of cane cultivation. But sugarcane agriculture in Matanzas suffered from the general scarcity of investment capital. Available capital resources were devoted to the industrial sector. Although the labor base of agriculture was transformed by the abolition of slavery, the development of different types of colonias, and the beginnings of a free rural labor market, agricultural yields per land unit or laborer experienced no improvements in the 1880s and 1890s.

There is no question that the end of servitude resulted in the more productive long-term use of land, labor, and capital. In this sense, abolition released previously stifled productive forces. A separate question is whether the sugar economy could have continued functioning in the short term with its stodgy, tradition-bound ways had slavery not been abolished. Was the crisis of the 1880s caused by structural difficulties endemic to the sugar economy that could be resolved only by a radical transformation of the labor and capital bases of the industry? Or was the crisis the result of abolition?

It is clear that the levels of Cuban sugar production in the early 1890s could not have been achieved without the more productive division of labor forthcoming in the aftermath of abolition. In this sense, from a broad economic point of view, the end of servitude was revolutionary indeed. However, much evidence indicates that the slave-based sugar economy could have survived intact into the 1880s, if not for the destructive impact of abolition. Economically, slave labor seems to have continued yielding profits through the Ten Years' War. Clearly the capital-intensive mills and large-scale colonias of the 1880s and 1890s were more efficient and profitable. But this does not mean that old, slave-based ingenios could not have produced at smaller profit margins well into the 1880s had abolition not been imposed on the plantation owners. Abolition may have resulted in an economic leap forward for the industry as a whole, but from a social point of view it severely weakened the old, sugar-producing elite.

Labor scarcity was the single most important variable that determined the emerging forms of the post-abolition Matanzas sugar economy. The main characteristic of the industry was the concentration of processing and the dispersion of growing. The chief reason that there was no concentration of sugar agriculture was the inability to develop a free rural labor market on a broad enough scale to support the emergence of extensive latifundia. Direct ownership over large estates would have been a logical way of guaranteeing the enormous supplies of cane needed to satisfy the installed capacity of a modernized industrial sector. But this was impossible because the anticipated rural-proletarianization process did not take place after abolition. It was one thing to abolish slavery; but the emergence of a free labor market was something entirely different. Too much land was available in frontier zones to the east, thus offering potential workers alternatives for survival other than plantation labor.

Objective conditions were not the only reasons why freed men and women did not coalesce into a rural labor force in the 1880s and 1890s. Former slaves loathed plantation labor in the rural zones identified with their former condition of oppression and human degradation. The alternative pursued by the elites was to use the land itself as a lure to attract renters and smallholders, thus shifting the onus of agricultural labor to a newly emerging sector of Cuban rural society. The proliferation of the colonato ensued, the sugar economy's response to the failure to develop a broad-based free labor market in the aftermath of abolition.

To understand fully the 1878–1895 period, the social dimensions of abolition in Matanzas rural society must be considered; and the broader, long-term socioeconomic impact must be weighed as well. Slaves, of course, were the principal beneficiaries of emancipation, and despite the fact that little social mobility or amelioration of material life followed for most blacks or mulattoes, abolition did end the most destructive and degrading of all human conditions. Despite theoretical legal equality, the structures of social, economic, and political power kept blacks and mulattoes at the bottom of the socioeconomic heap. Freedom did not generally translate into opportunities for upward mobility, and the pervasiveness of racism and social inequality lasted through much of the twentieth century. The domination of white elites over the institutions that controlled the lives of blacks continued; and, in many ways, it has persisted despite radical changes in race relations and power structures effected by the socialist revolution.

Abolition also resulted in the development of social sectors between elites and unskilled laborers. The emergence of the colonato, of renters and owners of farms of all sizes, meant the partial opening of the Matanzas social structure for the first time in the nineteenth century. A rather diverse cross section of society was presented with opportunities to survive in other ways than as mere plantation laborers. Free Cuban whites, blacks, and mulattoes, as well as peninsular immigrants who had formerly shunned labor in the Cuban countryside, took advantage of opportunities to participate in the sugar economy because now they could cultivate their own plots of land. This system was remarkably successful. The dislocations of the immediate aftermath of abolition in the 1880s were overcome by the early 1890s, and sugar monoculture was revitalized within the new productive parameters. Another social process paralleled abolition. The old, sugar-producing elite was no longer Matanzas rural society's dominant social class. Families descended from the eighteenth-century nobility were the most glaring casualties. By the 1890s, not one of the titled families that had opened the frontier and built the provincial railroad system remained in Matanzas. There are many Montalvos, O'Farrills, Pedrosos, and Herreras in rural Matanzas today, largely the descendants of former slaves who assumed the surnames of their masters after abolition. But the great planter families of the late eighteenth and early nineteenth centuries had faded from the historical stage.

The immigrants of the 1830s and 1840s fared no better. Several descendants of the most powerful family groups remained, among them the Zuluetas, the Barós, and the Torrientes. But most were swept away by the radical changes in productive structures that accompanied abolition. The capital resources needed to convert obsolete ingenios over to modern centrales were available to only a handful of entrepreneurs by the mid-1880s. Buffeted and battered by the crisis of the early 1880s, few remained solvent by the end of the decade. Once prosperous estates, such as Flor de Cuba, San Martín, and Echevarría, fell into disrepair and were lost through foreclosure or were sold cheaply to newcomers. The aftermath of abolition was destructive to the former slaveholders, who collapsed along with the institution that had sustained them. They had prospered within the old productive system, which rested on a constantly shifting frontier and African slavery. When both disappeared, and the challenge of adjusting to a totally different set of objective and subjective circumstances was presented, the old families ceded their place at center stage to new actors.

The new system was in the process of consolidation when it was interrupted by the war for independence. The destruction of war swept away all but the most resilient entrepreneurs. Those who survived were confronted with a situation totally alien to that which greeted their predecessors. Nineteenth-century Matanzas elites operated within the confines of a colonial system in which they were the most dynamic element. The neocolonial order emerging in the early twentieth century was altogether different. Controlled in all but name by the most dynamically expanding nation in the world, Cubans could barely catch their collective breath before the economy began marching ahead as if the war that claimed so many lives had not even taken place. Before recovery from the devastation of war and revolution was consummated, Matanzas was revived by new infusions of capital and entrepreneurial skills. Some of the old families remained, but most were distant memories before the close of the first decade of the twentieth century.

There is an enduring sense of pride and dignity in the *bateys* of the old mills that still produce sugar in Matanzas, that ubiquitous mainstay of rural society in the late twentieth century. The workers of España, Álava, Tinguaro, and Australia talk with ease, cordiality, and typical rural humility. Most know how to read and write, and their children are all enrolled in schools, something emphasized to visitors with great pride. They have access to free medical care and decent housing, and there is a collective awareness that, despite the material limitations imposed by monoculture, they are somehow in control of their own destinies. They smile a great deal and, though hardly naive, they seem to be genuinely content with their future prospects.

It is exhilarating to walk among them, listening to their stories and talking to their laughing children who so theatrically pose for pictures. To know their past—that they are in large part the descendants of Africans brutally wrenched from faraway shores, forced to serve the needs of a product that generated both wealth and poverty—cannot but help create a cautious optimism for peoples who confront the weight of similar historical circumstances. The old, nineteenth-century slave-trading entrepreneurs who created the system inherited by these energetic and optimistic men, women, and children could never have envisioned a future in which the organization of Cuban rural society would serve the needs of the once downtrodden and exploited.

In many ways, contemporary matanceros continue to struggle against the legacy of the past described in this book; for it has been nearly impossible to diversify an economy so finely tuned for so long to serve the needs of a single crop, despite the sweeping transformations in political structure during the contemporary period. However, masters no longer summon them to the fields. Sugar remains, dominating the landscape in every direction and defining the rhythms of daily life. But it is no longer a source of wealth to so few and of suffering to so many, as it was in the not too distant past.

NOTES

Chapter 1

1. For the early history of Matanzas, see Carlos M. Trelles, *Matanzas y su puerto desde 1508 hasta 1693* (Matanzas: Imp. Estrada, 1932); Francisco J. Ponte y Domínguez, *Matanzas: biografía de una provincia* (Havana: Imp. El Siglo XX, 1959), pp. 1–30; Levi Marrero, *Cuba: economía y sociedad*, vol. 1 (Río Piedras: Ed. San Juan, 1972), p. 115, and vol. 2 (Madrid: Ed. Playor, 1974), pp. 37, 329; and Irene A. Wright, *The Early History of Cuba, 1492–1586* (New York: Macmillan, 1916), pp. 36, 193.

Marrero, *Cuba: economía y sociedad*, vol. 2, p. 329, reproduces the 1570 census conducted by Juan del Castillo. Bernal Díaz del Castillo wrote about the origins of the name Matanzas in his famous *Historia verdadera de la conquista de la Nueva España* (Mexico: Ed. Porrua, 1968). Matanzas first appears in the official cartography in 1541 (as "Portus Matanças") on a map of Cuba drawn by the Italian G. Benzoni and reproduced in Trelles, *Matanzas y su puerto*, between pp. 12 and 13.

2. Power to award grants of land and Indians (*encomienda*) was originally entrusted to the first royal governor of Cuba, Diego Velázquez, in 1514. However, this authority passed to the seven *cabildos*, or town councils, by the 1550s, thus transferring a great deal of authority to local elite groups. Most of these cabildos were established in the east or on the southern coast (Bayamo, Santiago, Baracoa, Trinidad, Sancti Spíritus, and Puerto Príncipe). The Havana cabildo had jurisdiction over almost all of the western half of Cuba, including the Matanzas region. This local-level authority over usufruct land lasted for nearly two centuries. Cabildos were stripped of their power to award land rights only in 1729.

It should be emphasized that these "mercedes de tierra" did not confer legal property rights, but only usufruct rights. Although private property was not legally established in Cuba until 1819, functionally these grants seem to have conferred inalienable property rights to recipients and their heirs *if* a presence was maintained.

For a discussion of the early system of land grants in Cuba, see Francisco Pérez de la Riva, *Origen y régimen de la propiedad territorial en Cuba* (Havana: Imp. El Siglo XX, 1946); and Duvon C. Corbitt, "Mercedes and Realengos: A Survey of the Public Land System in Cuba," *Hispanic American Historical Review* 19:3 (1939), pp. 262–285. It should be noted that land grants in Cuba were more important as a source of early colonial wealth and power than encomienda grants—especially in the Matanzas region, where few indigenous peoples were found by the second half of the sixteenth century. Marrero, *Cuba: economía y sociedad*, vol. 1, pp. 177–178, found no *encomenderos* in the Matanzas region during the mid-sixteenth century.

3. One Cuban league measures 4,227 meters; 5,000 "varas cubanas"; 208 cordeles, 8 varas; or 2 English miles, 1,159 yards, and 8 inches. The area of an hato is 1,684 caballerías, or 22,616.12 hectares, or 56,582.4 acres. The area of a corral is 421 caballerías, or 5,654.03 hectares, or 14,145.6 acres. One caballería equals 33.6 acres or 13.43 hectares.

For a complete account of Cuban measurements, see Esteban Pichardo, *Geografía de la isla de Cuba* (Havana: Est. Tip. de D. M. Soler, 1854), vol. 1, pp. vii–xv. For the areas of hatos and corrales, see Pérez de la Riva, *Origen y régimen*, p. 52.

4. For a listing of usufruct land grants made by the Havana cabildo, see Rodrigo de Bernardo y Estrada, *Prontuario de mercedes o sea índice por orden alfabético de las mercedes concedidas por el escmo. ayuntamiento de la Habana en cuanto concierne a las haciendas de crianza de animales* (Havana: Est. Tip. La Cubana, 1857).

5. By the late sixteenth century important shipyards had been built in Havana, as well as foundries to manufacture cannon, anchors, and hardware. These foundries used copper from mines in Santiago. On early copper mining in Cuba, see Irene A. Wright "Los origenes de la minería en Cuba. Las minas del Prado hasta 1600," *La Reforma Social* 7 (April–July 1916), pp. 450–462.

Thousands of people often jammed the streets of Havana when the fleet was docked, and the great demand for food supported high prices for agricultural and cattle products. Commercial opportunities were extensive. See Heinrich Friedlaender, *Historia económica de Cuba* (Havana: Ediciones de Ciencias Sociales, 1978), vol. 1, p. 4.

6. The development of agriculture on the perimeter of Havana pushed Cuban cattle ranching to the south and east. It should be reiterated that before the spread of sugar in the eighteenth and nineteenth centuries, most of the island was covered by forest. Cattle grazed on natural pastures in various regions, among them Matanzas, and had to be eliminated from the environs of Havana in order to protect developing crop farms.

7. Antón Recio was an early settler on the island. He founded one of Cuba's first sugar mills, Guaicanamar, on the outskirts of Havana (Regla today), and he was active in the cattle economy of the Matanzas region. Although legitimately married to a Spaniard, Catalina Hernández, he had no children by her. However, Antón did have two children with the daughter of the Indian *cacique* of Guanabacoa, Cacanga. These offspring continued the Recio lineage in Cuba. The sixth generation of the Havana Recios was headed by Gonzalo Recio de Oquendo, who was bestowed the title "Marqués de la Real Proclamación" by Charles III in 1760. Gonzalo Recio held the position of "Teniente de Gobernador Político de Cuba" during the English occupation of Havana in 1762. He also owned two haciendas in Guamutas, Cimarrones and Cayamas.

For the lineage of the Recio family, see Rafael Nieto y Cortadellas, *Dignidades nobiliarias en Cuba* (Madrid: Ediciones de Cultura Hispánica, 1954) (herafter *DN*), pp. 420–426; and Francisco Xavier de Santa Cruz y Mallen (Conde de San Juan de Jaruco y de Santa Cruz de Mopox), *Historia de familias cubanas* (Havana: Ed. Hércules, 1940) (hereafter *HFC*), vol. 3, pp. 358–383.

8. See Bernardo y Estrada, *Prontuario de mercedes*, pp. 14, 28; and Ponte y Domínguez, *Matanzas*, p. 51.

9. Julio LeRiverend, *Historia económica de Cuba* (Havana: Instituto Cubano del Libro, 1971), p. 31.

10. During the 1620s and 1630s the Havana cabildo awarded two mercedes in the Guamacaro region and three in Guamutas. In April 1621 Luis de Soto was granted the "paso de Guamacaro," and in November 1631 Melchor Pérez Borroto was granted permission to graze cattle on the "corral Guamacaro."

In February 1626 the "sabana de Guamutas" was granted to García Fernando de Córdoba. In June 1628 the "sitio de Guamutas" was bestowed upon Francisco Sánchez; and in August 1629 Martín Oquendo was granted access to the same "sitio de Guamutas." See Bernardo y Estrada, *Prontuario de mercedes*, p. 28.

11. Several eighteenth-century maps of Cuba show the approximate location of all major roads, and from seventeenth-century descriptions these seem to be similar with respect to general itineraries. See "Carte rediute de l'isle de Cuba, 1762" and "Carte de l'ile de Cuba redigee sur les observations astronomiques des navigateurs espagnols et sur celles de M' de Humboldt, 1826" (which was composed by Humboldt in 1801), Map Division, NYPL.

Two early nineteenth-century works also describe the general itinerary and condition of the Cuban road system. See José Antonio Saco "Memoria sobre caminos en la isla de Cuba," in José Antonio Saco, *Colección de papeles científicos, históricos, políticos, y de otros ramos sobre la isla de Cuba* (Havana: Dirección General de Cultura, 1960), pp. 61–176; and Esteban Pichardo, *Itinerario general de los caminos principales de la isla de Cuba* (Havana: Imp. de Palmer, 1828).

12. There are many accounts of the famous Dutch capture of the "Flota de Plata" in Matanzas Bay in 1628, and there is a famous painting (*Verovering Vande Silvervloot Inde Bay Matanca*) that accompanies nearly every one. For an excellent consideration of this episode within the context of Dutch designs in the Caribbean, see Cornelio Ch. Goslinga, *Los holandeses en el caribe* (Havana: Casa de las Americas, 1983), esp. pp. 157–181.

13. See Provincia de Matanzas, Excma. Diputación Povincial, Sección de Fomento y Estadística, *Censo agrícola. Fincas azucareras. Año de 1881* (Matanzas: Imp. Aurora de Yumurí, 1883), which gives a brief history of the sugar industry in the province. Also see Trelles, *Matanzas y su puerto*, pp. 7–8; Ponte y Domínguez, *Matanzas*, pp. 53–54; and Bernardo y Estrada, *Prontuario de mercedes*, pp. 20–21.

14. Ponte y Domínguez, *Matanzas*, pp. 57–58.

15. See "Planta de la bahía de Matanzas en la Hauvana [*sic*], 1682," reproduced after p. 29 in Trelles, *Matanzas y su puerto*.

16. There are numerous folkloric accounts of the founding of Matanzas. For the straight facts, see Jacobo de la Pezuela, *Crónica de las Antillas* (Madrid: Rubio, Grilo y Vitturi, 1871), pp. 159–160.

The practice of selling land or urban parcels "a censo" was to become fundamental when "haciendas comuneras" were broken up from the late eighteenth through the mid-nineteenth centuries. Censos were legal monetary obligations that could be imposed on purchasers of any type of property. A capital value was set by the owner, and the buyer had to pay a percentage of that value each year, usually 5 percent. Sometimes the censos were in perpetuity, other times a fixed time limit was set. Censos could be imposed on highly valued land even when purchasers actually paid the full purchase price. This was a mechanism whereby those without large capital resources could acquire land; it was also a means of providing income to owners of unutilized land, usually absentees with noble titles living in Havana. See Pérez de la Riva, *Origen y régimen de la propiedad territorial*, chap. 6 ("Censos y gravámenes"), pp. 76–92, which also recounts the story of the founding of Matanzas.

17. For an account of the early history of tobacco cultivation in Matanzas, see José Rivero Muñiz, *Tabaco. Su historia en Cuba* (Havana: Instituto de Historia, 1964) vol. 1, pp. 67–68, 146–148.

18. The Jústiz family appears in every account mentioning anything about the history of Matanzas. Much of the corral de Matanzas became part of the family's property together with the corral de Yumurí, which was donated to the town in the late eighteenth century. The role of the two brothers in the development of the eighteenth-century tobacco economy has been emphasized only by Rivero Muñiz, *Tabaco*. For a history of the family lineage, see *DN*, pp. 294–297; and *HFC*, vol. 2, pp. 227–240.

In 1860 Samuel Hazard visited the location of the Jústiz mills, called "Los Molinos" by locals, and drew a picturesque sketch of the region. See Hazard, *Cuba with Pen and Pencil* (Hartford, Conn.: Hartford Publishing Co., 1871).

19. The imposition of the first tobacco monopoly was met by open revolts on the part of tobacco farmers. The revolt of 1717 succeeded in driving the functionaries of the Real Factoría back to Spain. There were also revolts in 1718, 1720, and 1723, although these were based in the Havana region, where vegueros were more affected by actual attempts to enforce the monopoly. Matanzas, distant from the center of power, was hardly affected by the first monopoly. See José Rivero Muñiz, *Las tres sediciones de los vegueros en el siglo xviii* (Havana: Academia de la Historia de Cuba, 1951).

20. For a brief description of the Real Compañía de Comercio, see Friedlaender, *Historia económica de Cuba*, vol. 1, pp. 80–81. For a more detailed account, see Marrero, *Cuba: economía y sociedad*, vol. 12, pp. 2–16.

21. See Ponte y Domínguez, *Matanzas*, p. 78, for an account of this episode. Also see Marrero, *Cuba: economía y sociedad*, vol. 11, pp. 9–10.

22. For a scathing contemporary indictment of the tobacco monopoly, see the 1808 speech of Francisco Arango y Parreño "Abolición de la factoría: libertad en la siembra, fabricación, y comercio del tabaco," in Francisco Arango y Parreño, *De la factoría a la colonia* (Havana: Dirección de Cultura, 1936), pp. 114–145. Also see Arango's famous 1792 speech "Discurso sobre la agricultura de la Habana y medios de fomentarla," pp. 21–113 in the same volume.

23. See Manuel Moreno Fraginals, *El ingenio. Complejo económico social cubano del azúcar* (Havana: Ed. de Ciencias Sociales, 1978), vol. 1, pp. 52–62.

24. For a graphic locational display of Cuban sugar ingenios in 1766, see Marrero, *Cuba: economía y sociedad*, vol. 10, p. 139.

25. See the 1773 "Padrón de haciendas ganaderas en la jurisdicción de la Habana," reproduced in Marrero, *Cuba: economía y sociedad*, vol. 10, p. 109. At that time, three partidos that would become part of the jurisdicción of Matanzas in 1815 were administratively part of Havana. These were Guamutas, Macuriges, and Guamacaro. Almost every one of the thirty-nine haciendas with known owners (this includes Matanzas as well) were the property of Havana-based families.

26. For the genealogy of the Montalvo clan, see *DN*, pp. 143–148, 308–313; and *HFC*, vol. 3, pp. 289–324. Ignacio Montalvo y Ambulodi was also one of the founding members of the Havana Sociedad Económica de Amigos del País. See "Catálogo general alfabético de los individuos que componen la real sociedad patriótica de la Habana desde su erección hasta diciembre del año de 1795," in Fernando Ortíz, *Recopilación para la historia de la Sociedad Económica Habanera* (Havana: Imp. y Lib. El Universo, 1930), vol. 1, pp. 115–120.

27. The O'Farrill family history is traced in *HFC*, vol. 3, pp. 334–339. For the location of the O'Farrill's Matanzas mills, see Map 3; and AHPM, Mapas y Planos, leg. 34, exp. 179, "Plano de la ciudad, puerto, y jurisdicción de Matanzas." Also see Moreno Fraginals, *El ingenio*, vol. 1, p. 29.

Juan Manuel O'Farrill was vice-director of the Sociedad Patriótica de la Habana, and his brother Rafael was vice-contador. See *Calendario manual y guía de forasteros de la isla de Cuba para el año de 1795* (Havana: Imp. de la Capitanía General, 1795), pp. 96–97. Also see Ponte y Domínguez, *Matanzas*, p. 102.

28. It should be stressed that these data cannot be used to assess the *total* population in the entire region that would become a separate jurisdiction in 1815 and a province in 1878. In 1774, and in the census of 1792, most of the Matanzas area was controlled by Havana. This area included the partidos of Guamacaro, Macuriges, and Guamutas. It is impossible to assess the population or economic resources of these three important partidos because the data for Havana were not disaggregated but were included under a category "La Habana y sus partidos." Yet, even though they may not indicate total population in 1774 and 1792, the data listed here do reflect the demographic expansion taking place in the region.

It also should be noted that there is no indication of rural/urban population distribution. Because of the then rudimentary development of agriculture, however, it is likely that a substantial share of the total population lived in the port city.

29. "Distribución de los tipos de fincas, por jurisdicciones, en 1778 y 1792," in Marrero, *Cuba: economía y sociedad*, vol. 10, p. 87. This chart was prepared by Marrero from the manuscript *padrones* found in the Archivo General de Indias, Indiferente General, 1527.

30. AHPM, ME, Estadística, leg. 6, no. 121, fol. 7. One box generally contained between 16 and 22 arrobas of sugar (1 arroba = 25 pounds), or between 400 and 550 pounds.

31. Biblioteca Nacional José Martí, Colección Cubana, Fondo C. M. Morales, tomo. 79, no. 4, fols. 13–16ᵛ, "Algunas noticias de la jurisdicción de la Habana de población rural y particularmente la de los ingenios de fabricar azúcar. 20 de abril 1799." These data (* = Matanzas partidos) are reproduced below:

Partido	Ingenios	Slaves	Slaves/Ingenio
Bahía Honda	13	379	29.2
Batabanó	11	347	31.5
Bauta	12	1,342	111.8
Buenaventura	9	1,122	124.7
Calvario	1	95	95.0
Cano	3	176	58.7
Gabriel	4	107	26.8
Gibacoa	12	641	53.4
Guara	6	231	38.5
Guatao	7	674	96.3
Jubajay	2	138	69.0
Macuriges*	5	661	132.2
Managua	18	1,542	85.7
Quemado	1	92	92.0
Río B. del Sur	22	1,826	83.0
Santa Ana*	5	125	25.0
San Gerónimo	15	1,425	95.0
Tapaste	9	986	109.6
Yumurí*	9	381	42.3
TOTAL	164	12,290	74.9

32. AHPM, ME, Estadística, leg. 8, no. 143, fols. 1–14, "Expediente relativo a la geografía física y política de Matanzas, 1846"; this document has a "Memoria histórica" attached. Also see Marrero, *Cuba: economía y sociedad*, vol. 11, p. 100.

33. Marrero, *Cuba: economía y sociedad*, vol. 10, p. 86. This document lists farmland in caballerías, while hacienda land is designated in "leguas." According to Esteban Pichardo, 1 "legua corralera" was equal to 105.3 caballerías. See Pichardo, *Geografía de la isla de Cuba*, vol. 1, p. xvi. The data presented here have been transformed into caballerías for uniformity.

Chapter 2

1. See the 1800 report of Antonio del Valle Hernández reproduced in Levi Marrero, *Cuba: economía y sociedad* (Madrid: Ed. Playor, 1984), vol. 10, pp. 160–161. Del Valle was the secretary of the Real Consulado and a collaborator of Francisco Arango y Parreño.

2. O'Farrill stated that in 1766 forests had receded to a distance of nearly 16 miles from Havana; by 1797, he estimated, there were no forests within 42 miles of the capital; and, in an 1828 report, José Antonio Saco estimated that there were no forests within 100 miles of Havana. See José Antonio Saco, "Montes o bosques en la isla de Cuba," in his *Colección de papeles científicos, históricos, políticos, y de otros ramos sobre la isla de Cuba* (Havana: Dirección General de Cultura, 1960), vol. 1, pp. 46–47.

Also see a reproduction of another O'Farrill report on woodlands in Marrero,

Cuba: economía y sociedad, vol. 10, p. 203; and Moreno Fraginals, *El ingenio. Complejo económico social cubano del azúcar* (Havana: Ed. de Ciencias Sociales, 1978), vol. 1, pp. 157–167. Moreno estimates (pp. 157–158) that the sugar sector consumed 500 caballerías (16,800 acres) of forests per year at the end of the eighteenth century; 1,000 caballerías (33,600 acres) in 1819; and 4,000 caballerías (134,400 acres) in 1844.

The first steam engine was introduced in Cuba in 1797 by the Conde de Mopox y Jaruco, Joaquín de Santa Cruz, on his Ingenio Ceibabo. By 1828, there were 20 ingenios using steam engines in Cuba.

Distances are listed in Cuban leagues, which have been converted to miles at 2.66 miles per league. For measurements, see Esteban Pichardo, *Geografía de la isla de Cuba* (Havana: Est. Tip. de D. M. Soler, 1854), vol. 1, p. xv.

3. For sugar prices in the 1790s and early 1800s, see ANC, Junta de Fomento, leg. 93, no. 3953, "Negociado de Agricultura, 1807." By 1804, prices for sugar had declined to 1790 levels.

4. Thus, sugar expansion outside of Havana was financed by Cuban capital. This is a critical fact that should be emphasized, for it meant that total dependence on foreign sources of capital was avoided and control of production remained in Cuban hands in the early nineteenth century. It does not mean, however, that foreign capital was absent in early-nineteenth-century Cuba; nor should the importance of foreign capital be minimized. What should be underscored is the internal process of capital accumulation during the second half of the eighteenth century and the ability of Cuban-born entrepreneurs to control production.

The Güines Valley offers a clear example of this expansion: 4 ingenios ground cane in 1784; 9 in 1792; and 26 in 1804. See Moreno Fraginals, *El ingenio*, vol. 1, p. 140.

5. A report written in 1796, attached to a map of Corral de Matanzas, indicates the resentment that local residents felt toward outsiders. An anonymous author wrote of "el miserable estado en que se hallaba esta ciudad por las escases de sus propios y por las usurpaciones de las tierras hechas por varios poderosos de la Habana" (the miserable state in which this city finds itself because of the shortage of funds and the abuse of the land perpetrated by various powerful Havana families). See ANC, Junta de Fomento, leg. 185, exp. 8347.

Francisco J. Ponte y Domínguez, *Matanzas: biografía de una provincia* (Havana: Imp. El Siglo XX, 1959), p. 79, reports that in the 1790s tobacco *vegueros* were abandoning their farms to seek work on developing sugar ingenios.

6. The information on early-nineteenth-century Matanzas sugar-mill owners comes from AHPM, Mapas y Planos, leg. 34, exp. 179, "Plano de la ciudad, puerto, y jurisdicción de Matanzas." This is reproduced as Map 2. Unfortunately there is no date on this map, although (thanks to later information) there can be little doubt that it was rendered in the final years of the eighteenth century or the first years of the nineteenth century, probably no later than 1805. Justo G. Cantero, *Los ingenios. Colección de vistas de los principales ingenios de azúcar de la isla de Cuba* (Havana: Litografía de Luis Marquier, 1857), cites a Matanzas cabildo report stating that there were 39 ingenios grinding cane in 1802 and 10 "en fomento." This is repeated by Marrero, *Cuba: economía y sociedad*, vol. 10, p. 161, and earlier by Pedro Antonio Alfonso, *Memorias de un matancero. Apuntes para la historia de la isla de Cuba* (Matanzas: Imp. de Marsal y Cía., 1854), p. 182. This is plausible, but I have not

come across any documentary evidence to support this claim. The next date when reliable statistical data on the number of ingenios in Matanzas are available is 1817, when the region supported 76 mills.

I have not been able to trace the lineage of the other three Yumurí ingenio owners. For the lineage of the Jústiz family, see *HFC*, vol. 2, pp. 227–240; and *DN*, pp. 294–297. For the Junco clan, see *HFC*, vol. 7, pp. 219–241.

7. The Lamar brothers both served as alcaldes ordinarios of Matanzas at different times. For the Lamar family lineage, see *HFC*, vol. 2, pp. 242–251, which also includes information on Manuel del Portillo. For a notation of Luis Lamar as a Matanzas surveyor in 1780, see Alfonso, *Memorias de un matancero*, p. 174. I have been unable to trace the family histories of the other two ingenio owners in this region, Luis Caravallo and Gabriel Santoyo.

8. The Garros owned ingenios in the Havana partido of Sibarimar (Jesús María in 1786) and in the Güines Valley. See Marrero, *Cuba: economía y sociedad*, vol. 10, p. 140; and Moreno Fraginals, *El ingenio*, vol. 1, p. 57. Teresa Garro was married to José María Herrera y Herrera, Conde de Fernandina and Conde de Jibacoa. The Zequeiras held the title Conde de Lagunillas. For the lineage of the Zequeiras, see *HFC*, vol. 6, pp. 366–382; and *DN*, pp. 300–305.

9. For an excellent history of the Sociedad Económica, see Rafael Montoro, "Historia de la Sociedad Económica de Amigos del País de la Habana," *Revista Bimestre Cubana* 4:1–2 (1910), pp. 11–48 and pp. 113–138. Volumes 1–3 of the *Revista Bimestre* were published in 1832, when the journal folded—only to be resurrected by Fernando Ortíz, who became its editor in 1910.

Also see Fernando Ortíz, *Recopilación para la historia de la Sociedad Económica Habanera* (Havana: Imp. y Lib. El Universo, 1930), esp. "Catálogo general alfabético de los individuos que componen la real sociedad patriótica de la Habana desde su erección hasta diciembre del año de 1795" in vol. 1, pp. 115–120.

10. Free trade had first been proclaimed in 1778, but between 1784 and 1789 Cuba's ports were closed once again to legal foreign trade. See Marrero, *Cuba: economía y sociedad*, vol. 12, p. 12. Also see AHPM, ME, Estadística, leg. 7, no. 126, fols. 65–71.

11. The following trade data from Matanzas are listed in AHN, Ultramar, leg. 4602, "Comercio y navegación de Matanzas":

Year	Boxes of Sugar
1806	16,112
1807	28,392
1808	20,007
1809	27,761
1810	17,794
1811	18,507
1812	18,253
1813	14,859
1814	21,235
1815	21,202
1816	21,866

12. Heinrich Friedlaender, *Historia económica de Cuba* (Havana: Ediciones de Ciencias Sociales, 1978), vol. 1, p. 180.

13. Francisco Pérez de la Riva, *Origen y régimen de la propiedad territorial en Cuba* (Havana: Imp. El Siglo XX, 1946), pp. 138–147.

14. Ibid., pp. 150–151.

15. I have not discovered any maps that delineate the boundaries of these partidos in the early nineteenth century or before.

16. See Jacobo de la Pezuela, *Crónica de las Antillas* (Madrid: Rubio, Grilo y Vitturi, 1871), p. 160; and Jacobo de la Pezuela, *Diccionario geográfico, estadístico, histórico de la isla de Cuba* (Madrid: Imp. del Establecimiento de Mellado, 1863), vol. 4, p. 18. For administrative partidos in 1817, see AHPM, ME, Estadísticas, leg. 1, no. 2, "Estadística de Matanzas y los cinco partidos de su jurisdicción."

17. For a general consideration of the growth of U.S.–Caribbean trade, see Douglass C. North, *The Economic Growth of the United States, 1790–1860* (New York: W. W. Norton & Co., 1966).

18. These different areas of economic activity will be discussed in more detail below.

19. For notices of Latting & Glen, see Alfonso, *Memorias de un matancero*, p. 181; and Ponte y Domínguez, *Matanzas*, p. 89.

Zacarias Atkins, from an old Massachusetts Bay Colony family, was one of the most important early Matanzas slave traders; his activities will be discussed below. See AHPM, Esclavos, Bozales, leg. 21. For a family history of the Atkins clan, see William Howell Reed, *Reminiscences of Elisha Atkins* (Boston: privately printed, 1890).

For the Rhodes and Otis coffee plantation, see ANC, PN, Matanzas, Luis López Villavicencio, 1810, fols. 229–230ᵛ.

For information on John Forbes and Ingenio Reunion Deseada, see AHPM, ME, Estadística, leg. 6, no. 115, fols. 1–1ᵛ.

20. See AHN, Ultramar, leg. 4602, "Comercio y navegación de Matanzas," and Pezuela, *Crónica de las Antillas*, p. 160, for the story of Spanish entrepreneurs settling in Matanzas in 1808 because of the impossibility of returning to Spain.

For information on Joaquín Madan as an early merchant and slave trader, see AHPM, Esclavos, Bozales, leg. 21. The Madan family came to Havana from Ireland in the second half of the eighteenth century. Joaquín generated the family fortune through slave trading. His son Cristóbal Madan, born in Havana in 1806, would become one of the most powerful merchants, planters, slave traders, and railroad builders in nineteenth-century Cuba. See *HFC*, vol. 5, pp. 164–170, for the Madan family lineage.

21. See AHPM, Mapas y Planos, leg. 25, exp. 145, "Plano relativo a las ciénagas que rodeaban la ciudad de Matanzas, 1815."

22. A detailed analysis of the regional economy of Ceiba Mocha in 1817 will be presented below.

23. In 1843, as part of an administrative redivision of the region, Camarioca became part of the jurisdiction of Cárdenas. A detailed analysis of the regional economy in 1817 will be presented below. The major town in Guamacaro, which took its name from an old corral, was Limonar.

24. This was calculated by including all of the future province's partidos, not only those included in the jurisdiction of Matanzas. Thus, in addition to data on Yumurí, Ceiba Mocha, Santa Ana, Guamacaro, Camarioca, and Sabanilla, which constituted the tenencia de gobierno of Matanzas, data on Alacranes, Cimarrones, Guamutas, Lagunillas, Macuriges, and Palmillas have been added. Prior to 1843 these partidos were part of the jurisdiction of Havana. However, data were rarely collected separately. All of these partidos, with the exception of Alacranes, were included in the tenencia de gobierno, or jurisdicción, of Cárdenas when it was formed in 1843. Thus, the total population of the official jurisdicción of Matanzas was 85,040. Another 61,322 people lived in the other partidos. See AHPM, ME, leg. 1, nos. 5, 7.

25. The data for this manuscript census are contained in AHPM, ME, leg. 81, no. 137, fols. 17–64. They have been organized into data files and analyzed using SPSS. The results differ somewhat from the statistics on Ceiba Mocha shown in Tables 2.1 and 2.2, which were derived from a different source.

26. For a history of the Drake family in Cuba, see Roland T. Ely, *Comerciantes cubanos del siglo xix* (Havana: Ed. Librería Martí, 1961), chap. 4, "La Casa Drake."

27. Martin Averhoff migrated from Germany to the Matanzas region in the late eighteenth or early nineteenth century. See *HFC*, vol. 7, pp. 37–40. There was another German coffee farmer in Ceiba Mocha in 1817: John Yinker, owner of San Cirilio, 18 caballerías and 74 slaves. Nothing more is known about this early Matanzas coffee farmer.

28. See José A. Benítez, *Las Antillas: colonización, azúcar, e imperialismo* (Havana: Casa de las Américas, 1976), pp. 232–233. Early North American coffee planters included Joseph Wilson, Robert Davis, Martin Denney, Martin Folch, Nathan Thomas, Cornelio Roberts, and John Booth. Little is known about these early U.S. investors, who were no doubt drawn to the island by the surge in U.S.–Cuban commerce.

29. AHPM, ME, Estadística, leg. 6, no. 115, fol. 3, "Estadística rural del partido o distrito de Camarioca."

30. For a history of the Cuban coffee industry, see Francisco Pérez de la Riva, *El café. Historia de su cultivo y explotación en Cuba* (Havana: Jesús Montero, 1944).

31. Industrial yields could not have accounted for this difference, since the same technology was employed on the ingenios in both regions.

32. The 1817 Matanzas-wide census lists 21 ingenios in Yumurí. However, an 1817 manuscript slave census, by farm type, lists 23 ingenios. See AHPM, Gobierno Provincial, leg. 34, "Estado que manifiesta los esclabos de ambos sexsos que se hallan en este partido de Yumurí–marzo primero de 1817."

33. The Montalvo family was discussed above. For the lineage of the Zequeiras, see *HFC*, vol. 6, pp. 366–382; for the Marquesado de Arcos, see *DN*, pp. 31–35; and for the history of the Zayas family, see *HFC*, vol. 4, pp. 401–447.

34. AHPM, Miscelánea de Libros, Estadísticas, leg. 6, no. 115, fols. 6–14ᵛ. Guamutas also had 54 sitios and 8 potreros in 1826, while Cimarrones had 25 cafetales, 66 sitios, and 13 potreros.

35. See Ricardo V. Rousset, *Historial de Cuba* (Havana: Lib. Cervantes de Ricardo Veloso, 1918), for dates of official town foundings.

36. For information on the early history of Cárdenas, see Carlos Hellberg, *His-*

toria estadística de Cárdenas, 1893 (Cárdenas: Comité Pro-Calles de Cárdenas, 1957); and Marrero, *Cuba: economía y sociedad,* vol. 9, p. 237.

Chapter 3

1. For the location of Corral San Pedro, see Levi Marrero, *Cuba: economía y sociedad* (Madrid: Ed. Playor, 1984), vol. 10, p. 60. For this transaction, see ANC, PN, Matanzas, Santiago López Villavicencio, 1804, fols. 309–309ᵛ.

2. José Canuto Cabrera purchased this land for 3,900 pesos from Juan de Dios Aguiar. See ANC, PN, Matanzas, Luis López Villavicencio, 1810, fols. 56ᵛ–57ᵛ.

3. See AHPM, Anotaduría de Hipotecas, libro 1, partidas 20–23, fol. 5ᵛ. Undeveloped land was also being sold in Santa Ana and Yumurí for between 250 and 300 pesos/caballería in 1817.

4. ANC, PN, Matanzas, Joaquín de la Fuente, 1826, fols. 118, 128–129ᵛ. Also see the 1829 land mortgages for Lagunillas recorded in AHPM, Anotaduría de Hipotecas, libro 5, partida 21 fol. 5ᵛ. For 1835 and 1840, see AHPM, Anotaduría de Hipotecas, libros 7 and 10.

5. See ANC, PN, Matanzas, Santiago López Villavicencio, 1804, fols. 368ᵛ–369ᵛ and fol. 344, for transactions of developed estancias in Yumurí at 1,000 pesos/caballería. In Santa Ana, estancia land was sold at the same price in the early nineteenth century (see fol. 191). Also see AHPM, Gobierno Provincial, Ingenios, leg. 1, no. 1, fols. 3–7.

6. ANC, PN, Matanzas, Joaquín de la Fuente, 1818, fols. 13, 86–86ᵛ. Also see fol. 56 for the sale of one caballería for 3,000 pesos in an unknown Matanzas partido.

7. AHPM, Anotaduría de Hipotecas, libro 1, partida 490, fol. 122.

8. ANC, PN, Matanzas, Joaquín de la Fuente, 1823, fols. 145–146.

9. ANC, PN, Matanzas, Joaquín de la Fuente, 1826, fols. 191–191ᵛ. An advertisement in the newspaper *La Aurora de Matanzas,* July 9, 1829, p. 4, confirms the price of roughly 1,750 pesos/caballería for coffee land. Juan Francisco Ruiz placed an advertisement for the sale of a 10-caballería coffee farm in Camarioca (36,000 coffee trees and 5 slaves) that was assessed at 23,400 pesos. The value of the coffee trees was roughly 3,600 pesos, the slaves were worth 2,200 pesos, and the land was valued at 1,758 pesos/caballería.

10. ANC, PN, Matanzas, Joaquín de la Fuente, 1826, fols. 116–116ᵛ. Although land transactions involving most types of rural property are abundant in Matanzas protocol records and in the collection of the Anotaduría de Hipotecas, I have not been able to find a single notation of a transaction involving an ingenio before the 1830s, despite constant searching that included an examination of Havana protocol transactions. Thus, values for ingenios before the 1830s cannot be noted here.

11. Examples include Tinguaro (today Sergio Ramírez), founded by the Diagos in the 1830s; España and Álava (today España Republicana and Méjico), founded by Julián Zulueta in the 1840s; and Santa Rita (today René Fraga), built by José Baró in the 1840s.

12. For the activities of Simon Poey Lacasse and his two brothers Juan Bautista and Juan Andrés, see Manuel Moreno Fraginals, *El ingenio. Complejo económico*

social cubano del azúcar (Havana: Ed. de Ciencias Sociales, 1978), vol. 1, pp. 267–268. For a brief biography of Juan Poey Lacasse, see vol. 3, pp. 249–250.

Las Cañas was a visiting place for nearly all of the many travelers passing through Cuba during the nineteenth century, some of whom chronicled their journeys. See, for example, "Un joven francés visita el ingenio Las Cañas en 1865," in Juan Pérez de la Riva, ed., *La isla de Cuba en el siglo xix vista por los extranjeros* (Havana: Ed. de Ciencias Sociales, 1981), pp. 143–180, which includes a brief biography of Poey; and Antonio Gallenga, *The Pearl of the Antilles* (London: Chapman & Hall, 1873).

For a description of Las Cañas in the 1870s, see Fermín Rosillo y Alquier, *Noticias de dos ingenios. Datos sobre la producción azucarera de la isla de Cuba* (Havana: Imp. El Iris, 1873).

13. According to colonial property laws dating from 1529 and referred to as the "privilegio de los ingenios," ingenio land, slaves, animals, and fixed property could not be mortgaged or embargoed. However, creditors could attach liens to harvests, which became the common guarantee for credit. Ingenio privileges were repealed in 1860. For a nineteenth-century discussion of the "privilegio's" economic impediments to the development of credit, see Vicente Vázquez Queipó, *Informe fiscal sobre fomento de la población blanca en la isla de Cuba* (Madrid: Imp. Alegría, 1845). Also see Francisco Pérez de la Riva, *Origen y régimen de la propiedad territorial en Cuba* (Havana: Imp. El Siglo XX, 1946), pp. 70–71; and Roland T. Ely, *Comerciantes cubanos del siglo xix* (Havana: Ed. Lib. Martí, 1961), pp. 51–82.

14. For the transactions involving Poey's purchase of Las Cañas and accompanying inventories, see ANC, Anotaduría de Hipotecas, La Habana, libro 57, 1832–1833, fols. 225ᵛ–226; ANC, PN, La Habana, Francisco Valerio, 1833, fols. 9ᵛ–15; and ANC, Anotaduría de Hipotecas, La Habana, 1835, fol. 313.

15. Zulueta recounted a fictionalized version of his early life to Antonio Gallenga, claiming to have been the son of a rural worker arriving in Cuba "without a farthing, without education. . . . [T]he height of his ambition was to scrape together a sum of 25,000 dollars." See Gallenga, *The Pearl of the Antilles*, pp. 100–101. This version of Zulueta's life, in the absence of any other information on his early career, has been accepted by other scholars. See Franklin W. Knight, "Origin of Wealth and the Sugar Revolution in Cuba, 1750–1850," *Hispanic American Historical Review* 57:2 (1977), p. 251.

Hugh Thomas, *Cuba: The Pursuit of Freedom* (New York: Harper & Row, 1970), pp. 136–137, writes about Zulueta. Without citing sources, Thomas claims that Zulueta did indeed arrive in Cuba penniless but was left a fortune by an uncle, who is not named. This must have been Tiburcio Zulueta with whom Julián purchased Ingenio San Francisco (see below). Thomas states that Julián was a cousin of Pedro de Zulueta, the slave trader who had merchant houses in London, Seville, and Liverpool. Pedro's father, clearly Julián's uncle, was president of the Spanish Cortes. These family connections, and Julián Zulueta's meteoric rise to wealth and prominence, certainly indicate that he was well endowed very soon after his arrival in Cuba.

16. See Pedro de Zulueta, *Trial of Pedro de Zulueta, Jun., on a Charge of Slave Trading* (London: C. Wood & Co., 1844).

17. For data on this sale, see ANC, PN, La Habana, Francisco Valerio, 1835, fols.

454ᵛ–468ᵛ; and ANC, Anotaduría de Hipotecas, La Habana, 1835, fols. 318–319. Manuela Teresa Caraballo also owned the 30-caballería Ingenio Nuestra Señora de la Merced (known as Anguila) in Guamutas that was sold in 1835 for 168,462.87 pesos. See ANC, Anotaduría de Hipotecas, La Habana, 1835, fols. 239–239ᵛ.

18. Zulueta's activities in the 1840s will be discussed below. For the lineage of Julián Zulueta and his descendants, see *HFC*, vol. 4, pp. 448–456; and *DN*, pp. 17–19, 119–120. For an account of his fortune from the 1840s through the 1870s, see "El imperio azucarero de Julián de Zulueta en tierras de Banagüises," in Marrero, *Cuba: economía y sociedad*, vol. 10, pp. 269–271. For information on the Samá family, see Moreno Fraginals, *El ingenio*, vol. 1, pp. 221, 268–269.

19. For the Diago family lineage, see *HFC*, vol. 1, pp. 132–138. See Moreno Fraginals, *El ingenio*, vol. 1, p. 267, for information on the Compañía de Seguros Marítimas de la Habana.

20. Most accounts of Ingenio Amistad in the mid-nineteenth century refer to it as the property of Ayestarán. See, for example, the information accompanying the lithograph of Amistad in Justo G. Cantero, *Los ingenios. Colección de vistas de los principales ingenios de azúcar de la isla de Cuba* (Havana: Litografía de Luis Marquier, 1857). However, letters from the Diagos and references to Amistad by merchants corresponding with Moses Taylor & Co. of New York make it clear that the ingenio was owned by the Diagos and Ayestarán. See NYPL, Moses Taylor Collection, case B, drawers 2 and 3, box 6, letter of Feb. 27, 1847, from Drake & Coit of Matanzas to Moses Taylor.

21. For the location of Ingenio Santa Rita, see Esteban Pichardo, *Isla de Cuba. Carta geotopográfica* (Havana: Dirección de la Capitanía General, 1860–1872), plate 4B. Also see ANC, Anotaduría de Hipotecas, La Habana, libro 62, Fincas, 1838, fols. 178ᵛ–179, for information on the financing of Santa Rita, and libro 57, 1832–1833, fol. 32ᵛ, for data on Ingenio Cambre.

22. See the information on Ingenio Tinguaro in Cantero, *Los ingenios*; and the letters of Apr. 5, 1840, and Dec. 27, 1840, from Pedro Diago to Moses Taylor ordering machinery from the West Point Foundry for Ingenio Tinguaro (NYPL, Moses Taylor Collection, case B, drawers 2 and 3, box 6).

23. ANC, Anotaduría de Hipotecas, La Habana, libro 62, Fincas, 1838, fol. 60ᵛ. The Torriente family lineage is discussed in *HFC*, vol. 1, pp. 372–381.

24. See Cuba, Centro de Estadística, *Noticias estadísticas de la isla de Cuba en 1862* (Havana: Imp. del Gobierno, Capitanía General y Real Hacienda, 1864), "Estadística territorial. Caballerías de tierra."

25. For an excellent summary of railroad development in Cuba, see Gert J. Oostindie, "La burguesía cubana y sus caminos de hierro, 1830–1868," *Boletín de Estudios Latinoamericanos y del Caribe*, no. 37 (December 1984), pp. 99–115. The most detailed study of Cuban railroads is Oscár Zanetti and Alejandro García, *Caminos para el azúcar* (Havana: Ed. de Ciencias Sociales, 1987). Railroad construction will be discussed in more detail in Part Three.

26. ANC, Anotaduría de Hipotecas, La Habana, libro 57, 1832–1833, fols. 44–45, 63–63ᵛ, 132, 177–177ᵛ, 281, 310–310ᵛ.

27. ANC, Anotaduría de Hipotecas, La Habana, libro 62, 1838, fols. 30ᵛ–31, 39ᵛ–40ᵛ, 45ᵛ–48, 90–90ᵛ, 125ᵛ–126.

28. It should be stressed that data on early-nineteenth-century Matanzas merchants are fragmentary. One reason is that these early merchant houses did not play a role in providing credit to sugar and coffee planters, who secured working capital from Havana merchants. Only when local credit facilities emerged in the 1820s do better data on Matanzas commercial interests become available in documentary sources.

29. See the report on the 1827 census in Francisco Jimeno Fuentes, "Matanzas, estudio histórico estadístico dedicado a la Exma. Diputación Provincial de Matanzas," reproduced in *Revista de la Biblioteca Nacional* 7:1 (January-March 1957), pp. 11–99.

30. USNA, DUSCM, roll 1, vol. 1, Oct. 24, 1820–Dec. 21, 1838, "Commerce of Matanzas for the Year 1823"; PRO, FO 72/347, copy of *Balanza general del comercio de la isla de Cuba en el año de 1826* (Havana: Oficina del Gobierno y Capitanía General, 1827).

31. See USNA, DUSCM, letter of Feb. 1, 1822, from J. W. Padone to John Quincy Adams, Secretary of State.

32. PRO, FO 72/347, *Balanza general del comercio de la isla de Cuba en el año de 1838* (Havana: Imp. del Gobierno y de la Real Hacienda, 1839).

33. *Balanza general . . . 1826.*

34. See NYPL, Moses Taylor Collection, Letters, 1838, box 9, letter of Jan. 10, 1838, from Drake & Coit of Matanzas to Moses Taylor.

35. *Balanza general . . . 1826*; USNA, DUSCM, "Commerce of Matanzas for the Year 1823."

36. NYPL, Moses Taylor Collection, letter of Aug. 2, 1838, from Drake Hermanos to Moses Taylor.

37. During the summer of 1985, Armando Fernández Soriano and I hiked to the site of the ruins of the old embarcadero on the Canimar. Listed on nineteenth-century Cuban maps such as Pichardo's as "Tumbadero," its massive walls remain but are covered with tropical plant growth. The site is in horrible condition, but it is possible to climb and stumble through the brush to the outer perimeter of the warehouses. Although I had no measuring implements, the size of this ruin was stunning; it must have had a tremendous storage capacity. Unfortunately, I have run across no documentary materials indicating who built this embarcadero or when it declined. It was probably built jointly by the merchants of Matanzas during the 1810s and 1820s and slowly declined in the 1840s and 1850s, when its function was preempted by railroad construction.

38. See *Aurora de Matanzas*, April 6, 1835, for advertisements by local lancha owners.

39. The announcement by Sarah Echevarría reads as follows: "Mrs. Sarah Echevarría respectfully informs her friends and strangers coming to this Island for the recovery of their health, that she has her house made entirely new and comfortable for invalids, and is delightfully situated on the river Canimar about four miles from town, and one from the ferry. Its proximity to the city makes it very advantageous, and the steamboat can leave passengers at the landing place on her estate" (*Aurora de Yumurí*, March 22, 1835).

40. These contracts will be discussed below.

41. USNA, DUSCM, roll 1, vol. 1, trade report of Feb. 8, 1824, and Dec. 30, 1823–June 30, 1824. Latting, Adams & Stewart issued one of the first printed trade reports from Matanzas for Stateside-based merchant establishments. For the sale of their Yumurí warehouse in 1837, see ANC, PN, Matanzas, Joaquín de la Fuente, 1837, fols. 275^v–276^v.

42. See José A. Benítez, *Las Antillas: colonización, azúcar, e imperialismo* (Havana: Casa de las Américas, 1976), p. 232; AHPM, Anotaduría de Hipotecas, libro 2, partida 703; AHPM, Esclavos, Bozales, leg. 21, exp. 12.

43. See Pedro Antonio Alfonso, *Memorias de un matancero. Apuntes para la historia de la isla de Cuba* (Matanzas: Imp. de Marsal y Cía., 1854), p. 183. Forbes continued operating his cafetal in the late 1820s. For its location, see the map reproduced in Marrero, *Cuba: economía y sociedad*, vol. 11, p. 110.

44. USNA, DUSCM, roll 1, vol. 1, trade report of Feb. 8, 1824; AHPM, Anotaduría de Hipotecas, libro 1, partida 501, fol. 124^v, concerning Simpson's Feb. 21, 1821, purchase of 29.5 caballerías in Canimar from the Conde de Lagunillas.

45. See AHPM, Esclavos, Bozales, leg. 21, exp. 5; ANC, PN, Matanzas, Joaquín de la Fuente, 1819, fols. 281^v–282.

46. *HFC*, vol. 5, pp. 164–170, and vol. 3, pp. 8–17.

47. *HFC*, vol. 1, pp. 132–138.

48. See the correspondence of Levi Coit in NYPL, Manuscript Division, Levi Coit Letter Book, vol. 1, 1796–1804.

49. See Roland T. Ely, *Cuando reinaba su majestad el azúcar* (Buenos Aires: Ed. Sudamericana, 1963), p. 175. Moses Taylor, the New York merchant who would help form First National City Bank, was first employed by the Howland brothers before embarking on his own. For the location of El Dorado, directly north of the town of Sagua, see Pichardo, *Isla de Cuba*, plate 4C.

50. For the complete story of the Drakes, see Ely, *Comerciantes cubanos*, "La Casa Drake," pp. 83–140. For an account of the career of Henry A. Coit, see Ely, *Cuando reinaba*, pp. 156–172.

51. See *Aurora de Matanzas*, 1829–1835, for notices of Bartlett, Harris, and Shoemaker; and USNA, DUSCM, letter of Feb. 24, 1829. George Bartlett and his brother Richard owned a small cafetal in Guamacaro, 4 caballerías and 24 slaves. It was sold after Bartlett's death to another North American, Thomas Gibbs. See ANC, PN, Matanzas, Joaquín de la Fuente, 1830, fols. 275^v–276^v.

52. Examples of Havana capital financing large- and small-scale planters are numerous in the notarial protocols of Matanzas and in the mortgage notaries of both Matanzas and Havana. See, for example, the contract between Miguel de Cárdenas, whose Ingenio Intrépido, one of Cuba's largest, was financed by Pedro Martínez y Cía. of Havana, one of the island's notorious slave traders. Intrépido's zafras during the early 1830s were mortgaged to Martínez. See ANC, Anotaduría de Hipotecas, La Habana, libro 57, 1832–1833, fols. 248^v–249. Also see "Algunas de las firmas refaccionistas de la Habana, 1836–1853," in Marrero, *Cuba: economía y sociedad*, vol. 12, p. 256.

53. ANC, PN, Matanzas, Joaquín de la Fuente, 1834, fols. 9^v–12^v.

54. See AHPM, ME, Estadística, leg. 6, no. 114, fols. 43–47^v, "Noticias de las tiendas, tabernas, y almacenes que exsisten en este partido y puntos en que se hallan

situados con inmediación a los fundos en que estan y nombres de estos. Santa Ana 1827." The largest merchant was Juan Mansarret who ran a warehouse "abundantamente surtida de víveres y generos" (well stocked with food and sundries). For Ceiba Mocha, see the same collection, leg. 8, no. 139, fols. 28–31ᵛ; and for Guamacaro in 1835, see leg. 8, no. 141, fol. 11.

Chapter 4

1. These partidos were Alacranes, Cimarrones, Guamutas, Lagunillas, Palmillas, and Macuriges. With the exception of Alacranes, the other partidos would be included in the jurisdiction of Cárdenas in 1843. By 1856 there was a general administrative redivision of these partidos to create the jurisdicción of Colón. Alacranes remained administratively apart from the rest of Matanzas province through most of the nineteenth century.

See AHPM, Me, Estadísticas, leg. 1, no. 2, "Estadística de Matanzas y los cinco partidos de su jurisdicción. 15 de febrero 1817"; leg. 1, no. 7, "Población de Matanzas en el censo general de 1841," "Distribución de habitantes 1841," and "Población de los partidos de la jurisdicción de la Habana (1841) que hoy (1846) pertenecen a la provincia de Matanzas," fols. 3–4ᵛ. For 1827, see Cuba, Gobernador y Capitán General, *Cuadro estadístico de la siempre fiel isla de Cuba correspondiente al año de 1827* (Havana: Imp. del Gobierno y Capitanía General, 1829), "Estado de población."

2. Crude estimates stressing natural rates of decline among Cuba's slave population can be found in Jack E. Eblen, "On the Natural Increase of Slave Populations: The Example of the Cuban Black Population, 1775–1900," in Stanley L. Engerman and Eugene D. Genovese, eds., *Race and Slavery in the Western Hemisphere: Quantitative Studies* (Princeton: Princeton University Press, 1975), pp. 211–248. Also see David Eltis, "The Nineteenth-Century Transatlantic Slave Trade: An Annual Time Series of Imports into the Americas Broken Down by Region," *Hispanic American Historical Review* 67:1 (1987), pp. 109–138, who estimates a −2.1 percent growth rate between 1826 and 1847.

3. Free urban blacks and mulattoes also enjoyed a measure of cultural independence that should be stressed. Cabildos, which maintained African religious and cultural forms, flourished from the early nineteenth century. In 1818 the first Matanzas cabildo, Virgen de Belén, was founded by freedmen from Congo Luango ethnic groups. See AHPM, Religiones Africanas, leg. 1.

4. In 1803 the most important members of the Havana nobility, many of whom had begun to penetrate Matanzas, formed the Compañía Africana de la Habana with the purpose of cornering the Cuban slave market and guaranteeing labor supplies to the expanding economy. Among them were the Conde de Jibacoa, Conde de Lagunillas, Marqués de Jústiz de Santa Ana, Marqués de la Real Proclamación, Conde de Buenavista, and the Marqués Cárdenas de Monte Hermoso. Their efforts failed, and control over the Cuban slave trade remained in the hands of merchants, most of whom were of immigrant origin. See Levi Marrero, *Cuba: economía y sociedad* (Madrid: Ed. Playor, 1983), vol. 9, pp. 24–25, for information on the "Compañía Africana."

For brief biographies of the most important Havana slave traders in the early nineteenth century, such as Pancho Marty, Pedro Blanco, Pedro Martínez, Joaquín Gómez, see José Luciano Franco, *Comercio clandestino de esclavos* (Havana: Ed. de Ciencias Sociales, 1985). The most famous of all, Pedro Blanco Fernández de Trava, was the subject of an extensive "fictionalized" biography that is extremely informative on the mechanisms of the Cuban slave trade. See Lino Novas Calvo, *El negrero. Vida novelada de Pedro Blanco Fernández de Trava* (Madrid: Espasa-Calpe, 1933). For more information on slave-trading families, see Manuel Moreno Fraginals, *El ingenio. Complejo económico social cubano del azúcar* (Havana: Ed. de Ciencias Sociales, 1978), vol. 1, pp. 265–269.

5. See AHPM, Esclavos, Bozales, leg. 21. In 1819 notices of Madan's imports between March and July indicate the carrying capacity of slave vessels. Four ships were received, carrying 343, 256, 280, and 363 Africans. On August 23, 1819, Atkins's ship the *Serenade* landed with 540 bozales. This would place Matanzas slave traders in league with the largest carriers landing in Cuba. According to data compiled by Herbert S. Klein, only 17 percent of all ships involved in the Cuban trade between 1790 and 1820 carried 201 or more slaves, while 49 percent carried 50 or fewer. See Klein, "The Cuban Slave Trade in a Period of Transition, 1790–1843," in Klein, *The Middle Passage: Comparative Studies in the Atlantic Slave Trade* (Princeton: Princeton University Press, 1978), p. 218. It is well known that the 1817 treaty banning the slave trade to Cuba had little meaning. Local slave traders worked closely with government officials; for example, in 1819 Madan sold 18 "piezas" to the Governor of Matanzas, Juan Tirry y Lacy. See ANC, PN, Joaquín de la Fuente, Matanzas, 1819, fols. 281^v–282.

6. My analysis of slave prices between 1804 and 1837 is based on slave sales recorded by Matanzas notaries and preserved in the Archivo Nacional de Cuba. There were several notaries working in Matanzas, and those whose records were chosen for scrutiny were picked randomly. The years chosen—1804, 1810, 1818, 1823, 1826, 1830, 1834, and 1837—were also selected randomly, although factors such as legibility and completeness of a protocol volume were important in choosing a particular year. All sales appearing in each protocol volume examined were recorded. In all, 703 transactions between 1804 and 1837 were analyzed. Data were consistent but not ideal. Most transactions listed sex, origin, price, and age; however, there were no consistent data on occupations, skills, or infirmities.

7. Figure 4.9 was derived from the data on estimated slave imports to Cuba between 1811 and 1837 provided by Eltis, "The Nineteenth-Century Transatlantic Slave Trade," pp. 122–123. The raw data from 1804 through 1810 were derived from David R. Murray, *Odious Commerce: Britain, Spain, and the Abolition of the Cuban Slave Trade* (Cambridge: Cambridge University Press, 1980), p. 18. However, to make them consistent with the manner in which Eltis calculated imports from 1811 to 1837, 33.3 percent was added to Murray's statistics, which were largely from Alexander von Humboldt, *Ensayo político sobre la isla de Cuba* (Havana: Cultural, 1959). See the Eltis article for the rationale behind the one-third increase from official statistical estimates of slave imports.

8. The epidemic first appeared in the Yumurí Valley on March 4, 1833, and gradually spread through Matanzas. José Antonio Saco described it as follows: "De los

pueblos de Cuba atacados hasta ahora, ninguno, ninguno ha sufrido tantos estragos como Matanzas, y las escenas horribles que se representan en las pequeñas poblaciones de su distrito'' (Of all the towns in Cuba attacked until now, none has suffered such havoc as Matanzas, and the horrible scenes of the city are generalized in the smaller towns of the Matanzas administrative district). Saco, *Colección de papeles científicos, históricos, políticos, y de otros ramos sobre la isla de Cuba* (Havana: Dirección General de Cultura, 1960), pp. 280–281.

Also see Ricardo Vázquez Pérez, "Un modesto obrero de la ciencia: Don Francisco de Jimeno y Fuentes. Notas biográficas," *Cuadernos de Historia Matancero* 5 (1961), pp. 1–32, located in the NYPL. Vázquez Pérez notes that the cholera epidemic of 1833 caused many families to emigrate from Matanzas.

9. For local sugar prices in 1835 and 1836, see the newspaper *Aurora de Matanzas*, February 12, 1835, and March 12, 1836.

10. Data on the age structure of the Matanzas slave population in the first four decades of the nineteenth century are almost nonexistent in the archival collections I have examined. The only manuscript census data available are for Camarioca and are summarized here. Although Camarioca was not a sugar-producing region, there is no reason to believe that the demographic structure of slave populations in the frontier zones of Matanzas would be substantially different in the second decade of the nineteenth century, regardless of crop specialization.

11. AHPM, ME, Estadística, leg. 8, no. 137, fols. 17–64.

12. One reason for the development of closely guarded slave barracks was security. A number of slave rebellions broke out in Matanzas in the mid-1820s and early 1830s (see below), and planters responded by concentrating slave populations. For the best treatment of the barracón, see Juan Pérez de la Riva, "El barracón de ingenio en la época esclavista," in Pérez de la Riva, *El barracón y otros ensayos* (Havana: Ed. de Ciencias Sociales, 1975), pp. 15–74.

13. Ingenio inventories always listed a wide variety of crops, including plantains, rice, and tubers, that clearly were cultivated by slaves. For examples, see AHPM, Gobierno Provisional, Ingenios, leg. 1, no. 1, fols. 3–7; and no. 2, fol. 9. In addition, there were numerous notices about slaves marketing produce that could only have come from provision grounds.

14. AHPM, Gobierno Provincial, Esclavos, Generalidades, leg. 23, nos. 10, 12, 13, 22: "Comunicación al gobernador de Matanzas quejandose de que en las tabernas les vendan licores e les compren frutos a los esclavos"; "Comunicaciones denunciando que los taberneros venden aguardientes a los negros a cualquier hora del día y de la noche"; communication on "el abusivo desorden que se nota en los negros que de las fincas bajan de noche al pueblo a vender efectos, la mayor parte robados"; and "Comunicaciones sobre circular del Capitán General prohibiendo que los esclavos puedan vender mercancías sin la autorización de su dueño."

15. AHPM, Gobierno Provincial, Esclavos, Generalidades, leg. 23, no. 16.

16. AHPM, Gobierno Provincial, Esclavos, Generalidades, leg. 23, nos. 22, 43.

17. ANC, PN, Matanzas, Joaquín de la Fuente, 1830, fols. 85–86.

18. For an early discussion of coartación, see Hubert Aimes, "Coartación: A Spanish Institution for the Advancement of Slaves into Freedmen," *The Yale Review* 17 (1909), pp. 412–431.

19. Data on manumissions recorded in Matanzas notarial records do not permit an accurate analysis of the price of freedom in any particular year. The amount of money paid by a slave on the specific date freedom was legally declared was noted, but documentation never made clear whether the amount represented the last payment or the total amount of manumission. Thus, it is impossible to calculate accurate coartación prices for any year.

20. The years include 1804, 1810, 1818, 1823, 1826, 1830, 1834, and 1837. Along with the 133 manumissions, 704 slave sales were recorded as well as 39 payments by coartados on their hoped-for future freedom. Together, coartación payments and manumissions represented 24.4 percent of total slave sales.

21. All data were derived from manumissions noted in the following sources: ANC, PN, Matanzas, Santiago López Villavicencio, 1804; Luis López Villavicencio, 1810; and Joaquín de la Fuente, 1818, 1823, 1826, 1830, 1834, and 1837.

22. ANC, PN, Matanzas, Joaquín de la Fuente, 1830, fols. 273ᵛ–275ᵛ.

23. AHPM, ME, Estadísticas, leg. 1, no. 5.

24. For a general consideration of cabildos in Cuba, see Fernando Ortíz, "Los cabildos afro-cubanos," *Revista Bimestre Cubana* 16 (January–February 1921), pp. 5–39.

25. ANC, PN, Matanzas, Joaquín de la Fuente, 1823, fols. 117–118ᵛ.

26. The word *cimarrón*, or maroon, was first applied to the Indian peoples of the Caribbean who fled from sixteenth-century Spanish domination in Santo Domingo, Puerto Rico, and Cuba. For a general consideration of palenques, see José Luciano Franco, *Los palenques de los negros cimarrones* (Havana: Colección Histórica, 1973). Also see Rafael Duharte Jiménez, "Palenque: Economy and Society," *Cimarrón* 1:2 (1986), pp. 37–48; and Zoila Danger Roll, *Los cimarrones de El Fríjol* (Santiago: Ed. Oriente, 1977).

27. AHPM, Gobierno Provincial, Cimarrones, leg. 12, no. 5a.

28. AHPM, Gobierno Provincial, Cimarrones, leg. 12, nos. 23, 23a, 29, 30, 33.

29. AHPM, Gobierno Provincial, Cimarrones, leg. 12, no. 25a.

30. AHPM, Gobierno Provincial, Cimarrones, leg. 12, nos. 29, 30. Also see Cirilo Villaverde, *Diario del rancheador* (Havana: Ed. Letras Cubanas, 1982), which recounts the experiences of the slave bounty hunter Francisco Estévez in Matanzas during the early 1840s.

31. PRO, FO 72/304, report of Jul. 6, 1825; Fernando Ortíz, *Hampa afro-cubana. Los negros esclavos* (Havana: Revista Bimestre Cubana, 1916), p. 432.

32. See Ortíz, *Los negros esclavos*, p. 433.

33. PRO, FO 72/468, p. 50.

34. "El miserable estado en que se encuentra la negrada del Yngenio llamado La Lima, tanto en su desnudez como en la estremida escasez de alimentos" (AHPM, Gobierno Provincial, Esclavos, leg. 20, no. 4).

Chapter 5

1. Cuba, Gobernador y Capitán General, *Cuadro estadístico de la siempre fiel isla de Cuba correspondiente al año de 1846* (Havana: Imp. del Gobierno y Capitanía General, 1847); Cuba, Centro de Estadística, *Noticias estadísticas de la isla de Cuba*

en 1862 (Havana: Imp. del Gobierno, Capitanía General, y Real Hacienda, 1864); Spain, Instituto Geográfico y Estadístico, *Censo de la población de España según el empadronamiento hecho en 31 de diciembre de 1877* (Madrid: Imp. de la Dirección General del Instituto Geográfico y Estadístico, 1883).

2. Data on population by place of residence are not available for 1877.

3. The partido data listed here and included in Table 5.8 were derived from the published 1877 census. Fé Iglesias García, in her article "El censo cubano de 1877 y sus diferentes versiones" (*Santiago* 34 [June 1979], pp. 167–214), convincingly argues that the 1881 and 1882 versions published by the *Boletín Oficial de Hacienda* are more accurate. They list a total population of 250,728, while the official census lists 288,868 including all categories. If only "presentes" are counted, then the total declines to 277,637, a figure about 10 percent higher than the 1881 and 1882 count. The data listed here are derived from the official census because it lists detailed information at the partido level.

4. The formula $Pn = Po (1 + r)^n$ has been used to calculate annual population growth rates, where *Po* is the initial population, *Pn* the population after *n* years, *n* the number of years between census counts, and *r* the growth rate. See A. H. Pollard, Farhat Yusuf, and G. N. Pollard, *Demographic Techniques* (Rushcutters Bay, Australia: Pergamon Press, 1974), pp. 15–16.

5. See David Eltis, "The Nineteenth-Century Transatlantic Slave Trade: An Annual Time Series of Imports into the Americas Broken Down by Region," *Hispanic American Historical Reveiw* 67:1 (1987), pp. 122–123.

6. See Juan Poey, *Informes presentados al excm. capitán general gob. superior civil de la isla de Cuba sobre el proyecto de colonización africana y al Ilmo. Sr. intendente de Hacienda de la propia isla sobre derecho de los azúcares* (Madrid: Imp. D. A. Aurial, 1862), p. 144; and letter of Jan. 28, 1848, Jos. T. Crawford to Viscount Palmerston, PRO, FO 72/748.

7. This rate was derived from data in Rebecca Scott, *Slave Emancipation in Cuba: The Transition to Free Labor, 1860–1899* (Princeton: Princeton University Press, 1985), p. 87, which lists a Matanzas slave population of 87,858 in 1871 and 70,849 in 1877.

8. There were substantial administrative changes during this period. The jurisdiction of Matanzas remained intact except for the partido of Camarioca, which became part of Cárdenas in 1843. These calculations include Camarioca with Matanzas for comparative purposes.

9. In 1843 Cárdenas became a separate jurisdiction; in 1856 Colón, which had been part of Cárdenas, was formed. These calculations include the rural areas of Cárdenas in 1846 (excluding Camarioca) and those of Colón and Cárdenas (excluding Camarioca) for 1862.

10. In 1877 and 1878 the province of Matanzas was officially constituted, and the old jurisdictions of Matanzas, Cárdenas, and Colón were administratively divided into twenty-four ayuntamientos, which brought Alacranes into the province. The old Matanzas and Cárdenas partidos remained by and large intact, although Colón was subdivided into the ayuntamientos listed below. Jovellanos (Soledad de Bemba) was formerly part of Colón. These data are based for the ayuntamientos of Corral Nuevo (formerly Yumurí), Ceiba Mocha, Guamacaro, Santa Ana, Sabanilla, Cabe-

zas, and Camarioca. For the administrative divisions in 1878 and the creation of provinces, see Juan Styuck y Reig, *División territorial de la isla de Cuba y nomenclator de sus poblaciones* (Madrid: Imp. de la Viuda e Hija de Peñuelas, 1880). The following list shows the administrative subdivisions of Matanzas province from 1846 to 1878:

1846	1862	1878
Matanzas	Matanzas	Matanzas
Yumurí	Corral Nuevo	Corral Nuevo
Guanábana	Cabezas	Cabezas
Ceiba Mocha	Ceiba Mocha	Ceiba Mocha
Guamacaro	Guamacaro	Guamacaro
Sabanilla	Sabanilla	Sabanilla
Santa Ana	Santa Ana	Santa Ana
Camarioca		
Cárdenas	Cárdenas	Cárdenas
Lagunillas	Lagunillas	Lagunillas
Cimarrones	Cimarrones	Cimarrones
Hanábana	Guanajayabo	Guanajayabo
Guamutas	Guamutas	Guamutas
Macuriges	Camarioca	Camarioca
Palmillas	La Villa	
Ceja de Pablo		
Guásimas		
	Colón	Colón
	Jíquimas	Colón
	Macuriges	Macuriges
	Hanábana	Hanábana
	Macagua	Macagua
	Palmillas	Palmillas
Alacranes was	Alacranes was part	Alacranes
part of Güines.	of Güines. Ceja de	Alacranes
	Pablo became part of	Bolondrón
	Sagua la Grande.	Estante
		Güira
		La Unión
		Jovellanos
		Jíquimas
		Roque

NOTE: Cárdenas was created as a separate jurisdiction in 1843; Colón in 1856; Alacranes and Jovellanos in 1878.

11. These calculations include Lagunillas, Cimarrones, Guanajayabo, and Guamutas.

12. These calculations include the Colón partidos of Macagua, Palmillas, Hanábana, Macuriges, and Jíquimas in 1862; Colón, Macagua, Cuevitas, Jovellanos, Perico, San José de los Ramos, Roque, and Macuriges in 1877. The urban area of Colón had to be included in these calculations, since it was not separated from a large rural area in 1877. It was a small village, rather than a city such as Matanzas or Cárdenas.

Chapter 6

1. In 1862 the jurisdiction of Colón produced 25 percent of total Cuban white-sugar production. See Cuba, Centro de Estadística, *Noticias estadísticas de la isla de Cuba en 1862* (Havana: Imp. del Gobierno, Capitanía General, y Real Hacienda, 1864), "Estadística territorial."

2. On the Güines canal project, see "Expediente instruido a excitación del Sr. Síndico don Francisco Arango con el fín de que se efectue el antiguo proyecto del Sr. Conde de Macuriges de abrir un canal que reunise los ríos de los Güines y de la prensa," ANC, Real Consulado, 115/4844; Levi Marrero, *Cuba: economía y sociedad* (Madrid: Ed. Playor, 1984), vol. 11, pp. 147–149; and Manuel Moreno Fraginals, *El ingenio. Complejo económico social cubano del azúcar* (Havana: Ed. de Ciencias Sociales, 1978), vol. 1, p. 150.

3. On the need to improve the Cuban road system in the 1790s, see Nicolás Calvo y O'Farrill, *Memoria sobre los medios que convendría adoptar para que tuviese la Habana los caminos necesarios* (Havana: Imp. de la Capitanía General, 1795). Also see José Antonio Saco "Memoria sobre caminos en la isla de Cuba," in Saco, *Colección de papeles científicos, históricos, políticos, y de otros ramos sobre la isla de Cuba* (Havana: Dirección General de Cultura, 1960), vol. 1, pp. 61–176. For a complete account of all Cuban roads *before* railroad construction was initiated, see Esteban Pichardo, *Itinerario general de los caminos principales de la isla de Cuba* (Havana: Imp. de Palmer, 1828). This should not be confused with Pichardo's later, two-volume work: *Caminos de la isla de Cuba. Itinerarios* (Havana: Imp. Militar de M. Soler, 1865). Also see Julio LeRiverend, *Historia económica de cuba* (Havana: Instituto Cubano del Libro, 1971), chap. 13, "La nueva era en las comunicaciones."

4. As early as 1838, even before railroad construction had begun in Matanzas, the Matanzas merchants Drake & Coit, were ordering regular shipments of Pennsylvania Lehigh Valley coal to be used on ingenios. See NYPL, Moses Taylor Collection, M. T. & Co., Letters, 1838 (formerly box 9), letter of June 10, 1838.

5. For the most recently revised estimates of total slave imports to Cuba, see David Eltis, "The Nineteenth-Century Transatlantic Slave Trade: An Annual Time Series of Imports into the Americas Broken Down by Region," *Hispanic American Historical Review* 67:1 (1987), pp. 109–138. Between 1831 and 1840 an average of 18,160 slaves were imported to Cuba each year.

6. See *Extracto de las memorias y acuerdos de la junta de caminos de hierro* (Havana: Imp. Fraternal, 1831).

7. Marrero, *Cuba: economía y sociedad*, vol. 11, p. 165.

8. The most important work on Cuban railroads is a book by Oscár Zanetti and

Alejandro García, *Caminos para el azúcar* (Havana: Ed. de Ciencias Sociales, 1987). For a succint summary of Cuban railroad development, see Gert J. Oostindie, "La burguesía cubana y sus caminos de hierro, 1830–1868," *Boletín de Estudios Latinoamericanos y del Caribe*, no. 37 (December 1984), pp. 99–115. Also see Marrero, *Cuba: economía y sociedad*, vol. 11, chap. 7 ("La revolución del transporte: navegación a vapor y ferrocarril"), pp. 139–219.

The following works also contain information on railroads in Cuba: Duvon C. Corbitt, "El primer ferrocarril construido en Cuba," *Revista Cubana* 12 (1938), pp. 179–195; Fernando Ortíz, "Las perspectivas económico-sociales del primer ferrocarril de Cuba," *Revista Bimestre Cubana* 40:2 (November-December 1937), pp. 161–176.

9. ANC, PN, La Habana, Juan de Entralgo, 1844, fols. 583–584.

10. By January 1837 the project's directors had raised an initial 241,000 pesos by issuing 482 "acciones," or shares of stock, at 500 pesos/share. For a complete list of original shareholders, see AHN, Ultramar, Fomento, leg. 52 (no ex. no.), "Expediente sobre la construcción de un ferrocarril desde Cárdenas a Bemba y prolongación del mismo por medio de diferentes ramales. Lista de subscripción por la empresa del camino de hierro desde el puerto de Cárdenas al territorio de Soledad de Bemba."

11. AHN, Ultramar, Fomento, leg. 52, hojas sueltas, "Solicitud del Conde de Peñalver y otros de privilegio por 20 años para el establecimiento de un camino de hierro desde el Júcaro hasta Macuriges . . . 1840."

12. See LeRiverend, *Historia económica de Cuba*, pp. 201, 251.

13. ANC, PN, La Habana, Juan de Entralgo, 1844, fols. 959–960.

14. See Marrero, *Cuba: economía y sociedad*, vol. 11, pp. 198–199; and AHPM, ME, Ferrocarriles, leg. 1, no. 8, "Ferrocarril de la Sabanilla, 1845," and leg. 1, no. 43, fols. 1–2.

15. For an account of the sale of the railroad see Zanetti and García, *Caminos para el azúcar*, pp. 42–46. See David R. Murray, *Odious Commerce: Britain, Spain and the Abolition of the Cuban Slave Trade* (Cambridge: Cambridge University Press, 1980), pp. 114–132, for an account of the abolitionist movement and of pressures in Cuba in the late 1830s. Also see Arthur F. Corwin, *Spain and the Abolition of Slavery in Cuba, 1817–1886* (Austin: University of Texas Press, 1967), pp. 47–68.

16. For this interpretation, see Marrero, *Cuba: economía y sociedad*, vol. 11, p. 186.

17. For a succinct general account of the transfer of the Havana-Güines railroad from the Junta de Fomento, see ibid., pp. 185–191; for a list of accionistas in the private company, see p. 190. Also see Real Junta de Fomento de Agricultura y Comercio, *Documentos relativos a la enagenación del camino de hierro de la Habana a Güines* (Havana: Imp. del Gobierno y Capitaniá General, 1839).

18. The financial details of Schroeder & Company's loan to the Fesser group, which owned the Ferrocarril de la Bahiá de la Habana a Matanzas, is found in AHPM, Libros de la Antigua Anotaduría de Hipotecas, no. 20, fols. 1–6. The original loan was for 1.25 million pesos. In 1863 a second loan of half a million pesos was advanced, and in 1865 a third loan of 2 million pesos was extended.

19. For a report on the shareholders and financial status of the Matanzas railroad

system in 1873, see *Informe que debe leerse a nombre de la junta directiva de la compañía del ferrocarril de Matanzas en la general ordinaria de accionistas* (Matanzas: Imp. Aurora de Yumurí, 1872), found in AHN, Ultramar, Fomento, leg. 4736.

Chapter 7

1. Cuba, Gobernador y Capitán General, *Cuadro estadístico de la siempre fiel isla de Cuba correspondiente al año de 1846,* (Havana: Imp. del Gobierno y Capitanía General, 1847), pp. 68, 76; Cuba, Centro de Estadística, *Noticias estadísticas de la isla de Cuba en 1862* (Havana: Imp. del Gobierno, Capitanía General y Real Hacienda, 1864), "Registro general de fincas rústicas"; "Noticias de las fincas azucareras en producción que existían en toda la isla de Cuba al comenzar el presupuesto de 1877–1878," *Revista Económica*, June 7, 1878, pp. 7–24.

2. The history of land ownership in Banagüises is found in the record of the transaction whereby Julián de Zulueta purchased the land from the Conde de Peñalver on which he would construct the Ingenios Álava, Habana, and Vizcaya. See ANC, PN, La Habana, Juan de Entralgo, 1844, fols. 1195–1198.

3. ANC, Anotaduría de Hipotecas, La Habana, libro 62, Fincas, 1838, fol. 213^v.

4. See the description of Flor de Cuba and the lithograph drawn by Eduardo Laplante in Justo G. Cantero, *Los ingenios. Colección de vistas de los principales ingenios de azúcar de la isla de Cuba* (Havana: Litografía de Luis Marquier, 1857), which is reproduced in Levi Marrero, *Cuba: economía y sociedad* (Madrid: Ed. Playor, 1984), vol. 10, pp. xviii–xix.

5. The following debts were recorded for Flor de Cuba by the Cárdenas Anotaduría de Hipotecas on June 20, 1849:

Antonio Yerrau y Cía. (Havana)	16,432 pesos
Drake Hermanos (Havana)	8,300 pesos
Zangroni Hermanos (Havana)	36,863 pesos
Souberville de París (Paris)	2,500 pesos
Real Hacienda (Havana)	15,339 pesos
Frederick Hut & Company (London)	289,533 pesos

See AHPM, Anotaduría de Hipotecas, Fincas, Cárdenas, libro 3, partida 17, fols. 14^v–16^v.

6. ANC, ME, leg. 4120, no. M, "Repartos municipales de la jurisdicción de Colón, 1859"; ANC, Gobierno General, leg. 405, no. 19209, "Padrón de fincas rústicas de la jurisdicción de Colón, 1865"; ANC, Gobierno General, leg. 270, no. 13563, "Padrón general de fincas rústicas de este distrito, año de 1875 a 1876."

7. See ANC, Anotaduría de Hipotecas, La Habana, libro 62, Fincas, 1838, fols. 178^v–179, for reference to Ingenio Santa Rita. The Diagos must have sold this mill shortly thereafter, for it is never mentioned later in connection with the family.

8. For information on the purchases in Banagüises, see ANC, Anotaduría de Hipotecas, La Habana, libro 64, Fincas, 1840, fol. 278^v. Information on purchase prices is available for the 40-caballería tract on which Tinguaro was built, which was acquired from the Conde de Peñalver for 28,198 pesos, or 705 pesos/caballería. The

Diagos were listed as owners of Ingenio Tinguaro, 40 caballerías, and as owners of 30 caballerías of Hacienda Altamisal and 10 caballerías of Laguna Grande.

For the 1843 purchase, see ANC, PN, La Habana, Juan de Entralgo, 1843, fols. 867–869ᵛ. Also see ANC, PN, Escribano Mayor de la Real Hacienda, 1842–1843, fols. 438–439. The 34 caballerías on which Ponina was constructed were purchased from the Peñalvers for 20,851 pesos. See ANC, Anotaduría de Hipotecas, La Habana, libro 67, 1843, fols. 329–329ᵛ; also see fol. 255ᵛ for a notation on the 1840 sale of Tinguaro.

9. ANC, Anotaduría de Hipotecas, La Habana, libro 70, Fincas, 1846, fols. 458ᵛ–459ᵛ.

10. NYPL, Moses Taylor Collection, case B, drawers 2 and 3, box 6, letters of Dec. 27, 1840, and Feb. 1, 1841.

11. NYPL, Moses Taylor Collection, case B, drawers 2 and 3, box 6, letter of Dec. 27, 1840. In 1852 a census of foreign mechanics was conducted in Matanzas jurisdiction. There were 41 in all, including 19 from the United States; 1 German; 3 Frenchmen; 9 Scots; 4 Englishmen; 1 Irishman; 2 Mexicans; and 2 of unknown origin. See AHPM, Gobierno Provincial, Ingenios, leg. 6, no. 90, "Estado que manifiesta los maquinistas extrangeras que residen en los partidos de esta jurisdicción . . . 1853."

12. NYPL, Moses Taylor Collection, case B, drawers 2 and 3, box 6, letter from Pedro Diago to Henry Coit, March 15, 1841.

13. On February 17, 1849, Fernando Diago sold a strip of land on Ponina to the Ferrocarril de Júcaro, which had already constructed tracks across this stretch that were destined for Julián de Zulueta's adjacent plantation, Ingenio Álava. See AHPM, Anotaduría de Hipotecas, Cárdenas, libro 2, Fincas, partida 349, fols. 204ᵛ–206.

14. PRO, FO 72/760, report of Jos. J. Crawford, Havana, Jan. 3, 1849. One of Pedro Diago's principal concerns in the early 1840s was that the English campaign to curb the Cuban slave trade would be successful. He wrote to Henry Coit on March 15, 1841:

> Una cosa nos tiene ahora un poco inquietos y es que el gobierno Español se dispone a tomar medidas eficaces a fin de impedir la introducción de negros de Africa . . . medidas que apesar de que todos conocemos que es util al pays porque le dará mas seguridad política, me deja de ser sentida por algunos como yo que no han podido completar todavía su dotación de negros; y que quitada la trata, tendra que pagar $1,000 por cada negro cuando ahora se pueden comprar for $400 [One of the things that has us a little preoccupied is the fact that the Spanish government seems disposed to take efficient measures to impede the introduction of slaves from Africa . . . measures that we all know are useful to Cuba because they would yield more political security, but that are damaging to people like me who have not yet completed building up their slave populations; if the slave trade is eliminated, I would have to pay $1,000 pesos for each slave while now they can be purchased for $400 pesos].

See NYPL, Moses Taylor Collection, case B, drawers 2 and 3, box 6.

15. NYPL, Moses Taylor Collection, case B, drawers 2 and 3, box 6, letter from Francisco Diago to Henry Coit, May 22, 1849.

16. NYPL, Moses Taylor Collection, case B, drawers 2 and 3, box 6, letter from Fernando Diago to Henry Coit, Apr. 27, 1850.

17. NYPL, Moses Taylor Collection, case B, drawers 2 and 3, box 6, letters of Aug. 26, 1850, Sept. 6, 1850, Nov. 20, 1850, Jan. 9, 1851, Feb. 24 and 26, 1851, March 1, 1851.

18. See Marrero, *Cuba: Economía y sociedad*, vol. 12, p. 291, for a listing of "sociedades anónimas" formed between March and July 1857. More than 55 million pesos were invested in 36 joint-stock companies through this period.

19. This strategy will be discussed below.

20. The following list of shareholders in La Perseverancia accompanied the sale of Ponina in 1863 to Rafael Rodríguez Torices:

Shareholder	No. Shares
Francisco Diago	378
Gabriel López Martínez y Cía.	663
Crédito Industrial	5
Rafael Rodríguez Torices	321
Torices, Puente y Cía.	206
Compañía de Seguros Marítimas de la Habana	118
Cayetano Ortíz	234
Simón Pérez de Ferán	127
José Fernández Jaime	124
Francisco de Zayas	40
María de la Trinidad de Zayas	145
Tomás de Juara Soler	40
Francisco Arrieta	30
TOTAL	2,431

See AHPM, Anotaduría de Hipotecas, Cárdenas, Fincas, 1863, libro 14, partida 62, fols. 81–95ᵛ.

21. See AHN, Ultramar, Fomento, leg. 69, "Memoria de Cipriano del Mazo al Ministerio de Ultramar"; and leg. 66, "Informe del Conde de Pozos Dulces, Juan Poey, y Alvaro Reynoso al Capitán general Domingo Dulce . . . 1863," parts of which are reproduced in Marrero, *Cuba: economía y sociedad*, vol. 12, p. 304, and vol. 10, pp. 255–257.

22. See ANC, Gobierno General, leg. 405, no. 19209. "Año de 1865. Padrón de fincas rústicas de la jurisdicción de Colón"; and "Noticias de las fincas azucareras en producción que existían en toda la isla de Cuba al comenzar el presupuesto de 1877–1878," *Revista Económica*, June 7, 1878, pp. 7–24. For the lineage of María Luisa Diago y Tirry, see *HFC*, vol. 1, pp. 133–134.

I visited Tinguaro in June 1986. It is now called Central Sergio González and bears little resemblance to the ingenio built by the Diagos. Few of the old buildings remain, although there is an old church that seems to date from the late nineteenth century rather than from the period of the mill's original construction. I spent two hours there on a Sunday afternoon interviewing more than thirty people, none of whom had heard of the Diagos. Tinguaro passed to the U.S.-owned "Cuban-American Company" in the early twentieth century, and one worker told me that it was once owned by Coca-Cola. The Cuban sugar baron Julio Lobo owned Tinguaro at the time of the triumph of the revolution in 1959, after which it was confiscated by the socialist government.

23. See ANC, Gobierno General, leg. 405, no. 19209, "Año de 1865. Padrón de fincas rústicas de la jurisdicción de Colón"; and "Noticias de las fincas azucareras en producción que existían en toda la isla de Cuba al comenzar el presupuesto de 1877–1878," *Revista Económica*, June 7, 1878, pp. 7–24.

24. See AHPM, Anotaduría de Hipotecas, Cárdenas, Fincas, 1863, libro 14, partida 62, fols. 81–95ᵛ; ANC, Gobierno General, leg. 405, no. 19209, "Año de 1865. Padrón de fincas rústicas de la jurisdicción de Colón"; and "Noticias de las fincas azucareras en producción que existían en toda la isla de Cuba al comenzar el presupuesto de 1877–1878," *Revista Económica*, June 7, 1878, pp. 7–24.

25. NYPL, Moses Taylor Collection, case C, drawers 3 and 4, box 10, ship manifest of the bark *Rapid*, Aug. 26, 1836.

26. Zulueta, who had just begun his career as a sugar producer and slave trader, purchased 10 "acciones" in the company (led by Pedro Martínez, Joaquín Gómez, and Pedro Blanco) in an attempt to gain control of this first Cuban railroad line. See Marrero, *Cuba: economía y sociedad*, vol. 11, p. 185.

27. ANC, PN, Juan de Entralgo, La Habana, 1844, fols. 1195–1198. Justo Cantero, in *Los Ingenios*, mistakenly wrote that Álava was constructed on the site of the "demolido" Ingenio San Francisco; this error has been repeated by Marrero, *Cuba: economía y sociedad*, vol. 10, pp. 269–271. Cantero was confused by Zulueta's original ownership of Ingenio San Francisco de Paula, which was in distant Corral Nuevo, adjacent to Matanzas bay. Zulueta's own account of the founding of Álava makes it clear that it was a piece of virgin land when purchased. See AHN, Ultramar, Fomento, leg. 67 (no exp. no.), "Don Julián de Zulueta, vecino y del comercio de la Habana."

28. For Zulueta's claim of a 20,000-box total production for 1849, see AHN, Ultramar, Fomento, leg. 67 (no exp. no.), "Don Julián de Zulueta, vecino y del comercio de la Habana." It is certain he was producing that much in 1855 and 1856, which made Álava the largest producing mill in Cuba. See Félix Erenchun, *Anales de la isla de Cuba. Diccionario administrativo, económico, estadístico, y legislativo* (Havana: Imp. de la Antilla, 1855–1857), p. 1963, for production data in 1856. For the 1848 report of Crawford, see PRO, FO 72/760.

29. AHN, Ultramar, Fomento, leg. 67 (no exp. no.). For the 1859 data, see ANC, ME, leg. 4120, no. M, "Repartimientos municipales de la jurisdicción de Colón, 1859."

30. See ANC, Gobierno General, leg. 405, no. 19209. "Año de 1865. Padrón de fincas rústicas de la jurisdicción de Colón." For a description of Ingenio España in 1873, see Fermín Rosillo y Alquier, *Noticias de dos ingenios. Datos sobre la producción azucarera de la isla de Cuba* (Havana: Imp. El Iris, 1873), pp. 33–46.

Ingenios Vizcaya and Habana disappeared sometime in the 1880s. Álava and España are two of Cuba's largest centrales today; however, the names have been changed to Méjico and España Republicana. I visited both mills during the summer of 1986.

The visit to España was remarkable. The mill was bombed by counterrevolutionaries during the Bay of Pigs invasion, and the story of that event was recounted to me by the local administrators. Some could recall the name Zulueta, but there was no detailed knowledge of the family or of the mill's founding. I was permitted to walk around the grounds adjacent to the central and was attracted by a section of ramshackle housing inhabited exclusively by Afro-Cubans. One old man in his nineties was particularly fascinating, and I began a long conversation with him. He told me that the area where he was living was called Barrio África and that it was the site of the old slave quarters. His father was a Lucumí slave, and most of his childhood contemporaries were Lucumís or Carabalís. He was born and raised on España, where he had worked all of his life, and he told me that no white man or woman had ever lived in Barrio África. The revolution has given the people of Barrio África dignity and security, and has guaranteed their children a brighter future. But the material limitations of daily life were evident in the poor housing conditions, which possessed an element of timelessness that with a little imagination could help conjure up images of more than a century ago, when Julián de Zulueta was lord of the land.

Álava, its name faintly visible on the old smokestack of today's Central Méjico, also generated images of the past. The nineteenth-century campanario, the bell tower used to call the slaves to and from the fields, still stands at the entrance to a barrio of workers, all of them Afro-Cubans, the descendants of Julián de Zulueta's slaves. I stopped at three residential communities on Álava and was invited to lunch by one family with typical Cuban rural hospitality. No one could recall the name Zulueta, and all agreed that life was much better since the revolution. I asked whether they recognized the names of mills called "Vizcaya" or "Habana," and they found this amusing; none had ever heard of such names.

31. David R. Murray, *Odious Commerce: Britain, Spain, and the Abolition of the Cuban Slave Trade* (Cambridge: Cambridge University Press, 1980), p. 249.

32. See the report in AHN, Ultramar, Esclavitud, leg. 3547, caja 2, exp. 49, "Estado que manifiesta el número de esclavos que han sido desembarcados en Cuba en 1858 y el de los apresados por las autoridades."

33. This incident is recounted in Justo Zaragoza, *Las insurrecciones en Cuba. Apuntes para la historia política de esta isla en el presente siglo* (Madrid: Imp. de Manuel G. Hernández, 1873), vol. 2, pp. 124–125. Also see Murray, *Odious Commerce*, p. 313.

34. AHN, Ultramar, Esclavitud, leg. 3552.

35. See British Parliamentary Papers, Slave Trade, vol. 43, 1857, p. 437, and PRO, FO 72/878, for lists of Cubans involved in the Chinese trade.

36. For the project to build a railway system from Placetas to Caibarién, see the long *expediente*, complete with maps, in AHN, Ultramar, Fomento, leg. 200 (no exp. no.), "Expediente instruido a solicitud de E. S. Dn. Julián de Zulueta para hacer la declaratoria de utilidad pública en el tramo de f.carril que de vía estrecha constituye y que ha de ocupar las calles de Caibarién. Año 1878."

37. See Hugh Thomas, *Cuba: The Pursuit of Freedom* (New York: Harper & Row, 1970), p. 264. For a narrative account of the invasion of Las Villas, which began in January 1875, see Ramiro Guerra y Sánchez, *La guerra de los diez años, 1868–1878* (Havana: Cultural, 1952), vol. 2, pp. 283–330.

38. See the report of Consul General Cowper to the Marquis of Salisbury, Ha-

vana, May 13, 1878, PRO, ZHC/4108. One of the reasons that Cowper was so distressed was because of the reduction of the labor force, owing to the abolition law of 1870, slave desertions to the rebels, and the imminent emancipation law of 1880. A concerted effort to address the labor problem was undertaken by Zulueta and the Sociedad de Hacendados by intense negotiations with the Chinese over reviving the "coolie" trade. See AHN, Ultramar, Fomento, leg. 103 (no exp. no.), "Año de 1877. Expediente promovido por D. Julián Zulueta a nobre de la Sociedad de Hacendados de la isla de Cuba en solicitud de autorización exclusiva para introducir en dicha isla, colonos asiáticos del Imperio Chino y del Reyno de Annan."

Between Placetas and Remedios, along the comtemporary railway line, there are two towns that bear Zulueta's name: Zulueta del Sur and Zulueta. To the northeast of Zulueta is Central Chiquitico Fabregat, which I believe is the old Ingenio Zaza. See Instituto Cubano de Geodesia y Cartografía, *Atlas de Cuba* (Havana: 1978), pp. 120–121, map coordinates B–8.

39. Every major transaction involving San Martín and Echevarría was effected by González Solar, who had power of attorney for Francisca Pedroso y Herrera.

40. Ingenio San Martín has been written about extensively, although much of the information presented here derives from documentary sources and has not appeared before. See the lithographs depicting San Martín's barracón and a map of the mill's layout in Cantero, *Los ingenios*; they have been reproduced in Marrero, *Cuba: economía y sociedad*, vol. 10, pp. 237–238. Also see H. B. Auchinloss, "Sugar Making in Cuba," *Harper's New Monthly Magazine* 30:178 (March 1865), pp. 440–453, for a contemporary description of the mill; José Miguel González Jiménez, "El ingenio San Martín," *Revista de la Biblioteca Nacional José Martí* 9:1 (January-March 1967), pp. 71–100; and Juan Pérez de la Riva, "Riesgo y ventura del San Martín," in Pérez de la Riva, ed., *La isla de Cuba en el siglo xix vista por los extranjeros* (Havana: Ed. de Ciencias Sociales, 1981), pp. 183–192.

41. This account is based on the correspondence of Antonio González Solar with Moses Taylor & Company, found in NYPL, Moses Taylor Collection, case A, drawers 1 and 2, box 2, letters of Oct. 21, 1853, Nov. 21, 1853, Jan. 20, 1854, March 20, 1854, Feb. 8, 1855, Nov. 27, 1855, and Feb. 7, 1856.

42. For the lineage of the Benítez family, see *HFC*, vol. 3, pp. 88–93.

43. This transaction is recorded in AHPM, Anotaduría de Hipotecas, Cárdenas, Fincas, libro 8, Anotador Joaquín Ma. Casanova, Sept. 7, 1857–Aug. 26, 1858, partida 318, fols. 205ᵛ–208ᵛ.

44. AHPM, Anotaduría de Hipotecas, Cárdenas, Fincas, libro 8, Anotador Joaquín Ma. Casanova, Sept. 7, 1857–Aug. 26, 1858, partida 167, fols. 106ᵛ–110ᵛ.

45. The general partners of Noriega, Olmo y Cía. were José B. Noriega, Rosendo Noriega, Manuel García de Olmo, Benito Gutiérrez de Olmo, José Melgares, and José E. de la Cámara. Little has been written about these men who played such an important role in Cuba's sugar economy during the late 1850s and early 1860s.

46. For the purchases of Belfast, Victoria, Socorro, and Fundador, see AHPM, Anotaduría de Hipotecas, Cárdenas, Fincas, libro 8, Anotador Joaquín Ma. Casanova, Sept. 7, 1857–Aug. 26, 1858, partida 77, fols. 51ᵛ–52, 73–76ᵛ, 89–91. For the aquisition of Arco Iris, La Perla, and Santa Cruz, see AHPM, Antigua Anotaduría de Hipotecas, libro 16, Fincas, fols. 389ᵛ–390, 392–392ᵛ, 404–404ᵛ, 427–427ᵛ. For

additional data on Victoria and Fundador, see AHPM, Esclavos y Semovientes, Cárdenas, libro 2, fols. 198ᵛ–200, 203–203ᵛ.

47. I have not been able to locate information on the purchase of Apuros, Chumba, San Joaquín, and Destino. For the company's assets in 1863, as bankruptcy proceedings progressed, see NYPL, Microfilm Collection, TLH, p.v. 52–55, vol. 55, no. 7, "Proyecto para la venta de las propiedades de la Compañía Territorial Cubana aprobado en Junta General de accionistas celebrada el día 20 de mayo del corriente año. 1863."

48. See Marrero, *Cuba: economía y sociedad*, vol. 12, p. 275, for a list of the Banco Español's shareholders; and pp. 291–292 for data on the Sociedad General de Crédito Mobiliario y Fomento Cubano.

49. The assets of Benítez, Dirón y Cía. are listed in Sociedad en Comandita La Gran Azucarera, *Balanza general y memoria* (Havana: Imp. La Universal, 1866), p. 19.

La Alianza, Compañía de Crédito y Seguros was formed in 1858 by consolidating four existing companies: La Positiva, Caja Central de Comercio, Banco de Pinar del Río, and Crédito Agrícola de Cárdenas. See Marrero, *Cuba: economía y sociedad*, vol. 12, p. 301.

50. For a discussion of the "privilegio," see Francisco Pérez de la Riva, *Origen y régimen de la propiedad territorial en Cuba* (Havana: Imp. El Siglo XX, 1946), pp. 70–75.

51. Every mortgage recorded in the Cárdenas Anotaduría de Hipotecas in the mid-1850s included the clause "y renunciando el privilegio de ingenios." See AHPM, Cárdenas, Anotaduría de Hipotecas, Fincas, libro 6, fols. 170ᵛ–171., where Ingenio Isabelita in Sabanilla was mortgaged in a refacción contract.

52. Documentation on the bankruptcy of the Gran Azucarera is contained in a large *legajo* titled "Gran Azucarera. Quiebra," in ANC, Escribanías, leg. 311. See no. 2, 1861, "Copia de la cuenta de los Sres. Pedroso y Ca. con la Gran Azucarera por la refacción de los ingenios S. Martín y Echevarría en la zafra de 1861 a 1862"; and leg. 444, no. 9, "La imperiosa y urgente necesidad de alimentar las dotaciones de los ingenios San Martín y Echevarría, y de atender estas fincas en lo que fuera absolutamente preciso y indispensable," Aug. 29, 1863.

53. Sociedad en Comandita La Gran Azucarera, *Balanza general y memoria*.

54. Profits were derived by subtracting "refacción" expenses from gross income and dividing the resulting net income by the costs of the mills. The total cost of San Martín and Echevarría, was 3,032,046 pesos, while Santa Susana and Santísima Trinidad cost 2,797,598 pesos. See Sociedad en Comandita La Gran Azucarera, *Balanza general y memoria*.

55. The demise of La Perseverancia was discussed above. For documents on the sale of the Compañía Territorial Cubana, see NYPL, Microfilm Collection, TLH, p.v. 52–55, vol. 55, no. 7, "Proyecto para la venta de las propiedades de la Compañía Territorial Cubana aprobado en Junta General de accionistas celebrada el día 20 de mayo del corriente año. 1863." In 1866 Francisco Feliciano Ibáñez purchased a three-quarters interest in two of the Compañía Territorial Cubana's mills, Arco Iris and Santa Cruz; Luis Díez de Ulzurrun purchased the other quarter-share for a total price of 2,472,090.81 pesos. See AHPM, Anotaduría de Hipotecas, libro 18, Fincas,

partida 1224, fols. 222ᵛ–224. For the 1878 auction of Santísima Trinidad and Santa Susana to Eugenio Moré, see ANC, Escribanías, leg. 14, no. 98.

Chapter 8

1. The data for San Antonio de Cabezas and Sabanilla in 1852 are found in AHPM, ME, Estadística, leg. 6, no. 116. For Sabanilla in 1855, see AHPM, ME, Estadística, leg. 8, no. 145, fols. 28–31. Sabanilla's principal ingenios were owned by the most noted families of Cuba's sugar and slave-trading elite. Domingo Aldama operated the ingenios Santa Rosa, Santo Domingo, and San José in the partido (104 total caballerías); while his father-in-law Gonzalo Alfonso owned San Gonzalo and Concepción (94 caballerías). Drake Hermanos of Havana owned Ingenio Saratoga (59 caballerías).

2. AHPM, ME, Estadística, leg. 6, no. 118, fols. 1–42, "Padrón de predios del partido de Corral Nuevo formado en 17 de noviembre de 1854."

3. This will be discussed in more detail below, in the context of land-tenure structures.

4. See the map "Croquis del distrito de Colón en la isla de Cuba," Nov. 9, 1858, in AHN, Ultramar, Fomento, leg. 4657.

5. All of these data were derived from the farm-census materials found in ANC, ME, leg. 4120, no. M, "Repartos municipales de la jurisdicción de Colón, 1859"; ANC, Gobierno General, leg. 405, no. 19209, "Padrón de fincas rústicas de la jurisdicción de Colón, 1865"; ANC, Gobierno General, leg. 270, no. 13563, "Padrón general de fincas rústicas de este distrito, año de 1875 a 1876"; ANC, Gobierno General, leg. 945, no. 16724, "Padrón general de la riqueza rústica para regir en los años económicos de 1866 a 1867"; and ANC, Gobierno General, leg. 269, no. 13554, "Jurisdicción de Cárdenas. Padrón general de la riqueza rústica de esta ciudad y su jurisdicción formado para los años económicos de 1875 a 1876."

6. AHPM, PN, Manuel Vega Lavarría, 1872, fols. 71–73ᵛ.

7. AHPM, PN, Manuel Vega Lavarría, 1868, fols. 828–829.

8. Land cultivation will be discussed in more detail below. The data cited here for 1860 were derived from Carlos Rebello, *Estados relativos a la producción azucarera de la isla de Cuba* (Havana: Imp. del Gobierno, 1860); those for 1878 come from the 1877/78 sugar plantation census published in "Noticias de las fincas azucareras en producción que existían en toda la isla de Cuba al comenzar el presupuesto de 1877–1878," *Revista económica*, June 7, 1878, pp. 7–24.

9. For the most complete description of milling machinery, see Manual Moreno Fraginals, *El ingenio. Complejo económico social cubano del azúcar* (Havana: Ed. de Ciencias Sociales, 1978), vol. 1, pp. 214–226.

10. See Fé Iglesias García, "The Development of Capitalism in Cuban Sugar Production, 1860–1900," in Manuel Moreno Fraginals, Frank Moya Pons, and Stanley L. Engerman, eds., *Between Slavery and Free Labor: The Spanish-Speaking Caribbean in the Nineteenth Century* (Baltimore: The Johns Hopkins University Press, 1985), p. 70.

11. These data are found in AHN, Ultramar, Fomento, leg. 17, no. 8, "Informe presentado a la Real Junta de Fomento de Agricultura y Comercio de esta isla por el

Sr. D. Wenceslao de Villaurrutia sobre los resultados de la zafra que este año ha hecho su ingenio en un tren de Derosne, 1843." They are reproduced in Moreno Fraginals, *El ingenio*, vol. 1, p. 248.

12. This changed ratio between white and quebrado sugars resulted in a significant rise in income. For example, for the harvest of 1843 this ingenio was paid average prices of 2.8 cents/pound for quebrados and 4.5 cents/pound for whites.

13. On efforts to mechanize plowing and cane cutting, see Moreno Fraginals, *El ingenio*, vol. 1, pp. 182–196, which includes reproductions of lithographs depicting the Fowler plow and other machines employed in cane agriculture.

14. Labor-force organization will be discussed in more detail below.

15. For a discussion of internal rail systems utilized by Cuban sugar plantations in the 1870s, see Patria Cok Márquez, "La introducción de los ferrocarriles portátiles en la industria azucarera, 1870–1880," *Santiago* 41 (March 1981), pp. 137–147.

16. "Noticias de las fincas azucareras en producción que existían en toda la isla de Cuba al comenzar el presupuesto de 1877–1878," *Revista Económica*, June 7, 1878, pp. 7–24.

Chapter 9

1. ANC, ME, leg. 4120, no. M, "Repartos municipales de la jurisdicción de Colón, 1859"; ANC, Gobierno General, leg. 405, no. 19209, "Padrón de fincas rústicas de la jurisdicción de Colón, 1865"; ANC, Gobierno General, leg. 270, no. 13563, "Padrón gral. de fincas rústicas de este distrito, año de 1875 a 1876."

2. ANC, Gobierno General, leg. 945, no. 16724. "Padrón general de la riqueza rústica para regir en los años económicos de 1866 a 1867"; ANC, Gobierno General, leg. 270, no. 13563, "Padrón general de fincas rústicas de este distrito, año de 1875 a 1876."

3. It should be emphasized that after 1870 there was rampant inflation in Cuba because of the Banco Español's policy of printing paper money in order to finance the colonial government's efforts to contain rebellion in the east. A dual system of economic transactions emerged: prices were quoted either in gold, which did not reflect inflation, or in "billetes," paper currency that did. Sugar prices—and, indeed, most transactions regarding any kind of property were quoted in gold.

The data presented here were subjected to a variety of tests to determine whether or not income data were quoted in gold. The most important was an examination of gross income per ingenio in 1865, (before inflation) and in 1876 (when inflation had been rampant). The average gross income per plantation remained constant, and sugar prices had changed very little. If inflation were a factor, a radical change in income would have been forthcoming. Since this was not the case, these data clearly reflect real increases in revenue because of new ingenio construction.

4. These salary levels were prevalent on Cosme de la Torriente's Ingenio La Isabel. See AHPM, Gobierno Provincial, Ingenios, leg. 2, no. 23.

5. These mills were Ramón de LLanos's Ingenio Buen Suceso; Dolores Ugarte's Buen Amigo; Juan Zequeira's Ingenio El Pan; and Manuel del Portillo's (a Matanzas notary) Ingenio Candelaria. See AHPM, ME, Estadística, leg. 9, no. 148, fols. 26–42.

Chapter 10

1. For complete schedules of the different Cuban railway lines in the late 1850s, see Jacobo de la Pezuela, *Diccionario geográfico, estadístico, histórico de la isla de Cuba* (Madrid: Imp. del Establecimiento de Mellado, 1863), vol. 2, pp. 334–359.

2. For a brief discussion of the development of telegraph and mail services in Cuba, see Julio LeRiverend, *Historia económica de Cuba* (Havana: Instituto Cubano del Libro, 1971), p. 406. Also see Levi Marrero, *Cuba: economía y sociedad* (Madrid: Ed. Playor, 1984), vol. 11, pp. 212–213; and *Book of the Telegraph* (Boston: Daniel David, 1851). A map of Cuba's telegraph stations in 1857 is contained in *Memoria instructivo formado por D. Juan Poey y D. Antonio Carillo socios y representantes de la minoría de los accionistas de la Compañía de los Caminos de Hierro de la Habana* (Madrid: Imp. Benigno Carranza, 1872), "Ferrocarriles, vapores, y estaciones telegráficas en el departamento Occidental, 1857." For a notice of the international cable system linking Cuba with Florida, see the trade report of Dec. 31, 1867 in PRO, FO 72/1189.

3. In 1845 the British consul in Matanzas noted that London was the major brokerage center for sugar imported by Russia, Prussia, Germany, Holland, and Belgium. Systematic data on shipping from Matanzas are missing from the historical record. In 1845 there was the following breakdown of ships trading with Matanzas: Britain, 63 ships, 10,737 tons; United States, 535 ships, 94,793 tons; Spain, 572 ships, 85,992 tons. See PRO, FO 72/682, p. 64.

4. On the Drakes' history, see Roland T. Ely, *Comerciantes cubanos del siglo xix* (Havana: Ed. Lib. Martí, 1961), chap. 4 ("La Casa Drake"), pp. 83–140. For Drake, Kleinwort & Cohen, see NYPL, Moses Taylor Collection, case A, drawer 1, box 1, notice of March 24, 1860.

5. AHPM, Anotaduría de Hipotecas, Cárdenas, Fincas, libro 14, 1863, no. 96, fols. 128ᵛ–130.

6. Pezuela, *Diccionario*, vol. 4, p. 40.

7. For notices of the Fessers, see NYPL, Moses Taylor Collection, case A, drawer 1, box 1.

8. NYPL, Moses Taylor Collection, Letters, 1840–1841 (formerly boxes 11 and 12), notice of Schweyer & Day, Dec. 1, 1839.

9. An excellent source for identifying the merchants of Matanzas is the local newspaper *Aurora de Yumurí* (or *La Aurora* or *Aurora de Matanzas*, which were different names for the same paper). Advertisements for products, or for space on docked ships appear in every issue. The full collection is housed in Matanzas in the Biblioteca Gener y del Monte. Unfortunately, it is more difficult to find biographical data on most of the above-mentioned merchants, and the careers and connections of most remain enigmatic.

10. NYPL, Moses Taylor Collection, case A, drawers 1 and 2, box 2, letter from Cárdenas, Cornelius O'Callaghan to Moses Taylor, Dec. 12, 1851.

11. The sale of Hacienda Banagüises by the Peñalver family, discussed in Chapter 7, is a prime example of a titled Havana family playing a major role in the development of the sugar economy through land sales. See Chapter 7 for a discussion of land sales "a censo."

12. AHPM, libro 1, Cárdenas, Registro de la Propiedad de Colón, Partido de Ma-

curiges, no. 162, fols. 55–55ᵛ. The same transaction was recorded in AHPM, Anotaduría de Hipotecas, Cárdenas, libro 6, fols. 163–163ᵛ.

13. AHPM, Anotaduría de Hipotecas, Cárdenas, Fincas, libro 8, Sept. 1, 1857–Aug. 26, 1858, no. 11, fols. 5ᵛ–6; no. 16, fols. 9–9ᵛ; no. 19, fols. 10ᵛ–11.

14. AHPM, PN, Manuel Vega Lavarría, 1867, Indice, fols. 230ᵛ, 344ᵛ, 346, 411, 714ᵛ.

15. ANC, PN, Cárdenas, Carlos Acosta Espou, 1852, fols. 849–852ᵛ

16. AHPM, libro 1, Cárdenas, Registro de la Propiedad de Colón, Partido de Macuriges, no. 113, fols. 33–34; AHPM, Anotaduría de Hipotecas, Cárdenas, Fincas, libro 6, fols. 250–251.

17. Sometimes, early in their careers, capital was borrowed in small amounts from friends and business associates. For example, in 1838 Pedro Diago, in the process of acquiring the land for the construction of Ponina, Santa Elena, and Tinguaro, borrowed 9,600 pesos from his friend and neighbor Tomás Juara Soler. ANC, Anotaduría de Hipotecas, La Habana, Fincas, libro 62, 1838, fols. 178–179ᵛ.

18. Throughout the Moses Taylor Collection in the New York Public Library, copies of the *Mercantile Weekly Report* appear regularly. See, for example, case C, drawers 3 and 4, box 10, for issues appearing in the 1850s. Another important publication was the *Havana Prices Current*.

19. NYPL, Moses Taylor Collection, case B, drawer 4, and case C, drawer 1, box 8, *Mercantile Weekly Report*, Apr. 3, 1849, June 8, 1849, Aug. 11, 1849, Nov. 8, 1849.

20. NYPL, Moses Taylor Collection, case A, drawer 1, box 1, letter of Jan. 11, 1853, from Aviles y Leblanc to Moses Taylor.

21. NYPL, Moses Taylor Collection, Cuban Sugar Trade (no box no.), invoices from Apr. 1861.

22. He also operated Zulueta, Hermanos y Cía. (with his brothers Gregorio and Salvador) in the Cuban port of Trinidad; Julián Zulueta y Cía. in Havana; and Zulueta y Sobrino (with his nephew Pablo Gamiz) in Havana. Tomás de Goyri was Zulueta's partner in Julián Zulueta y Cía., and Andrés Isasi was his partner in Zulueta e Isasi in Andoain. See the letter of May 20, 1878, announcing Zulueta's death on May 4, in NYPL, Moses Taylor Collection, case A, drawers 2 and 3, box 3.

23. Each time a new company was formed, or an old one reorganized, the custom was to mail a printed official notice to major clients with whom the company expected to be transacting business. These listed the names of partners and those having power of attorney. If a company had been reorganized, old and new partners were listed. Throughout the Moses Taylor Collection, literally hundreds of these notices are interspersed among correspondence and invoices. For the Barós, see NYPL, Moses Taylor Collection, case A, drawer 1, box 1, letters of Jan. 24, 1852, and May 1, 1859; case B, drawers 2 and 3, box 6, letters of Jan. 1, 1870, and Jul. 15, 1871; and Miscellaneous and Individual Files, A–J, 1872 (formerly box 87).

24. For a concise account of the founding of the Banco de Fernando VII, see Marrero, *Cuba: economía y sociedad*, vol. 12, pp. 262–265.

25. See D. A. Bachiller y Morales, *Memoria de los trabajos de la caja de ahorros, descuentos y depósitos de la Habana durante el año económico de 1859 a 1860* (Havana: Imp. La Antilla, 1860).

26. For a complete list of shareholders, see the *Gaceta de la Habana*, May 18, 1855, which is reproduced in Marrero, *Cuba: economía y sociedad*, vol. 12, pp. 272–273.

27. See Heinrich Friedlaender, *Historia económica de Cuba* (Havana: Ed. de Ciencias Sociales, 1978), p. 417.

28. For the biography of the Gumá family, see *HFC*, vol. 7, pp. 183–187. These transactions are found in ANC, PN, Matanzas, Manuel Padró, 1865, fols. 4v–8, 780–788. The Banco de San Carlos de Matanzas provides an example of an eminently successful local bank. It was one of many founded during the speculative fever accompanying the rise of sugar prices in 1857, with capital resources of 2,825,000 pesos. The crisis of 1858 reduced assets to 847,000 pesos; by 1863, however, capital had increased to 5,790,735 pesos, and annual dividends of 13 percent had been paid to shareholders. See Marrero, *Cuba: economía y sociedad*, vol. 12, pp. 283–284.

29. Slave traders will be discussed in Chapter 12.

30. ANC, PN, Matanzas, Manuel Portillo, 1875, fols. 205–211v.

31. See ANC, PN, Matanzas, Manuel Portillo, 1875, fols. 456–457v. For a contract involving Rionda's financing of Ingenio San Pedro for the zafra of 1874/75. For information on the marriage of Rionda to Elena Torriente, see *HFC*, vol. 4, p. 328.

Chapter 11

1. PRO, FO 72/1576, letter of Oct. 2, 1880. In a recent article, Louis Pérez has left the impression that the war "profoundly disrupted Cuba's economy." This was clearly the case in eastern Cuba, but the Matanzas sugar sector was hardly affected by the war. See Louis A. Pérez, Jr., "Vagrants, Beggars, and Bandits: Social Origins of Cuban Separatism, 1878–1895," *American Historical Review* 90:5 (Dec. 1985), pp. 1092–1121.

2. Aug. and Sept. of 1870 were months of severe drought in rural Matanzas, and on Oct. 7–8, 1870, a hurricane swept through the region causing substantial damage to the cane crop, which had already been stunted by the prolonged absence of rain. See the letters of Smith & Company of Cárdenas to Moses Taylor, in NYPL, Moses Taylor Collection, Individual Letters, 1870 (formerly boxes 86 and 123), Aug. 25, 1870, Sept. 16, 1870, and Oct. 13, 1870. José Baró wrote to Moses Taylor on Nov. 2, 1870, describing the hurricane: "ha causado en lo general bastantes desgracias. Las jurisdicciones de Matanzas y Cárdenas son las que esperimentan mayor daño en sus campos de caña" (has generally caused a great deal of damage. The cane fields of the jurisdictions of Matanzas and Cárdenas have suffered the greatest damage). NYPL, Moses Taylor Collection, Individual Letters, 1870 (formerly boxes 86 and 123).

3. NYPL, Moses Taylor Collection, Cuban Revolution, box 1, letter from Emilio Rubio to Pedro M. Amoy c/o Moses Taylor, May 12, 1876.

4. Ramiro Guerra y Sánchez, *La guerra de los diez años 1868–1878* (Havana: Cultural, 1950), vol. 1, pp. 149–150.

5. Central Australia served as Fidel Castro's command post during the Bay of Pigs invasion in 1961. I visited the mill in July 1986 and would like to thank Noel Mar-

tínez Martínez, director of the mill's "Museo 'La Comandancia de las FAR,' " for his accounts of revolutionary activities in the region during the Ten Years' War.

The Moras' mill was confiscated by the colonial government in the aftermath of the insurrection, and Máximo was condemned to death for financing the rebellion. However, he was a U.S. citizen and was able to avoid the death penalty through intervention of the U.S. consul.

6. See Guerra y Sánchez, *Guerra de los diez años*, vol. 2, pp. 319–320. Henry Reeve, a close associate of Gómez, was killed in combat on Aug. 4, 1876.

7. For a discussion of the breakdown of mechanisms of control within plantations, see Rebecca Scott, *Slave Emancipation in Cuba: The Transition to Free Labor, 1860–1899* (Princeton: Princeton University Press, 1985), pp. 45–62.

8. This decree is found in PRO, ZHCI/4108, p. 222.

9. Dispatch of Apr. 1, 1877, Consul General Cowper to the Earl of Derby, PRO, ZHCI/4108. The assessment of rural violence around Colón as being perpetrated principally by gangs of runaway slaves, rather than by insurgents, was also made by Rafael Torices, the owner of Ingenio Ponina, in Banagüises. See letter of May 12, 1876, NYPL, Moses Taylor Collection, Cuban Revolution, box 1.

10. There are four folders from the U.S. Treasury Department listing owners of government bonds payable at 6 percent interest in NYPL, Moses Taylor Collection, Individual Letters, 1870 (formerly boxes 86 and 123).

11. For a succinct summary of reformist efforts that preceded the Ten Years' War, see Hugh Thomas, *Cuba: The Pursuit of Freedom* (New York: Harper & Row, 1971), chap. 19 ("Reformism"), pp. 233–244.

12. The Aldama mills that were embargoed, built by his father Domingo Aldama, included the ingenios Concepción, Santo Domingo, Santa Rosa, Armonía, and San José. See AHPM, Gobierno Provincial, Ingenios, leg. 6, no. 86, fol. 8, "Relación de los operarios y dotaciones que ecsisten en la actualidad en los Yngenios embargados de este partido de D. Domingo Aldama."

Both father and son fled to New York in 1869, and Miguel became one of the principal exile leaders of the rebellion. Domingo Aldama died in New York City on April 11, 1870. He resided at 43 W. 47th Street and was buried at Greenwoods Cemetery. For a copy of his death certificate, see ANC, PN, Matanzas, Manuel de Portillo, 1870 "Testamento de Domingo Aldama," fols. 1–6, and 40ᵛ.

13. Torices wrote to Moses Taylor after the invasion of Matanzas: "Esas partidas se componen en su mayor parte de negros y otras gentes de color y también se asegura que hay una partida de bastante fuerzas en la Ciénaga de Zapata. Ya Usted comprenderá que esta gente no entiende de autonomía, ni de reforma alguna política sino de hacer una vida aventurera amenazando promover la guerra de raza para convertir esto en otro Santo Domingo" (These gangs are mostly composed of blacks and other people of color, and you can also be certain that there is a large gang in the Zapata swamp. You should understand that these people understand little of "autonomy," nor of political reform, but rather prefer lives of adventure, threatening to promote a race war and to convert Cuba into another Santo Domingo). NYPL, Moses Taylor Collection, letter of May 12, 1876.

Chapter 12

1. For the most complete English-language consideration of the abolition of the slave trade to Cuba, see David R. Murray, *Odious Commerce: Britain, Spain, and the Abolition of the Cuban Slave Trade* (Cambridge: Cambridge University Press, 1980). Also see Arthur F. Corwin, *Spain and the Abolition of Slavery in Cuba, 1817–1886* (Austin: University of Texas Press, 1967).

2. The pioneering work on the question of slavery and the Ten Years' War is Raúl Cepero Bonilla, *Azúcar y abolición* (Havana: Ed. Cenit, 1948). The best consideration of linkages between the insurrection, slavery, and the Moret Law is Rebecca Scott, *Slave Emancipation in Cuba: The Transition to Free Labor, 1860–1899* (Princeton: Princeton University Press, 1985).

3. Scott, in *Slave Emancipation in Cuba*, emphasizes the gradual demise of slavery, between 1870 and 1886, as a process involving the interaction of various historical actors and in which slaves played an active role.

4. These data were derived from Cuba, Gobernador y Capitán General, *Cuadro estadístico de la siempre fiel isla de Cuba. correspondiente al año de 1846* (Havana: Imp. del Gobierno y Capitanía General, 1847), "Estado general de la población del departamento occidental de la isla de Cuba, en fín del año de 1846," between pp. 41 and 42, and p. 59. For a complete census of the Cuban slave population in 1857, see AHN, Ultramar, Cuba, Esclavitud, leg. 3551.

5. Data for the slave population in 1862 are derived from Cuba, Centro de Estadística, *Noticias estadísticas de la isla de Cuba en 1862* (Havana: Imp. del Gobierno, Capitanía General y Real Hacienda, 1864), "Partidos pedaneos, con expresión de los cuartones que cada uno contiene y la particular de cada pueblo aldea y caserío que se halla en ella." The 1871 data for Matanzas are noted in Scott, *Slave Emancipation in Cuba* p. 87; the 1877 data are from Fé Iglesias García, "El censo cubano de 1877 y sus diferentes versiones," *Santiago* 34 (June 1979), pp. 167–211.

6. For 1862, see Cuba, Centro de Estadística, *Noticias estadísticas . . . 1862*. For 1871 data, see AHPM, Gobierno Provincial, provisional leg. 60, exp. 1731.

7. It is not known whether the example of Guanajayabo is typical of regions where slave imports had by and large ceased. A contrasting image is provided by the Cienfuegos partido of Lajas studied by Rebecca Scott. There, the slave population did not decline between 1862 and 1875, and Scott suggests that this may have been because of the presence of slaveowners who were slave traders. Also evident was a distorted age pyramid, since working-age slaves made up the major share of the enslaved population. See Scott, *Slave Emancipation in Cuba*, pp. 92–96.

8. See Manuel Moreno Fraginals, *El ingenio Complejo económico social cubano del azúcar* (Havana: Ed. de Ciencias Sociales, 1978), vol. 1, pp. 278–287; and Murray, *Odious Commerce*, p. 306.

9. For brief biographies of the major Cuban slave traders Joaquín Gómez, Pancho Marty, Pedro Blanco, Julián Zulueta, and Salvador Samá (Zulueta's brother-in-law) and for a discussion of other families, see José Luciano Franco, *Comercio clandestino de esclavos* (Havana: Ed. de Ciencias Sociales, 1985), chap. 6 ("La oligarquía negrera"), pp. 203–256.

On the life of Pedro Blanco, and for valuable descriptive materials on aspects of the African end of the trade, see Lino Novas Calvo, *El negrero. Vida novelada de Pedro Blanco Fernández de Trava* (Madrid: Espasa-Calpe, 1933).

See Moreno Fraginals, *El ingenio,* vol. 1, pp. 265–269, for descriptions of six family slave-trading consortiums.

10. Information on these points of slave disembarkation is located in AHPM, Esclavos, Bozales, leg. 21. This is an extremely rich legajo, and notices of slave smuggling from the points discussed above are numerous. See, for example, exp. 29a, which describes a slave landing at Canimar in 1842: "he tenido noticia que por el río de Canimar se hayan introducido negros de Africa . . . por las lanchas que entran de noche en el río para transportar azúcar de los almacenes de Canimar" (I have had notices that slaves from Africa have been introduced through the Canimar River . . . by means of barges that enter the river during the night to transport sugar from the warehouses on the Canimar).

11. AHPM, Esclavos, Bozales, leg. 21, exp. 93, "Comunicaciones sobre desembarco de bozales organizado por la Sociedad Noriega, Olmo y Compañía frustrado por las autoridades."

12. AHPM, Esclavos, Bozales, leg. 21, exp. 95.

13. AHPM, Esclavos, Bozales, leg. 21, exp. 107.

14. AHPM, Esclavos, Bozales, leg. 21, exp. 144.

15. In 1853 a circular was sent to Matanzas noting: "Este gobierno tiene suficientes datos para estar convencido de que los que se ocupan en el reprovada tráfico de negros no pueden realizar los desembarcos sin contar anticipadamente o con la apatiá or con la aquiescencia de las autoridades de las jurisdicciones en que quieren verificarlos" (This government has sufficient data to be convinced that those who engage in the banned slave trade cannot effect successful landings without the prior acquiescence or apathy of officials in the jurisdictions where these landings take place). AHPM, Esclavos, Bozales, leg. 21, exp. 54.

16. In June 1857 a communiqué was sent from Havana to the governor of Matanzas listing the principal slave traders of Matanzas. These included the following:

José Carbó	Sres. Amezaga Arenas y Compa.
Félix Cabarroca	Bartolomé Casañas
Francisco Abally	Pablo Hernández
José N. Tolosa	Fidel Juarnaba
Esteban Centeno	Cosme de la Torriente
Juan Sentelles	Salvador Baró
José Baró	Bartolomé Rodríguez
Joaquín Andricaín y dos hermanos	H. Rosiguol
Manuel Aguabella	Joaquín Ferrer
Juan Soler y sus dos hermanos	Juan Capó y su sobrino
José Magarolas	José el Mallorquín

Incredibly, Julián de Zulueta, the most notorious of them all, was omitted from the list.

See AHPM, Esclavos, Bozales, leg. 21, exp. 90, "Comunicación al Gobernador de Matanzas adjuntado relación de individuos que, según noticias confidenciales pueden dedicarse al tráfico de bozales."

17. For the statistics on slave seizures along the Cuban coast from 1824 through

1866, see AHN, Ultramar, Cuba, Esclavitud, leg. 3549, exp. 181, "Estado de las expediciones de negros bozales capturados en las costas de la Ysla de Cuba."

In addition, between 1819 and 1860, 165 Spanish ships bound for Cuba with 45,191 slaves were seized off the African coast by British patrols, and their captains and crews were judged before the Mixed Court of Sierra Leone. See AHN, Ultramar, Cuba, Esclavitud, leg. 3547, exp. 32, 33.

18. The most recent estimates of slave imports to Cuba, published by David Eltis, list 457,700 slaves imported between 1824 and 1866. See Eltis "The Nineteenth-Century Transatlantic Slave Trade: An Annual Time Series of Imports into the Americas Broken Down by Region," *Hispanic American Historical Review* 67:1 (1987), pp. 109–138. Also see David R. Murray, "Statistics of the Slave Trade to Cuba, 1790–1867," *Journal of Latin American Studies* 3:2 (November 1971), pp. 131–149.

19. The best discussion of the emancipados is to be found in Murray, *Odious Commerce*, chap. 13 ("A New Class of Slaves"), pp. 271–297.

20. See AHN, Ultramar, Cuba, Esclavitud, leg. 3549 (no exp. no.), for a list of *patronos* contracting emancipados.

21. Unless otherwise noted, data for slave sales included in the text, tables, and figures have been based on the following sources: ANC, PN, Matanzas, Joaquín de la Fuente, 1840; ANC, PN, Matanzas, Manuel Morales, 1843; ANC, PN, Matanzas, Manuel Morales, 1846; ANC, PN, Manuel Morales, 1850; ANC, PN, Matanzas, Manuel Morales, 1854; ANC, PN, Matanzas, Clemente Mihoura, 1857; ANC, PN, Matanzas, Clemente Mihoura, 1860; ANC, PN, Matanzas, Manuel Padrón, 1865; ANC, PN, Matanzas, Manuel del Portillo, 1870; ANC, PN, Matanzas, Manuel del Portillo, 1875; AHPM, PN, Colón, Manuel Vega Lavarría, 1863, 1864, 1867, 1870, 1872, 1875.

All values were listed in pesos. The 1875 data, however, were listed in "billetes" (paper money) or "oro" (gold). In order to finance the Spanish military during the Ten Years' War (1868–1878), the Banco Español de la Habana began printing paper money in the early 1870s, which resulted in rampant inflation by the middle of the decade. For 1875 I have determined that the value of billetes was half that of gold; 2 pesos in billetes were worth 1 peso in gold. This was done by separately analyzing transactions in each type of currency. The mean prices for different categories of slaves (males, females, Africans, creoles, various age groups) were compared by type of currency utilized. In almost every category the value rate was 2 pesos in paper for every 1 peso in gold. Thus, for the 1875 mean prices, billetes have been converted to gold at the 2:1 rate. It should be noted that since specific age data are unavailable for the 1840s, trends can be indicated only by the average price of all slaves by sex and origin. Much of this has appeared in Laird W. Bergad, "Slave Prices in Cuba, 1840–1875," *Hispanic American Historical Review* 67:4 (1987), pp. 631–655.

22. Sugar production increased from 205,608 to 397,713 metric tons between 1846 and 1854 (93.4 percent). See Moreno Fraginals, *El ingenio*, vol. 3, p. 36. This expansion was largely a result of the founding of new mills and the planting of virgin land in sugarcane. For example, there were 9,150 caballerías of land cultivated in 1846, but 15,877 in 1862 (73.5 percent). See Cuba, Gobernador y Capitán General,

Cuadro estadístico . . . 1846, pp. 41–42; and Cuba, Centro de Estadística, *Noticias estadísticas . . . 1862*, "Estadística territorial. Caballerías de tierra."

23. See Eltis, "The Nineteenth-Century Transatlantic Slave Trade," pp. 122–123; and Murray, *Odious Commerce*, p. 244, who lists slightly lower statistics. This decline in imports reflects low levels of demand on the Cuban slave market because of high imports during the 1830s.

24. Prices peaked later in Colón because almost all slaves in this jurisdicción were employed on ingenios where the demand for slaves continued even after the Moret Law was decreed in 1870. In Matanzas, a large portion of the slave population lived in the city or on other types of farms where demand for labor was not so strong.

In 1876, for example, 94 percent of Colón's slaves lived on sugar estates. See ANC, Gobierno General, leg. 270, no. 13563, "Padrón general de fincas rústicas de este distrito, año de 1875 a 1876." In 1862, when similar data are available for Matanzas, 64.1 percent of all slaves lived on ingenios. See Cuba, Centro de Estadística, *Noticias estadísticas . . . 1862*, "Distribución de la población en los pueblos y fincas de la isla."

It should be noted that Manuel Moreno Fraginals, Herbert S. Klein, and Stanley Engerman ("The Level and Structure of Slave Prices on Cuban Plantations in the Mid-Nineteenth Century: Some Comparative Perspectives," *American Historical Review* 88:5 [1983], pp. 1201–1218), found that prices for prime-age slaves peaked in 1859 (see p. 1207). My findings for prime-age slaves (to be discussed below) confirm this for Matanzas, but in Colón prices for this category peaked in 1870.

25. See Eltis, "The Nineteenth-Century Transatlantic Slave Trade," pp. 122–123. Murray, *Odious Commerce*, p. 244, offers higher figures based on the British consular estimates that have been revised downward by Eltis. For 1859, when British consuls estimated 30,473 African imports (Murray), Eltis lists 25,000; for 1860 Murray cites 24,895 imports, while Eltis lists 21,000; for 1861 Murray cites 23,964 imports, Eltis a substantially lower 13,800.

26. David Eltis found an absence of slave price rises on the African coast. See his *Economic Growth and the Ending of the Transatlantic Slave Trade* (New York: Oxford University Press, 1987), app. 3, fig. 1. This is supported by E. Phillip LeVeen, "A Quantitative Analysis of the Impact of British Suppression Policies on the Volume of the Nineteenth-Century Atlantic Slave Trade," in Stanley L. Engerman and Eugene Genovese, eds., *Race and Slavery in the Western Hemisphere: Quantitative Studies* (Princeton: Princeton Univeristy Press, 1975), pp. 51–81, who found that slave prices in Africa declined between 1820 and 1860. However, LeVeen (p. 56) found a considerable rise in the shipping and distribution costs of the Cuban trade during the 1850s and 1860s. I thank Professor Eltis for pointing out the role of increased bribes in pushing up slave costs.

27. Murray, *Odious Commerce*, pp. 304–305. Also see Corwin, *Spain and the Abolition of Slavery in Cuba*, pp. 129–151.

28. For sugar prices, see the respective years of *La Aurora de Matanzas* (also published under the name *La Aurora* or *Aurora de Yumurí*). The Biblioteca Gener y del Monte, in the town of Matanzas, has a complete collection of this valuable provincial newspaper from 1828 through 1895. I thank Mirta Martínez of the library's "Fondos Raros y Valiosos" for helping me locate and examine these news-

papers. For monthly sugar prices in Havana from 1857 through 1866, see PRO, FO 72/1153.

29. Moreno Fraginals, *El ingenio*, vol. 3, pp. 36–37.

30. For example, Colón sugar planters experienced a 55.7 percent increase in income between 1865 and 1876, from 5,396,337 to 8,402,088 pesos. See ANC, Gobierno General, leg. 405, no. 19209, "Padrón de fincas rústicas de la jurisdicción de Colón, 1865"; and ANC, Gobierno General, leg. 270, no. 13563, "Padrón general de fincas rústicas de este distrito, año de 1875 a 1876." Data on income for Colón and Cárdenas are summarized in Laird W. Bergad, "Land Tenure, Slave Ownership, and Income Distribution in Nineteenth Century Cuba: Colón and Cárdenas, 1859–1876," *Social and Economic Studies* 37:1–2 (March–June 1988), pp. 301–340.

31. For a statistical look at Chinese labor in Cuba, see Juan Pérez de la Riva, *El barracón y otros ensayos* (Havana: Ed. de Ciencias Sociales, 1975), "Demografía de los culíes en Cuba (1853–1874)," pp. 469–508. For more general treatment, see Duvon C. Corbitt, *A Study of the Chinese in Cuba, 1847–1947* (Wilmore, Ky.: Asbury College, 1971); and Denise Helly, *Idéologie et ethnicité: Les Chinois Macao à Cuba: 1847–1886* (Montreal: Les Presses de l'Université de Montréal, 1979).

32. The construction of new sugar mills, and accompanying demand for slave labor, continued right through the Ten Years' War in Matanzas province. For example, in Colón the largest sugar-producing jurisdicción in Cuba, 33 new ingenios were constructed between 1865 and 1876, a 45.2 percent increase in the number of mills. *All* were based on slave labor in this late period in the history of Cuban slavery. See ANC, Gobierno General, leg. 405, no. 19209, "Padrón de fincas rústicas de la jurisdicción de Colón, 1865"; and ANC, Gobierno General, leg. 270, no. 13563, "Padrón general de fincas rústicas de este distrito, año de 1875 a 1876."

33. Although the ratio of creole to African slaves shifted in favor of more and more creoles over time, this should not be confused with the demographic increase of the Cuban slave population based on natural reproduction. Obviously Cuban slaves reproduced, but not at rates that would lead to a naturally expanding slave population. For data on the Cuban slave population increase, see Jack Ericson Eblen, "On the Natural Increase of Slave Populations: The Example of the Cuban Black Population, 1775–1900," in Engerman and Genovese, eds., *Race and Slavery in the Western Hemisphere*, pp. 211–247.

Even on plantations with large African-born slave populations, age-structure differentiations between Africans and creoles were sometimes extreme. For example, in 1854 in the Matanzas partido of Sabanilla, the ingenio San Juan owned 197 creoles and 503 Africans. The mean age of the Africans was 44 years, while the creoles had a mean age of 15.9 years. See AHPM, Gobierno Provincial, Esclavos, leg. 6 (no exp. no.).

Although global nineteenth-century census data do not include the national origins of the Cuban slave population, surviving manuscript slave-census data do include this information. For example, in Guanajayabo, a major sugar-producing partido of Cárdenas, 75.5 percent of the 2,107 slaves registered in 1871 were creoles. See AHPM, Gobierno Provincial, provisional leg. 60, exp. 1731, "Provincia Matanzas. Término mpal. de Guanajayabo. Cuaderno para tomar razón de las certificaciones espedidas por la central sobre derechos de patronato."

34. Another factor was the increased demand for slaves by the sugar sector. There is evidence that high prices and plantation demand induced the late 1860s and early 1870s transfer of slaves from non-sugar-sector slaveholders to ingenios. For example, in Colón 83 percent of all slaves lived on ingenios in 1859; 94 percent did so in 1876. See ANC, ME, leg. 4120, no. M, "Repartos municipales de la jurisdicción de Colón, 1859"; and ANC, Gobierno General, leg. 270, no. 13563, "Padrón general de fincas rústicas de este distrito, año de 1875 a 1876."

35. For example, in 1834, when age data are available in the Matanzas protocol records, 43 of 54 Africans sold (79.6 percent) were between the ages of fifteen and forty; of 28 creoles sold, 53.9 percent fell into this category; and 42.9 percent were younger than fifteen. See slave sales in ANC, PN, Matanzas, Joaquín de la Fuente, 1834.

36. See AHPM, Gobierno Provincial, provisional leg. 60, exp. 1731, "Provincia Matanzas. Término mpal. de Guanajayabo. Cuaderno para tomar razón de las certificaciones espedidas por la central sobre derechos de patronato."

37. The one exception was in 1864, when only 58 percent of all Colón slave sales were in this category. In 1870, 79.7 percent of all slaves marketed in Colón were between the ages of fifteen and forty.

38. It should be noted that the prices listed for African males and females in Matanzas are based on very few transactions. They are presented here not as authoritative data, but because they are the only data available. Data on the other groups are more reliable, since they are based on a larger number of transactions.

The average slave prices presented here are significantly lower than the data presented by Moreno Fraginals, Klein, and Engerman in "The Level and Structure of Slave Prices on Cuban Plantations in the Mid-Nineteenth Century," p. 1207. Data are comparable for 1863. The average prices for 1863 presented here are 23.6 percent lower for creole males; 21.3 percent lower for creole females; 31.1 percent lower for African males; and 28.3 percent lower for African females.

Several explanations may account for these discrepancies. The first and most probable is that values presented for slaves in plantation assessments (the source material utilized by Moreno Fraginals, Klein, and Engerman) were inflated and did not reflect real market values. Motives for stating inflated prices were many, including fear of abolition and the thought of possible indemnification. Most slaves were also insured by various slave-life-insurance companies, such as José María Morales's La Protectora, Compañía General de Seguros Mutuos sobre la Vida de los Esclavos, which was founded in 1855. Thus, it was in a planter's interest to present high slave values. That slaves were assessed by "independent" assessors is of little importance, since they, like all Spanish officials, could be handsomely rewarded for presenting "correct" figures.

It is also possible that plantation slaves were generally more "seasoned" and thus worth more in the marketplace. Unfortunately, the data used to calculate average prices here do not indicate occupation or place of residence. It is therefore impossible to determine how many were plantation slaves. However, since more than 90 percent of all slaves in Colón during the 1860s lived on ingenios, it is very likely that Colón's slaves were destined for plantations. In addition, I doubt that the value of "seasoning" in an epoch of strong slave demand could account for 20-percent-plus higher values in each category. There is also the possibility that what planters considered to be the "value" of their slaves was inflated for many subjective reasons, including self-serving calculations of their own financial worth, and did not reflect the objective possibilities in the marketplace. In sum, I believe that the data presented here reflect the real prices for slaves on the Cuban slave market and are more reliable as a measure of slave value than plantation assessments.

39. See Scott, *Slave Emancipation in Cuba*, pp. 84–110, for a discussion of planter attempts to diversify labor forces.

40. This figure is derived from the data on Matanzas sugar ingenios listed in the sugar plantation census conducted in 1877. See "Noticias de las fincas azucareras en producción que existían en toda la isla de Cuba al comenzar el presupuesto de 1877–1878," *Revista Económica*, June 7, 1878, pp. 7–24. Much of this appears in Laird W. Bergad, "The Economic Viability of Sugar Production Based on Slave Labor in Matanzas, Cuba: 1859–1878," *Latin American Research Review* 24:1 (1989), pp. 95–113.

41. In the aftermath of the Ten Years' War and the final abolition of slavery, a period coinciding with a major decline in sugar prices on the international market, Cuban sugar production was substantially reorganized. The central factory emerged, refining cane but growing sugar only in small quantities. Cane for milling was largely provided by colonos, who specialized in growing cane but did not refine. The Cuban colonato was highly stratified: there were small-scale minifundia and large plantations. On the colonato, see the classic study by Ramiro Guerra y Sánchez, *Azúcar y población en las antillas* (Havana: Ed. de Ciencias Sociales, 1976).

42. So says the distinguished Cuban historian Manuel Moreno Fraginals, who emphasizes this position in *El ingenio* and in a series of articles, the most important of which are "El esclavo y la mecanización de los ingenios," *Bohemia*, June 13, 1969, pp. 98–99; and "Abolición o disintegración?" and "Plantaciones en el Caribe: el caso Cuba–Puerto Rico–Santo Domingo (1860–1940)," in Moreno Fraginals, *La historia como arma y otros estudios sobre esclavos, ingenios y plantaciones* (Barcelona: Ed. Crítica, 1983), pp. 50–55 and 56–117. A version of this last essay has appeared in English as "Plantations in the Caribbean: Cuba, Puerto Rico, and the Dominican Republic in the Late Nineteenth Century," in Moreno Fraginals, Frank Moya Pons, and Stanley L. Engerman, eds., *Between Slavery and Free Labor: The Spanish-Speaking Caribbean in the Nineteenth Century* (Baltimore: The Johns Hopkins University Press, 1985), pp. 3–22. For a more recent consideration of the theme, one that tempers his earlier views slightly, see "La esclavitud, a cien años del fin," *Revolución y Cultura*, no. 8 (Aug. 1986), pp. 2–11.

Fé Iglesias García varies her interpretation but also stresses the incompatibility of slave labor with the technological modernization of refining. See "The Development of Capitalism in Cuban Sugar Production, 1860–1900," in Moreno Fraginals, Moya Pons, and Engerman, eds., *Between Slavery and Free Labor*, pp. 54–76; "Formación del capitalismo en la producción de azúcar en Cuba (1860–1900)" (manuscript); and "Changes in Cane Cultivation in Cuba, 1860–1900" (paper presented at the Symposium on Caribbean Economic History, University of the West Indies, Jamaica, Nov. 7–8, 1986), published in *Social and Economic Studies* 37:1–2 (March–June 1988).

Rebecca Scott's *Slave Emancipation in Cuba* skillfully challenges this interpretation by examining the abolition process from a regional perspective within Cuba. Scott emphasizes the persistence of slavery in areas of intense sugar production after abolition began in 1870.

43. The data for Colón are to be found in ANC, ME, leg. 4120, no. M, "Repartos municipales de la jurisdicción de Colón, 1859"; ANC, Gobierno General, leg. 405, no. 19209, "Padrón de fincas rústicas de la jurisdicción de Colón, 1865"; and ANC, Gobierno General, leg. 270, no. 13563, "Padrón general de fincas rústicas de este distrito, año de 1875 a 1876."

The data for Cárdenas are in ANC, Gobierno General, leg. 945, no. 16724, "Padrón general de la riqueza rústica para regir en los años económicos de 1866 a 1867"; and ANC, Gobierno General, leg. 269, no. 13554, "Jurisdicción de Cárdenas. Padrón general de la riqueza rústica de esta ciudad y su jurisdicción formado para los años económicos de 1875 a 1876."

The 1877/78 sugar census is in "Noticias de las fincas azucareras en producción que existían en toda la isla de Cuba al comenzar el presupuesto de 1877–1878."

Unless otherwise indicated, all of the data and statistical tables presented below are derived from these sources.

44. "Refacción" contracts were the principal way that planters secured credit and supplies for their plantations at harvesttime. They were also the legal mechanism that tied planters to particular merchants for the marketing of sugar and molasses. These contracts included several important stipulations. First of all, merchants would supply the capital and supplies needed to maintain the ingenio. Included were salary disbursements for free workers; capital to purchase slaves if needed; food and clothing for the slave population; capital for the medical maintenance of the slave population; all types of supplies, from containers to hold processed sugar to such basic items as nails and lumber; and transportation services to move sugar from plantation to port (or the capital to pay for those services). Moreover, planters usually mortgaged a portion or all of their harvest to the merchant granting the "refacción" contract. They were forbidden to market their products to other merchant houses, but were usually paid the current price in port at the time of delivery. Warehousing fees, commissions on marketing, and transportation costs were deducted at this time.

The terms of these contracts are important to take into consideration, especially when the 1877/78 census is examined. That document listed "refacción" contract expenses for each plantation. Usually, 65 percent of gross income was deducted for "refacción" costs to determine net income, although in some cases 50 or 60 percent was deducted. The importance of this is that slave-maintenance costs were thus deducted from gross income, allowing us to factor those costs into the formula to determine net income per slave for 1877/78.

Unfortunately, the same formula used to calculate net income in 1878 cannot be applied to earlier years. To do so would be inappropriate, for it is important to stick closely to the archival source materials. In all of the documentary materials utilized for years prior to 1878 there is no mention of net income, nor is there any way to calculate it. The calculations on gross income presented here are accurate, especially with respect to documenting changes over time. While clearly net income data would be more desirable, these are simply not available for the years before 1878.

45. On inflation in the 1870s, see Fé Iglesias García, "Azúcar y crédito durante la segunda mitad del siglo xix en Cuba," *Santiago* no. 52 (1983), pp. 119–144.

46. For sugar prices in the middle of the 1859 zafra, see Biblioteca Gener y del Monte, Matanzas, *Aurora del Yumurí*, March 23, 1859; for 1878, see Biblioteca Nacional José Martí, *Gaceta de la Habana*, May 1, 1878.

Evidence that local-level sugar prices were quoted in gold rather than in paper money is contained in the invoices sent to U.S. importers of Cuban sugar. These invoices indicated prices in Cuban currency, but specifically noted that they were quoted in gold. See, for example, NYPL, Moses Taylor Collection, Individual Letters, 1870 (formerly boxes 86 and 123), invoice of Zaldo & Company to Moses Taylor, Jan. 1, 1870.

47. A fundamental problem in determining slave profitability is how to ascertain the ratio of productive, prime-age slaves to unproductive, very young and old slaves who contribute marginally to production. Unfortunately, data on the age structure of the slave population in these jurisdictions is lacking for the years under consideration.

48. Since calculations had to be made in order to determine the total work force for some years, clearly an unquantifiable margin of error exists in calculating income per worker. But even if an arbitrary margin of error as high as plus-or-minus 10 percent is used, it would not detract from the fundamental analyses outlined below.

The datum for Matanzas, 83.5 percent of all workers as slaves, is suspect. With the exception of Ceiba Mocha, Matanzas partidos did not report on rented or freed slaves. The only other category noted was Chinese contract laborers. Thus, the figure for slaves as a percentage of all workers was in all likelihood artificially inflated.

49. A large number of mills in Colón did not report information on their work forces for the 1877/78 census, while all mills reported income data. In order to calculate income per worker without statistical distortion, only those estates reporting data on their labor forces were utilized. They accounted for 70 of the 116 sugar ingenios.

50. In an economic report on the sugar industry sent by the British consul in Havana, Joséph Crawford, to Viscount Palmerston of the Foreign Office, on Jan. 28, 1848, Crawford stated that the average productive life of an individual slave was twenty years. He also noted a 5 percent yearly death rate among slave populations. Stanley Engerman has pointed out to me that these two statistics may not be compatible. Crawford made no attempt to explain this possible contradiction. See PRO, FO 72/748.

51. Although no data on income per worker are available for 1870, between 1865 and 1876 income per worker increased in Colón by 4.7 pesos/year, from 309.6 to 361.6 pesos. Thus, in the five years between 1865 and 1870 we can estimate an increase of 23.5 pesos, so that by 1870 income per worker was 333.1 pesos.

52. By 1876 the slave market had contracted for three basic reasons. First, supplies of new slaves ceased with the end of African imports. Second, since abolition had begun and other sources of labor en masse were not forthcoming to planters, slaves were zealously held on to rather than sold. Third, because of the drop in slave

prices, which was related to imminent emancipation rather than to conditions in the marketplace, slave values had declined well below the prices of previously purchased slaves, making marketing undesirable.

53. Estimates on profitability and costs were made by Juan Poey, owner of Ingenio Las Cañas, one of Cuba's largest mills in the early 1860s. He estimated a 2.5 percent depreciation of slave values (owing to death) and presented a detailed array of economic calculations that derived a final loss of 4.13 percent yearly on investment capital for an "average" ingenio cultivating 17 caballerías of cane with 132 workers. The figure of 7.7 workers/caballería is strikingly close to the estimates noted here. See Poey, *Informes presentados al excmo. Capitán general gob. superior civil de la isla de Cuba sobre el proyecto de colonización africana y al Illmo. Sr. intendente de Hacienda de la propia isla sobre derechos de los azúcares* (Madrid: Imp. D. A. Aurial, 1862), pp. 141–145.

However, these data must be viewed with caution, since one of Poey's purposes was to have Spain reduce taxes on sugar exports and imports and to garner support for his ill-fated project to import "free" African laborers. Planters were always complaining about losing money while they increased production, constructed lavish homes, and lived lives of luxury. Their printed testimonies on the internal economic dynamics of their estates cannot be used with confidence. Until detailed internal account books are located and scrutinized, rates of return on investments in slaves cannot be accurately ascertained.

54. See the accounts of Cosme de la Torriente's Ingenio La Reforma, from 1866 through 1871, in AHPM, Gobierno Provincial, Ingenios, leg. 3, no. 38; and those of Mauricio Alfonso's Ingenio la Vega, for 1874, in leg. 3, no. 37. Scott, in *Slave Emancipation in Cuba*, found wage rates in the late 1870s to be between 22 and 27 pesos monthly (p. 119).

55. For sugar prices, see the relevant issues of *Aurora de Yumurí* in the Biblioteca Gener y del Monte, Matanzas; and of the *Gaceta de la Habana* in the Biblioteca Nacional José Martí, Havana.

56. PRO, FO 72/748, letter of Jan. 25, 1848, from Crawford to Viscount Palmerston.

57. The 1852 farm census for Sabanilla is in AHPM, ME, Estadística, leg. 6, no. 116; for 1855, see leg. 8, no. 145. There were 20 sugar mills in 1852 and 24 in 1855.

58. AHPM, ME, Estadística, leg. 6, nos. 116, 118.

59. The most complete description of daily life at harvesttime on Cuban plantations is to be found in Moreno Fraginals, *El ingenio*, vol. 2, "La jornada de trabajo," pp. 29–38.

The great Cuban slave-poet, Juan Francisco Manzano (1797–1854), described the harvest in his poem "El Ingenio" as follows:

> Whoever spent a night on an estate
> In time of crop, and had endured of late
> Fatigue and toil, that amply might dispose
> A weary trav'ller to enjoy repose,
> And roused at midnight, heard the frightful bell,
> The dismal conch's loud blast at change of spell,
> The crack of whips, the hurried tramp of men,

The creaking mill, the driver's threats, and then
The sudden scream, the savage bloodhounds growl,
The shout prolonged, the "stokers" ceaseless howl;
All the dread noise that's requisite to keep
The jaded cattle and the slaves from sleep;
To rouse the weak, to down the women's cries,
And cause one deaf'ning uproar to uprise.
Whoever found this tumult at its height,
This Cuban's Babel's strife at dead of night;
Whoever listened to these horrid sounds,
And might not deem, hell had enlarged her bounds,
Made this plantation part of her domain,
And giv'n its owner, slaves, and lust of gain.

See Manzano, *The Life and Poems of a Cuban Slave* (Hamden, Conn.: Archon Books, 1981), p. 62.

Nicolás Tanco Armero, who traveled through Cuba in 1853 described the harvest as follows:

Las zafras empiezan por lo común en noviembre y duran hasta fines de mayo. Durante este largo período, la negrada trabaja diez y nueve horas diarias constantemente, contando apenas con unas cuatro horas de descanso. Los infelices esclavos, a manera del infortunado marinero, al toque de la campana y al chasquido del látigo, trabajan sin cesar, haciendo de la noche día, y sin tener minuto a su disposición para reposar sus fatigados miembros. [The sugar harvests generally begin in Nov. and last until the end of May. During this long period, the slave population works nineteen hours daily on a continual basis, with scarcely four hours of sleep. These unfortunate slaves, in the same way as an unfortunate sailor, at the ringing of the morning bell and the crack of the whip, work without stop, turning day into night without a moment at their disposition to rest their weary limbs].

See Nicolás Tanco Armero, "La isla de Cuba," in Juan Pérez de la Riva, ed., *La isla de Cuba en el siglo xix vista por los extranjeros* (Havana: Ed. de Ciencias Sociales, 1981), p. 121.

60. AHPM, ME, Estadística, leg. 8, no. 145, fols. 28–31.

61. PRO, FO 72/760, letter of Joséph Crawford, Jan. 3, 1849.

62. ANC, ME, leg. 4120, no. M, "Repartos municipales de la jurisdicción de Colón, 1859"; ANC, Gobierno General, leg. 405, no. 19209, "Padrón de fincas rústicas de la jurisdicción de Colón, 1865"; ANC, Gobierno General, leg. 270, no. 13563, "Padrón general de fincas rústicas de este distrito, año de 1875 a 1876."

63. For 1846, see Cuba, Cobernador y Capitán General, *Cuadro estadístico 1846*, pp. 71, 79; for 1862, see Cuba, Centro de Estadística, *Noticias estadísticas . . . 1862*, "Riqueza pecuaria."

64. For a description of changing settlement patterns within plantations, see Moreno Fraginals, *El ingenio*, vol. 2, pp. 67–75. For consideration of the barracón, see Juan Pérez de la Riva, "El barracón de ingenio en la época esclavista," in Pérez de la Riva, *El barracón y otros ensayos*, pp. 15–74.

65. The British consul wrote in 1875: "Negroes are now perfectly aware that the Cuban insurgents proclaimed their freedom, and the immediate abolition of slavery in 1868; thus their knowledge of the fact increases the danger." PRO, FO 72/1418, letter of March 17, 1875, from Graham Dunlop to the Foreign Office.

66. On many slaves fleeing Matanzas ingenios in the mid–1870s, see AHPM, Gobierno Provincial, Esclavos, leg. 20. In AHPM, Gobierno Provincial, Sublevaciones, leg. 11, there are numerous examples of slaves refusing to work, attacking abusive mayorales fleeing en masse from plantations, and generally sabotaging production by active resistance which, however, fell short of armed rebellion. Also see Scott, *Slave Emancipation in Cuba*, chap. 4 ("Adaptation, 1870–1879") and chap. 5 ("Challenge"), pp. 84–124.

67. See AHPM, Anotaduría de Hipotecas, Cárdenas, Fincas, libro 27, fols. 117–134, for a complete inventory of Ingenio Victoria in Guamutas which paid 20 pesos monthly to "varios esclavos acomodados" (various resident slaves).

68. The data for Matanzas and Colón were derived from the following sources: ANC, PN, Matanzas, Joaquín de la Fuente, 1840; ANC, PN, Matanzas, Manuel Morales, 1843; ANC, PN, Matanzas, Manuel Morales, 1846; ANC, PN, Manuel Morales, 1850; ANC, PN, Matanzas, Manuel Morales, 1854; ANC, PN, Matanzas, Clemente Mihoura, 1857; ANC, PN, Matanzas, Clemente Mihoura, 1860; ANC, PN, Matanzas, Manuel Padrón, 1865; ANC, PN, Matanzas, Manuel del Portillo, 1870; ANC, PN, Matanzas, Manuel del Portillo, 1875; AHPM, PN, Colón, Manuel Vega Lavarría, 1863, 1864, 1867, 1870, 1872, 1875.

69. Cuba, Gobernador y Capitanía General, *Cuadro estadístico . . . 1846*, table between pp. 41 and 42. This includes data from the partido of Alacranes and the jurisdictions of Matanzas and Cárdenas. Also see Cuba, Centro de Estadística, *Noticias estadísticas . . . 1862*, "Partidos pedaneos, con expresión de los cuartones que cada uno contiene y la particular de cada pueblo aldea y caserío que se halla en ella."

70. For extensive documentation on Matanzas cimarrones in the early nineteenth century, see AHPM, Gobierno Provincial, Cimarrones, leg. 12.

In 1829 a palenque of 300 cimarrones was reported near Nueva Florida, and in July 1830 notices were given of the "organización de una batida contra crecido número de cimarrones apalencados en el monte situado en el Bermejal" and of "rancherías organizadas para capturar 50 negros cimarrones entre los montes de Mocha y Aguacate" ("organization of an expedition against the growing number of maroons living in the mountains near Bermejal" and of "organized missions of slave hunters to capture 50 maroons in the mountains between Mocha and Aguacate"). See above leg., nos. 26, 29, 30.

In 1832 Corral Nuevo authorities noted having found "frente al ingenio Galindo un palenque de 21 ranchos donde capturaron 7 negros" as well as a "palenque de 80 negros en el Espinal junto al ingenio Cuatro Pasos" ("a maroon community of 80 slaves in Espinal adjacent to the Cuatro Pasos sugar mill"). See AHPM, Gobierno Provincial, Sublevaciones, leg. 7, nos. 6 and 7.

71. See Fernando Ortíz, *Hampa afro-cubana. Los negros esclavos* (Havana: Revista Bimestre Cubana, 1916), p. 432, for a brief account of these revolts.

72. Turnbull's antislavery diatribe, *Travels in the West: Cuba with Notices of Porto Rico and the Slave Trade* (London: Longman, 1840), was scorned in Havana.

73. David R. Murray gives a detailed account of Turnbull's activities in Cuba and the Spanish reaction, in *Odious Commerce*, chap. 8 ("The Turnbull Affair"), pp. 133–158.

74. See Murray, *Odious Commerce*, pp. 161–162, for the contradictory reports on this incident by the Spanish Captain General Valdés and by Turnbull, who reported on it to the British Foreign Office. Today the "Palacio Aldama" houses the Cuban Institute of History.

75. The March 1843 rebellion is described in detail by Joseph Crawford in his letter of Apr. 18, 1843, to the Earl of Aberdeen (PRO, FO 72/634, pp. 59–60). José María Morales also described the revolt in a letter to Henry Coit of Apr. 1, 1843 (NYPL, Moses Taylor Collection, case B, drawers 3 and 4, box 7).

76. On José Dolores, see AHPM, Gobierno Provincial, Sublevaciones, leg. 7, nos. 24, 25, 28, 29, 30, 32, 34. I thank Saúl Vento, the former director (now retired) of the Archivo Histórico Provincial de Matanzas, for pointing out the activities of José Dolores which are discussed in his pamphlet *Las rebeldías de esclavos en Matanzas* (Matanzas: Filial del Instituto de Historia del Partido Comunista de Cuba en la Provincia de Matanzas, 1976).

77. For the best summary of the different views, see Murray, *Odious Commerce*, chap. 9 ("The Escalera Conspiracy"), pp. 159–180. For other versions, see Franklin W. Knight, *Slave Society in Cuba during the Nineteenth Century* (Madison: University of Wisconsin Press, 1970), who argues that it had "no foundation in fact" (p. 71); Gwendolyn Hall, *Social Control in Slave Plantation Societies: A Comparison of Saint Domingue and Cuba* (Baltimore: The Johns Hopkins University Press, 1971), who argues that it was real (p. 57); and Corwin, *Spain and the Abolition of Slavery in Cuba*, who is convinced of its veracity. All Cuban historians who mention the revolt are absolutely certain that a conspiracy was in preparation. See Ortíz, *Los negros esclavos* as an example.

For a full-scale study of the uprising, see Robert L. Paquette, *Sugar Is Made with Blood: The Conspiracy of La Escalera and the Conflict between Empires over Slavery in Cuba* (Middletown, Conn.: Wesleyan University Press, 1988). Paquette, unfortunately, was denied permission to work in Cuban archives.

78. For complaints of British citizens jailed, see PRO, FO 72/664, pp. 154–171.

79. One prominent case involved the U.S. machinist Christopher Boone, who was employed on Ingenio Atrevido. On February 19, 1844, Boone was arrested and sent to the Andrea estate, where he was locked in the slave barracón for two days. He was then tied up, bound to a horse, and sent to Matanzas, some forty miles away. There he was locked in solitary confinement for fourteen days without being charged. He was finally freed through the intervention of the U.S. consul and subsequently wrote repeated letters to President John Tyler protesting his treatment. See USNA, DUSCM, 1820–1899, roll 4, vol. 4, Jan. 1, 1844–Dec. 7, 1850, letter of J. M. Rodney, Apr. 8, 1844.

80. Phinney's letter to Crawford, written on June 29, 1844, is located in PRO, FO 72/664, pp. 215–219^v.

The U.S. vice-consul in Cárdenas wrote on April 1, 1844, that "an alarming and extensive servile insurrection has just been discovered in this neighborhood and many persons have been implicated black and white." He also noted the involvement of many U.S. citizens, the widespread arrest of ingenio mechanics on the basis of hearsay, and the fact that they were sent off to jail and placed in stocks without apparent reason. See USNA, DUSCC, 1843–1845, roll 1 (vol. 20 of Havana Dispatches), June 10, 1843–June 4, 1845.

81. USNA, DUSCM, 1820–1899, roll 4, vol. 4, Jan. 1, 1844–Dec. 7, 1850, letter of J. M. Rodney, June 4, 1844.

82. See AHPM, Gobierno Provincial, Cimarrones, leg. 12.

83. See AHPM, Gobierno Provincial, Sublevaciones, leg. 11.

Chapter 13

1. The *memorias* of the Real Consulado in the 1790s were dominated by the fear of slave revolt and the need to maintain racial equilibrium by encouraging white immigration to Cuba. See Duvon C. Corbitt, "Immigration in Cuba," *Hispanic American Historical Review* 22:2 (1942), pp. 289–290.

2. See Heinrich Friedlaender, *Historia económica de Cuba* (Havana: Ed. de Ciencias Sociales, 1978), vol. 1, pp. 187–189; and Levi Marrero, *Cuba: economía y sociedad* (Madrid: Ed Playor, 1984), vol. 10, pp. 34–39. This project was resurrected in a slightly different form by the Conde de Pozos Dulces, Francisco de Frías Jacott in the 1850s, similarly without success.

3. Rebecca Scott, in *Slave Emancipation in Cuba: The Transition to Free Labor, 1860–1899* (Princeton: Princeton University Press, 1985), has skillfully discussed the adaptation of planters to abolition and the emergence of a mosaic of labor systems during the 1870s (pp. 84–110).

4. The notarial archives of Matanzas, Colón, and Cárdenas are filled with records of land purchases by smallholders even in the late 1860s. See for example, AHPM, PN, Manuel Vega Lavarría, 1867, Indice, on the parcelization of Hacienda Amarillas in 1867, where land was sold for as little as 250 pesos/caballería.

5. PRO, FO 72/748, letter of Crawford to Palmerston, Jan. 25, 1848.

6. AHPM, Gobierno Provincial, Ingenios, leg. 2, no. 23, fol. 8.

7. See the accounts listed in AHPM, Gobierno Provincial, Ingenios, leg. 7, no. 108, "Comunicaciones referentes a salarios de obreros azucareros"; and leg. 2, no. 23, fol. 8, the accounts of "Ingenio La Isabel de los herederos del Sr. D. Cosme de la Torriente."

8. ANC, PN, La Habana, Juan de Entralgo, 1844, fols. 583–584. For an excellent study of labor on Cuban railroad lines, see Oscár Zanetti Lecuono, "Esclavitud i treball lliure. El problema laboral dels ferrocarrils cubans, 1837–1867," *L'Avenc*, no. 101 (January 1987), pp. 17–23. I thank Rebecca Scott for sending me a copy of this article.

9. See, for example, the elaborate plan drawn up by the Junta de Fomento in the aftermath of La Escalera to promote white immigration by offering planters a series of awards for the use of immigrant labor on sugar ingenios. This is discussed in Friedlaender, *Historia económica de Cuba*, vol. 1, p. 186.

For later attempts, see Urbano Feijoo Sotomayor, *Isla de Cuba. Inmigración de trabajadores españoles* (Havana: Imp. de Eleizegui, 1853), who was intent on bringing laborers from his native Galicia to rural Cuba.

10. On the Chinese in Cuba, see Juan Pérez de la Riva, *El barracón y otros ensayos* (Havana: Ed. de Ciencias Sociales, 1975), "Demografía de los culíes en Cuba (1853–1874)," pp. 469–508; "La situación legal del culí en Cuba," pp. 206–246; and "Aspectos económicos del tráfico de culíes chinos a Cuba 1853–1874," pp. 255–281. Also: Duvon C. Corbitt, *A Study of the Chinese in Cuba, 1847–1947* (Wilmore, Ky.: Asbury College, 1971); Denise Helly, *Idéologie et ethnicité: Les Chinois Macao à Cuba: 1847–1886* (Montreal: Les Presses de l'Université de Montréal, 1979); *Report of the Commission Sent by China to Ascertain the Condition of Chinese Coolies in Cuba* (Shanghai: Imperial Maritime Customs Press, 1876); Juan Jiménez Pastrana, *Los chinos en las luchas por la liberación cubana (1847–1930)* (Havana: Instituto de Historia, 1963); Manuel Moreno Fraginals, "Migraciones asiáticos a Cuba: 1849–1959," in Moreno Fraginals, *La historia como arma y otros estudios sobre esclavos, ingenios y plantaciones* (Barcelona: Ed. Crítica, 1983), pp. 118–144; and Marrero, *Cuba: economía y sociedad*, vol. 9, pp. 123–136.

11. For a complete statistical summary of the Chinese landing in Cuba between 1847 and 1873, see PRO, ZHCI/3831, P.6, report of the British Consulate General, Havana, Sept. 1, 1873. On slave imports, see David Eltis, "The Nineteenth-Century Transatlantic Slave Trade: An Annual Time Series of Imports into the Americas Broken Down by Region," *Hispanic American Historical Review* 67:1 (1987), pp. 122–123.

12. For a statistical recapitulation of the Chinese trade up to 1859, including data on importing firms, see Félix Erenchun, *Anales de la isla de Cuba. Diccionario administrativo, económico, estadístico, y legislativo* (Havana: Imp. de la Antilla, 1858), Año de 1856, B-E, pp. 1329–1334.

13. For the participation of Zulueta's La Alianza, see *Memoria de La Alianza. Compañía de Crédito y Seguros* (Havana: n.p., 1866).

14. See AHPM, Gobierno Provincial, Político Militar, Negociado de Colonización, which has numerous Chinese colono contracts. The following clauses were standard in the contracts effected by Joaquín Pedroso:

> Me comprometo a trabajar en la isla de Cuba a las órdenes de dichos señores o de cualquiera otra persona a quien traspasen este contrato, para lo cual doy mi consentimiento. . . . Las horas de trabajo me serán fijadas por el patrono a cuyas órdenes se me ponga, y dependerá del género de trabajos en que me ocupe. En todo caso, cada 24 horas se me deberá conceder cierto tiempo para descansar; y ademas, el preciso para mis comidas el cual se arreglará tomando por norma el que se acostumbra dar par este objeto a los demas trabajadores asalariados en Cuba [I promise to work on the island of Cuba at the orders of said men or any other person to whom they transfer this contract, a condition to which I give my consent. . . . The hours of labor will be fixed by the contractor, at whose orders I place myself, and these hours will depend on the type of work in which I will be employed. In any case, each 24 hours I should be conceded a certain time to rest; and, additionally, my dietary needs will be arranged taking into consideration those conditions which are the custom for salaried workers in Cuba].

These clauses were repeated in Chinese.

15. Cuba, Centro de Estadística, *Noticias estadísticas de la isla de Cuba en 1862*

(Havana: Imp. del Gobierno, Capitanía General y Real Hacienda, 1864), "Censo de población según el cuadro general de la comisión ejecutiva de 1861," p. 1; and Fé Iglesias García, "El censo cubano de 1877 y sus diferentes versiones," *Santiago*, no. 34 (June 1979), pp. 198, 212.

16. ANC, ME, leg. 4120, no. M, "Repartimientos municipales de las jurisdicciones de Colón, 1859."

17. ANC, Gobierno General, 269/13554.

18. "Noticias de las fincas azucareras en producción que existían en toda la isla de Cuba al comenzar el presupuesto de 1877–1878," *Revista Económica*, June 7, 1878, pp. 7–24.

19. PRO, ZHCI/3831, letter of Crawford to Earl of Granville, Sept. 3, 1878.

20. See PRO, FO 72/1013, pp. 212^v–213^v, letter of Charles Rebello, British vice-consul at Cárdenas, Nov. 1, 1861; and FO 78/878.

21. See AHPM, Gobierno Provincial Colonial, provisional leg. 61, exp. 1787, "Jurisdicción de Matanzas. Partido de Alacranes. Padrón de asiáticos prófugos. Feb. 29, 1872," which lists 148 runaways in the month of February alone.

22. NYPL, Moses Taylor Collection, Cuban Revolution, box 1, letter of May 12, 1876.

23. The fantasy of importing nominally free African labor to Cuba in order to avoid the crusading British was first developed in the late 1850s. See José Suárez Argudín, *Proyecto de inmigración africana. Para las islas de Cuba y Puerto Rico y el imperio del Brasil. Presentado a los respectivos gobiernos por los Sres. Suárez Argudín, Cunha Reis y Perdones* (Havana: Imp. La Habanera, 1860).

The 1873 plan was detailed in a report to the British Foreign Office in a letter of Aug. 4, 1873, from Juan Carbonell y Martí. The Earl of Granville reported in a letter of October 3, 1878, that this scheme, "if carried into effect, would, in my opinion be tantamount to a renewel of the Slave Trade on the West Coast of Africa, as it would be impossible to procure labourers except by purchasing them as slaves from the native Chiefs on the coast" (PRO, ZHCI/3831).

24. PRO, ZHCI/4108, letter of Consul General Cowner to the Earl of Derby, May 8, 1877.

25. See Fé Iglesias García, "The Development of Capitalism in Cuban Sugar Production, 1860–1900," in Manuel Moreno Fraginals, Frank Moya Pons, and Stanley L. Engerman, eds., *Between Slavery and Free Labor: The Spanish-Speaking Caribbean in the Nineteenth Century* (Baltimore: The Johns Hopkins University Press, 1985), pp. 65–66.

26. AHPM, Gobierno Provincial, provisional leg. 76, exp. 2878.

27. ANC, Gobierno General, 269/13554.

28. See Marrero, *Cuba: economía y sociedad*, vol. 10, pp. 252–253.

29. This is discussed by Scott, *Slave Emancipation in Cuba*, pp. 208–212. The classic study of the Cuban colonato is Ramiro Guerra y Sánchez, *Azúcar y población en las Antillas* (Havana: Ed. de Ciencias Sociales, 1976).

30. AHPM, Anotaduría de Hipotecas, Cárdenas, libro 30, Fincas, no. 18, fols. 32–34.

31. AHPM, PN, Manuel Vega Lavarría, 1870, Colón, contrato 64, and fol. 498^v.

Chapter 14

1. Different versions of the 1877 census were published by Cuban authorities, and these have been discussed in Fé Iglesias García, "El censo cubano de 1877 y sus diferentes versiones," *Santiago*, no. 34 (June 1979), pp. 167–214. She concludes that the version published in 1881 and 1882 by the *Boletín Oficial de Hacienda* is the most reliable; it lists 250,728 inhabitants in the province. The published census itself lists 278,991 inhabitants present and another 9,877 residents either absent for various reasons or living there as transients, a total population of 288,868. There is no way to verify the accuracy of any version. For the purposes of this section I rely on Iglesias's estimates, since her knowledge of the historical sources available for the study of nineteenth-century Cuba is unparalleled.

The 1887 data are contained in the national census of Spain for that year and have not been questioned by scholars. See Spain, Instituto Geográfico y Estadístico, *Censo de la población de España según el empadronamiento hecho en 31 de diciembre de 1887* (Madrid: Imp. de la Dirección General del Instituto Geográfico y Estadístico, 1892), vol. 1, pp. 764–767.

The next published census was the one carried out under the auspices of the U.S. War Department in 1899, but it does not list provincial populations just before the outbreak of the war for independence. However, I have located a manuscript census (carried out in 1894) in the Matanzas municipal archives. Unfortunately, there is no disaggregation of population by race or sex, and only total population statistics are available by municipal district. See AHPM, ME, Estadística, leg. 9, no. 171, fol. 2.

2. The rural partidos of Matanzas included in these calculations are Canasí, Guamacaro, Santa Ana, Sabanilla, and Cabezas; for Cárdenas, they are Lagunillas, Cimarrones, Guanajayabo, and Guamutas; and for Colón they are Jovellanos, Roque, San José de los Ramos, Macuriges, Macagua, and Cuevitas.

3. In 1880 the zafra declined to 618,654 metric tons, and by 1881 it stood at 580,894 tons, which was smaller than every harvest during the Ten Years' War except that of 1877, when 516,268 metric tons were produced. These data are from Manuel Moreno Fraginals, *El ingenio. Complejo económico social cubano del azúcar* (Havana: Ed. de Ciencias Sociales, 1978), vol. 3, p. 37.

4. AHPM, ME, Estadística, leg. 9, no. 166, fol. 2. These mills included the ingenios San Rafael, Feliz, Jicarita, Atrevido, Armonía, San Francisco, Juan Bautista, Mercedes, Reglita, Pura y Limpia, and José Montelo.

5. See Rebecca Scott, *Slave Emancipation in Cuba: The Transition to Free Labor, 1860–1899* (Princeton: Princeton University Press, 1985), pp. 127–140, for the most complete discussion of the patronato.

6. There were 70,849 slaves in Matanzas in 1877 and 38,620 slaves and patrocinados in 1883, an overall decline of more than 45 percent. See Scott, *Slave Emancipation in Cuba*, p. 194, for these data.

7. The reports of U.S. and British consular agents emphasized this fact. As early as 1880 the U.S. consul in Matanzas, George Roosevelt wrote: "The negroes show already symptoms of restlessness and planters assert that it is impossible to get from them the same amount of labor as formerly. . . . The spirit of unrest and longing for change must continue and increase, and the effect will doubtless be seen in a diminished yield and in less careful cultivation." See USNA, DUSCM, roll no. 14,

letter of Dec. 31, 1880, George W. Roosevelt to John Hay, Assistant Secretary of State.

The British consul in Havana reported in 1883 that slaves, in spite of the patronato, "roam at will over the country," and he characterized remaining slaves as "uncontrolled." See PRO, FO 72/1656, letter of Apr. 20, 1883, from A. de C. Crow to the Foreign Office.

8. See Jean Stubbs, *Tobacco on the Periphery: A Case Study in Cuban Labour History, 1860–1958* (Cambridge: Cambridge University Press, 1985), pp. 85–93.

9. USNA, DUSCM, roll no. 15, letter of March 5, 1886, Frank H. Pierce to James D. Porter.

10. USNA, DUSCM, roll no. 14, letters of Jul. 3, 1883, and Oct. 24, 1883, David Vicker to John Davis.

11. USNA, DUSCM, roll no. 14, letter of Oct. 24, 1883, David Vicker to John Davis. He wrote: "Merchants . . . heavily involved through previous failures of planters and knowing the condition of the country have refused to give more credit."

12. USNA, DUSCM, roll no. 14, letter of Oct. 24, 1883, David Vicker to John Davis.

13. A detailed account of taxes paid by mill owners is to be found in USNA, DUSCM, roll no. 15, letter of Aug. 11, 1887, Frank H. Pierce to James D. Porter.

Chapter 15

1. The widespread misconception that North American capital moved decisively into Cuba during this period is absolutely erroneous for Matanzas. Although Cuban-born entrepreneurs who had acquired U.S. citizenship were operating in the province during the 1880s and 1890s, not one mill or "central" came under the ownership of North American interests; nor is there any evidence that any U.S.-owned commercial houses supplied credit to the provincial economy. Matanzas sugar was marketed almost exclusively to the United States, but there was little direct U.S. investment until after the war. For the continuation of these mistaken generalizations, even in the most recent works, see the otherwise excellent political study of the period by Louis A. Pérez, Jr., *Cuba between Empires, 1878–1902* (Pittsburgh: University of Pittsburgh Press, 1983), pp. 18–31; repeated in Louis A. Pérez, Jr., "Vagrants, Beggars, and Bandits: Social Origins of Cuban Separatism, 1878–1895," *American Historical Review* 90:5 (Dec. 1985), pp. 1092–1121.

2. The detailed accounts of Ingenio Isabel in the refacción contract of Dec. 5, 1885 (AHPM, PN, Colón, Manuel Vega Lavarría, 1885, fols. 910–953) indicate wage levels.

3. For these and many more examples of the total breakdown of plantation discipline in the 1880s, see AHPM, Gobierno Provincial, Sublevaciones, leg. 11, nos. 10–36. Also see AHPM, Gobierno Provincial, provisional leg. 61, exp. 1766, for the flight of patrocinados.

4. See, for example, the maps of these settlement colonias contained in AHN, Ultramar, Fomento, leg. 173, "Relación de las colonias agrícolas de inmigrantes y número de familias que las pueblan." These colonias were located in Puerto Príncipe and Santiago de Cuba and were created by the colonial government on land largely

donated for the purpose of recruiting immigrants from Spain. On the Xagua Bay colony, see Levi Marrero, *Cuba: Economía y sociedad* (Madrid: Ed. Playor, 1983), vol. 9, p. 229.

5. United States War Department, Office of the Director of the Census of Cuba, *Report on the Census of Cuba, 1899* (Washington, D.C.: Government Printing Office, 1900), p. 560.

6. AHPM, Registro no. 1 del Notario Comercial de esta Plaza, Dn. Pedro G. Magriña y Olano, Años 1892, 1893, 1894, 1895, fols. 3–4.

7. Concerning these agreements, see the elaborate testimony of Patricio Ponce de León on the prewar economics of sugar production, contained in USNA, RG 76, entry 352, Spanish Treaty Claims Commission, case no. 476.

8. USNA, RG 76, entry 352, Spanish Treaty Claims Commission, case no. 476.

9. USNA, RG 76, entry 352, Spanish Treaty Claims Commission, case no. 100.

10. AHPM, PN, Colón, Manuel Vega Lavarría, 1880, fols. 7–10.

11. AHPM, PN, Colón, Manuel Vega Lavarría, 1892, fols. 1655–1659.

12. See León Crespo's last will and testament in ANC, PN, Bonifacio Domínguez, Matanzas, 1885, fols. 600–628. For his death notice, see Biblioteca Gener y del Monte, Matanzas, *Aurora del Yumurí*, May 4, 1885.

13. ANC, PN, Juan Bolet y Durán, Matanzas, 1894, fols. 551–560, 820–846.

14. The use of public railways is considered in a manuscript by Fé Iglesias García, "Formación del capitalismo en la producción de azúcar en Cuba (1860–1900)"; and in Hugh Thomas, *Cuba: The Pursuit of Freedom* (New York: Harper & Row, 1970), pp. 273–274. According to Thomas, the price of steel rail dropped from 166 dollars per hundred pounds in 1867 to below 30 dollars in the 1880s.

15. See Junta de Agricultura, Comercio e Industria de la Provincia de Matanzas, *Memoria descriptiva de los trabajos realizados durante el año fiscal de 1900 a 1901* (Matanzas: Lib. La Pluma de Oro, 1901), pp. 42–61, for a list of all the mills in Matanzas and the types of equipment they used. This is to be found in USNA, RG 140, Military Government of Cuba, Letters Received, 1901, box 207, no. 4532.

16. See Rebecca Scott, *Slave Emancipation in Cuba: The Transition to Free Labor, 1860–1899* (Princeton: Princeton University Press, 1985), pp. 227–254, for a discussion of these problems and of the options available to former slaves.

17. See United States War Department, *Report on the Census of Cuba, 1899*, p. 195. The Matanzas black and mulatto population declined from 117,538 in 1887 to 80,321 in 1899. Mortality preceding and during the war will be discussed in Chapter 17.

18. Ibid., pp. 556–557, 560.

19. USNA, DUSCM, letter of Jan. 3, 1881, George W. Roosevelt to John Hay, Assistant Secretary of State.

20. United States War Department, *Report on the Census of Cuba, 1899*, p. 478.

21. P. M. Beal, who ran this estate (owned by Edwin Atkins) reported that the best field workers were black women, whom he preferred to all others because of their reliability. They were paid the same wages as men. Native blacks and whites performed field labor while immigrants worked loading cane cars, plowing, and ditching, as well as on roads and railroads. See ibid., pp. 529–530. For a description

of life on plantations after abolition, see Esteban Montejo, *The Autobiography of a Runaway Slave* (New York: Vintage Books, 1973), pp. 63–171.

22. Data on Spanish migration were compiled by the Instituto Geográfico y Estadístico, beginning in 1882. See Spain, Instituto Geográfico y Estadístico, *Estadística de la emigración y inmigración de España en el quinquenio 1896–1900* (Madrid: 1903). Data on the slave trade are from David Eltis, "The Nineteenth-Century Transatlantic Slave Trade: An Annual Time Series of Imports into the Americas Broken Down by Region," *Hispanic American Historical Review* 67:1 (1987), pp. 122–123.

23. Spain, Instituto Geográfico y Estadístico, *Estadística de la emigración y inmigración de España en el quinquenio 1896–1900*, charts 67, 68.

24. United States War Department, *Report on the Census of Cuba, 1899*, pp. 442–443.

Chapter 16

1. This report is the most reliable document I have encountered on the pre-1895 state of the sugar industry. It was prepared by Cuban authorities headed by Serafín Fontela and B. Pichardo (the son of the great Matanzas cartographer Esteban Pichardo) and included the name of each mill, its extension in caballerías, location, and its status: "demolido," having ceased grinding cane; "destruido," destroyed during the war; "reconstruido," reconstructed since the war's end; "destruido y por reconstruir," destroyed and in the process of being rebuilt; and "no destruido," not destroyed. Even though it is the most detailed account of the status of the prewar sugar industry, there are contradictory data. One prewar document in the Matanzas archive indicates that there were 99 mills in 1895. See AHPM, Gobierno Provincial, Estadísticas, leg. 8, no. 9. It has been cited by Fé Iglesias García, "The Development of Capitalism in Cuban Sugar Production, 1860–1900," in Manuel Moreno Fraginals, Frank Moya Pons, and Stanley L. Engerman, eds., *Between Slavery and Free Labor: The Spanish Speaking-Caribbean in the Nineteenth Century* (Baltimore: The Johns Hopkins University Press, 1985), p. 73; and by Manuel Moreno Fraginals "Plantaciones en el Caribe: el caso Cuba–Puerto Rico–Santo Domingo (1860–1940)," in Moreno Fraginals, *La historia como arma y otros estudios sobre esclavos, ingenios y plantaciones* (Barcelona: Ed.Crítica, 1983). Another document in the Matanzas archive lists 118 prewar mills. See AHPM, ME, Estadísticas, leg. 7, no. 129, fol. 24. Still another very detailed document prepared by Matanzas authorities lists a total of 213 mills in 1899, 25 of which are classified as centrales and 188 as ingenios; there is no indication of how many were "demolidos." See AHPM, ME, leg. 7, nos., 128, 130, 131, 132.

Because of its great detail and the fact that it was supervised by Matanzas residents who knew the intricacies of the local sugar economy, I think that the figure of 150 functioning provincial mills on the eve of the insurrection is the most accurate. See Military Government of Cuba, Department of Agriculture, Commerce, and Industry, *Report of the Work Accomplished by This Department during the Fiscal Year Which Commenced on the 1st of July 1899, and Ended on the 30th of June, 1900* (Washington, D.C.: 1900). Also see Bureau of Insular Affairs Library, USNA,

"Estado no. 25 Secretaria de Agricultura, Comercio e Industria. Provincia de Matanzas. Ingenios existentes en 31 de diciembre de 1899, con expresión del estado en que se hallaban en esa fecha," pp. 240–243.

2. The data referred to here are contained in AHPM, ME, Estadística, leg. 7, no. 128, fols. 12–23, 34– 35; no. 130, fols. 1–15, 40–58; no. 131, fols. 25–91; no. 132, fols. 1–19. They are substantially different from those found in the 1899 census conducted by the United States War Department (*Report on the Census of Cuba, 1899* [Washington, D.C.: Government Printing Office, 1900]). The War Department census found a total of 1,955 farms, while the census cited here counted 2,912 farms. The War Department census also noted a much more intense fractionalization of land; for example, it found that 74 percent of all farms were less than 1 caballería in extension, while the census cited here noted 26.7 percent in that category. With respect to the sugar sector, the data also differ from the Department of Agriculture, Commerce, and Industry report cited in note 1, above.

While there is no way to account for these differences, it is my opinion that the manuscript census cited here (and in subsequent tables) can be used with more accuracy to determine land-tenure patterns. These data were compiled by local officials in the exact same manner as all previous agricultural censuses through the nineteenth century. Because this was a manuscript source that listed each farm, I was able to transcribe all of the raw data and submit them to numerous computer analyses to verify their accuracy. The War Department census did not list any information at the farm level, but included only summary results. Thus, there is no way to determine its accuracy. Additionally, there is no disaggregation of farms larger than 10 caballerías.

3. For the 1860 and 1878 data, see Table 8.8; for the 1899 data, see Table 16.1, which aggregates the data for centrales and ingenios.

4. This was done by first identifying the owners of all mills listed in the 1877/78 sugar census of Matanzas ("Noticias de las fincas azucareras en producción que existían en toda la isla de Cuba al comenzar el presupuesto de 1877/78," *Revista Económica*, June 7, 1878, pp. 7–24).

Then the 1899 Matanzas sugar mill census (Military Government of Cuba, *Report of the Work Accomplished by This Department*) was examined. Only the mills listed as "destruido," "reconstruido," "por reconstruir," or "no destruido" were included, for those labeled "demolido" had ceased grinding cane by 1895. This document does not list the owners of these mills, but it does note name, size, and location. The 150 mills falling in the above category were next located in J. C. Prince, *Cuba Illustrated* (New York: Napoleon Thompson & Co., 1893–1894), which lists all sugar mills in Cuba, their location, and the names of their owners. In this way, the owners of 120 mills were identified for both 1878 and 1895.

5. Junta de Agricultura, Comercio e Industria de la Provincia de Matanzas, *Memoria descriptiva de los trabajos realizados durante el año fiscal de 1900 a 1901* (Matanzas: Lib. La Pluma de Oro, 1901); USNA, RG 140, Military Government of Cuba, Letters Received, 1901, box 207, no. 4532, pp. 42–43, 59–60. Both of these mills were operated by Julián Zulueta's heirs through the early twentieth century, and they continue grinding cane in today's socialist Cuba. For a listing of Matanzas mills in 1913, see AHPM, Gobierno Provincial, Ingenios, leg. 3, no. 39.

6. A detailed account of Rosell's assets is in USNA, RG 76, entry 349, Spanish Treaty Claims Commission, 1901, case no. 268.

7. See *HFC*, vol. 3, pp. 217–225, for the lineage of the Matanzas Hernández family.

8. USNA, RG 76, entry 349, Spanish Treaty Claims Commission, 1901 case no. 478.

9. For the history of the Baró and Soler families see *HFC*, vol. 1, pp. 32–35, and vol. 6, pp. 332–335.

10. AHPM, PN, Colón, Manuel Vega Lavarría, 1888, fols. 497–502.

11. AHPM, PN, Colón, Manuel Vega Lavarría, 1888, fols. 713–717. On March 15, 1896, a column of Spanish troops under the command of General Luis Prats arrived at Colonia Francesa and destroyed the entire farm by burning all of the structures and cane fields. See the April 9 deposition given by Dahetz in AHPM, PN, Colón, Manuel Vega Lavarría, 1896, fol. 181.

12. ANC, PN, Matanzas, Juan Bolet y Durán, 1894, fols. 219–221^v.

13. AHPM, PN, Colón, Manuel Vega Lavarría, 1885, fols. 412–414v.

14. USNA, RG 76, entry 352, Spanish Treaty Claims Commission, 1901, case no. 76. It should be noted, however, that another branch of the Alfonso family continued owning the San Cayetano estate into the twentieth century. Echarte was married to Cristóbal's sister, Josefa María Alfonso. See *HFC*, vol. 2, pp. 123–126.

15. AHPM, PN, Colón, Manuel Vega Lavarría, 1885, fols. 910–953. Prince's *Cuba Illustrated* lists Isabel as a functioning estate in 1893, and the plantation is noted in 1900 as "reconstruido" in Military Government of Cuba, *Report of the Work Accomplished by This Department*.

Pérez de la Riva also acquired the debt-ridden Ingenio Elena (also known as Cuanabaco), in Corral Nuevo, from the Torrientes. See ANC, PN, Bonifacio Domínguez, Matanzas, 1885, fols. 31–39.

16. Louis A. Pérez, Jr., *Cuba between Empires 1878–1902* (Pittsburgh: University of Pittsburgh Press, 1983), pp. 22–23.

17. For the lineage of the Beas, see *HFC*, vol. 7, pp. 47–49. See ANC, PN, Bonifacio Domínguez, Matanzas, 1885, fols. 1627–1635^v, for a full listing of the partners in Bea, Bellido y Cía., which included Ramón Pelayo y Torriente and Juan Landeta y Lavin.

18. ANC, PN, Bonifacio Domínguez, Matanzas, 1885, fols. 945–953.

19. I have been unable to locate significant biographical materials on any of these firms. All were newcomers (with the exception of Rosell, who was discussed above), for there are no notices of any before the 1880s. An inquiry made by the occupying U.S. military authorities in 1899 revealed that approximately one-half of the Matanzas sugar crop was purchased by local merchants before the zafra. However, Cárdenas merchants reported that most of the sugar in the Cárdenas region had been purchased by Havana merchants. See USNA, RG 140, Military Government of Cuba, Letters Received, 1902, box 244, no. 1074, "Summary of Reports of Banking Firms on Letter Sent Them Requesting Information as to Amount of Sugar Pledges as Security for Loans, etc. etc."

20. ANC, PN, Bonifacio Domínguez, Matanzas, 1885, fols. 1058–1066.

21. ANC, PN, Juan Bolet y Durán, Matanzas, 1890, fols. 202–261, 748–758^v.

22. AHPM, PN, Manuel Vega Lavarría, Colón, 1880, fols. 615–624.
23. ANC, PN, Juan Bolet y Durán, Matanzas, 1890, fols. 481–502^v.

Chapter 17

1. Phillip S. Foner, *The Spanish-Cuban-American War and the Birth of American Imperialism* (New York: Monthly Review Press, 1972), vol. 1, p. 51.

2. The prewar provincial population can only be estimated, although summary statistics found in the Matanzas provincial archives indicate a total population of 253,616 in 1894. For population by partido in 1894, see Table 14.2.

General James H. Wilson, the military governor of Matanzas and Santa Clara in the aftermath of the U.S. occupation, estimated the 1894 population to be 271,960 and the 1899 population to be 190,560, a decline of 29.9 percent. See USNA, RG 140, Military Government of Cuba, Letters Received, 1899, no. 2594, James H. Wilson, "Report on the Industrial, Economical, and Social Conditions Existing in the Territory Covered by His Department." Between 1895 and 1898 there were 60,927 recorded deaths in Matanzas province (see Table 17.1 and Figure 17.1), 24 percent of total inhabitants found in the 1894 census (Table 14.2).

For a description of the military campaigns in Matanzas during the war, see Carlos M. Trelles y Govín, *Matanzas en la independencia de Cuba* (Havana: Imp. Avisador Comercial, 1928), pp. 45–94.

3. See the discussion in Louis A. Pérez, Jr., *Cuba between Empires, 1878–1902* (Pittsburgh: University of Pittsburgh Press, 1983), pp. 51, 55.

4. For an account of the repression, see USNA, DUSCM, roll 16, Jan. 22, 1889–Apr. 28, 1896, letters of March 8, Apr. 9, and Aug. 21, 1895, from Alex C. Brice to Edwin F. Uhl.

5. For example, about 600 people abandoned the village of Jovellanos after 40 people were arrested for suspected revolutionary sympathies in early 1895. See Pérez, *Cuba between Empires*, p. 120.

6. USNA, DUSCM, roll 16, Jan. 22, 1889–Apr. 28, 1896, letter of Jan. 7, 1896, from Alex C. Brice to Edwin F. Uhl.

7. USNA, Bureau of Insular Affairs Library, *Report of Brig. Gen. James H. Wilson, U.S. Volunteers, Commanding the Department of Matanzas and Santa Clara, Aug. 1, 1899*.

8. USNA, DUSCM, roll 16, Jan. 22, 1889–Apr. 28, 1896, letter of Jan. 27, 1896, from Alex C. Brice to Edwin F. Uhl.

9. USNA, Bureau of Insular Affairs Library, *Report of Brig. Gen. James H. Wilson, U.S. Volunteers, Commanding the Department of Matanzas and Santa Clara, Aug. 1, 1899*, p. 144.

A report from Matanzas in early Nov. 1898 is worth quoting at length:

No one who has not been here and seen their wretchedness can appreciate at all the dreadful condition of a large part of the entire suburban population. Starvation, disease, and death everywhere, without the means of warding them off. . . . It is hard to see the grown people here, but a sight of the little ones would soften the hearts of the most indifferent. The legs and arms of many of them are not larger than your thumb, and when their bodies are exposed you can see every bone. Colorless, hollow-eyed, and sunken-cheeked, they are indeed wrecks of the pitiless barbarity of Gen. Weyler and the inhumanity of the Cuban government.

Foner, *The Spanish-Cuban-American War*, vol. 2, pp. 385–386.

10. USNA, roll 16, DUSCM, Jan. 22, 1889–Apr. 28, 1896, letters of Sept. 20, 1895, Dec. 24, 1895, and Jan. 7, 1896, from Alex C. Brice to Edwin F. Uhl.

11. See Pérez, *Cuba between Empires*, pp. 52–54.

12. USNA, RG 76, entry 352, Spanish Treaty Claims Commission, case nos. 199, 210.

13. USNA, RG 76, entry 349, Spanish Treaty Claims Commission, case no. 468.

14. USNA, RG 76, entry 349, Spanish Treaty Claims Commission, case no. 478.

15. It is likely that 121 of these were not grinding cane by the beginning of the insurrection in 1895. See Military Government of Cuba, Department of Agriculture, Commerce, and Industry, *Report of the Work Accomplished by This Department during the Fiscal Years Which Commenced on the 1st of July 1899, and Ended on the 30th of June, 1900* (n.p., 1900).

16. USNA, RG 76, entry 349, Spanish Treaty Claims Commission, case no. 268.

17. These data were noted in two reports submitted by James H. Wilson, the Matanzas military governor, in the aftermath of the war. See USNA, RG 140, Military Government of Cuba, Letters Received, 1899, no. 2594; and USNA, Bureau of Insular Affairs Library, *Report of Brig. Gen. James H. Wilson, U.S. Volunteers, Commanding the Department of Matanzas and Santa Clara, Aug. 1, 1899*.

18. USNA, RG 140, Military Government of Cuba, Letters Received, 1900, box 100, no. 3624.

Chapter 18

1. For a summary of all this see Louis A. Pérez, Jr., *Cuba between Empires, 1878–1902* (Pittsburgh: University of Pittsburgh Press, 1983), chaps. 7 and 8, pp. 140–178.

2. See Phillip S. Foner, *The Spanish-Cuban-American War and the Birth of American Imperialism* (New York: Monthly Review Press, 1972), vol. 2, pp. 426–427.

3. USNA, RG 140, Military Government of Cuba, Letters Received, entry 1, no. 1670, letter of February 3, 1900, from Fred S. Foltz, Captain, 2nd Cavalry, Acting Inspector General to the Adjutant General, Department of Matanzas and Santa Clara.

4. USNA, RG 140, Military Government of Cuba, Letters Received, entry 1, no. 1670, report of Dec. 9, 1899, 1st Lieutenant Ralph Harrison, 2nd Cavalry, Matanzas.

5. United States War Department, Office of the Director of the Census of Cuba, *Report on the Census of Cuba, 1899* (Washington, D.C.: Government Printing Office, 1900), p. 558. There was an interesting racial dichotomy to this renting population which reflected the legacy of slavery. White renters occupied average-size

plots of .89 caballerías, while the average-size plots of "colored" renters were less than half that size, .39 caballerías.

6. See USNA, RG 140, Military Government of Cuba, Letters Received, 1900, box 100, no. 3624, which indicates clearly that the U.S. Military Government actively distributed oxen and agricultural implements to indigent families.

7. Foner, *The Spanish-Cuban-American War*, vol. 2, p. 474; Pérez, *Cuba between Empires*, p. 348; David F. Healy, *The United States in Cuba, 1898–1902* (Madison: University of Wisconsin Press, 1963), p. 93. Also see Louis A. Pérez, Jr., "Insurrection, Intervention, and the Transformation of Land Tenure Systems in Cuba, 1895–1902," *Hispanic American Historical Review* 65:2 (1985), pp. 234–235. Pérez errs when he claims there were 434 mills in Matanzas before the war (p. 230).

8. See the letter by John Murphy of New Orleans, "manufacturer of sugar machinery, double and triple effects, vacuum pan evaporators, pumps, boilers, engines, centrifugal machines, mixers, the Nason steam traps, Blacke's steam pumps," who wrote to Wilson "I would be thankful to have you favor me, at your earliest convenience, with a list of the sugar plantations in your district, giving their locations and the names of their proprietors." AHPM, ME, Estadísticas, leg. 8, no. 133, fol. 3.

9. Registro de Propiedad, Matanzas, libro 328, Finca no. 9535, fols. 236–247.

10. This is noted verbatim in Foner, *The Spanish-Cuban-American War*, pp. 476–477; Pérez, *Cuba between Empires*, p. 360; and Jules Robert Benjamin, *The United States and Cuba: Hegemony and Dependent Development, 1880–1934* (Pittsburgh: University of Pittsburgh Press, 1977), pp. 8, 14.

11. On Cuban rural banditry between the Ten Years' War and the war for independence, see Louis A. Pérez, Jr., "Vagrants, Beggars, and Bandits: Social Origins of Cuban Separatism, 1878–1895," *American Historical Review* 90:5 (December 1985), pp. 1092–1121. Also see Rosalie Schwartz's comments on this article and Pérez's response, in the *American Historical Review* 91:3 (June 1986), pp. 786–788.

12. On December 4, 1900, a report from Matanzas stated: "The increase in the number of bandits is alarming, many armed gangs traversing various parts of the province, and their work is having considerable effect. Several kidnapings have been committed within the past fifteen days for the purpose of demanding ransom. . . . [N]ewspapers and officials endeavor to conceal their real extent." USNA, RG 140, Military Government of Cuba, Letters Received, 1899, box 119, no. 6390.

13. USNA, RG 140, Military Government of Cuba, Letters Received, 1900, box 119, no. 6380.

14. See the reports on early-twentieth-century banditry in USNA, RG 140, Military Government of Cuba, Letters Received, 1901, box 123, no. 41.

15. Production for 1898/99 is noted in Military Government of Cuba, Department of Agriculture, Commerce, and Industry, *Report of the Work Accomplished by This Department during the Fiscal Years Which Commenced on the 1st of July 1899, and Ended on the 30th of June, 1900* (n.p., 1900), p. 244. In that year, 757,401 sacks of 325 pounds each were produced. Production for 1881 was noted in Provincia de Matanzas, Excma. Diputación Provincial, Sección de Fomento y Estadística, *Censo agrícola. Fincas azucareras. Año de 1881* (Matanzas: Imp. Aurora del Yumurí, 1883). Sugar output was listed in arrobas (18,110,609), which were converted

to pounds by multiplying by 25 and then to metric tons by dividing total pounds by 2,232. There are no data on provincial sugar output in the intervening years.

16. USNA, RG 140, Military Government of Cuba, Letters Received, 1899, entry 1, no. 1670.

17. For a complete list of the equipment utilized by each of the 47 Matanzas mills grinding cane in 1901, see USNA, RG 140, Military Government of Cuba, Letters Received, 1901, box 207, no. 4532; Junta de Agricultura, Comercio e Industria de la Provincia de Matanzas, *Memoria descriptiva de los trabajos realizados durante el año fiscal de 1900 a 1901* (Matanzas: Lib. La Pluma de Oro, 1901), pp. 42–61.

18. In 1901 Matanzas mills processed 194,064,713 arrobas of sugarcane and produced 18,656,690 arrobas of sugar. These figures are listed by mill in USNA, RG 140, Military Government of Cuba, Letters Received, 1902, box 244, no. 1074, "Provincia de Matanzas. Zafra de 1900 a 1901." For a discussion of industrial yields from the 1830s through the 1870s, see Manuel Moreno Fraginals, *El ingenio Complejo económico social cubano del azúcar* (Havana: Ed. de Ciencias Sociales, 1978), vol. 1, pp. 248–255.

19. Agricultural yields in 1901 are indicated in USNA, RG 140, Military Government of Cuba, Letters Received, 1902, box 244, no. 1074, "Provincia de Matanzas. Zafra de 1900 a 1901."

Yields in 1830 were estimated by Alejandro Dumont, *Guía de ingenios que trata de la caña de azúcar desde su origen de su cultivo y de la manera de elaborar sus jugos* (Matanzas: Imp. del Gobierno, a Cargo de Campé, 1832). Moreno Fraginals, *El ingenio*, vol. 1, p. 190, questions Dumont's assertion without offering any evidence to the contrary.

Yields in 1850 were estimated by José Luis Casaseca, "Memoria sobre el rendimiento en caña y azúcar de los ingenios de esta isla," *Gaceta de la Habana,* June 15, 1851, and are summarized in Moreno Fraginals, *El ingenio*, vol. 1, p. 190. There is an error in the "promedio," which is listed as 86,666 arrobas of cane/caballería but is actually 90,402 arrobas/caballería.

Agricultural yields in the mid-1880s are estimated by Fé Iglesias García, "The Development of Capitalism in Cuban Sugar Production, 1860–1900," in Manuel Moreno Fraginals, Frank Moya Pons, and Stanley L. Engerman, eds., *Between Slavery and Free Labor: The Spanish-Speaking Caribbean in the Nineteenth Century* (Baltimore: The Johns Hopkins University Press, 1985), p. 71; although the figure noted (74,649 arrobas cane/caballería) may be suspect, since it is exactly the same figure noted by Dumont for 1830. Cuban agronomists may simply have used this figure, rather than conducting any scientific observations.

20. USNA, RG 140, Military Government of Cuba, Letters Received, entry 1, no. 1670, report of Feb. 3, 1900, by Fred S. Foltz. These statistics were also generated independently in the United States War Department Census of 1899, which notes 42,697 laborers in agriculture and 3,827 caballerías in cane (*Report on the Census of Cuba, 1899* [Washington, D.C.: Government Printing Office, 1900], p. 442–443; 558–559).

21. Thus, the fact that in 1881 the greatest productivity in the province was achieved in Alacranes—where 2,213 arrobas of sugar were produced per caballería of land, compared with 6,909 arrobas/caballería in 1901 on the most productive

land—tells us nothing about sugar agriculture. This increase was entirely because of increased efficiency in industrial yields, rather than improvements in agriculture.

With respect to sugar yields per planted caballería of cane in Matanzas, there are some fundamental errors made in the only published work on this subject (Iglesias García, "The Development of Capitalism in Cuban Sugar Production, 1860–1900," p. 70), although those errors do not detract from the valuable arguments made in the essay. Iglesias lists the following yields of sugar, in arrobas per caballería:

	1860	1881
Cárdenas	2,177	1,612
Colón	2,358	1,887
Matanzas	2,895	2,049

The corrected figures are:

Cárdenas	2,177	1,614
Colón	2,317	2,073
Matanzas	1,691	1,848
Alacranes	—	2,213
Province	2,092	1,960

The most glaring difference between the two sets of data was for Matanzas jurisdiction, the oldest area of sugar exploitation in the province. Intuitively, there is little possibility that Matanzas could have had the highest yields in 1860: land there was exhausted, and there were no great technological innovations in processing that could have made mills there more productive than those in Colón, the most capital-intensive area of the provincial sugar industry.

Iglesias' 1860 data were derived from Carlos Rebello, *Estados relativos a la producción azucarera de la isla de Cuba* (Havana: Imp. del Gobierno, 1860). Rebello did not supply these data; they had to be calculated, and that is where Iglesias' error originates. Rebello reported production and caballerías of land planted in cane by jurisdiction. To arrive at yields per caballería, several mathematical operations had to be performed. Sugar production was listed in two forms: "cajas" and "bocoyes," both of which had be converted to arrobas. One caja averaged 17 arrobas of sugar, and one bocoy averaged 54 arrobas in the mid-nineteenth century. The corresponding figures for each measure of productive output were multiplied and then added together to arrive at gross production in arrobas. These figures were then divided by the number of caballerías in cane to arrive at the above statistics.

The 1881 data are to be found in Provincia de Matanzas, *Censo agrícola . . . 1881*. Data are listed in arrobas of sugar per cultivated caballería by *municipio*. To determine yields in the four jurisdictions, the yields in the municipal districts of each were averaged. For Matanzas, the municipios included Matanzas, Canasí, Guamacaro, and Santa Ana. For Alacranes, they were Alfonso XII, Cabezas, Bolondrón, Unión de Reyes, and Sabanilla. For Cárdenas, municipios included Cárdenas, Cimarrones, Guanajayabo, Guamutas, and Lagunillas. And for Colón, they were Colón, Jovellanos, Macuriges, Macagua, Perico, Roque, San José de los Ramos, Cuevitas, and Palmillas.

By way of comparison, Alejandro Dumont estimated sugar yields in 1830 to be 3,200 arrobas on the best land; 2,400 arrobas on second-rate land; and 1,600 arrobas on third-rate land. See Dumont, *Guía de ingenios que trata de la caña de azúcar desde su origen de su cultivo y de la manera de elaborar sus jugos*, p. 86.

In 1901 the sugar yields per caballería were 6,909 arrobas on the best land; 4,007 arrobas on second-rate land; and 3,118 arrobas on third-rate land. These higher yields had little to do with agriculture and were linked solely to industrial improvements. See USNA, RG 140, Military Government of Cuba, Letters Received, 1902, box 244, no. 1074.

22. For the notice of Rionda, Ceballos & Company, see Iglesias García, "The Development of Capitalism in Cuban Sugar Production, 1860–1900," p. 74.

GLOSSARY

a censo: method of selling land; imposed a yearly monetary obligation, usually a percentage of assessed value paid in perpetuity

accionista: shareholder in a company

agrimensor: surveyor

aguardiente: cane brandy

almacén: warehouse

apalancado: runaway slave living in a palenque (q.v.)

arroba: 25 pounds

asiento: monopoly granted by the Spanish Crown for slave trading

ayuntamiento: town council

bagazo: cane stock after juice has been extracted; used for fuel

barracón: slave quarters resembling barracks

billete: paper currency

bocoy: hogshead; container used to hold sugar or molasses

bohío: thatched-roof hut; peasant dwelling

boyero: cattle tender

bozal: African-born slave

bramadero: marker that denoted the center of an hato (d.v.)

caballería: land area equal to 33.6 acres

cabildo: town council; same as ayuntamiento

cabildos de nación: African cultural organizations

cacique: tribal chief of indigenous population of Cuba

cafetal: coffee farm

caja: box; container used to hold sugar

camino: road

camino real: royal road

caminos de hierro: railroads

caminos vecinales: local roads; usually little more than bridle paths

campanario: bell tower used to summon slaves to work or from the fields

cañaveral: cane field

carreta: cart, usually drawn by oxen

cédula: royal decree

central: central factory specializing in sugar production rather than in cane growing

cimarrón: runaway slave

coartación: legal mechanism through which slaves could purchase their freedom by making a down payment that fixed the price; when total price was paid, the slave was freed

coartado: slave who has entered into a coartación contract fixing the price of freedom

colonato: term used collectively to refer to colonos; see colono

colonia: farm on which sugarcane was grown to sell to a central factory; could be operated by a renter or a landowner

colono: grower of sugarcane who sold cane to a central factory; could be a renter or a landowner

comerciante: merchant

contador: accountant

contrabandista: smuggler

contramayoral: assistant foreman, under the supervision of a mayoral

conucos: provision grounds for slaves

corral: circular extension of land granted in usufruct and measuring 1 league in radius, or 421 caballerías, for raising ganado menor (q.v.)

costurera: seamstress

cuadrilla: gang

cuartón: administrative subdivision of a partido (q.v.)

defecadora: huge vat utilized at sugar mill to clarify guarapo (q.v.) by applying heat

demolición: partition of a rural property; refers to the conversion of hatos and corrales (q.v.) into private property or to the breakup of ingenios (q.v.)

dotación: total slave population on a rural property

emancipado: slave theoretically freed by authorities after capture from illegal slave traders, at sea or within Cuba; in fact, usually distributed to plantation owners and treated exactly as slaves

embarcadero: point for import or export of products; usually on the coast, but also on river banks

empadronamiento: the act of taking a census, usually in reference to slaves

empleomanía: quest for jobs in government bureaucracy; usually associated with the twentieth century

encargado: person in charge of administering a plantation; usually a trusted associate of the owner

envase: container used to hold sugar or molasses; usually a box (caja) or a hogshead (bocoy)

factoría: royal monopoly on tobacco production and marketing

florete: top-grade white sugar

fondo: documentary collection in library or archive

ganado mayor: bovine cattle

ganado menor: pigs

gremio: guild

guarapo: syrup extracted from sugarcane

hacienda; hacienda comunera: corral or hato (q.v.) held in usufruct; legally the property of the Crown and could have multiple legal users

hacienda demolido: hacienda that has been partitioned into private property

hato: circular extension of land granted in usufruct and measuring 2 leagues in radius, or 1,624 caballerías, for raising ganado mayor (q.v.)

horma: conical mold used to dry and drain crystallized sugar

informe: written report

ingenio: sugar mill, usually powered by steam

insurrecto: insurgent during the Ten Years' War (1868–1878) and the Cuban war for independence (1895–1898)

jurisdicción: administrative subdivision of Cuba before provincial subdivisions were established in 1878; same as tenencia de gobierno

lancha: flat-bottom barge used to transport sugar on rivers to export centers

látigo: whip

lavandera: washerwoman

macheteros: cane cutters

maquinista: machinist

mata: coffee bush

mayoral: foreman

mayordomo: chief foreman

memoria: a report

merced: land grant; sing. of mercedes de tierra

mercedes de tierra: land grants that conferred usufruct rights

molino: mill

municipio: municipality

muscovado: inferior-grade yellow sugar

negrero: slave trader

obligación: legal debt

padrón: census

palenque: community of runaway slaves

paradero: train station

partido: administrative subdivision of a jurisdicción

pastos artificiales: planted pastures

patrocinados: slaves freed by the emancipation law of 1880 but obligated to enter into work contracts with property owners

patronato: system of labor, established by the emancipation law of 1880, whereby slaves were obligated to enter into work contracts with property owners

patronos: property owners contracting emancipados (q.v.); after 1880 refers to contractors of patrocinados (q.v.)

pedaneo: administrative official in charge of a cuartón (q.v.)

peninsular: native of Spain

poblado: small population center

poblador: settler

polvillo: snuff

potrero: stock-raising farm

privilegio: legal code forbidding mortgage and alienation of sugar-mill property; repealed in the 1850s

pulpería: small-scale, rural retail store selling a variety of merchandise

pulpero: operator of a pulpería

quebrados: brown sugars

quintal: 100 pounds

rancho: small rural dwelling

rancheador: bounty hunter; scoured countryside searching for runaway slaves

ranchería: bounty-hunting gang organized to track and round up runaway slaves *rapé*: snuff

recogedor: marker that denoted the center of a corral (q.v.)

reconcentrados: people herded into fortified villages and towns as part of Spanish counterinsurgency policies during the Ten Years' War and the war for independence

refacción contract: legal device used by planters to secure credit from merchants; used by merchants to guarantee sugar supplies at harvesttime

sacarocracía: sugar-producing elite

sitiero: owner of a sitio

sitio; sitio de labor: small-scale subsistence farm

tahona: coffee-milling center

tenencia de gobierno: administrative subdivision of Cuba before provinces were formed in 1878; same as jurisdicción

tiempo muerto: "dead season"; period between June and November after one zafra had been completed and the next was about to begin

tienda: general store

trapiche: primitive sugar mill, usually animal-powered

trata: transatlantic slave trade

trata amarilla: trade in Chinese contract laborers (virtual slaves)

trocha: trench; armed ditch constructed across Cuba by Spanish autorities during Ten Years' War to prevent invasion of western Cuba by rebel army

vecinal: see caminos vecinales

vega: tobacco farm

veguero: tobacco farmer

venta de terreno: land sale

verdín: type of green tobacco grown in Matanzas for snuff

viandas: tubers; food crops grown by small-scale farmers

volante: horse-drawn carriage

zafra: sugar harvest

BIBLIOGRAPHY

Manuscript Sources

This book is based principally on manuscript sources located in various archival collections, the most valuable of which are located in Cuba. These are indicated below, in order of importance.

Archivo Histórico Provincial de Matanzas (AHPM). Located in the center of the port city of Matanzas, this well-organized provincial archive provided the richest materials for the present study. The collection is organized into more than thirty *fondos*, and there is a great deal of material now in the process of being catalogued. The most important used for this study were Bandoleros, Gobierno Provincial; Bandoleros Insurrectos; Conspiraciones; Esclavos; Esclavos Sublevaciones; Ingenios; Estadística; Ferrocarriles; Gobierno Provincial; Religiones Africanas; and Mapas y Planos.

    The archive of the nineteenth-century notary Manuel Vega Lavarría of Colón is largely uncatalogued, but I was graciously permitted to make use of the collection at my discretion. There is also an uncatalogued collection of the Cárdenas Anotaduría de Hipotecas, which recorded land mortgages, and a similar collection titled Esclavos y Semovientes, which noted mortgages that used slaves as collateral.

Archivo Nacional de Cuba (ANC). The Cuban national archives in Havana contain a number of fondos utilized for this study. The most important were the notarial archives of Cárdenas, Matanzas, and Havana which recorded a wide variety of legal transactions, including land sales, slave sales, last wills and testaments, "refacción" contracts, mortgage notes, and rental agreements. The Anotaduría de Hipotecas of Havana was another valuable collection, which recorded mortgages contracted by Matanzas entrepreneurs. Other collections at the ANC include Miscelánea de Expedientes; Miscelánea de Libros; and Gobierno General, which contained a wide range of materials on a variety of topics.

Biblioteca Gener y del Monte. This is the Matanzas city library. Its Fondos Raros y Valiosos contain many nineteenth-century Matanzas publications. The most important is a complete collection of the local newspaper *Aurora de Matanzas*, which was sometimes published under the name *Aurora de Yumurí* or simply *Aurora*.

Biblioteca Nacional José Martí. The Cuban national library in Havana naturally holds one of the largest extant collections of nineteenth-century Cuban materials. These are conserved in the Colección Cubana. The collection of maps was particularly valuable.

New York Public Library (NYPL). The Manuscript Division of the New York Public Library holds the complete collection of the Moses Taylor Papers, one of the major

New York merchant houses that had extensive business contacts with Matanzas merchants and planters. This is a vast collection, largely uncatalogued. Hundreds of letters between the firm and the Matanzas elite were valuable for this study. The NYPL is also a repository for secondary materials on Cuban history.

Public Records Office (PRO). Located in London, the PRO is the principal depository for British consular reports from Cuba. The Foreign Office 72 record group contains the reports from Havana consuls used in the present book.

National Archives of the United States (USNA). The most important collection consulted here was Record Group 76, entries 348–354, which contains the depositions made to the Spanish Treaty Claims Commission concerning reparations to U.S. citizens for damages incurred during the war for independence (1895–1898). These yielded valuable insights into the economic and social dynamics of the prewar and wartime periods.

Also of importance were the U.S. consular reports from Matanzas, on microfilm, and the records of the Military Government of Cuba conserved in Record Group 140. The Bureau of Insular Affairs Library contains many bound volumes on Cuba that were also utilized.

Archivo Histórico Nacional (AHN). Located in Madrid, the Spanish national archive's Ultramar Collection is the principal depository for nineteenth-century Cuban materials in Spain. The two most useful fondos for the present study were Esclavitud and Fomento. Materials in Gobierno and Gracia y Justicia were also consulted.

Published Sources

Aimes, Hubert. "Coartación: A Spanish Institution for the Advancement of Slaves into Freedmen." *The Yale Review* 17 (1909), pp. 412–431.

Alfonso, Pedro Antonio. *Memorias de un matancero. Apuntes para la historia de la isla de Cuba*. Matanzas: Imprenta de Marsal y Cía., 1854.

Arango y Parreño, Francisco. *De la factoría a la colonia*. Havana: Dirección de Cultura, 1936.

Auchincloss, H. B. "Sugar Making in Cuba." *Harper's New Monthly Magazine* 30:178 (March 1865), pp. 440–453.

Bachiller y Morales, D. A. *Memoria de los trabajos de la caja de ahorros, descuentos y depósitos de la Habana durante el año económico de 1859 a 1860*. Havana: Imprenta La Antilla, 1860.

Balanza general del comercio de la isla de Cuba en el año de 1826. Havana: Oficina del Gobierno y Capitanía General, 1827.

Balanza general del comercio de la isla de Cuba en el año de 1838. Havana: Imprenta del Gobierno y de la Real Hacienda por S. M., 1839.

Beato, Jorge J. *Cuba en 1830. Diario de viaje de un hijo del Mariscal Ney*. Miami: Ediciones Universal, 1973.

Benítez, José A. *Las Antillas: colonización, azúcar, e imperialismo*. Havana: Casa de las Américas, 1976.

Benjamin, Jules Robert. *The United States and Cuba: Hegemony and Dependent Development, 1880–1934*. Pittsburgh: University of Pittsburgh Press, 1977.

Bergad, Laird W. "The Economic Viability of Sugar Production Based on Slave Labor in Cuba: 1859–1878." *Latin American Research Review*, 24:1 (1989), pp. 95–113.

———. "Land Tenure, Slave Ownership, and Income Distribution in Nineteenth Century Cuba: Colón and Cárdenas, 1859–1876." *Social and Economic Studies* (University of the West Indies) 37:1–2 (March–June 1988), pp. 301–340.

———. "Slave Prices in Cuba, 1840–1875." *Hispanic American Historical Review* 67:4 (1987), pp. 631–655.

Bernardo y Estrada, Rodrigo de. *Prontuario de mercedes o sea índice por orden alfabético de las mercedes concedidas por el escmo. Ayuntamiento de la Habana en cuanto concierne a las haciendas de crianza de animales.* Havana: Est. Tip. La Cubana, 1857.

Book of the Telegraph. Boston: Daniel David, 1851.

Calendario manual y guía de forasteros de la isla de Cuba para el año de 1795. Havana: Imprenta de la Capitanía General, 1795.

Calvo y O'Farrill, Nicolás. *Memoria sobre los medios que convendría adoptar para que tuviese la Habana los caminos necesarios.* Havana: Imprenta de la Capitanía General, 1795.

Cantero, Justo G. *Los ingenios. Colección de vistas de los principales ingenios de azúcar de la isla de Cuba.* Havana: Impreso en la Litografía de Luis Marquier, 1857.

Cepero Bonilla, Raúl. *Azúcar y abolición.* Havana: Editorial de Ciencias Sociales, 1971 (originally published 1948).

Cok Márquez, Patria. "La introducción de los ferrocarriles portatiles en la industria azucarera, 1870–1880." *Santiago* 41 (March 1981), pp. 137–147.

Corbitt, Duvon C. "Immigration in Cuba." *Hispanic American Historical Review* 22:2 (1942), pp. 280–308.

———. "Mercedes y Realengos: A Survey of the Public Land System in Cuba." *Hispanic American Historical Review* 19:3 (1939), pp. 262–285.

———. "El primer ferrocarril construido en Cuba." *Revista Cubana* 12 (1938), pp. 179–195.

———. *A Study of the Chinese in Cuba, 1847–1947.* Wilmore, Ky.: Asbury College, 1971.

Corwin, Arthur F. *Spain and the Abolition of Slavery in Cuba, 1817–1886.* Austin: University of Texas Press, 1967.

Cuba, Centro de Estadística. *Noticias estadísticas de la isla de Cuba en 1862.* Havana: Imprenta del Gobierno, Capitanía General y Real Hacienda, 1864.

Cuba, Gobernador y Capitán General. *Cuadro estadístico de la siempre fiel isla de Cuba correspondiente al año de 1827.* Havana: Imprenta del Gobierno y Capitanía General, 1829.

———. *Cuadro estadístico de la siempre fiel isla de Cuba correspondiente al año de 1846.* Havana: Imprenta del Gobierno y Capitanía General, 1847.

Danger Roll, Zoila. *Los cimarrones en El Fríjol.* Santiago: Editorial Oriente, 1977.

Deschamps Chapeaux, Pedro. *El negro en la economía habanera del siglo xix.* Havana: Unión de Escritores y Artistas de Cuba, 1971.

Díaz del Castillo, Bernal. *Historia verdadera de la conquista de la Nueva España*. 2 vols. Mexico: Editorial Porrua, 1968.

Duharte Jiménez, Rafael. "Palenque: Economy and Society." *Cimarrón* 1:2 (1986), pp. 37–48.

Dumont, Alejandro. *Guía de ingenios que trata de la caña de azúcar desde su origen de su cultivo y de la manera de elaborar sus jugos*. Matanzas: Imprenta del Gobierno, a Cargo de Campe, 1832.

Eblen, Jack E. "On the Natural Increase of Slave Populations: The Example of the Cuban Black Population, 1775–1900." In Engerman and Genovese, eds., *Race and Slavery in the Western Hemisphere*, pp. 211–248.

Eltis, David. *Economic Growth and the Ending of the Transatlantic Slave Trade*. New York: Oxford University Press, 1987.

———. "The Nineteenth-Century Transatlantic Slave Trade: An Annual Time Series of Imports into the Americas Broken Down by Region." *Hispanic American Historical Review* 67:1 (1987) pp. 109–138.

Ely, Roland T. *Comerciantes cubanos del siglo xix*. Havana: Editorial Libreria Martí, 1961.

———. *Cuando reinaba su majestad el azúcar*. Buenos Aires: Editorial Sudamericana, 1963.

Engerman, Stanley L., and Eugene D. Genovese, eds. *Race and Slavery in the Western Hemisphere: Quantitative Studies*. Princeton: Princeton University Press, 1975.

Erenchun, Félix. *Anales de la isla de Cuba. Diccionario administrativo, económico, estadístico, y legislativo*. 3 vols. Havana: Imprenta de la Antilla, 1855–1857.

Extracto de las memorias y acuerdos de la junta de caminos de hierro. Havana: Imprenta Fraternal, 1831.

Feijoo Sotomayor, Urbano. *Isla de Cuba. Inmigración de trabajadores españoles*. Havana: Imprenta de Eleizegui, 1853.

Foner, Phillip S. *The Spanish-Cuban-American War and the Birth of American Imperialism*. 2 vols. New York: Monthly Review Press, 1972.

Franco, José Luciano. *Comercio clandestino de esclavos*. Havana: Editorial de Ciencias Sociales, 1985.

———. *Ensayos históricos*. Havana: Editorial de Ciencias Sociales, 1974.

———. *Los palenques de los negros cimarrones*. Havana: Colección Histórica, 1973.

Friedlaender, Heinrich. *Historia económica de Cuba*. 2 vols. Havana: Ediciones de Ciencias Sociales, 1978 (originally published 1944).

Gallenga, Antonio. *The Pearl of the Antilles*. London: Chapman & Hall, 1873.

González Jiménez, José Miguel. "El ingenio San Martín." *Revista de la Biblioteca Nacional José Martí* 9:1 (January–March 1967), pp. 71–99.

Goslinga, Cornelio Ch. *Los holandeses en el caribe*. Havana: Casa de las Américas, 1983.

Guerra y Sánchez, Ramiro. *Azúcar y población en las Antillas*. Havana: Editorial de Ciencias Sociales, 1976 (originally published 1944).

———. *La guerra de los diez años, 1868–1878*. 2 vols. Havana: Cultural, 1950–1952.

Hall, Gwendolyn. *Social Control in Slave Plantation Societies: A Comparison of Saint Domingue and Cuba.* Baltimore: The Johns Hopkins University Press, 1971.

Hazard, Samuel. *Cuba with Pen and Pencil.* Hartford, Conn.: Hartford Publishing Co., 1871.

Healy, David F. *The United States in Cuba, 1898–1902.* Madison: University of Wisconsin Press, 1963.

Hellberg, Carlos. *Historia estadística de Cárdenas, 1893.* Cárdenas: Comité Pro-Calles de Cárdenas, 1957.

Helly, Denise. *Idéologie et ethnicité: Les Chinois Macao à Cuba: 1847–1886.* Montreal: Les Presses de l'Université de Montréal, 1979.

Humboldt, Alexander von. *Ensayo político sobre la isla de Cuba.* Havana: Cultural, 1959.

Iglesias García, Fé. "Azúcar, esclavitud y tecnología (segunda mitad del siglo xix)." *Santiago*, no. 61 (1986), pp. 113–131.

———. "Azúcar y crédito durante la segunda mitad del siglo xix en Cuba." *Santiago*, no. 52 (1983), pp. 119–144.

———. "El censo cubano de 1877 y sus diferentes versiones." *Santiago*, no. 34 (June 1979), pp. 167–214.

———. "Changes in Cane Cultivation in Cuba, 1860–1900." *Social and Economic Studies* (University of the West Indies) 37:1–2 (March–June 1988).

———. "The Development of Capitalism in Cuban Sugar Production, 1860–1900." In Moreno Fraginals, Moya Pons, and Engerman, eds., *Between Slavery and Free Labor*, pp. 54–76.

———. "Formación del capitalismo en la producción de azúcar en Cuba (1860–1900)." Manuscript.

Informe que debe leerse a nombre de la junta directiva de la compañía del ferrocarril de Matanzas en la general ordinaria de accionistas. Matanzas: Imprenta Aurora de Yumurí, 1872.

Instituto Cubano de Geodesia y Cartografía. *Atlas de Cuba.* Havana: Instituto Cubano de Geodesia y Cartografía, 1978.

Jiménez Pastrana, Juan. *Los chinos en las luchas por la liberación cubana (1847–1930).* Havana: Instituto de Historia, 1963.

Jimeno Fuentes, Francisco. "Matanzas, estudio histórico estadístico dedicado a la Exma. Diputación Provincial de Matanzas." *Revista de la Biblioteca Nacional* 7:1 (January–March 1957), pp. 11–99.

Junta de Agricultura, Comercio e Industria de la Provincia de Matanzas. *Memoria descriptiva de los trabajos realizados durante el año fiscal de 1900 a 1901.* Matanzas: Librería La Pluma de Oro, 1901.

Klein, Herbert S. *The Middle Passage: Comparative Studies in the Atlantic Slave Trade.* Princeton: Princeton University Press, 1978.

Knight, Franklin W. "Origin of Wealth and the Sugar Revolution in Cuba, 1750–1850." *Hispanic American Historical Review* 57:2 (1977), pp. 231–253.

———. *Slave Society in Cuba during the Nineteenth Century.* Madison: University of Wisconsin Press, 1970.

LeRiverend, Julio. *Historia económica de Cuba*. Havana: Instituto Cubano del Libro, 1971.

LeVeen, E. Phillip. "A Quantitative Analysis of the Impact of British Suppression Policies on the Volume of the Nineteenth-Century Atlantic Slave Trade." In Engerman and Genovese, eds., *Race and Slavery in the Western Hemisphere*, pp. 51–81.

Manzano, Juan Francisco. *The Life and Poems of a Cuban Slave*. Edited by Edward J. Mullen; trans. by R. R. Madden. Hamden, Conn.: Archon Books, 1981.

Marrero, Levi. *Cuba: economía y sociedad*. Vols. 9–12. Madrid: Editorial Playor, 1983–1985.

Memoria instructivo formado por D. Juan Poey y D. Antonio Carillo socios y representantes de la minoría de los accionistas de la Compañía de los Caminos de Hierro de la Habana. Madrid: Imprenta Benigno Carranza, 1872.

Memoria de La Alianza. Compañía de Crédito y Seguros. Havana: n.p., 1866.

Military Government of Cuba, Department of Agriculture, Commerce, and Industry. *Report of the Work Accomplished by This Department during the Fiscal Year Which Commenced on the 1st of July 1899, and Ended on the 30th of June, 1900*. Washington, D.C.: n.p., 1900. In USNA, Bureau of Insular Affairs Library.

Montejo, Esteban. *The Autobiography of a Runaway Slave*. Edited by Miguel Barnet; trans. by Jocasta Innes. New York: Vintage Books, 1973.

Montoro, Rafael. "Historia de la Sociedad Económica de Amigos del País de la Habana." *Revista Bimestre Cubana* 4:1–2 (1910), pp. 11–48, 113–138.

Moreno Fraginals, Manuel, ed. *Africa en América Latina*. Mexico: Siglo XXI, 1977.

———. *La historia como arma y otros estudios sobre esclavos, ingenios y plantaciones*. Barcelona: Editorial Crítica, 1983.

———. "La esclavitud, a cien años de fin." *Revolución y Cultura*, no. 8 (August 1986), pp. 2–11.

———. "El esclavo y la mecanización de los ingenios." *Bohemia*, June 13, 1969, pp. 98–99.

———. *El ingenio. Complejo económico social cubano del azúcar*. 3 vols. Havana: Editorial de Ciencias Sociales, 1978.

Moreno Fraginals, Manuel, Herbert S. Klein, and Stanley L. Engerman. "The Level and Structure of Slave Prices on Cuban Plantations in the Mid-Nineteenth Century: Some Comparative Perspectives." *American Historical Review* 88:5 (1983), pp. 1201–1218.

Moreno Fraginals, Manuel, Frank Moya Pons and Stanley L. Engerman, eds. *Between Slavery and Free Labor: The Spanish-Speaking Caribbean in the Nineteenth Century*. Baltimore: The Johns Hopkins University Press, 1985.

Murray, David R. *Odious Commerce: Britain, Spain, and the Abolition of the Cuban Slave Trade*. Cambridge: Cambridge University Press, 1980.

———. "Statistics of the Slave Trade to Cuba, 1790–1867." *Journal of Latin American Studies* 3:2 (November 1971), pp. 131–149.

Nieto y Cortadellas, Rafael. *Dignidades nobiliarias en Cuba*. Madrid: Ediciones de Cultura Hispánica, 1954.

North, Douglass C. *The Economic Growth of the United States, 1790–1860*. New York: W. W. Norton & Co., 1966.

"Noticias de las fincas azucareras en producción que existían en toda la isla de Cuba al comenzar el presupuesto de 1877–1878." *Revista Económica*, June 7, 1878, pp. 7–24.

Novas Calvo, Lino. *El negrero. Vida novelada de Pedro Blanco Fernández de Trava.* Madrid: Espasa-Calpe, 1933.

Oostindie, Gert J. "La burguesía cubana y sus caminos de hierro, 1830–1868." *Boletín de Estudios Latinoamericanos y del Caribe* no. 37 (December 1984), pp. 99–115.

Ortíz, Fernando. "Los cabildos afro-cubanos." *Revista Bimestre Cubana* 16 (January-February 1921), pp. 5–39.

————. *Hampa afro-cubana. Los negros esclavos.* Havana: Revista Bimestre Cubana, 1916.

————. "Las perspectivas económico-sociales del primer ferrocarril de Cuba." *Revista Bimestre Cubana* 40:2 (November–December 1937), pp. 161–176.

————. *Recopilación para la historia de la Sociedad Económica Habanera.* 4 vols. Havana: Imprenta y Librería El Universo, 1930.

Paquette, Robert L. *Sugar Is Made with Blood: The Conspiracy of La Escalera and the Conflict between Empires over Slavery in Cuba.* Middletown, Conn.: Wesleyan University Press, 1988.

Pérez, Louis A., Jr. *Cuba between Empires, 1878–1902.* Pittsburgh: University of Pittsburgh Press, 1983.

————. "Insurrection, Intervention, and the Transformation of Land Tenure Systems in Cuba, 1895–1902." *Hispanic American Historical Review* 65:2 (1985), pp. 229–254.

————. "Vagrants, Beggars, and Bandits: Social Origins of Cuban Separatism, 1878–1895." *American Historical Review* 90:5 (December 1985), pp. 1092–1121.

Pérez de la Riva, Francisco. *El café. Historia de su cultivo y explotación en Cuba.* Havana: Jesús Montero, 1944.

————. *Origen y régimen de la propiedad territorial en Cuba.* Havana: Imprenta El Siglo XX, 1946.

Pérez de la Riva, Juan. *El barracón y otros ensayos.* Havana: Editorial de Ciencias Sociales, 1975.

————, ed., *La isla de Cuba en el siglo xix vista por los extranjeros.* Havana: Editorial de Ciencias Sociales, 1981.

Pezuela, Jacobo de la. *Crónica de las Antillas.* Madrid: Rubio, Grilo y Vitturi, 1871.

————. *Diccionario geográfico, estadístico, histórico de la isla de Cuba.* 4 vols. Madrid: Imprenta del Establecimiento de Mellado, 1863.

Pichardo, Esteban. *Caminos de la isla de Cuba. Itinerarios.* 2 vols. Havana: Imprenta Militar de M. Soler, 1865.

————. *Geografía de la isla de Cuba.* 4 vols. Havana: Est. Tip. de D. M. Soler, 1854.

————. *Isla de Cuba. Carta geotopográfica.* Havana: Dirección de la Capitanía General, 1860–1872.

————. *Itinerario general de los caminos principales de la isla de Cuba.* Havana: Imprenta de Palmer, 1828.

Poey, Juan. *Informes presentados al excmo. capitán general gobierno superior civil*

de la isla de Cuba sobre el proyecto de colonización africana y al Illmo. Sr. inten-
dente de Hacienda de la propia isla sobre derechos de los azúcares. Madrid: Imprenta D. A. Aurial, 1862.

Pollard, A.H., Farhat Yusuf, and G. N. Pollard, *Demographic Techniques.* Rushcutters Bay, Australia: Pergamon Press, 1974.

Ponte y Domínguez, Francisco J. *Matanzas: biografía de una provincia.* Havana:
Imprenta El Siglo XX, 1959.

Prince, J. C. *Cuba Illustrated.* New York: Napoleon Thompson & Co., 1893–1894.

Provincia de Matanzas, Excma. Diputación Provincial, Sección de Fomento y Estadística. *Censo agrícola. Fincas azucareras. Año de 1881.* Matanzas: Imprenta Aurora de Yumurí, 1883.

Real Junta de Fomento de Agricultura y Comercio. *Documentos relativos a la enagenación del camino de hierro de la Habana a Güines.* Havana: Imprenta del
Gobierno y Capitanía General, 1839.

Rebello, Carlos. *Estados relativos a la producción azucarera de la isla de Cuba.*
Havana: Imprenta del Gobierno, 1860.

Reed, William Howell. *Reminiscences of Elisha Atkins.* Boston: privately printed,
1890.

*Report of the Commission Sent by China to Ascertain the Condition of Chinese
Coolies in Cuba.* Shanghai: Imperial Maritime Customs Press, 1876.

Ribera, Nicolás Joseph de. *Descripción de la isla de Cuba.* Havana: Instituto Cubano
del Libro, 1973.

Rivero Muñiz, José. *Tabaco. Su historia en Cuba.* 2 vols. Havana: Instituto de Historia, 1964–1965.

––––––. *Las tres sediciones de los vegueros en el siglo xviii.* Havana: Academia de
la Historia de Cuba, 1951.

Rosillo y Alquier, Fermín. *Noticias de dos ingenios. Datos sobre la producción azucarera de la isla de Cuba.* Havana: Imprenta El Iris, 1873.

Rousset, Ricardo V. *Historial de Cuba.* Havana: Librería Cervantes de Ricardo Veloso, 1918.

Saco, José Antonio. *Acerca de la esclavitud y su historia.* Havana: Editorial de Ciencias Sociales, 1982.

––––––. *Colección de papeles científicos, históricos, políticos, y de otros ramos sobre
la isla de Cuba.* 2 vols. Havana: Dirección General de Cultura, 1960.

Santa Cruz y Mallen, Francisco Xavier de. *Historia de familias cubanas.* 8 vols.
Havana: Editorial Hércules, 1940.

Scott, Rebecca. "Gradual Abolition and the Dynamics of Slave Emancipation in
Cuba, 1868–86." *Hispanic American Historical Review* 63:3 (1983), pp. 449–477.

––––––. *Slave Emancipation in Cuba: The Transition to Free Labor, 1860–1899.*
Princeton: Princeton University Press, 1985.

––––––. "The Transformation of Sugar Production in Cuba after Emancipation,
1880–1900: Planters, Colonos and Former Slaves." In Bill Albert and Adrian
Graves eds., *Crisis and Change in the International Sugar Economy, 1860–1914*
(Norwich and Edinburgh: ISC Press, 1984), pp. 111–119.

Sociedad en Comandita La Gran Azucarera. *Balanza general y memoria.* Havana:
Imprenta La Universal, 1866.

Spain, Instituto Geográfico y Estadístico. *Censo de la población de España según el empadronamiento hecho en 31 de diciembre de 1877.* 2 vols. Madrid: Imprenta de la Dirección General del Instituto Geográfico y Estadístico, 1883.

————. *Censo de la población de España según el empadronamiento hecho en 31 de diciembre de 1887.* 2 vols. Madrid: Imprenta de la Dirección General del Instituto Geográfico y Estadístico, 1892.

————. *Estadística de la emigración y inmigración de España en los años 1882 a 1890.* Madrid: Instituto Geográfico y Estadístico, 1891.

————. *Estadística de la emigración y inmigración de España en los años de 1891–1895.* Madrid: Instituto Geográfico y Estadístico, 1898.

————. *Estadística de la emigración y inmigración de España en el quinquenio 1896–1900.* Madrid: Instituto Geográfico y Estadístico, 1903.

Stubbs, Jean. *Tobacco on the Periphery: A Case Study in Cuban Labour History, 1860–1958.* Cambridge: Cambridge University Press, 1985.

Styuck y Reig, Juan. *División territorial de la isla de Cuba y nomenclator de sus poblaciones.* Madrid: Imprenta de la Viuda e Hija de Peñuelas, 1880.

Suárez Argudín, José. *Proyecto de inmigración africana. Para las islas de Cuba y Puerto Rico y el imperio del Brasil. Presentado a los respectivos gobiernos por los Sres. Suárez Argudín, Cunha Reis y Perdones.* Havana: Imprenta La Habanera, 1860.

Tanco Armero, Nicolás. "La isla de Cuba." In Juan Pérez de la Riva, ed., *La isla de Cuba en el siglo xix vista por los extranjeros,* pp. 107–139.

Thomas, Hugh. *Cuba: The Pursuit of Freedom.* New York: Harper & Row, 1971.

Trelles y Govín, Carlos M. *Matanzas en la independencia de Cuba.* Havana: Imprenta Avisador Comercial, 1928.

————. *Matanzas y su puerto desde 1508 hasta 1693.* Matanzas: Imprenta Estrada, 1932.

Turnbull, David. *Travels in the West: Cuba with Notices of Porto Rico and the Slave Trade.* London: Longman, 1840.

United States War Department, Office of the Director of the Census of Cuba. *Report on the Census of Cuba, 1899.* Washington, D.C.: Government Printing Office, 1900.

Vázquez Pérez, Ricardo. "Un modesto obrero de la ciencia: Don Francisco de Jimeno y Fuentes. Notas biográficas." *Cuadernos de Historia Matancero* 5 (1961), pp. 1–32.

Vázquez Queipó, Vicente. *Informe fiscal sobre fomento de la población blanca en la isla de Cuba.* Madrid: Imprenta Alegría, 1845.

Vento, Saúl. *Las rebeldías de esclavos en Matanzas* (pamphlet). Matanzas: Filial de Instituto de Historia del Partido Comunista de Cuba en la Provincia de Matanzas, 1976.

Villaverde, Cirilio. *Diario del rancheador.* Havana: Editorial Letras Cubanas, 1982.

Vives, Francisco Dionisio. *Cuadro estadístico de la siempre fiel isla de Cuba correspondiente al año de 1827.* Havana: Imprenta del Gobierno y Capitanía General, 1829.

Wright, Irene A. *The Early History of Cuba, 1492–1586.* New York: Macmillan, 1916.

Wright, Irene A. "Los origenes de la minería en Cuba. Las minas del Prado hasta 1600." *La Reforma Social* 7 (April–July 1916), pp. 450–462.

Zanetti Lecuono, Oscár. "Esclavitud i treball lliure. El problema laboral dels ferrocarrils cubans, 1837–1867." *L'Avenc*, no. 101 (January 1987), pp. 17–23.

Zanetti, Oscár, and Alejandro García. *Caminos para el azúcar*. Havana: Editorial de Ciencias Sociales, 1987.

Zaragoza, Justo. *Las insurrecciones en Cuba. Apuntes para la historia política de esta isla en el presente siglo*. 2 vols. Madrid: Imprenta de Manuel G. Hernández, 1872–1873.

Zulueta, Pedro de. *Trial of Pedro de Zulueta, Jun., on a Charge of Slave Trading*. London: C. Wood & Co., 1844.

INDEX